This Book's Special Elements

Note: Notes offer supplementary information that doesn't fit within the structure of the current chapter.

Textbook Tip: Textbook Tips are formal methods and guidance. For example:

The syntax of the InStr function is

InStr(*start*,*search_string*,*find_string*)

Developer's Tip

Developer's Tips are hints, descriptions, and rules of thumb that are gleaned from experience rather than formal learning. For example:

Punching out your customers will have a detrimental effect on your future income.

Showstopper: Showstoppers are warnings and cautions about things to watch out for or avoid. For example:

If you stick the CD-ROM in the floppy disk drive, you will probably break the disk drive.

The CD icon indicates that whatever is being discussed in that paragraph can be found on the CD-ROM that is included with this book.

At the end of each chapter are two special sections. **Modification Notes** describes the differences you would expect to apply to the process if you were modifying an existing application instead of creating one from scratch. **Debugging the Process** describes possible problems to watch out for at this stage of the design and indicates some solutions.

Develop a Professional Visual Basic™ Application in 14 Days

Develop a Professional Visual Basic™ Application in 14 Days

William J. Orvis

SAMS
PUBLISHING

201 West 103rd Street
Indianapolis, Indiana 46290

For Liz, Scott, and Nate. Good friends are hard to find.

Copyright © 1995 by Sams Publishing

FIRST EDITION

All rights reserved. No part of this book shall be reproduced, stored in a retrieval system, or transmitted by any means, electronic, mechanical, photocopying, recording, or otherwise, without written permission from the publisher. No patent liability is assumed with respect to the use of the information contained herein. Although every precaution has been taken in the preparation of this book, the publisher and author assume no responsibility for errors or omissions. Neither is any liability assumed for damages resulting from the use of the information contained herein. For information, address Sams Publishing, 201 W. 103rd St., Indianapolis, IN 46290.

International Standard Book Number: 0-672-30596-8

Library of Congress Catalog Card Number: 94-67083

98 97 96 95   4 3 2 1

Interpretation of the printing code: the rightmost double-digit number is the year of the book's printing; the rightmost single-digit, the number of the book's printing. For example, a printing code of 95-1 shows that the first printing of the book occurred in 1995.

Composed in AGaramond, Helvetica, and MCPdigital by Macmillan Computer Publishing

Printed in the United States of America

Trademarks

All terms mentioned in this book that are known to be trademarks or service marks have been appropriately capitalized. Sams Publishing cannot attest to the accuracy of this information. Use of a term in this book should not be regarded as affecting the validity of any trademark or service mark.

Visual Basic is a trademark of Microsoft Corporation.

Publisher
Richard K. Swadley

Acquisitions Manager
Greg Wiegand

Managing Editor
Cindy Morrow

Acquisitions Editor
Grace Buechlein

Development Editor
Bradley L. Jones

Software Development Specialist
Tim Wilson

Production Editor
Gayle L. Johnson

Editorial Coordinator
Bill Whitmer

Editorial Assistants
Carol Ackerman
Sharon Cox
Lynette Quinn

Technical Reviewer
Discovery Computing, Inc.

Marketing Manager
Gregg Bushyeager

Assistant Marketing Manager
Michelle Milner

Cover Designer
Tim Amrhein

Book Designer
Alyssa Yesh

Manufacturing Coordinator
Paul Gilchrist

Imprint Manager
Kelly Dobbs

Team Supervisor
Katy Bodenmiller

Support Services Supervisor
Mary Beth Wakefield

Production Analysts
Angela Bannan
Dennis Clay Hager
Bobbi Satterfield

Graphics Image Specialists
Becky Beheler
Steve Carlin
Jason Hand
Clint Lahnen
Cheri Laughner
Mike Reynolds
Laura Robbins
Craig Small
Jeff Yesh

Page Layout
Charlotte Clapp
Aleata Howard
Louisa Klucznik
Ayanna Lacey
Jill Tompkins
Tina Trettin
Mark Walche
Dennis Wesner
Michelle Worthington

Proofreading
Michael Brumitt
Michael Henry
Donna Martin
Cheryl Moore
Brian-Kent Proffitt
Beth Rago
Erich J. Richter
SA Springer
Tim Taylor
Holly Wittenberg

Indexer
Chris Cleveland

Overview

		Introduction	xix
Part I		**Systems Analysis and Design**	**1**
Day	1	Whose Project Is This?	3
	2	Specifying the Application	29
	3	Structured Design	61
	4	Database Design	103
	5	Creating the Program Structure Chart	155
	6	Procedure Design	183
	7	Forms Design	205
Part II		**Construction**	**249**
Day	8	Coding the Application, Part 1	251
	9	Coding the Application, Part 2	301
	10	Adding Error Trapping to the Application	343
	11	Debugging and Testing	361
Part III		**Documentation**	**393**
Day	12	Documenting the Application	395
Part IV		**Implementation**	**423**
Day	13	Manufacturing and Sales	425
	14	Support, Upgrades, and Phaseout	455
Appendixes			
	A	Glossary	469
	B	Using the CD-ROM	479
		Index	485

Contents

		Introduction	**xix**
		Developing an Application xix	
		Database Developer's Guide xx	
		The Layout of a Chapter xx	
		The Parts of the Development Process xx	
		Part I: Systems Analysis and Design xxi	
		Part II: Construction xxii	
		Part III: Documentation xxii	
		Part IV: Implementation xxii	
		This Book's Conventions xxii	
		Time to Go for It xxiii	
Part I		**Systems Analysis and Design**	**1**
Day	**1**	**Whose Project Is This?**	**3**
		The Goal of Day 1 4	
		Define the Customer 5	
		You Are the Customer 5	
		You Work for the Customer 6	
		Someone Else Is the Customer 6	
		Define the Project 7	
		Planning 8	
		Creating a Task List 10	
		Estimating Time 12	
		Creating a Gantt Chart 13	
		Cost Estimates 14	
		The Proposal 14	
		The Contract 15	
		You Are an Independent Developer 16	
		You Are Employed as a Developer 16	
		You Are a Contractor or Consultant 16	
		Things to Consider 16	
		Protecting Your and Your Customer's Property 17	
		You Are an Independent Developer 17	
		You Are Employed as a Developer 17	
		You Are a Contractor or Consultant 18	
		Who Owns the Results? 18	
		You Are an Independent Developer 18	
		You Are Employed as a Developer 19	
		You Are a Contractor or Consultant 19	
		The Decision Support Application Project 19	
		Define the Customer 19	
		Define the Project 20	

	Planning	21
	The Proposal	25
	The Contract	27
	The Nondisclosure Agreement	27
	Modification Notes	27
	Debugging the Process	28
	Summary	28

2 Specifying the Application — 29

The Goal of Day 2	30
Background Study	31
Define the Scope of the Project	31
List the Program's Features	32
Usability Enhancements	33
Sketch Some Possible Forms	33
Draw a High-Level Data Flow Diagram	34
Write Down the Questions	35
The Survey	35
Make Changes Now	37
Get Away from the Office	37
Don't Get Away from the Office	38
What Form Is the Data In?	38
Where Will New Data Come From?	38
Can You Translate the Data to a New Form?	38
What Security Is Necessary?	39
Take Lots of Notes	39
The Analysis	39
Prepare the Final Specification	39
Write Down the Design	40
Get Approval from the Customer	40
The Decision Support Application Project	40
Background Study	40
The Survey	49
The Analysis	52
Modification Notes	58
Debugging the Process	59
Summary	59

3 Structured Design — 61

The Goal of Day 3	62
Creating the Data Flow Diagram	63
Data Flows	66
Processes	67
Data Stores	67
Objects	68
Partitioning Processes	68
When to Stop Partitioning	70

	The Mechanics of Creating a Data Flow Diagram	71
	Creating the Data Dictionary	71
	The Mechanics of Creating a Data Dictionary	73
	Creating the Process Specifications	75
	The Decision Support Application Project	76
	Creating the Data Flow Diagram	76
	Creating the Data Dictionary	85
	Creating the Process Specifications	94
	Modification Notes	99
	Debugging the Process	100
	Summary	101
4	**Database Design**	**103**
	The Goal of Day 4	104
	What Is a Database?	105
	Flat Versus Relational Databases	105
	Database Terminology	106
	Joining Tables	109
	Accessing Data: Queries	111
	The Rules of Database Design	113
	One Property per Field	114
	Attributes Have Consistent Values	114
	Each Table Contains a Single Independent Entity Class	115
	Each Entity Appears in a Database Only Once	115
	At Least One Identifier per Record	115
	Designing a Database	116
	Entity-Relation Diagrams	116
	Relational Table Diagram	116
	Access Database Applications	117
	Accessing a Database with Visual Basic	120
	Connecting to a Database	120
	Persistent Versus Virtual Database Objects	121
	Using Database Tables	122
	Accessing a Database with SQL	123
	The Decision Support Application Project	124
	Attaching the Tables	128
	Creating Rollup Tables	130
	Year-To-Date Total Sales	130
	Sales by Product Category	134
	Sales by Market Segment	135
	Sales by Sales Region	137
	Average Gross Margin	137
	Margins by Product Category	138
	Year-To-Date Orders	138
	Orders by Product Category	139
	Orders by Market Segment	139

Develop a Professional Visual Basic Application in 14 Days

Orders by Sales Region	140
Monthly Backlog	140
Backlog by Product Category	140
Backlog by Market Segment	141
Backlog by Sales Region	141
Average Order Cycle	142
Order Cycle by Market Segment	142
Order Cycle Frequency Distribution	143
Monthly Ending Inventory	144
Inventory by Product Category	148
Inventory Turnover by Product Category	148
Automatically Running the Monthly Queries	148
The Definitions Table	152
Modification Notes	152
Debugging the Process	153
Summary	153

5 Creating the Program Structure Chart — 155

The Goal of Day 5	156
The Program Structure Chart	156
Modules	158
Connections: Normal and Pathological	160
Couples	161
Evaluating the Structure	161
Coupling	161
Cohesion	162
Partitioning from the Data Flow Diagram	163
Transform Analysis	165
Transaction Analysis	167
The Conversion of Real Systems	168
The Decision Support Application Project	170
Modification Notes	180
Debugging the Process	180
Summary	181

6 Procedure Design — 183

The Goal of Day 6	184
Designing the Procedures	184
Partitioning the Structure Chart	185
Pseudocode or Flowcharts	189
Combining Procedures into Modules	193
Testing Algorithms	193
Test Programs	193
Testing Queries	194
Testing Procedures	194
The Decision Support Application Project	195
Specifying the *DrawChartAndGrid* Procedure	195

	Specifying the *Class* and *Type* Event Procedures	196
	Specifying the *ResizeChartAndGrid* Procedure	197
	Specifying the *DrawPieChart* Procedure	198
	Specifying the *ToggleGraphVisible* Procedure	198
	Specifying the *DisplayDDOptions* Procedure	199
	Specifying the *DisplayDDData* Procedure	199
	Specifying the *PrintVisibleChart* Procedure	200
	Specifying the *Save*, *Copy*, and *Exit* Procedures	201
	Specifying the Initialization Procedures	202
	Modification Notes	203
	Debugging the Process	203
	Summary	204

7 Forms Design 205

The Goal of Day 7	206
User Interface Design Rules	207
Stifle Your Creativity and Keep Things Simple	207
Obvious Operations	210
Maintain Internal Consistency	210
Use Familiar Design Elements	211
Designing Forms with Visual Basic	213
What Is the Goal of the Form?	213
What Commands Do You Need?	213
What Data Do You Need?	213
Walk Through the Design	213
Creating Special Controls	214
Creating a Toolbar	215
Creating a Toolbox	216
Creating Button Pictures	217
Creating Pop-Up Button Labels	218
Adding Hot Spots to Controls	220
The Decision Support Application Project	222
The Main MDI Parent Form	222
The Graphs Form	234
The Drill-Down Grid Form	240
The Drill-Down Options Form	242
Modification Notes	245
Debugging the Process	246
Summary	247

Part II Construction 249

Day 8 Coding the Application, Part 1 251

The Goal of Day 8	252
Use Good Programming Practice	252
Make Procedure Functions Obvious	253
Make Code Readable	253

xiii

	Make Code Maintainable	255
	The Decision Support Application Project	255
	Creating the Chart Definitions Table	256
	The Program Files	260
	The Program's Global Variables	262
	Chart Class and Type Button Procedures	271
	The *CreateNewGraph* Procedure	273
	Drawing the Chart and Grid	274
	Creating the SQL Statement	280
	Setting and Disabling the Type Buttons	282
	Managing the Grid	283
	Adding a Legend	292
	Selecting a Month for the Pie Chart	293
	Drawing the Pie Chart	295
	Hiding Everything	297
	Positioning the Graph and Grid	298
	Summary	300
9	**Coding the Application, Part 2**	**301**
	The Decision Support Application Project	302
	Exploding a Pie Wedge	302
	Getting the Drill-Down Data	307
	Creating the Drill-Down Tables	316
	Restoring the Pie Chart	320
	The Printing Procedures	320
	Copying and Saving a Chart	332
	Handling the Pop-Up Labels	332
	Selecting a Chart Using the Menus	334
	Viewing the Detail Grid Using the Menus	335
	Initialization	335
	Ending the Program	338
	The About Menu	339
	Using the Test Forms	339
	Resizing Things	341
	Modification Notes	341
	Debugging the Process	342
	Summary	342
10	**Adding Error Trapping to the Application**	**343**
	The Goal of Day 10	344
	Understanding Error Trapping	344
	Control Flow in an Error Situation	347
	Common Locations for Error Trapping	349
	The Decision Support Application Project	350
	The *DEBUGON* Global Constant	351
	Error Trapping in the Main Procedure	351
	Error Trapping in the *DrawMonthlyChartAndGrid* Procedure	353

		Error Trapping in the *SetGridCrossfoot* Procedure 354
		Error Trapping in the *Form_Load* Procedure 355
		Error Trapping in the *DisplayDDData* Procedure 356
		Modification Notes 358
		Debugging the Process 358
		Summary 359
	11	**Debugging and Testing** **361**
		The Goal of Day 11 362
		Using the Built-In Debugger 363
		Adding Debugging Code 364
		Testing the Procedures 366
		Testing 367
		Alpha Testing 368
		Beta Testing 368
		Nondisclosure Agreements 369
		Stress Written Reports 371
		Dr Watson 371
		Microsoft's MSD Program 371
		Time Bombs 371
		Release Candidate Testing 372
		The Decision Support Application Project 372
		A Beta Tester's Notebook 373
		Fixing Bugs in Your Own Programs 389
		Modification Notes 390
		Debugging the Process 390
		Summary 390

Part III Documentation **393**

Day	12	**Documenting the Application** **395**
		The Goal of Day 12 396
		Documentation Options 396
		Printed Documents 397
		Online Documents 397
		Online Help 398
		Designing a Help System 398
		Determine What Information Is Needed 399
		Break the Information into Modular Topics 399
		Determine the Connectivity Between Topics 399
		Design the Document's Structure 400
		Create the Document 400
		The Windows Help System 401
		Creating Help Topic Files 402
		Creating Help Project Files 406
		Compiling the Help File 407
		Linking the Help System with Visual Basic 407

The Decision Support Application Project	408
Designing the Help System	408
Converting the Design to a Topic File	413
Creating the Project File	416
Compiling the Help File	417
Linking the Help File to the Application	418
Modification Notes	421
Debugging the Process	421
Summary	422

Part IV Implementation — 423

Day 13 Manufacturing and Sales — 425

The Goal of Day 13	426
You Are the Customer	426
Someone Else Is the Customer	426
A Third Person Is the Customer	427
Preparing an Application for Manufacturing	427
Adding a Program Icon	427
Scanning for Viruses	428
Creating a Distribution Set	429
Manufacturing: You Do It	430
Subcontract It	431
Use a Publisher	432
Shareware	432
Disk Selection Considerations	433
Apple Macintosh Distributions	433
MS-DOS/Windows Distribution	433
CD-ROM	433
Distribution Options	434
Legal Issues	434
Disclaimers and Limits of Liability	435
License or Sale	435
Copyrights	436
Patents	438
Warranties	439
Registration	439
Distributing Code Owned by Others	439
The Decision Support Application Project	440
Adding an Icon to the Application	440
Scanning for Viruses	441
Creating a Setup Program	441
The Setup Package	441
Creating a Setup Package	442
Using the Setup Wizard	442
Modifying the Setup1 Program	446

		Adding the New SETUP1.EXE to the Setup	452
		Testing the Setup	452
	Modification Notes		452
	Debugging the Process		453
	Summary		453
14	**Support, Upgrades, and Phaseout**		**455**
	The Goal of Day 14		456
	Support		456
		No Support	458
		Written Support	458
		Fax Support	459
		Telephone Support	459
		Video Support	459
		Online Support	460
		On-Site Support	461
	Upgrades		462
		Maintenance Upgrades	463
		Features Upgrades	463
		Damage Control Upgrades	464
		Competitive Upgrades	464
	Phaseout		464
	The Decision Support Application Project		465
	Modification Notes		466
	Debugging the Process		466
	Summary and Conclusion		467

Appendixes

A	**Glossary**	**469**
B	**Using the CD-ROM**	**479**
	What's on the CD-ROM	480
	Installing the Final Version and the Database Files	481
	The Source Code Files	482
	The Sample Databases	482
	Using the Databases Directly from the CD-ROM	483

Index   **485**

Acknowledgments

There is no way this book could have been put together in the time available without the considerable help and constant encouragement from the folks at Sams. Especially Greg Croy, who stuck with me as due date after due date slipped quietly by, and actually let me take time off to sleep once in a while. I need to thank Roger Jennings for letting me borrow the beginnings of a database application to mold into the sample problem used to demonstrate all the steps and techniques in this book. If you look closely, Roger, you will see the skeleton of your application hidden in the example. I also want to thank Gayle Johnson, Brad Jones, David Freriks, and Grace Buechlein (Beek-line—I'll get it right eventually, Grace), who made everything come together.

I want to thank Julie for putting up with the long hours it takes to make a project like this work, and B.J., Skye, Sierra, and Shane for understanding Daddy's distracted looks and apparent lack of attention as he searched for better ways to present difficult concepts.

Thank you, all. I could not have done it without you.

William J. Orvis
Livermore, California

About the Author

William J. Orvis is an electronics engineer at the University of California's Lawrence Livermore National Laboratory. There he is actively developing large-scale numerical models of electron transport in semiconductor devices and quantum mechanical properties of materials and devices. He is an active member of the Computer Incident Advisory Capability (CIAC), the Department of Energy's emergency response team for computer-related incidents such as break-ins and viruses. Orvis has written several books, including *Do It Yourself Visual Basic* (Sams Publishing, 1992) and *Visual Basic for Applications by Example* (Que, 1994). His books are available worldwide, with translations in Japanese, Italian, and Greek. He has also written for *Computer in Physics* and *IEEE Circuits and Devices* magazines. He received his bachelor's and master's degrees in physics and astronomy at the University of Denver in Colorado.

Introduction

The purpose of *Develop a Professional Visual Basic Application in 14 Days* is to teach you the process of software development from conception and contract negotiation through analysis, design, coding, documentation, manufacturing, sales, support, and phaseout. With that lofty goal in mind, you must realize that this is not a two-year graduate course in software design and development, but a single book designed to be read in about two weeks. However, this book will expose you to all the bits and pieces of software development and lead you through the development process by showing you all the steps necessary to develop a fully-functional, commercial-quality application.

The application itself is a database front end designed to obtain data from a company database and turn it into understandable graphs and tables that can be used to support the decision making processes required by company management. The application is akin to what a software developer would create under contract for a private company. A large sample of the company database is included on the CD-ROM to use for testing the application.

The CD-ROM provided with this book contains all the files generated during the development process for this application. Appendix B lists the files contained on the CD and gives instructions for installing the application on your hard disk. As you work through this book, examine the relevant examples at the same time and try to work through the processes yourself. To make changes to any of the applications, you must copy the application files onto your hard disk. Otherwise, you can't save any of your changes. Appendix B contains instructions for copying the application to your hard disk and changing the database files so that they can be accessed.

Developing an Application

The development of commercial software is a multistep process, with tasks that range from business management to application engineering and programming. A software developer must understand all of these steps as well as the goals of application development to be effective in any of the individual steps. In other words, he must know how the whole process fits together so that he can make his piece or pieces fit into the development scheme. In a large software development company, different departments handle different parts of this process. In a small consulting firm, one person probably does it all.

The main goals of commercial software development are to satisfy the customer and to receive a reasonable compensation for providing that satisfaction. Each step in the process has its own special goals that build toward those main goals in a repeatable, structured way. This book will teach you those goals and the process involved in achieving them.

This book's title states that you can learn to develop an application in 14 days. If you manage to read a chapter a day, you will make it, but don't be discouraged if it takes a little longer. Also, while you might be able to learn the process in 14 days, don't expect to be able to develop commercial-quality applications in that amount of time. It takes a lot more work to perform these steps and to do a good job performing them than it takes to read and learn about them.

Database Developer's Guide

A special feature of this book is that the sample application is adapted from one in Roger Jennings's book *Database Developer's Guide with Visual Basic 3* (Sams Publishing, 1994). All the code necessary to create the sample application and the descriptions of how that code works appear in this book, but readers interested in more details about accessing and manipulating a database with Visual Basic should read Jennings's book.

The Layout of a Chapter

Each chapter (or day) has essentially the same structure: it describes one of the steps involved in developing an application. Each chapter starts with the day's goals and proceeds to explain how to achieve those goals. The second half of the chapter describes in detail one particular process that achieves those goals as part of the development of the decision support application.

Following the example is a section titled Modification Notes. It describes the differences you would expect to apply to the process if you were modifying an existing application instead of creating one from scratch. After Modification Notes is Debugging the Process, which describes possible problems to watch out for at this stage of the design and indicates some solutions.

The Parts of the Development Process

The development process is broken into four parts: Systems Analysis and Design, Construction, Documentation, and Implementation.

Systems Analysis and Design is the planning part where you collect information, analyze the system that the program will automate, and design the application. This stage includes working with the customer to determine his needs, negotiating the contract, and planning manpower and facilities needs. In addition, it includes structured analysis of the process being automated and structured design of the application.

Construction is where you take your carefully-crafted designs and turn them into code. Construction includes creating the visual interface by drawing the forms, and debugging and testing the code.

Documentation is where you tell the user how to install and use the application. Documentation can be either a written manual, an online manual, or a Windows online help file.

Implementation is where you prepare the application for manufacturing and consider sales, support, new versions, and eventual phaseout.

This book is laid out according to these four parts of the development process.

Part I: Systems Analysis and Design

Day 1: Whose Project Is This?

Define the customer and the application, plan the project, write the proposal, and negotiate the contract.

Day 2: Specifying the Application

Perform the background study, interview the client, and obtain information about the system you are to automate with a program. Use structured analysis methods to specify exactly what the application will do.

Day 3: Structured Design

Use structured design methods to create the data flow diagram, the data dictionary, and the process specifications.

Day 4: Database Design

Examine database design and access, write SQL statements to create queries for the database, and create rollup tables to speed database access.

Day 5: Creating the Program Structure Chart

Using the results of the structured analysis, create the program structure chart.

Day 6: Procedure Design

Using the program structure chart and the process descriptions, specify the individual procedures.

Day 7: Forms Design

Design the forms to use with the application.

Develop a Professional Visual Basic Application in 14 Days

Part II: Construction

Day 8: Coding the Application, Part 1

Code the main procedures in the application to access the database and create the charts and tables.

Day 9: Coding the Application, Part 2

Code the support procedures that create the drill-down tables and handle printing, saving, and ending the program.

Day 10: Adding Error Trapping to the Application

Add error trapping routines to capture errors instead of letting the program crash.

Day 11: Debugging and Testing

Perform alpha and beta testing of the application and debug any problems found.

Part III: Documentation

Day 12: Documenting the Application

Consider documentation options and create a context-sensitive Windows help file to work with the WinHelp application.

Part IV: Implementation

Day 13: Manufacturing and Sales

Prepare the application for manufacturing by adding an icon, scanning for viruses, and creating a set of installation disks. Consider different sales options.

Day 14: Support, Upgrades, and Phaseout

Consider different support options, upgrades, and what to do to eventually phase out an application.

This Book's Conventions

The visual design of this book includes several formatting conventions designed to make it easier to discern different elements of the book. Code elements such as variable names and functions appear in monospace type when they are included within a paragraph. For example, the function `Command1_Click()` is in monospace type. If the code contains one or more full lines, they are set off from the main text and formatted in monospace type like the following:

```
'Toggle the grid.
'
Sub ToggleGrid ()
   If fShowGrid Then
      fShowGrid = False
      frmMDIMain.mnuViewDetails.Checked = False
      frmMDIGraph.grdMonthly.Visible = False
   Else
      fShowGrid = True
      frmMDIMain.mnuViewDetails.Checked = True
      frmMDIGraph.grdMonthly.Visible = True
   End If
   'Resize the graph.
   Call ResizeChartAndGrid

End Sub
```

Code lines that are longer than can be printed on one line of this book are broken at a convenient place. The remaining part of the line is preceded by a code continuation character (➥). For example:

```
frmMDIGraph.imgColor(intCtr).Left = intMargin + (frmMDIGraph.ScaleWidth -
➥intMargin) * (intCtr - 1) / frmMDIGraph.chtMonthly.NumSets
```

When typing these lines into a program, you would type them as one long line without the continuation character.

Pseudocode also appears in monospace. **`Bold monospace`** is used in listings to indicate text to type or change. `Italic monospace` is used to indicate placeholders for variables in code. *Italic* indicates the definitions of new words, most of which are included in the Glossary (Appendix A).

Menu options are separated by a vertical bar. For example, File | Open means to access the File menu and choose Open.

Time to Go for It

Now that the preliminaries are out of the way, you can start learning the development process by beginning with Day 1.

Systems Analysis and Design

PART I

Part I of this book concerns designing the application. As in all forms of engineering—be it machine, electronic, or software—doing an adequate job of designing a project before actually trying to build it saves a tremendous amount of effort and grief. In addition, it simplifies the remaining steps in the development cycle by clarifying their tasks.

Whose Project Is This?

Whose Project Is This?

Whose project is this, anyway? That might seem like an obvious question, and usually it is, but you should know the answer before starting a new project. Especially if this project is for someone else, you need to do some formal planning and paperwork to smooth the development process and prevent problems of ownership and contract compliance in the future.

Today you will learn

- who the customer is
- how to define a project and its ultimate goals
- what to consider when proposing the project
- planning the project and allocating resources
- who owns the project

The Goal of Day 1

When you start a new programming project, you don't sit down at the computer and start cutting code. If you do so, you're either incredibly intelligent or you're headed for a lot of grief. Supposedly, Mozart could write a whole symphony in his head and wrote it down on paper only when he was done. I expect there are people who can do the same thing with computer programs, but the rest of us are not so capable. To do a good job, we must specify and design all but the simplest projects before actually trying to build them.

Before any project of any significant duration gets underway, certain questions must be answered to make it obvious to all involved what is to be done, who is to do it, and who owns the results. Misunderstandings about the answers to these questions often lead to major difficulties later in a project. These difficulties can even expand into litigation that serves no one but the lawyers.

As a software developer—or a businessperson, for that matter—you want to be a partner with your customer, not an adversary. Get everything out into the open at the beginning so that there will be no surprises later to give you grief. If there are any known or possible "showstoppers," let your customer know so that he can make a decision before committing a large amount of time and money to a project. The more your customer believes you're being straight with him, the more likely he is to send more projects and more responsibility your way.

Therefore, the goal of Day 1 is to learn to define and answer the following questions to everyone's satisfaction:

- Who is the customer?
- What is the project?
- What resources are necessary to complete the project?
- Who owns the results?

To answer these questions, the first day's tasks include defining the customer and the project, planning the project to determine the resources needed, and creating the proposal and contract. Defining the customer must be done first, because it strongly influences the rest of your planning.

Defining the project is necessary both for the customer and for you, the developer. The customer must understand what he is paying for, and you, the developer, must understand what you are being asked to build. When the project has been defined, you can plan the project to determine the resources needed so that reasonable estimates can be made as to the project's cost and duration. Once the project is specified and planned, a proposal should be written, detailing what is to be done. This proposal then becomes a specification of what will be done to guide the work and measure the final performance. The proposal also becomes the basis for any contract.

Define the Customer

The first step is to define the customer and your relationship with him. Defining the customer generally is straightforward, but not always. The customer usually is the person who wants the work done or who is paying the bills. Very often this is the same person, which makes it very easy to specify the customer. If not, it's still not too difficult to determine who the customer is. However, keep in mind that you might have more than one customer, especially if you're developing code that will be sold to someone else.

There are three situations you will find yourself in when trying to define your customer. Actually, there are many different situations, but they should be reducible to these three:

- ☐ You are the customer.
- ☐ Someone else is the customer.
- ☐ A third person is the customer.

You Are the Customer

If you're creating code for yourself, much of the rest of this chapter is unneeded. You may still want to specify the project, but you don't normally write a contract with yourself, because you know what you want. If you don't know what you want, maybe you should go through this chapter and write yourself a proposal just to get things straight as to what you want to do.

Write Yourself a Proposal
For any large programming project you're creating for yourself, it's a good idea to write a proposal so that you can better organize your thoughts as to what you want

Whose Project Is This?

to do. Writing things down has the effect of forcing you to formalize your ideas. This not only helps you confine your project to a reasonably sized task, but it also helps you spot any holes that would cause you problems later.

You Work for the Customer

A very common situation is to be working for the customer as an employee, contractor, or consultant. Your project is something that the customer or his people will use. This is a good situation, because you have direct contact with those who are going to use your work, and they are also the ones who are paying the bills. There should be no conflict between what the customer needs or wants and what your employer wants.

Someone Else Is the Customer

If you work for a commercial software house, you're writing code that will be sold to someone else. This can be a difficult situation, because your employer isn't the one who will use the software. Hopefully, their desires are the same. If not, you have a problem that must be resolved before you start the project.

Try to find out as much as you can about the customers. Find out what they want, what they have, and what they need. A company's marketing department should be able to define the customer's demographics for you and give you a good indication as to what they want and need and what they're willing to pay for. Marketing should also be able to tell you what kind of hardware your customer has. Keep these facts in mind as you design and plan a project, because any significant deviation could render a project unsellable.

If your employer has a different concept of what the customer wants, discuss that with him at the outset and see if you can come to an understanding. Maybe he has specific reasons for disregarding the marketing results. Maybe he will share them with you, and maybe he won't. Some employers are known for their ability to predict successful software titles even when they contradict marketing results. In the end, though, the Golden Rule applies, and you have to do it his way.

Note: I have been reminded by a thoughtful editor that there are several "Golden Rules" out there and that you might not be familiar with the one I'm referring to. In business situations, the Golden Rule is this: He who has the gold makes the rules. You can see that this is appropriate in this situation.

Define the Project

This step is very important, because here is where you first describe just what it is you're planning to do. There are three good reasons to do this. First, the customer must know that the project will fill his need. If it doesn't, both of you are just wasting time and money.

The second reason is that when the project is complete, the customer believes he got what he asked for. Although he might be disappointed with the result, he shouldn't think that it was your design and execution that led to that disappointment. This is important to you, because disappointment can lead to lawsuits over what you promised and what you delivered, and lawsuits serve no one but lawyers.

The third reason is that you, the developer, must have a clear vision of what you are going to create. The clearer you are about that creation, the easier it is to create. Even if you're creating a project for yourself, you will find that taking the time to write down a clear vision of what you want to do more than pays for itself in time saved later in the project.

The project itself may come from your own pipe dreams, or it may be given to you by an employer or customer. No matter where it comes from, write down a clear, concise description of what you want to do. Don't worry about the details at this point; you're only interested in the overall goals of the project. Later, in conjunction with the customer, you will determine the specifics.

For example, the sample problem being developed in this book is a decision support application for a fictional company. It takes no more than a paragraph or two to define the project.

The project is to create a decision support application for the Orco Company that displays data from the company's database in a series of graphs. Graphs will be created in the following five classes: Sales, Orders, Margins, Order Cycle, and Inventory. Initially, a high-level total or average is displayed for each class, giving a global view of the data.

The project then has *drill-down* capability so that the user can get at the details of the data presented in a graph by simply clicking on it. The first level of drill-down shows the initial data broken down according to product category, market segment, and market region. Each of these types of graphs can be further broken down into a graph of a single month and a table of the data needed to create the graph.

Textbook Tip: The terms *drill down* and *roll up* are used in business to describe a layering of company sales (or other) data. Starting with the records of individual sales, the data is rolled up by averaging or totaling by product or salesman. These totals are rolled up again into averages or totals by product type or sales region, and then again into global totals and averages that give the big

Whose Project Is This?

> picture of what's going on. A drill-down application displays the top-level totals or averages first. Clicking on the chart or a button displays the next level of detail. Clicking on the button again moves down yet another level, until you reach the bottom-most level. Hence, you *roll up* the data from the details to the high-level averages or totals and *drill down* from the high-level averages and totals to the more detailed data.

As you can see, this definition isn't terribly long or detailed, but it's sufficient for you to build a mental picture of what is to be done. You could also include a few sketches of the user interface. A project that has a lot of data manipulation should have that manipulation described in the project definition.

Planning

Once a project is defined, you begin planning for its creation. Planning is the task of determining and allocating the resources needed to support all the activities necessary to create the project. The duration to plan for depends on the particular project and your involvement with it. It may only extend to the delivery of the code in its final form, or it may include distribution, sales, and support activities.

> **Textbook Tip:** Some of the activities to plan for include the following:
>
> *Systems analysis:* Analysis of the current system and planned changes to that system. Preparation of the specification for the software to be developed.
>
> *Software design:* Application of structured design techniques to lay out the application, partition it into modules, and specify what the modules do.
>
> *Construction:* Writing the code and drawing the forms according to the results of the design, and testing the code.
>
> *Documentation:* Documenting the application with either a written manual, on-line help files, or both.
>
> *Implementation:* Manufacturing, distribution, sales support, and so on. Everything that comes after the code package is complete.

Initial planning activities are very rough because you don't yet have a complete project description. Without all the project details, you can't explicitly state how much time and personnel it will take to do the work, but you should be able to make reasonable estimates. The more explicit the project definition is, the better your planning estimates will be.

Planning for programming projects is concerned primarily with people and time. Availability of equipment usually isn't a consideration, unless access to special equipment is needed, such as time on a Cray supercomputer. Most other equipment can be purchased or leased as needed.

Planning needs to consider the customer's needs. While almost every customer wants everything done yesterday at the lowest price, work with him to determine what he really needs and what his primary considerations are. How soon does he need it, and how much does he want to pay? If he needs the program sooner, can it be reasonably broken into parts that can be worked on simultaneously? Will he accept beta-level code as an interim solution? If cost is the primary consideration, is the customer willing to wait for the code so that you can use it as fill-in work between your other projects? Is he willing to accept rough documentation?

Textbook Tip: Unreleased code usually is labeled *alpha-* or *beta-level*, or *release candidate*, depending on its state of completion.

Alpha-level code has most of its pieces in place, but many are not implemented yet, and there are still lots of bugs. Alpha-level code doesn't usually leave the lab.

Beta-level code has almost everything in place, and most of the bugs are fixed. Beta-level code is usually made available to a select group of users for testing—hence the term *beta testing*.

Release candidate code has everything in place and working. Testing is concerned with locating any remaining bugs.

Testing is covered in more detail on Day 11.

Maintain Your Professional Reputation

Your reputation as a developer is very important, so be careful. Delivering shoddy code or documentation to save the customer money might backfire, because you might become perceived as someone who creates shoddy products. It's better to delay parts of the project that the customer doesn't need right away and do a better job on those that he does need. You also could leave out some of the project's special features so that you can spend more time on the core features that he really needs. Special features can be added in a later version.

In some cases, you might need to put in a little "free" time to ensure that a delivered product is of good quality. A willingness to put in free time distinguishes the professional developer from a programming technician.

Whose Project Is This?

Sometimes the customer just wants too much for too little time and money. Tell him that—diplomatically, of course—and then explain to him why what he wants isn't in his best interest. Try to work out a project that fits what he wants and that you can do with the resources you have. If you can't work it out, you might have to refuse the project.

Refusing Projects

Take care when refusing or accepting projects. Refusing or accepting projects is another place where your reputation can be damaged. Although you don't want to accept a project you know you can't deliver, you also don't want to be perceived as someone who refuses all the hard projects. Try to work things out with the customer, or possibly accept the work but subcontract it to someone else. Occasionally, for a good customer, you might need to throw in a "freebie" just to maintain good relations.

You can plan a project by hand or by using one of several software tools. Software tools greatly speed the planning process if you do enough planning to warrant their purchase. Microsoft Project is one such tool. It allows you to work with a project plan, assign resources, and view changes to the final cost and date of completion.

Creating a Task List

When planning a project, start with a list of *tasks* to perform. Specify each task with a positive, definite statement such as "design the modules" or "code the input module." List the tasks in order. Put the tasks that must be done first at the top of the list, followed by those that must be done second, and so on.

In addition to the tasks, include some major milestones for the project in the task list. A *milestone* is an event (rather than a task) that signifies the completion of an important task or group of tasks. Initially, state only global tasks. Later, when you have more information, break the global tasks into subtasks.

As you write down the list of tasks, you will find that some tasks can't be performed until other tasks are complete. This connection between the completion of one set of tasks and the start of another is called a *link*. Keep track of links as you develop your task list, either by listing the numbers of the tasks that must be completed before another can start, or by drawing lines from the tasks that must be completed to the ones that can't start until the others are done.

A good way to create a task list is to create a table with the following columns:

Task number
Task name
Duration
Links
Start date
End date
Resources

The task number is simply a sequential numbering of the tasks that makes it easier to refer to the task in other statements. The task name is a descriptive name for the task. The links are a list of the task numbers of tasks that must be completed before this task can start. You use the rest of the columns later in this chapter as you estimate the project's cost and duration.

For example, Table 1.1 contains a partial task list for the sample project we will develop in this book.

Table 1.1. A partial task list for the decision support application.

Task Number	Task Name	Duration (Days)	Links (Task)	Resources
1	Define Customer	1		wjo
2	Define Project	1		wjo
3	Preliminary Plan	1		wjo
4	Proposal	5	1, 2, 3	wjo
5	Contract	2	4	wjo
6	Plan	1	4	bj
7	Contract Signed	0	5, 6	
8	Background Study	5	7	wjo
9	Survey	1	8	wjo
10	Analysis	5	9	wjo
11	Specification Complete	0	10	

In this table, task 4, the proposal, can't be started until tasks 1, 2, and 3 are completed. Thus, tasks 1, 2, and 3 are linked to the beginning of task 4. Tasks 7 and 11 are milestones, signified by the 0 in the Duration column.

Whose Project Is This?

Estimating Time

The hardest part of planning is estimating the duration of the tasks. The only good tool you have for estimating is experience. Be sure the tasks in the task list are of a low-enough level that you can extrapolate the time necessary to complete them from the time it took to perform similar tasks in a previous project. Estimate most tasks in full days (eight hours), and don't consider weekends or holidays.

For example, if it takes you an average of a day to code a module, and there are 20 modules in a new project, estimate 22 days to write the modules. Here I added 10 percent for unexpected problems, but this might be a low estimate. Ten percent extra is probably the lowest you should consider.

There are several rules of time estimation. One engineering rule says to multiply by 10 for experimental research. However, a factor of 10 is unreasonable for a professional developer creating an application similar to one he has created in the past. What you use depends on your experience and your success at estimating previous projects. If you find that you consistently underestimate the time necessary to complete a project by half, multiply your next estimate by a factor of 2.

Good Estimates Are Important

Good project estimates are important for professional developers. You should be able to estimate project durations and costs within about 10 percent of the actual time needed. If you consistently underestimate your projects by a large amount, either your customers will be dissatisfied, or you will have to absorb the cost of much of the overage. Although it's good to overestimate a little, if you consistently overestimate your projects by a lot, you'll have satisfied customers only if you can find any willing to pay your inflated costs. If you're not good at estimating project durations, you might want to consider contracting with someone who is.

The time estimates are added to the task list as shown in Table 1.1. In addition to these estimates, place any resources needed in the Resources column. In most cases, the resource is the person who will do the work, but it could be hardware availability if that is a constraint on how quickly the project is completed. If you have two resources applied to a project, the assumption is that each works half the time in the Duration column and that the task will be completed in half the time. Using more than two people divides the duration accordingly. Keep in mind that many tasks don't lend themselves to being split among several people.

Creating a Gantt Chart

The next step in creating the project plan is to create a *Gantt chart*. A Gantt chart is a timeline for the project, with each task drawn as a line or rectangular box on the chart in its respective location. The chart has days as its horizontal axis and tasks as the vertical. The first task is drawn as a line or rectangular box across the top of the chart. It starts at the project's starting date and extends for the number of days in the duration (excluding weekends and holidays). If the next task can run in parallel with the first task, it is placed immediately below the first task. If it must follow the first task, its starting date coincides with the ending date of the first task and proceeds to the right for its duration. All the other tasks are added in a similar manner.

You can draw a Gantt chart by hand, as shown in Figure 1.1, but have a large eraser handy, because you will be moving things around a lot as you rearrange your plan to use your resources more efficiently and reduce costs and time. Removable drafting tape, or anything you can cut to the length of a task and stick to and remove from the chart, is useful when you create a Gantt chart by hand.

Figure 1.1.
A Gantt chart for the data in Table 1.1.

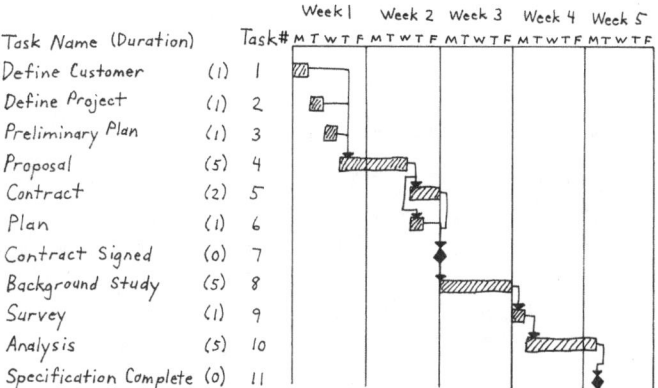

Alternatively, you could use a drawing program to draw a Gantt chart. You probably also could do it with a spreadsheet program with a little work. The easiest way is to use a project tool that creates a Gantt chart automatically. Figure 1.2 shows a Gantt chart created by Microsoft Project for the same data.

Something to watch for as you draw the Gantt chart is overcommitted resources. Having the same person work on two different tasks at the same time generally is impossible, so watch for the same person appearing on parallel tasks. If you find an overcommitted resource, you have two options: change the resource for one of the tasks or change the starting times to allow the two tasks to run in series. Changing the starting times to account for overcommitted resources is known as *resource leveling*.

Figure 1.2.
The Gantt chart created by Project.

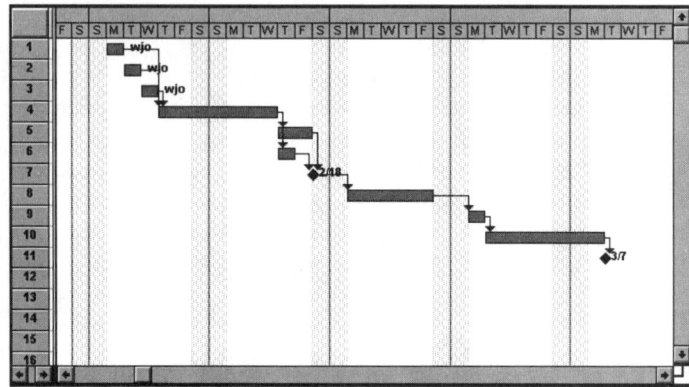

For example, tasks 1, 2, and 3 in Figures 1.1 and 1.2 could have the same starting date and could be done in parallel, but because they're performed by the same resource, their starting dates must be adjusted. Tasks 5 and 6, on the other hand, have different resources, so they can proceed in parallel. Tasks 7 and 11 are milestones. Once you complete the Gantt chart, you can fill in the starting and ending dates in the task table.

Cost Estimates

Once you have a good time estimate, cost estimates are relatively easy. You know what resources are working how many days from the time estimates and the Gantt chart, so simply multiplying by the cost of each resource gives the manpower costs of the projects. Add any procurements and overhead, and you have a reasonable cost estimate. Realize, though, that cost estimates are only as good as the time estimates they're based on.

The Proposal

The proposal is the first formal document relating to the project. It doesn't matter whether the project is your own creation or is handed to you by an employer or customer. A written proposal is necessary to specify, to everyone involved, what is to be done and who will do it. If a contract is involved, the proposal forms the basis for that contract.

A proposal is a series of definite statements that describe something to be done and who will do it. For example: "Developer will create a decision support program. The cost to the customer will be a rate of $55 per hour." A proposal is a fluid document that changes as different points are negotiated. Specify as much as possible in the proposal. Don't assume anything. Just because a customer did something last time, don't expect him to do it again this time. If the customer paid travel expenses last time and you want them paid this time, put it in the proposal. If you're planning to do something different from the way you usually do it, put it in the proposal. Try to put as much as possible in the proposal up front so that there will be no surprises later.

> **Don't Assume Anything**
>
> Fight the urge to assume you know how the customer would answer a question. Get on the phone and ask. Put it in the proposal. Write it down and negotiate it. Do whatever it takes to find out for sure, but don't assume anything.

This doesn't mean that a project can't be changed in the middle, but the proposal ensures that such changes will be recognized as additions to the original proposal. Hopefully, your customer won't make significant changes after you've started writing code, but be advised that it will happen and that you must be able to handle it. Since the changes aren't in the proposal, the customer must expect to pay for the changes, either in cash or in delays in a program's delivery dates.

This works the other way as well. You might run into unexpected delays or difficulties that you will have to absorb. You might even run into the ominous "brick wall" that all engineers (developers included) try to avoid. If you can't finish a project, your customer has to have some recourse, and that recourse is spelled out in the contract.

The Contract

First the disclaimer: The following sections deal with legal things, but I am *not* a lawyer, nor am I an expert in contract law. Therefore, don't treat the following sections as legal opinion. Instead, treat them as a list of things to consider when working with your lawyer to create a contract. You should also keep in mind that the law in this respect is different in various parts of the country and is subject to change day by day.

With any project, you should strongly consider having a written contract. For any agreement with a duration of more than a year or involving more than $500, a contract is required in order for the agreement to be enforceable. Two individuals can make a contract with a handshake, but a written contract should be used to ensure that both parties know what is to be done and what is expected of them. No one should be upset if you ask for a written contract to cover an agreement. If someone is upset about having a written contract, I suggest you refuse to continue without one.

Whose Project Is This?

You Are an Independent Developer

If you are your own customer, you can write a contract if you want to, but it's unlikely that you would sue yourself over a noncompliance issue. (If you do, drop me a line. I would like to know how it turns out.)

You Are Employed as a Developer

If the customer is your employer, the contract (your employment contract) is already in place and there isn't much you can do about it. That contract might be a written document that you signed, or it might be implicit in your employment. Your employee handbook or personnel department should be able to answer any questions you have.

You Are a Contractor or Consultant

If you are a contractor or consultant, a contract is usually required. Large organizations generally have their own standard contract. Depending on the organization, this contract can be fair or extremely biased toward the organization. There is nothing that says you must accept the standard contract without modification. However, there is nothing that says you should not accept it, either.

Things to Consider

You can write your own standard contract or buy a computer program such as It's Legal, which creates many types of legal documents. However, you should still have a lawyer look over the contract.

When someone presents you with a contract, take the time to read it and make sure you understand every clause. Then have your lawyer read it. You should have your lawyer look over any contract and explain what it means. Once you've executed a few contracts and understand all the parts, you might not need to have your lawyer look them over. However, you should inform him if you have a new contract so that he can warn you of any changes to the law that might apply.

Things might happen that make it impossible for you to complete a project, or to complete it on time as specified in the proposal. The customer can also go out of business and not be able to pay you. The contract should cover what happens in these situations. Your lawyer will explain the risks involved.

Protecting Your and Your Customer's Property

During the course of a project, you may have access to critical or confidential data about your customer's company. In addition, your customer will have access to prerelease versions as well as final versions of your software. Your software may contain methods for efficiently doing things that you want protected.

Long-term protection, including patents and copyrights, should be specified in the contract. Short-term protection is afforded with a nondisclosure agreement. Although simple ethical behavior insists that you not divulge any information given to you in confidence, a nondisclosure agreement spells out what is protected and gives you or your customer some recourse if confidential data is divulged.

You Are an Independent Developer

If you're an independent developer, you won't need a nondisclosure agreement for the same reason you won't need a contract. If you can't trust yourself to protect your own data, you need to find another line of business.

You Are Employed as a Developer

If you're employed as a developer, the nondisclosure between you and your employer is spelled out in your employment contract. Nondisclosure is implicit in any company, even without a written contract. You don't give outsiders sensitive internal information. The only things abrogating that implicit agreement are illegal operations by the company or operations that subject outsiders to unacceptable risk of harm without their knowledge.

If your company is working with another company on a project, and you sign a nondisclosure with that other company, and you aren't an officer of your company with the authority to bind your company with a contract, realize that the nondisclosure you sign binds only you, not your company. Because only you are bound, speaking with other people within your own company about the other company's information is a breach of the nondisclosure. Only certain individuals within a company have the authority to bind that company with a nondisclosure. When an authorized individual binds the company with a nondisclosure, all of the company's employees are likewise bound, and they may now discuss the information among themselves, unless the agreement specifically prohibits that.

Whose Project Is This?

You Are a Contractor or Consultant

If you're a contractor or consultant, you will use nondisclosure agreements often. A nondisclosure agreement usually is executed between you and your customer before you begin your preliminary discussions. This happens when you or your customer needs to show the other any sensitive data or confidential prototypes during the negotiation process. Nondisclosure is also used to hide a new project to protect it from being re-engineered by a competitor before it's ready for release.

Nondisclosure is also the first step in protecting intellectual property as a trade secret. Intellectual property refers to intangible properties that you develop with your intellect rather than with your hands. You might think that you created a computer program with your hands, but you only typed the code with your hands. The research, design, analysis, and data that lead to the development of a project are intellectual properties. Trade secret law requires that you actively protect the knowledge of the internal workings of your projects in order to be afforded any protection.

In addition protecting intellectual property, nondisclosure is used to control a customer's property that you have in your possession and governs its eventual return to the customer at the completion of the development cycle. It also covers any of your property that your customer has in his possession during project development. Nondisclosure usually doesn't cover any transfer of money, but it covers the protection of intellectual and tangible property that must temporarily change hands while a project is being proposed and during its execution.

Who Owns the Results?

Determining who owns the work tends to get a bit murky in the absence of a written contract. Even if you develop the work on your own time at home on your own computer, your employer might still own the result, or possibly the right to use the result royalty-free. If you're employed to develop certain applications, ownership is determined by your employment contract, which generally gives it to the employer. If you're a consultant, your consulting contract should define who owns what.

You Are an Independent Developer

If you're developing code for yourself, ownership is relatively straightforward. However, if at the same time you're employed to develop similar software, your new work might belong to your employer. Again, it depends on your employment contract.

If you've been working on a project before you accept employment, be sure to have that project and any additional work on that project excluded from your employment contract—unless, of course, you're being employed to bring that work into your employer's company.

You Are Employed as a Developer

If you're employed to develop software of a specific type, that work belongs to your employer. That particular stipulation generally is found in any employment contract. However, if you're working on your own time, and you develop some software that is in a totally different area from that which you're being employed to work on, it usually belongs to you.

You Are a Contractor or Consultant

As a contractor or consultant, you might work for many different companies, so your employment contract should stipulate who owns the resultant work. That stipulation should limit ownership to the specific derivative of the software that you're creating for a specific company.

For example, if you're creating a decision support program that reads a database and displays the data, you would want to hold title to the general framework of the program while passing ownership or a license to use the specific variation of the software to your employer. You could then use the same framework to create a similar application for another company with a different database.

The Decision Support Application Project

The decision support application, a fictional project for a fictional organization, is used throughout this book to demonstrate the principles described in each chapter. Any resemblance to a real company is purely coincidental.

Define the Customer

The Orco Company is a small manufacturer of computer cables. Although the company is small, it sells its cables throughout the world (though most of its sales are in the U.S. and Canada). Its motto is "Connecting the world together." Recently, Mr. Orco, the president and owner of the company, decided that he needed a formal decision support application to try to make some sense of the mass of raw data stored in the company's database. To create this program, he hired you, an independent consultant, to develop it for him.

In this case, the primary customer is obviously Mr. Orco, but he's not the only one who will use the decision support application. Mr. Orco is a very busy man, so his two vice presidents will spend the most time with you, determining what they want your application to do.

Whose Project Is This?

Define the Project

The project you have been selected to create is a decision support application. A decision support application takes raw data from a company's database and then averages, totals, and reformats it into numerous graphs and tables, as shown in Figure 1.3. A standard decision support application has six classes of data: sales, margin, orders, backlog, order cycle, and inventory. Each of these classes has one or more types of graphs, depending on the class. The highest-level type is the total or average of the data. Below that are several other types that break up the single total or average graph into its component parts. Charts are commonly broken down by product category, by market segment, and by sales region.

Figure 1.3.
The charts of a decision support program.

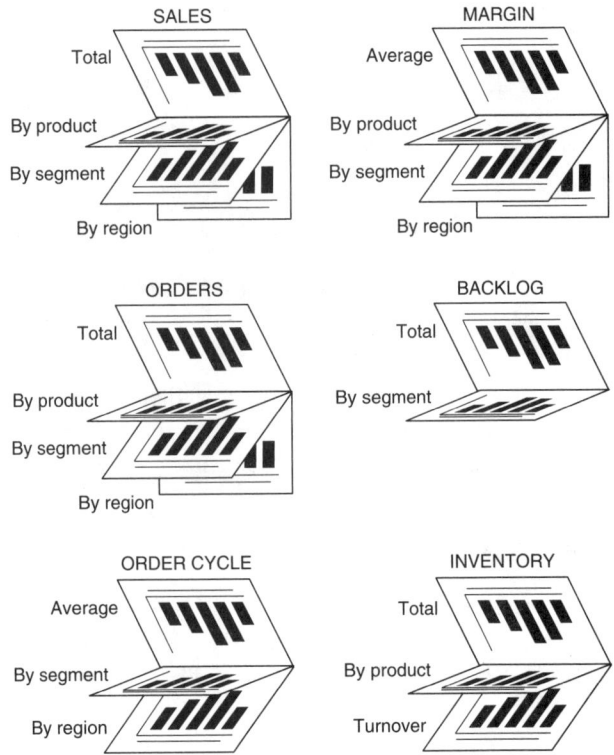

The graphs and tables are created to help the company's executives better understand their market and its changes. The application will have drill-down capabilities. In other words, a person can obtain the detailed data that was used to create a chart or table simply by clicking on the chart or table heading.

The company database is in Microsoft Access format and resides on a networked file server. This fact tremendously simplifies the project, because if the data were in a proprietary format, it would be difficult or impossible to extract. By being in one of the industry-standard formats such as Access, dBASE, xBase, Btrieve, or Paradox, the database can be read directly by the JET database engine included with Visual Basic. A copy of a couple of years' worth of data for that database will be available for you to experiment with while developing the application.

The company uses IBM-compatible computers running Windows 3.1 as its standard desktop workstation. This is also good, because it means that you can use Visual Basic for Windows to develop the application. If some other computer had been the company standard, you would have to choose a development environment that runs on that standard.

Planning

Initial planning is rough, because you don't have anywhere near the amount of data necessary to make a very accurate estimate. However, as more data becomes available, you can revise the plan and better estimate the completion date and total cost. The revised plan can also be used to track the project's progress. Table 1.2 contains the task list, and Figure 1.4 shows the Gantt chart. Figure 1.5 shows a Gantt chart created with a commercial planning package.

Table 1.2. The task list for the Orco decision support application development project.

Task Number	Task Name	Duration (Days)	Links (Task)	Resources
1	Define Customer	1		wjo
2	Define Project	1		wjo
3	Plan	1		wjo
4	Proposal	5	1, 2, 3	wjo
5	Contract	2	4	wjo
6	Contract Signed	0	5	
7	Background Study	5	6	wjo
8	Survey	1	7	wjo
9	Analysis	20	8	wjo
10	Specification Complete	0	9	
11	Database Design	2	10	wjo
12	Data Flow Diagram	5	10	wjo
13	Module Design	5	10	wjo

continues

Whose Project Is This?

Table 1.2. continued

Task Number	Task Name	Duration (Days)	Links (Task)	Resources
14	Structure Chart	1	10	wjo
15	Structured Design Complete	0	11, 12, 13, 14	
16	Design Forms	2	15	wjo
17	Mockup Forms	2	16	wjo
18	Preliminary Forms to Customer	0	17	
19	Code Modules	20	15	wjo
20	Alpha Application Complete	0	19, 18	
21	Debug and Test	10	20	wjo
22	Beta Application to Customer	0	21	
23	Debug and Test	10	22	wjo
24	Application Complete	0	23	
25	Add Help File	5	24	wjo
26	Create Installer	5	24	wjo
27	Complete Application to Customer	0	26, 25, 24	

In Table 1.2, the first three items—Define Customer, Define Project, and Plan—are each given a day. Actually, defining the project and the customer takes a morning, and planning takes a day or two, so allocating three days for these three activities should be more than adequate. Task 4 is the proposal, and five days are allocated for it. The proposal for a project as straightforward as this could probably be written in a day or two, but different points might need to be negotiated with the customer, requiring extra time.

Note: All of the items listed in the plan will be described in detail later.

Figure 1.4.
The Gantt chart for the decision support application project.

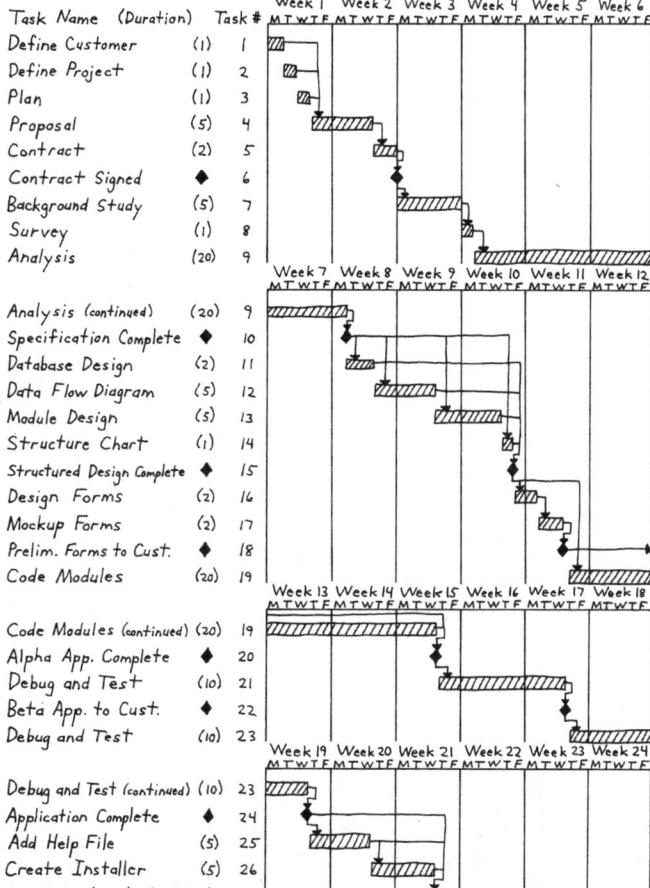

Figure 1.5.
The Gantt chart created with Microsoft Project. This chart has been overlapped on itself to make it fit on a single page.

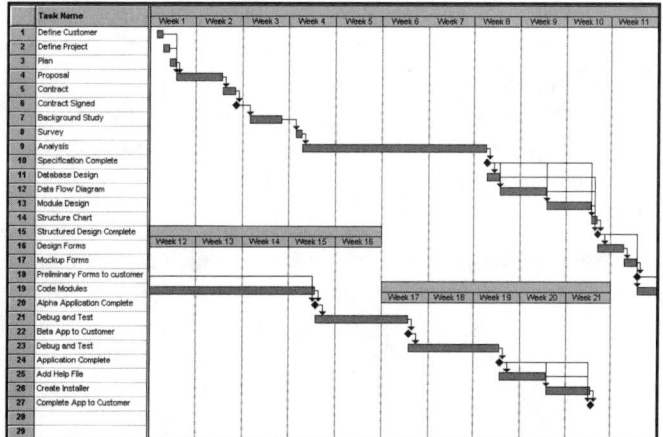

Whose Project Is This?

Task 5 is the contract. It should be straightforward if the proposal was well done, so two days are allocated to complete it. Task 6 is the first milestone: a signed contract. This is the go/no-go point for the whole project, making it a major milestone.

Tasks 7, 8, and 9 comprise the detailed analysis of the project, which includes a preliminary background study, a meeting with the customer to determine his needs and ask questions about his current system, and a final analysis phase (discussed on Day 2). The result of the analysis is the specification for the project, which is milestone task 10. The analysis task is where you find out all the details of the project and lay them out for the design phase. You need to do a good job here. Twenty-six days are allocated for these three tasks—six days to do the background study and survey, and four weeks to do the analysis.

Tasks 11 through 14 comprise the project's structured design (discussed on Days 3 through 6). In structured design, all the data structures are laid out, the data flow diagram is drawn, the data dictionary is created, and the modules are designed. The data flow diagram is a drawing showing how the data flows within the application. The data dictionary is a detailed specification of the contents of each of the data flows on the data flow diagram. Each data item and group of data items is named and detailed in the data dictionary. Module design is where you describe in detail exactly what each procedure and module does. The structure chart shows the application's code structure. The result is the structured design (task 15). A week each is allocated for the data flow diagram and the module design, and a day is allocated for the structure chart. Only two days are allocated for database design because the database is already in existence and only changes need to be determined. If you were creating a new database from scratch, you would allocate a lot more time here (five to 10 days) to do it right.

In addition to designing the code, you also need to draw and test the forms, which is done in tasks 16 and 17, with the resulting mockups taken to the customer in task 18 (discussed on Day 7). There are only about three forms in this application, so two days are allocated to design the forms and two days to prepare the mockups.

Task 19 is to code the modules and do preliminary testing (discussed on Days 8 through 10). Four weeks are allocated for this phase, which results in the alpha test version of the application (milestone task 20). After two weeks of debugging and testing (task 21), the beta test version of the application is ready to go to the customer for review and real-life testing at his facility (milestone task 22). Another two weeks of debugging and testing (task 23) results in the completed application (milestone task 24, discussed on Day 11). In general, you will spend about the same amount of time or more time debugging and testing as you do coding the actual modules.

With the application complete, you need to create a help file (task 25, discussed on Day 12) and an automated installer (task 26, discussed on Day 13). A week is allocated for each of these activities. The final result is the complete application package (milestone task 27).

Determining the cost estimate for the project is easy, because only one resource is doing all the work. Calculate the total number of hours worked (93 × 8) and multiply that times the contract's negotiated hourly cost. Don't include the first 10 days spent negotiating the contract, because that is an overhead cost to you. In a larger project, different hourly rates would apply. For example, contract programming runs about $55 per hour, while expert consulting and system design starts around $100 per hour and goes up from there. In this case, the Orco company is a good customer, so we offer an average hourly cost of $80 per hour for the whole project. Multiply the hours times the hourly cost to get the total cost estimate of $59,520. Because no special procurements have to be made, this amount comprises the total cost estimate.

Figure 1.6 shows the resource summary from Microsoft Project, from which you can get the total project duration and cost estimate. Precontract work is accounted for by creating a pseudo-resource that has no cost for those tasks.

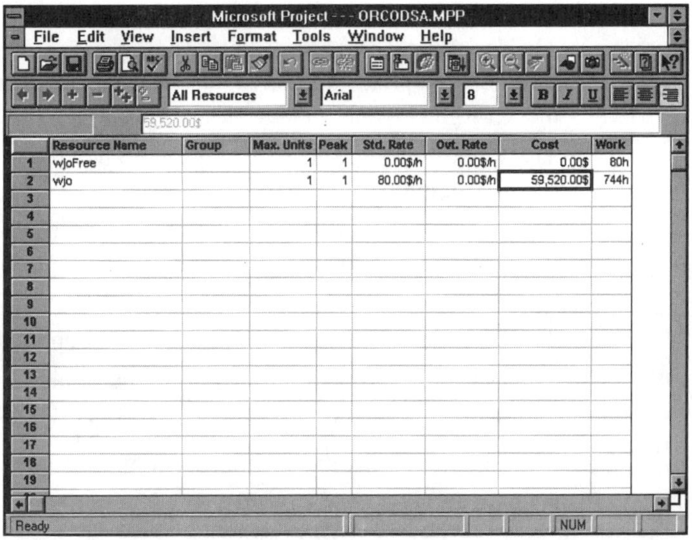

Figure 1.6.
The resource usage summary, showing the total estimated duration and cost of the project.

The Proposal

The proposal should now follow directly from the definitions of the project and the planning activities. The following is a possible proposal for the work being described here.

> *A PROPOSAL to Develop a Decision Support Application for Orco Co. by the Local Area Consultants Co. (LAC Co.)*
>
> The Orco Company, a local distributor of quality computer interconnection products, is in need of a decision support application to help them understand the sales data accumulating in the company database.

Whose Project Is This?

The LAC Co. will endeavor to create such an application for Orco Co. to run on Orco's management workstations.

Orco Co. will compensate LAC Co. for the cost of developing that software at the current going rate of $80 per hour for approximately 800 hours. Payment will be made monthly on invoices provided by LAC Co.

The company database is in Microsoft Access format and is available via a file server to the executive workstations.

The company will supply a couple of years' worth of data to use for development purposes by LAC Co.

The LAC Co. will develop a decision support application that runs under the Windows 3.1 operating system.

The decision support application will display the following classes of data: Sales, Margins, Orders, Backlog, Order Cycle, and Inventory.

The decision support application will display the following types of graphs for each class, as appropriate: monthly totals or averages, total by product category, total by market segment, and total by sales region.

The application will allow the user to drill down to more detailed data from the monthly graphs.

The Orco Co. executives will make themselves available at appropriate times to discuss their exact needs and to examine and comment on the designs and prototypes presented to them.

The LAC Co. will create a detailed design for approval by Orco Co.

The LAC Co. will create a rough prototype application for approval by Orco Co.

The method of implementation and the language used is entirely up to the LAC Co.

The completed software, including a copy of the source code, will become the property of Orco Co. to use with any or all company data on any or all company computers, but it may not be sold by the company except as part of a sale of the company as a whole. Orco Co. will not distribute the software outside of the company and will protect the source code as valuable company data.

The LAC Co. retains the right to use the source code to create similar applications for other concerns without payment to Orco Co.

The LAC Co. will install the software at the Orco Co. offices and conduct a technical training session for Orco computer support personnel.

The LAC Co. will provide two training sessions at the Orco Co. for users of the software.

The LAC Co. will supply free phone support for up to two years after delivery of the software.

The LAC Co. will protect any company data made available to them and will not divulge that data to any source outside of LAC Co. without Orco Co.'s permission.

Of course, everything in the proposal is negotiable between the customer and the developer and should be discussed until both parties are happy with the result. Once both parties are happy with the proposal, it is formally presented to the customer, and a contract is drawn up.

The Contract

At this point, a lawyer is needed to draw up the contract based on the proposal. While the proposal takes a page or two to detail the planned project, the contract takes a dozen. For example, the contract to write this book took 11 pages. It briefly covered what was to be done and then covered, in detail, what would happen if either I or the publisher did not fulfill the contract.

The Nondisclosure Agreement

A nondisclosure agreement could be initiated in this case so that the developer could have access to some of the company data to use when writing the proposal. However, since the developer can be given some old data to work with, a nondisclosure agreement probably isn't needed. Only if the customer believes that the data has intrinsic value to a competitor would nondisclosure be required.

Modification Notes

Modification Notes is a section common to all the chapters in this book. It examines how you would do things differently if you were modifying an existing application instead of creating a new one from scratch.

If the decision support application is an existing program at your customer's place of business, you could be hired to modify it. If you're lucky, you wrote the original program and still have all your notes and design drawings. If not, you must decipher someone else's code. If the code is modularized, commented, and well documented, it shouldn't take too long to figure it out. If it's undocumented and contains few comments, it might take a lot longer. If it has been heavily modified, it might be very difficult to understand, because the modifications might not follow good programming practices. In many cases, it's simpler and faster to just write a new application instead of trying to modify an old one.

Whose Project Is This?

Rewrite a Program When Necessary

It's not improper to rewrite a program that can't easily be modified. Rewriting a program is often simpler than trying to figure everything out. Plus, if you rewrite code, you can fix all the problems and inconsistencies in the original program and apply good programming practice to make it easier to change in the future.

When modifying an existing application, you still need to create a proposal and write a contract. You're probably still doing a significant amount of work for a significant amount of money and need to detail the work to be done and to bind you to the customer.

Debugging the Process

Debugging the Process, like Modification Notes, is a section common to all the chapters in this book. It examines special problems that you should watch out for while performing the tasks in the current chapter.

There's not much in the way of debugging in this chapter because you haven't yet written any code. Debugging at this point involves trying to find points you forgot to put in the proposal and the contract. As I stated earlier, you don't want to assume anything when doing the proposal and the contract. Leaving out a point is implicitly making an assumption about that point. Spelling out the project also can be overdone. If every minute detail of the project is included in the proposal, there's no need to do the project, because it's already done.

Summary

The main goal of today's work was to ensure that everyone involved with the project understands what is to be done and who is to do it. The aim of this initial work is to ensure that there are no surprises for anyone involved as the project proceeds. Most of this chapter was spent figuring out the project's background and logistics and completing the initial planning. In particular, you learned to specify the customer and the project and created a project plan. From the plan, you created a proposal and a contract. In addition, you considered who owns the results of your labors and the different types of relationships between a developer and a customer.

Now that much of the paperwork is out of the way, you will actually start designing the project in the next chapter. The design includes interviews with the customer, as well as how to create drawings and prototype applications.

The files generated during the planning process are in the directory \PLANNING on the included CD.

Specifying the Application

Specifying the Application

The next step in this project is to specify the application. Here is where you perform a detailed analysis of the application and specify exactly what it is you want to do. This step is the final preparation for actually designing the application.

Today you will learn

- to perform a background study
- to prepare for the survey
- to perform the survey
- to perform the analysis
- to create the project specification

The Goal of Day 2

The goal of Day 2 is to learn to create the application's *specification*—a detailed description of exactly what the application is supposed to do. The specification deals with the low-level details of how the application will work. Contrast this with the proposal, which deals with the high-level description of what the application should do. This is still not the lowest level of specification. That will be discussed in the next chapter, where you actually start designing the application.

The specification is created in three steps, as shown in Figure 2.1—the background study, the survey, and the analysis. The background study is a preparatory step before you interview the customer during the survey. Here you specify, to the best of your knowledge, how the application should look and work and get a good understanding of what can be done and what can't.

Figure 2.1.
The specification is created in three steps.

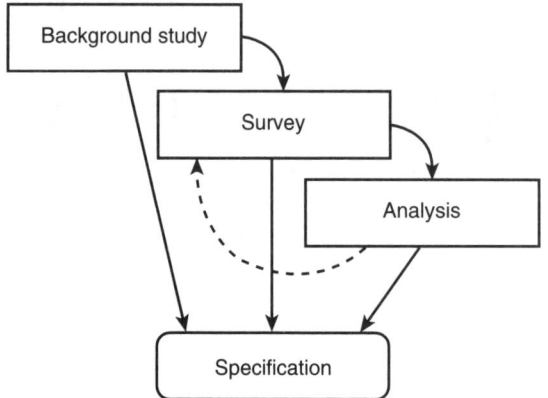

The second step is the survey. In the survey, you interview the customer to determine exactly what he wants done. Using all the designs and sketches you prepared during the background study, you and the customer decide exactly what is to be done and make decisions concerning any trade-offs that need to be made.

The final step is to take the results of the background study and the survey and combine them into the detailed specification. This final specification needs to be as clear and detailed as possible, because it guides all the design work to come.

Realize that, as shown in Figure 2.1, you may perform the last two steps more than once for a particular project. During the analysis, you invariably discover things you missed during the survey, which raises new questions. Many of these questions can be answered with a simple phone call, but the more complex ones require another interview with the customer. Large development projects require multiple surveys spaced over several weeks or months.

Background Study

In the background study, you prepare for the survey. If you go to an interview unprepared, you're not only likely to sound like a fool, you're apt to make promises you can't keep. In any business or engineering situation, preparing for an important meeting generally means the difference between your success or failure at that meeting. You need to know beforehand what you want to talk about and what questions you need answered. Trying to do this off the top of your head is likely to be a waste of your time and your customer's time.

Keep the Customer Informed of Your Needs

As you perform this background study, start sending questions to the customer so that he can be thinking about them before the survey. This allows the customer to better prepare for the interview. Not only does this make your interview go more smoothly, but it also makes your customer feel involved and knowledgeable, which he will appreciate.

Define the Scope of the Project

The scope of a project is a determination of the project's limits. These limits include not only software options, but also hardware and data options. Software options include the number and type of commands the program has, how large it can be, and how fast it must run. Hardware options include the range of machines that the program must work on and what options those machines have. The data scope includes where the data actually resides, how much space it takes

Specifying the Application

up, and how you access it. All of these limits help define how a project fits into the general scheme of things at the customer's location.

Using the proposal, develop a preliminary cut as to what the project should do and how it will look to the user. Consider how the project will work, what it needs in terms of data, and what it does with the data it gets.

Try to get a feel for how much work the application needs to do to the data it gets. Is this going to take a lot of time? Is the amount of time acceptable? If this is a number-crunching application, running it overnight might be acceptable. If this is a *real-time* application, it's not acceptable to have the customer sitting around waiting for results. If this is the case, you need to consider other ways to approach the problem. Is it possible to precalculate some or all of the data so that it doesn't have to be done while the customer is waiting at the screen? Can it run in batch mode and display all the results at the end?

Pay close attention to the scope of a project. Especially consider what happens when a project is out of scope. Do you scrap or revise the project or adjust the scope? You might not be able to adjust the scope. For example, if it concerns the amount of memory needed to run the program, you must back up and redesign the project to fit. On the other hand, if it will take longer to develop the application than you originally estimated, your customer might be willing to extend the due date, which is extending the scope.

List the Program's Features

Develop a list of program features. Features are those little extra commands and capabilities that make a program easier to use. Beware: features can cause a program to become unmanageable and make using the code extremely difficult. Some features are very easy to implement, while others might take weeks of coding. For example, cut, copy, and paste commands are often very simple to implement in Visual Basic, because most of the code is already done. On the other hand, implementing undo can be a real nightmare. As you select features for your application, keep in mind what the user has asked for, and try to limit yourself to that list. Keep a list of all your good ideas for new features so that you can suggest them to the customer at a later time. Next year, when the customer has had some experience with the application and wants a revision, you can suggest them, but let your customer pick the features he wants or suggest others based on his experience.

Keep the Feature Count Under Control

No doubt you can think of lots of useful and exciting features for your application that the customer will just love. However, unless they're necessary for the basic operation of the application, or the customer just can't live without them, leave

them out for now. A simple, straightforward program that does what it's supposed to and is easy to use will get you more appreciation than one that is loaded with all the latest features. Leave the feature wars to the big corporate developers who must add features so that their marketing departments can make feature list comparisons with the competition.

Usability Enhancements

Features tend to be one of two different types: bells and whistles or usability enhancements. Bells and whistles are features that make great marketing presentations and that are great for showing off to your friends but that you will never use in a real-world situation. Up until the last few years, most features were of this type. Usability enhancements are features that take into account how you use an application and try to streamline that process. As you might expect, usability enhancements are a lot more difficult to come up with, because you must examine your users' work habits over a long period of time to see how they do things and then figure out something that will make their tasks smoother or easier. A second problem with usability enhancements is that they generally aren't flashy and don't show off your genius for design. The user usually won't see them as features; he will just note that things seem easier to do.

For example, moving the controls that execute the most-used commands closer to where they are used is a great feature. This is done with toolbars and floating drop-down menus or key combinations you can press with the left hand while the right hand moves the mouse. Another good feature that few people notice is prioritized updates, in which the mouse or keyboard is allowed to make changes before the other parts of a program have completely updated the screen. For example, when you're scrolling the screen in a graphics application, it can be really frustrating to have to wait for the screen to be completely updated before you can scroll another screen. Prioritized updating allows the mouse to scroll the screen even though the system hasn't finished redrawing the current screen. Drop-down button labels are another good feature. I can never remember what all the icons stand for, and the labels keep me from having to look up the button in the manual. Given two similar applications, a user might not notice exactly what the usability enhancements are, but he will notice that the application that has them is easier to use.

Usability enhancements aren't usually included in the first version of an application, because you must study how the application is used to learn what would be useful. They are also often hard to implement compared to bells and whistles.

Sketch Some Possible Forms

As you get a feel for what the customer wants or needs to see on-screen, start sketching some prototype *forms*. Do this with pencil and paper or with Visual Basic, whichever is easier. If you

Specifying the Application

have several reasonable variations for a form design, draw them all and let the customer decide which one he wants. (The rules of good form design are covered on Day 7.) Write all this stuff down, then gather the sketches of the forms and take the best ones to the survey.

Stick-On Notes Simplify Form Design

When sketching forms on sheets of paper, draw the buttons and other controls on Post-it™ notes and stick them on a sheet of paper that represents the form. Because Post-it™ notes are removable, you can move the buttons around to see how they look in different places. When you take these paste-ups of the forms with you to the survey, you can move things around until they make the most sense to the customer. Although you could draw the forms using Visual Basic, it's usually easier to use paper drawings in a meeting. An alternative to Post-it™ notes is pieces of paper attached with drafting tape. (Drafting tape isn't as sticky as other tapes and can be removed without tearing the paper.)

Draw a High-Level Data Flow Diagram

Data flow diagrams are discussed in detail on Day 3. High-level data flow diagrams use a few simple functional blocks connected with directed lines (lines with points) to indicate where data comes from and where it goes. Use these diagrams to determine what data is needed and where you think it comes from. Verify all this with the customer during the survey.

A basic data flow diagram consists of data stores, data flows, and transforms. A data store is a temporary storage place for data, such as a file on disk. The user is considered to be a data store. A data store is represented on a data flow diagram as a straight line. A data flow is a line indicating the transfer of data between data stores and data transforms. A data flow is represented by a curved line with arrows that indicate the direction the data moves. A data transform is a module that changes its input data in some way. A data transform is represented by a circle. Figure 2.2 shows the high-level data flow diagram for an order entry system. The client number flows from the user to the Get Client Data transform, which locates and returns the client data. The client data is passed to the Create New Order transform, which combines it with the order data from the user and passes a new order to the company database for storage.

Figure 2.2.
A high-level data flow diagram.

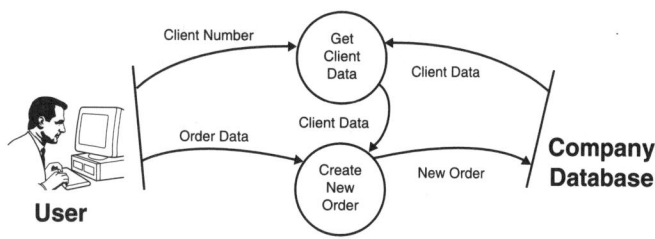

Write Down the Questions

As I mentioned in the last few sections, you should write down all the questions you have for the customer. List all the questions you come up with while doing this preparation. Add any other questions needed to define the scope of the project—How big? How fast? and so forth. Collect all the questions and drawings in preparation for the survey. Send the list of questions to the customer well before the survey so that he'll know what information you need and can prepare.

> **Bring in the Technical People Early**
>
> The survey likely will begin with a high-level manager but end with you working with his technical people. Try to bring the technical people in on the project as early as possible so that they can be thinking about the technical questions you need answered. If you know you're going to start with management and then move to the technical people, structure your questions so that the questions the manager must answer are handled first. If you do technical stuff first, the manager will pass you off to the technical people and then leave. Later, when you need answers he must provide, he won't be available.

The Survey

The survey is where you sit down with the customer and discuss the details of the project. Here is also where you and he decide all the external details. External details are not concerned with how the code works but with how the code interacts with its environment, including the customer. Where is the data? What form is the data in? How do you access the data? How should the data be transformed at each step in the application? Try to nail down the final form of how the user interface will look.

Specifying the Application

You are well prepared for this meeting, with a list of questions that your customer has had time to find the answers to, so structure the meeting to start answering the questions right away. You will undoubtedly come up with new questions during the discussions, but try to keep the survey on track. If it looks like a question can't be answered today, list it as an action item for a later meeting or phone call. If you don't keep the meeting structured and on track, it's unlikely that you will get through it all, and you'll have to come back again.

Leave the Customer Something to Do

Although it's useful to second-guess what the customer wants, and to have available variations of the designs he might select, don't make the decisions for him. If you've already decided how everything is going to be done, why have a meeting with him? If the customer thinks he has participated in the development of this project rather than just signing the checks, he will tend to be more committed to the project and to future revisions he might ask you to do.

Let the Customer Choose from a List

When getting the customer's advice on the layout of a form or some other design element, have him select from two or more options rather than having him design it on the spot. By giving him a selection, you can ensure that each of the choices uses good design practice (see Day 7 for more information on forms). If he designs a form for you at the last minute, he might create something that is difficult to use or wrong.

Don't Let the Customer Tell You How to Write the Code

Although the customer rightfully should tell you what he wants the application to do and what it should look like, try to stay away from implementation questions. Implementing the project is your area of expertise. The less direction you have on how to implement the solution, the more flexibility you have to do it in the most efficient way. You can change your mind and do it differently without having to review the change with the customer.

Make Changes Now

The survey is a good place to make changes in the project. If you want to make changes, you generally can't do so unilaterally—the customer must approve each change. If you happen to also be the customer, you probably will get along just fine with yourself and agree to any and all changes. In all other situations, you must be ready to show the customer that the changes make the project work better or cheaper, or that the original specifications are wrong or won't work.

Encourage the customer to make any changes he wants here as well. It's much easier to insert changes now, while the project is being planned, than later, when everything's done. It's also easier to plan for future changes here. The customer might have something he eventually wants inserted in the application. By planning for it now, you can make it easier to insert at a later date.

> **Textbook Tip:** In the life of a project, the later you make a change in the design, the greater the impact and cost to implement it.

Get Away from the Office

When dealing with company executives, it's a good idea to get them away from their office if possible, or at least away from their phones. To do a good job of designing this application, they need to focus on it with you, examining how it will be used and what it should look like. You can't do that if there are a lot of interruptions.

> **Have Them Show You**
>
> Many people treat software like Kleenex®. In other words, every soft tissue that you wipe your nose with is Kleenex®, even if it says Puffs® on the box. If the customer tells you his company uses a certain piece of software, ask to see it or at least to see the manual, ostensibly to see what version it is. Even knowledgeable people (some with PhDs) sometimes say they have a specific brand of software when in fact they have a totally different one. For example, one person called all spreadsheets 123, when the one he actually used was Excel.

Specifying the Application

Don't Get Away from the Office

When you deal with the technical people, you need to be in their offices so that you can see the terminals and networks you have to work with. Seeing what they have can often save you a lot of aggravation. If they say the company data is available on every terminal, have them show you exactly what steps they have to go through to get access to the data. What passwords or security measures are required? Is there any security? (If not, this could be your next project for the company.) Take notes, get screen dumps that you can take with you, or take pictures.

What Form Is the Data In?

Find out what form the data is in. Is it online, on tape or disk, or on printed pages? If the data is available in machine-readable form, you probably don't need to include a data input capability in your application. If the data is on paper, you need to figure out how to get it into the computer so you can use it. Find out if you are expected to do this or if the company will provide this service.

Where Will New Data Come From?

In the same vein as the last point, find out what form the new data is in. If it is on printed pages, is your application expected to be able to input it, or will it be input by someone else? Find out who will do it and when.

Can You Translate the Data to a New Form?

If you're dealing with a company database that's in a proprietary format, see if you can change it to a standard format. Visual Basic can handle most standard database formats, but not proprietary formats. If a proprietary database format is used, you will need to obtain an ODBC driver from the database developer in order to access it directly.

Textbook Tip: If the data is in Access, dBASE, xBase, Btrieve, or Paradox form, Visual Basic can read it directly. If the data is available on an SQL server, Visual Basic can communicate with that server and obtain data when it's needed.

If a driver isn't available, the existing database program might be able to export a copy of its data in some standard form such as a tabbed list. You could then create a new database to use with your application. This isn't an optimal solution, because the exported data would always be out of sync with the main company database.

Explore with the technical people what can be done to make the data available and to keep it up to date. Try to push them toward more-standard formats to increase their flexibility and to decrease their reliance on the company that owns the proprietary format.

What Security Is Necessary?

Are only certain people allowed to use the application and see the data? If so, you must build some sort of log-in procedure into the program to restrict the access and to *authenticate* the allowed users. A database program may also have security protections, and your application must be able authenticate itself to the database so that it can get the data. Find out what protections are in place and get access to the data if possible.

Take Lots of Notes

Take lots of notes during the survey. Whenever possible, get copies of screen dumps showing the available data and the steps necessary to make it available. Take pictures and get samples of the data. It doesn't have to be current data; it only has to be representative of what you would expect to find in the current year's data. Anything you can take back with you that will answer future questions is worthwhile. If possible, get an account on the customer's machine for testing purposes.

The Analysis

When you finish the survey, immediately go find a quiet place to write your notes, filling in any details you missed and adding your candid impressions. It's important that you do this as soon as the survey is over and not wait until the next day. You will forget too much if you wait overnight.

Prepare the Final Specification

The next step is to combine everything you've done so far and convert it into a specification for the application. Include descriptions and drawings of the user interface and the command structure. Describe the form of the data, how it's accessed, and what is to be done with the data. Specify what processing should be done and what the results should be.

At this point, you probably have discovered a dozen questions that you forgot to ask during the survey. If they're relatively simple questions, call the customer and get the answers. If you have a lot of questions, or if the answers will be more detailed than can be given over the phone, schedule another meeting. It may take many meetings before you finally are ready to start designing the project.

Day 2 — Specifying the Application

> **Don't Assume Anything**
>
> Call the customer and get answers from him for any questions. Don't guess at the answers for important questions about the design, or you might find yourself with a lot of code that can't do anything because you assumed something instead of asking. Even if it seems obvious that the company should have something or should do something in a specific way, don't count on it until you ask or see it for yourself. For example, two networked machines in the same room might not be on the same network and might not have access to the same data. If you assume they do, you will end up with an application that runs but has no data and no way to get it.

Write Down the Design

When you think the specification is complete and accurate, write it all down and review it. Make sure it fits the original specification, and that any changes in the original specification are clearly marked, along with their cost, if any. If everything looks good, it's time to take the specification to the customer.

Get Approval from the Customer

Take a copy of the specification to the customer for approval. If he approves it, it's time to start designing the application. If he doesn't, continue working on the specification until he's happy. If you're concerned about any changes from the original contract, have the customer sign an approval agreeing to the preliminary designs and any changes in the contract requirements. How much legal work you insert here is determined by how much you can afford to lose versus how much trouble it is to do the legal work. Hopefully, the consequences of changes are covered in the contract, including such things as additional costs and delays.

The Decision Support Application Project

Here you are again with the decision support application. The proposal was accepted and the contract is signed. It's time to do the detailed program specification.

Background Study

You know the customer wants a decision support application to display different charts and graphs of his company's data. The first thing you do is dig out your copy of Roger Jennings's

Database Developer's Guide with Visual Basic 3 (Sams Publishing, 1994) and review database design and access methods. Next, you scope the project to lay out the different charts the customer wants so that you can determine what data is needed.

Define the Scope of the Project

In the contract and proposal, the customer indicated that he wanted six categories of data displayed: sales, margin, orders, backlog, order cycle, and inventory. For each graph, he wants to be able to see the numbers as well as the graph. For each class of graph, the initial graph type should be a monthly total or average, depending on the class.

The second type of graph is to split the initial data into its component parts according to some criteria such as product type or market segment. The sum of these parts always equals the totals on the initial graph. The criteria to consider are by product category, by market segment, and by sales region. These types don't make sense for all classes of graph, however, especially inventory, where turnover is important.

For each of the graph types, you want to be able to see the actual numbers as well as the graph, and you want to be able to select a single month's worth of data and display it as a pie chart. From that pie chart, you want to be able to select a single segment and see a table of the data that makes up that segment. An application of this type is known as a drill-down application because you drill down through each chart to more and more detailed data. Table 2.1 is a list of the graphs needed to do this.

Table 2.1. The graph classes and types for the decision support application.

Sales	Margin	Orders	Backlog	Order Cycle	Inventory
Year-to-date total sales	Average gross margin	Year-to-date orders	Monthly backlog	Average order cycle	Monthly ending inventory
Sales by product category	Margins by product category	Orders by product category	Backlog by product category	Order cycle by market segment	Inventory by product category
Sales by market segment		Orders by market segment	Backlog by market segment	Order cycle frequency distribution	Inventory turnover by product category
Sales by sales region		Orders by sales region	Backlog by sales region		

Specifying the Application

Figure 2.3 shows the breakdown of the total sales graph class. The top-level graph is a plot of the total sales since the beginning of the year. The totals are calculated and plotted monthly. From the graph of total sales, you can branch to a table of the actual data that is plotted in the graph. You can break down this top-level graph into one of three graph types: by category, by segment, and by region. Each of these second-level graphs can also branch to a table of values for that graph.

Figure 2.3.
The breakdown of the graph type for the total sales graph class. The full drill-down is shown only for the product category type.

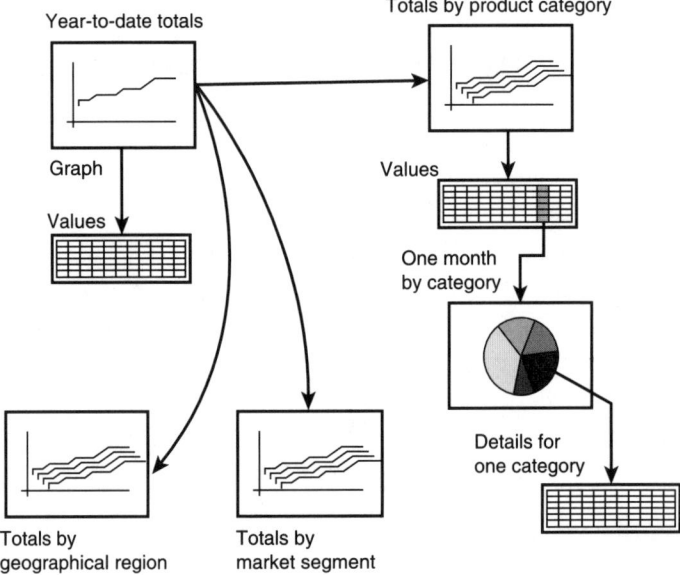

From each second-level graph or table, you can select a month and see that month's data displayed in a pie chart. Selecting a segment of the pie chart displays the option to display the data that was used to create the pie chart ordered by salesperson or by individual product.

To create all these plots, you need a lot of data, twisted and turned in different ways by a *database engine*. All of these charts need rollup data rather than the raw data from the database. *Rollup data* is the stored sums and averages of the raw data from the database. Table 2.2 lists the data needed for each chart type.

Table 2.2. The data needed for the charts.

Chart	Data
Year-to-date total sales	For each month, the sum of the sales from the beginning of the year to that month.

Chart	Data
Sales by product category	For each month and product category, the sum of the sales from the beginning of the year to that month.
Sales by market segment	For each month and market segment, the sum of the sales from the beginning of the year to that month.
Sales by sales region	For each month and sales region, the sum of the sales from the beginning of the year to that month.
Average gross margin	The sum of difference between the sales price and the cost of each sale in a month divided by the number of items sold in a month.
Margins by product category	For each product category, the sum of the difference between the sales price and the cost of each sale in a month divided by the number of items sold in a month.
Year-to-date orders	For each month, the sum of the number of orders placed from the beginning of the year to the current month.
Orders by product category	For each month and product category, the sum of the orders from the beginning of the year to that month.
Orders by market segment	For each month and market segment, the sum of the orders from the beginning of the year to that month.
Orders by sales region	For each month and sales region, the sum of the orders from the beginning of the year to that month.
Monthly backlog	For each month, the number of orders that are unfilled at the end of the month.
Backlog by product category	For each month and product category, the number of orders that are unfilled at the end of the month.

continues

Specifying the Application

Table 2.2. continued

Chart	Data
Backlog by market segment	For each month and market segment, the number of orders that are unfilled at the end of the month.
Backlog by sales region	For each month and sales region, the number of orders that are unfilled at the end of the month.
Average order cycle	For all orders shipped in a month, the average time between the order date and the shipping date.
Order cycle by market segment	For all orders in each market segment that are shipped in a month, the average time between the order date and the shipping date.
Order cycle frequency distribution	A frequency plot of the number of orders shipped versus the order cycle time.
Monthly ending inventory	The inventory at the end of each month.
Inventory by product category	For each product category, the inventory at the end of each month.
Inventory turnover by product category	For each product category and month, the sum of the number of products sold divided by total number of products in a product category in the inventory.

Sketch Some Possible Forms

The user interface for this application is relatively simple, consisting only of charts or tables. Figures 2.4 through 2.9 show some sketches of what the user interface could look like. The main differences are in the placement and size of the button bar and the tables of numbers. The first possibility is a full-screen graph (Figure 2.4), followed by a full-screen table when you click on the graph (Figure 2.5). A more compact interface lets the graph and table share the form (Figure 2.6). Start with a full-screen graph, and when the user double-clicks on the graph, shrink the graph and insert the table at the bottom.

The addition of a button bar simplifies the application's use by making all the chart classes and types available at the push of a button (see Figure 2.7). Add drop-down labels to identify the buttons whenever the mouse pointer is over a button. Without the button bar, graph classes and types must be selected from a menu.

Figure 2.4.
The graph displayed full-screen.

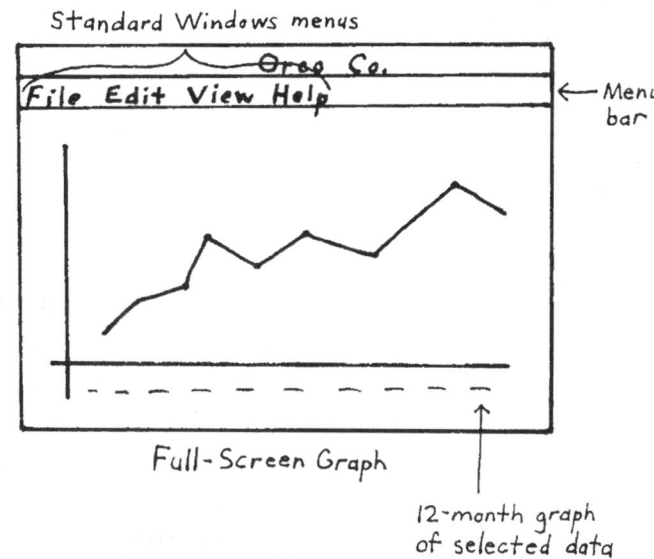

Figure 2.5.
The full-screen table replaces the graph.

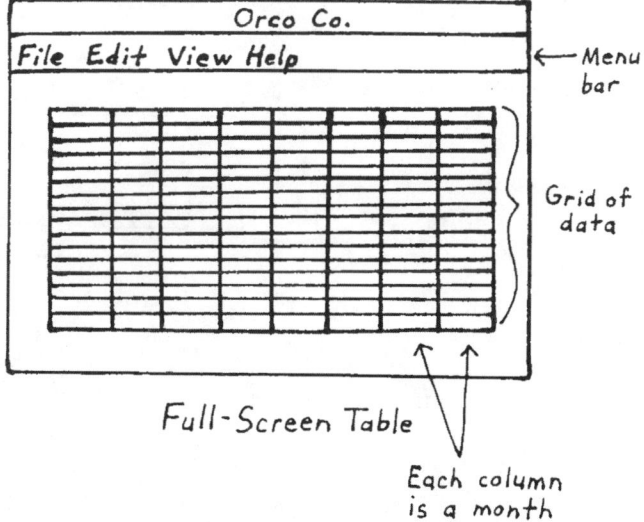

DAY 2
Specifying the Application

Figure 2.6.
The graph and the table could share the form.

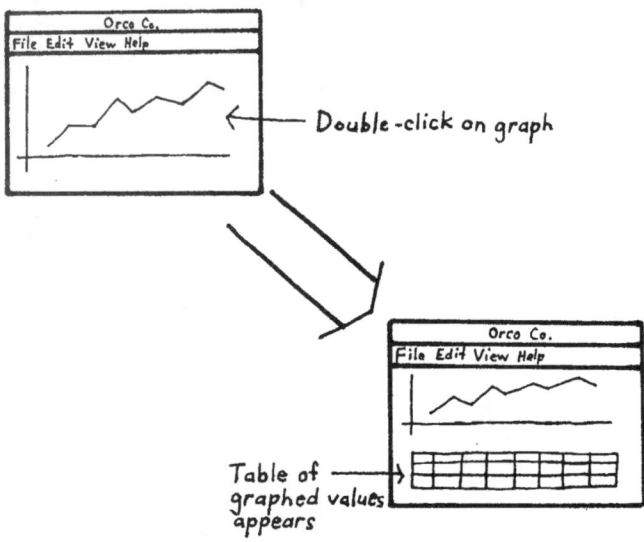

Figure 2.7.
A button bar eases the selection of graph class and type.

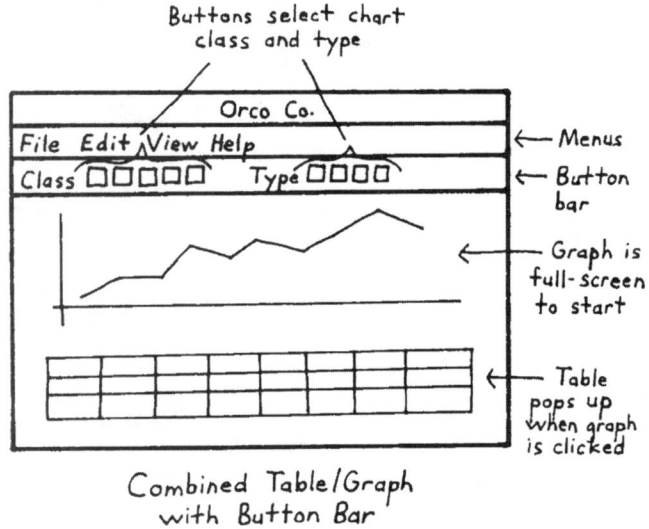

Selecting a month on a graph or table causes a pie chart to be displayed, showing the data for that month only (see Figure 2.8). Clicking on one of the pie segments causes the segment to move out, and a table appears, showing the detail data for that segment (see Figure 2.9). There are many other possible variations, but these charts show most of the features.

Figure 2.8.
A pie chart displays a single month.

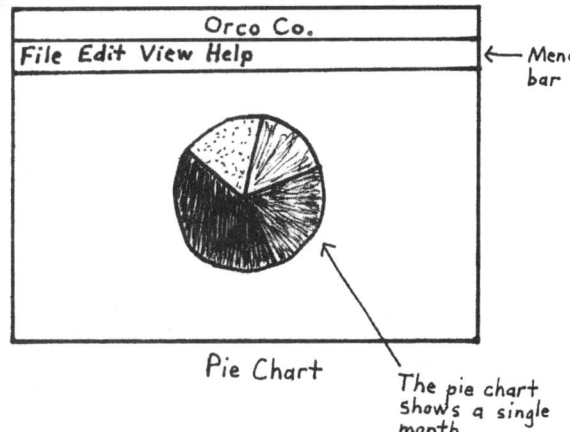

Figure 2.9.
Expanding a pie segment to see the detail data.

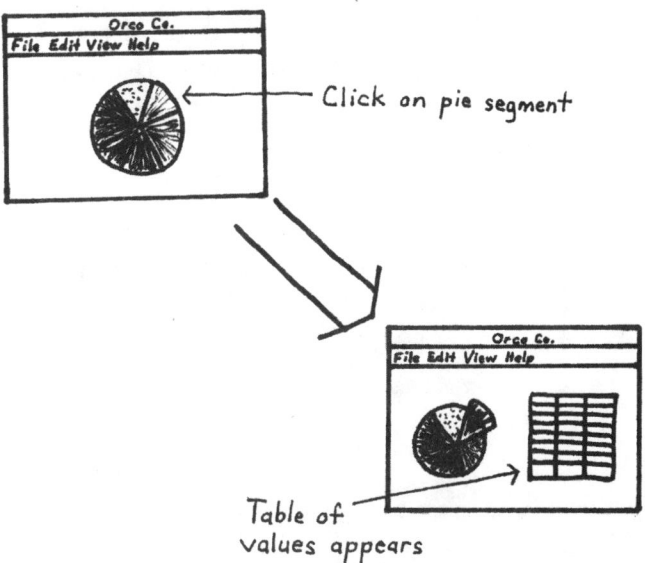

Draw a High-Level Data Flow Diagram

The high-level data flow diagram (see Figure 2.10) shows the data paths between the user and the database. The user sends the graph class and type to the create criteria module, which creates an SQL statement to select the appropriate data. The SQL statement is passed to the database engine, which selects the requested data from the database. The selected data is passed to the Make Graph and Make Table processes, which put the data in visual form for the user.

Specifying the Application

Figure 2.10.
The high-level data flow diagram.

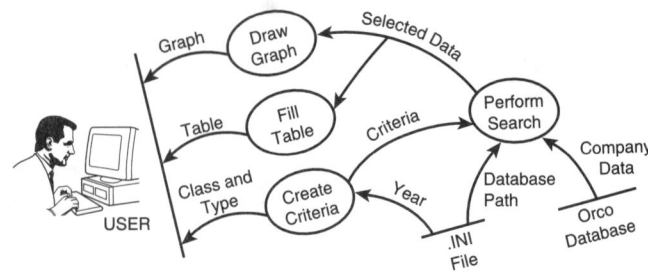

Data flows from the Orco database to the database search engine. The search engine selects the data according to the criteria set by the user and sends that data to the graphing transform and the table-filling transform. From there, the data is passed to the user. Other flows on the diagram take data to the database search engine.

Write Down Your Questions

You have lots of questions for Mr. Orco and his people, so write them down in preparation for the meeting.

1. Would you like to make any changes to the original proposal?
2. How do you want the data displayed? One chart or table per form, or both on a single form?
3. Do you want a button bar? Tradeoff: It reduces the space available for the chart but makes access easier.
4. Is the data listed in Table 2.1 the correct data to display?
5. Can we get a sample of the data?
6. Where is the data stored?
7. Does each person who will use this application have access to the data?
8. How do the users get access to the data?
9. Is access to the database restricted? How do we get access?
10. Who is responsible for adding new data?
11. What is the layout and joining of the tables in the database? What data is in each of the tables?

Note that in questions 2 and 3 the customer is given a choice between two alternatives instead of being asked how he wants the interface to look. Here you are ensuring that good design practices are used in the user interface by controlling the customer's choices. The customer still gets to choose what he wants from a set of well designed options. If he doesn't like the options, get a feeling for what he wants and ask to come back with some new designs rather than trying to design on the spot. In this way, you ensure that he selects a well designed interface.

The Survey

You go to your first interview with Mr. Orco and his people, secure in the knowledge that you are well prepared and have some good designs to show them. You have brushed up on database design, and you have all your sketches and tables with you. But you can't get him out of the office. He can't stand to be away from his phone during business hours. With a little persuasion, you get him to move to a conference room so that you can spread out your designs for him to see (which also gets him away from the phone.)

Do You Have Any Changes?

Pulling out your list of questions, you start with the first one and see if he has any changes he wants to put in the original proposal. This can be a little scary, because he might want to change things so significantly that none of what you have to show him is of any use anymore. But grit your teeth and do it now. There's no sense in going through all your stuff if you're just going to have to change it all. The worst that can happen is that you'll have to postpone your meeting while you incorporate his changes into the design. Hopefully, he won't change much and you can get on with your presentation.

How Do You Want the Data Displayed?

Next, spread your user interface designs in front of Mr. Orco and ask him to pick the layout for the visual display of the data. Note again that you don't ask him what he wants the display to look like; you give him some good options and ask him to select one. Designing a good user interface takes careful thought and study. It's not something you can sketch on-the-fly and obtain a good result. Unlike a sketch artist drawing some ideas for an ad campaign, where how it looks is the only important factor, a user interface must be designed to work as well as look good, and that takes time.

Mr. Orco selects Figure 2.7, a combination of a graph and table on one form with a button bar. He comments that it looks a lot like the interfaces for Word and Excel, with which he is very familiar.

Is the Data in Table 2.1 the Correct Data to Plot?

You lucked out. The data is exactly what he wants.

Can We Get a Sample of the Data?

Ask Mr. Orco if you can have a sample of the data. If you clear this one up front with the boss, you shouldn't have any problem getting sample data from the technical people. If you wait and ask the technical people, they will most likely have to clear it with him anyway. He says yes and directs his technical people to copy a couple of years of data for you and put it on a CD-ROM that you can take with you.

Specifying the Application

　This data is in the \ORCO directory on the included CD.

Where Is the Data Stored and How Do We Access It?

Here, Mr. Orco turns to his technical people. He knows the data is on the computer somewhere, but they have all the details. Note that at this point, we have finished with all the questions that require executive decisions. The following questions are all for the technical people to answer, so shake his hand, thank him for helping you, and let him escape if he wants to.

You and the technical people can now get down to business and talk tech stuff while you determine the details of where the data is and how to access it. In this case, the data is on a shared volume on a file server on an in-house network. There is no read protection, because only company people have physical access to the data. The data is available to all networked computers in the company. Orco is a very progressive company that sees its employees as partners in its enterprise. They are encouraged to see what is selling and where, and to make suggestions on how to do things better. Some companies hide their data, allowing people to see only sales data that is directly related to their jobs. If this were the case, you would have to build in a log-in procedure to get access information from the users before getting data from the database. You would also have to restrict the chart type and data according to who the user is. Happily, that is not required here.

The data is write-protected, and only authorized individuals in the sales, accounting, and shipping and receiving departments can make changes to the database. These departments make changes whenever they make a transaction, such as taking or shipping an order. As mentioned earlier, the database is in Access format so that most Microsoft mainline applications can access it.

What Is the Layout of the Database?

When you ask about the layout of the database and what information it contains, the technical people open it with Access and display the tables and connectivity. You quickly grab the screen dump of the table, as shown in Figure 2.11. Figure 2.12 shows the same layout using Microsoft Query, which is included with Microsoft Excel. Using Visual Basic, you can load and run the sample program VisData. Although it doesn't have a nice graphic display of the tables and connectivity, you can open each table and see the names and contents of the fields. Any of these applications can be used to examine the layout of the database. Access is by far the easiest, because it's a major application dedicated to database design and manipulation. Query isn't far behind.

Figure 2.11.
The layout of the Orco database in Microsoft Access.

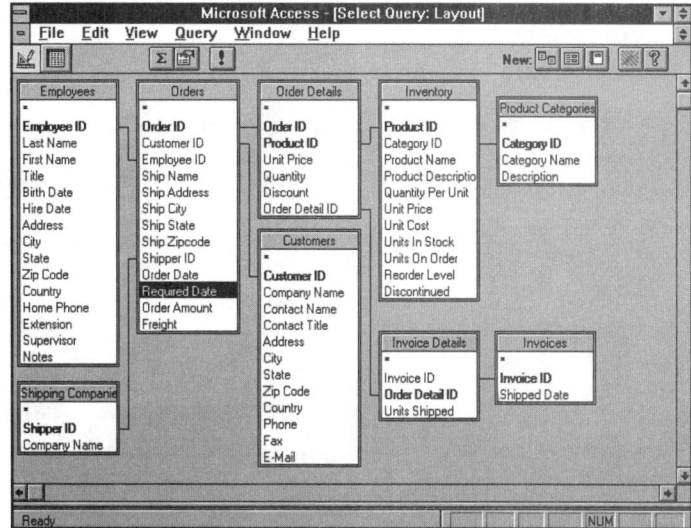

Figure 2.12.
The layout of the Orco database in Microsoft Query.

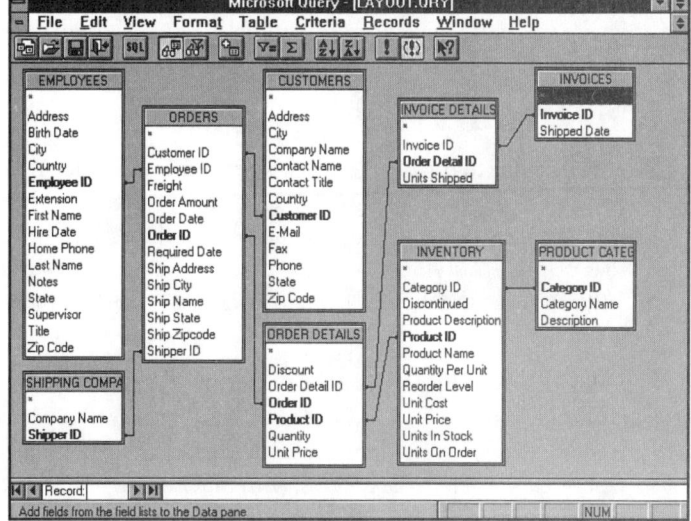

These figures show each table as a boxed list of the field names in each table. Bold field names are *indexed fields*, and lines connect the *links* between the tables. Each table can be thought of as a spreadsheet of data, with the field names across the top and the values of the fields in each row. For example, Figure 2.13 shows the product categories table displayed with VisData. The table has nine records—one for each product category. Each record is made up of three fields that describe the category: Category ID, Category, and Description. The Category ID field,

Specifying the Application

which is indexed, is used to link the Product Categories table with the Inventory table. You will look more closely at databases during the design phase of this project. Roger Jennings's book *Database Developer's Guide with Visual Basic 3* also is a good reference for database design and analysis.

Figure 2.13.
The product categories table of the Orco database displayed with the VisData sample program.

This completes the survey for this project. You collect phone numbers from all the technical people and thank them for their help. You have taken notes all this time, but they're a bit sketchy because you had to participate and write at the same time. So you head for a local coffee shop, where you write up your notes, filling in any missing details.

The Analysis

Now it's time to try to put everything together into a detailed specification for the project. How you do this depends largely on your personal preferences, but the more closely the specification matches the structured analysis you'll do in the design part of this project, the easier it is to do that design. Most importantly, you must understand what it means to write the specification. When writing the specification, use drawings, tables, structured English—whatever it takes to get the point across.

Drawings and tables are good for listing the forms and data elements a program will have, and structured English is a good way to describe what each processing step will do. *Structured English* is a cross between English and code. In other words, clipped English sentences are used to describe each step in the process, with indentation to indicate the block structuring of the data. For example, the following is structured English for calculating overtime in a payroll program:

```
If the employee is paid hourly then
    If the hours are greater than 40 then
        Pay equals the HourlyRate times 40
            plus (hours - 40) times the HourlyRate
            times 1.5
    else
        Pay equals the HourlyRate times hours
end
```

As you can see, the English isn't very good, but the statements make it obvious what is to be done. When it's time to write code, the structure is already very close to what the code will look like. For example, the code specified by the preceding structured English could be the following:

```
If employee.hourly = True Then
    If employee.hours > 40 Then
        thePay = Rate * 40 + (employee.hours - 40) * Rate * 1.5
    Else
        thePay = Rate * employee.hours
    End If
End If
```

Prepare the Final Specification

Here is what your final specification might look like:

SPECIFICATION

A Decision Support Program for Orco Co.

The decision support application for the Orco Co. is specified as follows:

The application obtains data from the company database with the structure shown in exhibit 1 (Figure 2.14).

The data obtained from the database is used to compute the values shown in exhibit 2 (Table 2.3).

The values are initially plotted on a graph like that shown in exhibit 3 (Figure 2.15).

Double-clicking on the chart displays a table along the bottom of the form that contains the data used to create the graph, as shown in exhibit 4 (Figure 2.16). Double-clicking on the chart again removes the table.

Clicking on one of the month labels at the bottom of the graph or clicking on one of the columns of the table displays the selected month's data in a pie chart.

Specifying the Application

Clicking on one of the pie chart's wedges displays a menu for you to select the ordering of the data used to calculate the value displayed by the wedge. The options are by product, by customer, and by salesman. Selecting one and clicking on OK displays a table of the data used to calculate the value for the wedge of the pie ordered according to the selected option.

The button bar will have five chart class buttons: Sales, Margins, Orders, Backlog, and Inventory.

The button bar will have four chart type buttons: Total, By Product Category, By Market Segment, and By Sales Region. Not all buttons will be available for all chart classes. Some of the button names will change according to the chart class.

Pop-up labels will appear when the cursor is over any button.

Menu items will follow the Windows standard.

A Print command will be on the File menu to print the chart.

A Save command will be on the File menu to save a chart as a picture document.

A Copy command will be on the Edit menu to copy the chart to the clipboard.

A View menu will include the same chart selections as the buttons on the button bar.

A Help menu will access the on-line help system. The project will have regular help and context-sensitive help.

The company database is an Access database available with read-only access to any company computer.

Company computers are all MS-DOS machines with Windows 3.1 and 14-inch VGA monitors.

Figure 2.14.
Exhibit 1: the layout of the company database.

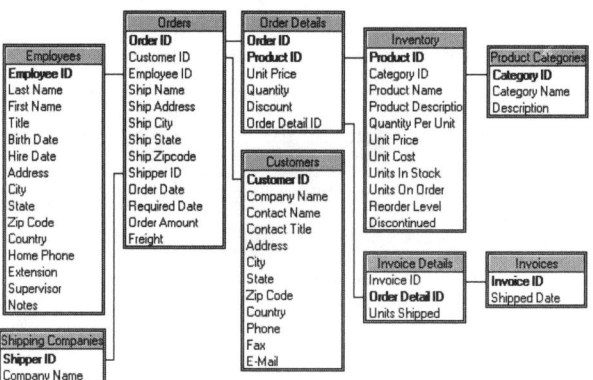

Table 2.3. Exhibit 2: the data values to calculate for the charts.

Chart	Data
Year-to-date total sales	For each month in the current year Sum the sales from the beginning of the year to the month.

Sales by product category	For each month in the current year
	    For each product category
	        Sum the sales.

Sales by market segment	For each month in the current year
	    For each market segment
	        Sum the sales.

Sales by sales region	For each month in the current year
	    For each sales region
	        Sum the sales.

Average gross margin	For each month in the current year
	    For each sale in the month
	        Sum the difference between the sales price and the cost
	    Divide the sum by the number of sales in the month.

Margins by product category	For each month in the current year
	    For each product category
	        Sum the difference between the sales price and cost
	    Divide the sum by the number of items sold in the month.

Year-to-date orders	For each month in the current year Sum the number of orders placed from the beginning of the year to the month.

Orders by product category	For each month in the current year
	    For each product category
	        Sum of the number of orders from the beginning of the year to the month.

continues

Specifying the Application

Table 2.3. continued

Chart	Data

Orders by market segment	For each month in the current year
	  For each market segment
	    Sum the number of orders from the beginning of the year to the month.

Orders by sales region	For each month in the current year
	  For each sales region
	    Sum the number of orders from the beginning of the year to the month.

Monthly backlog	For each month in the current year The number of orders that are unfilled at the end of the month.

Backlog by product category	For each month in the current year
	  For each product category
	    The number of orders that are unfilled at the end of the month.

Backlog by market segment	For each month in the current year
	  For each market segment
	    The number of orders that are unfilled at the end of the month.

Backlog by sales region	For each month in the current year
	  For each sales region
	    The number of orders that are unfilled at the end of the month.

Average order cycle	For each month in the current year
	  For all orders shipped in a month
	    The sum of the difference between the shipping date and the order date
	  Divide the sum by the number of orders shipped in a month.

Chart	Data

Order cycle by market segment	For each month in the current year
	  For each market segment
	    For all orders shipped in a month
	      The sum of the difference between the shipping date and the order date
	      Divide the sum by the number of orders shipped in a month.

Order cycle frequency distribution	For each order cycle time Tally the number of shipped orders in the current year with that cycle time.
Monthly ending inventory	For each month in the current year The value of the inventory at the end of the month.

Inventory by product category	For each month in the current year
	  For each product category
	    The value of the inventory at the end of each month.

Inventory turnover by product category	For each month in the current year
	  For each product category
	    The sum of the number of products sold divided by the total number of products in that product category in the inventory.

Figure 2.15.
Exhibit 3: the prototype form with only a chart showing.

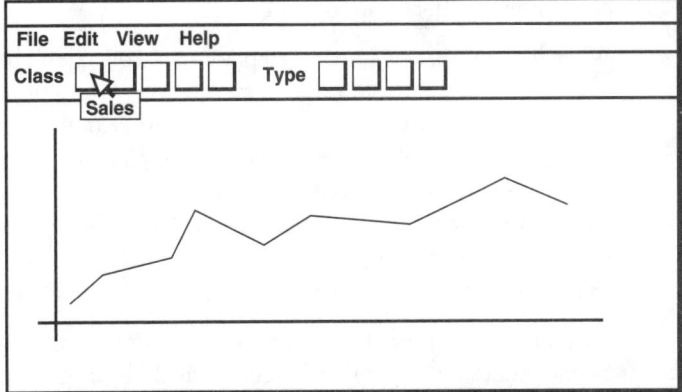

Specifying the Application

Figure 2.16.
Exhibit 4: the prototype form with a chart and a table showing.

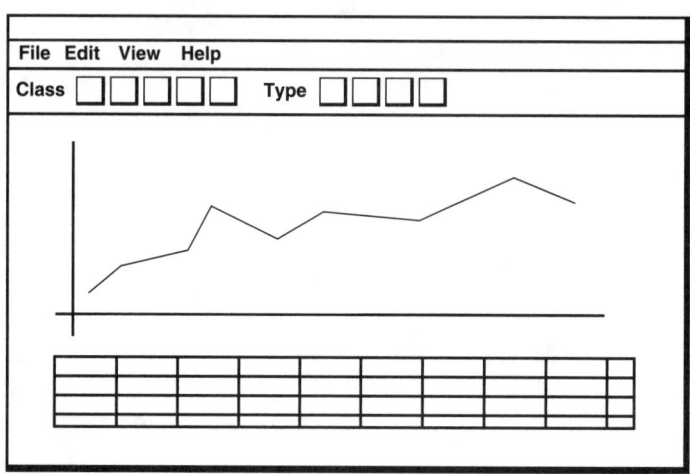

Get Approval from the Customer

Take the completed specification and show it to the customer to ensure that what you remember and wrote down during the survey is what your customer remembered. Sketch the forms to give him a good idea of what they will look like. It doesn't hurt to check with the customer one last time before starting to design the application.

Modification Notes

The survey and analysis steps take on an added dimension if the new application will replace an existing system. The existing system might be manual, automated, or a combination of both. A *manual system* is one in which the system's functions are performed by people, and an *automated system* performs the functions with a machine. Before you analyze the new system, you must analyze the existing system to see how it works. Then you analyze the new system and define how it differs from the old one.

When designing a new system to replace an old one, don't be afraid to completely throw out the old system and start over. Often it's easier to rewrite a system than to figure out how to revise it. This is especially true if the change isn't visible to the customer. Keep in mind, though, that if the change *is* visible to the customer, changing to a completely new system might bother a customer who is comfortable with an old one. You might need to defend the changes and show the customer how the new system accomplishes the same tasks with less work on his part. Or you might need to compromise a little and include some parts of the old system, even if they aren't really necessary from a functional point of view.

For example, if in the old system the user fills out a form and stores that form in his desk, he might be uncomfortable with a new system in which the form is filled out automatically by the system

and stored on disk. The pile of filled-out forms is the user's measure of accomplishment, and it's also his assurance that the data won't get lost. Without the forms, there is nothing tangible he can hold in his hand to show what he has done. One option in this case would be to print a copy of the form for him to store in his desk. Once the user is comfortable with the new system, he can drop this option. Alternatively, you might print some statistics at the end of each day for him, perhaps comparing his work yesterday with his work today or with his previous best day. What you eventually do is totally dependent on your current situation. You must work with your customer and negotiate something that makes him happy.

Debugging the Process

Debugging at this point is still directed at eliminating any misconceptions between what the customer wants and what you're trying to create for him. It is implemented by continually going back to him with drawings and designs to ensure that both you and he understand exactly what it is you're going to do.

Additionally, you should be looking at the data and the processing of that data to ensure that the needed data is available and that the processing is possible. There is a hole in the data requirements for the Orco project. Do you see it? Look at the layout of the database and the calculations needed to create the charts. The problem doesn't jump out at you here, but it will become very evident when you do the database design on Day 4.

Summary

As on Day 1, the main goal of today's work was to ensure that your vision of the project and your customer's vision are the same. You accomplish this by doing a survey and analysis to get the information necessary to create the specification for a project. The project specification is the input to the design phase of the project, so it must be much more detailed than the proposal. The specification indicates exactly what is to be done, what calculations are done to what data, how the data is displayed, and where the data comes from. To do the specification, you first do a background study to check the project's feasibility and prepare for the survey. In the survey, you work with the customer to answer all the questions necessary to specify the project. In the analysis phase, you take the data from the background study and the survey and create the specification.

The sample Orco database is in the \ORCO directory on the included CD.

Structured Design

Structured Design

The discipline of structured design has its roots in the '60s and early '70s, when people realized that a rational approach to the design of computer programs was necessary to understand the operation of a computer program before trying to code it. Most of the methodology of structured design came together in the middle '70s in the work of Ed Yourdon of Yourdon, Inc. This understanding not only makes it easier to write code, but it also makes the code provable and maintainable. Provable code is code whose operation can be proven to do what it is supposed to do. Maintainable code is code whose operation is sufficiently easy to understand that anyone can make corrections and changes.

Today you will learn

- how to create data flow diagrams
- how to create the data dictionary
- how to create the process definitions

The Goal of Day 3

Today you will learn the basics of structured design. *Structured design* is the methodology used by software engineers to analyze a data processing system that will be converted fully or partially into a computer program. With structured design, you create an abstract model of the system and use that model to comprehend the system and organize it into an efficient, understandable design. With structured design, you break down a system into its most basic parts and then recombine those parts in a way that can be efficiently converted to a computer program.

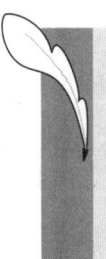

Note: The study of structured design occupies whole books, so I can't begin to show that level of detail in a single chapter. However, the basics of structured design are straightforward and will be covered here. To learn more about structured design, locate some good books on the subject. A dated but very readable book on the subject is Tom DeMarco's *Structured Analysis and System Specification* (Yourdon: New York, 1978). Although I doubt that this book is still in print, it's probably available at the library.

Structured design starts with a data flow diagram. *Data flow diagrams* are a method of analyzing how data flows and is processed within an application. Once you draw a data flow diagram, it's usually relatively obvious how to break an application into procedures and modules. At the same time you create the data flow diagram, you also create the data dictionary and the process descriptions.

Textbook Tip: A *data flow diagram* is a drawing that models the data flow paths, data transformations, and data storage locations in a data processing system.

A *data dictionary* is a document in which you specify the name and type of data contained in each of the data flows on a data flow diagram.

A *process description* is a document in which you specify what happens to the data in each of the processes on a data flow diagram.

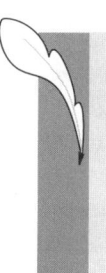

Note: The use of the term *process* here is different than that used in reference to executing programs. When a computer operating system starts a program running, that program and its associated execution environment are known as a process. This term is most meaningful in time-shared systems where multiple processes can be in memory and executing at the same time. Here, a process is an abstract data process on the data flow diagram and is more akin to a function or procedure.

Creating the Data Flow Diagram

Starting with the system specification in the last chapter, you begin to trace the paths of data within the application. Starting at data stores, data flows out to processes, where one or more data elements are combined in some way to produce one or more new data flows. These new data flows pass out of the process to other processes or other data stores. As mentioned in the last chapter, a data store is a temporary storage place for data, such as a data file. The user is also considered a data store.

Textbook Tip: A *data flow* is a flow of data from one element in a data flow diagram to another. Data is only transported in a data flow; it is not processed or changed in any way. Symbol: curved arrow.

A *process* or *data transform* is where data is used. Data may be used in a complex calculation, or it may simply be rearranged into a new data flow. Symbol: circle.

A *data store* is a place where multiple data elements are stored for a certain length of time. A data store is usually a disk file, but it can be a document, a file in memory, or a block of data in memory. The distinction between a data flow

Day 3

Structured Design

> and a data store is that a data flow passes any data placed at the input to the process at the output, and a data store holds the data until it is extracted by a data flow and passed to a process. Symbol: slanted line.
>
> A *data source* or *sink* is an object where data appears or disappears. This differs from a data store in that data passed to a data sink can't be retrieved by a data flow. A random-number generator is a data source. Data sources and sinks are also used to describe sources and sinks of information that are outside of the system being modeled. Symbol: rectangle.

By diagramming data flows rather than just describing them with text, you create a visual representation of an application's function. The diagramming method used is known as *directed graphs,* or *digraphs.* Long before there were computers, digraphs were developed as a way of modeling the operation of complex systems. Digraphs have flows, storage, and transformation of things—data, fluids, machinery, and so forth. Digraphs are also purely abstract representations of systems, because they don't contain the restrictions presented by the physical contrivance that contains the system. By fully abstracting a system, you divorce yourself from the hardware to see what is really being done in a system. Digraphs are still used to analyze complex systems, including computer programs.

A data flow diagram is made up of data flows, signified by directed lines (lines with arrows); data stores, signified by slanted straight lines; and processes, signified by circles. For example, the process of structured design could be described using the data flow diagram shown in Figure 3.1. In this figure, the program specification and hardware description come into the process from the Specification document (data store).

The program specification reaches the Codify Specification process, where it is converted into four data flows: the Data Flow Diagram, the Process Specification, the Data Dictionary, and the Database Structure. The Design Modules process receives the Data Flow Diagram, the Data Dictionary, the Process Specification, and Program Structure data flows. It then creates the functional specifications for the modules as the Module Description data flow.

The Create Structure Chart process receives the Data Flow Diagram as input and outputs the Program Structure. The Design Forms process receives the Program Structure data flow and creates the Form Designs data flow. The last process is the Package Design process, where all of the other data flows are combined into a Package Design and a test plan that go into the Design document (data store).

Something you don't see in this figure are *control flows.* Control flows indicate the flow of execution and control in an application. Control flows are not allowed on a data flow diagram because they are related to the physical structure of the program, and here we are interested only in how the data flows. For example, a flow named Read Next Record is a control statement, not a data flow.

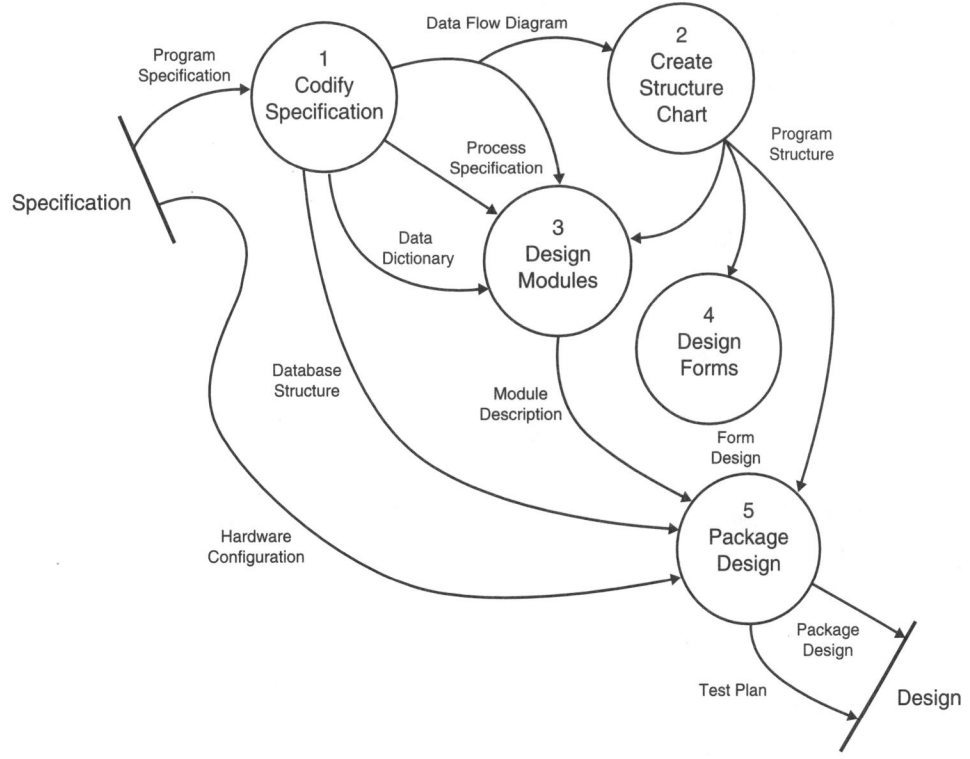

Figure 3.1. *The process of structured design presented as a data flow diagram.*

Textbook Tip: Control flows and timing information aren't allowed in a data flow diagram.

No Control Flows

Probably one of the hardest things for an experienced programmer to learn when creating data flow diagrams is to keep control flows out of the diagram. This is because most programmers are used to thinking in terms of how a program executes and not where the data goes.

Structured Design

Another thing you don't see are *timing flows*. That is, there is no timing information on the diagram to indicate connections between incoming and outgoing flows. If receiving a flow causes a process to emit data in a flow, that fact isn't included on the data flow diagram. The data part of the flows is included, just not the connection between the timing of the incoming and outgoing flows.

Data Flows

Data flows don't actually represent pipelines of data. They represent the interfaces between processes or between processes and files. The information contained in a data flow is strictly structured, so you don't define a single flow that contains one kind of data one time and a completely different type of data another time. However, you do pass multiple linked pieces of data in the same flow if they normally travel together. For example, you don't create a single flow that contains a salesman's name one time and his monthly sales another. You do create a data flow that passes the salesman's name and monthly sales together at the same time. If you're passing two or more different types of data between two processes at different times, draw two flows instead of trying to put all the data into a single flow. As another example, consider data flows between a user and an accounting process. These flows include invoices, payments, and account information (name and address). The invoices and payments could probably share the same flow, because they're both transfers of funds. However, the account information consists of name, address, and phone number, which should be a separate flow.

Naming Data Flows

You should give a data flow a name that describes what it contains. If you can't think of a name for a flow, maybe you don't really have a data flow and should restructure your chart. As you draw data flows, you enter their names and definitions in the data dictionary as explicit lists of data elements.

Data flows are drawn on the data flow diagram as curved lines with an arrowhead on the end, signifying the direction in which the data moves. If the same type of data moves both ways in a data flow, place an arrowhead on both ends. A data flow starts on a process or data store and ends on another process or data store. There is no processing in a data flow, only a transfer of data between two places where the data is stored or processed.

Data flows shouldn't cross each other. If you need to cross two data flows to correctly specify a system, try to restructure your diagram to make the crossing unnecessary. Occasionally this is impossible, such as with two parallel flows that split and connect to two different processes.

Note: There's a good reason for not allowing data flows to cross. If data flows don't cross, the structure of the data transport is much more apparent, and key processes are much easier to identify. This occurs because the restructuring of the chart moves processes with a lot of connectivity to the center of the chart, identifying them as key processes. It also moves processes with a lot of connectivity closer to the processes they connect to. Later, when you break the system into functional modules, the grouping you see in the data flow diagram helps you know what processes to group into procedures.

Processes

Processes, or data transforms, are where calculations are performed in our model. The calculations may combine multiple data elements in a complex formula or may simply rearrange the elements into a different order. For example, the database engine process shown in Figure 3.2 receives data records from the database file, but selects only records that match the criteria for inclusion in the output flow. It doesn't change the data; it only sets the arrangement.

Figure 3.2.
Data flows around a database engine process.

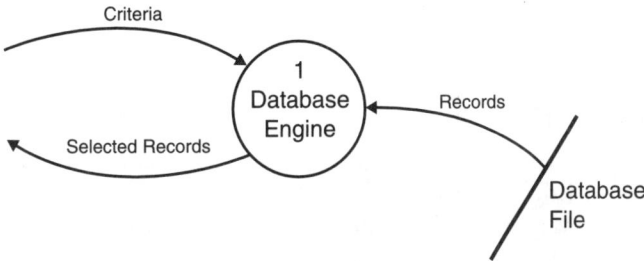

Processes are drawn on the data flow diagram as circles containing the name of the process. They are also numbered to make them easier to locate.

Data Stores

The Specification and Design shown in Figure 3.1 are both temporary data storage areas. Most temporary data stores are files on disk, but they may also be documents or the user. All files and file-like data stores are represented with an angled straight line on the data flow diagram. Included as data stores are human beings if they pass stored data to a program or read the results of a program's calculations.

Structured Design

> **Data Sources and Sinks**
>
> Another object used on a data flow diagram is the *data source* or *sink*. (I tend to use data stores instead.) A data source or sink is a place where data is created or disappears. It is represented as a square box on the data flow diagram, and it can have either data flowing out of it or into it, but not both. Very few things are truly data sources or sinks. For example, a random-number generator is a data source because it manufactures data out of nothing. A null printing device is a data sink. A null printing device is a system device driver that appears to be connected to a printer but isn't really connected to anything. You print to it, and as far as your program is concerned, it's printing data, but the data really just disappears. I tend to ignore data sources and sinks and represent everything as a data store, but you can use them if they make sense to you.
>
> Data sources and sinks are also used to represent data objects that are outside of the system being modeled. Instead of having a data flow appear from out of nowhere or disappear off the side of your diagram, you can terminate the dangling end of the data flow with a data source or sink that represents where the data is coming from or going to. Again, use them if you think they make the data flow diagram more understandable.

Objects

Visual Basic, along with many modern programming languages, is object-oriented. An object-oriented programming (OOP) language combines data and the code that manipulates that data into a programming object. For example, when you draw a button on a form, that button is a programming object. It contains data that describes its position and how it looks (properties) and contains code to manipulate it (methods). Objects are modeled as a data store and one or more processes. The data store contains the object's properties, and the processes are the methods that manipulate the properties.

Partitioning Processes

Processes can themselves be broken down or partitioned into lower-level data flow diagrams that describe just the operation of the process. You usually do this to make a whole data flow diagram fit on a single page. A diagram that takes more than a single page is difficult to understand because you can't see the whole diagram at one time. Of course, you can use a larger piece of paper, but that quickly becomes unwieldy.

An easier way is to start with a high-level description of a system, known as a *context chart*. You then partition the data transforms in the context chart into first-level charts that each describe the operation of one of the processes on the context chart. For example, the database engine in Figure 3.2 could be partitioned into several parts, as shown in Figure 3.3.

Figure 3.3.
Partitioning the database engine in Figure 3.2.

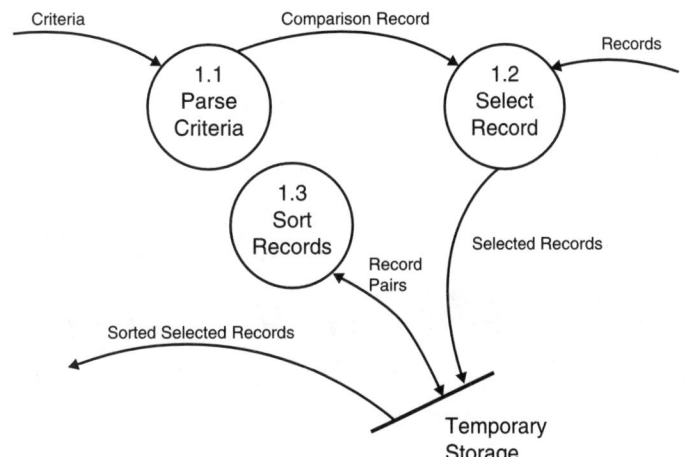

In Figure 3.3, the criteria is first parsed into a form that can be compared to a record from the database file and then passed to the comparison process. The comparison process gets records from the database, compares them to the criteria, and passes to the temporary file any records that match. The records in the temporary file are sorted by a sorter and returned to the temporary file. The sorted records are then passed to the output.

If these first-level charts start getting larger than a page, describe some of the processes in a functional manner and then create a set of second-level diagrams that partition the processes in the first-level diagrams. Continue creating levels of diagrams until the processes are all functional primitives. A *functional primitive* is a process that can't be partitioned again. For example, the Sort Records process in Figure 3.3 could be partitioned as shown in Figure 3.4.

Figure 3.4.
Partitioning the Sort Records process in Figure 3.3.

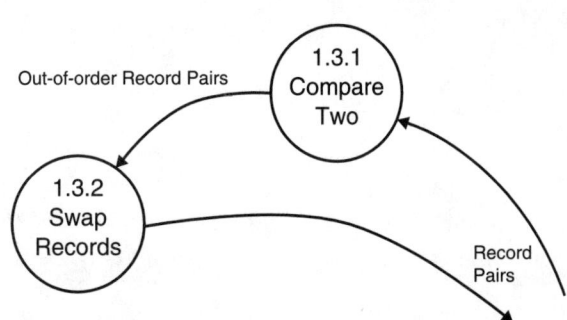

Structured Design

The Sort Records process performs a bubble sort on the records by comparing two records from the file. If the records are in the sort order, nothing is done. If they are not in the sort order, they are swapped and written back to the file. At this point, it's not necessary to partition the sort anymore. Note that in a bubble sort process, you would have a loop that loops over all the records and an If statement to make the comparison and branch to the swap process if the records were out of order. All of these functions are control flows, not data flows, so they aren't included in Figure 3.4.

Processes that are integral parts of a higher-level process are numbered with the number of the upper, parent process, followed by a dot and another number. For example, process 3.2 is part of process 3, and process 5.3.4 is part of process 5.3, which is part of process 5. The swap process in Figure 3.4 carries the number 1.3.2 because Swap Records is a part of Sort Records (1.3) in Figure 3.3, and Sort Records is a part of Database Engine (1) in Figure 3.2.

When to Stop Partitioning

When partitioning a system, you could partition it all the way down to the Visual Basic statements necessary to implement the code, or even carry it down to the machine language codes that drive the microprocessor. Clearly, there is no need to go that far with partitioning. In fact, if you specify language elements on a data flow diagram, you are adding implementation-specific information to the diagram, which is not allowed. You partition a diagram until the processes are functional primitives. Functional primitives rarely represent more code than a single process.

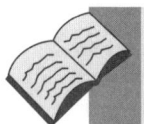

Textbook Tip: A data flow diagram is abstract in nature and thus can't contain any implementation-specific information.

Textbook Tip: A *functional primitive* is a process that performs an easy-to-understand task that doesn't need to be partitioned any more to understand how it works.

When to Stop Partitioning
A good rule of thumb when partitioning a process is that the process description should take less than a page to write. If it takes more than a page to describe what a

> process does, break it down into two or more subprocesses. You don't have to stop partitioning when the description reaches a page in length. Just don't have descriptions longer than a page. You always continue partitioning processes until they are functionally obvious, no matter how short the description gets. Many of Visual Basic's language statements are extremely powerful, so a process description might consist of a single line, far less than a full page.

The Mechanics of Creating a Data Flow Diagram

Creating a data flow diagram is relatively simple—just draw it on a piece of paper. Use a pencil, and have a big eraser available because you will revise the diagrams many times before you get them right. Programs are available to create these diagrams, but they're rarely as fast as simple, hand-drawn diagrams. Removable Post-it™ notes save you a lot of time when creating the diagrams. If you draw a process on a removable note, you can move it around as you revise the diagrams instead of redrawing it. The names of the data flows also can be placed on removable notes and moved when you revise the lines.

As you draw data flow diagrams, keep the one-page limit in mind and partition the diagrams accordingly. By suitably partitioning the diagrams, you reduce the amount of redrawing you have to do when you revise a diagram, because you have to revise only the page where you need to make changes and not the whole diagram.

Creating the Data Dictionary

The data dictionary is created along with the data flow diagram. It contains the complete specifications for all the data flows in the data flow diagram. When you draw a data flow on a data flow diagram, create an entry for it in the data dictionary and decompose it into its constituent parts. Next, create an entry for each of the parts, naming any subparts. Continue until you can specify individual data elements and their contents.

For example, in Figure 3.3, the criteria data flow consists of a database name and an SQL SELECT statement. The SELECT statement consists of table and field names, combined with relational operators. The criteria data flow would generate the following entries in the data dictionary:

```
criteria = database + SELECT
SELECT = table name + field name + operators
database = string(filename)
Table name = string
Field name = string
Operators = [>,<,=,>=,<=,<>]
```

Structured Design

The operators in the data dictionary aren't mathematical operators, but are used to show the composition of a data flow. There are many more operators you can use in a data dictionary to specify specific relationships between data elements. Table 3.1 shows some of these operators.

Table 3.1. Relational operators for specifying data element relationships.

Symbol	Operator	Meaning
=	IS EQUIVALENT TO	Equality or equivalence between two objects.
+	AND	Concatenation or sequence of data elements.
[ ]	EITHER-OR	Selection of one element from a list of elements. Separate elements with vertical bars.
{ }	ITERATIONS OF	Multiple iterations of the selected objects.
( )	OPTIONAL	Indicates an optional component.

The equivalence operator is used primarily to equate a data flow and its composition. Unlike a formula, in which the equivalence operator stores the result of the formula in a variable on the left, or a logical expression, in which the equivalence operator tests the equivalence of two data objects, the equivalence operator in the data dictionary declares that the data flow and its composition are the same, defining the data flow.

The concatenation operator combines several data elements into a group that can be assigned to a data flow. Unlike the mathematical addition operator, the data items themselves are combined, not their contents. The data elements are defined in a list of elements that are carried along together in a data flow.

Textbook Tip: When implementing a multielement data flow in Visual Basic, define its structure with a `Type` statement and then define a variable with that type.

The selection operator presents a list of objects to select from. Individual elements are separated by vertical bars or line feeds. That is, each element is placed on a separate line. Only one element is selected from such a list. For example, the following statement declares that the variable `intIndex` is a single integer in the range from 1 to 9:

```
intIndex = [1¦2¦3¦4¦5¦6¦7¦8¦9]
```

which is entirely equivalent to the following:

```
intIndex = [1
           2
           3
           4
           5
           6
           7
           8
           9]
```

The iterations operator indicates that the selected element is to be repeated a certain number of times. Often the limits of the iteration counter are appended to the brackets. For example, the following specifies Last-name as a string of from 1 to 12 characters:

$$\text{Last-name} = {}^{12}_{1}\{\text{character}\}$$

Optional data elements are just that: they may or may not appear in a data flow. For example, the following defines the variable Full-name as a sequence of a First-name, an optional Middle-initial, and a Last-name:

```
Full-name = First-name + (Middle-initial) + Last-name
```

Simplifying Complex Logic

When trying to figure out how to write a complex data description, say what the options are, then write down what you say. Statements that appear to need complex logic often can be specified as a selection list of several objects. For example, if you want Obj1 or Obj2 or the combination of Obj1 and Obj2, you don't need a lot of complex logic between the two objects. Simply write it down as it was specified: [Obj1|Obj2|Obj1+Obj2].

The Mechanics of Creating a Data Dictionary

A simple way to make a data dictionary is to use index cards. Place one entry on each card with the information shown in Figure 3.5 or 3.6, depending on whether you're describing a data flow or a data element. Data dictionary programs are available, but they tend to be expensive. An automated way of creating a dictionary is to use a word processor or a spreadsheet program. In a word processor, define each entry in a single paragraph or a row in a table, then use the word processor's sort capability to put the entries in alphabetical order. In a spreadsheet program, place entries in rows, then use the sort capabilities of the spreadsheet to keep things organized.

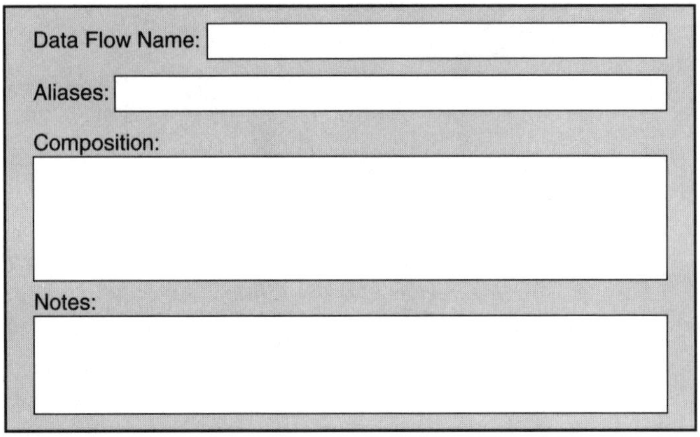

Structured Design

Figure 3.5.
A data flow card for the data dictionary.

| Data Flow Name: |
| Aliases: |
| Composition: |
| Notes: |

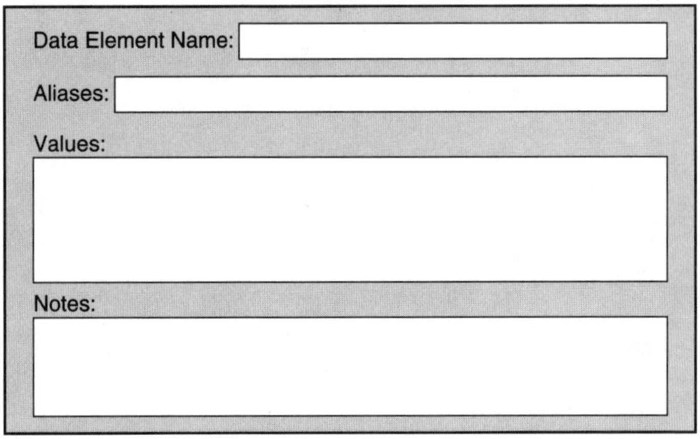

Figure 3.6.
A data element card for the data dictionary.

| Data Element Name: |
| Aliases: |
| Values: |
| Notes: |

In addition to data flows and data elements, you also place descriptions of the data content of files and databases in the data dictionary (see Figure 3.7).

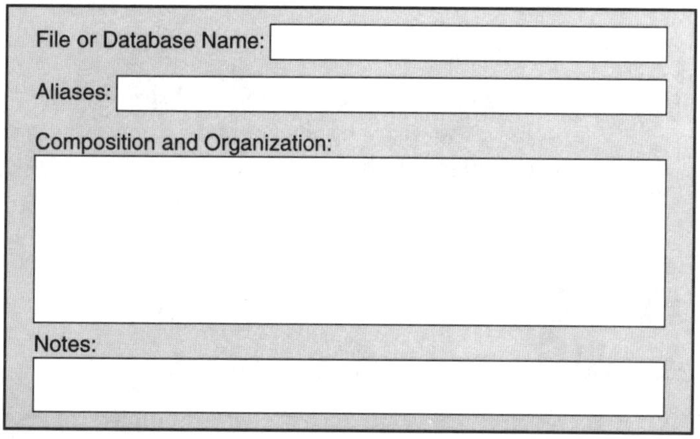

Figure 3.7.
A data file or database card for the data dictionary.

Creating the Process Specifications

Process specifications must explicitly specify what is done in the processes. However, they're not written in Visual Basic code, but in pseudocode or as a flowchart. Use whichever method is most meaningful to you. The process specifications also can be stored in the data dictionary, as shown in Figure 3.8. In this way, the data dictionary contains most of the data and code structure data needed to create the application.

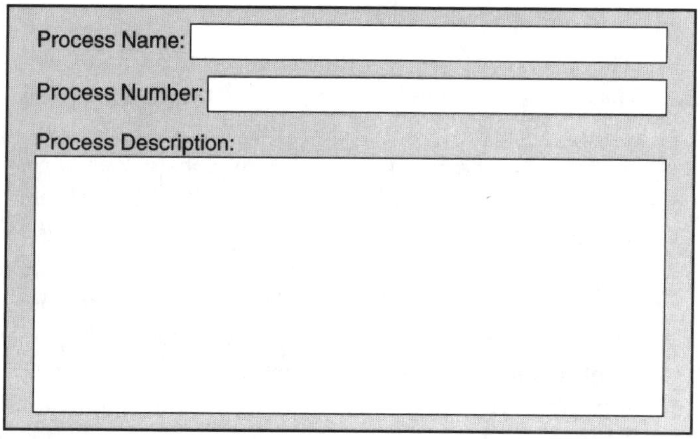

Figure 3.8.
A process card for the data dictionary.

Day 3

Structured Design

Specification Methods

Although any method can be used to specify processes, I find that pseudocode is the easiest to write and the closest in form to the code that will eventually be written to match the specifications.

The Decision Support Application Project

In the last chapter, we specified the decision support application for the Orco company. Using that specification and a whole pad of Post-it™ notes, we create the data flow diagram, the data dictionary, and the process specifications.

Creating the Data Flow Diagram

The first step is to create the data flow diagram. The diagram shown in Figure 3.9 describes all the processes and flows necessary to make this project work. Although this chart might look a little complicated at first, if you follow the data flows you will see that it is very straightforward. The major tasks are retrieving data from the database, drawing the charts, filling the grid, and printing the charts and grids.

The data flow diagram starts in the center of the figure with processes 1 and 2—database search engines that, given some criteria, search the database files and return any matching values. The two database files, GRAPHS.MDB and ORCO.MDB, are attached to the application in process 11 and stored in the program globals. *Program globals* is another name for the global variable list for the application. The file ORCO.MDB is the Orco company's database file, which contains all of the company's data. The GRAPHS.MDB file is a new database that contains the tblDefinitions table. The tblDefinitions table contains one record for each chart class and type, and each record contains the information necessary to re-create a chart. For example, records contain the chart labels, title, data types, and chart type. Records also contain information on how to obtain the data from the Orco database, such as field names and parts of SQL statements. The Graphs database makes it easier to make changes to this application when the need arises. If the customer wants to change something, all you have to do is to change the record in the database, and the existing code creates the new chart. We will look more closely at database files in the next chapter.

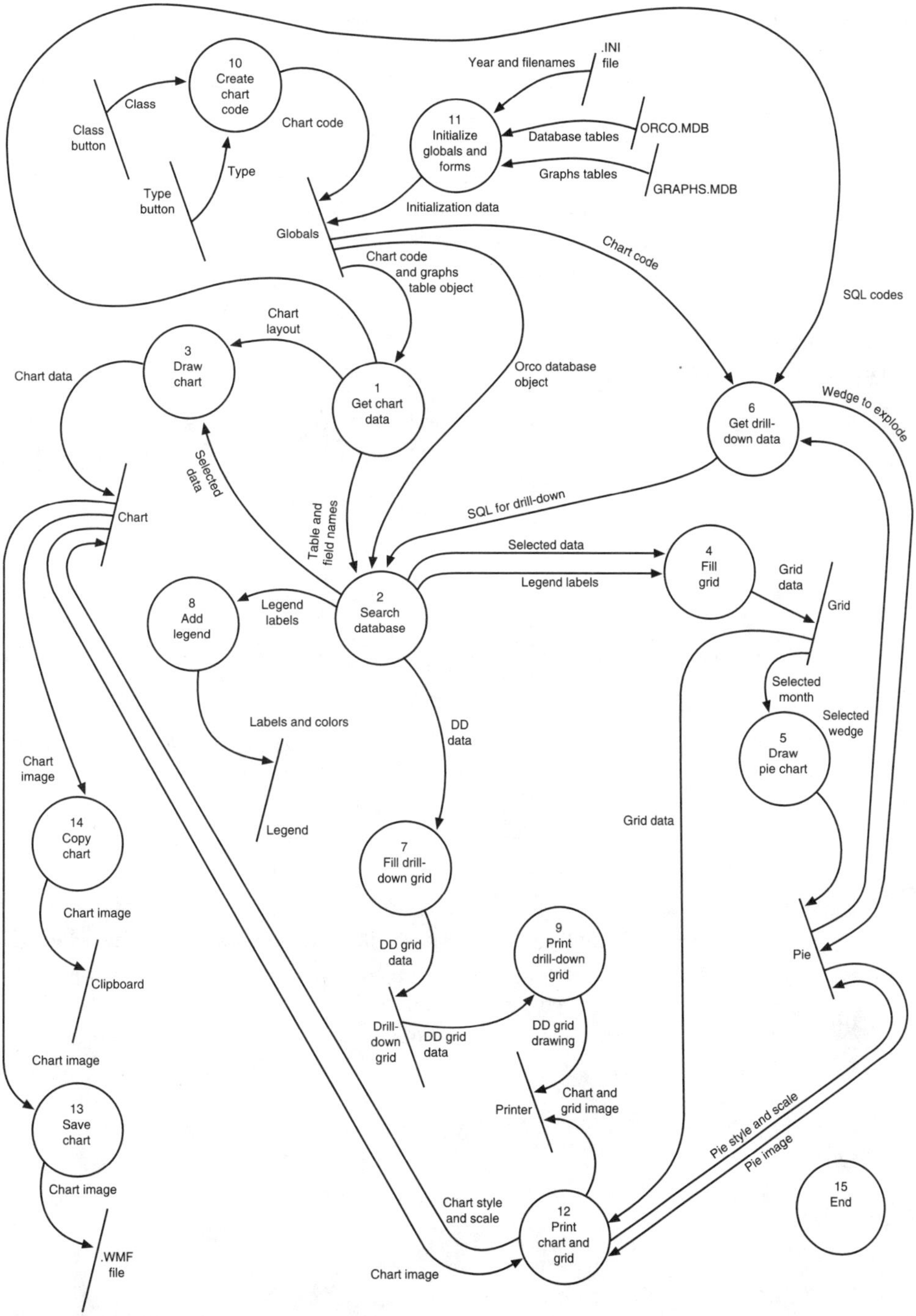

Figure 3.9. *The data flow diagram for the decision support application.*

Figures 3.10 and 3.11 show the partitioning of processes 1 and 2. In Figure 3.10, the chart code is used to select the appropriate record from the tblDefinitions table. Then, depending on what's needed, either the chart layout data, the SQL codes, or the table and field names for the Orco database are extracted from that record. In Figure 3.11, the table and field names are used to select a table from the Orco database, from which either the legend labels or the data for a chart is extracted. At the bottom of the figure, the same database tables are combined and pivoted using an SQL statement to create the data for the drill-down grids. A grid is a two-dimensional table of numbers on a form, much like a spreadsheet.

Figure 3.10.
The partitioning of the 1.0 Get Chart Data process.

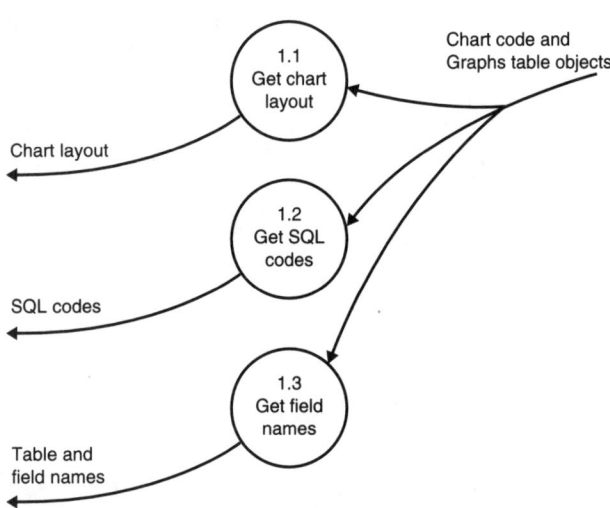

Note: Figure 3.11 has a crossing of a data flow. In a situation like this where there are parallel flows, both branching to the same two processes, there is no way to prevent a crossing. In a context diagram, you can go around the outside, but level diagrams have flows passing into and out of the process, preventing you from going around the outside. A way around this would be to combine the two flows with one process, and then to feed the combined flow to the two processes on the other side. However, that would tend to confuse what is really going on.

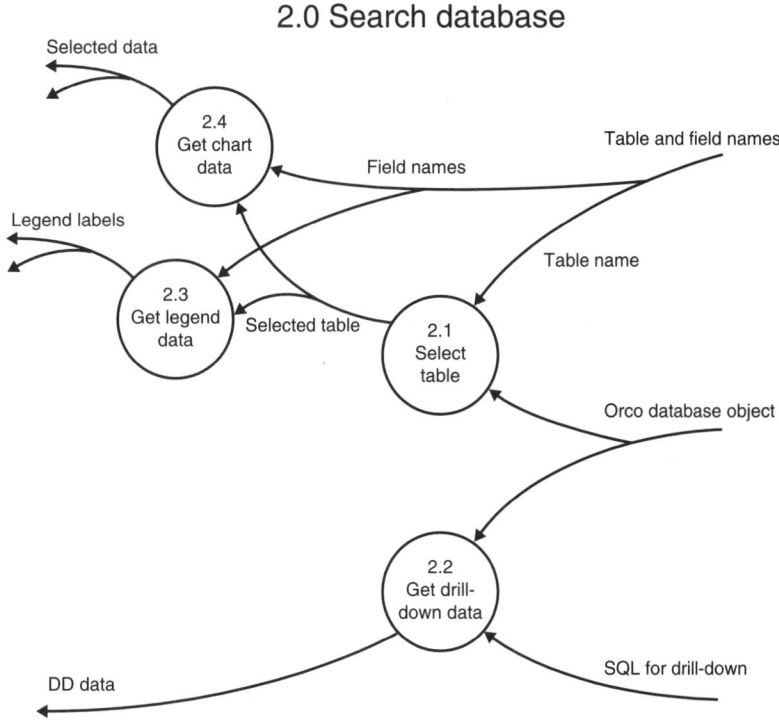

Figure 3.11. *The partitioning of the 2.0 Search Database process.*

The selected data from each of the search engines is passed to the 3.0 Draw Chart, 4.0 Fill Grid, 6.0 Get Drill-Down Data, 7.0 Fill Drill-Down Grid, and 8.0 Add Legend processes. Figure 3.12 shows the partitioning of the 3.0 Draw Chart process, which consists of two subprocesses. The 3.1 Set Chart Layout process applies the chart layout data to the chart to set its type and layout, while the 3.2 Set Chart Data process passes the actual data to plot to the chart.

Figure 3.13 shows the 4.0 Fill Grid process, which has much the same structure as the 3.0 Draw Chart process. It has one subprocess to set the layout of the grid and one to put in the data. In this case, though, most of the layout is static and doesn't need to get information from the Graphs database. It does need to get the legend labels from the Orco database. All of the processes that create charts or grids share this basic structure.

Structured Design

Figure 3.12.
The partitioning of the 3.0 Draw Chart process.

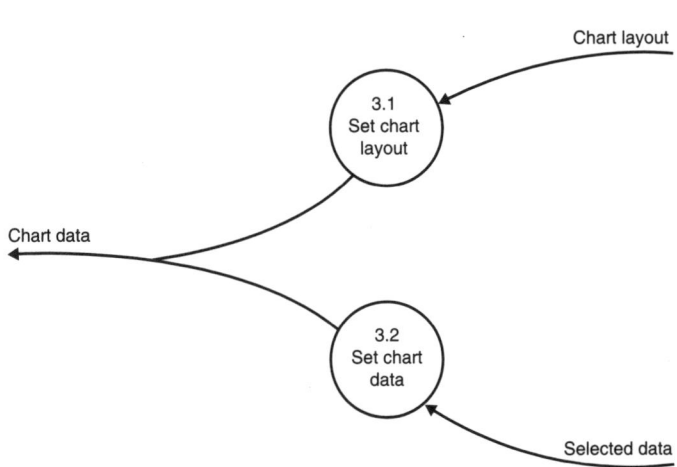

Figure 3.13.
The partitioning of the 4.0 Fill Grid process.

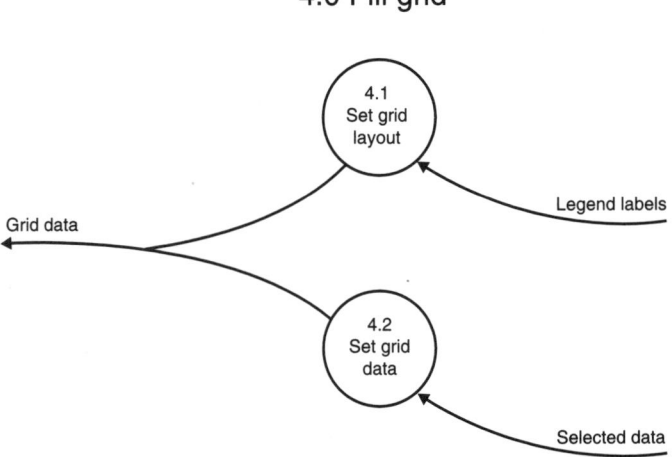

Figure 3.14 shows the subprocesses for the 6.0 Get Drill-Down Data process. The 6.1 Explode Wedge process gets information from the pie chart about the wedge that the user double-clicked on and sets the wedge to explode. The exploded wedge is used in combination with the SQL codes and the Chart code to produce the SQL statement to request the data associated with the exploded wedge for the drill grid. Those SQL statements are passed back to the 2.0 Search Database process, which selects the data from the database.

Figure 3.14.
The partitioning of the 6.0 Get Drill-Down Data process.

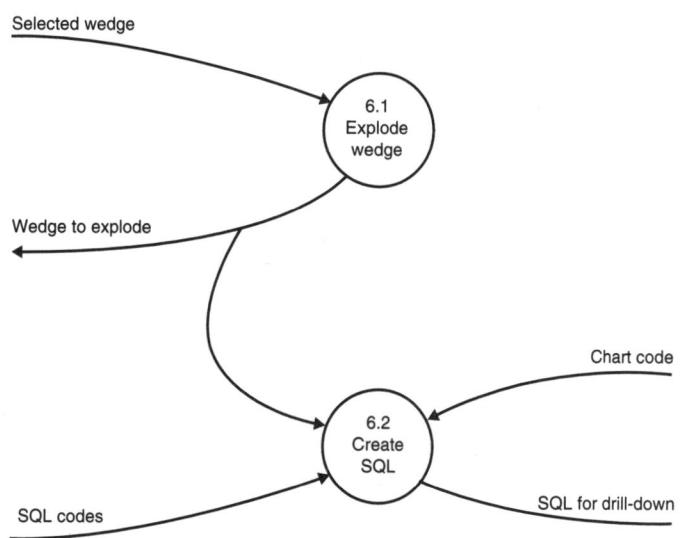

Figure 3.15 shows the subprocesses for the 7.0 Fill Drill-Down Grid process. As with the other processes that fill graphs or grids, this contains two subprocesses—one to set the layout and one to insert the data.

Figure 3.15.
The partitioning of the 7.0 Fill Drill-Down Grid process.

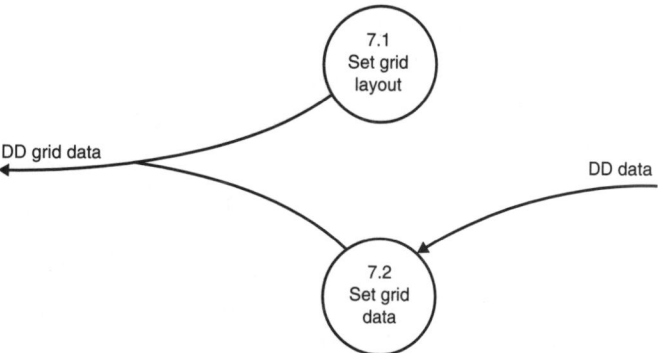

Structured Design

Figure 3.16 shows the subprocesses for the 8.0 Add Legend process. This process has two subprocesses—one to fill the legend with colored squares that match the colors on the chart, and one to insert the labels for the legends. In this case, the labels must come from the Orco database, because they are the names of the products, market segments, or market regions that are being charted.

Figure 3.16.
The partitioning of the 8.0 Add Legend process.

The 5.0 Draw Pie Chart process, shown in Figure 3.17, works slightly differently from the other draw processes. Since the pie chart displays a month's worth of data from the existing year-long chart, it gets its data from the grid that holds the chart data. We could go back to the database and retrieve the data again, but it's much faster to simply copy it from the grid control.

Figure 3.17.
The partitioning of the 5.0 Draw Pie Chart process.

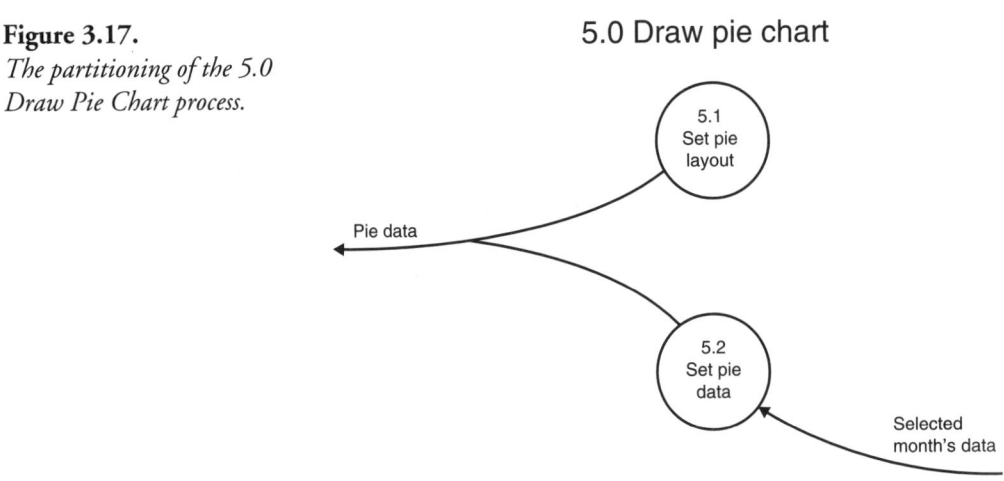

All of these processes pass the layout and selected data to the Chart, Pie, Grid, Drill-Down Grid, and Legend data stores. These data stores are the data display objects that display the data for the user. The data is stored in the properties of the data display objects.

The print processes obtain their data from the data display objects. The 9.0 Print Drill-Down Grid process prints the current contents of the drill-down grid. Its subprocesses, shown in Figure 3.18, consist of 9.1 Draw Grid on Printer and 9.2 Print Data on Grid. The first process uses line-drawing commands to draw a grid on the printer object, and the second gets the data from the drill-down grid and prints it in the grid just drawn on the printer.

Figure 3.18.
The partitioning of the 9.0 Print Drill-Down Grid process.

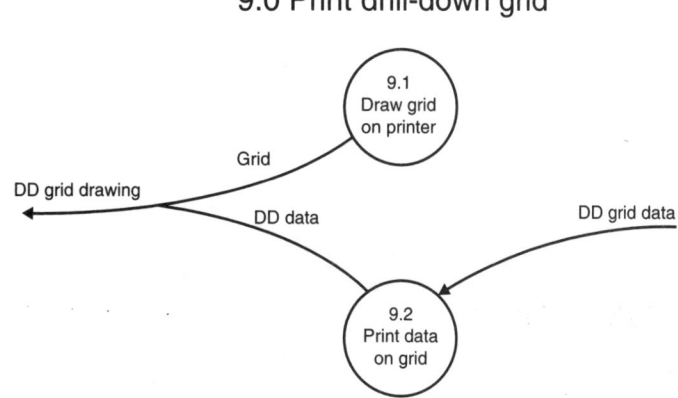

Figure 3.19 shows the subprocesses of the 12.0 Print Chart and Grid process. The process consists of three separate parts. Subprocesses 12.1 and 12.2 rescale the chart object to fit the printer's page and change it to black-and-white. Subprocesses 12.6 and 12.7 rescale the pie chart object to fit the printer's page and change it to black-and-white. The rest of the subprocesses import the image from the chart or pie object and pass it to the printer. If a chart is being printed, they also draw a grid on the printer and copy the data from the grid object to the new grid drawn on the printer.

The 10.0 Create Chart Code process isn't broken into subprocesses because it simply combines the chart class and type codes into a combined chart code.

The subprocesses of the 11.0 Initialize Globals process are shown in Figure 3.20. Subprocess 11.1 reads the year and filename from the project .INI file and stores them in the program globals. It also passes the filenames to process 11.3, which opens the databases and stores database and table objects in the globals for the other processes to use. Process 11.2 loads some text arrays with the names of months and so forth. Process 11.4 loads the initial chart class and type into the globals.

Structured Design

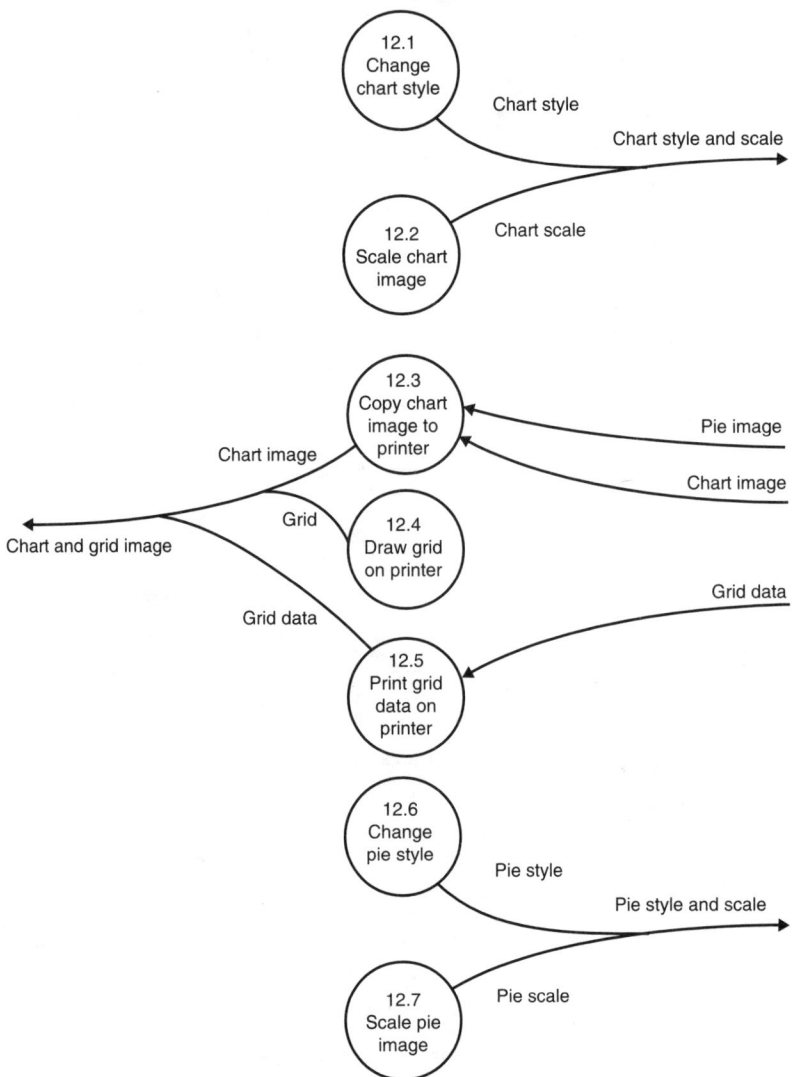

Figure 3.19. *The partitioning of the 12.0 Print Chart and Grid process.*

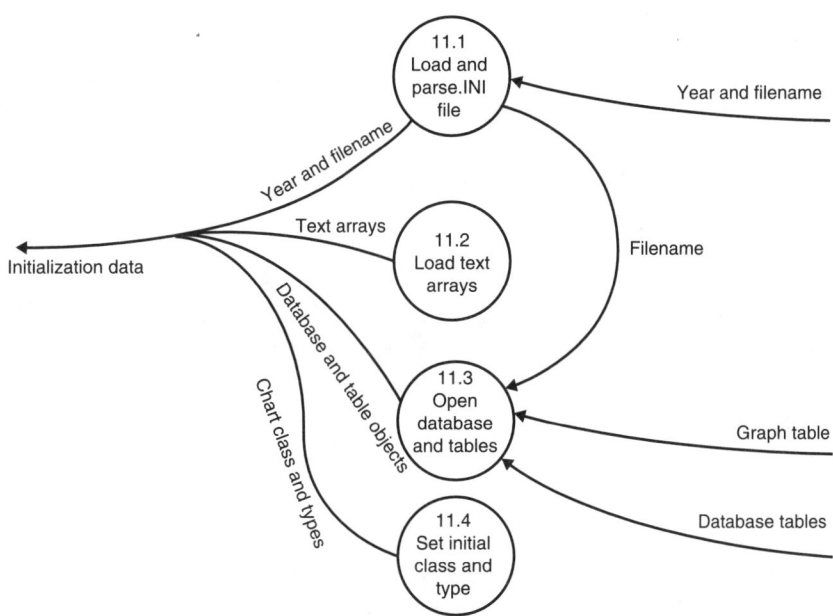

Figure 3.20. *The partitioning of the 11.0 Initialize Globals process.*

The 14.0 Copy Chart and 13.0 Save Chart processes work much the same way. 14.0 Copy Chart copies the chart to the clipboard, and 13.0 Save Chart copies it to a file. The last process is also disconnected from the body of the data flow diagram. The 15.0 End process simply ends the program.

This completes the data flow diagrams. Now we identify all the data flows by creating the data dictionary.

Creating the Data Dictionary

The next step in this process is to create the data dictionary. For this project, a table in Microsoft Word was used to hold and sort the entries in the data dictionary (see Table 3.2). Data flows are typed first, followed by the components of the data flows. When all of the components and flows are in the table, the Sort command in Word is used to sort the table. A similar process could have been accomplished with a spreadsheet program such as Microsoft Excel.

Structured Design

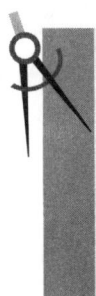

Creating the Data Dictionary with Word

The table structure in Microsoft Word is useful in that it can be sorted and searched to make it easy to locate needed data items. A drawback is that a word processor doesn't do any of the cross-referencing or checking of the flows and flow components that a commercial data dictionary does. However, for a project with this small a number of data flows, it doesn't make sense to invest a lot of money in a commercial data dictionary. If the project were a lot larger, you might consider it.

Table 3.2. The data dictionary for the decision support application.

Name	Type	Alias	Composition or Value	Notes
Chart and grid image	Flow		=Chart.image+ Grid+Grid data	
Chart class and type	Element	Chart code		
Chart code	Element	Chart class and type	=string:(Class+ Type)	The combined class and type codes converted to a string to use with the database.
Chart code and graphs table object	Flow		=Class+Type+ dbGraphs+ tblGraphs	
Chart data	Flow		=value1+value2+... +value12	The 12 data values plotted on the chart.
Chart image	Element		=WMF image	WMF image of the chart.
Chart layout	Flow		=chtMonthly.Top+ chtMonthly.Left+ chtMonthly.Height+ chtMonthly.Width	
Chart scale	Flow		=chtMonthly.Width+ chtMonthly.Height	

Name	Type	Alias	Composition or Value	Notes
Chart style	Flow		=chtMonthly.Style	
Chart style and scale	Flow		=Chart style+ Chart scale	
Chart.image				
chtMonthly.Height	Element		0-max twips, 1440 twips/inch	Height of chart in twips.
chtMonthly.Left	Element		0-max twips, 1440 twips/inch	Location of left edge of chart in enclosing form, measured from the left.
chtMonthly.Style	Element		=[MONO|COLOR]	Selects color or black-and-white for graphs.
chtMonthly.Top	Element		0-max twips, 1440 twips/inch	Location of top of chart, measured down.
chtMonthly.Width	Element		0-max twips, 1440 twips/inch	Width of chart in twips.
chtPie.Height	Element		0-max twips, 1440 twips/inch	Height of the pie chart.
chtPie.Style	Element		See chtMonthly.Style.	
chtPie.Width	Element		0-max twips, 1440 twips/inch	Width of the pie chart.
Class	Element		Chart class= 1=Sales 2=Margins 3=Orders 4=Backlog 5=Cycle 6=Inventory	
Colors	Element		=(Color picture boxes)=light blue| Light green|cyan| red|magenta|yellow| blue|green|blue-green	

continues

Structured Design

Table 3.2. continued

Name	Type	Alias	Composition or Value	Notes
Data field name	Element		=string: data field name	The name of the field containing the data for the current chart.
Data table	Element		=string: data table name	The name of the table containing the data for the current chart.
Database and table objects	Flow		=dbGraphs+ tblGraphs+dbOrco+ Database tables	
Database tables	Flow		Tables from Orco company database. See database design on Day 4.	
dbGraphs	Database		=graphs.mdb	Graphs database object. Database of graph settings.
dbOrco	Database		=ORCO.MDB	Orco database object.
DD Data	Flow	DD Grid data	=value1+value2+ ...+valueN	Data values for the drill-down grid.
DD Grid data	Flow	DD Data		
DD Grid drawing	Flow		=grid+DD Data	
Field names	Flow		=legend field+legend text field+data field	The name of the fields that contain the legend text and the field that contains the data to be graphed.

Name	Type	Alias	Composition or Value	Notes
Filenames	Element	strDataFile	See strDataFile.	
Graphs Table	Table		=graphs.table	Table of chart layout data.
Grid	Flow		=Line+Line+Line+...	Drawing of the grid.
Grid data	Flow		=value1+value2+...+valueN	
Initialization data	Flow		=Year and filenames+Text arrays+Database and table objects+Chart class and type	
Labels and colors	Flow		=Legend label text+Colors	
Legend field	Element		=string: legend field name	The name of the field containing the legends.
Legend label text	Element		=Strings	Text strings from the Orco database to use as labels for the chart legend. Use the Legend Table/Legend field entries in graphs to select the correct list of text strings.
Legend labels	Element	Legend label text	=strings: legend labels	
Legend table name	Element		=string: table name	The name of the table holding the legend label data.

continues

Structured Design

Table 3.2. continued

Name	Type	Alias	Composition or Value	Notes
Legend text field	Element		=string: legend text field name	The name of the field containing descriptions of the legends.
Line	Element		=object.Line	Line method for drawing lines on the printer or a form.
Orco database object	Database		=list of database tables	The company data database.
Pie data	Flow		=Selected Month data =value1+value2+... +valueN	Data values plotted with the pie chart. Number depends on specific chart class and type.
Pie image	Flow		=WMF image of the pie chart	
Pie scale	Flow		=chtPie.Width+ chtPie.Height	
Pie style	Element		=chtPie.Style	The style (color) of the pie chart.
Selected data	Flow		=value1+value2+... +valueN	Table of data values returned by the database engine in response to an SQL statement. Different SQL statements are used for the different charts.

Name	Type	Alias	Composition or Value	Notes
Selected month data	Flow		=value1+value2+...+valueN	Data values from one month on the grid.
Selected table	Table		=orco.Table	Table from the Orco database. Contains the legend labels or the data to be graphed.
Selected wedge	Flow		=Pie.wedge	Pie wedge selected for drill-down.
SQL codes	Flow		=string:codes	Codes from the Graphs table to use when building the drill-down SQL statements. See database design on Day 4.
SQL for drill-down	Flow		=string: SQL statement	SQL statement to select the data for the drill-down grid.
strDataFile	Element	Filenames	=string: path+filename	The path and name of a file.
strYear	Element		=string: year	The year to display data for.
Table and field names	Flow		=Table names+Field names	The name of the table and fields in the Orco database from which to get the data for the current legend.

continues

 **Structured Design**

Table 3.2. continued

Name	Type	Alias	Composition or Value	Notes
Table name	Element		=legend table name+ data table name	The name of the tables containing the legend text and the data to be graphed.
tblGraphs	Table		=Graphs.table object	Table of graph settings and labels.
Text arrays	Flow		=string:arrays	String arrays that hold such things as the months of the year, for use with the graph and grids.
Type	Element		Chart type. Number of types depends on the class. Class=1=Sales Type= 1=Year-to-date total 2=By product category 3=By market segment 4=By sales region Class=2=Margins Type= 1=Average gross 2=By product category Class=3=Orders Type= 1=Year-to-date total 2=By product category 3=By market segment 4=By sales region Class=4=Backlog	

Name	Type	Alias	Composition or Value	Notes
			Type=	
			1=Monthly	
			2=By product category	
			3=By market segment	
			4=By sales region	
			Class=5=Cycle	
			Type=	
			1=Average	
			2=By market segment	
			3=Distribution	
			Class=6=Inventory	
			Type=	
			1=Monthly ending	
			2=By product category	
			3=Turnover by product category	
value1...value12	Element		=single:numeric value	
Wedge to explode	Flow		=integer: pie.wedge	
Year and filenames	Flow		=strYear+strDataFfile	

In the table, the first entry is for the Chart and grid image data flow, which is passed from the Print Chart and Grid process to the Printer object. The Type column identifies records as data flows or elements. If an item is a data flow, it is made up of data elements that flow from one process to another. The data elements that make up a data flow are described elsewhere in the table. A data element may also flow from one process to another, but its composition is not broken down further in the table.

The composition of the Chart and grid image flow consists of the Chart image, the Grid, and the Grid data. Looking down in the table, you find that Chart.image is a Windows metafile (WMF) image of the current chart. The Grid is a list of lines that create the grid on the printer, and the Grid data are the numbers to be printed on the grid.

The second entry is the Chart class and type, which is a data element and also an alias of Chart code. Looking down, you find the Chart code, which is a string comprised of the chart class and the chart type. Here, the chart code is an element, because it is a single string, but it is comprised of two other data elements. The rest of the flows follow in much the same way.

Structured Design

Creating the Process Specifications

The next step in structured analysis is to create the process descriptions. Processes, as we are using the term here, are descriptions of how data is processed in our model of the data processing system. Table 3.3 contains the process descriptions for the processes in the data flow diagram.

Table 3.3. The process descriptions for the decision support application.

Process Name	Process Number	Description

Get chart data	1.0	For the current chart
		    Get the data from the Graphs
		    database that sets the layout
		    of the chart

Get chart layout	1.1	From the graphs table
		    Select the record where the chart
		    code equals the Code field
		    Extract and return the data fields
		    for chart layout

Get SQL codes	1.2	From the graphs table
		    Select the record where the chart
		    code equals the Code field
		    Extract and return the SQL code
		    fragments

Get field names	1.3	From the graphs table
		    Select the record where the chart
		    code equals the Code field
		    Extract and return the table names
		    and field names for the legend
		    data and the chart data

Search database	2.0	For the current chart or SQL
		    statement
		    Get the data from the database
		    tables

Select table	2.1	From the database tables
		    Get and return the table containing
		    the legend labels
		    Get and return the table containing
		    the chart data

Process Name	Process Number	Description
Get drill-down data	2.2	From the database tables Return the array of data selected with the SQL statement

Get layout data	2.3	From the legend table
		    Return the contents of the legend field
		    Return the contents of the legend text field

Get chart data	2.4	From the data table Return the contents of the data field
Draw chart	3.0	Draw a chart on the chart form

Set chart layout	3.1	With the chart layout data
		    Set the chart title
		    Set the chart height, width, and location
		    Set the chart type
		    Set the chart style

Set chart data	3.2	With the selected data Plot the data on the chart
Fill grid	4.0	Fill the grid with the same data plotted on the chart
Set grid layout	4.1	Set the number of rows and columns With the legend labels Set the legend column Set month names in the columns Shade the fixed rows and columns
Set grid data	4.2	With the selected data Insert the data in the grid
Draw pie chart	5.0	Draw a pie chart using one month's worth of data taken from the current chart
Set pie layout	5.1	Set the height, width, and location of the pie chart Add lines and labels for each piece

continues

Day 3: Structured Design

Table 3.3. continued

Process Name	Process Number	Description
Set pie data	5.2	With the selected month's data Insert the data in the pie chart
Get drill-down data	6.0	Get the selected wedge Explode the wedge Create an SQL statement to get the selected data
Explode wedge	6.1	Get the selected wedge Explode the wedge
Create SQL	6.2	Get the SQL codes for the current chart Combine the SQL codes, the exploded wedge, and the chart code to create an SQL statement to get the data
Fill drill-down grid	7.0	Draw and fill the drill-down grid
Set grid layout	7.1	Set the number of rows and columns for the grid Set the location, height, and width of the grid
Set grid data	7.2	With the DD data Insert the DD data into the grid
Add legend	8.0	Add a legend to the table
Set legend colors	8.1	Set the location and size of the color pictures that match the graph colors
Set legend labels	8.2	With the legend labels Insert the labels into the grid
Print drill-down grid	9.0	Re-create the drill-down grid on the printer
Draw grid on printer	9.1	Using the drawing commands Create the grid on the printer
Print data on grid	9.2	With the DD Grid data Write the grid data on the grid

Process Name	Process Number	Description

Create chart code	10.0	With the integer chart class
		    With the integer chart type
		        Turn the two integer codes into strings
		Combine the two code strings into a single string
		Store the string code in the globals

Initialize globals	11.0	Load the .INI file Parse the .INI file and extract the data Load the global string arrays Open the database and database tables Initialize the chart class and type

Load and parse .INI file	11.1	Open the DCSPT.INI file
		For each record in the file
		    Read a record
		    Extract the variable name
		    Extract the value
		    Store the value in the named global variable
		Next record
		If year is null or filename is null
		    Print "Error in .INI file"
		    End the program

Load text arrays	11.2	For each month in the year
		    Store the three-letter abbreviation for the month name in the global strMonths(n, 1)
		    Store the four-letter abbreviation for the month name in the global strMonths(n, 2)
		    Store the month number in the global strMonths(n, 3)
		For each quarter in the year
		    Store the name of the quarter in strQuarters(n)

continues

Structured Design

Table 3.3. continued

Process Name	Process Number	Description
Open database and tables	11.3	Open the Graphs database and create the database object dbGraphs Open the graph definitions table and store the object in tblGraphs Open the Orco database and create the database object dbOrco
Set initial class and type	11.4	Initialize any flags Set the initial chart class to 1 = sales Set the initial chart type to 1 = year-to-date
Print chart and grid	12.0	Change the style of the chart or pie chart to monochrome Resize the chart or pie Copy the chart or pie to the printer object Draw the grid on the printer Draw the data on the grid

Change chart style	12.1	Before printing
		    Set the chart style to monochrome
		After printing
		    Set the chart style to color

Scale chart image	12.2	Before printing
		    Set the chart height and width to fit in the printer window
		After printing
		    Set the chart height and width to fit the chart form

Copy chart image to printer	12.3	Get a handle to the Windows metafile for the current chart from the graphics server Copy the chart to the printer object

Process Name	Process Number	Description

Draw grid on printer	12.4	If this is a chart (not a pie)
		    For number of columns
		        Draw evenly-spaced vertical
		        lines on the printer
		    For number of rows
		        Draw evenly-spaced horizontal
		        lines on the printer

Print grid data on printer	12.5	If this is a chart (not a pie)
		    For each data value in the grid
		        Print the data value on the
		        printer

Change pie style	12.6	Before printing
		    Set the pie style to monochrome
		After printing
		    Set the pie style to color

Change pie scale	12.7	Before printing
		    Set the pie height and width to fit
		    in the printer window
		After printing
		    Set the pie height and width to fit
		    the chart form

Save chart	13.0	Get a filename Open the file for printing Copy the current chart or pie to the file Close the file
Copy chart	14.0	Copy the current chart or pie to the clipboard
End program	15.0	Close the database and tables Exit the program

Modification Notes

If you're modifying an existing program, you should go through the design process twice—once to model the current system as it exists, and a second time to add the changes. If the changes are extensive, you might have to model it a third time to reengineer the project to fit the new criteria.

Day 3: Structured Design

Redoing a Project

Whenever you make extensive changes to a design, it's often easier to redesign a program than to modify the old one. There's nothing wrong with starting from scratch, especially if the rewrite results in well-modularized, extensible code. Code usually isn't rewritten often enough, resulting in legacy codes that no one knows how to fix.

The down side to rewriting code is that you invariably introduce new bugs into the program and eliminate a lot of the fine-tuning that has been done in the past to speed the procedures. Realize, though, that you don't have to throw everything out when you do a rewrite. Use whatever parts are reasonable.

You will run into a lot of "cultural inertia" when trying to rewrite existing code. This inertia, which seeks to prevent you from rewriting the code, has three origins. First, no matter how difficult it is to use a piece of code, people who know how to use it will prefer it over new code that they don't yet know how to use. Second, people hate to throw out working code. Just as most people wouldn't throw away a perfectly good car just because they wanted a different color, they don't want to throw away working code, especially since code doesn't wear out like a car. Finally, people as a whole don't recognize that it's often easier to rewrite a complex piece of code than it is to figure out an existing one. Your gut feeling is that the opposite should be true, even when experience proves otherwise.

A little diplomacy is necessary to overcome people's objections to throwing out old code.

Debugging the Process

Debugging at this point consists of ensuring that the model you're creating has no missing pieces and is consistent with itself. As you create the data dictionary or write the process descriptions, you will invariably find problems with the data flow diagram. Things are out of place, missing data, or just plain missing. Realize that this is normal. This is why you create the data flow diagram, the data dictionary, and the process descriptions at the same time. You find yourself rotating between the diagram, the dictionary, and the specifications as you correct errors and add missing pieces. You will find many more missing pieces as you start to write the code, but hopefully, nothing important, because it's much more difficult to make changes after the code is written.

Summary

Today you learned the basics of structured design. As you progress in your programming career, you should devote a lot more time to this topic, because it's well worth the effort. It is with good engineering and design that you create excellent software. And, most importantly, the next time you or someone else has to work on your system, they will find the software to be straightforward and understandable.

In this chapter, you learned the first three steps of structured design: creating data flow diagrams, creating the data dictionary, and creating the process specifications. But the structured design started in this chapter isn't yet complete. You must still design the modules and procedures and the visual interface. Also required for this project is database design, which is the topic of the next chapter.

The data dictionary and process descriptions are in the \DESIGN directory on the included CD.

Database Design

Day 4: Database Design

An important part of the sample application being developed in this book concerns accessing a database and extracting information from it. To help you better understand that capability, this chapter describes databases and how to access them with Visual Basic and Microsoft Access. You don't need Access to complete this chapter's work, but it would make things easier.

Today you will learn

- what a database is
- how to design a database
- how to access a database with Visual Basic

The Goal of Day 4

Today you will examine what databases are and how to access them. However, the treatment of databases here is relatively cursory. Like structured design, database design is a field unto itself, with whole books devoted to it. If you expect to learn everything about databases here, you'll be disappointed. There just isn't enough room in a single chapter to give more than an overview. You *will* learn enough about databases in this chapter to understand the principles of database design and to design uncomplicated databases on your own. You need this capability to be able to understand the sample application being developed in this book. To learn all about databases, read Roger Jennings's book *Database Developer's Guide with Visual Basic 3* (Sams Publishing, 1994).

The simplest description of a database is that it's a file of data that has been organized to make it easy to locate specific values. For example, a telephone book is a database optimized for manually looking up phone numbers. This is actually an overly simplistic description of modern databases. A modern, well-designed database minimizes the amount of data that must be stored while enhancing the capability to locate lists of values matching complicated criteria.

A Visual Basic developer can access a database in many ways. Visual Basic contains statements and controls that can access and manipulate most modern database files directly. Visual Basic can also communicate with a remote SQL database server to obtain needed data. In addition, Visual Basic contains the Data Manager, which gives you a glimpse of the structure of a database's tables and allows you to change data there. To do more complicated things with a database, you should use a dedicated database application such as Microsoft Access, or the VisData sample application included with Visual Basic.

Using Specialized Database Applications

You might be wondering, "Why use a specialized database application to store and extract information? Why not just use one of the Visual Basic file formats and store the data with it?" You could do this, but why go to all the work of creating a new database engine to handle the organization and storage of data and extract the data requested by the database commands when it has already been done? The database engine in Visual Basic is well tested and validated. The expense isn't high, so why go to all the trouble of creating a custom database application when you don't have to?

What Is a Database?

As I mentioned, a database is a collection of data that has been ordered in such a way to make it easy to search and retrieve data. The database is only the collection of data; it doesn't include the program that manipulates the data. The program that manipulates the data in the database is known as the *search engine*. A simple table of numbers is a database. If you scan those numbers to locate specific values, you are the search engine.

This definition doesn't really tell you much about a database, or how it differs from other databases or why those differences are important. How a database stores data determines how fast it can locate data and how efficiently it can store data.

Flat Versus Relational Databases

Two major database types are in use today: flat and relational. The most common database is the *flat file database system*—a single table of data arranged in a two-dimensional grid, much like the cells in a spreadsheet. Because there is a single table, data can't be segregated according to type to more efficiently store information. The biggest benefit of a flat file database is that it's simple to implement. A *relational database system* is a multitable database in which the tables are related to one another using special key fields. A key field is a set of identifiers in a field that uniquely identifies a record in a table.

Although many things can be represented with flat file database systems, they have some serious disadvantages. The biggest is that everything related to a single entity must be in each record. If you have a table of orders, and the same customer orders more than once, you must include his complete name and address in each record. If your customer changes his address, you must change it everywhere it appears in your database. With a multitable database, the address would be in one table and the orders in another. The tables would then be joined to attach the address to the order.

Day 4: Database Design

The second problem with flat file database systems is what to do with repeating entries. A customer often doesn't order just one thing. To handle several items ordered at the same time, you need to include enough slots in each record of your database to handle the largest number of items ordered. Doing this wastes a lot of space. Also, what do you do when a customer orders more items than you have slots for in your database? In a multitable database, each item is placed in an order items table that is joined to the order in the orders table.

As you might guess, a multitable relational database is much more efficient at storing and updating data. As a consequence, it's a much more complicated system to create. A relational database consists of multiple tables joined through specific identifiers. It may all be in one file, as is done in Access databases, or it may be in multiple files, one for each table, as is done with a dBASE database.

The rest of this chapter is devoted to relational databases.

Database Terminology

Before you can understand a database, you need to learn the terminology used to describe it. As with most science and engineering disciplines, database terminology has evolved into a jargon that appears cryptic to those who aren't versed in the field. However, as you learn the jargon of databases, you should start to understand how they work, and you will learn that they aren't so complicated to use after all. Figures 4.1 and 4.2 are tables from a database containing a car inventory and a list of employees. They should help you understand the definitions that follow.

Figure 4.1.
A car inventory table that shows the different parts of a database.

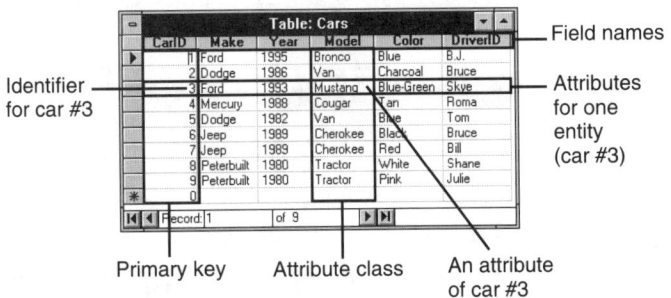

Database: The file or collection of files that contains the data being stored. The files also contain information on the structure of the files and indexes to make it easier to locate data.

Table: A database consists of one or more tables of data. A table is a two-dimensional arrangement of cells, much like the cells in a spreadsheet. Figure 4.1 shows such an arrangement.

Figure 4.2.
A car inventory table joined to an employee table.

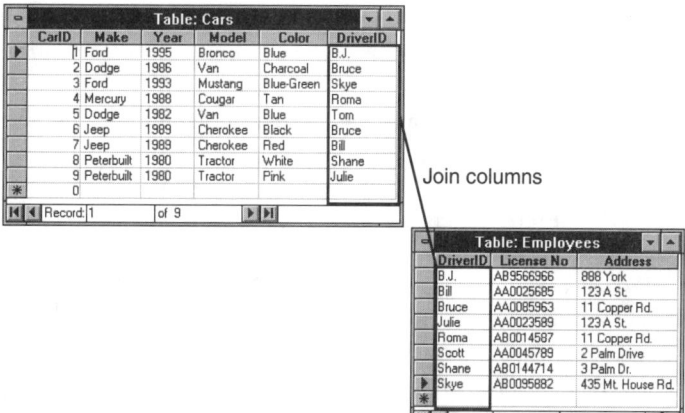

Join columns

Record: Each row in a table, known as a record, contains attributes that describe a single entity or object. For example, in the Cars table in Figure 4.1, row 7 describes car 7, a red Jeep Cherokee. Row 5 describes a different car, a blue Dodge van.

Field: Each column of the table, known as a field, contains a specific characteristic for each of the entities. Each field has a name that isn't physically part of the table but that describes the table.

Attribute: Each cell in a table contains an attribute of the entity described by the record (row) containing the cell. Thus, the data in a record is known as the attributes of the entity described by the record. A column in the table is known as the attribute class for all the entities. In Figure 4.1, Mustang is the Model attribute of car entity number 3. The other attributes for car number 3 are 3, Ford, 1993, Blue-Green, and Skye.

Entity: An entity is the object described by a single row in a table. For example, car number 3 is the entity described by the third row in the table.

Identifier, entity identifier: An identifier or entity identifier is the one or more attributes in a record that uniquely identify that record. For example, the CarID field in Figure 4.1 uniquely identifies each record. None of the other fields or combinations of fields can be depended on to always uniquely identify a record.

Primary key: The field or group of fields in a database that contain the identifier. In Figure 4.1, the CarID field is the primary key for the car table.

Joining: A method of producing a new table. You connect two tables by comparing the values in a field in the first table to a field in the second. Only fields that have matching values can be joined. For example, in Figure 4.2, the DriverID field in the Cars table is joined to the DriverID field in the Employees table. There are three ways to join two tables: inner joins (equijoins), outer joins, and cross-product joins.

107

Day 4 Database Design

Inner join: Records in the two tables that have the same value in the joined fields are connected. The inner join or equijoin is the most common way of joining two tables. For example, in Figure 4.2, if you want to know the license number of the driver of each car, do an inner join between the Cars table and the Employees table. Figure 4.3 shows the table resulting from an inner join of the tables in Figure 4.2. Note that car number 5 isn't included in the join because it doesn't have a matching record in the Employees table.

Figure 4.3.
The joined table that results from joining the tables in Figure 4.2 using an inner join.

CarID	Make	Year	Model	Color	Cars.Drive	Employe	License No	Address
1	Ford	1995	Bronco	Blue	B.J.	B.J.	AB9566966	888 York
2	Dodge	1986	Van	Charcoal	Bruce	Bruce	AA0085963	11 Copper Rd.
3	Ford	1993	Mustang	Blue-Green	Skye	Skye	AB0095882	435 Mt. House Rd.
4	Mercury	1988	Cougar	Tan	Roma	Roma	AB0014587	11 Copper Rd.
6	Jeep	1989	Cherokee	Black	Bruce	Bruce	AA0085963	11 Copper Rd.
7	Jeep	1989	Cherokee	Red	Bill	Bill	AA0025685	123 A St.
8	Peterbuilt	1980	Tractor	White	Shane	Shane	AB0144714	3 Palm Dr.
9	Peterbuilt	1980	Tractor	Pink	Julie	Julie	AA0023589	123 A St.

Equijoin: Same as inner join.

Outer join: Includes all the records in one table, plus any matching records in the joined table. Because of this, an outer join has a direction that points from the table that includes all the records to the table that includes only the matching records. For example, in Figure 4.2, if the Cars table is outer-joined to the Employees table, the top table in Figure 4.4 results. All the cars in the Cars table are included, but only employees with matching records are joined to the car records. Car number 5 is included in the table even though its driver isn't in the Employees table. Employee Scott isn't included because he isn't the driver of any of the cars. The bottom table in Figure 4.4 shows the resulting table if the join goes the other way, with the Employees table outer-joined to the Cars table.

Figure 4.4.
The joined table that results from joining the tables in Figure 4.2 using an outer join. The top table is an outer join of the Cars table to the Employees table, and the bottom one is an outer join of the Employees table to the Cars table.

Select Query: Outer Join L

CarID	Make	Year	Model	Color	Cars.Drive	Employe	License No	Address
1	Ford	1995	Bronco	Blue	B.J.	B.J.	AB9566966	888 York
2	Dodge	1986	Van	Charcoal	Bruce	Bruce	AA0085963	11 Copper Rd.
3	Ford	1993	Mustang	Blue-Green	Skye	Skye	AB0095882	435 Mt. House Rd.
4	Mercury	1988	Cougar	Tan	Roma	Roma	AB0014587	11 Copper Rd.
5	Van	1982	Blue	Tom				
6	Jeep	1989	Cherokee	Black	Bruce	Bruce	AA0085963	11 Copper Rd.
7	Jeep	1989	Cherokee	Red	Bill	Bill	AA0025685	123 A St.
8	Peterbuilt	1980	Tractor	White	Shane	Shane	AB0144714	3 Palm Dr.
9	Peterbuilt	1980	Tractor	Pink	Julie	Julie	AA0023589	123 A St.

Select Query: Outer Join R

CarID	Make	Year	Model	Color	Cars.Drive	Employe	License No	Address
1	Ford	1995	Bronco	Blue	B.J.	B.J.	AB9566966	888 York
7	Jeep	1989	Cherokee	Red	Bill	Bill	AA0025685	123 A St.
2	Dodge	1986	Van	Charcoal	Bruce	Bruce	AA0085963	11 Copper Rd.
6	Jeep	1989	Cherokee	Black	Bruce	Bruce	AA0085963	11 Copper Rd.
9	Peterbuilt	1980	Tractor	Pink	Julie	Julie	AA0023589	123 A St.
4	Mercury	1988	Cougar	Tan	Roma	Roma	AB0014587	11 Copper Rd.
						Scott	AA0045789	2 Palm Drive
8	Peterbuilt	1980	Tractor	White	Shane	Shane	AB0144714	3 Palm Dr.
3	Ford	1993	Mustang	Blue-Green	Skye	Skye	AB0095882	435 Mt. House Rd.

Cross-product join: A cross-product join isn't really a join, because no fields are joined between the two tables. By not joining the tables, you create a new table that combines every record in the first table with every record in the second. Figure 4.5 shows a fragment of the cross-product of the tables in Figure 4.2. Note how each single record in the Cars table is combined with every record in the Employees table. A cross-product table can get very large if you're not careful.

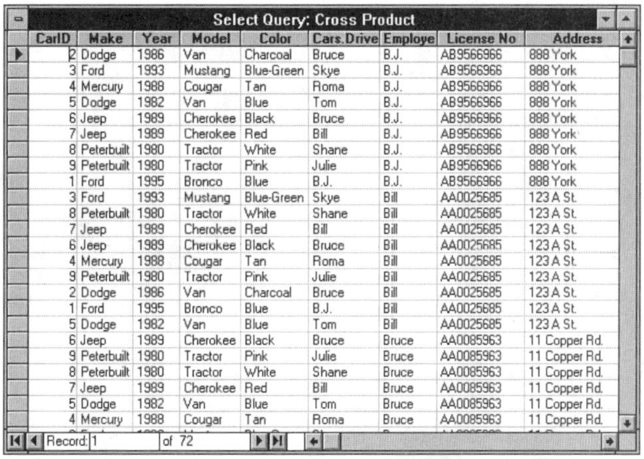

Figure 4.5.
The joined table that results from joining the tables in Figure 4.2 using a cross-product join.

Index: A data structure created on a particular column of a table to make it easier to locate specific values in that column. For example, a dictionary is a database of word definitions that is indexed by placing the words in alphabetical order. Although it isn't required, an index significantly speeds up search operations involving large tables. A problem with an index is that it uses up a lot more space on disk, so you don't normally index every field.

Query: A request passed to a database engine, asking it to do something such as select and return a table of values or create a new table.

Joining Tables

Although I've discussed the joining of tables in a relational database as part of the definitions of database technology, we need to examine this concept more closely. The joining of tables is where the "relational" part comes from in "relational databases," and it has a lot to do with their ultimate behavior.

When two tables are joined, the relationship between the records in one table and those in the table they're joined to can be one-to-one, one-to-many, or many-to-many. In a *one-to-one* join, each record in one table is joined to exactly one record in another table. You would think that

109

Database Design

one-to-one-joined tables should be combined into a single table. You could do that, but one-to-one joining has its uses. For example, if some of the fields in a record are optional, you would place them in a separate table to save space. In another scenario, some fields of a table have their access restricted to specific users. Personnel information often has data of this type. The restricted fields are put in a separate table with a one-to-one link to the rest of the table. The restricted table could then be protected without protecting all the unrestricted data. For example, imagine that the address of each employee is confidential, but the license number is public information. An Access database has security on a table-by-table basis, but not on a field-by-field basis. To protect the employee's address but still make the license number available, split the Employees table into two tables joined with DriverID, as shown in Figure 4.6. Access to the Addresses table would be password-protected to prevent unauthorized access.

Figure 4.6.

A one-to-one join to protect employee information from unauthorized access.

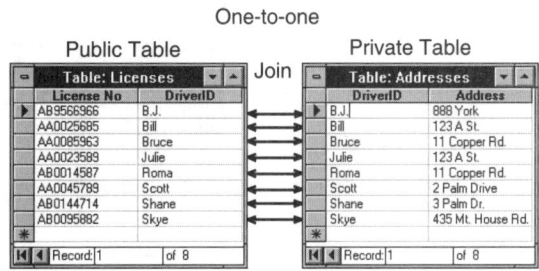

A *one-to-many* join, the more common join in most databases, has single records in one table joined to multiple records in another table. The Cars table/Employees table example shown in Figure 4.7 is a one-to-many join. In this example, each employee except Tom is joined to one or more cars, which satisfies the one-to-many relation. Tom can be joined to a car as soon as he gets his license back.

Figure 4.7.

A one-to-many join connecting single drivers to multiple cars.

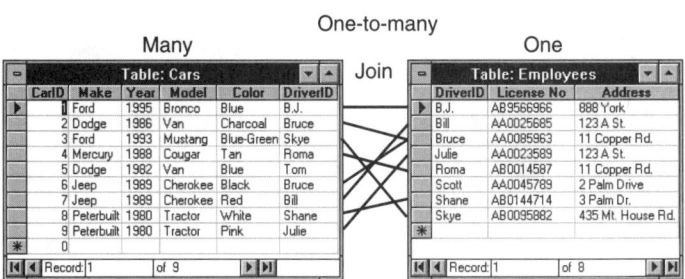

A *many-to-many* join isn't possible directly between two tables using a relational database. Creating a many-to-many join requires an intervening table. For example, consider the Cars table/Employees table example. If each car can have one or more drivers and each driver can drive one or more cars, you have a many-to-many relationship. To model that relationship using a relational database, insert a third table between the Cars table and the Employees table, as shown in Figure 4.8. The new table has two fields, CarID and DriverID, plus a primary key field, CarDriverID, and each record describes a possible car/driver combination. Thus, every car could be joined to multiple drivers, and each driver could be joined to multiple cars.

Figure 4.8.
A many-to-many join between cars and drivers using an intermediate table.

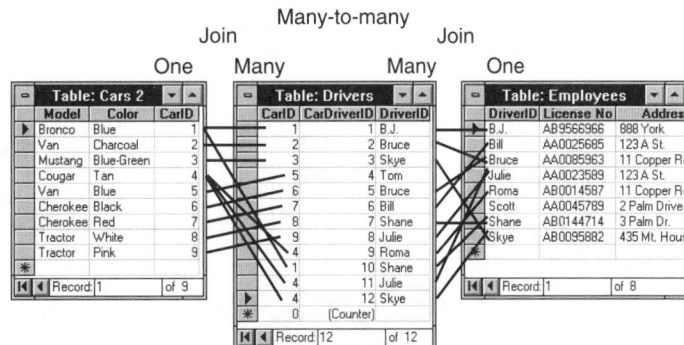

Accessing Data: Queries

Accessing data is what a database is all about, and you do that with queries. A *query* is a statement that lists the tables to use, the joins to make, the fields to return, and any criteria to apply to the records before returning a result. For example, a query to list the blue cars would specify the Cars table with no joins, return the CarID field and the Color field, and specify that the color equals blue. The result of this query would be cars 1 and 5. Another example would be to list the license number for the driver of each car. The query would specify the Cars table and the Employees table, with an outer join of the Cars table to the Employees table between the DriverID fields in both tables. The query would return the CarID field and the License No field. The result would be a table of cars 1 through 9 and the license numbers. Car number 5 would be listed without a license number because the driver isn't in the Employees table.

How you create a query depends on the application. In Access, a query is made with an SQL statement, but you don't have to learn SQL to make one. In Access, you create the query graphically, and Access writes the SQL statement for you. For example, to perform the second query in the preceding paragraph, you would open a new query, add the two tables to it, draw the link (if Access hasn't already done so) and set its type, select the output fields, and run the query. Figure 4.9 shows the query as it is set up, and Figure 4.10 shows the result of running the query. The two tables are placed on the query window, and an arrow is drawn between the fields to be linked. The arrowhead on the end of the line indicates that this is an outer join of the Cars table on the Employees table. At the bottom of the query window are the columns to return. Once a query is set up, you can see the SQL statement by opening the SQL window, as shown in Figure 4.11. The SQL statement starts with the SELECT command, followed by the list of columns to return. The clause starting with FROM indicates the tables to search and the join.

Database Design

Figure 4.9.
A query set up in Access.

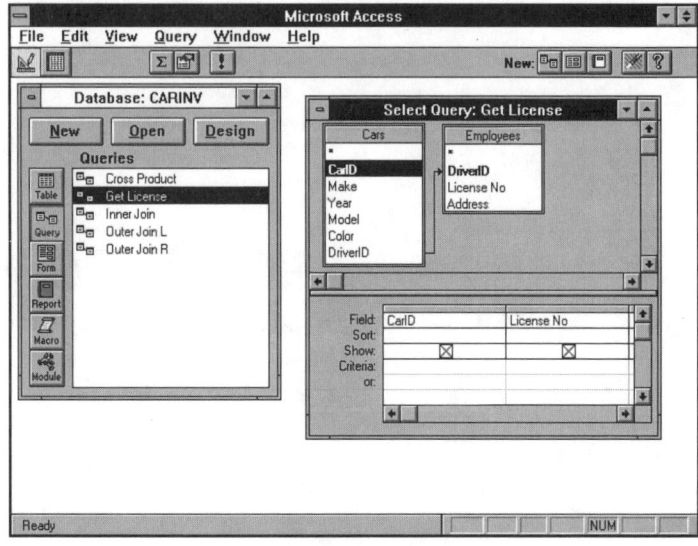

Figure 4.10.
The resulting table from the query set up in Figure 4.9.

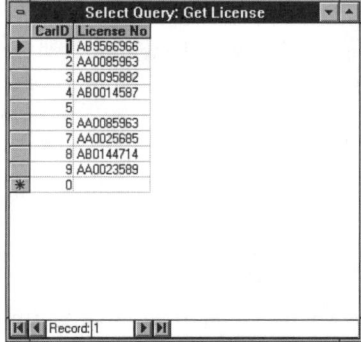

Figure 4.11.
The SQL statement created by Access to perform the query set up in Figure 4.9.

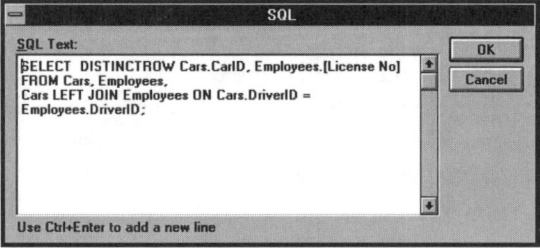

If you run the same search, but want to see the license numbers of the drivers of all the blue cars, add the Color column to the output and select all the records with the word "Blue" in them.

Figure 4.12 shows this setup, and Figure 4.13 shows the SQL statement. The SQL statement starts much the same as the previous statement. At the end is the criteria `Cars.Color="Blue"`, which selects only blue cars. If you need SQL statements, the easiest way to write them is to let Access or some other database application do it for you.

Figure 4.12.
A query to get the license numbers of all the drivers of blue cars.

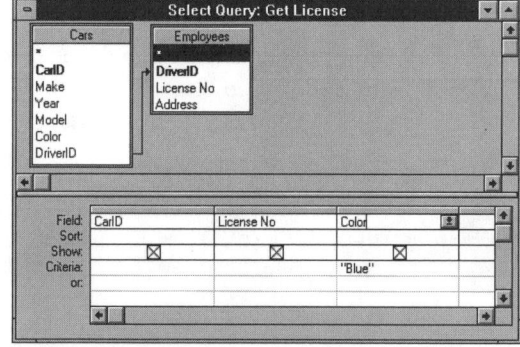

Figure 4.13.
The SQL statement created by Access to perform the query set up in Figure 4.12.

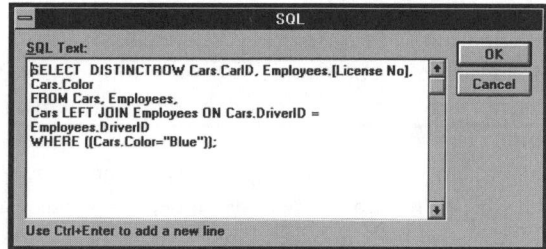

Note: Access uses the same object container model as Visual Basic for specifying tables and fields. The criteria in the SQL statement is `Cars.Color="Blue"`. As you can see, the Cars table is the container of the Color field, so they are specified by separating them with a period.

The Rules of Database Design

When designing a database structure, you should adhere to several rules to make your structure consistent and efficient. Although you can create workable databases without following the rules, they probably will have errors and might be difficult to expand as future needs arise. A well designed relational database is straightforward to extend and contains few blank records caused by storing empty fields of optional data.

Database Design

Textbook Tip: Here are some rules for good database design:

Store only one property per field. Don't combine multiple properties in a single field.

Attributes should have consistent values. Don't store different types of data in the same field.

Each table should contain a single independent entity class. Don't store data for different classes of objects, such as people and cars, in the same table.

Each entity should appear in a database only once. Don't store data describing an entity in more than one place.

There should be at least one identifier per record. You need to be able to uniquely identify each record.

One Property per Field

The first rule is that each field in a database contains a single property, and that property is *atomic*—it cannot be reasonably divided further. You have to be reasonable about applying this rule, however. You could divide a field into the individual letters in the field's contents, but that would be ridiculous in most cases. *Atomic* is in relation to how you use the data and what level of granularity you will need to use when querying the database for information. If you're a publisher with a subscriptions database, and you use the database only to print labels, you could make the whole name and address a single field. However, it's more likely that you'll want to query the database by name to see if the customer has paid his bills, or you might want to look at sales in different parts of the country. If so, you need to break the field into multiple fields containing the first name, last name, street address, city, state, and zip code. You could include a middle name with the first name since it's unlikely that you'll need them separately. If you're interested in querying the database by street name and number, you should divide the street address into street name and street number fields.

Attributes Have Consistent Values

When defining an attribute for a field, be sure that the definition allows only a single type of data. For example, don't store dollars and numbers in the same attribute. You can store two different kinds of the same type of data in a single attribute; they just need to be consistent with each other. For example, a check register contains debits and credits to an account. Both the debit amount and the credit amount could be stored in the same field of a check register database since they're the same kind of data and they're mutually exclusive in any one entry (you have one or the other

in a single entry, but never both). You wouldn't store the date or check number in that field, because those are different types of numbers.

Each Table Contains a Single Independent Entity Class

Each table should define a single class of independent entities. What this means is that a single record in a table should define a single thing. Don't try to squeeze multiple independent entities into the same table. For example, don't describe cars and people in the same table; that is, don't have one record describe a person and the next describe a car. Put them in two separate tables and then join them if necessary. However, if you find yourself creating a large number of joins between two tables, they might not be truly independent and should be combined. Again, what you do depends on your particular application and what degree of granularity you think you'll need when doing table lookups. For example, if you have a database of cars and their drivers, and each driver always drives the same car, you could put the car and driver descriptions in the same record because they are dependent. However, if a driver ever changes cars or drives more than one car, you have repeated information, which must be avoided.

Each Entity Appears in a Database Only Once

When designing a database, try to ensure that the description for any entity appears in the database only once. If the description of an entity appears more than once and part of that description changes, you must be sure to make the changes in each location—a situation prone to errors. A better idea is to have each piece of information in a single place so you have to change it only once. If you repeat descriptions, you've actually combined two independent entities into one. To fix this, put the two entities into two separate tables. For example, if you have a table in which each record describes a car and a driver, and some drivers drive more than one car, or some drivers change cars, or some cars have more than one driver, you'll find yourself repeating information in multiple records. You either have a single driver described in multiple records, or you have a car described in multiple records, or both. Avoid this situation by splitting the table into a table of cars and a table of drivers, and then join the car and driver tables to connect the cars and drivers.

At Least One Identifier per Record

Each record should have at least one unique identifier. An identifier doesn't have to be a single attribute, but it tends to be easier to use if it is. Without a unique identifier, it's difficult to link to records in other tables, because there's no way to ensure that you're accessing a specific record.

115

Database Design

Designing a Database

When it's time to actually design a database, many methods are available that can help you lay out your tables and declare their links. The most-used design method is to draw the database tables and fields by hand, drawing the different joins between the tables.

Entity-Relation Diagrams

Entity-relation (or *E-R*) *diagrams* describe not only the linkage but the logical relationship between any two fields. Figure 4.14 shows the parts of an entity-relation diagram drawn for the Cars table/Employees table from Figures 4.2 and 4.8. The table names are placed in rectangles, with the field name in an oval just above them. The relationship is placed in a diamond. A 1 and an m are placed on each side to indicate which side of the relationship is the "one" side and which is the "many."

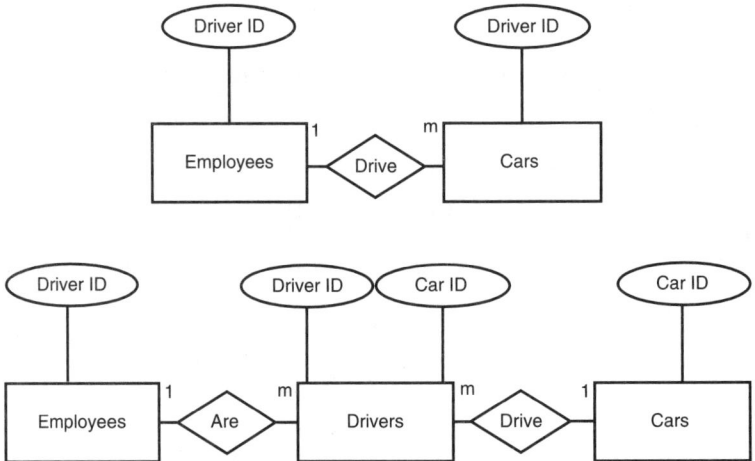

Figure 4.14. *An E-R diagram for the Cars table/Employees table example from Figure 4.2 (top) and the many-to-many example from Figure 4.8 (bottom).*

Relational Table Diagram

The most-used method of diagramming a small, uncomplicated database is the *relational table diagram*. Access and Query use the relational table diagram to specify the joins in a query. This type of diagram shows the field names of each table in a box, and lines drawn from table to table indicate the joins. For inner joins, a line is drawn between the joined fields. Figure 4.15 shows an inner join of the Cars table and the Employees table. For outer joins, the tables are connected with arrows that point from the table that includes all its records to the table that joins with any matching records. Figure 4.12 shows an outer join between two tables.

Figure 4.15.
An inner join between the Cars table and the Employees table, done with Access.

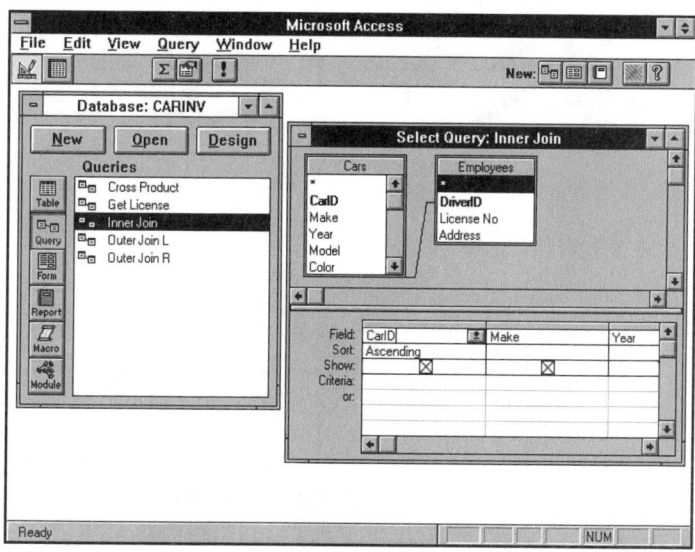

Access Database Applications

You can use three Microsoft applications to manipulate Access databases: Access, Query, and Visual Basic's Data Manager. All three use the Microsoft Jet database engine, which can manipulate the Access databases and most of the standard database file formats as well. In addition to these applications, the VisData program is included with Visual Basic as a sample application.

Although these three applications all use the same database engine, they have very different levels of capability. Access is a full-featured database application with all the capabilities necessary to create or modify a database. Figure 4.15 shows Access with a query that joins the Cars table and the Employees table. When you run the query, the Select Query window is replaced with the data returned by the query. Queries are created graphically by drawing joins between tables and selecting the fields to return from a list at the bottom of the query.

Textbook Tip: The following are the Microsoft database applications:

Access is a full-featured database application. You can easily perform most database manipulation with Access.

VisData is a sample program included with Visual Basic. It's not as powerful as Access, but it does a credible job. It's also filled with sample code.

Database Design

> **Query** is included with Excel for extracting data from a database. Queries are easy, but other manipulations such as adding fields are more difficult than using Access or VisData.
>
> **DataManager** is a Visual Basic add-in tool. It's very difficult to use because you must know SQL.

Microsoft Query is an add-in application included with Excel for obtaining information from a database and passing it to a worksheet. Query is best for retrieving information from a database, not creating a database. (Figure 4.16 shows Query performing the same query that Access performed in Figure 4.15.) You create queries much like you do in Access—by drawing the joins and selecting the fields to return. When you run a query, the data is returned to the bottom of the query window instead of being replaced. Although you can manipulate a database with Query, it's not well-suited for that task. Simple things such as adding a field to an existing table can't be done as easily in Query as they can in Access.

Figure 4.16.
An inner join between the Cars table and the Employees table, done with Query.

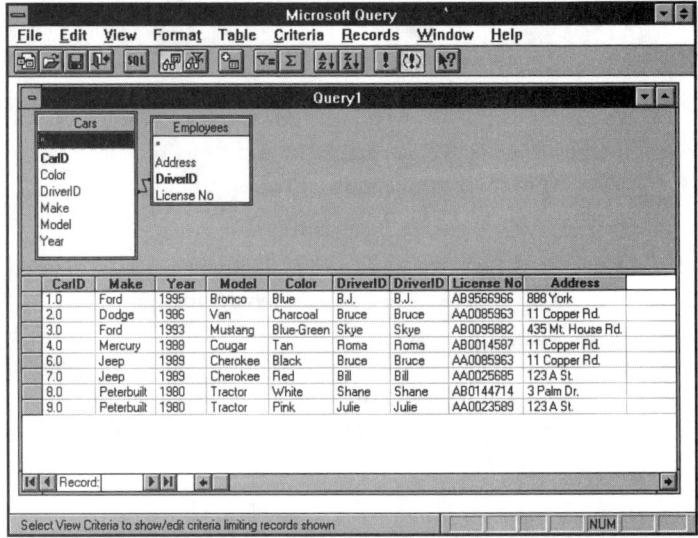

The Visual Basic Data Manager is also optimal for accessing information, not for manipulating a database. It has even fewer capabilities than Query. Figure 4.17 shows the Data Manager performing the same query that Access and Query performed in Figures 4.15 and 4.16. With the Data Manager, you create a query by typing an SQL statement into the SQL window. You must know SQL to create a query with the Data Manager, because that application has no graphical or other query creator.

Figure 4.17.
An inner join between the Cars table and the Employees table, done with the Data Manager.

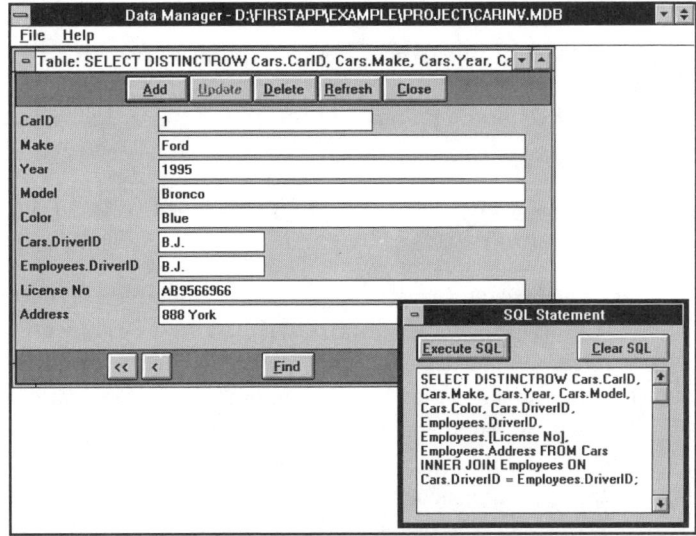

Also included with Visual Basic is the VisData sample application. Although it's just a sample application, VisData is a much more complete database manipulation program than the Data Manager. Figure 4.18 shows VisData performing the same query as the other three programs. Although it doesn't have a graphical query creator, it does have a Query Builder form that lets you create a query by selecting tables and fields from lists. When you run the query, the query builder writes the SQL statement and sends it to the database engine. The result appears in a separate table, as you can see in the background of Figure 4.18.

Figure 4.18.
An inner join between the Cars table and the Employees table, done with VisData.

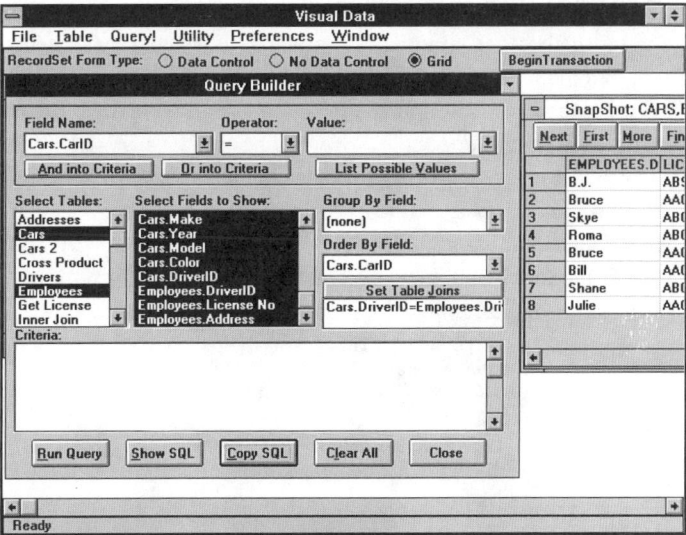

Database Design

Most of the database manipulation in this book is done with Access, but it can be done with Query or VisData if you don't have a copy of Access; it just takes more patience to get some things done. The Data Manager is useful when you want to look at or add data to a table, but it's not very useful for more-complicated manipulations unless you know SQL.

Accessing a Database with Visual Basic

Visual Basic itself is well-suited for creating a front end for a database. It has several database-aware controls and a full suite of database enhancements for the Visual Basic language. You can write a reasonably well-featured database application with Visual Basic, as evidenced by the VisData sample database application included with Visual Basic (shown in Figure 4.18). Examine the source code for this application to see several examples of accessing a database with Visual Basic. Another good place to see examples is Roger Jennings's book *Database Developer's Guide with Visual Basic 3*. Many of the examples in this section, with full credit to Roger, are adapted from his book.

Connecting to a Database

Before you can do anything with a database using Visual Basic, you must first connect to it and open a communication path. Although you will appear to be opening a data path to the database file, you're actually opening a connection to the Jet database engine, and it is actually communicating with the database file.

A Direct Connection

Probably the most common way to connect to a database is to simply open a connection to it using the OpenDatabase function. The OpenDatabase function operates much like the Open statement in Visual Basic. You specify the filename, driver, and level of access in the OpenDatabase function. You also include any security information needed to access the database, such as a username and password. The OpenDatabase function then returns a database object that you use to access and manipulate the database. Once the database is open, you use the OpenTable function to open a table in the database and to return a table object that you can then use for other forms of database access. For example, to open the Graphs database and then open the TblDefinitions table, you could use the following:

```
Dim dbGraphs As Database
Dim tblGrafDefs As Table
  Set dbGraphs = OpenDatabase("D:\firstapp\example\graphs.mdb")
  Set tblGrafDefs = dbGraphs.OpenTable("tblDefinitions")
```

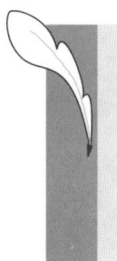

Note: In this book's examples, I use tagged variable names to make it easier to keep track of the type of a variable. These tags are two or three lowercase letters prefixed to the variable name, which starts with an uppercase letter. For example, strName is a string variable and intCounter is an integer. It's easy to tell which datatype the tags portray. For database objects such as those shown in this section, I use db for database and tbl for table.

When this code is executed, the variables are defined first, and then the database is opened and the variable dbGraphs is equated to a database object. The OpenTable method is then applied to the dbGraphs database object to open a table, which is returned to the variable tblGrafDefs. This table object can then be used to access the parts of the table, to obtain data, or to change data.

A Registered Database

The second way to access a database in Windows is to register it and access it by name. You register the name in Windows with the ODBC Control Panel. After it's registered, Visual Basic can open the database by name using the OpenDatabase method. The difference between this method and opening a database directly is that your Visual Basic program doesn't have to know where the database is; it only has to ask for it by name.

Persistent Versus Virtual Database Objects

After you've opened a database, you access one or more of the database's tables to obtain the data you need in a particular instance. How you access that table and the type of object you obtain from the database determines how you can use the object and how it responds to changes in the original database. A *persistent* database object is physically part of the database file rather than something that is adapted from the database file. Tables and QueryDefs are both persistent objects, because they are items that are actually stored in the database. A QueryDef is the SQL statement necessary to produce the query.

Textbook Tip: Here are the Visual Basic data access table objects:

TableDef contains descriptions of the tables in a database, including field names, number of fields, access, and so forth.

QueryDef contains a persistent query stored in the database.

Table contains a table from the database. Changes to the Table object affect changes in the database itself.

121

Database Design

> `Dynaset` contains a virtual table that is stored in memory. Changes in the database are reflected in the dynaset, and changes in the dynaset are reflected in the database.
>
> `Snapshot` contains a static virtual table. Data in a snapshot can't be changed and doesn't change if the data in the database changes.

Virtual database objects are created in memory from a database but aren't actually stored in the database file. A *dynaset* is a virtual database table. It can be created by copying all or part of an existing database table into memory, or it can be the result of a query. For the most part, it behaves exactly like a database table, but a dynaset isn't actually stored in the database file. Changes in the data stored in the database file are reflected in the dynaset, and changes in the dynaset are reflected in the database file.

A snapshot, like a dynaset, is a virtual table object. The difference is that it's not connected to the underlying data file. Changes in the snapshot or the database aren't propagated to the other object. A snapshot is simply a picture of the selected data from the database at the instant that the snapshot is created.

Using Database Tables

After you've defined a database and a table object, you can obtain two different types of data with them: the database and table properties data, and the table data. The properties are

- ☐ a description of the database or table
- ☐ the number and names of tables contained in the database
- ☐ the number, names, and types of fields in a table
- ☐ other attributes that indicate if a table can be updated, when it was created and changed, and the number of records

The table data is the data actually stored in the fields in the table.

The database properties are obtained using the `TableDef` object and the `TableDefs` collection of the `Database` object, or the `ListTables` method. When you know the names of the tables, use them to open a table object and apply the `ListFields` method to it to get the names and types of all the fields.

When you know the field names, use them and the table objects to actually extract the data from the fields. To access the contents of a table, you first select the record and then select the contents of the fields in that record. To select a record in a table, apply the `MoveFirst` method to select the first record in the table, then apply the `MoveNext` method to move to the next record. To back up one record, apply the `MovePrevious` method to the table object. The `MoveLast` method moves to the last record in the table. Using these methods, you can step through the records of a table. Complementing these methods is the `Seek` method, for use with tables, and the `FindFirst`, `FindNext`, `FindPrevious`, and `FindLast` methods, for use with dynasets and snapshots. These methods allow you to search for records with fields that match some criteria.

To read the contents of a record, apply the `Fields` collection to the table object. The `Fields` collection takes a single argument, which is either the name or number of the field to read. The `Value` property of the field is assumed, so you can leave it out and still get the contents of the field. For example, the following code opens a database, opens the first table, and gets the value of the third field of the fifth record:

```
Dim dbGraphs As Database
Dim tblFirstTable As Table
Dim strTableName As String
Dim intCtr As Integer
Dim intNumRecs As Integer
Dim strFieldName As String
Dim theValue As Variant
  'Open the database.
  Set dbGraphs = OpenDatabase("D:\firstapp\example\graphs.mdb")
  'Get the name of the first table.
  strTableName = dbGraphs.TableDefs(1).Name
  'Open the first table.
  Set tblFirstTable = dbGraphs.OpenTable(strTableName)
  'Find out how many records are in the table.
  'This is required to get an accurate count.
  tblFirstTable.MoveLast
  intNumRecs = tblFirstTable.RecordCount   'The number of records.
  tblFirstTable.MoveFirst   'Move to the first record.
  If intNumRecs >= 5 Then   'Make sure there are at least five records.
    For intCtr = 1 To 5     'Move down five records.
      tblFirstTable.MoveNext
    Next intCtr
  End If
  'Get the name of the third field.
  strFieldName = tblFirstTable.Fields(3).Name
  'Get the contents of the field.
  theValue = tblFirstTable.Fields(strFieldName).Value
```

Accessing a Database with SQL

The second way to access the records in a database is to use SQL statements to return a snapshot. Use the `CreateSnapshot` function with the SQL statement as the argument. What returns is a snapshot object that you can then apply the `MoveFirst`, `MoveNext`, `MoveLast`, and `Search` methods to locate records and the `Fields` collection to obtain the contents of a field. For example, the following code gets a snapshot of the inner join of the Cars table and the Employees table and returns the car number and the driver's license number:

Day 4

Database Design

```
Dim strSQL As String
Dim ssGraph As Snapshot
Dim dbGraphs As Database
  'Open the database.
  Set dbGraphs = OpenDatabase("D:\firstapp\example\graphs.mdb")
  'Create the SQL command string.
  strSQL = "SELECT DISTINCTROW Cars.CarID, Cars.DriverID,Emplyees.DriverID,
    ➥Employees.[License No] FROM Cars INNER JOIN Employees
    ➥ON Cars.DriverID=Employees.DriverID; "
  'Create a snapshot with the SQL string.
  Set ssGraph = dbGraphs.CreateSnapshot(strSQL)
```

Note: The square brackets you see in the SQL string are used to quote field names that contain blanks. Access databases allow blanks in field names, but they must be surrounded by square brackets. Field names without spaces don't need them.

The Decision Support Application Project

The decision support application currently contains two databases—the Orco database of company data and the Graphs database, which contains data about the graphs being displayed. Both are Access databases accessible over the company's network. The network is small and closed, so the databases don't require any security precautions. If there were security concerns, the capability to obtain usernames and passwords would be necessary so that the user could be authorized to use the database.

During the interview, I obtained the relational table diagram of the Orco company database (see Figure 4.19). During the analysis phase, I created Table 4.1 (a repeat of Table 2.3), which contains the list of tables needed for the decision support application. Looking at the relational table diagram, you can immediately see that there is a problem. The Order Details table has Order ID and Product ID chosen as the primary key instead of the Order Detail ID field. You also can see that the Invoice Details table is using the Order Detail ID as its primary key, which could be invalid for a partial shipment of an order. If part of an order is shipped on one invoice, the balance of the order will be shipped on another invoice, creating two Invoice Details records with the same Order Detail ID. Finally, if you execute the Edit | Relationships command and check the relationships, you find that referential integrity isn't being enforced. *Referential integrity* assures us that the joins we create remain valid as the users change the table. For example, an Order ID in the Orders table can't be changed, because that would break the join to the Order Details table.

Figure 4.19.
The layout of the Orco company database.

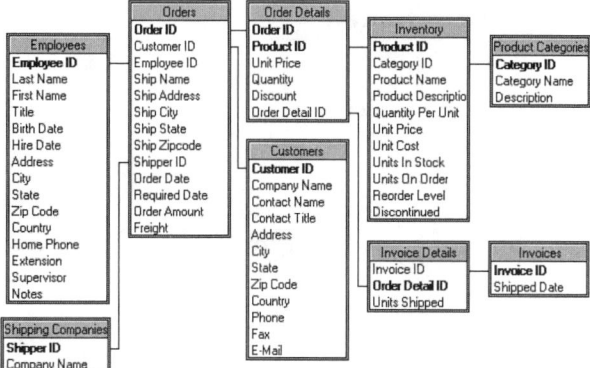

Table 4.1. Data tables needed for the decision support application.

Chart	Data

Year-to-date total sales	For each month in the current year
	    Sum the sales from the beginning
	    of the year to the month.

Sales by product category	For each month in the current year
	    For each product category
	        Sum the sales.

Sales by market segment	For each month in the current year
	    For each market segment
	        Sum the sales.

Sales by sales region	For each month in the current year
	    For each sales region
	        Sum the sales.

Average gross margin	For each month in the current year
	    For each sale in the month
	        Sum the difference between the
	        sales price and the cost
	    Divide the sum by the total sales
	    in the month.

Margins by product category	For each month in the current year
	    For each product category
	        Sum the difference between the
	        sales price and cost
	    Divide the sum by the total sales
	    in the month.

continues

Database Design

Table 4.1. continued

Chart	Data

Year-to-date orders	For each month in the current year
	    Sum the number of orders placed
	    from the beginning of the year to
	    the month.

Orders by product category	For each month in the current year
	    For each product category
	        Sum of the number of orders from
	        the beginning of the year to
	        the month.

Orders by market segment	For each month in the current year
	    For each market segment
	        Sum the number of orders from
	        the beginning of the year to
	        the month.

Orders by sales region	For each month in the current year
	    For each sales region
	        Sum the number of orders from
	        the beginning of the year to
	        the month.

Monthly backlog	For each month in the current year
	    The number of orders that are
	    unfilled at the end of the month.

Backlog by product category	For each month in the current year
	    For each product category
	        The number of orders that are
	        unfilled at the end of the month.

Backlog by market segment	For each month in the current year
	    For each market segment
	        The number of orders that are
	        unfilled at the end of the month.

Backlog by sales region	For each month in the current year
	    For each sales region
	        The number of orders that are
	        unfilled at the end of the month.

Chart	Data

Average order cycle	For each month in the current year
	    For all orders shipped in a month
	        The sum of the difference between the shipping date and the order date
	    Divide the sum by the number of orders shipped in a month.

Order cycle by market segment	For each month in the current year
	    For each market segment
	        For all orders shipped in a month
	            The sum of the difference between the shipping date and the order date
	        Divide the sum by the number of orders shipped in a month.

Order cycle frequency distribution	For each order cycle time Tally the number of shipped orders in the current year with that cycle time.
Monthly ending inventory	For each month in the current year The value of the inventory at the end of the month.

Inventory by product category	For each month in the current year
	    For each product category
	        The value of the inventory at the end of each month.

Inventory turnover by product category	For each month in the current year
	    For each product category
	        The sum of the number of products sold divided by the total number of products in that product category in the inventory.

Using Access (or the VisData application), you can fix these problems by adding the Invoice Detail ID field to the Invoice Details table, by changing the primary keys of the Order Details and Invoice Details tables, and by preserving referential integrity for all of the joins. An Access diagram of the relationships, shown in Figure 4.20, contains the corrections just described. These changes should be transparent to the users but make the database more robust.

Database Design

Figure 4.20.
The revised layout of the Orco company database.

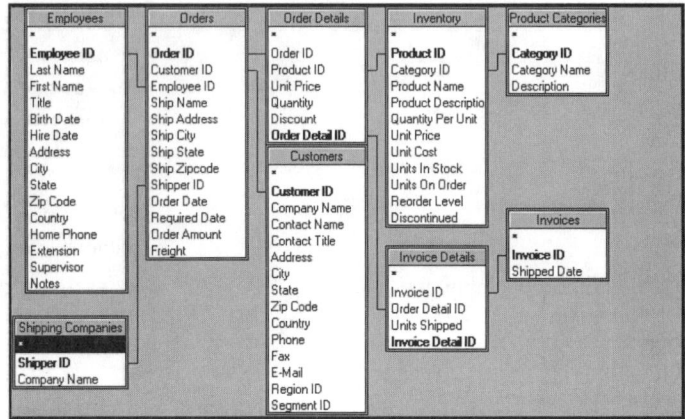

Attaching the Tables

To simplify access to the Orco database, we will attach the tables in the Orco database to the Graphs database. By doing this, you have to open only a single database to get access to both. Tables are attached to an Access database using the Attach Tables command in Access, Query, or VisData, as shown in Figure 4.21. Not all the tables are attached—only those needed for the decision support application.

Figure 4.21.
Attaching the Orco database tables to the Graphs database.

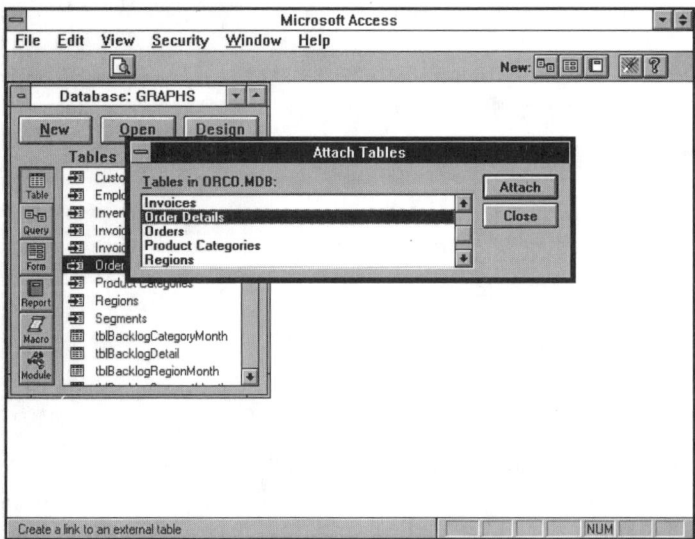

Attaching these tables changes the data flow diagram to that shown in Figure 4.22. The main changes are in the area of the database tables, where the Orco data now passes through the Graphs database on its way to the application.

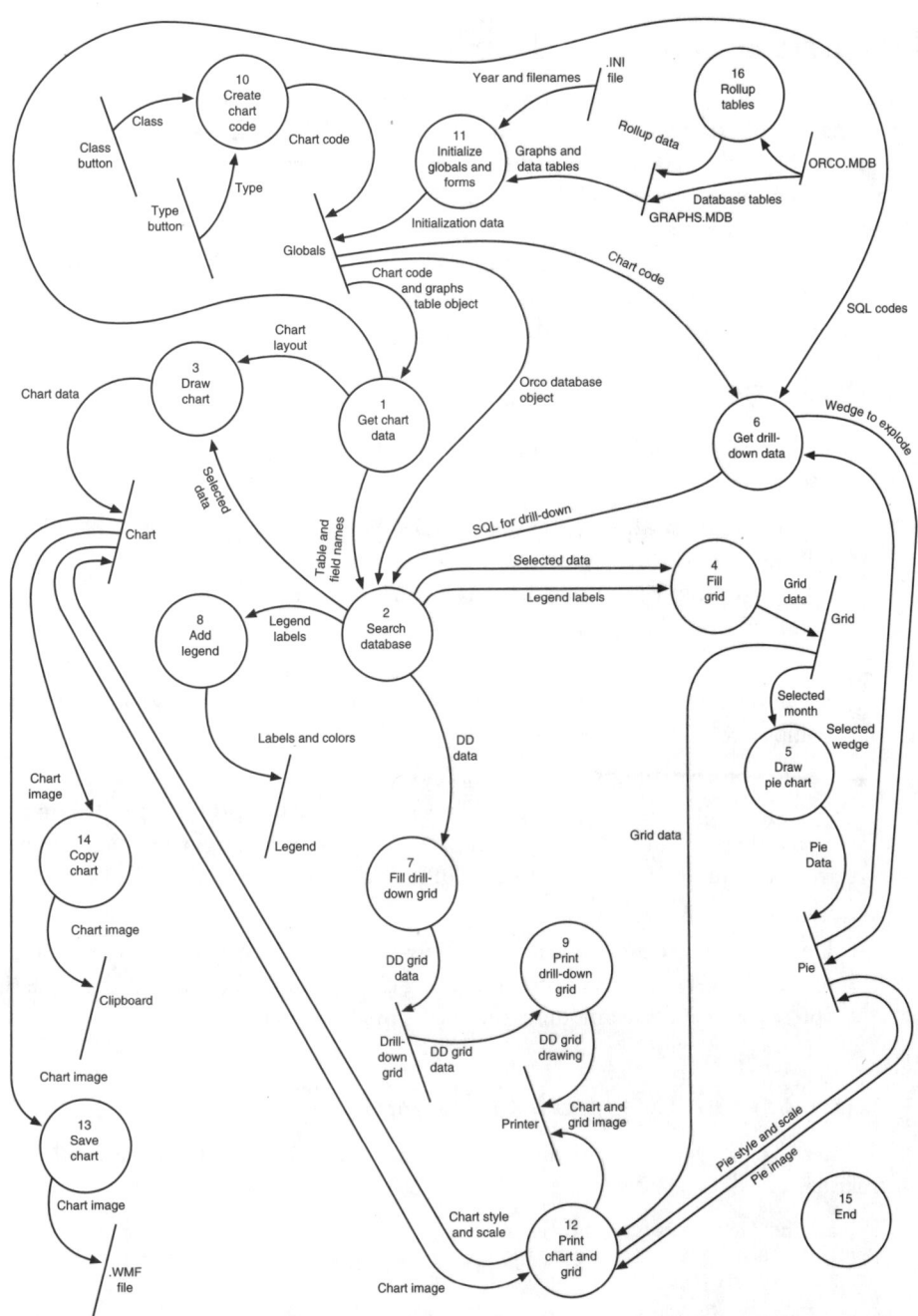

Figure 4.22. *The revised data flow diagram, with the Orco tables attached to the Graphs database.*

Database Design

Creating Rollup Tables

Each graph that is plotted requires only a small amount of data, but those data values represent summations of a relatively large amount of data from the database—summations that take time to create. Since the data for all but the current month is fixed, you can create rollup tables for each of the needed queries and then simply select the data you need from the rollup tables. A *rollup table* contains the completed summations and averages needed for the graphs. In addition to the rollup table, also save the query that was used to create the rollup table. At the end of each month, the rollup query is run again, updating all the rollup tables. Rollup tables do represent a break from the rules of database design, but they aren't really part of the database. They're an intermediate step the data takes as it moves from the database to the decision support application. The creation of the rollup tables is process 16 in Figure 4.22.

You should keep in mind some guidelines when doing rollups to maintain the consistency of your data:

1. Try to avoid cascading rollups. A *cascaded rollup* is when you calculate a rollup of a rolled-up value. If changes occur in the underlying data after the first value is rolled up, using it to further roll up data is inconsistent with the underlying data. Always try to roll up from the operational data.

2. Select rollup times that aren't likely to be subject to retroactive changes. If the operational data that was rolled up changes for any reason, such as an audit, all the rollups have to be recalculated.

3. Try to not have rollups in the operational data. This comes from our rule of having data appear in only one place in the operational database. If data is rolled up in an operational field, the data appears in two places—in the original field and as part of the rolled-up total. If changes occur in the original amount, the rolled-up amount must be recalculated.

4. Do the rollups at times when other transactions are unlikely to occur, such as at night or on the weekend. If someone is making changes to the database at the same time you're rolling up the amounts, the results might be inconsistent.

Year-To-Date Total Sales

The first chart is the year-to-date sales. According to Table 4.1, the data has the following structure:

```
For each month in the current year
  Sum the sales from the beginning
  of the year to the month.
```

To create the rollup table for this, you need a Create Table query that finds and totals the appropriate data. Looking at the database structure chart, you see that the Order Amount and

Order Date are in the Orders table. However, the order amount is already a roll-up amount, being the product of the quantity sold times the cost per item. The actual sales in a month depend on what is actually shipped and not on what was ordered, so what should be used are the Shipped Date from the Invoices table and the Units Shipped in the Invoice Details table. Units Shipped is then multiplied by Unit Price and then discounted to get the sales on the Shipped Date. These sales are then totaled by the month to give the total sales-to-date for each month.

To build the table named tblSalesTotalMonth, you first need to create a table called tblMonths that contains only the year and month. This table will then be used with the Order Details and Invoices tables to calculate the year-to-date sales. Figure 4.23 shows the query used to create tblMonths, and Figure 4.24 shows part of the table. The SQL statement that creates the table is as follows:

Query: qryMonths

```
SELECT Format(Invoices.[Shipped Date],"yyyy") AS Year,
Format(Invoices.[Shipped Date],"mm") AS Month INTO tblMonths
FROM Invoices
GROUP BY Format(Invoices.[Shipped Date],"yyyy"),
Format(Invoices.[Shipped Date],"mm");
```

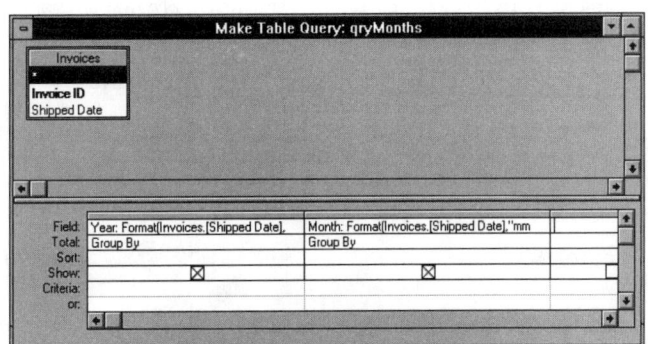

Figure 4.23.
The Access query to create the tblMonths *table.*

Figure 4.24.
Part of the completed tblMonths *table.*

Database Design

The table is created by extracting the month and year from the Shipping Date field in the Invoices table and then grouping them to eliminate any redundant values. Following the SELECT keyword are two format statements that select the year and month from the Shipping Date field and create new fields named Year and Month. The INTO clause indicates that a new table named tblMonths is to be created to contain these new fields. The FROM clause indicates that the data comes from the Invoices table, and the GROUP BY clause groups the results by the same values that were used to create the Year and Month fields.

The next step is to use tblMonths in a query named qrySalesTotalMonth to create the tblSalesTotalMonth needed for the first graph. Save the query so that it can be rerun every month to update the table with the new month's data. The query, created in Access, is shown in Figure 4.25. Running the query creates the table shown in Figure 4.26. The following is the SQL statement created by Query that creates the table:

Query: qrySalesTotalMonth

```
SELECT tblMonths.Year, tblMonths.Month,
Sum([Order Details].[Unit Price]*[Invoice Details].[Units Shipped]*
(1-[Order Details].Discount)) AS Sales, Count(Orders.[Order ID]) AS Orders,
Sum([Invoice Details].[Units Shipped]) AS Units
INTO tblSalesTotalMonth
FROM tblMonths, Invoices INNER JOIN ((Orders INNER JOIN [Order Details] ON
Orders.[Order ID] = [Order Details].[Order ID]) INNER JOIN
[Invoice Details] ON [Order Details].[Order Detail ID] =
[Invoice Details].[Order Detail ID]) ON Invoices.[Invoice ID] =
[Invoice Details].[Invoice ID]
WHERE (((Format([Invoices].[Shipped Date],"yyyy"))=[tblMonths].[Year]) AND
((Format([Invoices].[Shipped Date],"mm"))<=[tblMonths].[Month]))
GROUP BY tblMonths.Year, tblMonths.Month;
```

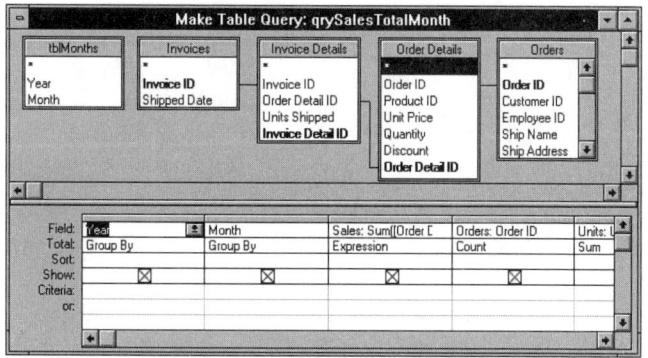

Figure 4.25.
The Access query to create the tblSalesTotalMonth *table.*

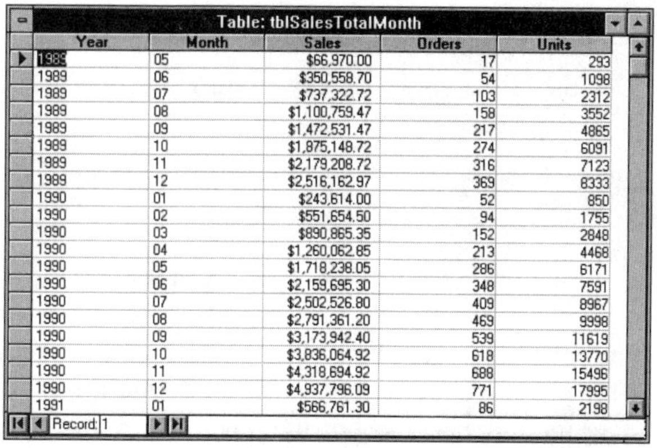

Figure 4.26.
Part of the completed `tblSalesTotalMonth` *table.*

Year	Month	Sales	Orders	Units
1989	05	$66,970.00	17	293
1989	06	$350,558.70	54	1098
1989	07	$737,322.72	103	2312
1989	08	$1,100,759.47	158	3552
1989	09	$1,472,531.47	217	4865
1989	10	$1,875,148.72	274	6091
1989	11	$2,179,208.72	316	7123
1989	12	$2,516,162.97	369	8333
1990	01	$243,614.00	52	850
1990	02	$551,654.50	94	1755
1990	03	$890,865.35	152	2848
1990	04	$1,260,062.85	213	4468
1990	05	$1,718,238.05	286	6171
1990	06	$2,159,695.30	348	7591
1990	07	$2,502,526.80	409	8967
1990	08	$2,791,361.20	469	9998
1990	09	$3,173,942.40	539	11619
1990	10	$3,836,064.92	618	13770
1990	11	$4,318,694.92	688	15496
1990	12	$4,937,796.09	771	17995
1991	01	$566,761.30	86	2198

The SELECT clause lists the fields that will be part of this new table. They consist of the Year and Month fields of the `tblMonths` table, a calculated field named Sales, a calculated field named Orders, and a calculated field named Units. The last two calculated fields aren't needed for the first graph. The Sales calculated field equals the product of Units Shipped times Unit Price times 1 minus Discount, which gives the total value of this particular invoice item. Those values are then summed over the grouping of the table. The FROM clause shows a Cartesian join of the `tblMonths` to the INNER JOIN of the Invoices, Orders, Order Details, and Invoice Details tables. The WHERE clause limits the selected records to those in which the year in the shipping date equals the year in the `tblMonths` table and where the month in the Shipping Date is less than or equal to the month in the `tblMonth` table. Finally, the GROUP BY clause groups the results by the Year and Month. The grouping determines which records are combined for summing or counting in the calculated fields.

This query operates by creating a Cartesian join of the `tblMonths` table and the joined tables Orders, Order Details, Invoice Details, and Invoices. The Cartesian join combines each of the year-month combinations with every record in the joined tables. These combined records are then filtered by keeping only those for the same year and for months that are less than or equal to the month in the `tblMonths` table. You do this because the values you want are the year-to-date sales, so the sales amounts must appear in the selected records multiple times, once for each following month being summed for. That is, the sales values for January are summed 12 times, once for each month of the year, while those for December are summed only once in the December total. If you did an inner join of all the tables instead of a Cartesian join, the sales amounts would each appear only once and you would calculate the sales per month instead of the year-to-date sales.

Because of the large number of records created as part of this calculation, you might want to write a new query for future months that only appends the current values to the table instead of recreating the whole table.

Database Design

Sales by Product Category

The second chart is the sales by product category chart. According to Table 4.1, the data has the following structure:

```
For each month in the current year
  For each product category
    Sum the sales.
```

The rollup data for the Sales by Product Category graph is simpler to create than the year-to-date sales, because each total involves only one month instead of all the months since the beginning of the year. By grouping the data by the product categories in the Product Categories table and then by the month and year, you get a crosstab table of monthly values for each category. The query is shown in Figure 4.27, and the resulting table is shown in Figure 4.28.

Query: qrySalesCategoryMonth

```
SELECT Format(Invoices.[Shipped Date],"yyyy") AS Year,
Format(Invoices.[Shipped Date],"mm") AS Month,
[Product Categories].[Category ID],
Sum([Order Details].[Unit Price]*[Invoice Details].[Units Shipped]*
(1-[Order Details].[Discount])) AS Sales
INTO tblSalesCategoryMonth
FROM ((((Orders INNER JOIN [Order Details] ON Orders.[Order ID] =
[Order Details].[Order ID]) INNER JOIN Inventory ON
[Order Details].[Product ID] = Inventory.[Product ID]) INNER JOIN
[Product Categories] ON Inventory.[Category ID] =
[Product Categories].[Category ID])
INNER JOIN [Invoice Details] ON [Order Details].[Order Detail ID] =
[Invoice Details].[Order Detail ID]) INNER JOIN Invoices ON
[Invoice Details].[Invoice ID] = Invoices.[Invoice ID]
GROUP BY Format(Invoices.[Shipped Date],"yyyy"), Format(Invoices.[Shipped
Date],"mm"), [Product Categories].[Category ID];
```

Figure 4.27.
The Access query to create the tblSalesCategoryMonth *table.*

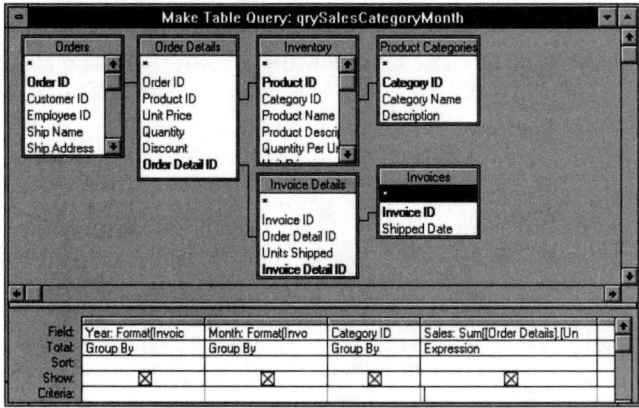

Figure 4.28.
Part of the completed `tblSalesCategoryMonth` *table.*

Sales by Market Segment

The query to create the sales by market segment is nearly identical to that for the sales by product category. You just group by the market segment instead of the product category. However, there is no table of market segments in the Orco database. In order to make this work, you must add a new table named Segments to the database and join it to the table of customers. At the same time, add a table of Regions as well, because that is needed for the query following this one. Figures 4.29 and 4.30 show the two new tables added to the Orco database, and Figure 4.31 shows the new Relations diagram with the new tables joined to the Customers table. Adding these tables amounts to a lot of work, because the record for every customer must be examined and its segment and region determined. You could handle part of the regions by writing a query that scans for specific ranges of zip codes and then uses that to select the region. The Segments and Regions tables also contain a field named Activated. This field indicates whether the specific market or region actually has any customers. It can be tested to determine whether there is any data to scan for. The first time the specific region or market segment is used, the Activated flag should be changed to Yes.

Figure 4.29.
The Segments table added to the Orco database.

135

Database Design

Figure 4.30.
The Regions table added to the Orco database.

Figure 4.31.
The new Relations diagram showing the new joins to the Customers table.

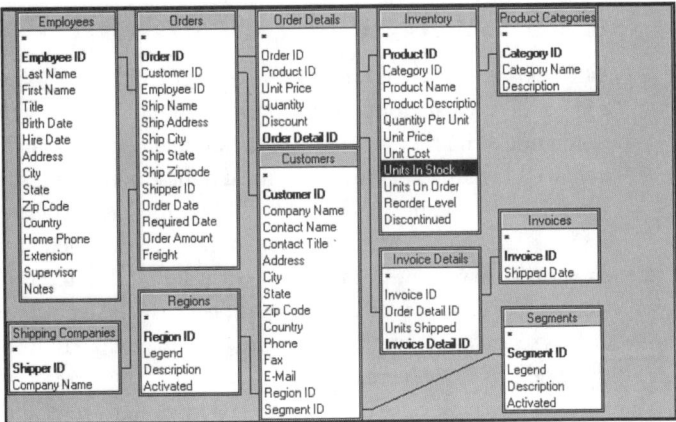

Now that you have a Segments table available, you can write a query to create the `tblSalesSegmentMonth` table. As you can see, the following SQL statement is nearly identical to the previous one, except that the Segment ID in the Customers table is used to group the summations by market segment.

Query: qrySalesSegmentMonth

```
SELECT Format(Invoices.[Shipped Date],"yyyy") AS Year,
Format (Invoices.[Shipped Date],"mm") AS Month, Customers.[Segment ID],
Sum([Order Details].[Unit Price]*[Invoice Details].[Units Shipped]*
(1-[Order Details].Discount)) AS Sales INTO tblSalesSegmentMonth FROM Invoices
INNER JOIN ((Customers INNER JOIN (Orders INNER JOIN [Order Details] ON
Orders.[Order ID] = [Order Details].[Order ID]) ON Customers.[Customer ID] =
Orders.[Customer ID]) INNER JOIN [Invoice Details] ON
[Order Details].[Order Detail ID] = [Invoice Details].[Order Detail ID])
ON Invoices.[Invoice ID] = [Invoice Details].[Invoice ID]
GROUP BY Format(Invoices.[Shipped Date],"yyyy"),
Format(Invoices.[Shipped Date],"mm"), Customers.[Segment ID];
```

The query creates a table containing year, month, and Segment ID columns, and then calculates the total sales by multiplying the number of units delivered times the cost and then applying any discount. The records included in the summation part of the formula are selected by the grouping of the data. The summation is calculated for all records that fall within a single group specified by the GROUPED BY clause of the SQL statement. In this case, all records that shipped on a specific month of a specific year with a single market segment are selected and summed. Records in a different month or segment are summed separately as part of that other segment.

Sales by Sales Region

The SQL statement for the Sales by Sales Region query is identical to the Sales by Market Segment query, except that the Segment ID is replaced with the Region ID.

Query: qrySalesRegionMonth

```
SELECT Format(Invoices.[Shipped Date],"yyyy") AS Year,
Format(Invoices.[Shipped Date],"mm") AS Month, Customers.[Region ID],
Sum([Order Details].[Unit Price]*[Invoice Details].[Units Shipped]*
(1-[Order Details].Discount)) AS Sales INTO tblSalesRegionMonth FROM Invoices
INNER JOIN ((Customers INNER JOIN (Orders INNER JOIN [Order Details] ON
Orders.[Order ID] = [Order Details].[Order ID]) ON Customers.[Customer ID] =
Orders.[Customer ID]) INNER JOIN [Invoice Details] ON
[Order Details].[Order Detail ID] = [Invoice Details].[Order Detail ID]) ON
Invoices.[Invoice ID] = [Invoice Details].[Invoice ID]
GROUP BY Format(Invoices.[Shipped Date],"yyyy"),
Format(Invoices.[Shipped Date],"mm"), Customers.Region ID];
```

Average Gross Margin

The average gross margin is calculated by subtracting the total cost of all sales from the total sales (Margin1) and then dividing by the total sales (Margin2) to get the average margin (Margin1/Margin2). The calculation has to be done in two parts because the formula is too long to fit in a formula cell in an Access query. As before, the grouping controls which records are included in each summation. The SQL statement to do this follows.

Query: qryMarginAverageMonth

```
SELECT Format(Invoices.[Shipped Date],"yyyy") AS Year,
Format(Invoices.[Shipped Date], "mm") AS Month, [Margin1]/[Margin2] AS Margin,
(Sum([Order Details].[Unit Price]*[Invoice Details].[Units Shipped]*
(1-[Order Details].[Discount]))-Sum([Inventory].[Unit Cost]*
[Invoice Details].[Units Shipped])) AS Margin1,
(Sum([Order Details].[Unit Price]*[Invoice Details].[Units Shipped]*
(1-[Order Details].[Discount]))) AS Margin2
INTO tblMarginAverageMonth
FROM Invoices, Inventory, Orders, [Order Details], [Invoice Details],
```

continues

Day 4: Database Design

Query: continued

```
Orders INNER JOIN [Order Details] ON Orders.[Order ID] =
[Order Details].[Order ID], Inventory INNER JOIN [Order Details]
ON Inventory.[Product ID] = [Order Details].[Product ID],
[Order Details] INNER JOIN [Invoice Details]
ON [Order Details].[Order Detail ID] = [Invoice Details].[Order Detail ID],
Invoices INNER JOIN [Invoice Details]
ON Invoices.[Invoice ID] = [Invoice Details].[Invoice ID]
GROUP BY Format(Invoices.[Shipped Date],"yyyy"),
Format(Invoices.[Shipped Date],"mm");
```

Margins by Product Category

The Margins by Product Category table is created by taking the Average Gross Margins query and adding the Category ID to the table and to the Group By phrase to separate the table into category groups.

Query: qryMarginCategoryMonth

```
SELECT Format(Invoices.[Shipped Date],"yyyy") AS Year,
Format(Invoices.[Shipped Date], "mm") AS Month,
Inventory.[Category ID], Margin1/Margin2 AS Margin,
(Sum([Order Details].[Unit Price]*[Invoice Details].[Units Shipped]*
(1-[Order Details].[Discount]))-Sum([Inventory].[Unit Cost]*
[Invoice Details].[Units Shipped])) AS Margin1,
(Sum([Order Details].[Unit Price]*[Invoice Details].[Units Shipped]*
(1-[Order Details].[Discount]))) AS Margin2
INTO tblMarginCategoryMonth
FROM Invoices, Inventory, Orders, [Order Details], [Invoice Details],
Orders INNER JOIN [Order Details] ON Orders.[Order ID] =
[Order Details].[Order ID], Inventory INNER JOIN [Order Details]
ON Inventory.[Product ID] = [Order Details].[Product ID],
[Order Details] INNER JOIN [Invoice Details]
ON [Order Details].[Order Detail ID] = [Invoice Details].[Order Detail ID],
Invoices INNER JOIN [Invoice Details]
ON Invoices.[Invoice ID] = [Invoice Details].[Invoice ID]
GROUP BY Format(Invoices.[Shipped Date],"yyyy"),
Format(Invoices.[Shipped Date],"mm"), Inventory.[Category ID];
```

Year-To-Date Orders

The Year-to-Date Orders query is created in the same way as the year-to-date sales, except that the units ordered are used instead of the units shipped to calculate the total amount. A Cartesian join is used again with the Months table to create combinations of all sales with all months and then to select only records that occur between the first of the year and the month in question.

Query: qryOrdersTotalMonth

```
SELECT tblMonths.Year, tblMonths.Month, Sum([Order Details].[Unit Price]*
[Order Details].Quantity*(1-[Order Details].Discount)) AS Sales
INTO tblOrdersTotalMonth
FROM tblMonths, Orders INNER JOIN [Order Details] ON Orders.[Order ID] =
[Order Details].[Order ID]
WHERE (((Format([Orders].[Order Date],"yyyy"))=[tblMonths].[Year]) AND
((Format([Orders].[Order Date],"mm"))<=[tblMonths].[Month]))
GROUP BY tblMonths.Year, tblMonths.Month;
```

Orders by Product Category

The Orders by Product Category query follows the same structure as the Sales by Product Category query. As with the year-to-date orders, the quantity ordered is used to calculate the totals instead of the units shipped.

Query: qryOrdersCategoryMonth

```
SELECT Format(Orders.[Order Date],"yyyy") AS Year,
Format(Orders.[Order Date],"mm") AS Month,
[Product Categories].[Category ID],
Sum([Order Details].[Unit Price]*[Order Details].[Quantity]*
(1-[Order Details].[Discount])) AS Sales INTO tblOrdersCategoryMonth
FROM [Product Categories] INNER JOIN (Inventory INNER JOIN
(Orders INNER JOIN [Order Details] ON Orders.[Order ID] =
[Order Details].[Order ID]) ON Inventory.[Product ID] =
[Order Details].[Product ID]) ON [Product Categories].[Category ID] =
Inventory.[Category ID]
GROUP BY Format(Orders.[Order Date],"yyyy"), Format(Orders.[Order Date],"mm"),
[Product Categories].[Category ID];
```

Orders by Market Segment

The Orders by Market Segment query is the same as the Orders by Product Category query, but the Category ID is replaced with the Segment ID to change the groupings. The SQL statement follows.

Query: qryOrdersSegmentMonth

```
SELECT Format(Orders.[Order Date],"yyyy") AS Year,
Format(Orders.[Order Date],"mm") AS Month, Customers.[Region ID],
Sum([Order Details].[Unit Price]*[Order Details].[Quantity]*
(1-[Order Details].Discount)) AS Sales INTO tblOrdersSegmentMonth
FROM Customers INNER JOIN (Orders INNER JOIN [Order Details] ON
Orders.[Order ID] = [Order Details].[Order ID]) ON Customers.[Customer ID] =
Orders.[Customer ID]
GROUP BY Format(Orders.[Order Date],"yyyy"), Format(Orders.[Order Date],"mm"),
Customers.[Segment ID];
```

Database Design

Orders by Sales Region

The Orders by Sales Region query is the same as the Orders by Market Segment query, but the Segment ID is replaced with the Region ID. The SQL statement follows.

Query: qryOrdersRegionMonth

```
SELECT Format(Orders.[Order Date],"yyyy") AS Year,
Format(Orders.[Order Date],"mm") AS Month, Customers.[Region ID],
Sum([Order Details].[Unit Price]*[Order Details].[Quantity]*
(1-[Order Details].Discount)) AS Sales INTO tblOrdersRegionMonth
FROM Customers INNER JOIN (Orders INNER JOIN [Order Details] ON
Orders.[Order ID] = [Order Details].[Order ID]) ON Customers.[Customer ID] =
Orders.[Customer ID]
GROUP BY Format(Orders.[Order Date],"yyyy"), Format(Orders.[Order Date],"mm"),
Customers.[Region ID];
```

Monthly Backlog

The Monthly Backlog table is a table of the value of all orders not yet shipped at the end of each month. You calculate the value of the orders in the same way as in the other tables, select all the tables in which the order date doesn't equal the shipping date, and then group the table by month and year. The SQL statement follows.

Query: qryBacklogTotalMonth

```
SELECT Format(Orders.[Order Date],"yyyy") AS Year,
Format(Orders.[Order Date],"mm") AS Month, Sum([Order Details].[Unit Price]*
[Order Details].Quantity*(1-[Order Details].Discount)) AS Backlog
INTO tblBacklogTotalMonth
FROM (Orders INNER JOIN [Order Details] ON Orders.[Order ID] =
[Order Details].[Order ID]) INNER JOIN (Invoices INNER JOIN [Invoice Details]
ON Invoices.[Invoice ID] = [Invoice Details].[Invoice ID])
ON [Order Details].[Order Detail ID] = [Invoice Details].[Order Detail ID]
WHERE (((Format([Invoices].[Shipped Date],
"mmyy"))<>Format([Orders].[Order Date],"mmyy")))
GROUP BY Format(Orders.[Order Date],"yyyy"), Format(Orders.[Order Date],"mm");
```

Backlog by Product Category

The Backlog by Product Category table is created from the Monthly Backlog table by adding the product category to the table and to the grouping. The SQL statement follows.

Query: qryBacklogCategoryTotalMonth

```
SELECT Format(Orders.[Order Date],"yyyy") AS Year,
Format(Orders.[Order Date],"mm") AS Month, Inventory.[Category ID],
Sum([Order Details].[Unit Price]*[Order Details].Quantity*
(1-[Order Details].Discount)) AS Backlog INTO tblBacklogCategoryMonth
FROM Invoices INNER JOIN ((Inventory INNER JOIN (Orders INNER JOIN
[Order Details] ON Orders.[Order ID] = [Order Details].[Order ID]) ON
Inventory.[Product ID] = [Order Details].[Product ID]) INNER JOIN
[Invoice Details] ON [Order Details].[Order Detail ID] =
[Invoice Details].[Order Detail ID]) ON Invoices.[Invoice ID] =
[Invoice Details].[Invoice ID]
WHERE (((Format([Invoices].[Shipped Date],
"mmyy"))<>Format([Orders].[Order Date],"mmyy")))
GROUP BY Format(Orders.[Order Date],"yyyy"), Format(Orders.[Order Date],"mm"),
Inventory.[Category ID];
```

Backlog by Market Segment

The Backlog by Market Segment is created from the Backlog by Market Category by replacing the Category ID with the Segment ID.

Query: qryBacklogSegmentMonth

```
SELECT Format(Orders.[Order Date],"yyyy") AS Year,
Format(Orders.[Order Date],"mm") AS Month, Customers.[Segment ID],
Sum([Order Details].[Unit Price]*[Order Details].Quantity*
(1-[Order Details].Discount)) AS Backlog INTO tblBacklogSegmentMonth
FROM Customers INNER JOIN (Invoices INNER JOIN ((Orders INNER JOIN
[Order Details] ON Orders.[Order ID] = [Order Details].[Order ID])
INNER JOIN [Invoice Details] ON [Order Details].[Order Detail ID] =
[Invoice Details].[Order Detail ID]) ON Invoices.[Invoice ID] =
[Invoice Details].[Invoice ID]) ON Customers.[Customer ID] =
Orders.[Customer ID]
WHERE (((Format([Invoices].[Shipped Date],
"mmyy"))<>Format([Orders].[Order Date],"mmyy")))
GROUP BY Format(Orders.[Order Date],"yyyy"), Format(Orders.[Order Date],"mm"),
Customers.[Segment ID];
```

Backlog by Sales Region

Finally, the Backlog by Sales Region is created by exchanging the Segment ID for the Region ID.

Database Design

Query: qryBacklogRegionMonth

```
SELECT Format(Orders.[Order Date],"yyyy") AS Year,
Format(Orders.[Order Date],"mm") AS Month, Customers.[Region ID],
Sum([Order Details].[Unit Price]*[Order Details].Quantity*
(1-[Order Details].Discount)) AS Backlog INTO tblBacklogRegionMonth
FROM Customers INNER JOIN (Invoices INNER JOIN ((Orders INNER JOIN
[Order Details] ON Orders.[Order ID] = [Order Details].[Order ID])
INNER JOIN [Invoice Details] ON [Order Details].[Order Detail ID] =
[Invoice Details].[Order Detail ID]) ON Invoices.[Invoice ID] =
[Invoice Details].[Invoice ID]) ON Customers.[Customer ID] =
Orders.[Customer ID]
WHERE (((Format([Invoices].[Shipped Date],
"mmyy"))<>Format([Orders].[Order Date],"mmyy")))
GROUP BY Format(Orders.[Order Date],"yyyy"), Format(Orders.[Order Date],"mm"),
Customers.[Region ID];
```

Average Order Cycle

The *order cycle* is the amount of time that elapses between the date an order is placed and the day it's shipped. Here, in the average order cycle, we use the `DateDiff` function to calculate the number of days between the order date and the shipping date, and the `Avg` function to calculate the average. In addition, we calculate the standard deviation and variance of the order cycle time.

Query: qryCycleAverageMonth

```
SELECT Format(Invoices.[Shipped Date],"yyyy") AS Year,
Format(Invoices.[Shipped Date],"mm") AS Month,
Avg(DateDiff("d",Orders.[Order Date],Invoices.[Shipped Date])) AS Days,
StDev(DateDiff("d",Orders.[Order Date],Invoices.[Shipped Date])) AS StDev,
Var(DateDiff("d",Orders.[Order Date],Invoices.[Shipped Date])) AS Variance,
Count("Orders") AS Orders INTO tblCycleAverageMonth
FROM Invoices INNER JOIN ((Orders INNER JOIN [Order Details] ON
Orders.[Order ID] = [Order Details].[Order ID]) INNER JOIN
[Invoice Details] ON [Order Details].[Order Detail ID] =
[Invoice Details].[Order Detail ID]) ON Invoices.[Invoice ID] =
[Invoice Details].[Invoice ID]
GROUP BY Format(Invoices.[Shipped Date],"yyyy"),
Format(Invoices.[Shipped Date],"mm");
```

Order Cycle by Market Segment

The Order Cycle by Market Segment query is created using the Average Order Cycle query and adding the Segment ID to the table and to the `GROUP BY` phrase.

Query: qryCycleSegmentMonth

```
SELECT Format(Invoices.[Shipped Date],"yyyy") AS Year,
Format(Invoices.[Shipped Date],"mm") AS Month, Customers.[Segment ID],
Avg(DateDiff("d",Orders.[Order Date],Invoices.[Shipped Date])) AS Days,
StDev(DateDiff("d",Orders.[Order Date],Invoices.[Shipped Date])) AS StDev,
Count("Orders") AS Orders INTO tblCycleSegmentMonth
FROM Invoices INNER JOIN (((Customers INNER JOIN Orders ON
Customers.[Customer ID] = Orders.[Customer ID]) INNER JOIN
[Order Details] ON Orders.[Order ID] = [Order Details].[Order ID])
INNER JOIN [Invoice Details] ON [Order Details].[Order Detail ID] =
[Invoice Details].[Order Detail ID]) ON Invoices.[Invoice ID] =
[Invoice Details].[Invoice ID]
GROUP BY Format(Invoices.[Shipped Date],"yyyy"),
Format(Invoices.[Shipped Date],"mm"), Customers.[Segment ID];
```

Order Cycle Frequency Distribution

The Order Cycle Frequency Distribution is quite a bit different from the previous tables. A *frequency distribution* is a histogram of the number of occurrences of a given order cycle throughout the year. To calculate this table, first calculate the order cycle by subtracting the ordered date from the shipped date, and then use this value to order the table. Figure 4.32 shows the query, and Figure 4.33 shows part of the resulting table. The Cycle column is the number of days in the order cycle, and the Frequency is the number of orders with the indicated cycle length. The SQL statement to create this table follows.

Query: qryCycleDistributionMonth

```
SELECT Format([Invoices].[Shipped Date],"yyyy") AS Year,
DateDiff("d",[Orders]![Order Date],[Invoices].[Shipped Date]) AS Cycle,
Count(Invoices.[Invoice ID]) AS Frequency INTO tblCycleDistribution
FROM Orders INNER JOIN ([Order Details] INNER JOIN (Invoices INNER JOIN
[Invoice Details] ON Invoices.[Invoice ID] = [Invoice Details].[Invoice ID]) ON
[Order Details].[Order Detail ID] = [Invoice Details].[Order Detail ID]) ON
Orders.[Order ID] = [Order Details].[Order ID]
GROUP BY Format([Invoices].[Shipped Date],"yyyy"),
DateDiff("d",[Orders]![Order Date],[Invoices].[Shipped Date])
ORDER BY Format([Invoices].[Shipped Date],"yyyy"),
DateDiff("d",[Orders]![Order Date],[Invoices].[Shipped Date]);
```

Figure 4.32.
The query to create the Order Cycle Frequency Distribution table.

Table: tblCycleDistribution

Year	Cycle	Frequency
1989	1	15
1989	2	24
1989	3	29
1989	4	31
1989	5	22
1989	6	34
1989	7	61
1989	8	27
1989	9	29
1989	10	19
1989	12	5
1989	13	5
1989	15	8
1989	18	13
1989	20	3
1989	22	1
1989	24	3
1989	25	6
1989	26	4
1989	28	1
1989	29	7
1989	31	4
1989	32	4

Record: 1

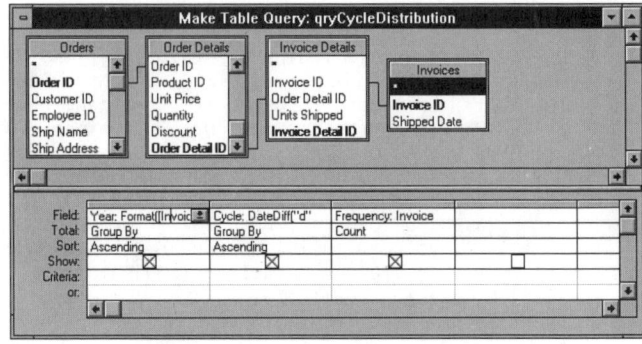

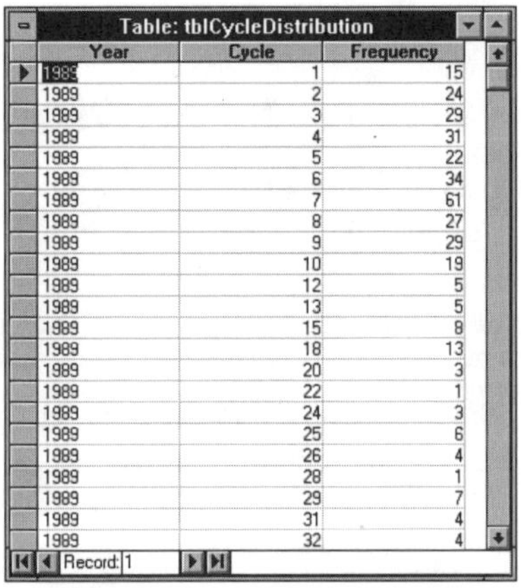

Figure 4.33.
Part of the Order Cycle Frequency Distribution table.

Monthly Ending Inventory

To create the Monthly Ending Inventory table, calculate the value of the inventory at the end of each month by multiplying the monthly inventory times the cost. Uh oh, guess what? There's no monthly inventory table. Apparently, the Orco company saw no need to store historical inventory data, so it stores only current inventory values in the Inventory table. The Orco database needs to be modified again to get this historical data, at least for any future queries.

At this point, there are two options. We can create an inventory transactions table that gets an entry every time items are added to or removed from the inventory, or we can simply store the current values of the inventory at the end of each month. We don't really need the added details of a transactions table, and the rollup tables are going to be updated once a month anyway, so simply add another query to copy the current values of the inventory to an inventory history table. We need to save enough details to be able to calculate the inventory by product category and the turnover rate by product category for the last two charts. The turnover rate needs the cost and the total number of units shipped each month, so we need to roll that up with the inventory data. You need to do an outer join, because you need to combine all the records from the inventory table with those that had units shipped. Since you can't do an outer join correctly on a group of inner-joined tables and limit the joining with a WHERE clause, first create an intermediate table with the sales data, then do an outer join of that table with the inventory table. The query to create the intermediate table is shown in Figure 4.34. The SQL statement created by it follows.

Figure 4.34.
The query used to create the intermediate inventory history table.

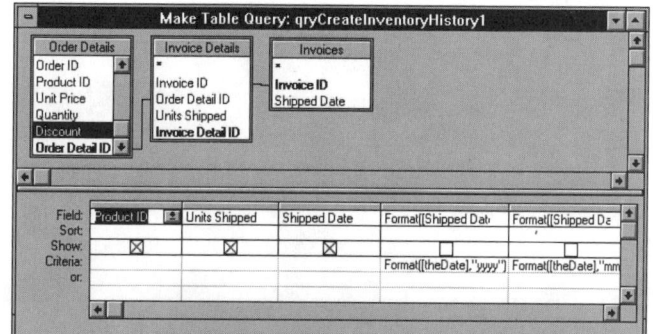

Query: `qryCreateInventoryHistory1`

```
PARAMETERS theDate DateTime;
SELECT [Order Details].[Product ID], [Invoice Details].[Units Shipped],
Invoices.[Shipped Date] INTO tblInventoryHistory1
FROM Invoices INNER JOIN ([Order Details] INNER JOIN [Invoice Details] ON
[Order Details].[Order Detail ID] = [Invoice Details].[Order Detail ID]) ON
Invoices.[Invoice ID] = [Invoice Details].[Invoice ID]
WHERE (((Format([Shipped Date],"yyyy"))=Format([theDate],"yyyy")) AND
((Format([Shipped Date],"mm"))=Format([theDate],"mm")));
```

The PARAMETERS clause allows you to insert a parameter when the query is executed. In this case, the parameter is named theDate, and it is of type DateTime. This parameter is used to specify the month to use when creating this table. The SELECT clause creates a new table named tblInventoryHistory1 and adds the columns Product ID, Units Shipped, and Shipped Date. The WHERE clause limits the records to those in which a product was shipped in the specified month. Part of the resulting table is shown in Figure 4.35. It has entries only for products that had shipments during the month.

Now, combine the Inventory table with this table to create one month's entry and store it in the Inventory History table. Figure 4.36 shows the query necessary to combine the two tables. The SQL statement for this combination follows.

Database Design

Query: qryCreateInventoryHistory

```
PARAMETERS theDate DateTime;
SELECT Format([theDate],"yyyy") AS Year, Format([theDate],"mm") AS Month,
Inventory.[Product ID], Inventory.[Unit Price], Inventory.[Unit Cost],
Inventory.[Units In Stock], Sum(tblInventoryHistory1.[Units Shipped]) AS
[Units Shipped] INTO tblInventoryHistory
FROM Inventory LEFT JOIN tblInventoryHistory1 ON Inventory.[Product ID] =
tblInventoryHistory1.[Product ID]
GROUP BY Inventory.[Product ID], Inventory.[Unit Price], Inventory.[Unit Cost],
Inventory.[Units In Stock];
```

Figure 4.35.

Part of the intermediate inventory history table.

Figure 4.36.

The query to combine the Inventory table and the Intermediate Inventory History table to create an entry for the current month for the inventory history.

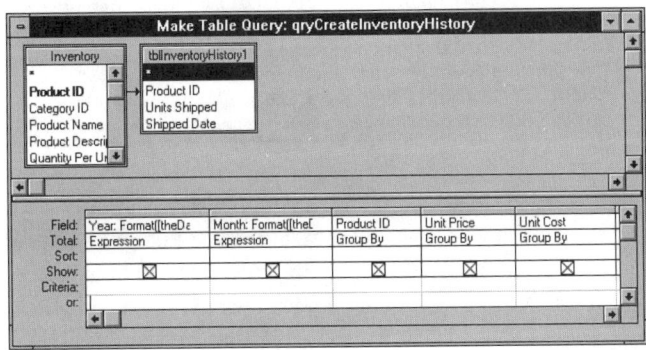

The date used as a parameter with this query should be the same one that was used with the previous one. The new tblInventoryHistory is created with the Year, Month, Product ID, Unit Price, Unit Cost, Units In Stock, and Units Shipped. The Units Shipped column is summed to roll up all orders for the same product during a single month. The left join of the Inventory table with the tblInventoryHistory table gets all the records from the Inventory table whether there was a sale or not. Figure 4.37 shows part of the table resulting from this query. Note that the Units Shipped column contains values for only products that had a shipment in the selected month.

Figure 4.37.
Part of a new entry for the Inventory History table.

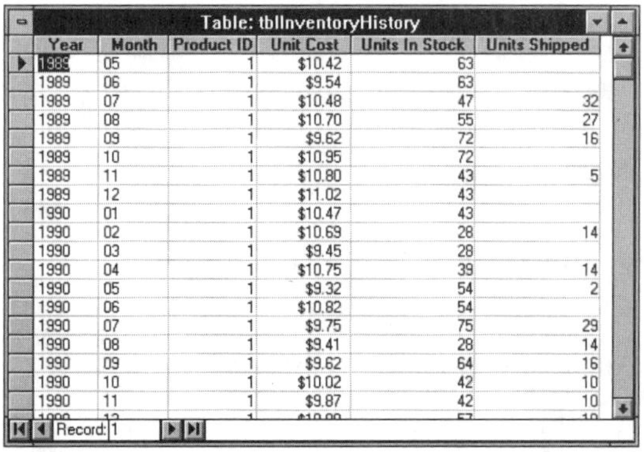

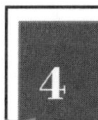

Table: tblInventoryHistory

Year	Month	Product ID	Unit Cost	Units In Stock	Units Shipped
1989	05	1	$10.42	63	
1989	06	1	$9.54	63	
1989	07	1	$10.48	47	32
1989	08	1	$10.70	55	27
1989	09	1	$9.62	72	16
1989	10	1	$10.95	72	
1989	11	1	$10.80	43	5
1989	12	1	$11.02	43	
1990	01	1	$10.47	43	
1990	02	1	$10.69	28	14
1990	03	1	$9.45	28	
1990	04	1	$10.75	39	14
1990	05	1	$9.32	54	2
1990	06	1	$10.82	54	
1990	07	1	$9.75	75	29
1990	08	1	$9.41	28	14
1990	09	1	$9.62	64	16
1990	10	1	$10.02	42	10
1990	11	1	$9.87	42	10

Record: 1

This query creates a new table, replacing an old one of the same name, but at the end of each month you really want to just append the current months data instead of recreating the whole table. To do this, remove the Into clause from the query and add the Insert Into clause shown below to the existing query. The rest of the query remains the same.

Query: qryAppendInventoryHistory

```
PARAMETERS theDate DateTime;
INSERT INTO tblInventoryHistory ( Year, Month, [Product ID], [Unit Price],
[Unit Cost], [Units In Stock], [Units Shipped] )
SELECT Format([theDate],"yyyy") AS Year, Format([theDate],"mm") AS Month,
Inventory.[Product ID], Inventory.[Unit Price], Inventory.[Unit Cost],
Inventory.[Units In Stock],
Sum(tblInventoryHistory1.[Units Shipped]) AS [Units Shipped]
FROM Inventory LEFT JOIN tblInventoryHistory1 ON Inventory.[Product ID] =
tblInventoryHistory1.[Product ID]
GROUP BY Inventory.[Product ID], Inventory.[Unit Price], Inventory.[Unit Cost],
Inventory.[Units In Stock];
```

Once you have a few months' data, you can use the following rollup query to create the table for the Total Monthly Inventory table.

Query: qryInventoryTotalMonth

```
SELECT tblInventoryHistory.Year, tblInventoryHistory.Month,
Sum([tblInventoryHistory].[Unit Cost]*[tblInventoryHistory].[Units In Stock])
AS [Value] INTO tblInventoryTotalMonth
FROM tblInventoryHistory
GROUP BY tblInventoryHistory.Year, tblInventoryHistory.Month;
```

This query creates a new table that contains the year and month, calculates the total value of sales for the month, and then divides that by the total value of inventory at the end of the month plus the sales during the month.

Database Design

Inventory by Product Category

You create the Inventory by Product Category table by adding the Category ID as a Group By field to the Total Inventory category and then adding the appropriate joins to connect the Category ID to the rest of the table.

Query: qryInventoryCategoryMonth

```
SELECT tblInventoryHistory.Year, tblInventoryHistory.Month,
Inventory.[Category ID], Sum([tblInventoryHistory].[Unit Cost]*
[tblInventoryHistory].[Units In Stock]) AS [Value]
INTO tblInventoryCategoryMonth
FROM tblInventoryHistory INNER JOIN Inventory ON
tblInventoryHistory.[Product ID] = Inventory.[Product ID]
GROUP BY tblInventoryHistory.Year, tblInventoryHistory.Month,
Inventory.[Category ID];
```

Inventory Turnover by Product Category

The Inventory Turnover is calculated by dividing the value of the inventory that was shipped during the month by the total inventory on hand during the month. The inventory on hand is estimated by adding the inventory at the end of the month to the amount sold. This method isn't exactly correct, because it doesn't take into account additions to the inventory, but it should be sufficient to show the trends in turnover rate.

Query: qryInventoryTurnsMonth

```
SELECT tblInventoryHistory.Year, tblInventoryHistory.Month,
Inventory.[Category ID], Sum([tblInventoryHistory].[Unit Cost]*
[tblInventoryHistory].[Units Shipped])/Sum([tblInventoryHistory].[Unit Cost]*
([tblInventoryHistory].[Units In Stock]+tblInventoryHistory].[Units Shipped]))
AS [Value] INTO tblInventoryTurnsMonth
FROM tblInventoryHistory INNER JOIN Inventory ON
tblInventoryHistory.[Product ID] = Inventory.[Product ID]
GROUP BY tblInventoryHistory.Year, tblInventoryHistory.Month,
Inventory.[Category ID];
```

Automatically Running the Monthly Queries

As the queries are created, save them in the Graphs database so that they can be recalled and rerun whenever the rollup tables need to be revised. Queries that are stored in the database file are known as *persistent queries*. Once a month, someone could run all the queries to update the rollup tables. However, it's more convenient to create a Visual Basic program to do the updates. This

program could be set to activate in the middle of the night so that none of the databases would be changed while the rollup tables were being created. To run a persistent query using a Visual Basic program, use the `OpenDatabase` function to open the database and then apply the `Execute` procedure to the database to run each of the queries.

The Do Rollups program, shown in Figure 4.38, contains the following single procedure attached to the RunQuerys command button. This procedure reruns all of the queries necessary to update the rollup tables.

Figure 4.38.
The Do Rollups program's visual interface, showing a completed rollup of all the tables.

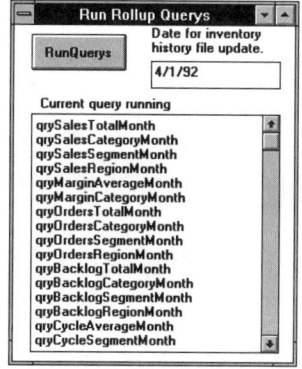

```
Sub RunQuerys_Click ()
  Dim dbGraphs As Database
  Dim qdfAQuery As QueryDef
  Dim EOL As String
  'MousePointer constants.
  Const DEFAULT = 0        '0 - Default.
  Const HOURGLASS = 11     '11 - Hourglass.

  EOL = Chr$(13) + Chr$(10)  'Carriage return + Linefeed.
  If Not IsDate(txtDate.Text) Then
    MsgBox "Insert a date in the date box first."
    Exit Sub
  End If
  'Change the mouse pointer to the hourglass.
  Screen.MousePointer = HOURGLASS
  'Open the database.
  Set dbGraphs = OpenDatabase("g:\rolupdat\graphs.mdb")
  'Run the persistent queries.
  txtLog.Text = txtLog.Text + "qrySalesTotalMonth" + EOL
  DoEvents
  'Delete the old table.
  dbGraphs.TableDefs.Delete "tblSalesTotalMonth"
  dbGraphs.Execute "qrySalesTotalMonth"   'Make the new table.
  txtLog.Text = txtLog.Text + "qrySalesCategoryMonth" + EOL
  DoEvents
  dbGraphs.TableDefs.Delete "tblSalesCategoryMonth"
  dbGraphs.Execute "qrySalesCategoryMonth"
```

Day 4

Database Design

```
txtLog.Text = txtLog.Text + "qrySalesSegmentMonth" + EOL
DoEvents
dbGraphs.TableDefs.Delete "tblSalesSegmentMonth"
dbGraphs.Execute "qrySalesSegmentMonth"
txtLog.Text = txtLog.Text + "qrySalesRegionMonth" + EOL
DoEvents
dbGraphs.TableDefs.Delete "tblSalesRegionMonth"
dbGraphs.Execute "qrySalesRegionMonth"
txtLog.Text = txtLog.Text + "qryMarginAverageMonth" + EOL
DoEvents
dbGraphs.TableDefs.Delete "tblMarginAverageMonth"
dbGraphs.Execute "qryMarginAverageMonth"
txtLog.Text = txtLog.Text + "qryMarginCategoryMonth" + EOL
DoEvents
dbGraphs.TableDefs.Delete "tblMarginCategoryMonth"
dbGraphs.Execute "qryMarginCategoryMonth"
txtLog.Text = txtLog.Text + "qryOrdersTotalMonth" + EOL
DoEvents
dbGraphs.TableDefs.Delete "tblOrdersTotalMonth"
dbGraphs.Execute "qryOrdersTotalMonth"
txtLog.Text = txtLog.Text + "qryOrdersCategoryMonth" + EOL
DoEvents
dbGraphs.TableDefs.Delete "tblOrdersCategoryMonth"
dbGraphs.Execute "qryOrdersCategoryMonth"
txtLog.Text = txtLog.Text + "qryOrdersSegmentMonth" + EOL
DoEvents
dbGraphs.TableDefs.Delete "tblOrdersSegmentMonth"
dbGraphs.Execute "qryOrdersSegmentMonth"
txtLog.Text = txtLog.Text + "qryOrdersRegionMonth" + EOL
DoEvents
dbGraphs.TableDefs.Delete "tblOrdersRegionMonth"
dbGraphs.Execute "qryOrdersRegionMonth"
txtLog.Text = txtLog.Text + "qryBacklogTotalMonth" + EOL
DoEvents
dbGraphs.TableDefs.Delete "tblBacklogTotalMonth"
dbGraphs.Execute "qryBacklogTotalMonth"
txtLog.Text = txtLog.Text + "qryBacklogCategoryMonth" + EOL
DoEvents
dbGraphs.TableDefs.Delete "tblBacklogCategoryMonth"
dbGraphs.Execute "qryBacklogCategoryMonth"
txtLog.Text = txtLog.Text + "qryBacklogSegmentMonth" + EOL
DoEvents
dbGraphs.TableDefs.Delete "tblBacklogSegmentMonth"
dbGraphs.Execute "qryBacklogSegmentMonth"
txtLog.Text = txtLog.Text + "qryBacklogRegionMonth" + EOL
DoEvents
dbGraphs.TableDefs.Delete "tblBacklogRegionMonth"
dbGraphs.Execute "qryBacklogRegionMonth"
txtLog.Text = txtLog.Text + "qryCycleAverageMonth" + EOL
DoEvents
dbGraphs.TableDefs.Delete "tblCycleAverageMonth"
dbGraphs.Execute "qryCycleAverageMonth"
txtLog.Text = txtLog.Text + "qryCycleSegmentMonth" + EOL
DoEvents
dbGraphs.TableDefs.Delete "tblCycleSegmentMonth"
dbGraphs.Execute "qryCycleSegmentMonth"
```

```
  txtLog.Text = txtLog.Text + "qryCycleDistribution" + EOL
  DoEvents
  dbGraphs.TableDefs.Delete "tblCycleDistribution"
  dbGraphs.Execute "qryCycleDistribution"
  'Update the inventory history table.
  txtLog.Text = txtLog.Text + "Inventory History table" + EOL
  DoEvents
  dbGraphs.TableDefs.Delete "tblInventoryHistory1"
  Set qdfAQuery = dbGraphs.OpenQueryDef("qryCreateInventoryHistory1")
  qdfAQuery!theDate = txtDate.Text
  qdfAQuery.Execute
  qdfAQuery.Close
  dbGraphs.TableDefs.Delete "tblInventoryHistory"
  Set qdfAQuery = dbGraphs.OpenQueryDef("qryAppendInventoryHistory")
  qdfAQuery!theDate = txtDate.Text
  qdfAQuery.Execute
  qdfAQuery.Close
  txtLog.Text = txtLog.Text + "qryInventoryTotalMonth" + EOL
  DoEvents
  dbGraphs.TableDefs.Delete "tblInventoryTotalMonth"
  dbGraphs.Execute "qryInventoryTotalMonth"
  txtLog.Text = txtLog.Text + "qryInventoryCategoryMonth" + EOL
  DoEvents
  dbGraphs.TableDefs.Delete "tblInventoryCategoryMonth"
  dbGraphs.Execute "qryInventoryCategoryMonth"
  txtLog.Text = txtLog.Text + "qryInventoryTurnsMonth" + EOL
  DoEvents
  dbGraphs.TableDefs.Delete "tblInventoryTurnsMonth"
  dbGraphs.Execute "qryInventoryTurnsMonth"
  dbGraphs.Close
  Screen.MousePointer = DEFAULT   'Reset the mouse pointer.
End Sub
```

First the procedure checks the value in the txtDate text box to be sure it's a date and exits the procedure if it isn't. Next, the procedure opens the Graphs database and starts the first rollup. Each rollup consists of four lines. The first adds a line to the txtLog text box to tell you what query is being processed, followed by a DoEvents call to let the system update the text box. Next, the procedure uses the TableDefs collection to select and delete the old table from the database. The fourth line uses the Execute method to run the query stored in the database.

Textbook Tip: The TableDefs collection contains descriptions of all the tables in the database, while the Tables collection contains the contents of the actual tables. Deleting a table from the TableDefs collection deletes the whole table. Applying Delete to the Tables collection doesn't delete the table, but deletes a value or values from the table.

All of the queries are executed this way except for the queries that update the Inventory History table. The two queries that update the Inventory History table both need to be sent a date so

Database Design

that they know what month to roll up. The `Parameters` collection is used to access `theDate` and supply it a value before the query is run.

The Definitions Table

There is one more important table in the Graphs database—the Definitions table. The Definitions table contains the information that is different for each graph in the decision support program—information such as the graph type and caption, the name of the table containing the information for the graph, and the name of the field in the table. By putting all this information in a database table, we can change the graphs in the application by simply changing the data in that table. Figure 4.39 shows part of the Definitions table. We will add to it as we determine what information we need to create the graphs.

Figure 4.39.
Part of the Definitions table for the graphs in the decision support application.

Code	Class	GraphCaption	Units	Type	GraphType	GraphStyle	
11	Sales	Year-to-Date Sales	$	Line	6	0	tblS
12	Sales	Sales by Product Category	$	AreaStacked	8	0	tblS
13	Sales	Sales by Market Segment	$	AreaStacked	8	0	tblS
14	Sales	Sales by Sales Region	$	AreaStacked	8	0	tblS
21	Margins	Average Gross Margin	%	Line	6	0	tblM
22	Margins	Margins by Product Category	%	LineMulti	6	0	tblM
31	Orders	Year-to-Date Orders	$	Line	6	0	tblO
32	Orders	Orders by Product Category	$	AreaStacked	8	0	tblO
33	Orders	Orders by Market Segment	$	AreaStacked	8	0	tblO
34	Orders	Orders by Sales Region	$	AreaStacked	8	0	tblO
41	Backlog	Monthly Backlog	$	Line	6	0	tblB
42	Backlog	Backlog by Product Category	$	AreaStacked	8	0	tblB
43	Backlog	Backlog by Market Segment	$	AreaStacked	8	0	tblB
44	Backlog	Backlog by Sales Region	$	AreaStacked	8	0	tblB
51	Cycle	Average Order Cycle (Days)	Days	Line	6	0	tblC
52	Cycle	Order Cycle by Market Segment	Days	LineMulti	6	0	tblC
53	Cycle	Order Cycle Distribution	Days	Histogram	3	0	tblC
61	Inventory	Monthly Ending Inventory	$	Line	6	0	tblI
62	Inventory	Inventory by Product Category	$	AreaStacked	8	0	tblI
63	Inventory	Inventory Turns by Product Category	$/Day	LineMulti	6	0	tblI

Modification Notes

This section is supposed to describe what to do differently when you're modifying an existing application rather than creating a new one. However, in this chapter, the database already existed and we made modifications to it to make available the data that the final application needed. Putting the variable parts of the application in a database table makes it much simpler to make updates and changes in the future, because you simply have to change the table to make changes in the application. The table doesn't necessarily have to be a database table. It could be some arrays in the application itself, filled with data from the application's .INI file or from some other file pointed to by an entry in the application's .INI file.

The more you can avoid building the variable parts of an application, but store them in a single location, the easier it is to make changes later.

Debugging the Process

At this stage, debugging consists of designing and running the queries to make sure they return the data you expect. Queries are most easily tested with Access or the VisData application. You simply run them and then examine the table they return. When you verify that a query works, you can save it in the database as a persistent query, or copy the SQL statement into the Visual Basic program and execute it there. We have already discovered several problems just by trying to create the queries and noting that the needed data is unavailable. We also can discover problems by running the queries and examining the resulting tables.

Another thing to check is if you're using all the data when running the queries. You could test this by putting fixed values in a copy of the database and seeing if the correct totals and averages are calculated.

Summary

Database use and design is a complicated science, but it might not be as complicated as you think. Once you understand the jargon of database design, designing database tables and queries is relatively straightforward. With a little practice, the needed elements of a query quickly become obvious. As I mentioned at the beginning, this chapter can't teach you everything about databases. I hope I've told you enough so that you can understand the application we're creating in this book. If you want or need to know more, examine the documents and help files that come with Visual Basic and Access. You can also consult Roger Jennings's book *Database Developer's Guide with Visual Basic 3,* which contains a wealth of information and examples.

The next step in the design process is to create the Program Structure Chart, which is the topic of the next chapter.

The queries and SQL statements are in the databases, which are stored in the \ORCO and \ROLUPS directories on the included CD.

Creating the Program Structure Chart

Day 5

Creating the Program Structure Chart

After a hard day's work like that in the preceding chapter, you deserve a rest, but this day's work won't wait. Luckily, creating the program structure chart isn't nearly as arduous as database design. The program structure chart is the final grouping of the processes identified in the data flow diagram into executable modules.

Today you will learn

- about program structure charts
- how to divide an application into modules
- how to create a program structure chart

The Goal of Day 5

Today you will take the data flow diagram and create the program structure chart. You don't create the program structure chart in order to create another chart that describes the operation of a program-to-be. The program structure chart is where the actual program starts to take shape, and the flows of data between modules are defined. Like the data flow diagram, the program structure chart helps you identify problems in a program before you actually build it.

Note: The term *module* used in structured analysis refers to a single-purpose code block that most closely resembles a procedure in Visual Basic. A module in Visual Basic is a container file for one or more procedures and possibly a form definition. It should be evident from the text which type of module is being discussed.

The Program Structure Chart

In classic program design, you chart the layout of a new program by creating a flowchart that begins with a start bubble and passes through several processes until it reaches the end bubble. This is very similar to how you would create a program if you just sat down and started typing. For example, if you were going to write a flowchart for installing a new disk drive in your computer, you might come up with something like Figure 5.1. When you design a process like this, you draw a start bubble, and then you consider what you should do first. Well, first you open the case, and then you insert the drive, attach the cables, close the case, change the CMOS settings, and initialize the drive. Sounds straightforward, right? Look closely at the flowchart in Figure 5.1. If you didn't know beforehand what this process was supposed to do, could you tell from the chart?

Figure 5.1.
A flowchart for installing a new disk drive in a computer.

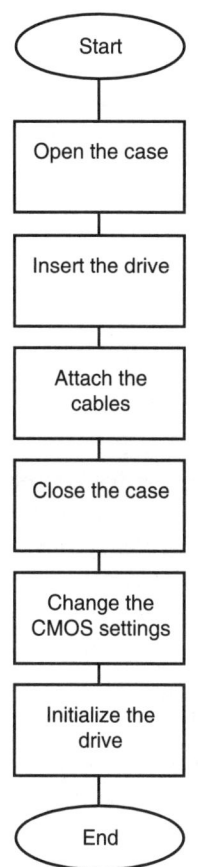

A design of this type is known as a *bottom-up design* because it starts with the details and works up to the program's function. Bottom-up design is fine for low-level module design, because there you must worry about details, but it has serious problems for any higher-level design. Chief among those problems is that you don't know where you're going when you draw a module on the chart, and you don't know exactly what the module is supposed to do because you don't yet know what the rest of the modules in the program need to have done. You end up having to go back to earlier modules to add things you forgot the first time. For example, with the process in Figure 5.1, as you try to open the case in the first module, you realize that you should have removed the monitor and taken out the screws before trying to pry open the box. These subtasks have to be added to the beginning of the module to open the case. As you get the case open and poke your fingers inside to insert the drive, you realize that you should have pulled the plug as well. You have to go back to the Open the Case module again and add another subtask to pull the plug, and so on.

Creating the Program Structure Chart

When you do a real bottom-up design, you generally have the goal and the whole process in your head before you start writing down the modules. If you don't, you won't know where you're going or what needs to be done to get there. For example, when creating Figure 5.1, the first thing I thought about was installing a disk drive. Next, I considered how to do that. Well, you can't get the disk in until you open the box, and then you can insert the drive, attach the wires, and close the box. Modeling the process using this strategy is known as *top-down design* since you start with the function of the process and then work your way down to the details of how to achieve it. Since you actually do this in your head before drawing the bottom-up flowchart model, why not draw the model in the same way that you think of it?

Top-down modeling is the essence of program design using a structure chart. A structure chart starts with the task to be accomplished, and then it moves to the subtasks necessary to complete the task. Figure 5.2 shows a structure chart for the same process as Figure 5.1. At the top of the chart is the top-level task. Below that are the subtasks necessary to achieve that top-level task. Connecting the top-level box and the subtasks are lines to show the subordination of the modules and small arrows (called *couples*) showing the flow of data between the modules. The top-level module is the top or *king* module. The modules directly below it are the first-level subordinated modules. As you discern more and more of the design's details, you add more levels of subtasks, as shown in Figure 5.3.

Figure 5.2.
A program structure chart for installing a new disk drive in a computer.

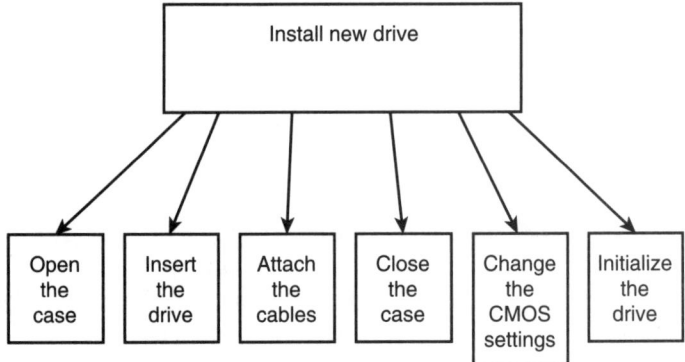

Modules

As you create the modules in the program structure chart, name them as explicitly as possible. Also, a module should depend only on the data passed to it from the procedures above and below it in the program hierarchy. If a module depends on the data in a neighboring module at the same level, redesign the project to put the neighbor module above or below the problem module.

Figure 5.3.
A program structure chart of Figure 5.2 with some subordinate submodules.

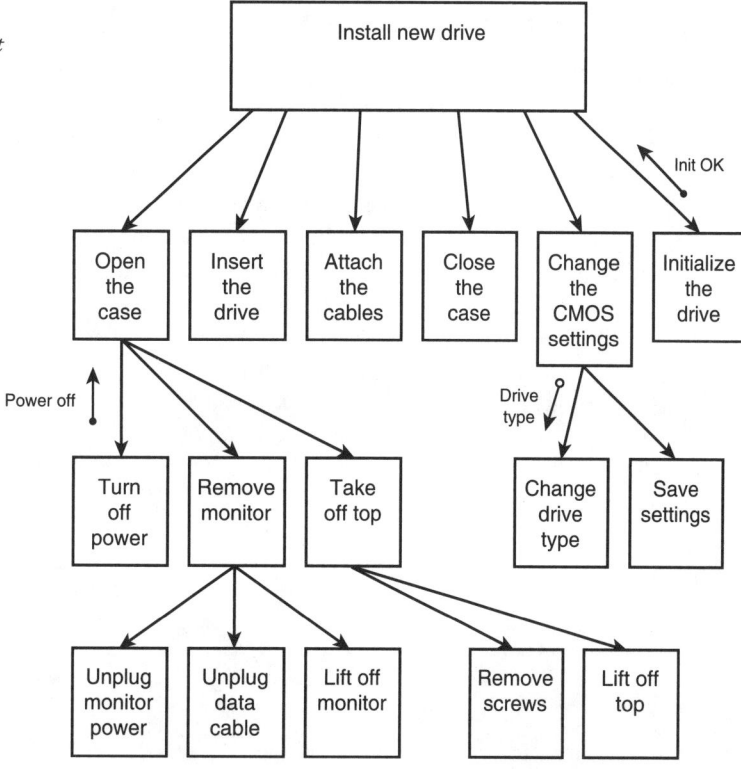

What's in a Name?

As you name the modules in your chart, try to be as explicit as possible as to what the module does. If you can't think of a good name, the module probably needs to be redesigned. The same goes for a name that consists of multiple nouns and verbs. If you can't get the name down to a single noun and verb, re-examine what you're planning to have the module do, and partition the work accordingly.

If you do a good job of partitioning the application, a module's function won't depend on what's going on elsewhere in the program. Thus, you can design each module independently of all the other modules in an application. You won't have to worry about the module's interactions with the other modules, except along the indicated connections. In addition, by making a module's function straightforward and as independent as possible from the program's other modules, you enormously simplify that module's coding.

Creating the Program Structure Chart

Connections: Normal and Pathological

As you draw your modules, you should connect them with arrows that point from the calling module to the called module. If each module connects to only one module above it, as shown in Figure 5.4, the lines are known as *normal connections*. However, if the lines connect like those in Figure 5.5, they are known as *pathological connections*. You should avoid pathological connections whenever possible. In Figure 5.5, module B is dependent on the data in module A, C is dependent on the data in module B, and A is dependent on C. The circle created is certain to cause problems in the final operating program, because a high-level module is subordinate to a low-level module. As an illustration, consider a company in which the boss's spouse works for the mail room manager. If the spouse exerts a lot of control over the boss, the pathological loop of control created (boss to manager to spouse to boss) could be destructive to the company's organization.

Figure 5.4.
A structure chart with normal connections.

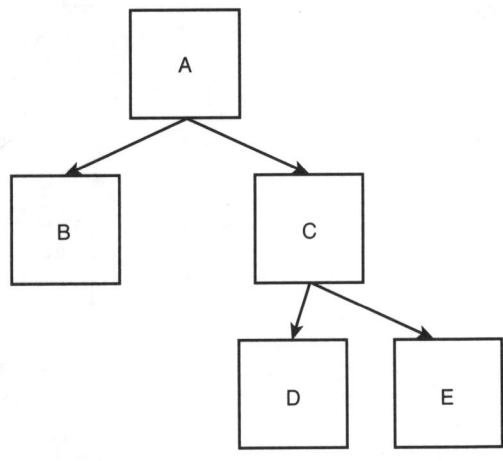

Figure 5.5.
A structure chart with pathological connections.

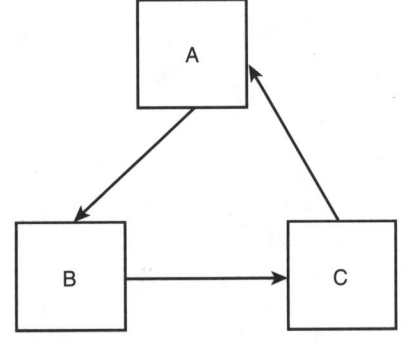

Couples

Couples are small arrows with a ball on one end. They represent data flow along the connection between a module and its subordinate. Thus, couples define the interface between the calling and the called modules. The direction of the arrow shows the direction of the data flow, and the circle tells if the data is a flag (filled) or a value (open). All couples should be explicitly named according to the data they carry, and the names and definitions should be put into the data dictionary. Every data flow that passes between two modules needs to be represented with a couple. For example, Figure 5.6 shows a simple hierarchy of procedures for dialing the telephone. The Lift Receiver module is called first, and then the Listen for Dial Tone procedure is called. When a dial tone is heard, the Got Tone flag is passed back to the Dial Phone procedure. The Dial Phone procedure calls the Dial Number procedure and sends it the phone number to dial. After the number is dialed, the Listen for Ring procedure listens for the ringing and passes back the Got Ring flag with a value of false. Finally, the Listen for Answer procedure listens for someone to answer the phone and passes back the Got Answer flag to the calling program.

Figure 5.6.
The structure chart for the Dial Phone task.

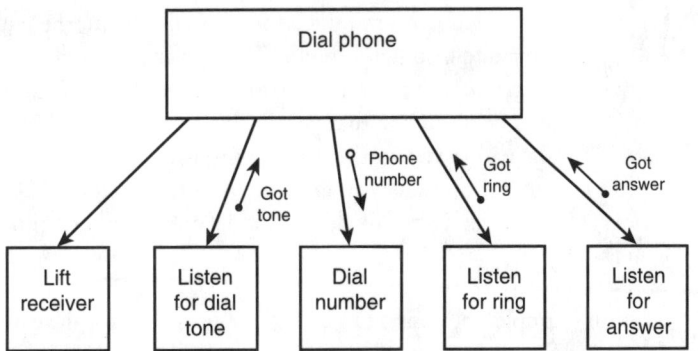

Evaluating the Structure

Once you have a program structure, how do you evaluate it to determine if it's a good design? You measure the coupling and cohesion.

Coupling

Coupling pertains to the number and type of connections between two modules in your design. A totally decoupled design has no connections to any other module, but a module with no connections at all doesn't do anything. A good design has as little coupling as possible between the modules above and below it and no coupling between the modules on either side. If two modules have many couples connecting them, they're probably part of the same task and should be combined into a single module.

Creating the Program Structure Chart

The reason you want weakly-coupled modules is to improve the modules' independence. The more heavily coupled two modules are, the less independent they are and the more likely that a change in one will have an unintentional effect on the other. The amount of coupling also has a strong effect on a module's readability. If a module is heavily coupled to another module, you'll have to continually flip to the other module to be able to read and understand the code.

Cohesion

The second measure is *cohesion*—a property of the statements and data that make up a module. In a strongly cohesive module, it's obvious to anyone reading the code that the code and data should be treated as a unit, and further subdivision into subunits doesn't make good sense. On the other hand, a module with poor cohesion likely has more than one independent task.

What's in a Name? Part 2

When you're examining a module's cohesion, the name is often a dead giveaway. If the name is something like "Do this and then do that," and "this" and "that" are unrelated, the module probably has poor cohesion. If you have such a hard time naming a module that you decide to call it "Sally," more than likely it should be repartitioned. On the other hand, if the name is "Do this part 1" and you have another module with lots of connections named "Do this part 2," you probably have over-partitioned your model and should combine these two modules.

For example, the design in Figure 5.7 stinks. The top-level module has a very general name that could fit any program you've ever written. The Lift Receiver or Dial Phone module contains two independent tasks. The Get Ring or Answer module contains two similar tasks. The Get Dial Tone module's task is similar to the two tasks in the Get Ring Or Answer module, and it shares the Listen for Something module with them. This connectivity suggests that the two modules should either be combined into one module or separated into three independent modules. Here's something else to consider: If you saw this chart without the figure caption, could you tell what it's doing?

Figure 5.7.
A poorly cohesive design for the Dial Phone task.

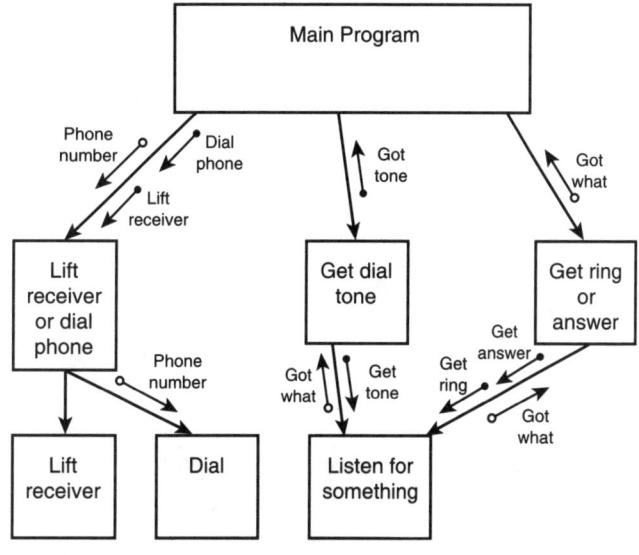

Switches

Another way to locate modules with poor cohesion is to look at the number of downward-passed switches that tell the module what to do. If a module needs several switches to know what to do, it probably has poor cohesion. For example, if you wrote a multipurpose trigonometry module to calculate the sine, cosine, or tangent of the argument, depending on which of three flags is true (or depending on the value of a single flag), the module has poor cohesion and should be broken into three separate modules to calculate each of the functions separately.

Partitioning from the Data Flow Diagram

As you might expect, there is a way to move from the data flow diagram to the structure chart. After all, why did you create the data flow diagram if it won't help you design the final program? Two forms of analysis are used to convert a data flow diagram into a program structure chart. Which one is used depends on the type of process your data flow diagram depicts. The two types of data flow diagram are a data transform and a transaction processor. A *data transform*, shown in Figure 5.8, is a linear stretch of data flows and processes that takes data as input, performs some sort of processing on it, and then spits out a result. A *transaction processor*, shown in Figure 5.9, is an area of parallelism in your program in which the data flow splits into several parts and later comes back together.

163

Creating the Program Structure Chart

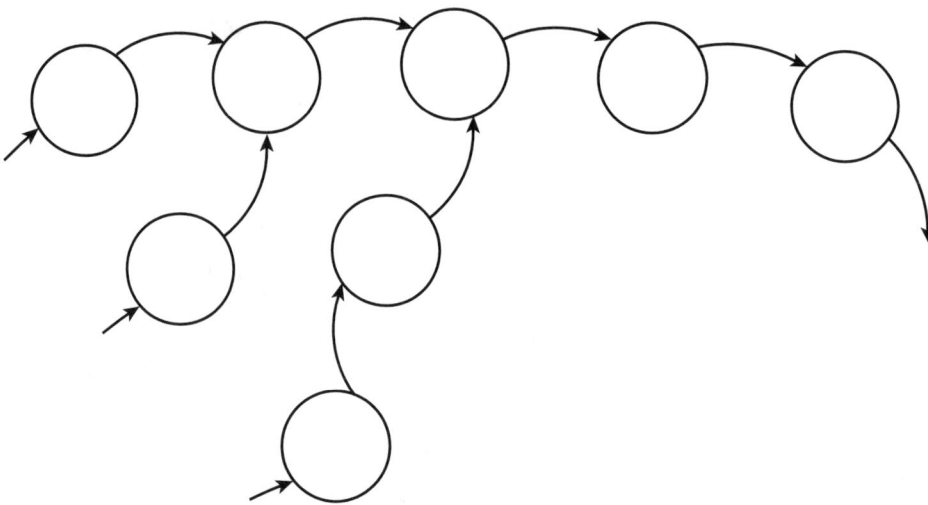

Figure 5.8. *The structure of a data transform in a data flow diagram.*

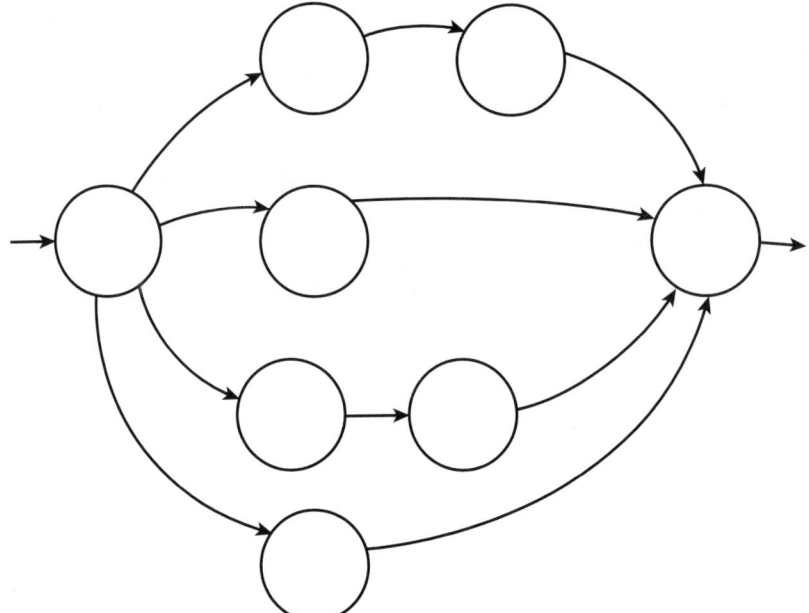

Figure 5.9. *The structure of a transaction processor in a data flow diagram.*

Transform Analysis

A simple example of a data transform is the stream of calculations performed in an income tax form (see Figure 5.10). Each calculation in the income tax form is based on the result of the previous calculation. When you convert this structure to a structure chart, you first locate the central transform. The *central transform* is usually the one that is not concerned with input or output, or the one most centrally located in terms of connectivity with other modules. Each input and output stream then gets a first-level module, plus one for the central process. The first-level input and output module then gets two second-level modules—one to get the data flow and one to convert it into the resulting flow that is passed up to the first-level module. Do the same for the second-level modules and so forth until you have accounted for all the processes and flows on the data flow diagram. Each data flow and process is transformed into a module on the structure chart. Figure 5.11 shows the conversion of the income tax data flow diagram into a program structure chart.

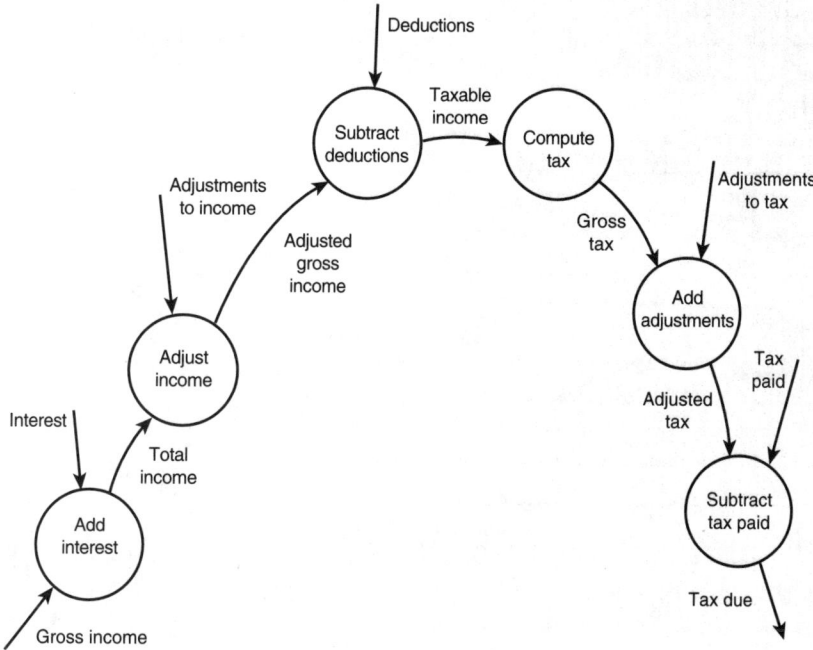

Figure 5.10. *A data flow diagram for a data transform-type task, calculating the values in an income tax form.*

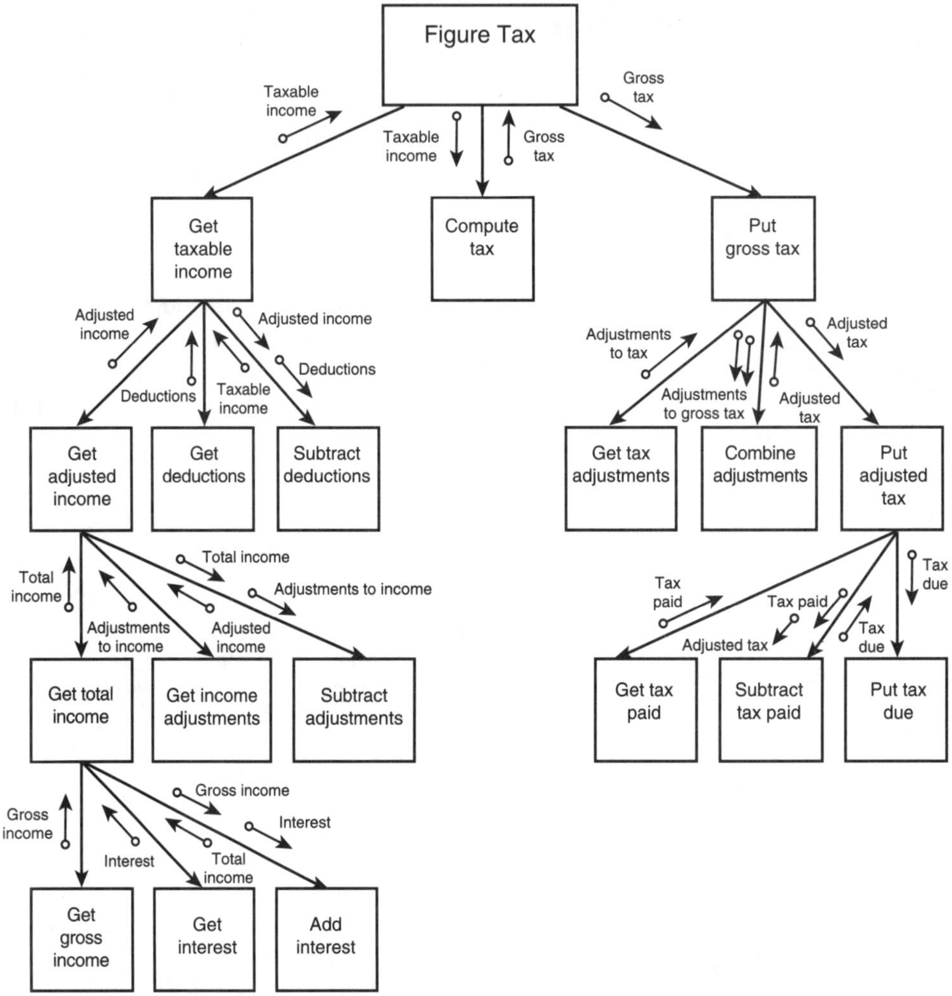

Creating the Program Structure Chart

[Figure: program structure chart diagram with modules including Figure Tax, Get taxable income, Compute tax, Put gross tax, Get adjusted income, Get deductions, Subtract deductions, Get tax adjustments, Combine adjustments, Put adjusted tax, Get total income, Get income adjustments, Subtract adjustments, Get tax paid, Subtract tax paid, Put tax due, Get gross income, Get interest, Add interest]

Figure 5.11. *A program structure chart for the data flow diagram in Figure 5.10.*

In Figure 5.10, the process that is not an input or output process is the Compute Tax process. It also represents what this whole calculation is about—calculating tax. Therefore, that module is pulled up as the top-level module in the structure chart. This top-level module has an input (Taxable Income), an output (Gross Tax), and a transform (Compute Tax). Each of these three items becomes a first-level module under the top module. In turn, the input and output modules have two inputs, an output, and a calculation. The modules on the input side pass their outputs up, while those on the output side pass their outputs down. The total effect is as if you grabbed the top-level process on the data flow diagram and draped the processes and flows across the structure chart.

Transaction Analysis

A simple example of a transaction processor is the calculation of the amount payable on a payroll check. As shown in Figure 5.12, the gross pay comes in as an input and is split into multiple parallel paths, because each of the calculations is dependent on the value of the gross pay and not on the amount left after the previous transaction.

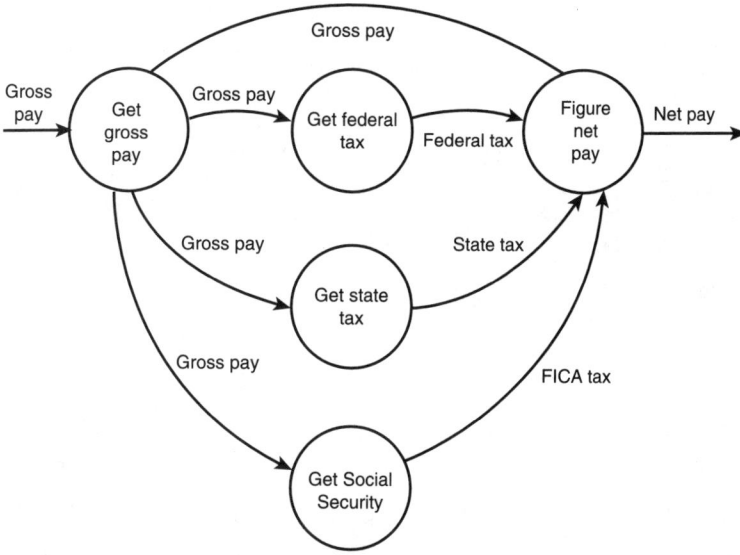

Figure 5.12. *A data flow diagram for the paycheck calculation.*

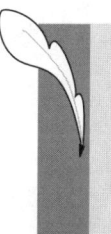

> **Note:** Many of the calculations in a business situation are of the form of a transaction process. Accounting is especially transaction-oriented, with multiple parallel data flows that operate on a single account. For example, a program that maintains bank accounts has multiple parallel processes that operate on the account. If money is deposited in the account, the credit process gets the account balance, adds the deposit to it, and then replaces the old balance with the new one. Similar calculations occur for the debit and interest processes.

Transaction analysis converts a data flow diagram of a transaction process into a program structure chart. If you examine the transaction process shown in Figure 5.12, you see that it could be changed into a single process in a data transform called Calculate Pay. Thus, the whole transaction process structure is modeled as a single top-level module, with first-level input and

Creating the Program Structure Chart

output modules plus a first-level module for each of the transactions. Each of the transactions then has a set of second-level action modules that perform the individual functions needed by the transactions, as well as a set of shared, third-level, detail modules. Figure 5.13 shows the conversion of the paycheck calculation into a structure chart.

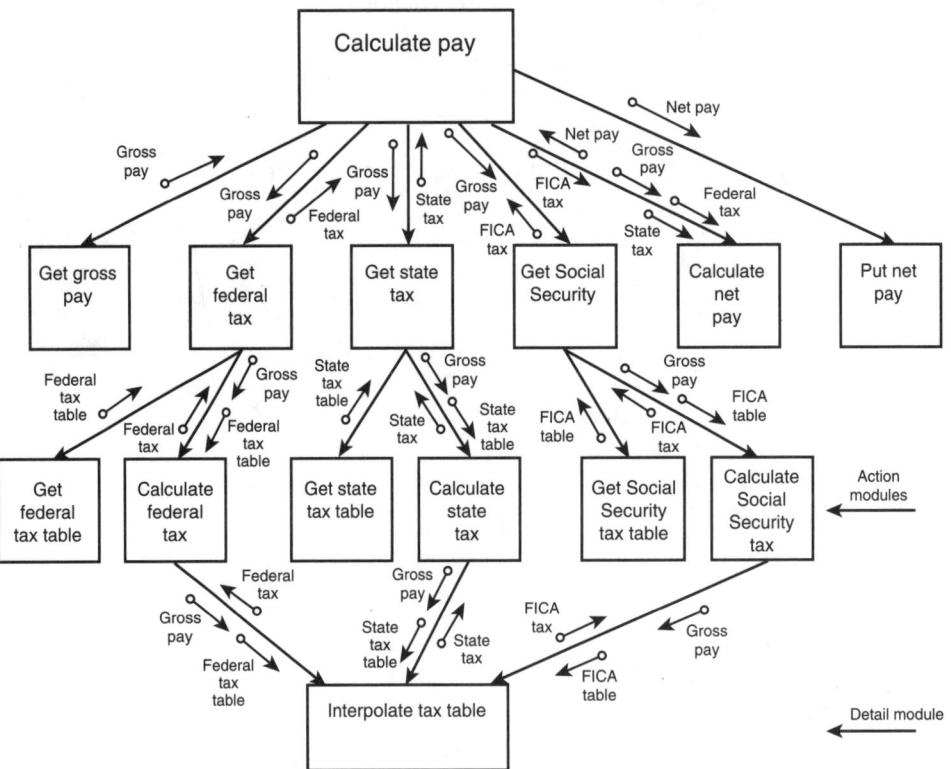

Figure 5.13. *A program structure chart for the paycheck calculation.*

The Conversion of Real Systems

The templates for converting a data flow diagram into a program structure chart aren't absolute, final forms for the final program structure chart. They're only a first cut of the conversion that then needs to be massaged to include the realities of the system the code is destined for and to eliminate unintelligent or trivial partitioning of the system. Here are some things to consider when revising the chart:

Trivial calculations: Often the rote conversion using transaction analysis or transform analysis results in modules that perform trivial calculations. For example, in Figure 5.11, many of the transforms are simple additions that don't rate a module all to themselves. They should be pulled up into the module above them.

Control flows: Data flow analysis completely ignores control flows, which must be incorporated at this level. A control flow (discussed on Day 3) is the step-by-step flow of calculations in a program that indicates the order in which the procedures are calculated. Event-driven procedures, such as those that are executed when a button is pressed or the value in a text box changes, especially cause changes in the structure.

Control points: Loops and decisions that occur in the real calculation have to be added, and that addition might change the structure to something other than the ideal. For example, if you don't always calculate state tax, your program needs to decide in the main module whether or not to select that calculation. If you're going to loop over many employees when calculating paychecks, the loop structure needs to be in a single module and encompass the whole of the paycheck calculation.

Packaging: Visual Basic has a fairly rigid packaging structure in that the event procedures must be in the form module that contains the object causing the event. Event procedures also create multiple starting points in a code because the event control structure is hidden from view in the Visual Basic system. For example, a form with multiple buttons and menus has starting points at each of the procedures attached to the buttons and menus. If one button is pressed, starting a procedure, and another button is pressed before the first procedure finishes, the procedure connected to the second button could start running before the first procedure finishes, further complicating the flow of control. (Note that this can occur only if the system gets control, such as by calling the `DoEvents` procedure.)

Error flows: Unlike a control flow, an error flow might need to traverse outside the normal procedure structure in order to get the system back to a stable location rather than letting it crash.

As you massage the program structure chart, it eventually starts to look like something you could turn into code and execute. When you're satisfied that you have an elegant solution to the problem, it's time to proceed to the next step.

Creating the Program Structure Chart

Deciding When to Go On

This is a difficult decision to make, because you can always design a little more or revise a procedure to make it more elegant. However, at some point you have to say that this design is good enough. Maybe it isn't perfect, but it will work as it was intended, and the cost to improve it isn't worth the expected gain. Keep in mind that the program must work. You're definitely not done if the program won't perform the job it was intended to do. However, once you reach that point, you need to consider the cost/benefit of any additional improvements.

The Decision Support Application Project

The decision support application is now starting to take shape. We have the data flow diagrams and process descriptions, so now it's time to arrange those flows and processes into an executable structure. Start with the data flow diagram shown in Figure 5.14. This is the same diagram that was developed on Days 3 and 4. The first thing you will notice is that process 16 is already done, so you don't have to worry about it in the current program structure.

The first thing you have to locate is the top-level module. Several processes in the figure seem to be somewhat central. Process 2 (Search Database) definitely has a lot of linkages, as do 6 (Get Drill-Down Data), 4 (Fill Grid), 1 (Get Chart Data), and 3 (Draw Chart). Process 2 has the most linkages, but it's not really part of the program. It's an interface to the database engine. To determine what the top-level module should be, consider what this program does: It draws charts. Therefore, 3 (Draw Chart) is a really good candidate for top module. One other thing to notice before making a final selection is that the flow of data from the database to the chart runs parallel to the flow of data from the database to the grid. These two flows are essentially the same flow until the end, where it is split so that the same data goes to both the chart and the grid. Since these two flows go together, it makes a lot of sense to combine them and make the top-level module Draw Chart and Grid, as shown in Figure 5.15.

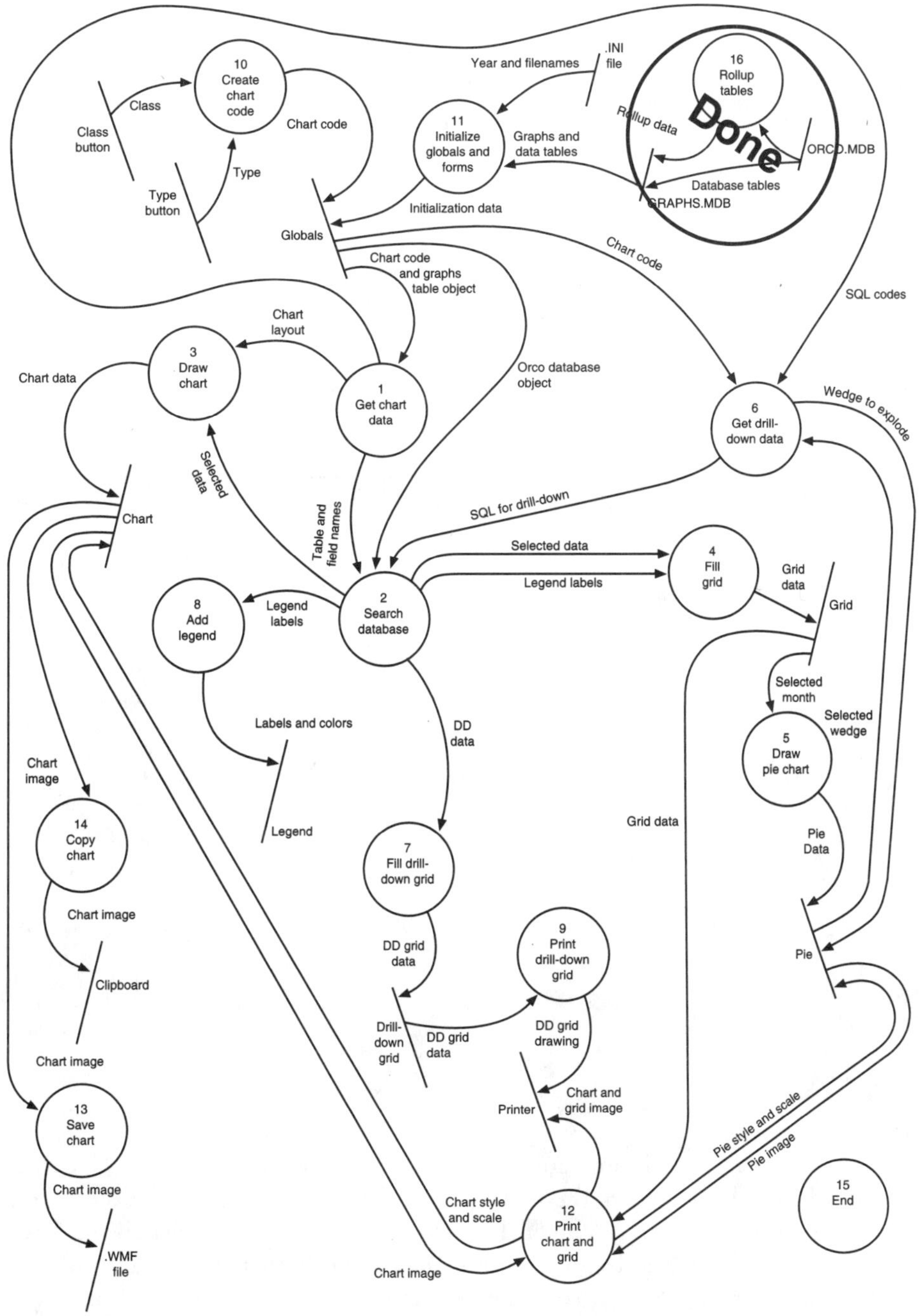

Figure 5.14. *The data flow diagram for the decision support application.*

Creating the Program Structure Chart

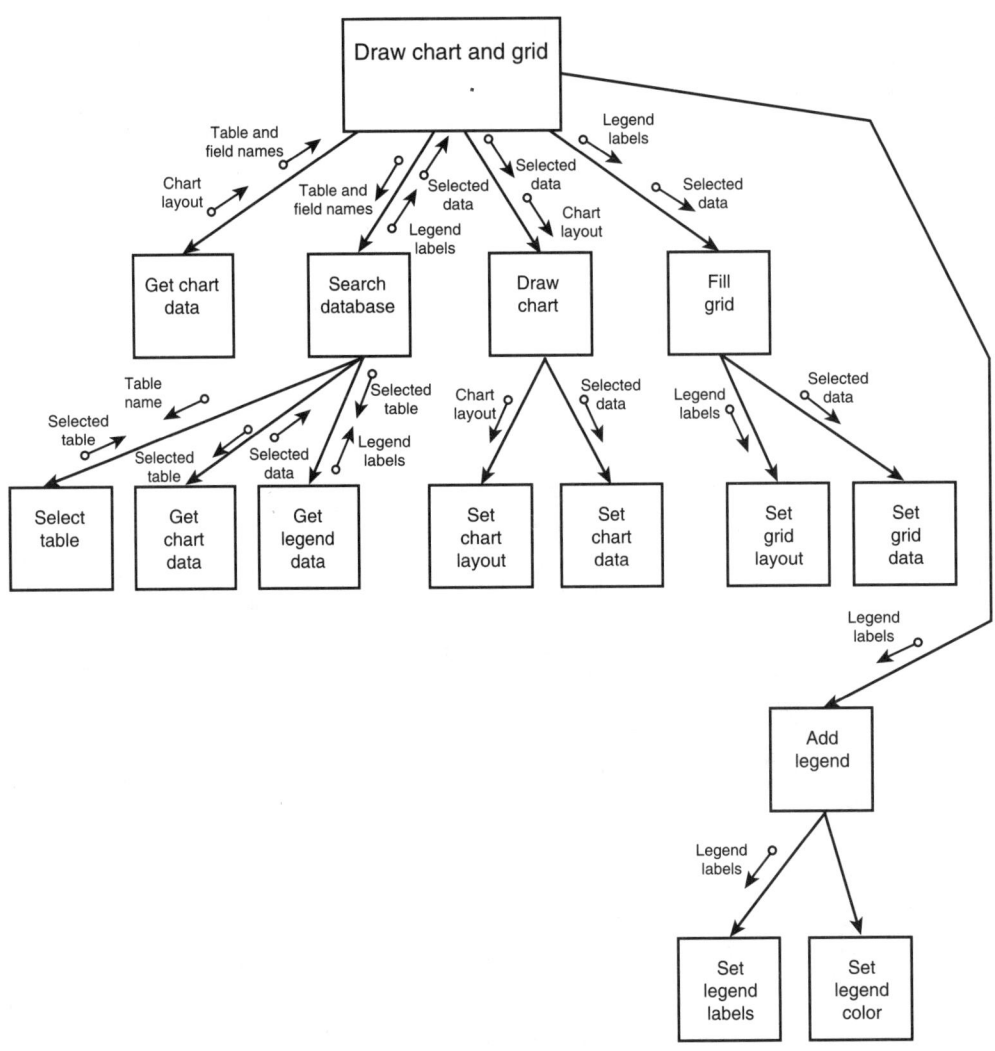

Figure 5.15. *The structure chart for drawing charts and grids.*

The Draw Chart and Grid module has five submodules: Get Chart Data, Search Database, Draw Chart, Fill Grid, and Add Legend. The Get Chart Data module searches the `tblDefinitions` table for the names of the table and field that contain the data for the chart being drawn. Those names are used to select and return from the database the data to be plotted and the legend labels. The data to be plotted is inserted in the chart and the grid, and the legend labels are put in the chart legend and on the grid. As soon as all this is done, the chart can be displayed for the user to examine.

Now that you have a set of modules to draw a chart, you need something to get it started. Visual Basic works with events, and those events are what you use to make code run. The events defined so far for this project are as follows:

1. Pressing the chart Class button to change the chart class.
2. Pressing the chart Type button to change the chart type.
3. Clicking on the chart to toggle the grid on and off.
4. Double-clicking on a month name on the chart to display a pie chart of the data for that month.
5. Double-clicking on a column of the grid to do the same as clicking on a month name on the chart.
6. Double-clicking on the form outside of a pie chart to switch back to a line or area chart.
7. Double-clicking on a pie wedge to explode it and display the drill-down options.
8. Selecting a drill-down option to display the drill-down grid.
9. Selecting File | Print to print the currently visible form or grid.
10. Selecting File | Save to save an image of the current chart.
11. Selecting Edit | Copy to place the current chart on the clipboard.
12. Selecting File | Exit to close the application.

Let's start with the first two events, the Class button and the Type button. In both cases, there will be a button array, and the button selected from the array will set the number of the chart class or type. When a new chart class is selected, you want to switch back to chart type 1. Figure 5.16 shows the two button arrays and their modules. Selecting the Class button sets the new class and then simulates pressing the type 1 button by calling its event procedure. When the type 1 button is pressed, the grid is toggled off, the chart code is created from the current chart class, and the type code is created from the Type button just pressed. The chart code is then stored in a global variable, and the Draw Chart and Grid procedure is called to draw the new chart.

When the chart is visible, you want to be able to click on it and have the grid appear or disappear. The structure shown in Figure 5.17 toggles the grid on or off whenever the chart is clicked and then calls a new module: Resize Chart and Grid. You could call the Draw Chart and Grid module again, but the data is already available, so the chart and grid need only to be resized to fit the current window.

Creating the Program Structure Chart

Figure 5.16.
The program structure chart for the Class and Type buttons.

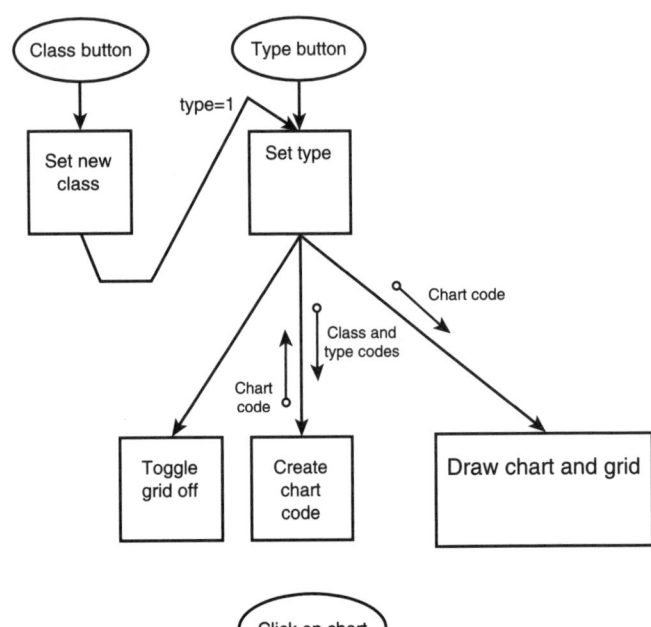

Figure 5.17.
The program structure chart for toggling the grid.

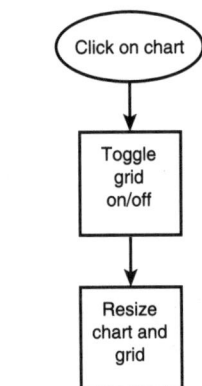

If you double-click on a month label instead of clicking on the body of the chart, you want to select that month and display a pie chart showing that single month's data. If a grid is visible, double-clicking on a column head should do the same thing. Figure 5.18 shows the structure chart to handle displaying the pie chart. Double-clicking on a month label simulates double-clicking on a grid column head by calling the grid's event procedure. The Double-Click on Column event calls the Draw Pie Chart module. Draw Pie Chart has to first find out what month or column was double-clicked on and copy the data out of the grid. You could run the query again and get a new copy of the data, but there's no sense in doing that when the data is available in the grid, even when the grid isn't showing. Next, the procedure has to set up the pie chart and fill it with the monthly data. Finally, it toggles the pie chart visible and the other chart and grid invisible.

Figure 5.18.
The program structure chart for the Draw Pie Chart module.

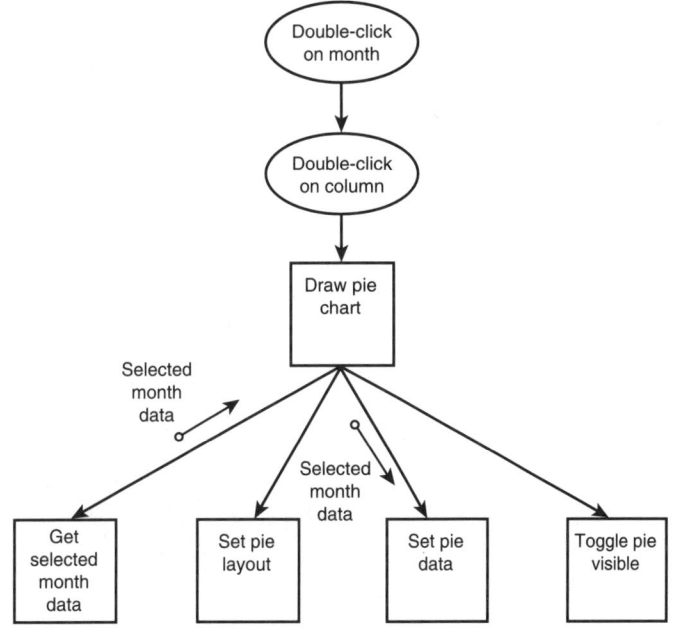

When the pie chart is visible and you double-click on the form outside of the pie chart, you want to switch back to the original form and grid. The structure shown in Figure 5.19 toggles the graph visible and the pie chart invisible to accomplish this task.

Figure 5.19.
The program structure chart for toggling the pie off and the graph visible.

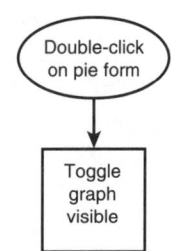

Next come the drill-down grids accessed from the pie chart. There are two steps to viewing a drill-down grid. First, you double-click on a pie wedge to select a specific category, segment, or region and display the drill-down options. Next, you select the specific option to display and then display the grid. Figure 5.20 shows the module that is executed when you double-click on a pie wedge. The module first determines which wedge was double-clicked, and then it explodes that pie wedge and displays the Drill-Down Options menu. The Drill-Down Options menu has options enabled that are appropriate to the selected pie wedge.

Creating the Program Structure Chart

Figure 5.20.
The program structure chart for displaying the drill-down options.

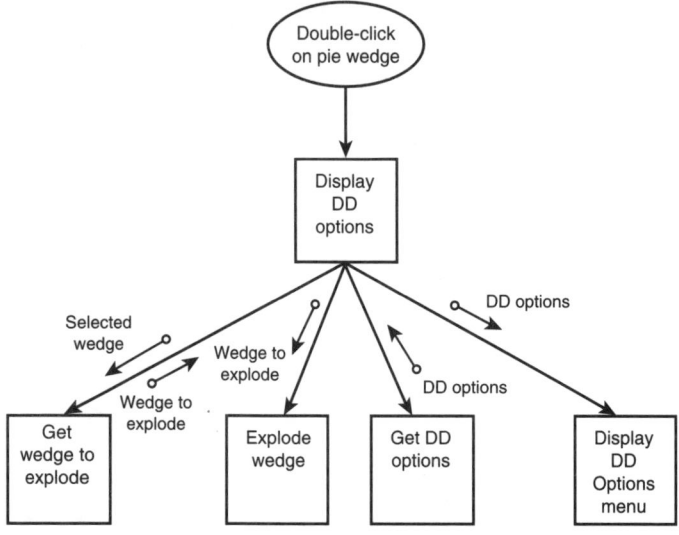

When the user has selected a drill-down option from the Drill-Down Options menu and clicked on OK, the module shown in Figure 5.21 is executed. The Display DD Data module first uses the selected date, category, segment or region, and drill-down option and creates an SQL statement to obtain the needed data from the database. When the data arrives, it is placed in the drill-down grid, and the grid is toggled visible while the other charts are hidden.

This completes the program's main structure, but some auxiliary commands still need to be included. First is the Print command on the application's File menu. The Print command (see Figure 5.22) must print the currently visible chart or grid, so the first thing it does is determine which chart or grid is visible. At this point, you could simply issue the PrintForm method of the currently active form and get an image of what is displayed. However, the graph control used to create the charts is capable of much higher resolution than that shown on-screen. To access this higher resolution, you must actively draw the image of the graph control onto the printer object. You do this by changing the chart style to black-and-white, scaling it to the size of a printed page, and copying the image of that chart to the printer. If the chart has a grid attached, that grid has to be explicitly drawn onto the printer, because the grid control doesn't have an image property that can be copied onto the printer. To draw the grid on the printer object, you first draw the grid lines, then print the numbers into the grid created by the lines. The pie chart is handled the same as the other charts, but without an attached grid, and the drill-down grid is handled like the attached grids, but without a chart.

The File | Save command saves the current color image of the chart on disk in the Windows metafile (.WMF) format. The metafile format is useful for placing images in other applications, because it is a picture description file rather than a bitmapped image. A picture description is a series of drawing commands that creates the picture. Since a metafile knows about the lines and boxes that make up the image, when that image is drawn on a higher-resolution screen, the resulting picture is also of a higher resolution. On the other hand, a bitmapped image can never be of a higher resolution than the original bitmap. As shown in Figure 5.23, the Save command first gets a filename from the user, using the Windows Save As common dialog box. The Save As dialog box returns a filename and path, which are used to save the current chart image.

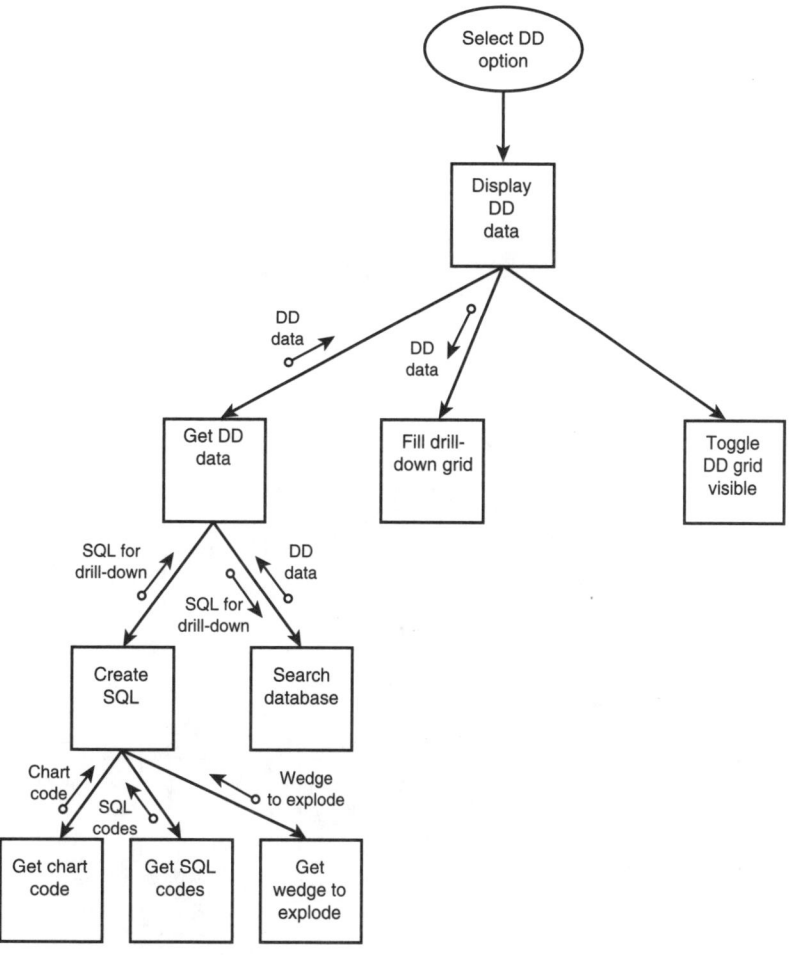

Figure 5.21. *The program structure chart for displaying the drill-down data.*

The Edit | Copy command works much like the Save command, except that the image is saved on the clipboard instead of in a file. Finally, the File | Exit command closes all files and ends the program.

One more event must be handled to make this program work. A startup module must be defined that runs when the program is first run. That startup module must initialize the application and set the defaults (see Figure 5.24). The module first loads and parses the .INI file. The .INI file

Creating the Program Structure Chart

has the same name as the application with the .INI extension. The .INI file is a plain text file that contains the startup options, such as the name and path to the database file. The module then loads some global text arrays used in the application. The text arrays contain things such as the names of the months of the year. The module opens the database file and the `tblDefinitions` table and stores them as global database and table objects. Thus, the database and graph definitions table are available throughout the application. Finally, the module sets the initial chart class and type by simulating a click of chart class button 1.

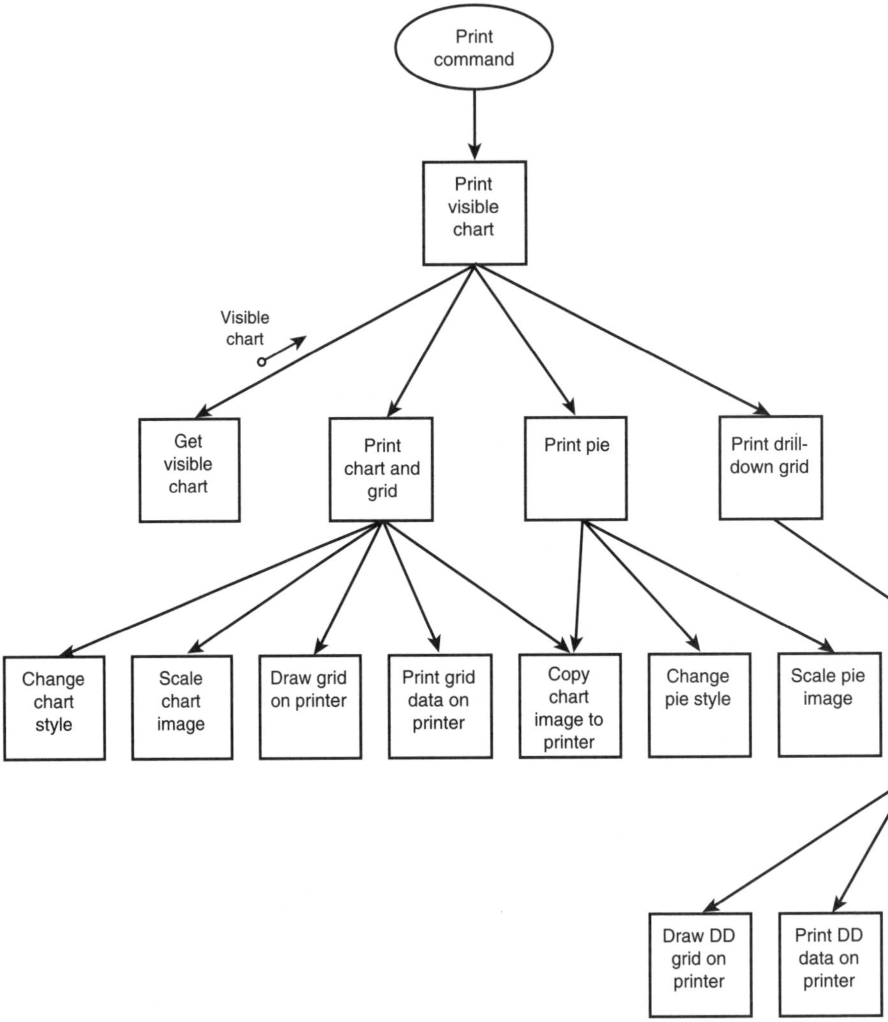

Figure 5.22. *The program structure chart for the Print command.*

This completes the program's structure chart for the decision support application.

Figure 5.23.
The program structure chart for the Save, Copy, and Exit commands.

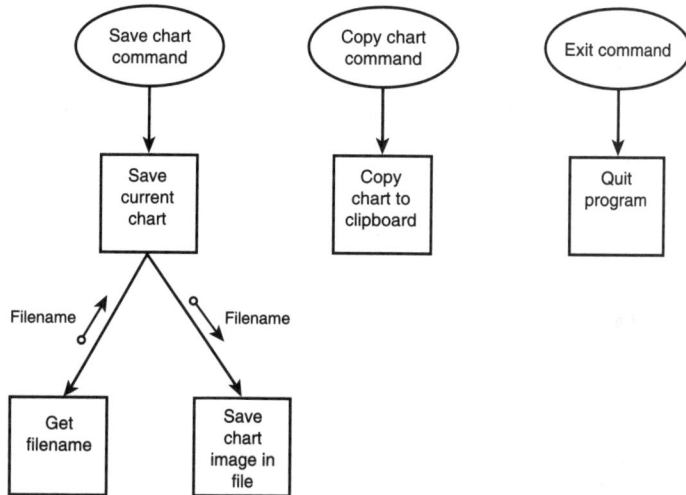

Figure 5.24.
The program structure chart for the startup module.

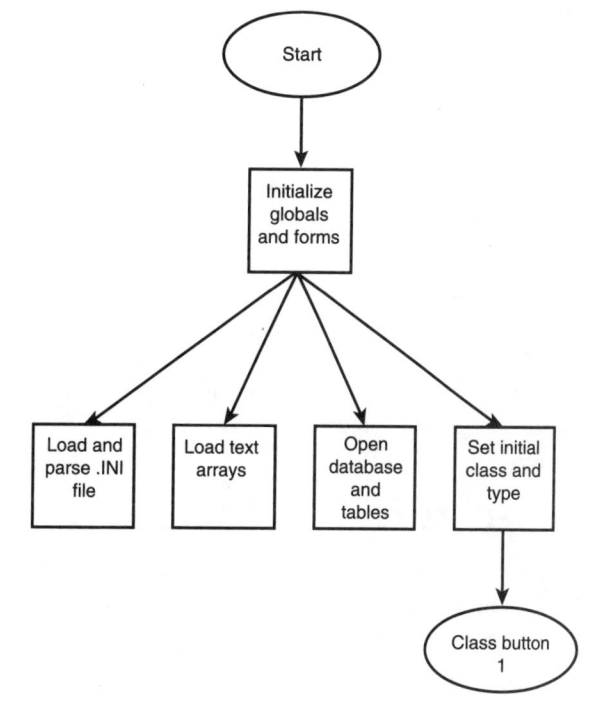

Creating the Program Structure Chart

Modification Notes

When modifying an existing application instead of creating a new one, you generally start with a program structure chart and then work your way back to the data flow diagram. The structure chart comes first because it can be easily created by simply listing the subprocedures that each procedure calls and the variables that are passed as arguments to the subprocedures. When you have the structure chart and the interfaces, you can create the data flow diagram by just reversing the processes described in this chapter for creating the structure chart.

Wanted: A Good Structure Chart

When you're making extensive modifications to an existing application, it's almost imperative that you have a good structure chart. Without it, you don't know the effect of your changes on other parts of the program. For example, a procedure used to debit amounts from a journal could also be used to credit amounts. If you change the procedure to place parentheses around every entry without checking the sign, you will change the credits into debits and thoroughly mess up your journal. On the other hand, if you have a structure chart, you immediately see that the procedure is shared and make your changes accordingly.

If the structure of a revised application needs some revision, you should consider the cost of doing the revision versus the gain achieved by having a consistent structure. If you're doing extensive revisions, you should be less hesitant to restructure the whole thing than if your changes are minor. In most situations, programs aren't revised often enough. Programmers often take the short-term view and patch a problem instead of fixing it. This doesn't mean that you should do a complete revision of a program every time you make a patch, but don't hesitate to do it if the program needs it and the program will be around long enough to benefit from the restructuring.

Debugging the Process

As in the other design steps, the debugging done at this step is to locate missing steps and holes in your program's logic. Additionally, at this step you're dealing with the program's implementation and the peculiarities of the hardware and software. For Visual Basic designs, the item most often neglected is an event procedure. Two important event procedures are missing from this application. They will become apparent as soon as we start testing. The other problem with event-driven applications is *event cascades,* in which an event causes an action that causes the event to happen again. You might see examples of this later in the book as well.

Summary

Today you learned about creating the structure chart for an application, using the data flow diagram to guide that structure into an understandable form. The main goal of the structure chart is to produce independent modules that can be designed and tested without regard to the rest of the application. While that is the goal, it can't be achieved in practice because a program made up of totally independent modules wouldn't do anything. Therefore, you create modules that are as independent as possible and then have a good structure chart to show you where the connections are so you can avoid making changes in one module that cause another module to break.

Now that you know the structure of the application, it's time to design the details of the procedures, which is the subject of the next chapter.

Procedure Design

Procedure Design

Yesterday you created the program structure chart that details the flow of control in an application. You have also created the data flow diagram to show where the data goes, and the process specifications to specify how the data is transformed. Today, you combine these specifications into procedures and specify what the procedures are supposed to do. You do this using either pseudocode or a flowchart.

Today you will learn to

- ☐ partition the program structure chart into procedures
- ☐ write procedure specifications in pseudocode
- ☐ write procedure specifications with a flowchart
- ☐ test algorithms before you design them into an application
- ☐ test the procedure designs

The Goal of Day 6

The goal of Day 6 is to take the program structure chart, the process specifications, and the data flow diagram and create the procedure specifications. Creating the procedure specifications is the final design step before actually writing the procedure in code. It's also your last chance to make significant changes in a program without having to rebuild it.

Until this point in the design process, the design has remained relatively abstract and could be implemented with almost any language or on any platform. However, at this point, you must consider the actual language you're programming in and how it interacts with its environment and the user.

Actually, much of the work for today has already been done. The process specifications contain most of the steps for performing a process, and the program structure chart shows how they fit together. The new stuff comes from determining how to partition the application into procedures. When this is done, you merely combine the process specifications that are to be included in each procedure and make them consistent. When the processes are designed, segment them into one or more program or form modules.

Designing the Procedures

The first step is to take the program structure chart and determine which modules should be combined into procedures and which should stand alone. The next step is to combine the process descriptions for each procedure to see that they are consistent and that they do indeed go together.

Partitioning the Structure Chart

The program structure chart contains all the program modules that are needed to make up an application. However, many modules are trivial in nature. In other cases, the modules are steps in a multistep process, such as the linear transforms discussed in the last chapter. In both of these cases, the modules should be combined when creating the procedures. For example, the Figure Tax example shown in Figure 5.11 has many modules that are trivial in nature. The Add Interest, Subtract Adjustments, Subtract Deductions, Combine Adjustments, and Subtract Tax Paid modules each would contain a single line of code performing a single addition or subtraction. It would be silly to write a special procedure to perform these calculations, so they would be combined with the modules above them, as shown in Figure 6.1. The revised structure chart is shown in Figure 6.2.

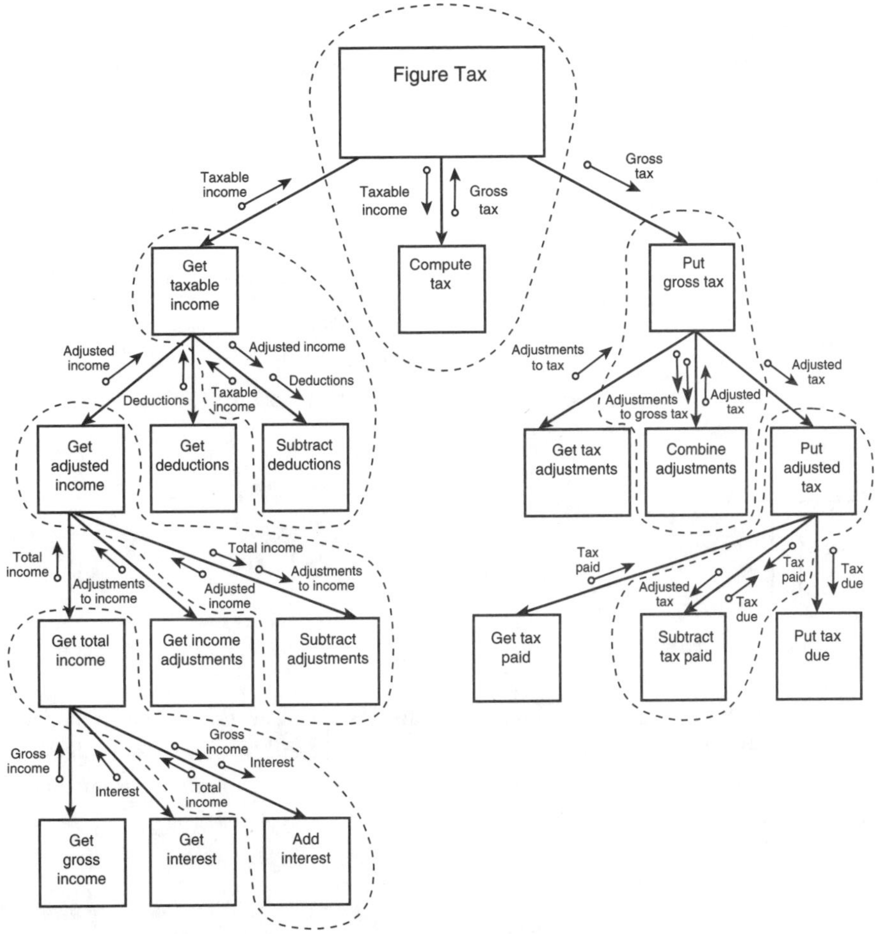

Figure 6.1. *Pulling up trivial modules in the program structure chart.*

Procedure Design

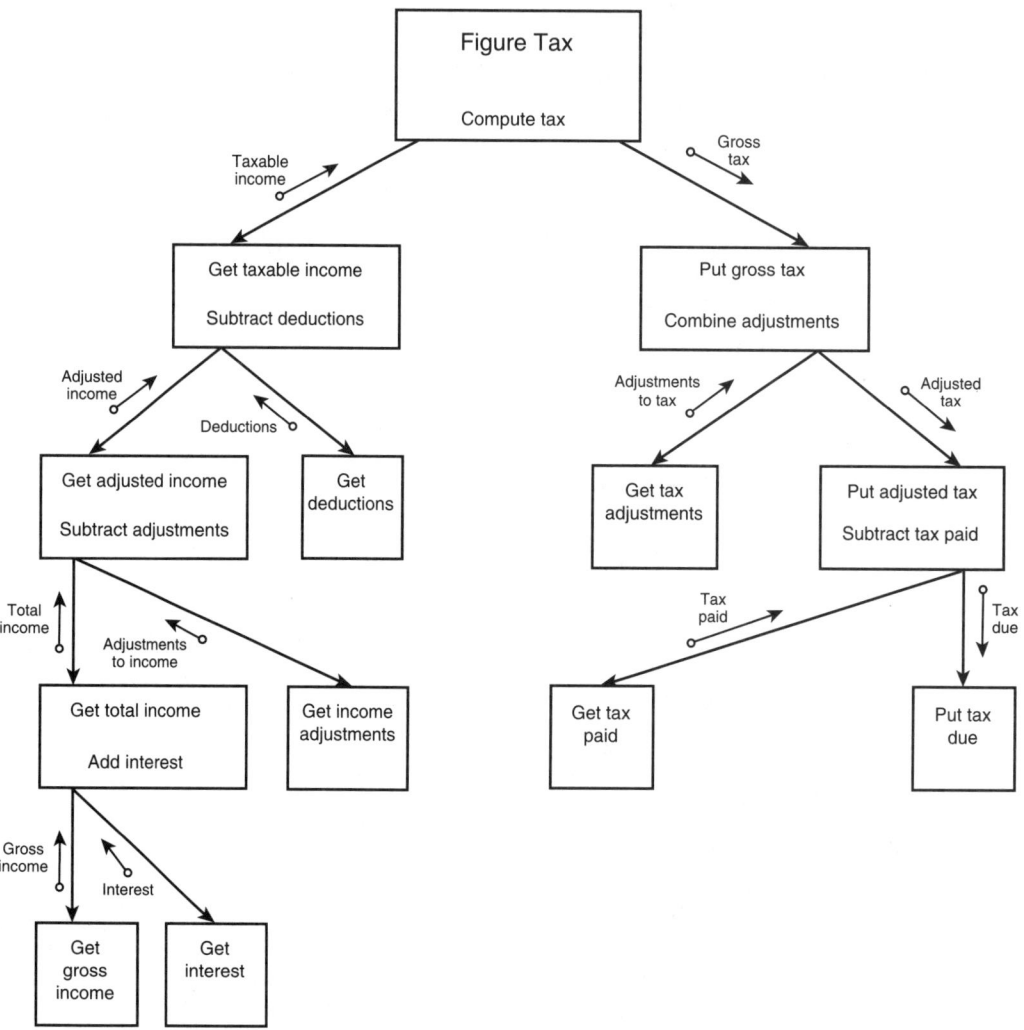

Figure 6.2. *The revised program structure chart for the Figure Tax task.*

Each of the modules required to figure the tax due is sequential and could be pulled up into the Figure_Tax procedure with calls to the Get Interest and Get Deductions modules. Thus, all of the Get and Put Income and Taxes procedures could be pulled up into the Figure Tax module, as shown in Figure 6.3.

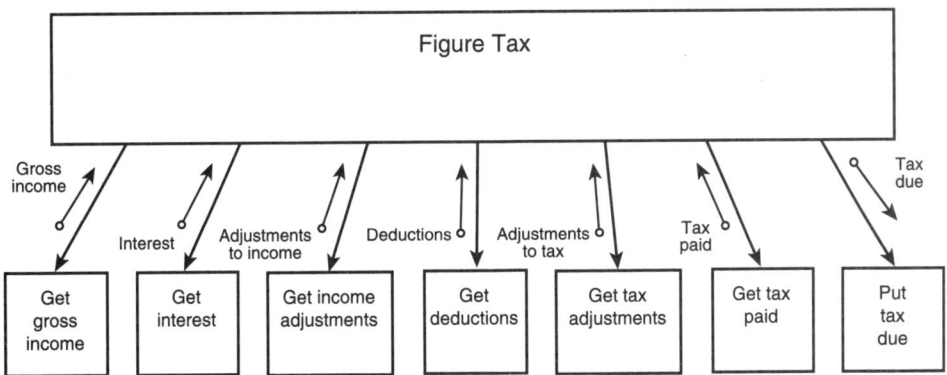

Figure 6.3. *Pulling up sequential modules into the program structure chart.*

The `Figure_Tax` procedure would then have the following procedure description:

```
'Figure Tax procedure
'
Procedure Figure_Tax(GrossIncome, TaxDue)
Call GetInterest to get the Interest
TotalIncome = GrossIncome + Interest
Call GetAdjustments to get the Adjustments
AdjustedIncome = TotalIncome - Adjustments
Call GetDeductions to get the Deductions
TaxableIncome = AdjustedIncome - Deductions
Call ComputeTax to calculate the GrossTax on TaxableIncome
Call GetTaxAdjustments to get the AdjustmentsToTax
AdjustedTax = GrossTax + AdjustmentsToTax
Call GetTaxPaid to get the TaxPaid
TaxDue = AdjustedTax - TaxPaid
End Sub
```

The Calculate Pay module in Figure 5.13 gets much the same treatment. The three Get Tax Rate modules in the figure are likely to be trivial in scope since they probably access a global table or open a file and read in a table. Therefore, they could be pulled up into the Get Tax modules. Likewise, the three Calculate Tax modules simply pass the tax table and the gross pay to the `InterpolateTaxTable` procedure, so they can simply be eliminated. The six first-level modules could also be pulled up into the Calculate Pay module, putting each module in a block `If` structure to determine whether the calculation is performed or not. The resulting structure chart would now look like Figure 6.4, with a procedure description like the following:

```
'Calculate Pay
'
Calculate Pay (GrossPay, NetPay, EmployeeInfo)
FedTax = StateTax = FICATax = 0
If EmployeeInfo.PaysFedTax is set
  Get the FedTaxTable
  Call InterpolateTaxTable to calculate FedTax on GrossPay
```

Procedure Design

```
If EmployeeInfo.PaysStateTax is set
  Get the StateTaxTable
  Call InterpolateTaxTable to calculate StateTax on GrossPay
If EmployeeInfo.PaysFICA is set
  Get FICATable
  Call InterpolateTaxTable to calculate the FICATax on GrossPay
NetPay = GrossPay - FedTax - StateTax - FICATax
End Sub
```

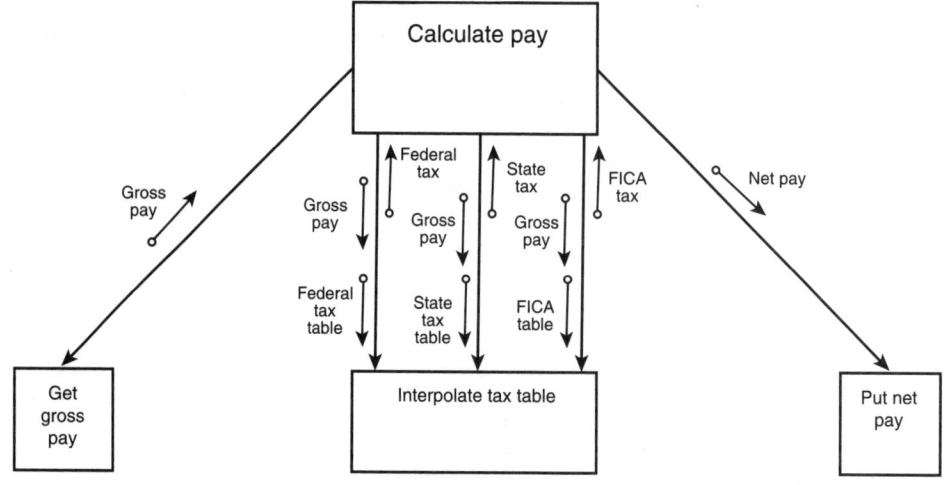

Figure 6.4. *The revised Calculate Pay structure chart.*

In creating the procedure description, it quickly becomes apparent that we have forgotten a critical piece of data: the employee info that tells us what taxes a particular employee pays. Note how the Get Gross Pay and Put Net Pay modules simply become the interface to the procedure.

> **Note:** You might wonder why you went to all the trouble of creating all the modules in the structure chart just so you could eliminate them to write the procedure descriptions. Well, you haven't eliminated them. They're still autonomous blocks of code. They're just stored together in a single procedure. When you create the procedure description, you should still see the modules as separate, well-defined blocks of code.

Pseudocode or Flowcharts

The procedure descriptions and process descriptions presented so far in this book have all been done in pseudocode, but that isn't the only way to specify a procedure. Flowcharts are also used to describe a procedure's operation. Both pseudocode and flowcharts have different strengths and weaknesses. You should use what is most meaningful to you. You can even use both. It depends on what you're modeling and what makes the most sense at the time.

Pseudocode

- ☐ is close in structure to the actual code that you will eventually write
- ☐ is written, so you can create and modify it with any word processor
- ☐ tends to be a lot shorter than flowcharts
- ☐ is easier to use if you prefer to write your descriptions
- ☐ has complex logical structures that might not be as easy to understand as flowcharts

Flowcharts

- ☐ are graphical, so the control structures are much easier to see and follow
- ☐ are easier to use if you prefer to draw your descriptions
- ☐ tend to be large and take up a lot of paper
- ☐ don't do a good job of showing the interface to called procedures
- ☐ don't look like the code in the actual procedure

Again, use the method you're most comfortable with.

> **My Personal Preference Is Pseudocode**
>
> Besides its smaller size and the fact that you can create it with any word processor, I find that by the time I get to the step of writing the procedure descriptions, I'm itching to write some code. Pseudocode is a lot closer to code than a flowchart. I also type well, so I can crank out pseudocode very quickly. Someone who doesn't type well might prefer to draw the descriptions instead of typing them.

Pseudocode

Pseudocode, which is also known as *structured English,* uses English words and simple formulas to describe what is being done in a procedure. There's more than one way to write pseudocode, but the structure I'm going to show you is fairly popular and easy to use.

DAY 6
Procedure Design

All variables have wordy names that are easy to understand, such as `GrossPay` or `StateTaxTable`. Structured data types use the *dot syntax* (.) to separate the structure name from the specific element. For example, if the data structure `EmployeeData` has the elements `Name` and `PayRate`, refer to them as `EmployeeData.Name` and `EmployeeData.PayRate`. This is the same syntax that is used in Visual Basic code. Do the same when referring to database tables and fields, using the structure `Table.Field`. Include the database name if more than one is open, as in `Database.Table.Field`.

Control structures and code blocks are delineated by indenting. Start each code block by indenting a couple of spaces or a tab. Most engineers do not use an `End` statement, but assume that the end occurs when the indenting changes. Use `End` statements if they make you more comfortable, or if they're needed to delineate a more complicated structure. For example, if you analyze the `Calculate Pay` procedure from earlier in this chapter, it is interpreted as follows:

Pseudocode	Description

`'`
`'Calculate Pay`
`'`
	Comments.

`Calculate Pay (GrossPay,` `NetPay, EmployeeInfo)`	The procedure header that specifies the interface to the calling procedure.
`FedTax = StateTax = FICATax = 0`	Zeros the three variables.

`If EmployeeInfo.PaysFedTax is set`
  `Get the FedTaxTable`
  `Call InterpolateTaxTable to`
    `calculate the FedTax on`
    `GrossPay`
	The first block `If`. If the `If` statement is True, the indented part of the block is executed. If the `If` statement is False, the indented statements are skipped, and execution continues with the next statement after them.

`If EmployeeInfo.PaysStateTax is set`
  `Get the StateTaxTable`
  `Call InterpolateTaxTable`
    `to calculate the StateTax`
    `on GrossPay`
	The second block `If` works the same as the first.

`If EmployeeInfo.PaysFICA is set`
  `Get the FICATable`
  `Call InterpolateTaxTable`
    `to calculate the FICATax on`
    `GrossPay`
	The third block `If` works the same as the other two.

```
        NetPay = GrossPay - FedTax -        A statement that calculates
            StateTax - FICATax              the net pay.
        End Sub                             An End statement to mark the
                                            end of the procedure.
```

The procedure could also be written like the following, which includes End statements much like Visual Basic does. Other languages such as C use brackets or semicolons instead of End statements to indicate the end of a block.

```
'
'Calculate Pay
'
Calculate Pay (GrossPay, NetPay, EmployeeInfo)
FedTax = StateTax = FICATax = 0
If EmployeeInfo.PaysFedTax is set
  Get the FedTaxTable
  Call InterpolateTaxTable to calculate FedTax on GrossPay
End If
If EmployeeInfo.PaysStateTax is set
  Get the StateTaxTable
  Call InterpolateTaxTable to calculate StateTax on GrossPay
End If
If EmployeeInfo.PaysFICA is set
  Get the FICATable
  Call InterpolateTaxTable to calculate FICATax on GrossPay
End If
NetPay = GrossPay - FedTax - StateTax - FICATax
End Sub
```

As you can see, the End statements don't add a lot here, but they could be useful if the structure were more complicated.

Flowcharts

Flowcharts were one of the first methods of diagramming the execution of computer code. They were originally used to diagram the operation of a whole program, but they're now used primarily to diagram a single procedure.

Flowcharts start and stop with ovals containing the words Start or Stop. Lines proceed from the Start oval to the next calculation to show the sequence of calculations. Rectangles contain calculations, and diamonds contain branches. I/O statements and procedure calls are placed in trapezoids. Branches that would take up a lot of room on the chart, or that would confuse things if they were drawn on the chart, are replaced with a letter in a circle. The assumption is that circles with the same letter are connected.

For example, Figure 6.5 shows the flowchart for the Calculate Pay procedure described earlier. The input data is in the first trapezoid. It's followed by the calculation to zero the three tax variables. The diamond holds the test of the PaysFedTax variable. The branch selected depends on the result of the test. If the test is True, the Get FedTaxTable I/O statement is executed,

Procedure Design

followed by a call to the InterpolateTaxTable procedure. Because the chart is getting long, it is split at this point and starts again at the top of the page. The assumed connection between the bottom of the first column and the top of the second is marked with a dashed line. Normally, the dashed line wouldn't be included in the chart, but I've included it here for greater clarity. The other two tax calculations proceed much the same as the first. Following the last tax calculation, the net pay is calculated and returned to the calling procedure.

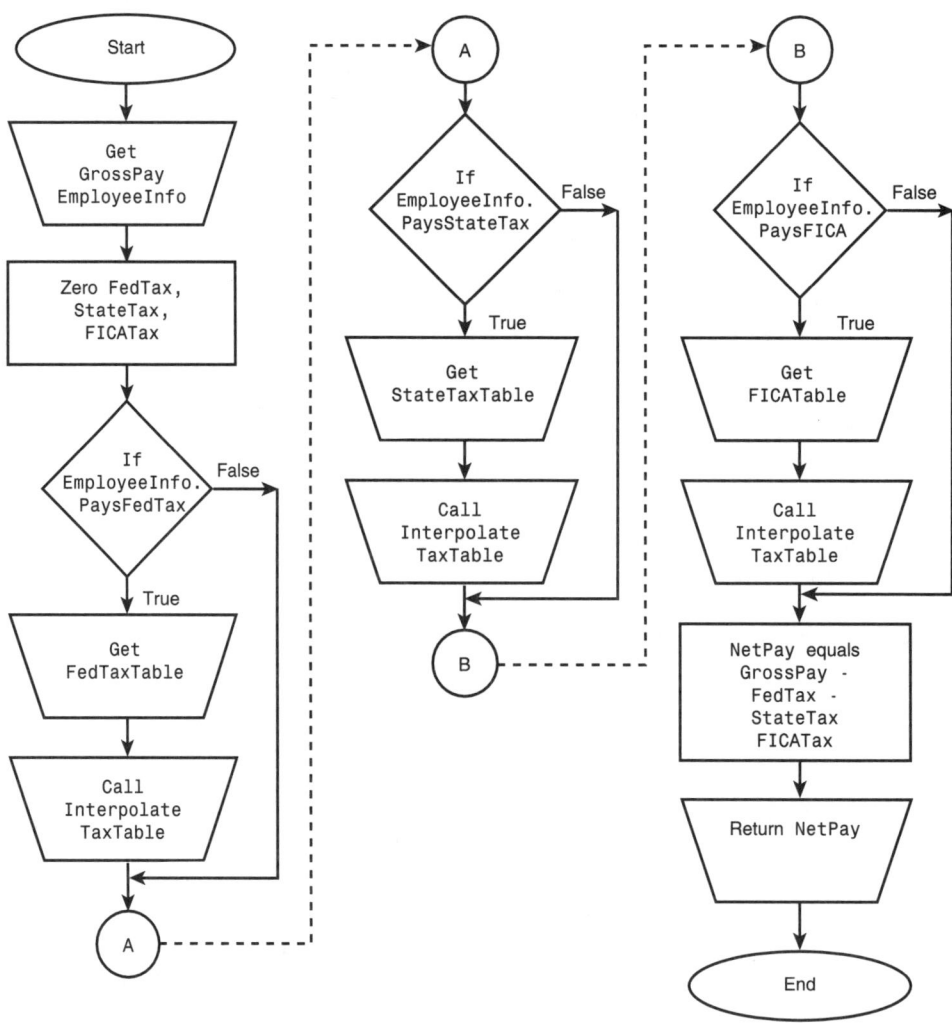

Figure 6.5. *The* Calculate Pay *procedure as a flowchart. The dashed lines show the connections implied by the circled letters.*

Combining Procedures into Modules

When you're programming in Visual Basic, all code must be contained in a form or module. The event procedures must be in the form containing the object that generated the event, but all the others can go just about wherever you want to put them. There are some restrictions, though. Any procedure that you want to be accessible to other procedures elsewhere in a program must be in a module. Procedures defined in a form are accessible only to other procedures in the same form. In Visual Basic 3.0, some database calls must be performed in a module because some database objects lose their definition in a form module, and only modules can have global error traps.

The number of forms for storing code is limited by the number of forms to be displayed. However, you can include as many modules as you need.

> **How Many Modules?**
>
> Don't put too many modules in an application. They'll just confuse things. Try to functionally group your procedures in the modules to make it easy to find things. For example, put all your printing procedures in the same module. Then, if you have a printing problem, you have to access only a single module to see all the code associated with printing.

Testing Algorithms

As you design your procedures, you invariably come up with new algorithms or unfamiliar code sequences. Before committing your application to depend on these algorithms and sequences, test them to be sure they work as you expect. Visual Basic has many capabilities for testing code sequences and functions to see how they work.

Test Programs

One of the simplest ways to test an algorithm or function is to write a short program that uses it and see if it works as expected. Use the `Debug.Print` statement to print the test results to the debug window, where you can examine them. It's also useful to create a short program to set up a problem and then examine the algorithm or function using debug window commands. Write a short program that declares the variables and does whatever other setup is needed, then insert a `Stop` statement to stop the execution and place the program in break mode. At this point, you can examine or change the values of the variables and execute subprocedures and formulas.

Procedure Design

For example, to examine the Visual Basic statements that access a database, create a short procedure like the following:

```
'
'Database Test Procedure
'
Sub Test1()
Dim dbDatabase As Database
Dim tblTable As Table
Set dbDatabase = OpenDatabase("D:\firstapp\example\rollups\graphs.mdb")
Set tblTable = dbDatabase.OpenTable("tblDefinitions")
Stop
End Sub
```

When you run this procedure by typing `Run "Test1"` in the debug window, the procedure opens a database and one of its tables, and then halts the procedure with all the variables still intact. In the debug window you can examine the effects of different functions applied to the database or table object variables by typing a question mark followed by a formula that results in a printable value. For example:

```
? dbDatabase.TableDefs(1).Name
```

prints the name of the first table in the database.

Testing Queries

By far the best way to test queries is to use a program such as Access or VisData (which is included with Visual Basic). In either program, you can create and execute queries and then view the results. When the results are what you expect, copy the query out of the SQL window and paste it into your program. You can also save the query as a persistent query in the database itself so that when you need it again, you simply execute the saved copy.

Testing Procedures

You should perform two tests on your procedure descriptions before actually coding them. First, do a walk-through to see if the procedure is doing what you expect. Second, check the interfaces to make sure they're consistent between the calling and called procedures. When you have completed a procedure description, imagine you're the computer and walk through the procedure one step at a time. At each step, say what you would do based on the description. Don't use general terms. Be explicit and tell all the details. Note the values of the variables at each step. Draw a line from statement to statement as you execute them in your mind so that you can keep track of the thread of execution. Try to follow each branch to make sure that they are all consistent. Any inconsistencies should be easy to spot.

The Decision Support Application Project

The decision support application is really starting to take shape. The procedures are in place, so now we'll create the procedure descriptions from the structure chart and process descriptions. The structure charts start with Figure 5.15, and the process descriptions are in Chapter 3.

Specifying the *DrawChartAndGrid* Procedure

The structure of the DrawChartAndGrid procedure has many subprocedures that need to be pulled up into the main procedure. In fact, most of the subprocedures are pulled up instead of being called separately. The second important fact is that the Set Chart Data and Set Grid Data modules will be intermixed instead of kept as separate modules. This is done because the data values that are placed in the chart are also placed in the grid, and it makes sense to put the data in both places when it's available instead of obtaining it twice.

First, combine the process descriptions for the processes that became modules in the program structure chart. Then, rearrange the process descriptions into a procedure structure, maintaining as much of the original modularity as possible. Delete any redundant tasks, as shown in the following:

```
Sub DrawChartAndGrid()
1.1 Get chart layout
   From the graphs table
      Select the record where the chart code equals the Code field.
      Extract and return the data fields for chart layout.
3.1 Set chart layout
   With the chart layout data
      Set the chart title.
      Set the chart height, width, and location.
      Set the chart type.
      Set the chart style.
4.1 Set grid layout
   Set the number of rows and columns.
   With the legend labels
      Set the legend column.
   Set month names in the columns.
   Shade the fixed rows and columns.
1.3 Get field names
   Extract and return the table name and field names
      for the legend data and the chart data.
2.1 Select table
   From the database tables
      Get and return the table containing the legend labels.
2.3 Get layout data
   From the legend table
```

Day 6: Procedure Design

```
      Return the contents of the legend field.
      Return the contents of the legend text field.
  8.1 Set legend colors
      Set the location and size of the color pictures that match the graph colors.
  8.2 Set legend labels
      With the legend labels
        Insert the labels into the grid.
  2.1 Select table
      From the database tables
        Get and return the table containing the chart data.
  2.4 Get chart data
      From the data table
        Return the contents of the data field.
  3.2 Set chart data
      With the selected data
        Plot the data on the chart.
  4.2 Set grid data
      With the selected data
        Insert the data in the grid.
End Sub
```

The procedure starts with process 1.1 and loads the record in the Graphs table that contains the data for the current chart class and type. Next, the procedure obtains the layout data and applies it to the chart in process 3.1 and to the grid in process 4.1.

Process 1.3 obtains the table and field names for the legend and for the chart and grid data. The first half of process 2.1 obtains the data table that contains the legend data. The legend data is obtained from the legend table in process 2.3 and then used to create the legend in processes 8.1 and 8.2. To obtain the data for the chart and grid, the second half of process 2.1 is used to obtain the table containing the data, and process 2.4 obtains the data from it. Process 3.2 then inserts this data into the chart, and process 4.2 inserts it into the grid. Processes 3.2 and 4.2 will be intermixed when the code is written so that the data can be obtained once and inserted into both the chart and the grid at the same time.

Specifying the *Class* and *Type* Event Procedures

The chart Class and Type buttons are two button arrays that change the class and type of the chart, as shown in Figure 5.16. Three procedures are specified with this structure chart. First, two event procedures are specified to detect the pressing of the Class and Type buttons and to create the class and type codes according to the button pressed. The Type procedure calls a procedure in a module to process the class and type codes. This doubling of procedures is needed because of a problem with Visual Basic 3.0, which loses the object quality of an object variable passed to a form. When this error occurs, you get a Variable not an array message. The two procedures to detect the pressing of the type and class buttons are as follows.

```
Sub Class_Click ()
Get class from button pressed
```

```
Call Type_Click (1) to simulate a click the first type button
End Sub

Sub Type_Click()
Get the type from the button pressed
Call CreateNewGraph ()
End Sub

Sub CreateNewGraph
10.0 Create chart code
  With the integer chart class
    With the integer chart type
      Turn the two integer codes into strings.
  Combine the two code strings into a single string.
  Store the string code in the globals.
  Toggle the grid off.
  Call DrawChartAndGrid.
End Sub
```

The class and type are both stored as global variables so that any procedure can access them as needed. Pressing a Class button changes the chart class and uses that to change the Type buttons that are enabled and then clicks on the type 1 chart type. Thus, you always start with a type 1 chart when you change the chart class. Pressing the Type button changes the chart type, toggles the grid off, and then calls the `DrawChartAndGrid` procedure to create the chart.

Specifying the *ResizeChartAndGrid* Procedure

The `ResizeChartAndGrid` procedure, shown in Figure 5.17, is called by the `ToggleGrid` procedure. The `ToggleGrid` procedure, which is executed whenever the chart is double-clicked on, simply toggles a flag that indicates whether the grid is visible or not. After toggling the flag, the `ToggleGrid` procedure calls the `ResizeChartAndGrid` procedure to redraw the chart with or without the grid. Since the grid was created when the chart was originally drawn, it doesn't need to be recreated here, only made visible on the form. The `ResizeChartAndGrid` procedure uses the parts of the `DrawChartAndGrid` procedure that set the chart position and make it visible without changing any of its data or attributes. Also included here is the code to redraw the pie chart if it happens to be the visible chart instead of the lone or area chart.

```
Sub Chart_DoubleClick ()
Call ToggleGrid
End Sub

Sub ToggleGrid ()
If the Grid is visible, make it invisible
  Else make it visible
Call ResizeChartAndGraph to resize it
End Sub

Sub ResizeChartAndGrid ()
```

Procedure Design

```
If the Pie Chart is not visible
  With the chart layout data
    Set the chart height, width, and location.
  If the grid is visible, display it.
    Else display the legend.
Else the pie chart is visible.
  Set the pie chart height, width, and location.
  Hide the grid and legend.
End Sub
```

Specifying the *DrawPieChart* Procedure

The DrawPieChart procedure is shown in Figure 5.18. Double-clicking on a month label or on a column of the grid selects the month associated with that label or column and displays a pie chart showing the data for that single month. Since clicking on the month or on the column does the same thing, the Month_Click procedure simply calls the Column_Click procedure, which calls the DrawPieChart procedure. The DrawPieChart procedure obtains its data from the existing grid and inserts it into the pie chart. It then toggles the pie chart visible and all the others invisible.

```
Sub Month_Click ()
  Determine what month was clicked on.
  Call the Column_Click procedure for that month.
End Sub

Sub Column_Click ()
  Determine what month was clicked on.
  Call DrawPieChart to draw the pie.
End Sub

Sub DrawPieChart ()
5.1 Set pie layout
  Set the height, width, and location of the pie chart.
  Add lines and labels for each piece.
Get the data for the selected month from the grid.
5.2 Set pie data
  With the selected month's data
    Insert the data in the pie chart.
    Attach labels to each wedge.
Toggle the pie chart visible.
Toggle the Chart and grid hidden.
End Sub
```

Specifying the *ToggleGraphVisible* Procedure

The ToggleGraphVisible procedure is shown in Figure 5.19. When the pie chart is visible, double-clicking on the form outside of the pie chart returns you to the previously displayed chart and grid. The graph doesn't need to be redrawn or resized, only made visible, along with the grid if it was visible before.

```
Sub PieForm_DoubleClick ()
Toggle pie hidden
Toggle graph visible
If the grid is enabled, toggle it visible
End Sub
```

Specifying the *DisplayDDOptions* Procedure

The DisplayDDOptions procedure is shown in Figure 5.20. When you double-click on a pie wedge, the wedge is exploded, the pie chart is moved over, and the drill-down options form is displayed beside it. The DDOptions form contains option buttons for the drill-down options allowed for the displayed pie chart.

```
Sub PieWedge_DoubleClick ()
Call DisplayDDOptions
End Sub

Sub DisplayDDOptions ()
6.1 Explode wedge
  Get the selected wedge.
  Explode the wedge.
Move the pie chart to the side.
Display the drill-down options form.
Get the available options for the displayed pie chart.
Disable the options on the form that are not available.
End Sub
```

Specifying the *DisplayDDData* Procedure

The DisplayDDData procedure is shown in Figure 5.21. When the user selects an option from the drill-down options form, the DisplayDDData procedure obtains the selected data and displays the drill-down grid.

```
Sub DDOption_Click ()
Call DisplayDDData
End Sub

Sub DisplayDDData ()
Get the selected wedge
1.2 Get SQL codes
  From the graphs table
    Select the record where the chart code equals the Code field.
    Extract and return the SQL code fragments.
6.2 Create SQL
  Get the SQL codes for the current chart.
  Combine the SQL codes, the exploded wedge, and the chart code
    to create an SQL statement to get the data.
2.2 Get drill-down data
  From the database tables
```

Procedure Design

```
        Return the array of data selected with the SQL statement.
7.1 Set grid layout
   Set the number of rows and columns of the grid.
   Set the location, height, and width of the grid.
7.2 Set grid data
   With the DD data
      Insert the DD data into the grid.
Toggle the DD form visible.
Hide the pie chart.
End Sub
```

Specifying the *PrintVisibleChart* Procedure

The File | Print command is used to print the currently visible chart and grid. The Print command calls the `PrintVisibleChart` procedure, as shown in Figure 5.22. The `PrintVisibleChart` procedure determines what chart is currently visible and then prints it. If the chart has a grid, the grid is printed also. Although we could use the `DrawMode` property of the Graph control to print the graph (setting it to 5 `G_PRINT` prints the current graph), the grid wouldn't be printed with it. If we used the `PrintForm` method to print both the graph and the grid, the graph would be printed at low resolution, and only the visible part would show. To print a high-resolution image of both, we get the Windows metafile image of the chart from the chart control and combine that with a drawing of the grid.

```
Sub Print_Click()
Call PrintVisibleChart to print whatever is visible on the screen
End Sub

Sub PrintVisibleChart ()
Get visible chart
If visible is Class and Type Chart, call PrintChartAndGrid
If visible is Pie chart, call PrintPie
If visible is DDGrid, call PrintDDGrid
End Sub

Sub PrintChartAndGrid ()
12.1 Change chart style
   Before printing
      Set the chart style to monochrome.
12.2 Scale chart image
   Before printing
      Set the chart height and width to fit in the printer window.
12.3 Copy chart image to printer
   Get a handle to the Windows metafile for the current chart
      from the graphics server.
   Copy the chart to the printer object.
12.4 Draw grid on printer
   For number of columns
      Draw evenly-spaced vertical lines on the printer.
   For number of rows
      Draw evenly-spaced horizontal lines on the printer.
12.5 Print grid data on printer
   For each data value in the grid
```

```
        Print the data value on the printer.
    12.1 Change chart style
      After printing
        Set the chart style to color.
    12.2 Scale chart image
      After printing
        Set the chart height and width to fit the chart form.
End Sub

Sub PrintPie ()
    12.6 Change pie style
      Before printing
        Set the pie style to monochrome.
    12.7 Change pie scale
      Before printing
        Set the pie height and width to fit in the printer window.
    12.3 Copy chart image to printer
      Get a handle to the Windows metafile for the current chart
          from the graphics server.
      Copy the chart to the printer object.
    12.6 Change pie style
      After printing
        Set the pie style to color.
    12.7 Change pie scale
      After printing
        Set the pie height and width to fit the chart form.
End Sub

Sub PrintDDGrid ()
    9.1 Draw grid on printer
      Using the drawing commands
      Create the grid on the printer.
    9.2 Print data on grid
      With the DD Grid data
        Write the grid data on the printer.
End Sub
```

Specifying the *Save*, *Copy*, and *Exit* Procedures

In addition to the Print and Print Setup commands, the File menu also has Save and Exit commands, as shown in Figure 5.23. The Save command gets a filename from the user using the standard file dialog and then stores a copy of the current chart in it. The Exit command quits the program. On the Edit menu is a Copy command. It places a copy of the current chart on the clipboard. All of these commands are implemented with the Graph control's built-in methods.

```
Sub Save_Click ()
    13.0 Save chart
      Get a filename using the standard file dialog.
      Open the file for printing.
      Copy the current chart or pie to the file.
```

Procedure Design

```
    Close the file.
End Sub

Sub Copy_Click ()
14.0 Copy chart
    Copy the current chart or pie to the clipboard.
End Sub

Sub Exit_Click
15.0 End Program
    Close the database and tables.
    Exit the program.
End Sub
```

Specifying the Initialization Procedures

The initialization procedures are shown in Figure 5.24. These procedures load and parse the .INI file, load some text arrays with the names of the months, open the database file, and display the initial chart. The first procedure run is set by Visual Basic using the Options | Project command. The default is to load the first form in the project and run the Form_Load procedure if it exists. You can change that to any form in the project or to a procedure named Main. The first step is to open the DCNSPT.INI file and load its contents. The following is that file's contents. The startup section starts with [startup] and ends with [end]. If you had a different database file or a secure Access database file, this .INI file would contain more sections relating to the specific database type. The standard location for this file in the final application is the C:\WINDOWS directory. This .INI file sets the path to the rollup database file GRAPHS.MDB and sets the year to display data for:

```
Decision Support Program INI File
[startup]
DataFile=D:\FIRSTAPP\EXAMPLE\ROLUPDAT\GRAPHS.MDB
Year=1991
[end]
```

The next step is to load some data arrays that contain the names of the months. These are used later in the program to label the graphs and grid. The Main program then opens the database and the graph description table and stores these objects as global variables. Finally, the Main program selects the Total Sales chart as the initial chart.

Note: In a standard bottom-up software design, the initialization procedures would be the first things designed. Here they are the last, which makes a lot more sense, because you don't know what needs to be initialized until you've designed the program.

```
Sub Main ()
Call LoadAndParseINIFile
11.2 Load text arrays
  For each month in the year
    Store the three-letter abbreviation for the month name in the global
      strMonths(n, 1).
    Store the four-letter abbreviation for the month name in the global
      strMonths(n, 2).
    Store the month number in the global strMonths(n, 3).
  For each quarter in the year
    Store the name of the quarter in strQuarters(n).
11.3 Open database and tables
  Open the Graphs database and create the database object dbGraphs.
  Open the Graph definitions table and store the object in tblGraphs.
11.4 Set initial class and type
  Initialize any flags.
  Set the initial chart class to 1 = sales.
  Set the initial chart type to 1 = year to date.
  Display the initial chart.
End Sub

Sub LoadAndParseINIFile ()
11.1 Load and parse .INI file
  Open the DCNSPT.INI file.
  For each record in the file
    Read a record.
    Extract the variable name.
    Extract the value.
    Store the value in the named global variable.
  Next record.
  If year is null or filename is null
    Print "Error in INI file".
    End the program.
End Sub
```

Modification Notes

If you're modifying an existing program, you can use the actual program code (with lots of comments) instead of pseudocode for the parts you aren't changing. If you make small modifications to the existing code, be sure to carefully mark the changes. When you remove parts, comment them out instead of deleting them so that you can put them back if they're really needed. You can delete them later, after you've verified that they're not needed. Design major changes to a procedure or new or replacement procedures first using pseudocode or flow charts.

Debugging the Process

There's still not a lot of debugging you can do other than looking for holes in your logic. You can test any algorithms you're planning to use to see if they work before designing them into your program. Create simple programs to try procedures. Set up an environment you can

Procedure Design

experiment in by writing a simple procedure to declare some variables, open a database, and then pause with a Stop statement. You can then experiment with procedures and statements using the debug window. If you're unsure if an algorithm will work, test it to make sure while you can still easily change it to something else.

Using the specification for the project, examine all the pseudocode to ensure that all the design requirements have been met. The project is supposed to do certain things, so you should be able to find the code that performs each task. Have other programmers walk through the code with you to try to spot any holes or missing steps. A walk-through is where you look at a chart showing the pseudocode and go through it step by step, explaining each step to someone else.

Walkthroughs

Walking through a program design is extremely useful for locating problems. In most cases, you will spot the errors as you try to explain the design to your listener. You are forced to explain things you would mentally skip over while reading the code. And, if you can't explain them, you have to assume that there's a problem and fix it.

Summary

Today you learned to combine the program structure chart, the data flow diagram, and the process specifications into the procedure specifications. You can now use the procedure specifications to start writing code. However, one more design step needs to be completed: the visual interface. Tomorrow you will design the forms that are the application's visual interface.

Some of the test procedures used today are in the \OTHER directory on the included CD.

7

Forms Design

Forms Design

The forms used in your application constitute the visual interface between your program and the user. The fine crafting of the design for the underlying code is wasted if the user interface is so poorly done that the user can't or won't use it. Designing a successful user interface isn't hard as long as you follow the simple design principles described in this chapter.

Today you will learn

- ☐ the rules for good user interface design
- ☐ how to apply those rules using Visual Basic
- ☐ how to create standard visual elements with Visual Basic controls

The Goal of Day 7

The goal of Day 7 is to learn how to design a well-crafted user interface. The user interface, as the name implies, forms the interface between the user and the computer code. Before Windows and the Macintosh, the user interface consisted of typed commands, typed results, and maybe a few simple menus. In less than 10 years, the user interface for computer programs has been transformed to the fully graphical interface seen in Windows applications, on the Macintosh, and on most UNIX-based workstations.

The phenomenal success of the Macintosh computer in a market dominated by the IBM PC can be only partly ascribed to its graphical user interface. I believe that the true success of the Macintosh and the subsequent Windows interface for PCs can be ascribed to a 57-page loose-leaf document prepared by Apple computer and distributed to all its developers. That document, *The Macintosh User Interface Guidelines,* describes how a Macintosh application should look and how the standard controls should work. This document forms a chapter of the first volume of *Inside Macintosh,* and it's the only chapter that doesn't contain any code. What it has are descriptions and drawings of every facet of the standard user interface. It specifies what the standard commands are, what menus they should be on, and what they should do. It also specifies how to edit text in any window or dialog box and how to select and manipulate things. Finally, it contains an admonishment to all developers to use the guidelines with the incentive that all the code needed to create the standard interface is built in.

The result is that all well-designed Macintosh programs work the same. No matter what program you're using, you do things the same way, and all similar commands and controls work the same way. To a developer, this might seem boring. You want to create the latest cutting-edge user interface. To a user, however, being able to immediately use a new program without having to read the manual is a tremendous incentive to use that program instead of the one with the cutting-edge interface and the 12-inch-thick manual.

The importance of consistent interface design isn't lost on Windows developers as they create Windows applications. The consistency you see between different Windows applications and between the same applications on the Windows and Macintosh platforms is an extremely strong

selling point. The largest benefit for the user is that it significantly reduces the training requirements needed for a new application.

Operating System Overload

As a scientist, developer, and author, I must continually switch between Windows, Macintosh, UNIX, and VMS platforms. As such, I feel as if I'm in a state of operating system overload as I try to remember what commands go with what system. Any consistency between platforms that reduces the number of new applications and languages that I must learn is a tremendous help.

To promote consistent interface design in Visual Basic applications, the *Visual Design Guide* is included in the professional version. It provides many useful suggestions and defines the size and shape of many visual elements seen in Microsoft applications.

User Interface Design Rules

The rules for visual interface design are straightforward, but you need a lot of self-discipline to implement them correctly. Although you strive to be creative and innovative, the design rules seek to restrain you and prevent you from using your creative ideas. There are only a few general rules:

- [ ] Keep it simple.
- [ ] Make it obvious.
- [ ] Make it internally consistent.
- [ ] Use familiar design elements (external consistency).

Stifle Your Creativity and Keep Things Simple

Even if you've designed the most wonderful user interface that allows you to do everything one-handed with a single form, forget it. Except for technofreaks who love to show off, your users will hate you. Make the interface simple and straightforward.

In a program like the decision support application, display only one type of data at a time. You could cover the screen with graphs, but that almost always confuses the issue. You should also be wary of placing tables and graphs on the same form. The decision support application has both a table and a graph on the same form, but the form always starts with only a graph on it. Only if the user wants to see the numeric data is the table displayed.

Forms Design

Textbook Tip: Here are some rules for keeping forms simple:

Make the object of the form straightforward.

Have only one topic per form.

Try not to mix charts and graphs on one form.

Use standard controls.

Make using the controls uncomplicated and obvious.

Keep the feature count within reason.

Make minimal use of color on unimportant items.

As you design the forms, you will undoubtedly think of several extra features you could add to the project. In general, you should leave them out and include only features that you contracted for. Including many unrequested features can actually complicate the user interface to the point that it loses its simplicity and becomes hard to use. You might actually decrease your application's usability by giving your customer extra features for free.

Make Feature Lists

Don't ignore or forget about those extra features that you come up with while designing an application. Write them in your notebook (you do keep a notebook, don't you?) so you won't forget about them. Use them when you're negotiating with your customer for an upgrade of this application, or use them to spice up another contract offer. As I mentioned, when writing custom applications, keep your feature count down, because a simple, straightforward application that does just what it should almost always makes your customer the happiest.

There's one case where you would add a new feature to an application. That's when your new feature significantly simplifies the user interface but is still obvious and easy to use—especially if this new feature replaces some of the required features. For example, to select a data item represented on a pie chart, you might place a list of items on a menu and have the user select from the list. A useful feature that replaces that capability is to simply click on the wedge of the pie chart that represents the item. This is much easier for the user to do, and it replaces an existing required feature. It also follows the other design rules in that it's simple, obvious, and similar to how other applications work.

Showstopper: Complicated forms are very difficult and confusing and probably won't get used.

When designing the form, keep in mind what the form is for and how a user perceives it. People tend to scan the form from left to right and from top to bottom (this differs in some cultures). The eyes are attracted to color more than black and white and to graphics more than characters. Keep these points in mind when designing the interface to ensure that the unimportant parts of the interface don't distract from the important ones. For example, if a form is to display a graph of data, the data is what you should emphasize, not the controls or the background of the form itself.

Showstopper: Overly colorful forms can make it difficult or impossible to separate the important information from the decorations.

Figures 7.1 and 7.2 show two displays of data. Figure 7.1 does it all wrong, emphasizing the background and the controls over the data. If this book could show the form's colors, it would look even worse. The form has large, strange-looking things in the button bar that might be buttons. It has a busy color background that makes the graph difficult to see. It has a grid on the same form as a graph and uses a difficult-to-read font on the command buttons on the right. Figure 7.2 isn't very fancy, but it follows the rules and therefore is much easier to read and use. The background is a neutral gray, and the form has small, simple buttons that are easy to find and that don't distract the eyes from the graph, which is in color. The grid is hidden until you press a button to make it visible.

Figure 7.1.
A poorly designed user interface that distracts the user from the chart, which is the reason for having the form.

Forms Design

Figure 7.2.
A much better designed user interface that doesn't detract from the chart.

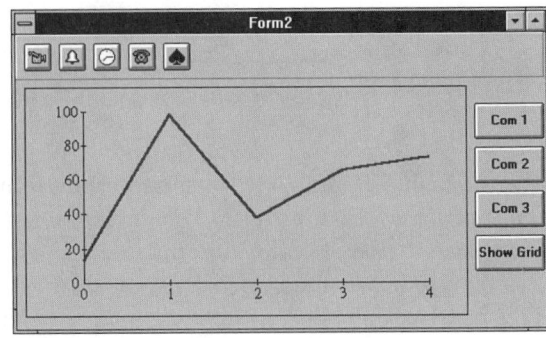

Obvious Operations

The second rule is to make the interface as obvious as possible. Make it possible for the user to run the application without having to read a manual. If the user can at least get started with an application without having to read instructions, he'll be much happier than if he must spend a day reading before he can even start it up. When naming menu items, be sure that the name strongly implies the function. The same applies to buttons. If at all possible, make the icon on the button imply the function. With buttons, be sure to identify the button by putting text on the top of the button or with a label that appears when the mouse pointer is over the button. Label everything that isn't obvious.

> **Textbook Tip:** Here are some hints on making forms obvious:
>
> Use design elements that the user has seen before and already knows how to use.
>
> Arrange design elements, such as buttons and text boxes, in the order in which they will be used (top to bottom, left to right).
>
> Use labels or other elements to guide the user. Toolbar buttons especially need labels to identify their function.

Maintain Internal Consistency

Internal consistency means to make the same or similar controls within an application work the same way. If two forms both have a button or menu item with the same name, they should both do the same thing. This doesn't mean that they have to work exactly the same way, but they should work in a way that you would expect. For example, on one form a string of text might be selected, and on another, a graphic might be selected. In both cases, the Cut command should copy the selection to the clipboard and then delete the selection. To only copy the selection in one case would break internal consistency.

Showstopper: Being inconsistent in your internal design is inviting disaster. For example, consider two buttons for deleting files, both named "Delete Files." One deletes a single file using a dialog box, and the other deletes all the files in the current directory without confirming that the user really wants to do it. The potential for disaster is obvious, but the user won't realize it until it's too late.

Use Familiar Design Elements

Using familiar design elements means to use the same controls and menus that mainstream applications use. By doing so, you maintain external consistency for your interface, which allows users to use their experience to guide them when using your application. Pick a mainstream application like Word or Excel and see what commands are on what menus and what they do. Make sure you include the same menu items that do the same things.

Showstopper: Familiar design elements that don't work in the standard way can frustrate your users or even cause disasters. An example is a File | Close command that doesn't warn you that you haven't saved the current document before closing it.

Don't Change the Standard Commands

Don't even think of using one of the common buttons or menu items to do something other than what it does in all the other Windows applications. Commands such as Open and Save on the File menu or Cut, Copy, and Paste on the Edit menu have well-established functions. Even if you think that the command should really do something else, its meaning has already been decided by its usage, and trying to change it will only get you complaints.

Most applications have File and Edit menus, a Help menu if they have online help (or an About menu if they don't), and a Window menu if they display multiple forms. The File menu handles

Forms Design

all I/O, including reading and writing files, creating new documents, and printing. The File menu also contains the Exit command to quit the application. The Edit menu contains the Undo, Cut, Copy, and Paste commands, and any other commands related to selecting and moving objects on an application's documents. Most applications at least have File and Edit menus, even if they don't have all the menu items.

Showstopper: Menus never directly execute a command; they always drop down a list of menu items that execute the commands. If you made a menu itself execute a command, people would accidentally execute that command when they attempted to pull down the menu to see what commands were on it.

In addition to using the same menu items to do the same things as mainstream applications, be sure to use the same access keys and shortcut keys as well. If you don't, you will again anger your users. For example, if C is the access key for the Clear command instead of the Copy command, people will delete things, thinking that they are copying them.

Showstopper: Consistency in commands is especially important for access and shortcut keys. Users learn to press certain keys to quickly execute commands. Unlike a menu item, which the user reads before selecting, keyboard-initiated commands are a conditioned response. If a key does something different, the user might not realize it until it's too late.

Use standard controls that the user will recognize. Don't make up your own controls, even if your controls look better. The same goes for the standard dialog boxes. In all possible cases, use the common dialogs' controls so that your dialog boxes will look the same as those in other Windows applications. Common dialog boxes exist for the Save As, Open, Print, Print Setup, Font, Color, and Help commands. Additionally, the common dialogs' controls save you the work of having to create your own dialog boxes to do the same things.

Designing Forms with Visual Basic

It's very easy to design forms for Visual Basic applications. In fact, it's easier to design them with Visual Basic than with pencil and paper. Simply open a new form and draw on it the controls and boxes that you need. If the controls are in the wrong place, select them and move them to where you want them.

What Is the Goal of the Form?

The first step in designing a form is to state its goal. What are you trying to do with this form? If it's serving as a command center, it should be designed differently than one that is for displaying data. Keep that goal in mind as you design the form to ensure that you don't stray from it.

What Commands Do You Need?

Determine which commands, menus, command buttons, button bars, or ribbon bars you need to achieve the form's goal. All commands should be available from the menus. If they are used often, they should also be available on a toolbar or button ribbon. Toolbars are becoming more common for heavily used commands and are very popular. Be sure the buttons are marked, either with text on the button or with a pop-up label.

What Data Do You Need?

Determine what data you need to display to and obtain from the user, and select the text boxes, labels, list boxes, option buttons, and check boxes necessary to perform those functions. Draw and label these items on the form.

Walk Through the Design

When you complete the form, imagine that you're using the application, and walk through the steps you would take when using the form. As you do so, ask yourself if the form's operation is obvious. Does the form achieve its goal? If not, redo it. Consider how the application switches from form to form. Is the flow logical and expected? Does the flow do anything unexpected? Again, redo the design if there's a problem.

Get another person who isn't familiar with your project and have her walk through the forms, asking the same questions. Are the forms obvious to her? Do the forms achieve their goals? Again, redo the forms if there's a problem.

Forms Design

Don't Blame the Testers

When people don't understand what you're trying to do in an application, you might be tempted to take that personally and blame them for being inattentive or careless. Don't do it. If they can't easily figure out what a form does or how to use it, other people will have the same difficulty. The problem lies with the form's design, not the people who test it, so fix it instead of blaming them. Try arranging things differently, or split things onto multiple forms if there's too much on one form. Try more or different wording for your labels. Do what it takes to get it right.

Creating Special Controls

Several commonly used control structures aren't available as single objects in Visual Basic, so they must be created from the existing list of controls. Toolbars and toolboxes are commonly used in modern applications. There isn't a big difference between these two controls. A toolbar is a gray bar across the top of a form that contains control buttons. A toolbox is usually a vertical bar or form that contains buttons that can be selected to initiate different tasks. As shown in Figure 7.3, Visual Basic uses a toolbox to select colors and to contain all the controls that can be selected and placed on a form. A toolbar can be seen across the top of the active part of the screen. The Microsoft Office toolbox is in the middle of the figure.

Figure 7.3.
Toolbars and toolboxes are used in Visual Basic itself to make the different controls available.

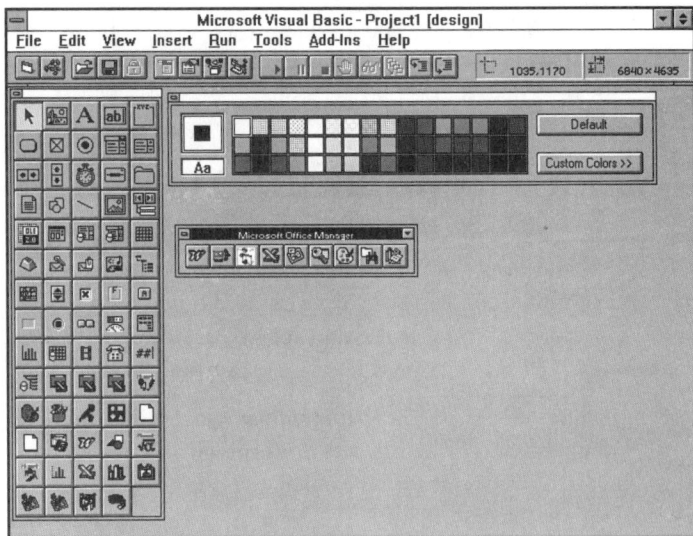

Creating a Toolbar

You create a toolbar on a standard form by placing a row of 3D command buttons or 3D group pushbuttons across the top of the screen. The buttons can be placed directly on the form itself, in a button group, on a picture box, or on a 3D panel. If the buttons are placed directly on a form, use the line drawing tool to draw a line below the buttons to separate them from the active part of the form.

If you're using an MDI parent form as the base for your application, you can't draw command or option buttons directly on the form. You must place a picture window or 3D panel on the form first and then place the buttons on the panel. When you draw a picture window or 3D panel on an MDI form, it's immediately attached across the top of the active area of the form and automatically reduces the active area to the area below it by changing the form's ScaleHeight and ScaleTop properties. The Align property controls this behavior.

Figure 7.4 shows a toolbar on an MDI form in the design stage, and Figure 7.5 shows a blowup of some buttons on a toolbar. The standard height of a toolbar is 28 pixels (420 twips,) including the black line across the bottom. The buttons are 24 pixels wide by 22 pixels high (360 by 330 twips). There are a black row and two light gray rows (45 twips) above the button, and two light gray rows and a black row below it. The image area on top of the 3D button for a bitmap is 16 by 15 pixels (240 by 225 twips.) The lateral spacing of buttons on the button bar is 0 pixels for buttons in a button group and 6 pixels (90 twips) between different button groups.

Figure 7.4.
The standard toolbar design.

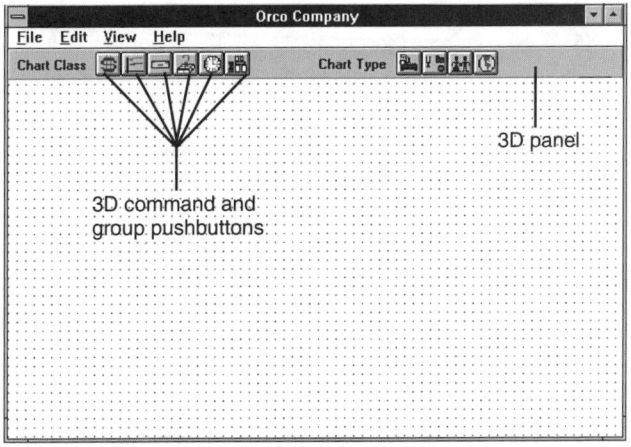

Figure 7.5.
A blowup of some buttons on a toolbar.

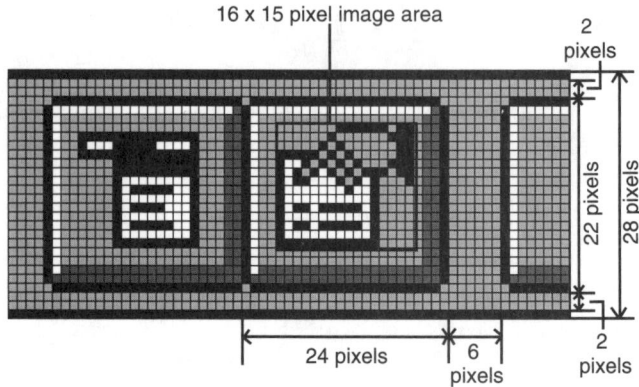

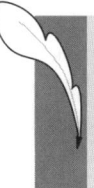

> **Note:** Since toolbar buttons are identified with pictures, and those pictures are bitmaps, the size of standard buttons and the button bar is measured in pixels instead of twips. The measurements in this section are for a standard VGA monitor with a 640x480 resolution. On that monitor, a pixel is 15 twips.

The toolbar in Figure 7.4 was created on an MDI parent form by drawing a 3D panel 420 twips tall across the top of the form. The buttons were created by drawing 3D group buttons or 3D command buttons on the 3D panel. The buttons were sized to 360x330 twips, and 16x15 pixel bitmaps created in Paintbrush were inserted in the `Picture` or `PictureUp` properties.

> **Note:** A larger button and a smaller button used in toolbars and toolboxes are also defined as Windows standards, but most applications use medium-sized buttons. The smaller button is 22x18 pixels with a 16x12 bitmap image on it. The larger one is 32x30 pixels with a 24x24 bitmap image.

Creating a Toolbox

A toolbox is created on a separate form. All the buttons are placed in a rectangular array, and the form is sized to contain just the array of buttons, as shown in Figure 7.6. These buttons are the same size as those used for a toolbar. In addition to being available as a floating form, a toolbox can also be docked to the left or right side of an MDI form, where it looks like a vertical toolbar. To do this, you must draw a 3D panel on the side of a form and put the buttons on that. Since the panel won't automatically resize itself in this position, you must write code to do it in response to a resize event of the MDI parent form.

Figure 7.6.
The standard toolbox design.

Note: A toolbar form should also have a reduced size heading, but there is no easy way to do that in Visual Basic.

Creating Button Pictures

The pictures placed on top of the buttons can be created in any drawing program that can create a bitmap (.BMP) file. The Paintbrush program included with Windows works just fine. To create a button picture with Paintbrush, start Paintbrush and execute the Options | Image Attributes command. As shown in Figure 7.7, change the image size to 16 by 15 pels (pixels) in the dialog box. Next, use the View | Zoom In command to expand the image, as shown in Figure 7.8, and use the fill tool to paint the whole image light gray. The picture is usually outlined with black and then filled with white, dark gray, or some other color. Don't use too much color here, or the buttons might detract from the more important parts of the form. Use color only to make it easier to recognize the button's function.

Figure 7.7.
Setting Paintbrush to create a 16x15 pixel image.

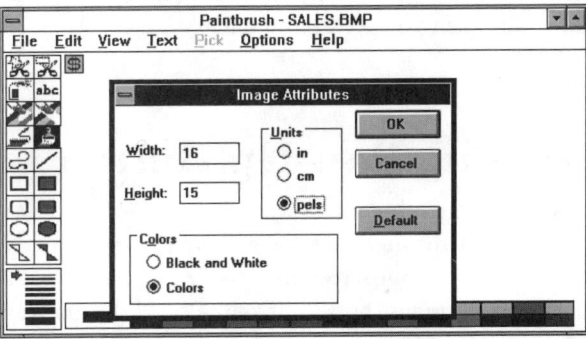

Forms Design

Figure 7.8.
Using Zoom In to draw the image a pixel at a time.

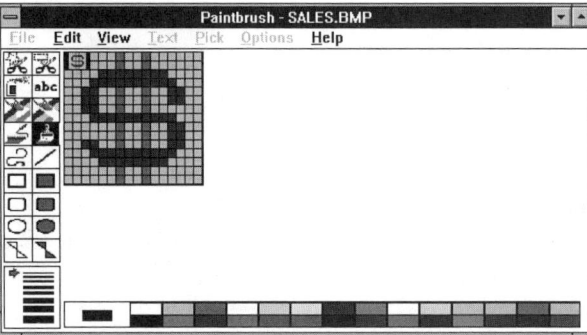

After you've saved the bitmap in a disk file, load the image into the button's `Picture` (3D command button) or `PictureUp` (3D group pushbutton) properties. Visual Basic comes with a large number of icons and bitmaps. If you want to use one of the existing icon pictures on a button, you must convert the icon to a bitmap. The IconWorks program is included as a sample program in Visual Basic. Use it to open and display an icon file. Select the icon and copy it to the clipboard. You can then open Paintbrush, paste the picture, and save it as a bitmap. Note that the image on an icon is larger than 16x15 pixels, so you will have to reduce it to fit on a button.

Showstopper: If you make an image larger than the allowed size for a button, the image will be reduced to fit the image area. Reducing such a small image is likely to make it unintelligible.

Creating Pop-Up Button Labels

Most people tend to forget what the toolbar buttons do, and they don't like to look them up in a manual, so you need to label them in some way. Older applications placed a message area at the bottom of the screen that displayed a button's function when you clicked on the button and held the mouse button. If you released the mouse button, the command was executed. If you moved off the button and then released the mouse button, the command was not executed. A problem with this method of identifying a button is that you have to look away from the button you're clicking on to the message at the bottom of the screen and then back to the button before you decide whether to use it or not. A better method of identifying buttons is to have pop-up labels.

A pop-up label appears whenever the mouse pointer is over the button. It's actually very simple to implement a pop-up label. As shown in Figure 7.9, first you add another small 3D panel below the toolbar to contain the labels. You must do this because you can't draw labels on an MDI form. Next, change the BevelOuter property of the 3D panel to 0-none to eliminate the line along its bottom. On the 3D panel, add labels for each of the buttons on the toolbar above it. Put the labels where you want them to appear when they pop up, even if they overlap in design mode, and set the label's Visible property to False. Add code like the following to the MouseMove event procedures for the buttons to make the appropriate label visible. In this example, the gpbGraphClass buttons are a button array whose index indicates the selected button and label. The MouseMove event procedure first calls the HidePopUpLabels procedure to hide all the labels in case one was already visible, and then it makes the selected label visible:

```
'
'Display the pop-up label when the pointer is over the button.
'
Sub gpbGraphClass_MouseMove (Index As Integer, Button As Integer,
↪Shift As Integer, X As Single, Y As Single)
    'Turn everything off, then turn one on.
    Call HidePopUpLabels
    lblPopUpClassLabels(Index).Visible = True
End Sub
'
'Turn off all button labels.
'
Sub HidePopUpLabels ()
    Dim intCtr
    For intCtr = 1 To NUM_CLASS_BUTTONS
        frmMDIMain.lblPopUpClassLabels(intCtr).Visible = False
    Next intCtr
End Sub
```

Figure 7.9.
Creating the pop-up labels.

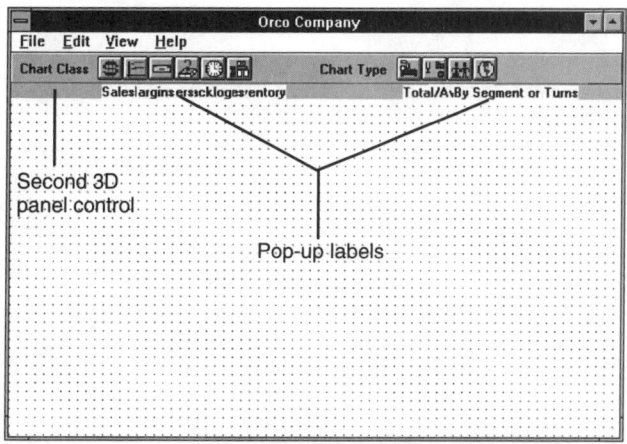

Add code like the following to the two 3D panels' MouseMove event procedures to hide all the buttons when the mouse moves off a button.

Forms Design

```
'
'Hide any button labels that were left visible when
'the user moved off the button bar too fast.
'
Sub Panel3D1_MouseMove (Button As Integer, Shift As Integer, X As Single,
➥Y As Single)
    Call HidePopUpLabels
End Sub
```

When you run the program, as shown in Figure 7.10, a label appears whenever the mouse moves over a button and disappears when you move off the button.

Figure 7.10.
A pop-up label appears when the mouse is over a button.

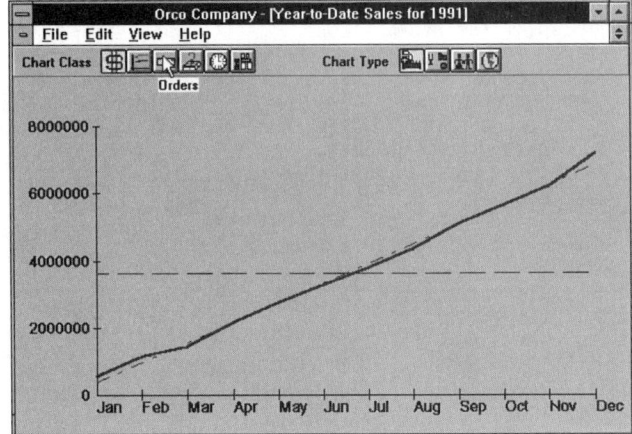

Turning Off the Pop-Up Labels

Turning on the pop-up labels is easy, but turning them off is often a problem. If the user is quick enough, he can move across the two 3D panels without registering a DragOver event. When that happens, the pop-up label isn't removed. It doesn't really hurt anything, but it's not pleasing from an aesthetic point of view. To fix this problem, add code to remove the labels to the MouseMove events of the MDI child forms that are displayed on the MDI form and to the ends of the event procedures that the buttons activate. This at least reduces the number of times that a pop-up label is left visible.

Adding Hot Spots to Controls

The graphical controls such as the graph control or the picture windows don't have hot spots on the individual picture elements. They have Click and DblClick events for when you click anywhere on the control, but the event procedures have no information on where you clicked. To select for an individual element or location on a control, combine a `MouseDown` event with a `Click` or `DblClick` event. The `MouseDown` event occurs first and provides the coordinates for where you clicked, and then the `Click` or `DblClick` event processes the event for that location. For example, to place hot spots on the month labels for the graph in Figure 7.10, add the two following event procedures to the project:

```
'
'Capture the mouse location when the user clicks on
'the left button on the chart. This works with the
'double-click event to select the drill-down chart.
'
Sub chtMonthly_MouseDown (intButton As Integer, intShift As Integer,
➥sngX As Single, sngY As Single)
    If intButton = LEFT_BUTTON Then
        'Left mouse button clicked
        sngMouseX = sngX
        sngMouseY = sngY
    Else
        sngMouseX = 0
        sngMouseY = 0
    End If
End Sub
'
'Display the grid when the chart is double-clicked on.
'
Sub chtMonthly_DblClick ()
    Dim intMonth As Integer          'The selected month
    Dim intActiveWidth As Integer    'Width of ordinate in twips
    Dim intStartX As Integer         'Position at left edge of "Jan"
    'intTestDblClickMonth: A global variable. The number of the selected month.
    'The double-click event doesn't return the location of the mouse,
    'so that data is supplied by the mouse-down procedure.
    intMonth = 0
    'Test vertical position of mouse on double-click.
    If sngMouseY >= .89 * frmMDIGraph.chtMonthly.Height Then
        'Mouse is below abscissa axis.
        If sngMouseY <= .94 * frmMDIGraph.chtMonthly.Height Then
            'Mouse is above bottom of labels.
            'See what label it is over.
            'Left edge of Jan is at 14% of the chart width.
            intStartX = .14 * frmMDIGraph.chtMonthly.Width
            'See if the click occurred in the area of the labels.
            If sngMouseX >= intStartX Then
                'Set width of ordinate. Right edge is at 86% of width.
                intActiveWidth = .965 * (.86 * frmMDIGraph.chtMonthly.Width)
                'The .965 is a trimming scaling factor.
                'Determine month corresponding to mouse x-coordinate as 1/12
                'of the distance to the edge of the graph.
                intTestDblClickMonth = Int((sngMouseX - intStartX) /
                ➥(intActiveWidth / 12)) + 1
            End If
        End If
    End If
```

Forms Design

```
    If intMonth > 0 Then
        'Process the monthly event with an If statement or Select Case.
    End If
End Sub
```

The first procedure processes the MouseDown event and saves the location of the mouse pointer for the second procedure, DblClick. In the DblClick procedure, code is used to determine if the event occurred within a rectangle surrounding a label. The actual month clicked is determined by breaking the area of the labels into 12 equal segments surrounding the labels. If it is within a label, the procedure processes the event. Otherwise, it ignores it.

The DblClick procedure contains several precise numbers that are used to locate things on the graph. For example, the x-axis labels range from 0.89 to 0.94 of the height of the graph. These numbers were found by creating a special test form that displays the location of mouse click events. The mouse can then be clicked around the screen to determine where things are and how that location changes when the form is resized.

The Decision Support Application Project

From the sketches you did on Day 2, you know you need two main forms—one with a graph and a grid and one with only a grid. The graph form needs to display a line graph, a pie chart, or a line graph and a grid. The grid form needs only to display the drill-down grid. To keep the controls the same, use an MDI parent form as the base, and display the other forms containing the charts and grids on it. Most modern Windows applications use the MDI interface because it creates a clean interface for the application, with all the common controls in view on the parent form. The MDI child forms contain the different documents opened by the application.

The Main MDI Parent Form

The object of frmMDIMain is to be the main control center for the decision support application. On it are the menus and the toolbar that control most of the decision support application's actions. It must have controls to accomplish the following tasks:

- ☐ Change the graph class between sales, margin, orders, backlog, order cycle, and inventory.
- ☐ Change the graph type between total, by product category, by market segment, and by market region, plus a couple of special types for the order cycle and inventory class.
- ☐ Toggle the display of the grid containing the details for the graph.
- ☐ Print the current graph.

- Save the current graph as an image.
- Copy the current graph to the clipboard.
- Supply a gateway into the Windows help system.

The frmMDIMain form is shown in Figures 7.9 and 7.10. It consists of an MDI parent form, two 3D panels, two groups of 3D pushbuttons, and some menus. The MDI parent form is a standard MDI form with only the caption changed, as shown in Table 7.1.

Table 7.1. MDI parent form. Type: MDI Form.

Property	Value
Name	frmMDIMain
File Name	MDI_MAIN.FRM
Caption	"Orco Company"
Height	6000
Width	8745

On the MDI parent form are two 3D panels—one to hold the class and type buttons and one to hold the pop-up labels. (See Table 7.2.) Both have a gray background and no caption. The lower one has the outer bevel turned off to eliminate the line at its bottom edge so that it will blend with the graph form that will be placed below it.

Table 7.2. 3D panels. Type: SSPanel.

Property	Value
Panel 1	
Top panel with buttons	
Name	Panel3D1
Align	1 'Align Top
BackColor	&H00C0C0C0&
Caption	""
Height	420
Left	0
Top	0
Width	8625

continues

Forms Design

Table 7.2. continued

Property	Value
Panel 2	
Bottom panel with labels	
Name	Panel3D2
Align	1 'Align Top
BackColor	&H00C0C0C0&
BevelOuter	0 'None
Caption	" "
Height	210
Left	0
Top	420
Width	8625

The upper 3D panel has two pushbutton groups—one named gpbGraphClass and one named gpbGraphType. There are six buttons in the class group and four buttons in the type group. (See Table 7.3.) The pictures shown on top of the buttons in Figure 7.10 were created using Paintbrush. Note that the Tag property for each button contains the number of the class or type activated by the button. The PictureDisabled property for the type buttons is a circle with NA in the center that is displayed when the button is disabled. This is necessary because some of the chart classes don't use all four chart type buttons.

Table 7.3. 3D group pushbutton. Type: SSRibbon.

Property	Value
These properties apply to all the class buttons.	
AutoSize	1 'Adjust picture size to button
BackColor	&H00C0C0C0&
GroupAllowAllUp	0 'False
Height	330
Name	gpbGraphClass
PictureDnChange	1 'Dither 'PictureUp' bitmap
Top	45
Width	360

Property	Value
Class button 1	
GroupNumber	1
Index	1
Left	1215
PictureUp	SALES.BMP
Tag	"1"
Class button 2	
GroupNumber	1
Index	2
Left	1575
PictureUp	MARGIN.BMP
Tag	"2"
Class button 3	
GroupNumber	1
Index	3
Left	1935
PictureUp	ORDERS.BMP
Tag	"3"
Class button 4	
GroupNumber	1
Index	4
Left	2295
PictureUp	BACKLOG.BMP
Tag	"4"
Class button 5	
GroupNumber	1
Index	5
Left	2655
PictureUp	CYCLE.BMP
Tag	"5"

continues

Day 7 Forms Design

Table 7.3. continued

Property	Value
Class button 6	
GroupNumber	1
Index	6
Left	3015
PictureUp	INVENTORY.BMP
Tag	"6"
These properties apply to all the type buttons.	
AutoSize	1 'Adjust picture size to button
BackColor	&H00C0C0C0&
GroupAllowAllUp	0 'False
Height	330
Name	gpbGraphType
PictureDnChange	1 'Dither 'PictureUp' bitmap
Top	45
Width	360
Type button 1	
GroupNumber	2
Index	1
Left	5400
PictureDisabled	DISABLE.BMP
PictureUp	TOTAL.BMP
Tag	"1"
Type button 2	
GroupNumber	2
Index	2
Left	5760
PictureDisabled	DISABLE.BMP
PictureUp	CATEGORY.PCX
Tag	"2"
Type button 3	
GroupNumber	2

	Property	Value
	Index	3
	Left	6120
	PictureDisabled	DISABLE.BMP
	PictureUp	SEGMENT.BMP
	Tag	"3"
Type button 4		
	GroupNumber	2
	Index	4
	Left	6480
	PictureDisabled	DISABLE.BMP
	PictureUp	REGION.BMP
	Tag	"4"

Two labels on the upper 3D panel identify the two button groups and a common dialog control. (See Table 7.4.) The location of the common dialog control on the panel is unimportant, because it's invisible in the running program. The control must be available on the form somewhere so that the Save As and Printer Setup dialog boxes can be displayed.

Table 7.4. Button labels. Type: Label and Common Dialog Control. Type: `CommonDialog`.

	Property	Value
Class label		
	Name	Label1
	BackColor	&H00C0C0C0&
	Caption	"Chart Class"
	Height	255
	Left	120
	Top	120
	Width	1095
Type label		
	Name	Label2
	BackColor	&H00C0C0C0&

continues

Forms Design

Table 7.4. continued

	Property	Value
	Caption	"Chart Type"
	Height	255
	Left	4320
	Top	120
	Width	975
Common dialog control		
	Name	cdgDialogs

On the second 3D panel are the 10 pop-up labels for the buttons above them. (See Table 7.5.) These buttons are invisible initially, and the caption text for the type labels is only placeholders that are replaced by the running program according to the chart class selected. The labels are combined in two control arrays with the Index property used to link the labels and the buttons. In other words, labels are activated for buttons with the same index property.

Table 7.5. Pop-up labels. Type: `Label`.

	Property	Value
These properties apply to all the class labels.		
	AutoSize	-1 'True
	BackColor	&H0000FFFF&
	Height	195
	Name	lblPopUpClassLabels
	Top	15
	Visible	0 'False
Class label 1		
	Caption	"Sales"
	Index	1
	Left	1275
Class label 2		
	Caption	"Margins"
	Index	2
	Left	1635

	Property	Value
Class label 3		
	Caption	"Orders"
	Index	3
	Left	2010
Class label 4		
	Caption	"Backlog"
	Index	4
	Left	2400
	TabIndex	6
Class label 5		
	Caption	"Cycles"
	Index	5
	Left	2715
Class label 6		
	Caption	"Inventory"
	Index	6
	Left	3045
These properties apply to all the type labels.		
	AutoSize	-1 'True
	BackColor	&H0000FFFF&
	Height	195
	Name	lblPopUpTypeLabels
	Top	15
	Visible	0 'False
Type label 1		
	Caption	"Total/Average"
	Index	1
	Left	5490
Type label 2		
	Caption	"By Product"
	Index	2
	Left	5850

continues

Forms Design

Table 7.5. continued

	Property	Value
Type label 3		
	Caption	"By Segment or Turns"
	Index	3
	Left	6210
Type label 4		
	Caption	"By Region"
	Index	4
	Left	6600

The MDI form has four menus on it: File, Edit, View, and Help. (See Table 7.6.) These menus provide a separate interface to the commands on the toolbar, and to other, less-used commands such as Print and Copy. On the View menu, each graph class has a submenu that contains a control array of menu items for each menu type. Note that the `Index` property of each of the control array items contains the chart code for that item. That code is used to identify what chart to create when the menu item is selected.

Table 7.6. Menus. Type: `Menu`.

Menu	Menu Item	Submenu Item	Property	Value
File			Menu Name	mnuFileMain
			Caption	"&File"
	Save		Menu Item Name	mnuFileSave
			Caption	"&Save..."
	-		Menu Item Name	mnuFileBar1
			Caption	"-"
	Print		Menu Item Name	mnuFilePrint
			Caption	"&Print..."
	-		Menu Item Name	mnuFileBar2
			Caption	"-"
	Exit		Menu Item Name	mnuFileExit
			Caption	"E&xit"
Edit			Menu Name	mnuEditMain

Menu	Menu Item	Submenu Item	Property	Value
			Caption	"&Edit"
	Copy		Menu Item Name	mnuEditCopy
			Caption	"&Copy"
View			Menu Name	mnuViewMain
			Caption	"&View"
	Details		Menu Item Name	mnuViewDetails
			Caption	"&Details"
	-		Menu Item Name	mnuViewBar
			Caption	"-"
	Sales		Submenu Name	mnuSales
			Caption	"&Sales"
		Totals	Submenu Item Name	mnuViewSales
			Caption	"&Totals"
			Index	11
		By Category	Submenu Item Name	mnuViewSales
			Caption	"By &Category"
			Index	12
		By Segments	Submenu Item Name	mnuViewSales
			Caption	"By &Segments"
			Index	13
		By Regions	Submenu Item Name	mnuViewSales
			Caption	"By &Regions"
			Index	14
	Margins		Submenu Name	mnuMargin
			Caption	"&Margins"
		Average Gross	Submenu Item Name	mnuViewMargins
			Caption	"&Average Gross"
			Index	21
		By Product	Submenu Item Name	mnuViewMargins
			Caption	"By &Product"
			Index	22

continues

Forms Design

Table 7.6. continued

Menu	Menu Item	Submenu Item	Property	Value
	Orders		Submenu Name	mnuOrders
			Caption	"&Orders"
		Totals	Submenu Item Name	mnuViewOrders
			Caption	"&Totals"
			Index	31
		By Category	Submenu Item Name	mnuViewOrders
			Caption	"By &Category"
			Index	32
		By Segment	Submenu Item Name	mnuViewOrders
			Caption	"By &Segment"
			Index	33
		By Region	Submenu Item Name	mnuViewOrders
			Caption	"By &Region"
			Index	34
	Backlog		Submenu Name	mnuBacklog
			Caption	"&Backlog"
		Totals	Submenu Item Name	mnuViewBacklog
			Caption	"&Totals"
			Index	41
		By Category	Submenu Item Name	mnuViewBacklog
			Caption	"By &Category"
			Index	42
		By Segment	Submenu Item Name	mnuViewBacklog
			Caption	"By &Segment"
			Index	43
		By Region	Submenu Item Name	mnuViewBacklog
			Caption	"By &Region"
			Index	44
	Cycle		Submenu Name	mnuCycle
			Caption	"&Cycle"

Menu	Menu Item	Submenu Item	Property	Value
		Average	Submenu Item Name	mnuViewCycle
			Caption	"&Average"
			Index	51
		By Segment	Submenu Item Name	mnuViewCycle
			Caption	"By &Segment"
			Index	52
		Distribution	Submenu Item Name	mnuViewCycle
			Caption	"&Distribution"
			Index	53
	Inventory		Submenu Name	mnuInventory
			Caption	"&Inventory"
		Totals	Submenu Item Name	mnuViewInventory
			Caption	"&Totals"
			Index	61
		By Category	Submenu Item Name	mnuViewInventory
			Caption	"By &Category"
			Index	62
		Turnover	Submenu Item Name	mnuViewInventory
			Caption	"&Turnover"
			Index	63
Help			Menu Name	mnuHelpMain
			Caption	"&Help"
	Contents		Menu Item Name	mnuHelpContents
			Caption	"&Contents"
	Search for Help on...		Menu Item Name	mnuHelpSearch
			Caption	"&Search for Help on..."
	About...		Menu Item Name	mnuHelpAbout
			Caption	"&About..."

This completes the MDI form. Next are the MDI child forms that are displayed on the MDI parent form.

Forms Design

The Graphs Form

Figure 7.11 shows the frmMDIGraphs form in design mode with the banner picture removed. The object of this form is to display the line or area graphs, the pie chart, and the monthly grid data whenever a user double-clicks on a graph. To do this, the form contains two graph controls, a grid control, a bunch of pictures (each containing a color), and a bunch of labels to use when creating a legend. Covering everything is a banner picture that covers all the controls at startup while the program is setting their size, location, and visibility.

Figure 7.11.
The frmMDIGraphs form in design mode with the banner picture removed.

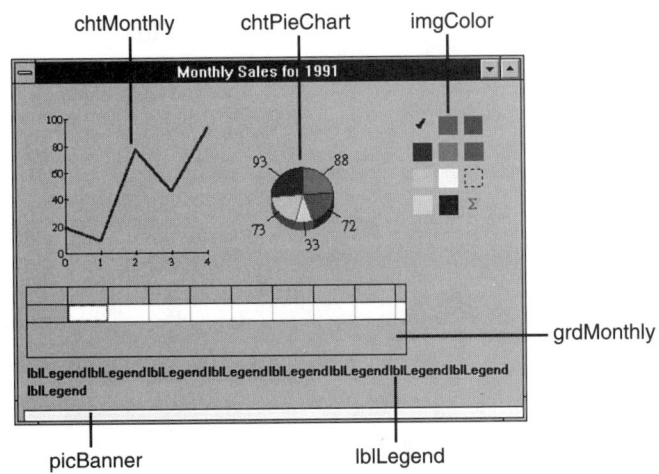

The frmMDIGraph form (see Table 7.7) is an MDIChild form with a light gray background, fixed boundaries, and no minimize button. The form is always used in its maximized state, so it fills the MDI parent form. The caption isn't really important here because it changes whenever you create a new chart.

Table 7.7. Graphs form. Type: Form.

Property	Value
Name	frmMDIGraph
File Name	MDI_GRAF.FRM
BackColor	&H00C0C0C0&
BorderStyle	1 'Fixed Single
Caption	"Monthly Sales for 1995"
MDIChild	-1 'True
MinButton	0 'False
WindowState	2 'Maximized

There are two graph controls on the form—one for the line and area charts and one for the pie chart (see Table 7.8). Figure 7.10 shows the line chart in operation, and Figure 7.12 shows the pie chart. Both chart types could have been displayed with a single graph control, but it's simpler to use two—one for the monthly data displayed as a line or area graph and one for a single month's data displayed as a pie chart. Another reason for having two graph controls is that double-clicking on the line graph and double-clicking on the pie chart do different things. Having two different controls gives you two sets of event procedures—one set for each graph control that you can then code differently.

Figure 7.12.
The `frmMDIGraphs` *form displaying the pie chart.*

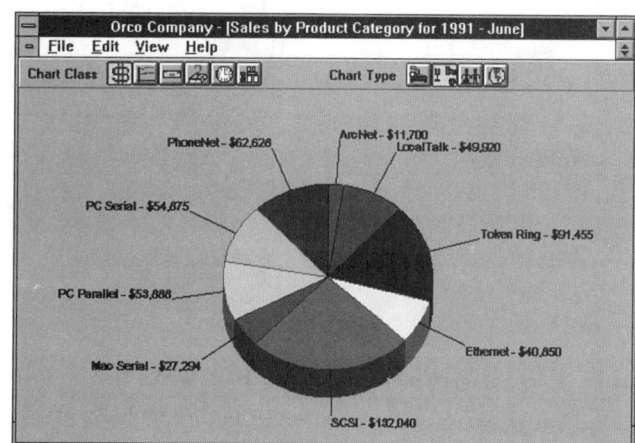

Table 7.8. Monthly and pie chart. Type: `Graph`.

	Property	Value
Monthly chart		
	Name	chtMonthly
	Background	7 'Light Gray
	BorderStyle	0 'None
	GraphType	6 'Line
Pie chart		
	Name	chtPieChart
	Background	7 'Light Gray
	BorderStyle	0 'None
	GraphType	2 '3D Pie

Forms Design

The monthly grid (see Table 7.9) is placed on the form to hold the same monthly data as the monthly graph. Normally it's hidden, then displayed when the user double-clicks on the monthly graph, as shown in Figure 7.13. Most of the properties are reset at runtime according to the type of graph that is being displayed.

Figure 7.13.
The frmMDIGraphs *form displaying an area chart and the details grid.*

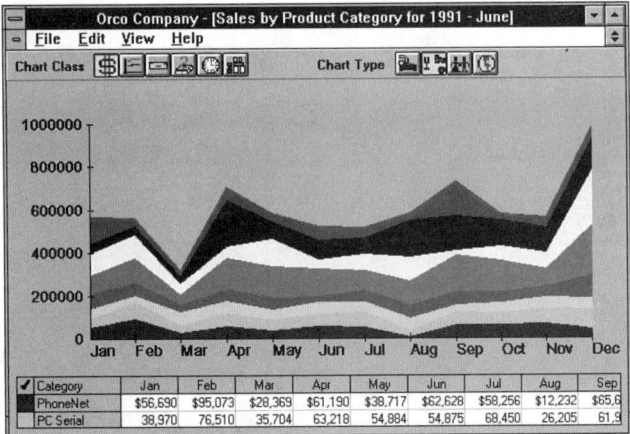

Table 7.9. Monthly grid. Type: Grid.

Property	Value
Name	grdMonthly
Cols	13
FontBold	0 'False
ScrollBars	0 'None
Visible	0 'False

There is a control array of 12 image controls on the form, and each image contains a symbol or a solid color. (See Table 7.10.) The pictures, 16x15 pixel images, were all created with Paintbrush. The colors are all available from Paintbrush's color bar. The nine image controls with solid colors match the colors and order of the colors used to differentiate the different lines or areas on a line or area graph. Thus, there are sufficient images to label nine lines or areas on a single graph, as shown in Figure 7.14. The images are also used in the first column of the grid, as shown at the bottom of Figure 7.13. The control array index is used to select the color for a legend such that an index of 1 selects the color used on the first line or area, an index of 2 selects the second, and so on. Index 0 is a check mark, index 10 is an empty image, and index 11 is a red Greek sigma.

Figure 7.14.
The frmMDIGraphs form displaying an area chart and a legend.

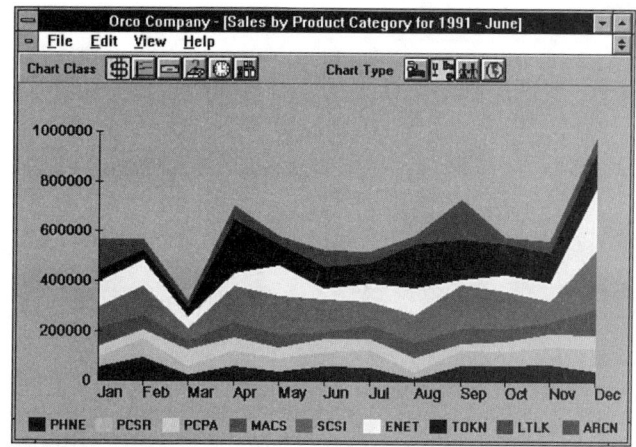

Table 7.10. Legend markers. Type: **Image**.

	Property	Value
These properties apply to all the image controls.		
	Height	255
	Name	imgColor
	Width	270
Image 0		
	Index	0
	Picture	CHECK0.BMP
Image 1		
	Index	1
	Picture	BLUE1.BMP
Image 2		
	Index	2
	Picture	LTGREEN2.BMP
Image 3		
	Index	3
	Picture	CYAN3.BMP
Image 4		
	Index	4
	Picture	RED4.BMP

continues

Forms Design

Table 7.10. continued

	Property	Value
Image 5		
	Index	5
	Picture	MAGENTA5.BMP
Image 6		
	Index	6
	Picture	YELLOW6.BMP
Image 7		
	Index	7
	Picture	DKBLUE7.BMP
Image 8		
	Index	8
	Picture	GREEN8.BMP
Image 9		
	Index	9
	Picture	DKCYAN9.BMP
Image 10		
	Index	10
	Picture	none
Image 11		
	Index	11
	Picture	SIGMA11.BMP

To match the nine colored images are nine legend labels to hold the names of the items being plotted on the graph, as shown in Figure 7.14. The nine labels (see Table 7.11) are a control array with the `Index` property used to link the legend labels to the legend markers and the lines or areas on the graph.

Table 7.11. Legend labels. Type: `Label`.

	Property	Value
These properties apply to all the labels.		
	AutoSize	True

	Property	Value
	BackColor	&H00C0C0C0&
	Caption	"lblLegend"
	Height	255
	Name	lblLegend
	Width	855
Legend label 1		
	Index	1
Legend label 2		
	Index	2
Legend label 3		
	Index	3
Legend label 4		
	Index	4
Legend label 5		
	Index	5
Legend label 6		
	Index	6
Legend label 7		
	Index	7
Legend label 8		
	Index	8
Legend label 9		
	Index	9

Last is the banner. (See Table 7.12.) It was pulled to the side in Figure 7.11, but it's shown in Figure 7.15. The banner is the topmost object on the form. It covers up the other controls at startup while the program is arranging things to display the first graph. Alternatively, you could make everything hidden while the arranging is done, but the banner gives the user something to look at instead of a gray screen. The banner is also used as the image that is displayed when the Help | About command is selected. The banner image was created in Paintbrush and then loaded into a `PictureBox` on the `frmMDIGraphs` form.

Day 7: Forms Design

Figure 7.15.
The decision support program showing the banner at startup.

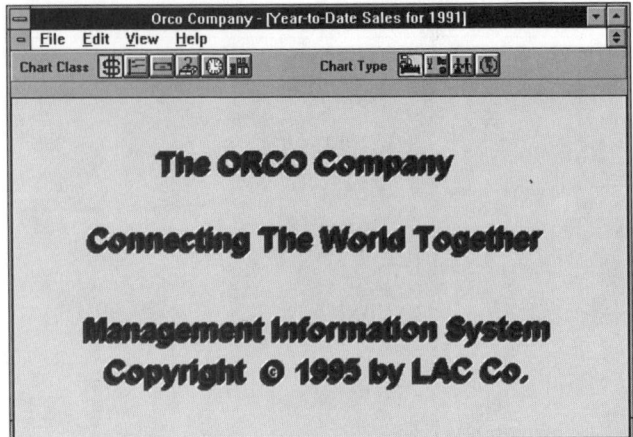

Table 7.12. Banner. Type: `PictureBox`.

Property	Value
Name	picBanner
BackColor	&H00FFFFFF&
FillColor	&H00FFFFFF&
FillStyle	0 'Solid
Height	5790
Left	0
Picture	BANNER.BMP
ScaleHeight	5760
ScaleWidth	8640
TabIndex	11
Top	0
Width	8670

The Drill-Down Grid Form

The object of the drill-down grid form is to display the detail drill-down data selected by the user. (See Table 7.13.) When the user has selected a wedge on the pie chart and selected the drill-down data he wants to view, the chart form is hidden and the drill-down grid is made visible to display the drill-down data. As such, the drill-down form is simply an MDI child form with a single grid control on it. It's shown in design mode in Figure 7.16 and in use in Figure 7.17.

Figure 7.16.
The drill-down grid form in design mode.

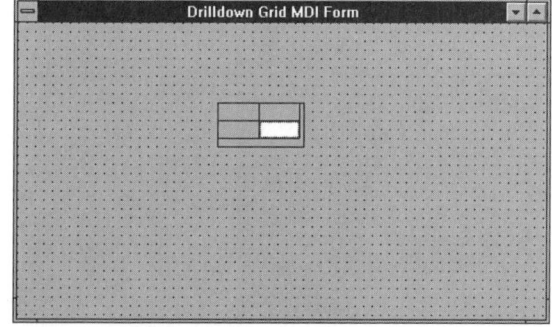

Figure 7.17.
The drill-down grid form in use, filled with data from the database.

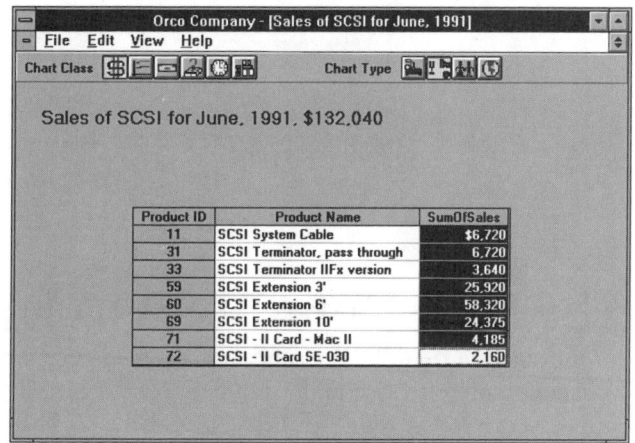

Table 7.13. Drill-down grid form. Type: Form.

Property	Value
Name	frmMDIGrid
File Name	MDI_GRID.FRM
BackColor	&H00C0C0C0&
Caption	"Drilldown Grid MDI Form"
MDIChild	-1 'True

On the form is a grid control and a label (see Table 7.14).

241

Forms Design

Table 7.14. Drill-down grid (type: `Grid`) and a caption (type: `Label`).

Property	Value
Drill-down grid	
Name	grdDetail
ScrollBars	0 'None
Visible	0 'False
Drill-down caption	
Name	lblCaption
BackStyle	0 'Transparent
FontSize	12
Height	375
Left	360
Top	120
Width	6735

The Drill-Down Options Form

The object of the drill-down options form (see Table 7.15) is to have the user select the detail data he wants displayed in the drill-down grid. The drill-down options form is displayed after the user has selected one of the wedges of the pie chart. The form lists the drill-down data available for the particular pie wedge as a group of option buttons. The form is shown in design mode in Figure 7.18, and in conjunction with the pie chart in Figure 7.19.

Figure 7.18.
The drill-down options form in design mode.

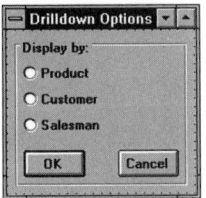

Figure 7.19.
The drill-down options form in use on the left, along with the pie chart with one wedge selected.

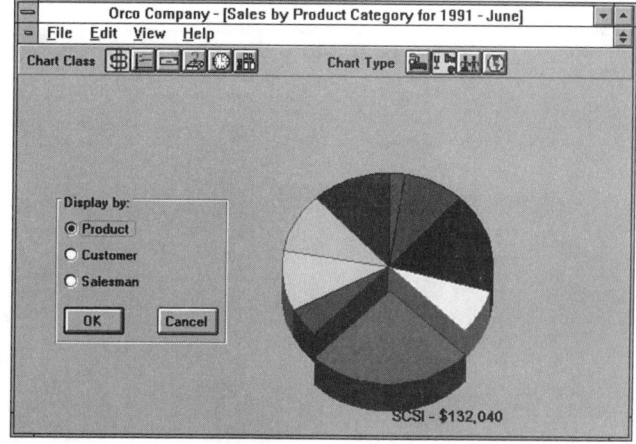

Table 7.15. Drill-down options form. Type: Form.

Property	Value
Name	frmDrillOptions
File Name	DDN_OPTS.FRM
BackColor	&H00C0C0C0&
BorderStyle	0 'None
Caption	"Drilldown Options"
Height	2715
Width	2790

On the drill-down options form is a frame with three option buttons and two command buttons (see Table 7.16).

Table 7.16. Option frame (type: SSFrame), drill-down option buttons (type: SSOption), and Cancel and OK buttons (type: CommandButton).

	Property	Value
Option frame		
	Name	Frame3D1
	Caption	"Display by:"
	Font3D	0 'None
	Height	2055

continues

Forms Design

Table 7.16. continued

Property	Value
Left	120
Top	120
Width	2415

Option button 1

Property	Value
Name	optDrill
Caption	"Product"
Font3D	0 'None
Height	255
Index	1
Left	120
Top	360
Width	1695

Option button 2

Property	Value
Name	optDrill
Caption	"Customer"
Font3D	0 'None
Height	255
Index	2
Left	120
Top	720
Width	1455

Option button 3

Property	Value
Name	optDrill
Caption	"Salesman"
Font3D	0 'None
Height	255
Index	3
Left	120
Top	1080
Width	1455

Property	Value
Cancel button	
Name	cmdCancel
Cancel	-1 'True
Caption	"Cancel"
Height	375
Left	1440
Top	1560
Width	855
OK button	
Name	cmdOK
Caption	"OK"
Default	-1 'True
Height	375
Left	120
Top	1560
Width	855

Modification Notes

When modifying the user interface of an existing program, pay close attention to the evolution of the interface and the skills of your user base. If you have a large user base that already knows how to use the old application, make sure they can start using the new one immediately. They'll be unhappy if they have to go through a lot of instruction to do things with your new application that they already know how to do with the old one.

Try to keep as much of the old interface intact as possible. Don't rearrange things unless you have a really good reason to do so. You're dealing with a group of users who expect to find things in a particular place, and if those things aren't there, at a minimum the users will be uncomfortable with your new program. If a user can apply her existing skill set to a new program and immediately start doing productive work, you will find that she is much happier, even if the interface isn't up to the highest standards of obviousness and usability. You can always add new functionality to an interface and have more than one avenue to execute a command. Just leave the old commands in place until your users get used to the new ones.

Forms Design

Toolbars are a good example. Before toolbars were available, most commands were executed using menus. When toolbars were added to mainline applications, the menu commands weren't removed. Users could learn a new application using the menu commands. As they became familiar with the toolbars, they could start using them instead of the menu commands.

On the other hand, if the old interface was incredibly hard to use, and your new application allows your users to do their work with a single command instead of a dozen, it might be better to make a clean break from the old application and simply replace the interface with a new one. Keep in mind, though, that your new way must be compelling enough to make the users of the existing application want to change. How you do that depends on what the changes are, but many avenues are available to you, such as pop-up help displays, wizards, and special help topics geared toward users of the previous program.

For example, Excel has a special help topic for users of Lotus 123 who are switching to Excel. The 123 user can simply type a 123 command, and Excel tells him which command to use to do the same thing in Excel.

Debugging the Process

At this point, debugging consists of ensuring that you haven't left out a needed command from the user interface. Generally it's a simple process to add a missed command to a menu when you discover it's missing. Walk through the user interface with another person, explaining how each control works and what you would see. You'll likely find all of your holes this way.

Now is a good time to get your customer involved again to take a look at the prototype interface. Do a walk-through with him, explaining what each command does and displaying an example of what he will see. He might spot missing things or unnecessary things that can be removed. Don't let him redesign the interface for you, though, for the same reasons you didn't let him design it in the first place. A short meeting isn't the place to create a well-thought-out interface. It's a place to get feedback and ideas that you can fold into a well-thought-out interface. If the customer wants lots of changes, offer to come back again with the redesigned interface after you've integrated his changes.

The biggest problem here is ensuring that the controls you're using are capable of producing the data and events you need. If they're not, you need to ensure that there is an alternative way to get the data. For example, if you click on the pie chart, the graph control can't tell you which pie wedge you clicked on. If you were depending on the existence of that capability, your project would be in trouble. In this case, you knew about the problem beforehand and devised a way around it before using that element in the user interface.

Note: An alternative graph control called ChartBuilder from Pinnacle Publishing in Kent, Washington has click events that return the data point, series, area, or bar that was clicked on.

Summary

Today you learned the rules of good user interface design:

- ☐ Keep it simple.
- ☐ Make it obvious.
- ☐ Make it internally consistent.
- ☐ Use familiar design elements.

In a nutshell, find a mainstream application with a good user interface and make your application look similar.

This ends the design phase of application engineering. The next part of the project is the actual construction of the application from the detailed design specifications you created in these first few chapters.

The code for today's work is part of the sample applications in the \DCNSPT, \DCNSPT1, and \DCNSPT2 directories on the included CD.

Construction

The construction step in the design process is where you actually start to build the application instead of designing it. Although you still might have to do some designing and experimenting, the main goal of the next few days is to create executable code.

PART II

Coding the Application, Part 1

Coding the Application, Part 1

All right! Time to start cutting code! If you thought you would never get around to writing code for this project, your worries are over. For the next two days, all you will do is write code. So limber up your fingers and let's get at it.

Today you will learn

- ☐ the rules of good programming practice
- ☐ how to implement working procedures from a structured design

The Goal of Day 8

Today's goal is to learn to code the procedures from the results of the structured design. For the most part, you will use the procedure specifications and the program structure chart to create the actual procedures. You will also learn to use good programming practice while creating these new procedures.

Since you already know how to write Visual Basic code and know how the different statements operate, don't expect to relearn these topics here. In the code shown in this and the next chapter, I concentrate primarily on how the different algorithms work, not on individual statements. If you've forgotten how some statements work (I forget all the time), pull out your manual or use the online help to look them up.

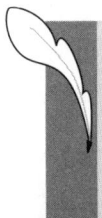

Note: If you're curious about the term *cutting code*, it comes from the use of punch cards to create computer programs. When you type characters on a punch card, the card punch cuts holes in the card that form a code for the character typed. Hence the cutting of holes in cards to create code, or "cutting code."

Those of us who learned to code using punch cards look back on them with nostalgia. You could really feel your code grow as it increased from a handful of cards to several boxes. The card punch itself was a relatively heavy piece of machinery that made a very satisfying thunk every time you pressed a key, especially when you pressed the exclamation point (why do you think they call it a bang?). However, none of us would ever consider going back to punch cards—no way.

Use Good Programming Practice

Using good programming practice is the difference between a professional programmer and an amateur. An amateur generally writes code only for himself, and delights in showing off to his friends what a complicated, convoluted piece of code he can create and still have it work. A

professional programmer writes straightforward, uncomplicated code that anyone can figure out, even a nonprogrammer. The result of a professional's work is well-written, understandable, maintainable code.

Writing Boring Code
You might think writing code like this is boring, but consider the stakes involved. If an amateur's code crashes, no big deal. If a professional's code crashes, his customer's business suffers, and, as a result, his customer might make him suffer. When your customer makes you suffer, that is decidedly nonboring.

Showstopper: Poorly-written, hard-to-understand code can bite you right in the pocketbook. Such code is really difficult to debug and change, and if you have a fixed contract to produce that code, you won't be paid for the extra time you have to put in to get it right.

The key word here for good programming practice is *understandable*. Everything else follows from that.

Make Procedure Functions Obvious

At the highest level of abstraction in code creation is the program. You already know what it's supposed to do, because it's in your contract. Code is made up of interrelated procedures that generally aren't specified in your contract, so you must make their function straightforward and obvious. A procedure whose function is obvious is much easier to debug or change, because you know what the procedure is supposed to do, and therefore you also know what the code that makes up the procedure is supposed to do. If your procedure is too complicated to figure out easily, whoever works on your code in the future (you, for example) might miss something and introduce a bug into the program.

Make Code Readable

As you write the code, do whatever it takes to make it readable. When you write a block of statements, make sure that you can read the block and easily understand what's going on. If you have to work at it for a while to figure out what's going on, you need to revise the code to make it easier.

Coding the Application, Part 1

The most important way to make code easier to read is to include lots of comments. Comment statements don't slow down the code, but they tremendously improve its readability. When writing code, you're restricted in what you can write by the syntax of the code statements. A comment statement is relatively unrestricted, so you can state exactly what the code is doing. You might consider it a waste of time to put lots of comments in code, but the time spent is paid back many times over when you have to search for a bug or revise a procedure and need to understand what a piece of code does.

The second most important technique is to use descriptive variable names that specify the variable type and its contents. The most current practice is to use one to four lowercase letters at the beginning of a variable name to specify the type of data the variable contains. For example, a string variable that is to contain the user's first name might be called `strUsersFirstName`. The `str` at the beginning indicates that this is a string variable, and the run-together words specify what it stores. Using upper- and lowercase characters in this manner makes the run-together words easier to read. Visual Basic makes no distinction between upper- and lowercase letters in a variable name.

Note: When Visual Basic creates a new procedure header, it doesn't use the convention I just mentioned to identify the types of the variables. In most cases, I've changed the variable names in the procedure headers to match the convention, but please excuse the few that I missed.

Use constants instead of numbers whenever possible. Don't use literal values in your code, but create a constant with that value and use it instead. The name will explain what it is and why you're using it. Generally, the numbers 1 and 2 are allowed in code, and often 3 or 4 as well, as long as the reason for using the number is obvious. Any other numbers should be declared as constants. Constants generally are written in all uppercase to distinguish them from variables.

Declare everything. Visual Basic will automatically declare variables the first time you use them in a program. Disable that capability by placing an Option Explicit statement in every module. You can automatically place an Option Explicit statement in every new module by selecting Tools | Environment Options and setting Require Variable Declaration to Yes. Having to explicitly declare every variable uncovers a lot of typing errors in a program that are otherwise extremely difficult to detect.

Showstopper: Misspelled variable names are really difficult to locate. If you don't require every variable to be declared, you can misspell one and not know it, except that your code won't work and you won't know why.

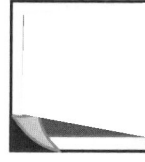

Make Code Maintainable

Maintainable code is easily revised or corrected. When you've finished writing an application, you will always have bugs in the code, or your customer will want changes. You need to make the code maintainable so that locating where a change goes is easy and making the change doesn't cause problems with other parts of the code.

The first step in making code maintainable is to make it readable. As I mentioned in the preceding section, readable code has lots of comments and descriptive variable and constant names.

The second step is to maintain as much independence for your procedures as possible. Procedure independence is one of the goals of structured design, and you need to make sure you don't lose that independence when you finally create the code.

The third step is to make the code as general as is reasonably possible. If you can create general-purpose procedures without unduly increasing an application's complexity, you should do it. General-purpose code has few custom statements in it and is applied to different data sets by simply changing a flag or a set of configuration data. For example, the decision support application uses a database table to set up all the graphs. The table contains the captions, graph type, scale, the name of the table, and the name of the field in the table that contains the data to be plotted. When a specific graph is to be created, the data for that graph is read from the table and is used to configure the procedures that actually draw the graph on the screen. If you need to change a graph, in most cases you simply change an entry in the table.

The Decision Support Application Project

Coding the decision support application will follow a functional order much like that used to create the structure chart and procedure specifications. Functional order proceeds from the button click to the event procedure to the code that completes the task assigned to the button. The first task, though, is to create the Definitions table that contains the data needed to create the graphs.

Note: The code development performed in this and the next chapter follows the structure charts developed on Day 5 and the module designs developed on Day 6. Be sure to follow the designs from Days 5 and 6 while you examine the code that was created from these designs. The forms designed on Day 7 are the starting point for the Visual Basic application.

Day 8

Coding the Application, Part 1

Creating the Chart Definitions Table

The tblDefinitions table, shown in Figures 8.1 through 8.5, is a standard Access database table in the Graphs database. It contains fields for all the different pieces of data needed to create a chart. The first column contains the chart code. This column is the primary index for the table and is used to locate the data for a specific chart. The Class, GraphCaption, Units, Type, GraphType, and GraphStyle fields specify the type of graph and the text labels used on it. The DataTable field contains the name of the database table in the Graphs database, and DataField contains the field name in that table that contains the data for the graph. Legend, LegendTable, LegendField, and LegendTextField contain the information needed to create a legend for the current graph.

Figure 8.1.

The tblDefinitions table, which contains a record for each chart class and type and fields that define all the variable parts of a graph.

Code	Class	GraphCaption	Units	Type	GraphType	GraphStyle
11	Sales	Year-to-Date Sales	$	Line	6	0
12	Sales	Sales by Product Category	$	AreaStacked	8	0
13	Sales	Sales by Market Segment	$	AreaStacked	8	0
14	Sales	Sales by Sales Region	$	AreaStacked	8	0
21	Margins	Average Gross Margin	%	Line	6	0
22	Margins	Margins by Product Category	%	LineMulti	6	0
31	Orders	Year-to-Date Orders	$	Line	6	0
32	Orders	Orders by Product Category	$	AreaStacked	8	0
33	Orders	Orders by Market Segment	$	AreaStacked	8	0
34	Orders	Orders by Sales Region	$	AreaStacked	8	0
41	Backlog	Monthly Backlog	$	Line	6	0
42	Backlog	Backlog by Product Category	$	AreaStacked	8	0
43	Backlog	Backlog by Market Segment	$	AreaStacked	8	0
44	Backlog	Backlog by Sales Region	$	AreaStacked	8	0
51	Cycle	Average Order Cycle (Days)	Days	Line	6	0
52	Cycle	Order Cycle by Market Segment	Days	LineMulti	6	0
53	Cycle	Order Cycle Distribution	Days	Histogram	3	0
61	Inventory	Monthly Ending Inventory	$	Line	6	0
62	Inventory	Inventory by Product Category	$	AreaStacked	8	0
63	Inventory	Inventory Turns by Product Category	$/Day	LineMulti	6	0

Figure 8.2.
The tblDefinitions *table continued.*

Code	DataTable	DataField
11	tblSalesTotalMonth	Sales
12	tblSalesCategoryMonth	Sales
13	tblSalesSegmentMonth	Sales
14	tblSalesRegionMonth	Sales
21	tblMarginAverageMonth	Margin
22	tblMarginCategoryMonth	Margin
31	tblOrdersTotalMonth	Sales
32	tblOrdersCategoryMonth	Sales
33	tblOrdersSegmentMonth	Sales
34	tblOrdersRegionMonth	Sales
41	tblBacklogTotalMonth	Backlog
42	tblBacklogCategoryMonth	Backlog
43	tblBacklogSegmentMonth	Backlog
44	tblBacklogRegionMonth	Backlog
51	tblCycleAverageMonth	Days
52	tblCycleSegmentMonth	Days
53	tblCycleDistribution	Frequency
61	tblInventoryTotalMonth	Value
62	tblInventoryCategoryMonth	Value
63	tblInventoryTurnsMonth	Value

Figure 8.3.
The tblDefinitions *table continued.*

Code	Legend	LegendTable	LegendField	LegendTextField
11	No			
12	Yes	Product Categories	Category ID	Category Name
13	Yes	Segments	Segment ID	Legend
14	Yes	Regions	Region ID	Legend
21	No			
22	Yes	Product Categories	Category ID	Category Name
31	No			
32	Yes	Product Categories	Category ID	Category Name
33	Yes	Segments	Segment ID	Legend
34	Yes	Regions	Region ID	Legend
41	No			
42	Yes	Product Categories	Category ID	Category Name
43	Yes	Segments	Segment ID	Legend
44	Yes	Regions	Region ID	Legend
51	No			
52	Yes	Segments	Segment ID	Legend
53	No			
61	No			
62	Yes	Product Categories	Category ID	Category Name
63	Yes	Product Categories	Category ID	Category Name

Coding the Application, Part 1

Figure 8.4.
The tblDefinitions *table continued.*

Code	GridRowHeader	UseActivated	DropLabelText	DDCaption	DDDataField
11		No	Total		
12	Category	No	By Product Categories	Sales of	Sales
13	Segment	Yes	By Market Segment	Sales to	Sales
14	Region	Yes	By Region	Sales to	Sales
21		No	Average		
22	Category	No	By Product Categories	Margins of	Margin
31		No	Total		
32	Category	No	By Product Categories	Orders for	Orders
33	Segment	Yes	By Market Segment	Orders from	Orders
34	Region	Yes	By Region	Orders from	Orders
41		No	Total		
42	Category	No	By Product Categories	Backlog of	Backlog
43	Segment	Yes	By Market Segment	Backlog for	Backlog
44	Region	Yes	By Region	Backlog for	Backlog
51		No	Average		
52	Segment	Yes	By Market Segment	Order Cycle Time of	Days
53		No	Distribution		
61		No	Total		
62	Category	No	By Product Categories	Ending Inventory for	Value
63	Category	No	Turns	Inventory Turnover fo	Value

Figure 8.5.
The tblDefinitions *table continued.*

Code	DDDataTable	DDFlag	DDTypeField	DDTypeName	DDTypeTable
11					
12	tblSalesDetail	PCS	[Category ID]	Category Name	Product Categories
13	tblSalesDetail	PCS	[Segment ID]	Legend	Segments
14	tblSalesDetail	PCS	[Region ID]	Legend	Regions
21					
22	tblMarginDetail	P	[Category ID]	Category Name	Product Categories
31					
32	tblOrdersDetail	PCS	[Category ID]	Category Name	Product Categories
33	tblOrdersDetail	PCS	[Segment ID]	Legend	Segments
34	tblOrdersDetail	PCS	[Region ID]	Legend	Regions
41					
42	tblBacklogDetail	PCS	[Category ID]	Category Name	Product Categories
43	tblBacklogDetail	PCS	[Segment ID]	Legend	Segments
44	tblBacklogDetail	PCS	[Region ID]	Legend	Regions
51					
52	tblCycleDetail	PCS	[Segment ID]	Legend	Segments
53					
61					
62	tblInventoryDetail	P	[Category ID]	Category Name	Product Categories
63	tblTurnsDetail	P	[Category ID]	Category Name	Product Categories

Note: The tblDefinitions table used in this application is an Access database table. Since this is already a database application, it makes sense to include this table along with the other tables. In a nondatabase application, you would probably put the data in this table into a setup or .INI file and read it into an array when you initialized the application.

The `GridRowHeader` field contains the text to use as a label in the first row second column of the grid. The `UseActivated` field indicates if the selected data has an activated field. When creating the market segment or region definitions, you might create definitions for segments or regions that aren't being used yet on the assumption that someday they will be needed. Use the `UseActivated` field to indicate if a definition is in use yet so you won't try to graph datasets that aren't yet in use.

The `DropLabelText` field contains the text for the pop-up labels on the graph type buttons. Because there are different graph types for the different graph classes, the labels need to change to identify the button's current use. The rest of the data fields concern the creation of the drill-down grid associated with a particular table.

Table 8.1 describes the usage of all the fields in the table.

Table 8.1. The use of the fields in the `tblDefinitions` table.

Field Name	Description
Code	The chart code used to locate data for a particular chart class and type.
Class	The name of the graph class.
GraphCaption	The caption used for the graph.
Units	The units for the data being displayed.
Type	The English name of the type of graph to be used.
GraphType	The code needed to create the specified graph type.
GraphStyle	The value to use for the `Style` property of the graph.
DataTable	The name of the table that contains the data.
DataField	The name of the field in the `dataTable` that contains the data.
Legend	A code to answer the question "Does the graph need a legend?"
LegendTable	The table containing the text for the legend.
LegendField	The field containing the text for the legend.
LegendTextField	The field containing a longer description of the object for use in the grid.
GridRowHeader	Text for the top cell in the second column of the grid.
UseActivated	A flag indicating if the data can contain inactive data types that should be skipped while plotting.
DropLabelText	The text for the graph type pop-up labels.
DDCaption	Caption text for the drill-down options grid.

continues

Day 8: Coding the Application, Part 1

Table 8.1. continued

Field Name	Description
DDDataField	The field containing the drill-down data.
DDDataTable	The table denoting the drill-down data.
DDFlag	A flag indicating which drill-down data types are available. P = By product, C = By product category, and S = By market segment.
DDTypeField	The field containing the descriptive data (legend data) for the drill-down table.
DDDTypeName	The field containing the longer descriptive text for the selected data.
DDTypeTable	The name of the table that contains the descriptive data.

The Program Files

Currently, 10 files make up the source code for the decision support application. These files are loaded whenever the make file (.MAK) for the application is loaded:

DCNSPT.MAK: The make file for the application.

MDI_MAIN.FRM: The MDI parent form containing all the menus and the toolbar. All the MDI child forms appear in the active area of this form.

MDI_GRAF.FRM: The MDI child form that contains all the graphs.

MDI_GRID.FRM: The MDI child form that contains the drill-down grid.

DDN_OPTS.FRM: The drill-down options form.

DCNSPT.BAS: The main code module for the project.

DRILL_DN.BAS: A code module containing the drill-down code.

PRINTING.BAS: A code module containing the printing code.

TESTMNTH.FRM: A special test form for locating the positions of the labels on the form.

TESTTRIG.FRM: A special test form for evaluating the code for selecting a wedge of the pie chart.

Table 8.2 shows which procedures are stored in which form or module.

Table 8.2. The locations of the procedures.

Form or Module Name	Procedure Name	Form or Module Name	Procedure Name
MDI_MAIN.FRM	gpbGraphClass_Click	DDN_OPTS.FRM	cmdCancel_Click
	gpbGraphClass_MouseMove		cmdOK_Click
	gpbGraphType_Click		Form_Load
	gpbGraphType_MouseMove		optDrill_Click
	MDIForm_Load	DCNSPT.BAS	AddLegends
	MDIForm_Resize		ClearGrid
	MDIForm_Unload		CreateNewGraph
	mnuEditCopy_Click		DrawChartAndGrid
	mnuFileExit_Click		DrawPieChart
	mnuFilePrint_Click		FillLegendArrays
	mnuFileSave_Click		GridColHeaders
	mnuHelpAbout_Click		GridColRowHeaders
	mnuHelpContents_Click		HideEverything
	mnuHelpSearch_Click		HidePopUpLabels
	mnuViewBacklog_Click		LoadAndParseINIFile
	mnuViewCycle_Click		Main
	mnuViewDetails_Click		ResizeChartAndGrid
	mnuViewInventory_Click		SetColWidths
	mnuViewMargins_Click		SetGraphPosition
	mnuViewOrders_Click		SetGridCrossfoot
	mnuViewSales_Click		SetGridPosition
	Panel3D1_MouseMove		SetGridValues
	Panel3D2_MouseMove		SetInitialTypeButtons
	SelectChartType		strCreateSQL
MDI_GRAF.FRM	chtMonthly_DblClick		ToggleGrid
	chtMonthly_MouseDown	DRILL_DN.BAS	DisplayDDData
	chtMonthly_MouseMove		intPieHotHit
	chtPieChart_DblClick		PopulateGrid
	chtPieChart_MouseMove		RestorePieChart
	chtPieChart_MouseUp	PRINTING.BAS	FindFont

continues

Day 8: Coding the Application, Part 1

Table 8.2. continued

Form or Module Name	Procedure Name	Form or Module Name	Procedure Name
MDI_GRAF.FRM	Form_DragOver	PRINTING.BAS	FindHeight
	Form_Load		FindWidth
	Form_Resize		PrintGrid
	grdMonthly_DblClick		PrintHatchLegend
	intTestDblClickMonth		PrintVisibleChart
	picBanner_Click ()	TESTMNTH.FRM	
MDI_GRID.FRM	Form_DblClick	TESTTRIG.FRM	
	grdDetail_DblClick		

The Program's Global Variables

Many of the variables used in this program are needed throughout the program, so there is a substantial group of system globals. Included in this group are constants used throughout the program. They were created for this program and were obtained from the CONSTANTS.TXT file included with Visual Basic. The following globals are from the DCNSPT.BAS module file. All the code and form modules begin with the `Option Explicit` statement to force all variables to be declared.

```
Option Explicit

'Test and debugging flags
Global Const DEBUGON = True           'Turn debugging mode on or off.
Global Const SHOW_TEST_FORMS = False  'Display test forms.

'Arrays for month names (short and long form), quarters, legends, etc.
Global strMonths(12, 3) As String
Global strLegendText(20) As String    'Long legends for grid.
Global strLegend(20) As String        'Short legends for graph.
Global strDDID(20) As String          'Pie chart segment ID strings.
                                      'for drill-down grid.
Global intLegendSets As Integer       'Number of data sets in the legend arrays.

'Other arrays ReDimed in code.
Global varRowTotals() As Variant      'Row totals array.
Global varColTotals() As Variant      'Col totals array.

'Object variables
Global dbGraphs As Database           'GRAPHS.MDB.
Global tblGraphs As Table             'tblDefinitions in GRAPHS.MDB.
Dim ssGraph As Snapshot               'Snapshot of tblGraphs.
Dim ssLegend As Snapshot              'Snapshot of table that serves as legend.
```

```
'Misc. variables
Global strYear As String              'The current year (set on Form_Load).
Global strYearStart As String         'Bookmark for beginning of year.
Global strDataFile As String          'Path to data file.

'Graph type and class
Global intGraphClass As Integer       'Current graph class.
Global intGraphType As Integer        'Current graph type.

'Flags
Global fInhibitResize As Integer      'Inhibit recursion.
Global fInhibit As Integer            'Inhibit button click handling.
Global fIsCrosstab As Integer         'Flag indicating a crosstab query.
Global fIsHistogram As Integer        'Flag indicating a histogram query.
Global fShowGrid As Integer           'Always display grid with graph.

'Constants for the number of chart classes and types
Global Const NUM_CLASS_BUTTONS = 6
Global Const NUM_TYPE_BUTTONS = 4
'Graph Type buttons
Global Const TOTAL_TYPE = 1
Global Const PRODUCT_TYPE = 2
Global Const SEGMENT_TYPE = 3
Global Const REGION_TYPE = 4
'Graph class buttons
Global Const SALES_CLASS = 1
Global Const MARGINS_CLASS = 2
Global Const ORDERS_CLASS = 3
Global Const BACKLOG_CLASS = 4
Global Const CYCLE_CLASS = 5
Global Const INVENTORY_CLASS = 6

'Other constants
Global Const GRID_BORDER = 100              'The width of the border around the grid.
Global Const LEGEND_HEIGHT = 100            'The height of the legend below the grid.
Global Const GRID_COL_WIDTH = 1000          'The width of the columns on the grid.
Global Const GRID1_COL_WIDTH = 1500         'The width of column 1 on crosstab charts.
Global Const GRID_LEGEND_LABEL_WIDTH = 600     'The width of a legend label.
Global Const GRID_LEGEND_LABEL_OFFSET = 300    'The offset of the legend labels.

'Constants from CONSTANT.TXT

' Show parameters
Global Const MODAL = 1
Global Const MODELESS = 0

' MsgBox parameters
Global Const MB_OK = 0                      'OK button only.
Global Const MB_OKCANCEL = 1                'OK and Cancel buttons.
Global Const MB_ABORTRETRYIGNORE = 2        'Abort, Retry, and Ignore buttons.
Global Const MB_YESNOCANCEL = 3             'Yes, No, and Cancel buttons.
Global Const MB_YESNO = 4                   'Yes and No buttons.
Global Const MB_RETRYCANCEL = 5             'Retry and Cancel buttons.

Global Const MB_ICONSTOP = 16               'Critical message.
Global Const MB_ICONQUESTION = 32           'Warning query.
Global Const MB_ICONEXCLAMATION = 48        'Warning message.
Global Const MB_ICONINFORMATION = 64        'Information message.
```

DAY 8: Coding the Application, Part 1

```
Global Const MB_APPLMODAL = 0          'Application modal message box.
Global Const MB_DEFBUTTON1 = 0         'First button is default.
Global Const MB_DEFBUTTON2 = 256       'Second button is default.
Global Const MB_DEFBUTTON3 = 512       'Third button is default.
Global Const MB_SYSTEMMODAL = 4096     'System modal.

' MsgBox return values
Global Const IDOK = 1         'OK button pressed.
Global Const IDCANCEL = 2     'Cancel button pressed.
Global Const IDABORT = 3      'Abort button pressed.
Global Const IDRETRY = 4      'Retry button pressed.
Global Const IDIGNORE = 5     'Ignore button pressed.
Global Const IDYES = 6        'Yes button pressed.
Global Const IDNO = 7         'No button pressed.


' WindowState
Global Const NORMAL = 0
Global Const MINIMIZED = 1
Global Const MAXIMIZED = 2

' MousePointer
Global Const DEFAULT = 0             '0 - Default
Global Const ARROW = 1               '1 - Arrow
Global Const CROSSHAIR = 2           '2 - Cross
Global Const IBEAM = 3               '3 - I-beam
Global Const ICON_POINTER = 4        '4 - Icon
Global Const SIZE_POINTER = 5        '5 - Size
Global Const SIZE_NE_SW = 6          '6 - Size NE SW
Global Const SIZE_N_S = 7            '7 - Size N S
Global Const SIZE_NW_SE = 8          '8 - Size NW SE
Global Const SIZE_W_E = 9            '9 - Size W E
Global Const UP_ARROW = 10           '10 - Up-arrow
Global Const HOURGLASS = 11          '11 - Hourglass
Global Const NO_DROP = 12            '12 - No drop

'Button parameter masks
Global Const LEFT_BUTTON = 1
Global Const RIGHT_BUTTON = 2
Global Const MIDDLE_BUTTON = 4

'Common Dialog Control
'Action Property
Global Const DLG_FILE_OPEN = 1
Global Const DLG_FILE_SAVE = 2
Global Const DLG_COLOR = 3
Global Const DLG_FONT = 4
Global Const DLG_PRINT = 5
Global Const DLG_HELP = 6

'File Open/Save Dialog Flags
Global Const OFN_READONLY = &H1&
Global Const OFN_OVERWRITEPROMPT = &H2&
Global Const OFN_HIDEREADONLY = &H4&
Global Const OFN_NOCHANGEDIR = &H8&
Global Const OFN_SHOWHELP = &H10&
Global Const OFN_NOVALIDATE = &H100&
```

```
Global Const OFN_ALLOWMULTISELECT = &H200&
Global Const OFN_EXTENSIONDIFFERENT = &H400&
Global Const OFN_PATHMUSTEXIST = &H800&
Global Const OFN_FILEMUSTEXIST = &H1000&
Global Const OFN_CREATEPROMPT = &H2000&
Global Const OFN_SHAREAWARE = &H4000&
Global Const OFN_NOREADONLYRETURN = &H8000&

'Color Dialog Flags
Global Const CC_RGBINIT = &H1&
Global Const CC_FULLOPEN = &H2&
Global Const CC_PREVENTFULLOPEN = &H4&
Global Const CC_SHOWHELP = &H8&

'Fonts Dialog Flags
Global Const CF_SCREENFONTS = &H1&
Global Const CF_PRINTERFONTS = &H2&
Global Const CF_BOTH = &H3&
Global Const CF_SHOWHELP = &H4&
Global Const CF_INITTOLOGFONTSTRUCT = &H40&
Global Const CF_USESTYLE = &H80&
Global Const CF_EFFECTS = &H100&
Global Const CF_APPLY = &H200&
Global Const CF_ANSIONLY = &H400&
Global Const CF_NOVECTORFONTS = &H800&
Global Const CF_NOSIMULATIONS = &H1000&
Global Const CF_LIMITSIZE = &H2000&
Global Const CF_FIXEDPITCHONLY = &H4000&
Global Const CF_WYSIWYG = &H8000&   'Must also have CF_SCREENFONTS
                                    'and CF_PRINTERFONTS.
Global Const CF_FORCEFONTEXIST = &H10000
Global Const CF_SCALABLEONLY = &H20000
Global Const CF_TTONLY = &H40000
Global Const CF_NOFACESEL = &H80000
Global Const CF_NOSTYLESEL = &H100000
Global Const CF_NOSIZESEL = &H200000

'Printer Dialog Flags
Global Const PD_ALLPAGES = &H0&
Global Const PD_SELECTION = &H1&
Global Const PD_PAGENUMS = &H2&
Global Const PD_NOSELECTION = &H4&
Global Const PD_NOPAGENUMS = &H8&
Global Const PD_COLLATE = &H10&
Global Const PD_PRINTTOFILE = &H20&
Global Const PD_PRINTSETUP = &H40&
Global Const PD_NOWARNING = &H80&
Global Const PD_RETURNDC = &H100&
Global Const PD_RETURNIC = &H200&
Global Const PD_RETURNDEFAULT = &H400&
Global Const PD_SHOWHELP = &H800&
Global Const PD_USEDEVMODECOPIES = &H40000
Global Const PD_DISABLEPRINTTOFILE = &H80000
Global Const PD_HIDEPRINTTOFILE = &H100000

'Help Constants
Global Const HELP_CONTEXT = &H1         'Display topic in ulTopic.
```

Day 8: Coding the Application, Part 1

```
Global Const HELP_QUIT = &H2              'Terminate help.
Global Const HELP_INDEX = &H3             'Display index.
Global Const HELP_CONTENTS = &H3
Global Const HELP_HELPONHELP = &H4        'Display help on using help.
Global Const HELP_SETINDEX = &H5          'Set the current index for
                                          'multi-index help.
Global Const HELP_SETCONTENTS = &H5
Global Const HELP_CONTEXTPOPUP = &H8
Global Const HELP_FORCEFILE = &H9
Global Const HELP_KEY = &H101             'Display topic for keyword in offabData.
Global Const HELP_COMMAND = &H102
Global Const HELP_PARTIALKEY = &H105      'Call the search engine in winhelp.

'Error Constants
Global Const CDERR_DIALOGFAILURE = -32768

Global Const CDERR_GENERALCODES = &H7FFF
Global Const CDERR_STRUCTSIZE = &H7FFE
Global Const CDERR_INITIALIZATION = &H7FFD
Global Const CDERR_NOTEMPLATE = &H7FFC
Global Const CDERR_NOHINSTANCE = &H7FFB
Global Const CDERR_LOADSTRFAILURE = &H7FFA
Global Const CDERR_FINDRESFAILURE = &H7FF9
Global Const CDERR_LOADRESFAILURE = &H7FF8
Global Const CDERR_LOCKRESFAILURE = &H7FF7
Global Const CDERR_MEMALLOCFAILURE = &H7FF6
Global Const CDERR_MEMLOCKFAILURE = &H7FF5
Global Const CDERR_NOHOOK = &H7FF4

'Added for CMDIALOG.VBX
Global Const CDERR_CANCEL = &H7FF3
Global Const CDERR_NODLL = &H7FF2
Global Const CDERR_ERRPROC = &H7FF1
Global Const CDERR_ALLOC = &H7FF0
Global Const CDERR_HELP = &H7FEF

Global Const PDERR_PRINTERCODES = &H6FFF
Global Const PDERR_SETUPFAILURE = &H6FFE
Global Const PDERR_PARSEFAILURE = &H6FFD
Global Const PDERR_RETDEFFAILURE = &H6FFC
Global Const PDERR_LOADDRVFAILURE = &H6FFB
Global Const PDERR_GETDEVMODEFAIL = &H6FFA
Global Const PDERR_INITFAILURE = &H6FF9
Global Const PDERR_NODEVICES = &H6FF8
Global Const PDERR_NODEFAULTPRN = &H6FF7
Global Const PDERR_DNDMMISMATCH = &H6FF6
Global Const PDERR_CREATEICFAILURE = &H6FF5
Global Const PDERR_PRINTERNOTFOUND = &H6FF4

Global Const CFERR_CHOOSEFONTCODES = &H5FFF
Global Const CFERR_NOFONTS = &H5FFE

Global Const FNERR_FILENAMECODES = &H4FFF
Global Const FNERR_SUBCLASSFAILURE = &H4FFE
Global Const FNERR_INVALIDFILENAME = &H4FFD
Global Const FNERR_BUFFERTOOSMALL = &H4FFC
```

```
Global Const FRERR_FINDREPLACECODES = &H3FFF
Global Const CCERR_CHOOSECOLORCODES = &H2FFF

'Grid
'ColAlignment, FixedAlignment Properties
Global Const GRID_ALIGNLEFT = 0
Global Const GRID_ALIGNRIGHT = 1
Global Const GRID_ALIGNCENTER = 2

'Fillstyle Property
Global Const GRID_SINGLE = 0
Global Const GRID_REPEAT = 1


'........................................
'Graph Control
'........................................
'General
Global Const G_NONE = 0
Global Const G_DEFAULT = 0

Global Const G_OFF = 0
Global Const G_ON = 1
'Graph DrawStyle
Global Const G_MONO = 0
Global Const G_COLOR = 1

'Graph Types
Global Const G_PIE2D = 1
Global Const G_PIE3D = 2
Global Const G_BAR2D = 3
Global Const G_BAR3D = 4
Global Const G_GANTT = 5
Global Const G_LINE = 6
Global Const G_LOGLIN = 7
Global Const G_AREA = 8
Global Const G_SCATTER = 9
Global Const G_POLAR = 10
Global Const G_HLC = 11

'Colors
Global Const G_BLACK = 0
Global Const G_BLUE = 1
Global Const G_GREEN = 2
Global Const G_CYAN = 3
Global Const G_RED = 4
Global Const G_MAGENTA = 5
Global Const G_BROWN = 6
Global Const G_LIGHT_GRAY = 7
Global Const G_DARK_GRAY = 8
Global Const G_LIGHT_BLUE = 9
Global Const G_LIGHT_GREEN = 10
Global Const G_LIGHT_CYAN = 11
Global Const G_LIGHT_RED = 12
Global Const G_LIGHT_MAGENTA = 13
Global Const G_YELLOW = 14
Global Const G_WHITE = 15
Global Const G_AUTOBW = 16
```

Day 8: Coding the Application, Part 1

```
'Patterns
Global Const G_SOLID = 0
Global Const G_HOLLOW = 1
Global Const G_HATCH1 = 2
Global Const G_HATCH2 = 3
Global Const G_HATCH3 = 4
Global Const G_HATCH4 = 5
Global Const G_HATCH5 = 6
Global Const G_HATCH6 = 7
Global Const G_BITMAP1 = 16
Global Const G_BITMAP2 = 17
Global Const G_BITMAP3 = 18
Global Const G_BITMAP4 = 19
Global Const G_BITMAP5 = 20
Global Const G_BITMAP6 = 21
Global Const G_BITMAP7 = 22
Global Const G_BITMAP8 = 23
Global Const G_BITMAP9 = 24
Global Const G_BITMAP10 = 25
Global Const G_BITMAP11 = 26
Global Const G_BITMAP12 = 27
Global Const G_BITMAP13 = 28
Global Const G_BITMAP14 = 29
Global Const G_BITMAP15 = 30
Global Const G_BITMAP16 = 31

'Symbols
Global Const G_CROSS_PLUS = 0
Global Const G_CROSS_TIMES = 1
Global Const G_TRIANGLE_UP = 2
Global Const G_SOLID_TRIANGLE_UP = 3
Global Const G_TRIANGLE_DOWN = 4
Global Const G_SOLID_TRIANGLE_DOWN = 5
Global Const G_SQUARE = 6
Global Const G_SOLID_SQUARE = 7
Global Const G_DIAMOND = 8
Global Const G_SOLID_DIAMOND = 9

'Line Styles
'Global Const G_SOLID = 0
Global Const G_DASH = 1
Global Const G_DOT = 2
Global Const G_DASHDOT = 3
Global Const G_DASHDOTDOT = 4

'Grids
Global Const G_HORIZONTAL = 1
Global Const G_VERTICAL = 2

'Statistics
Global Const G_MEAN = 1
Global Const G_MIN_MAX = 2
Global Const G_STD_DEV = 4
Global Const G_BEST_FIT = 8

'Data Arrays
Global Const G_GRAPH_DATA = 1
Global Const G_COLOR_DATA = 2
```

```
Global Const G_EXTRA_DATA = 3
Global Const G_LABEL_TEXT = 4
Global Const G_LEGEND_TEXT = 5
Global Const G_PATTERN_DATA = 6
Global Const G_SYMBOL_DATA = 7
Global Const G_XPOS_DATA = 8
Global Const G_ALL_DATA = 9

'Draw Mode
Global Const G_NO_ACTION = 0
Global Const G_CLEAR = 1
Global Const G_DRAW = 2
Global Const G_BLIT = 3
Global Const G_COPY = 4
Global Const G_PRINT = 5
Global Const G_WRITE = 6

'Print Options
Global Const G_BORDER = 2

'Pie Chart Options
Global Const G_NO_LINES = 1
Global Const G_COLORED = 2
Global Const G_PERCENTS = 4
Global Const G_NOT_EXPLODED = 0
Global Const G_EXPLODED = 1


'Bar Chart Options
'Global Const G_HORIZONTAL = 1
Global Const G_STACKED = 2
Global Const G_PERCENTAGE = 4
Global Const G_Z_CLUSTERED = 6

'Gantt Chart Options
Global Const G_SPACED_BARS = 1

'Line/Polar Chart Options
Global Const G_SYMBOLS = 1
Global Const G_STICKS = 2
Global Const G_LINES = 4

'Area Chart Options
Global Const G_ABSOLUTE = 1
Global Const G_PERCENT = 2

'HLC Chart Options
Global Const G_NO_CLOSE = 1
Global Const G_NO_HIGH_LOW = 2

'FontFamily
Global Const G_ROMAN = 0
Global Const G_SWISS = 1
Global Const G_MODERN = 2

'FontStyle
Global Const G_PLANE = 0
Global Const G_ITALIC = 1
```

Coding the Application, Part 1

```
Global Const G_BOLD = 2
Global Const G_UNDERLINES = 4

'FontUse
Global Const G_TITLE = 0
Global Const G_OTHER_TITLE = 1
Global Const G_LABELS = 2
Global Const G_LEGEND = 3
Global Const G_ALL_TEXT = 4
```

The following constants and declarations are from DRILL_DN.BAS:

```
Option Explicit

Global sngMouseX As Single              'Mouse position on mouse down.
Global sngMouseY As Single
Global fDblClick As Integer             'Area chart double-clicked.
Global hTaskGraph As Integer            'Task handle of graph.
Global hWndGraph As Integer             'Window handle of graph.

'Global variables for pie chart drill-down
Global fPieLoaded As Integer            'True if pie chart form loaded.
Global intPieChartLeft As Integer       'Left margin of pie chart.
Global strLabels() As String            'Labels of pie chart.
Global fDblClicked As Integer           'Flag for double-click.
Global intWedgeAngle As Integer         'Angle of middle of wedge (degrees).
Global intSelectedDDOption As Integer   'Selected drill-down option.
Global intDDReturnValue As Integer      'Return type from DD Options form,
                                        'OK or Cancel

'Global constants for drill-down
Global Const NUM_OPTS = 3
Global Const DDPRODUCT = 1
Global Const DDCUSTOMER = 2
Global Const DDSALESMAN = 3

'Global variables for grid
Global intFormWidth As Integer   'Width of form on loading.
Global intFormHeight As Integer  'Height of form on loading.

'Module-level variables
Dim intRow As Integer
Dim IntCol As Integer
```

The following declarations are from PRINTING.BAS:

```
Option Explicit

'Type definition for saving prior chart details
Type typSave
    intWidth As Integer
    intHeight As Integer
    intTop As Integer
    intLeft As Integer
End Type

'Declarations for Windows GDI functions used in PrintVisibleChart
```

```
Declare Function PlayMetaFile Lib "GDI" (ByVal hDC As Integer,
➥ByVal hMF As Integer) As Integer
Declare Function SetMapMode Lib "GDI" (ByVal hDC As Integer,
➥ByVal nMapMode As Integer) As Integer
Declare Function SetViewportOrg Lib "GDI" (ByVal hDC As Integer,
➥ByVal nX As Integer, ByVal nY As Integer) As Integer
Declare Function SetViewportExt Lib "GDI" (ByVal hDC As Integer,
➥ByVal nX As Integer, ByVal nY As Integer) As Integer
Declare Function GetDeviceCaps Lib "GDI" (ByVal hDC As Integer,
➥ByVal nIndex As Integer) As Integer

Declare Function GSGetMF Lib "GSWDLL.DLL" (ByVal nMode As Integer) As Integer


'Some constants for fPrintWhat in PrintVisibleChart, PrintGrid.
Const LEVEL1_CHART_AND_GRID = 1
Const LEVEL2_CHART_AND_GRID = 2
Const PIE_CHART = 3
Const DETAIL_GRID = 4
```

Chart Class and Type Button Procedures

Figure 5.16 shows the structure of the Chart Class and Type button procedures. The graph class and graph type buttons form two control arrays named gpbGraphClass and gpbGraphType. In both cases, the Click event procedure returns the Index property, indicating which button in the button array was pressed. The Tag property of each button contains the class or type code for the selected option, so indexing the Tag property with the button index gives the needed code.

Note: For this application, the value of the Index property and the code stored in the Tag property are the same, so we could have used the Index property directly to get the code. However, using the Tag property to hold the code makes the program more general. The Tag property is available for storing any text you want to put there.

The gpbGraphClass_Click event procedure that follows first tests the recursion flag fInhibit to see if it is set and sets it if it isn't. The fInhibit flag is cleared at the end of this procedure. This mechanism is needed to prevent the user from pressing another class or type button until the current one is processed. Otherwise, two call chains could be active, both trying to create a different chart using the same chart control. The procedure next calls HidePopUpLabels to hide the pop-up labels in case the user has moved the pointer off the class button too quickly for the program to register the event. You will see calls to this procedure in numerous locations to ensure that the labels are hidden when the user doesn't have the pointer over a button.

The next line sets the global variable intGraphClass to the class selected by pressing the class button. As I mentioned, the class for a particular button is stored in the button's Tag property.

Day 8
Coding the Application, Part 1

Every time the user selects a new class of graph, we want to change to the first graph type. The type code is obtained from the global constant TOTAL_TYPE and stored in the global variable intGraphType.

Some of the graph classes need only two or three of the four graph type buttons, so when the new graph class and type are set, SetInitialTypeButtons is called to set the pop-up labels and to activate or deactivate the type buttons. Once the buttons are set, CreateNewGraph is called to draw the graph, and the Show method is applied to the frmMDIGraph form to ensure that it's visible and that it's the topmost form. HidePopUpLabels is called again, and the fInhibit flag is cleared to complete the procedure.

Note: This procedure deviates slightly from the one that's shown in Figure 5.16 and described in the procedure specifications. This was caused by the need to enable or disable the type buttons before clicking on one. Since the graph type was already set, it was easier to go ahead and create the graph instead of simulating a click on a type button.

```
'
'Change the graph class and display the first type.
'
Sub gpbGraphClass_Click (intIndex As Integer, intValue As Integer)
    'The graph class is in the Tag property.
    Dim strCode As String

    'Prevent recursion.
    If fInhibit Then
      Exit Sub
    End If

    'Disable changing the graph class and type.
    fInhibit = True

    'Hide the pop-up labels.
    Call HidePopUpLabels
    DoEvents

    'Set the global graph class according to the button pressed.
    intGraphClass = gpbGraphClass(intIndex).Tag

    'Set the global type to the first graph type.
    intGraphType = TOTAL_TYPE

    'Set the type buttons.
    Call SetInitialTypeButtons

    'Create the graph.
    Call CreateNewGraph
```

```
        'Show the form in case another form is on top.
        frmMDIGraph.Show

        'In case the user moved the mouse before this procedure
        'finished, hide the pop-up labels.
        Call HidePopUpLabels

        fInhibit = False   'Clear the inhibit flag.

End Sub
```

Next is the event procedure for the graph type buttons, gpbGraphType_Click. This procedure is nearly identical to the gpbGraphClass_Click procedure, except that the graph class isn't changed, and the graph type is obtained from the Tag property of the button the user pressed.

```
'
'Set the graph type and display the graph.
'
Sub gpbGraphType_Click (intIndex As Integer, fValue As Integer)

    'Prevent recursion.
    If fInhibit Then
       Exit Sub
    End If

    fInhibit = True

    'Hide the pop-up labels.
    Call HidePopUpLabels
    DoEvents

    'The graph type number is stored in the button's Tag property.
    intGraphType = gpbGraphType(intIndex).Tag

    'Display the graph.
    Call CreateNewGraph
    DoEvents

    'Show the form in case another form is on top.
    frmMDIGraph.Show
    DoEvents

    'In case the user moved the mouse before this procedure
    'finished, hide the pop-up labels.
     Call HidePopUpLabels

    fInhibit = False   'Reset the inhibit flag.

End Sub
```

The *CreateNewGraph* Procedure

Both the graph class and graph type click event procedures call the CreateNewGraph procedure in the DCNSPT.BAS module to prepare to create a new graph. The procedure first combines

Coding the Application, Part 1

the graph class code and the graph type code to create the chart code and store it in the variable strCode. The variable strCode is then used with the Seek method to select the data for the current chart from the tblDefinitions table. Seek finds the record in the table where the value in the Code field matches the value in strCode. The table is available globally in the object variable tblGraphs, so any procedure that accesses fields in tblGraphs gets the data for the current graph.

The procedure then turns off the grid, hides everything, and calls DrawChartAndGrid to draw the new chart and grid. When that procedure returns, the new chart is displayed.

```
'
'Create a new graph.
'
Sub CreateNewGraph ()
   Dim strCode As String   'A string to hold the graph code.

   'Create the code that selects the chart to display.
   strCode = LTrim$(Str$(intGraphClass)) & LTrim$(Str$(intGraphType))
   'Set the graph code.

   'Load the graph description data for the new graph type.
   tblGraphs.Seek "=", strCode
   If tblGraphs.NoMatch Then
      'Should not occur; buttons for missing selections are disabled.
      MsgBox "Graph not available for this selection.", MB_ICONSTOP, "Developer
      ↪at Work"
      Exit Sub
   End If
   'Turn off the grid.
   If fShowGrid = True Then ToggleGrid

   'Hide everything.
   Call HideEverything

   'Draw the new graph on the form.
   Call DrawChartAndGrid

   'Unhide graph.
   frmMDIGraph.chtMonthly.Visible = True
   DoEvents
End Sub
```

Drawing the Chart and Grid

The DrawChartAndGrid procedure shown in Figure 5.15 is the primary procedure for drawing the charts and grids in this program. This procedure handles setting up the chart type, inserting labels and captions, obtaining data from the database, and inserting that data into both the chart and the grid. Because this procedure is somewhat lengthy, I've broken it into blocks, with explanations between each block.

The first block of the procedure declares the variables and checks for the existence of the data table needed to create the current graph. It gets the table name from the tblDefinitions table and checks to see that it is in the list of tables contained in the database. If not, the procedure is ended. Otherwise, the mouse pointer is changed to the hourglass, and the setup of the graph begins.

```
'
'Draw the monthly graph. If this is a crosstab chart,
'fill the grid with data. The grid is not displayed unless
'fShowGrid is true.
'
Sub DrawChartAndGrid ()

    'Local variables.
    Dim fPlotPoints As Integer      'Turn on plotting of points.
    Dim intDataSets As Integer      'Number of data sets.
    Dim intSet As Integer           'Data set counter.
    Dim intColStart As Integer      'Beginning column of query Snapshot.
    Dim intField As Integer         'Field counter in the database.
    Dim strSQL As String            'SQL statement for query.
    Dim intNullPoints As Integer
    Dim intCol As Integer           'The column in the grid.
    Dim intCtr As Integer           'Generic loop counter.

    'Check to see that the data table is available.
    fPlotPoints = False
    For intCtr = 0 To dbGraphs.TableDefs.Count - 1
       If dbGraphs.TableDefs(intCtr).Name = tblGraphs("DataTable") Then
          fPlotPoints = True
       End If
    Next intCtr
    If Not fPlotPoints Then
       MsgBox "Table '" & tblGraphs("DataTable") & "' not available.",
       ➥MB_ICONSTOP, "Programmer at Work"
       Exit Sub
    End If

    Screen.MousePointer = HOURGLASS   'Set the mouse pointer to the hourglass.
```

The second block prepares the chart layout by setting the caption, resetting the colors, and setting the GraphType and GraphStyle properties. The procedure next determines what type of chart this is—level 1 total or average chart, crosstab chart or histogram—and sets flags to indicate the type.

```
    'Set the title bar for the MDI child form.
    frmMDIGraph.Caption = tblGraphs("GraphCaption") & " for " & strYear

    'Set the GraphType and GraphStyle property values for the chart.
    frmMDIGraph.chtMonthly.DataReset = G_COLOR_DATA   'Reset the color data.
    frmMDIGraph.chtMonthly.GraphType = tblGraphs("GraphType")
    frmMDIGraph.chtMonthly.GraphStyle = tblGraphs("GraphStyle")

    'See if this is a crosstab or histogram table and set the flags.
    If tblGraphs("Legend") Then
       'Only crosstab queries have legends.
       fIsCrosstab = True
       fIsHistogram = False
```

Coding the Application, Part 1

```
ElseIf tblGraphs("Type") = "Histogram" Then
   'It's a histogram.
   fIsCrosstab = False
   fIsHistogram = True
Else
   fIsCrosstab = False
   fIsHistogram = False
End If
```

The third block calls the `strCreateSQL` function procedure to make an SQL statement appropriate for this graph class and type, and creates a snapshot of the data and stores it in `ssGraph`. When the data for the table is available, `FillLegendArrays` is called to load the descriptive text into the legend arrays for use when creating the legend and detail grid.

```
'Create an SQL string for the rollup table
'and create a snapshot with it.
strSQL = strCreateSQL()
Set ssGraph = dbGraphs.CreateSnapshot(strSQL)

'Fill the legend arrays for the grid and graph controls.
Call FillLegendArrays
```

The fourth block sets the chart and grid options, depending on the chart type. A large block `If` statement breaks this block into three parts—one for level 2 crosstab tables, one for histograms, and one for level 1 total or average charts. The options consist of line thickness, line stats (mean and linear fit), number of data sets, number of points in the data sets, and the labels for the horizontal axis. Depending on the graph type, either `GridColHeaders` or `GridColRowHeaders` is called to put the labels in the first row of the grid or in the first row and first two columns. Finally, `SetColWidths` is called to set the widths of the columns in the grid.

```
'Go to the last record to get record count (important).
ssGraph.MoveLast

'Set chart and grid options, depending on whether
'the data is from a crosstab table or not.
If fIsCrosstab Then
   'Set thin lines and turn off statistics.
   frmMDIGraph.chtMonthly.ThickLines = G_OFF
   frmMDIGraph.chtMonthly.LineStats = G_OFF

   'Set the number of data sets in the graph and the grid.
   frmMDIGraph.chtMonthly.NumSets = intLegendSets
   frmMDIGraph.grdMonthly.Rows = intLegendSets + 2
   frmMDIGraph.chtMonthly.NumPoints = 12
   intColStart = 1   'Column 0 = GROUP BY identifier.

   'Add the Month labels to the graph.
   For intCtr = 1 To 12
      frmMDIGraph.chtMonthly.ThisPoint = intCtr
      frmMDIGraph.chtMonthly.LabelText = strMonths(intCtr, 1)
   Next intCtr

   'Create the grid's column and row headers.
   Call GridColRowHeaders
ElseIf fIsHistogram Then
```

```
        'Set up a histogram plot.
        'Set thin lines and turn off statistics.
        frmMDIGraph.chtMonthly.ThickLines = G_OFF
        frmMDIGraph.chtMonthly.LineStats = G_OFF
        frmMDIGraph.chtMonthly.NumPoints = ssGraph.RecordCount

        'Set the number of data sets in the graph and the grid.
        'Histograms have only one data set.
        frmMDIGraph.chtMonthly.NumSets = 1
        frmMDIGraph.grdMonthly.Rows = 2
        intColStart = 2   'Column 0 = Year, Column 1 = Month.

        'Clear the image and text from the left box on the grid.
        Call ClearGrid(1, 0)

        'Create the grid column headers (only).
        Call GridColHeaders

    Else
        'Set thick lines and turn on statistics.
        frmMDIGraph.chtMonthly.ThickLines = G_ON
        'Add best fit and mean statistics.
        frmMDIGraph.chtMonthly.LineStats = G_BEST_FIT + G_MEAN

        'Set the number of data sets in the graph and the grid.
        'Monthly totals or averages have only one data set.
        frmMDIGraph.chtMonthly.NumSets = 1
        frmMDIGraph.grdMonthly.Rows = 2
        frmMDIGraph.chtMonthly.NumPoints = 12
        intColStart = 2   'Column 0 = Year, Column 1 = Month.

        'Add the Month labels to the graph.
        For intCtr = 1 To 12
            frmMDIGraph.chtMonthly.ThisPoint = intCtr
            frmMDIGraph.chtMonthly.LabelText = strMonths(intCtr, 1)
        Next intCtr

        'Clear the image and text from the left box on the grid.
        Call ClearGrid(1, 0)

        'Create the grid column headers (only).
        Call GridColHeaders

        'Test for January of "current" year.
        ssGraph.MoveFirst
        If ssGraph("Month") = "01" Then
            strYearStart = ssGraph.Bookmark
        Else
            'An error condition.
            MsgBox "No data found for January, " & strYear & ".", MB_ICONSTOP,
            ➥"Error in Rollup"
            ssGraph.Close
            Exit Sub
        End If
    End If

    'Set the grid column widths.
    Call SetColWidths
```

Coding the Application, Part 1

The fifth block begins loading the data into the graph and the grid. As before, it's broken into three separate parts with a large block If statement—one for crosstab tables, one for histograms, and one for the level 1 total or average graphs. The crosstab chart is processed in the first block by taking the first legend label from the grid and searching for it in the snapshot of the data table. This is necessary to keep the data in the chart and grid in sync with the labels on the chart and in the legend. When the data is located, it is copied into the graph and grid and added to the totals being calculated for each column. When all the data is copied into the graph and grid, SetGridCrossfoot is called to place the totals into the last row of the grid.

For the histogram plot, the process is simpler, because there is only one data set and you don't need to worry about synchronization with a legend. All the data in the snapshot is copied into the graph and grid. The cycle data is then copied into the horizontal labels of the graph and into the first row of the grid.

The class 1 total or average chart is handled much like the histogram plot. There is only one set of data to be plotted, so you don't need to worry about synchronization. The data is read from the snapshot and inserted into the graph and the grid.

```
'Load the data points and the grid explicitly.
If fIsCrosstab Then
    'Set up arrays to hold the row and column totals.
    ReDim varRowTotals(frmMDIGraph.chtMonthly.NumSets)
    ReDim varColTotals(frmMDIGraph.chtMonthly.NumPoints)

    'Process rows by column.
    'Select the first label from the label array.
    For intSet = 1 To intLegendSets
        'Find the legend label in the snapshot.
        ssGraph.FindFirst "[" & tblGraphs("LegendField") & "] = " & Chr$(34) _
        & strLegend(intSet) & Chr$(34)
        'The data for row intSet should now be selected.

        'Process rows.
        intCol = 1  'The point in the data set or the column on the grid.
        intNullPoints = 0
        'intCol is the column in the database table.
        For intField = intColStart To ssGraph.Fields.Count - 1
            'Set graph and grid columns and rows.
            frmMDIGraph.chtMonthly.ThisSet = intSet
            frmMDIGraph.grdMonthly.Row = intSet
            frmMDIGraph.chtMonthly.ThisPoint = intCol
            frmMDIGraph.grdMonthly.Col = intCol + 1

            'Test for null values (null causes an error)
            'and replace with the value 0.
            If IsNull(ssGraph.Fields(intField)) Then
                frmMDIGraph.chtMonthly.GraphData = 0
                frmMDIGraph.grdMonthly.Text = ""
                intNullPoints = intNullPoints + 1
            ElseIf ssGraph.NoMatch Then
                'No data found.
                frmMDIGraph.chtMonthly.GraphData = 0
```

```
                    frmMDIGraph.grdMonthly.Text = ""
                    intNullPoints = intNullPoints + 1
                Else
                    'Plot a data point.
                    frmMDIGraph.chtMonthly.GraphData = ssGraph.Fields(intField)
                    'Format and store the data in the grid.
                    Call SetGridValues(intField, intSet, intCol)
                    'Turn on plot pointing when the first
                    'non-null value is encountered.
                End If
                intCol = intCol + 1
                DoEvents
            Next intField
        Next intSet
        'Add the row and column totals.
        Call SetGridCrossfoot

    ElseIf fIsHistogram Then
        'Go here for the histogram chart.
        'Process each record in the histogram table
        '(1 record/cycle).
        frmMDIGraph.chtMonthly.ThisSet = 1

        'Move to the first record.
        ssGraph.MoveFirst
        'Set the point to 1.
        intCol = 1
        Do Until ssGraph.EOF
            frmMDIGraph.grdMonthly.Row = 1
            frmMDIGraph.chtMonthly.ThisPoint = intCol
            frmMDIGraph.grdMonthly.Col = intCol - 1
            'Replace null values with 0.
            If IsNull(ssGraph("Frequency")) Then
                frmMDIGraph.chtMonthly.GraphData = 0
                frmMDIGraph.grdMonthly.Text = ""
            Else
                'Add a data point to the chart.
                frmMDIGraph.chtMonthly.GraphData = ssGraph("Frequency")
                'Format the data and store it in the grid.
                Call SetGridValues(2, 1, intCol)   'Field = 2, Row = 1,
                                                   'Column = intCol.
            End If
            'Add the cycle labels to the graph.
            frmMDIGraph.chtMonthly.LabelText = ssGraph("Cycle")
            'Add the cycles.
            frmMDIGraph.grdMonthly.Row = 0
            frmMDIGraph.grdMonthly.Text = ssGraph("Cycle")

            'Move to the next record in the snapshot.
            ssGraph.MoveNext
            intCol = intCol + 1
        Loop
    Else
        'Go here if it is not a crosstab table.
        'Process each record in the monthly summary table
        '(1 record/month).
        frmMDIGraph.chtMonthly.ThisSet = 1
```

Coding the Application, Part 1

```
      'Set the point to the first month in the table (usually 1).
      ssGraph.MoveFirst
      frmMDIGraph.grdMonthly.Row = 1
      intCol = Val(ssGraph("Month"))
      Do Until ssGraph.EOF
         frmMDIGraph.chtMonthly.ThisPoint = intCol
         frmMDIGraph.grdMonthly.Col = intCol - 1
         'Replace null values with 0.
         If IsNull(ssGraph("SumOfData")) Then
            frmMDIGraph.chtMonthly.GraphData = 0
            frmMDIGraph.grdMonthly.Text = ""
         Else
            'Add a data point to the chart.
            frmMDIGraph.chtMonthly.GraphData = ssGraph("SumOfData")
            'Format the data and store it in the grid.
            Call SetGridValues(2, 1, intCol)   'Field = 2, Row = 1,
                                               'Column = intCol.
         End If
         'Move to the next record in the snapshot.
         ssGraph.MoveNext
         intCol = intCol + 1
      Loop
   End If
   ssGraph.Close
```

The sixth block calls procedures to position the grid and graph and then draws the graph by setting its DrawMode to the G_DRAW global constant. When the chart is drawn, the mouse pointer is reset to normal, and the procedure ends.

```
   'Set the position of the grid in the form.
   Call SetGridPosition

   'Set the position of the graph in the form.
   Call SetGraphPosition

   'Draw the graph.
   frmMDIGraph.chtMonthly.DrawMode = G_DRAW

   'Reset the mouse pointer.
   Screen.MousePointer = DEFAULT

End Sub
```

Creating the SQL Statement

The DrawChartAndGrid procedure calls the strCreateSQL function procedure to create and return an SQL statement that creates a data array containing the data needed for the current chart. The strCreateSQL procedure operates by creating a group of substrings, one for each of the parts of the SQL statement. At the end, the substrings are combined to create the SQL statement. Most of the strings are created in a "fill in the blanks" method in which names and strings are obtained from the tblDefinitions table and inserted into the string formulas. Which

substrings are created and combined into the SQL statement is determined by the type of graph being created. This procedure has a block If statement that breaks it into three parts. The first and largest part is for crosstab tables.

```
'
'Create the SQL statement for selecting the rollup data.
'Use the fields from the chart definitions database to
'create the statement.
'
Function strCreateSQL () As String
    Dim intCtr As Integer           'Generic loop counter.
    Dim strSQLTransform As String   'TRANSFORM clause.
    Dim strSQLSelect As String      'SELECT clause.
    Dim strSQLFrom As String        'FROM clause.
    Dim strSQLWhere As String       'WHERE criterion.
    Dim strSQLGroupBy As String     'GROUP BY clause.
    Dim strSQLPivot As String       'PIVOT clause.
    Dim strSQLIn As String          'IN predicate.

    'Create the basic FROM and WHERE clauses.
    strSQLFrom = "FROM " & tblGraphs("DataTable") & " "
    strSQLWhere = "WHERE Year = " & Chr$(34) & strYear & Chr$(34) & " "

    'Create the SELECT clauses for crosstab tables.
    If fIsCrosstab Then
        'Create the SELECT statement for the crosstab.
        strSQLSelect = "SELECT [" & tblGraphs("LegendField") & "] "

        'Define Access SQL crosstab clauses.
        strSQLTransform = "TRANSFORM Sum(" & tblGraphs("DataField") & ")
        ➥AS SumOfData "
        strSQLGroupBy = "GROUP BY [" & tblGraphs("LegendField") & "] "
        strSQLPivot = "PIVOT Month "

        'Create the IN predicate from the strMonths() array.
        strSQLIn = "IN ("
        For intCtr = 1 To 12
            strSQLIn = strSQLIn & Chr$(34) & strMonths(intCtr, 3) & Chr$(34)
            ➥& ", "
        Next intCtr
        strSQLIn = Left$(strSQLIn, Len(strSQLIn) - 2) & ")"

        'Concatenate the SQL clauses for the crosstab query.
        strCreateSQL = strSQLTransform & strSQLSelect & strSQLFrom &
        ➥strSQLWhere & strSQLGroupBy & strSQLPivot & strSQLIn & ";"
    ElseIf fIsHistogram Then
        'For histogram charts.
        strSQLSelect = "SELECT Year, Cycle, " & tblGraphs("DataField") & " "

        'Concatenate the SQL clauses for the SELECT query.
        strCreateSQL = strSQLSelect & strSQLFrom & strSQLWhere & ";"
    Else
        'For noncrosstab tables.
        'Create a conventional SELECT query statement.
        strSQLSelect = "SELECT Year, Month, " & tblGraphs("DataField") &
        ➥" AS SumOfData "
```

Coding the Application, Part 1

```
    'Concatenate the SQL clauses for the SELECT query.
    strCreateSQL = strSQLSelect & strSQLFrom & strSQLWhere & ";"
  End If
End Function
```

Setting and Disabling the Type Buttons

Depending on which of the graph class buttons is pressed, there are different numbers and different definitions for the graph type buttons. To handle this, every time a new graph class is selected, the SetInitialTypeButtons procedure is called to set the number and pop-up labels for the graph type buttons. The procedure first creates the graph code, and then locates the data for the graph in the tblDefinitions table. Next, the procedure stores a bookmark for the current position in tblDefinitions and disables all the graph type buttons. Starting at the current record in tblDefinitions, the code first searches backward, then forward, looking for more graphs of the same class as the selected one. Whenever the code finds a record for the same class, it sets the pop-up label for that button and enables the button. When complete, the code uses the bookmark to return to the same record that was selected when the procedure started, and ensures that the initial button is still pressed.

```
'
'Find the graph data and display the appropriate type buttons.
'
Sub SetInitialTypeButtons ()
   Dim strCode As String
   Dim intCtr As Integer   'Generic loop counter.
   Dim strBookmark As String
   Dim strClass As String
   Dim intType As Integer
   Dim intClass As Integer

   'Create the code that selects the chart to display.
   strCode = LTrim$(Str$(intGraphClass)) & LTrim$(Str$(intGraphType))

   'Load the graph description data for the new graph type.
   tblGraphs.Seek "=", strCode
   If tblGraphs.NoMatch Then
      'Should not occur; buttons for missing selections are disabled.
      MsgBox "Graph not available for this selection.", MB_ICONSTOP,
      ➥"Developer at Work"
      Exit Sub
   End If

   'Set a bookmark for the current record.
   strBookmark = tblGraphs.Bookmark

   'Turn all off, then turn on those that are needed.
   For intCtr = 1 To NUM_TYPE_BUTTONS
      frmMDIMain.gpbGraphType(intCtr).Enabled = False
   Next intCtr

   strClass = Left$(tblGraphs("Code"), 1)
   intClass = Val(strClass)
```

```
        'From the current record, search backward then forward in
        'the database to find all chart types of the selected class.

        'Search backward to enable buttons of the same class.
        Do While Left$(tblGraphs("Code"), 1) = strClass
          intType = Val(Right$(tblGraphs("Code"), 1))
          frmMDIMain.gpbGraphType(intType).Enabled = True
          'Set the text in the pop-up button labels.
           frmMDIMain.lblPopUpTypeLabels(intType).Caption =
          ➥tblGraphs("DropLabelText")
          tblGraphs.MovePrevious
          If tblGraphs.BOF Then
             Exit Do
          End If
        Loop
        'Return the current record.
        tblGraphs.Bookmark = strBookmark

        'Search forward to enable buttons of the same class.
        Do While Left$(tblGraphs("Code"), 1) = strClass
          intType = Val(Right$(tblGraphs("Code"), 1))
          frmMDIMain.gpbGraphType(intType).Enabled = True
          'Set the text in the pop-up button labels.
          frmMDIMain.lblPopUpTypeLabels(intType).Caption =
          ➥tblGraphs("DropLabelText")
          tblGraphs.MoveNext
          If tblGraphs.EOF Then
             Exit Do
          End If
        Loop

        'Return the current record.
        tblGraphs.Bookmark = strBookmark

        'Make sure the selected button is down.
        intType = Val(Right$(tblGraphs("Code"), 1))
        frmMDIMain.gpbGraphType(intType).Value = True
End Sub
```

Managing the Grid

Several procedures manipulate the grid. The grid is at the bottom of the frmMDIGraf form and is hidden initially. When the graph is created and filled with data, the grid is also filled with the same data, but it's hidden so that you see only the graph or the graph and a legend. When the user double-clicks on the graph, the grid is displayed and the graph is shrunk to fit.

The ClearGrid procedure clears a selected cell on the grid. When executed, it gets two arguments—the row number and the column number. These two numbers are used to locate the cell on the grid. Then an empty picture is stored in the cell to remove any existing picture in the background, and an empty text string is loaded into the Text property to clear it as well.

Coding the Application, Part 1

```
'
'Clear a cell on the grid.
'
Sub ClearGrid (intRow As Integer, intCol As Integer)

    'Select a cell.
    frmMDIGraph.grdMonthly.Row = intRow
    frmMDIGraph.grdMonthly.Col = intCol

    'Load an empty picture to clear the prior image.
    frmMDIGraph.grdMonthly.Picture = LoadPicture()
    frmMDIGraph.grdMonthly.Text = ""
End Sub
```

The `SetGridValues` procedure stores the contents of the selected database field into the control. The procedure first sums the current value if the table is a crosstab table. Next, it checks to see if this is the first row or a later row and formats the data accordingly. The procedure uses the `Units` field in the database to determine if the field is currency and needs a dollar sign or if it's some other unit. The first row in the grid is handled differently from the others in that a dollar sign precedes currency values and a percent sign follows percents. The other rows in the grid contain only numbers, not dollar and percent signs.

```
'
'Store the crosstab data in the grid and sum the rows and columns.
'
Sub SetGridValues (intField As Integer, intRow As Integer, intCol As Integer)
    'intField = field number in the database.
    'intRow = row number  on the grid.
    'intCol = column number on the grid.

    If fIsCrosstab Then
        'Sum only for crosstabs.
        varColTotals(intCol) = varColTotals(intCol) + ssGraph.Fields(intField)
        varRowTotals(intRow) = varRowTotals(intRow) + ssGraph.Fields(intField)
    End If

    'Format the data in accordance with the Units field.
    If intRow = 1 Then
        'First row has symbols determined by Definitions table.
        If tblGraphs("Units") = "$" Then
            frmMDIGraph.grdMonthly.Text = Format$(ssGraph.Fields(intField),
            ➥"$#,##0")
        ElseIf tblGraphs("Units") = "%" Then
            'Note: The percent format automatically multiplies by 100
            frmMDIGraph.grdMonthly.Text = Format$(ssGraph.Fields(intField),
            ➥"##0.0%")
        ElseIf tblGraphs("Units") = "Avg" Then
            frmMDIGraph.grdMonthly.Text = Format$(ssGraph.Fields(intField),
            ➥"#,##0.00")
        Else
            frmMDIGraph.grdMonthly.Text = Format$(ssGraph.Fields(intField),
            ➥"#,##0.00")
        End If
    Else
        'Remaining rows use standard formatting, except percents and averages.
```

```
        If tblGraphs("Units") = "%" Then
            'Provide right-alignment spacing for missing % symbol.
            frmMDIGraph.grdMonthly.Text = Format$(100 * ssGraph.Fields(intField),
            ➥"##0.0") & "    "
        ElseIf tblGraphs("Units") = "Avg" Then
            frmMDIGraph.grdMonthly.Text = Format$(ssGraph.Fields(intField),
            ➥"#,##0.00")
        Else
            frmMDIGraph.grdMonthly.Text = Format$(ssGraph.Fields(intField),
            ➥"#,##0.00")
        End If
    End If
End Sub
```

The ToggleGrid procedure changes the grid's Visible property from True to False or False to True, depending on its current value. It first tests to see if the grid is visible. If the grid is visible, the procedure toggles it hidden. If not, it toggles the grid visible. The procedure then calls the ResizeMonthAndGrid procedure to resize the graph to fill the whole form, or the graph and grid to share the form.

```
'
'Toggle the grid.
'
Sub ToggleGrid ()
    If fShowGrid Then
        fShowGrid = False
        frmMDIMain.mnuViewDetails.Checked = False
        frmMDIGraph.grdMonthly.Visible = False
    Else
        fShowGrid = True
        frmMDIMain.mnuViewDetails.Checked = True
        frmMDIGraph.grdMonthly.Visible = True
    End If
    'Resize the graph.
    Call ResizeChartAndGrid

End Sub
```

When all the data has been stored in the grid and totaled by the SetGridValues procedure, the SetGridCrossfoot procedure is called to write the totals across the bottom of the grid. This procedure first checks for a null value and replaces it in the grid with a blank since you don't want to count cells containing null values. The procedure then inserts data into the cells along the bottom and right edges of the grid and formats it according to the contents of the Units field in the database. If the field is of type Avg (average) or % (percent), the total is divided by the number of cells.

```
'
'Add the totals to the bottom of the grid.
'
Sub SetGridCrossfoot ()

    Dim intRow As Integer
    Dim intCol As Integer
    ReDim intNotNullRows(frmMDIGraph.chtMonthly.NumSets) As Integer
    ReDim intNotNullCols(frmMDIGraph.chtMonthly.NumPoints) As Integer
```

Day 8: Coding the Application, Part 1

```
        varColTotals(0) = 0

        'Count not-null ("") rows and columns for averaging.
        If tblGraphs("Units") = "%" Or tblGraphs("Units") = "Avg" Then
            For intRow = 1 To frmMDIGraph.chtMonthly.NumSets
                frmMDIGraph.grdMonthly.Row = intRow
                For intCol = 1 To frmMDIGraph.chtMonthly.NumPoints
                    frmMDIGraph.grdMonthly.Col = intCol + 1
                    If frmMDIGraph.grdMonthly.Text <> "" Then
                        intNotNullCols(intCol) = intNotNullCols(intCol) + 1
                        intNotNullRows(intRow) = intNotNullRows(intRow) + 1
                    End If
                Next intCol
            Next intRow
            'Since we must divide by this number, change any zeros to ones.
            For intRow = 1 To frmMDIGraph.chtMonthly.NumSets
                If intNotNullRows(intRow) = 0 Then
                    intNotNullRows(intRow) = 1
                End If
            Next intRow
            For intCol = 1 To frmMDIGraph.chtMonthly.NumPoints
                If intNotNullCols(intCol) = 0 Then
                    intNotNullCols(intCol) = 1
                End If
            Next intCol
        End If

        'Place column totals in last row of each column.
        frmMDIGraph.grdMonthly.Row = frmMDIGraph.grdMonthly.Rows - 1
        'Select last row.
        For intCol = 1 To frmMDIGraph.chtMonthly.NumPoints
            frmMDIGraph.grdMonthly.Col = intCol + 1    'Select column.
            Select Case tblGraphs("Units")
                Case "$"
                    frmMDIGraph.grdMonthly.Text = Format$(varColTotals(intCol),
                    ➥"$#,##0")
                Case "%"
                    frmMDIGraph.grdMonthly.Text = Format$(varColTotals(intCol) /
                    ➥intNotNullCols(intCol), "##0.0%")
                Case "Avg"
                    frmMDIGraph.grdMonthly.Text = Format$(varColTotals(intCol) /
                    ➥intNotNullCols(intCol), "##0.00")
                Case Else
                    frmMDIGraph.grdMonthly.Text = Format$(varColTotals(intCol),
                    ➥"#,##0.00")
            End Select
            varColTotals(0) = varColTotals(0) + varColTotals(intCol)
            'Total of all columns.
        Next intCol

        varRowTotals(0) = 0

        'Place row totals in last column of each row.
        frmMDIGraph.grdMonthly.Col = 14    'Select the last column.
        For intRow = 1 To frmMDIGraph.chtMonthly.NumSets
            frmMDIGraph.grdMonthly.Row = intRow    'Select a row.
            Select Case tblGraphs("Units")
                Case "$"
```

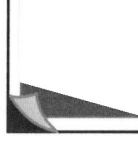

```
                    frmMDIGraph.grdMonthly.Text = Format$(varRowTotals(intRow),
                ➥"$#,##0")
            Case "%"
                frmMDIGraph.grdMonthly.Text = Format$(varRowTotals(intRow) /
                ➥intNotNullRows(intRow), "##0.0%")
            Case "Avg"
                frmMDIGraph.grdMonthly.Text = Format$(varRowTotals(intRow) /
                ➥intNotNullRows(intRow), "##0.00")
            Case Else
                frmMDIGraph.grdMonthly.Text = Format$(varRowTotals(intRow),
                ➥"#,##0.00")
        End Select
        varRowTotals(0) = varRowTotals(0) + (varRowTotals(intRow) /
        ➥frmMDIGraph.chtMonthly.NumSets)
    Next intRow

    'Select the last row.
    frmMDIGraph.grdMonthly.Row = frmMDIGraph.grdMonthly.Rows - 1

    'Use the arithmetic average for "%" and "Avg" values.
    If (tblGraphs("Units") = "%" Or tblGraphs("Units") = "Avg") Then
        varRowTotals(0) = varRowTotals(0) / frmMDIGraph.chtMonthly.NumPoints
        varColTotals(0) = varColTotals(0) / frmMDIGraph.chtMonthly.NumSets
        'Change the label to Averages
        frmMDIGraph.grdMonthly.Col = 1
        frmMDIGraph.grdMonthly.Text = "Averages"
    End If

    'Add crossfoot values to grid.
    'This is in the last column of the last row.
    frmMDIGraph.grdMonthly.Col = 14
    Select Case tblGraphs("Units")
        Case "$"
            frmMDIGraph.grdMonthly.Text = Format$(varRowTotals(0), "$#,##0")
        Case "%"
            frmMDIGraph.grdMonthly.Text = Format$(varRowTotals(0), "##0.0%")
        Case "Avg"
            frmMDIGraph.grdMonthly.Text = Format$(varRowTotals(0), "##0.00")
        Case Else
            frmMDIGraph.grdMonthly.Text = Format$(varRowTotals(0), "#,##0.00")
    End Select
    Exit Sub
End Sub
```

The SetColWidths procedure is called after the grid is filled with data to set the widths of the columns. Crosstab and histogram tables use the fixed column width stored in the global constant GRID_COL_WIDTH. The first-level total or average tables initially used a variable column width determined by dividing the width of the form by 12. However, that proved too small for some of the values to be displayed properly, so it was expanded to the same fixed width as the other type graphs. Note that the code to produce the variable widths is commented out. After the whole grid has been adjusted, the first two columns of a crosstab are readjusted. The first column is changed to a square to hold the color picture corresponding to the graph color, and the first column is enlarged to hold the description using the width in the global constant GRID1_COL_WIDTH.

Coding the Application, Part 1

```
'Set the column widths of the grid for numeric data.
'
Sub SetColWidths ()
    Dim intCtr As Integer   'Generic loop counter.
    For intCtr = 0 To frmMDIGraph.grdMonthly.Cols - 1
        If fIsCrosstab Then
            'Use fixed column widths for crosstabs.
            frmMDIGraph.grdMonthly.ColWidth(intCtr) = GRID_COL_WIDTH
        ElseIf fIsHistogram Then
            'Use fixed widths for the histogram.
            frmMDIGraph.grdMonthly.ColWidth(intCtr) = GRID_COL_WIDTH
        Else
            'Use fixed widths.
            frmMDIGraph.grdMonthly.ColWidth(intCtr) = GRID_COL_WIDTH
        End If
    Next intCtr
    If fIsCrosstab Then
        'Fix the first two column widths.
        frmMDIGraph.grdMonthly.ColWidth(0) = frmMDIGraph.grdMonthly.RowHeight(0)
        frmMDIGraph.grdMonthly.ColWidth(1) = GRID1_COL_WIDTH
    End If
End Sub
```

The FillLegendArrays procedure is called to load the global legend arrays strLegendText() and strLegend() with labels for the legend and the second column of the grid. The legend arrays apply only to crosstab charts, so the procedure is skipped if this isn't a crosstab chart. Each crosstab chart has two sets of text strings that describe the categories of data being displayed—a short string for the graph legend and a longer string for the grid. The table and field holding the strings are identified for each crosstab table in the tblDefinitions table. These names are used to query the database and create a snapshot containing the needed strings.

Some category description tables contain more descriptions than are actually in use to allow for easy expansion of the database in the future. For example, the Sales Region category of data contains descriptions of regions that cover most of the world, even though the company hasn't yet expanded into all of them. To eliminate categories that aren't in use yet, the tblDefinitions table contains a UseActivated field to indicate which tables have extra categories of data, and the description tables themselves contain an Activated field to indicate if a field is active or not. Inactive fields are then skipped.

```
'
'Fill the Legends and LegendText arrays from the database.
'
Sub FillLegendArrays ()
    'Put the grid legend labels in the strLegendText() array.
    'Put the graph legend labels in the strLegend() array.

    'Skip if this is not a crosstab table.
    If Not fIsCrosstab Then
        Exit Sub
    End If
    'Create the legends from the appropriate table.
```

```
    Set ssLegend = dbGraphs.CreateSnapshot(tblGraphs("LegendTable"))
    ssLegend.MoveFirst
    intLegendSets = 0    'Zero the set counter.
    Do Until ssLegend.EOF
        'Create a list of quoted, comma-separated strings.
        If tblGraphs("UseActivated") Then
            'Test if category is presently active.
            If ssLegend("Activated") Then
                'Add the category to the arrays.
                intLegendSets = intLegendSets + 1
                strLegendText(intLegendSets) =
                ➥ssLegend(tblGraphs("LegendTextField"))
                strLegend(intLegendSets) = ssLegend(tblGraphs("LegendField"))
            End If
        Else
            'Add all categories to the arrays.
            intLegendSets = intLegendSets + 1
            strLegendText(intLegendSets) = ssLegend(tblGraphs("LegendTextField"))
            strLegend(intLegendSets) = ssLegend(tblGraphs("LegendField"))
        End If
        ssLegend.MoveNext
    Loop
End Sub
```

Once the label arrays have been loaded, one of the two following procedures is called to insert the labels into the grid. The GridColHeaders procedure applies to the first-level total and average graphs and the histogram graph. Both of these graphs contain a single data series, so the grid contains only two rows. The first row contains the labels identifying the data, and the second contains the data. GridColHeaders inserts data in the first row of the grid. The following GridRowColHeaders procedure is for crosstab tables. Crosstab tables have multiple sets of data plotted, each with a different color. The grid is then set up with multiple rows, one for each data set, with a colored picture in the first column that matches the color used in the graph, a text description in the second, and a row of column labels across the top. In all cases, the rows and columns containing the labels are marked as fixed so that they don't scroll as you scroll the data on the grid.

The GridColHeaders procedure first checks to see if the data is from a histogram or a level 1 total or average graph. It then sets up the grid depending on the data type by setting the number of columns, the number of fixed rows and columns, and the alignment. The procedure then inserts the data from the label array.

The GridColRowHeaders procedure does substantially the same thing, except that it also inserts the pictures in the first column and the descriptions of the data sets in the second. The form has a set of colored squares that are picture boxes containing a single color. These boxes are copied into the background of the first column of the grid. The second column gets the descriptions of the items from the label arrays and inserts them into the array. The top row of the array contains the same things as the level 1 graphs—namely, the month names.

DAY 8
Coding the Application, Part 1

```
'Label the grid column headers for monthly total
'and histogram type grids.
'
Sub GridColHeaders ()
   Dim intCtr As Integer   'Generic loop counter.

   If fIsHistogram Then
      'Set no fixed column, one fixed row.
      frmMDIGraph.grdMonthly.FixedCols = 0
      frmMDIGraph.grdMonthly.FixedRows = 1
      frmMDIGraph.grdMonthly.Cols = ssGraph.RecordCount

      'Clear the prior picture and text from the grid.
      Call ClearGrid(0, 0)

      'Select the first row of the grid for the column headers.
      frmMDIGraph.grdMonthly.Row = 0
      'Set the remaining column headers.
      For intCtr = 1 To frmMDIGraph.grdMonthly.Cols
      'Set the alignment for nonfixed cells.
      frmMDIGraph.grdMonthly.ColAlignment(intCtr - 1) = GRID_ALIGNLEFT
      'Set the alignment for fixed cells.
      frmMDIGraph.grdMonthly.FixedAlignment(intCtr - 1) = GRID_ALIGNCENTER
   Next intCtr

   Else

      'Set 12 columns, no fixed column, one fixed row.
      frmMDIGraph.grdMonthly.FixedCols = 0
      frmMDIGraph.grdMonthly.FixedRows = 1
      frmMDIGraph.grdMonthly.Cols = 12

      'Clear the prior picture and text from the grid.
      Call ClearGrid(0, 0)

      'Select the first row of the grid for the column headers.
      frmMDIGraph.grdMonthly.Row = 0
      'Set the remaining column headers.
      For intCtr = 1 To 12
         'Set the alignment for nonfixed cells.
         frmMDIGraph.grdMonthly.ColAlignment(intCtr - 1) = GRID_ALIGNLEFT
         'Set the alignment for fixed cells.
         frmMDIGraph.grdMonthly.FixedAlignment(intCtr - 1) = GRID_ALIGNCENTER
         'Select a column.
         frmMDIGraph.grdMonthly.Col = intCtr - 1
         'Add the month abbreviations.
         frmMDIGraph.grdMonthly.Text = strMonths(intCtr, 1)
      Next intCtr
   End If
End Sub

'
'Insert the column headers into the Grid control.
'
Sub GridColRowHeaders ()
   Dim intCtr As Integer   'Generic loop counter.
```

```
        frmMDIGraph.grdMonthly.Cols = 15        'Fifteen columns.
        frmMDIGraph.grdMonthly.FixedCols = 2    'Two fixed columns.
        frmMDIGraph.grdMonthly.FixedRows = 1    'One fixed row.
        'Alignment for first fixed column.
        frmMDIGraph.grdMonthly.FixedAlignment(0) = GRID_ALIGNLEFT
        'Alignment for second fixed column.
        frmMDIGraph.grdMonthly.FixedAlignment(1) = GRID_ALIGNLEFT

        'Select the first row of the grid for the column headers.
        frmMDIGraph.grdMonthly.Row = 0
        'Set the alignment and insert labels in the column headers.
        For intCtr = 2 To 14
           frmMDIGraph.grdMonthly.Col = intCtr   'Select a column.
           'Set the alignment if the column is not fixed.
           frmMDIGraph.grdMonthly.ColAlignment(intCtr) = GRID_ALIGNRIGHT
           'Set the alignment if the column is fixed.
           frmMDIGraph.grdMonthly.FixedAlignment(intCtr) = GRID_ALIGNCENTER
           'Insert month names in columns 2 through 13 and totals in 14.
           If intCtr < 14 Then
              frmMDIGraph.grdMonthly.Text = strMonths(intCtr - 1, 1)
           Else
              frmMDIGraph.grdMonthly.Text = "Totals"
           End If
        Next intCtr

        'Insert pictures in the first column of the grid.
        frmMDIGraph.grdMonthly.Col = 0  'Select the first column.
        For intCtr = 0 To frmMDIGraph.grdMonthly.Rows - 2
           frmMDIGraph.grdMonthly.Row = intCtr   'Select the row.
           'Insert the picture (colored square).
           frmMDIGraph.grdMonthly.Picture = frmMDIGraph.imgColor(intCtr)
        Next intCtr
        'Select the last row.
        frmMDIGraph.grdMonthly.Row = frmMDIGraph.grdMonthly.Rows - 1
        'Insert a sigma in the last row.
        frmMDIGraph.grdMonthly.Picture = frmMDIGraph.imgColor(11)

        'Insert labels in the second column of the grid.
        'Problem here: the labels in the label array are not coordinated
        'with the labels in the data returned by the SQL statement.
        frmMDIGraph.grdMonthly.Col = 1  'Select the second column.
        For intCtr = 1 To frmMDIGraph.grdMonthly.Rows - 2
           frmMDIGraph.grdMonthly.Row = intCtr   'Select the row.
           'Insert the legend from the legend array.
           frmMDIGraph.grdMonthly.Text = strLegendText(intCtr)
        Next intCtr
        'In the first row, insert the table Type.
        frmMDIGraph.grdMonthly.Row = 0
        frmMDIGraph.grdMonthly.Text = tblGraphs("GridRowHeader")
        'In the last row, insert "Monthly Totals".
        frmMDIGraph.grdMonthly.Row = frmMDIGraph.grdMonthly.Rows - 1
        frmMDIGraph.grdMonthly.Text = "Monthly Totals"
End Sub
```

Coding the Application, Part 1

Adding a Legend

For crosstab tables, when the grid isn't showing at the bottom of the screen, a chart legend is shown in its place. The legend consists of the colored pictures and the text labels. Each colored picture is matched to a color on the graph, and a label is placed next to it to explain what you're seeing.

```
'
'Add a legend to the bottom of the form with color tabs
'that match the colors on the chart.
'
Sub AddLegends ()

    Dim strText As String
    Dim intWidth As Integer
    Dim intMargin As Integer
    Dim intCtr As Integer

    intMargin = (frmMDIGraph.ScaleWidth / (frmMDIGraph.chtMonthly.NumSets * 2))
➥- 300
    For intCtr = 1 To frmMDIGraph.chtMonthly.NumSets
        'Legend color keys
        frmMDIGraph.imgColor(intCtr).Width = 240
        frmMDIGraph.imgColor(intCtr).Height = 250
        frmMDIGraph.imgColor(intCtr).Top = frmMDIGraph.ScaleHeight - 365
        frmMDIGraph.imgColor(intCtr).Left = intMargin + (frmMDIGraph.ScaleWidth -
➥intMargin) * (intCtr - 1) / frmMDIGraph.chtMonthly.NumSets
        frmMDIGraph.imgColor(intCtr).Visible = True

        'Legend labels
        frmMDIGraph.lblLegend(intCtr).Width = GRID_LEGEND_LABEL_WIDTH
        frmMDIGraph.lblLegend(intCtr).Top = frmMDIGraph.ScaleHeight -
➥GRID_LEGEND_LABEL_OFFSET
        frmMDIGraph.lblLegend(intCtr).Left = frmMDIGraph.imgColor(intCtr).Left +
➥GRID_LEGEND_LABEL_OFFSET
        If InStr(strLegend(intCtr), "&") > 0 Then
            'Use a && to prevent underlining with & character in captions.
            strText = strLegend(intCtr)
            If InStr(strText, "&") = 1 Then
                strText = "&" & strText
            ElseIf InStr(strText, "&") = Len(strText) Then
                strText = strText & "&"
            Else
                strText = Left$(strText, InStr(strText, "&") - 1) & "&" &
➥Mid$(strText, InStr(strText, "&"))
            End If
            frmMDIGraph.lblLegend(intCtr).Caption = strText
        Else
            frmMDIGraph.lblLegend(intCtr).Caption = strLegend(intCtr)
        End If
        frmMDIGraph.lblLegend(intCtr).Visible = True
    Next intCtr
End Sub
```

Selecting a Month for the Pie Chart

As shown in Figure 5.18, when you double-click on one of the month labels on a crosstab chart, you want to see a pie chart with a single month's data in it. The graph control doesn't have a hot spot on the month labels, so use the techniques of Day 7 to add a hot spot to the grid. The chtMonthly_DblClick event procedure is executed whenever you double-click anywhere on a chart. To see where you are, a MouseDown event procedure is executed automatically first. The MouseDown event gets the location of the mouse when the event occurred. That data is saved in the global variables sngMouseX and sngMouseY. When the chtMonthly_DblClick procedure is executed, it gets the mouse location from the global variables and compares that location to the location of the chart labels. Through experimentation, the chart labels were found to be between 0.89 and 0.94 of the height of the chart. If the y location of the MouseDown event is between these extremes, the particular month is determined. The intTestDblClickMonth function determines the selected month by examining the x location of the MouseDown event.

When the selected month is known, the procedure selects the column on the grid for the same month and triggers the DblClick event on the grid.

```
'
'Display the grid when the chart is double-clicked.
'
Sub chtMonthly_DblClick ()
   Dim intMonth As Integer
   'The double-click event does not return the location of the mouse,
   'so that data is supplied by the MouseDown procedure.
   intMonth = 0
   'Test vertical position of mouse on double-click.
   If sngMouseY >= .89 * frmMDIGraph.chtMonthly.Height Then
      'Mouse is below abscissa axis.
      If sngMouseY <= .94 * frmMDIGraph.chtMonthly.Height Then
         'Mouse is above bottom of labels.
         intMonth = intTestDblClickMonth(sngMouseX, sngMouseY)
      End If
   End If

   If intMonth > 0 Then
      'Select the column corresponding to the month number.
      If fIsCrosstab Then
         frmMDIGraph.grdMonthly.SelStartCol = intMonth + 1
      Else
         frmMDIGraph.grdMonthly.SelStartCol = intMonth - 1
      End If
      frmMDIGraph.grdMonthly.SelStartRow = 1
      frmMDIGraph.grdMonthly.SelEndRow = frmMDIGraph.grdMonthly.Rows - 1

      'Call the event handler for the double-click on the grid.
      Call grdMonthly_DblClick
   Else
      'Toggle the grid if double-click occurs elsewhere.
      Call ToggleGrid
   End If
   fInhibitResize = False
End Sub
```

Coding the Application, Part 1

```
'Capture the mouse location when the user clicks
'the left button on the chart. This works with the
'double-click event to select the drill-down chart.
'
Sub chtMonthly_MouseDown (intButton As Integer, intShift As Integer,
↪sngX As Single, sngY As Single)
    If intButton = LEFT_BUTTON Then
        'Left mouse button clicked.
        sngMouseX = sngX
        sngMouseY = sngY
    Else
        sngMouseX = 0
        sngMouseY = 0
    End If
End Sub
```

DrawPieChart is actually called from the grdMonthly_DblClick event procedure, even if the grid is hidden. If the month label on the graph is double-clicked, the column for that month on the grid is selected and the grdMonthly_DblClick procedure is executed. If the grid is visible and a column is double-clicked, this procedure is also executed. The procedure itself is relatively simple. It checks to make sure a column was double-clicked and then hides everything and calls DrawPieChart. After the pie chart is drawn, the procedure makes sure that the pie chart is visible.

```
'Detect a double-click on the grid and display
'a pie chart with the detail data for that month.
'
Sub grdMonthly_DblClick ()
    If fIsCrosstab And grdMonthly.SelStartCol > 1 Then
        'Month column double-clicked.
        'You could also check here to see if a row is selected instead
        'of a column, and present individual product categories.
        'Hide all the charts and grids.
        Call HideEverything
        'Draw the pie chart.
        Call DrawPieChart
        'Display the pie chart.
        frmMDIGraph.chtPieChart.Visible = True
    End If
End Sub
```

The intTestDblClickMonth function procedure determines what month was clicked on. The numbers used in this procedure were determined experimentally by clicking on the form and comparing the position to the width of the form. The month is determined by trimming off the scale on the left side of the graph and dividing the remainder of the graph by 12. Each of the 12 regions just created corresponds to a month label, and the region clicked on determines what month the function procedure returns.

```
'Calculate the month number from the x position of the
'mouse. This procedure is called by a double click
'on chtMonthly. The mouse location is captured by the
'MouseDown event on the chart.
```

```
Function intTestDblClickMonth (sngMouseX As Single, sngMouseY As Single)
➥As Integer

    Dim intActiveWidth As Integer  'Width of ordinate in twips
    Dim intStartX As Integer        'Position at left edge of "Jan"

    'Left edge of Jan is at 14% of the chart width
    intStartX = .14 * frmMDIGraph.chtMonthly.Width

    If sngMouseX >= intStartX Then
        'Set width of ordinate, right edge is at 86% of width
        intActiveWidth = .965 * (.86 * frmMDIGraph.chtMonthly.Width)
        '(The .965 is a trimming scaling factor)

        'Determine month corresponding to mouse X coordinate
        intTestDblClickMonth = Int((sngMouseX - intStartX) / (intActiveWidth /
        ➥12)) + 1
    End If
End Function
```

Drawing the Pie Chart

The procedure to draw the pie chart is much simpler than the one to draw the main chart. The setup is much the same, but since there's only one type of chart to create, the procedure doesn't need to continually test for the chart type. The data for the chart is available in the graph and grid controls, so you don't have to extract it from the database.

As with the description of `DrawChartAndGrid`, I've broken down this procedure by code block, with an explanation preceding each block. The first block clears any previous data and then sets the properties of the pie chart control, using global constants to set the values.

```
'Draw a pie chart with the data for the selected
'month of a crosstab chart.

Sub DrawPieChart ()

    Dim dblTotal As Double
    Dim intPoints As Integer
    Dim intPoint As Integer
    Dim intCtr As Integer   'Generic loop counter.

    'Clear the prior chart.
    frmMDIGraph.chtPieChart.DrawMode = G_CLEAR

    'Set the size of the window if normal state.
    Call ResizeChartAndGrid

    'Set the captions.
    frmMDIGraph.Caption = tblGraphs("GraphCaption") & " for " & strYear & " - "
    ➥& strMonths(frmMDIGraph.grdMonthly.SelStartCol - 1, 2)
    frmMDIGraph.chtPieChart.AutoInc = G_OFF

    'Set font and graph characteristics
```

Coding the Application, Part 1

```
frmMDIGraph.chtPieChart.FontUse = G_ALL_TEXT
frmMDIGraph.chtPieChart.FontFamily = G_SWISS
frmMDIGraph.chtPieChart.FontStyle = G_BOLD
frmMDIGraph.chtPieChart.GraphStyle = G_DEFAULT
```

The next block reads the data from the chart control for the selected month and calculates the total for the month. It does this by setting the ThisPoint property to the number of the selected month and then looping over the data sets. The block loops over the data again and counts the number of values that are greater than one percent of the total and sets the number of points in the pie chart to the total. You do this so that you won't try to plot any small or zero values on a pie chart.

```
frmMDIGraph.chtMonthly.ThisPoint = frmMDIGraph.grdMonthly.SelStartCol - 1

'Get the total of the set.
For intCtr = 1 To frmMDIGraph.chtMonthly.NumSets
   frmMDIGraph.chtMonthly.ThisSet = intCtr
   dblTotal = dblTotal + frmMDIGraph.chtMonthly.GraphData
Next intCtr

'Get the number of points greater than 1% of total.
For intCtr = 1 To frmMDIGraph.chtMonthly.NumSets
   frmMDIGraph.chtMonthly.ThisSet = intCtr
   If frmMDIGraph.chtMonthly.GraphData > .01 * dblTotal Then
      intPoints = intPoints + 1
   End If
Next intCtr
frmMDIGraph.chtPieChart.NumPoints = intPoints
```

The next block loops over the data a third time, this time copying the data values greater than one percent of the total from the graph into the pie chart. In addition, the wedge is imploded and its caption is created by copying the caption from the grid control and then appending the value. The value is formatted according to the Units field in the tblDefinitions table.

```
'Reset all the data, then set the data.
frmMDIGraph.chtPieChart.DataReset = G_ALL_DATA
intPoint = 1
For intCtr = 1 To frmMDIGraph.chtMonthly.NumSets
   'Set the data point of the originating graph.
   frmMDIGraph.chtMonthly.ThisSet = intCtr

   'Don't display data for 0-value items.
   If frmMDIGraph.chtMonthly.GraphData > .01 * dblTotal Then
      'Set the data point of the pie chart.
      frmMDIGraph.chtPieChart.ThisPoint = intPoint
      frmMDIGraph.chtPieChart.GraphData = frmMDIGraph.chtMonthly.GraphData

      'Implode any exploded pie wedges.
      frmMDIGraph.chtPieChart.ExtraData = G_NOT_EXPLODED

      'Set the grid column and row for the label.
      frmMDIGraph.grdMonthly.Col = 1
      frmMDIGraph.grdMonthly.Row = intCtr
      'Save the ID field for the drill-down grid.
      strDDID(intPoint) = strLegend(intCtr)
```

```
            If tblGraphs("Units") = "$" Then
               frmMDIGraph.chtPieChart.LabelText = frmMDIGraph.grdMonthly.Text & _
               ➥" - " & Format(frmMDIGraph.chtMonthly.GraphData, "$#,##0")
            ElseIf tblGraphs("Units") = "%" Then
               frmMDIGraph.chtPieChart.LabelText = frmMDIGraph.grdMonthly.Text & _
               ➥" - " & Format(frmMDIGraph.chtMonthly.GraphData, "#0.##%")
            Else
               frmMDIGraph.chtPieChart.LabelText = frmMDIGraph.grdMonthly.Text & _
               ➥" - " & Format(frmMDIGraph.chtMonthly.GraphData, "#0.##")
            End If
            intPoint = intPoint + 1
        End If
    Next intCtr
```

The last block draws the chart and then stores a copy of the labels for use with the drill-down grid.

```
    DoEvents    'Let all above occur before showing form.

    'Draw the chart.
    frmMDIGraph.chtPieChart.DrawMode = G_DRAW


    'Fill the labels array (global) for the drill-down grid.
    ReDim strLabels(frmMDIGraph.chtPieChart.NumPoints)
    For intCtr = 1 To frmMDIGraph.chtPieChart.NumPoints
        frmMDIGraph.chtPieChart.ThisPoint = intCtr
        strLabels(intCtr) = frmMDIGraph.chtPieChart.LabelText
    Next intCtr

    'Save the position of the left margin of the chart (global).
    intPieChartLeft = frmMDIGraph.chtPieChart.Left
End Sub
```

Hiding Everything

The HideEverything procedure hides all the controls, including the main graph, the pie chart, and the grid. The controls are hidden while they are being updated to speed the update and to not confuse the user with partially drawn graphs.

```
'
'Hide all the charts and legends.
'
Sub HideEverything ()
    Dim intCtr As Integer    'Generic loop counter.

    'Hide the charts.
    frmMDIGraph.chtMonthly.Visible = False
    frmMDIGraph.chtPieChart.Visible = False

    'Hide the grid.
    frmMDIGraph.grdMonthly.Visible = False

    'Hide the legend pictures and labels.
    For intCtr = 1 To 9
        frmMDIGraph.lblLegend(intCtr).Visible = False
```

Coding the Application, Part 1

```
    Next intCtr
    For intCtr = 0 To 11
        frmMDIGraph.imgColor(intCtr).Visible = False
    Next intCtr
    DoEvents
End Sub
```

Positioning the Graph and Grid

The graph and grid are repositioned on the form whenever the graph changes. When the grid is displayed, the graph must be shrunk to fit. When the grid is hidden, the graph is enlarged to cover its position. The procedures that control all this positioning are `SetGraphPosition`, `SetGridPosition`, and `ResizeChartAndGrid`.

The `SetGraphPosition` procedure sets the position of the main graph. Everything is scaled to the width and height of the `chtMonthly` form. The graph is first positioned at the top of the form with its width set to be 10 percent larger than the form and its left edge shifted left by five percent. This results in a graph that better fills the form. The procedure next checks to see if the grid is visible and makes room for it if it is. If the grid isn't visible, the height is adjusted to make room for a legend at the bottom of a crosstab table or adjusted clear to the bottom for a level 1 graph.

```
'
'Position the graph on the form.
'
Sub SetGraphPosition ()
    'Set the top-left corner.
    frmMDIGraph.chtMonthly.Top = 0
    frmMDIGraph.chtMonthly.Left = -.05 * frmMDIGraph.ScaleWidth

    'Set the width.
    frmMDIGraph.chtMonthly.Width = 1.1 * frmMDIGraph.ScaleWidth

    'Set the height.
    'If the grid is visible, shrink the graph to fit.
    If fShowGrid Then
        frmMDIGraph.chtMonthly.Height = frmMDIGraph.ScaleHeight -
        ➥frmMDIGraph.grdMonthly.Height - 1.2 * GRID_BORDER
    Else
        'If the grid isn't visible, add a legend for crosstab tables.
        If fIsCrosstab Then
          frmMDIGraph.chtMonthly.Height = frmMDIGraph.ScaleHeight - LEGEND_HEIGHT
            ➥- 2 * GRID_BORDER
            'Add color keys and legends to the graph
            Call AddLegends
        Else
            frmMDIGraph.chtMonthly.Height = frmMDIGraph.ScaleHeight
        End If
    End If
    DoEvents
End Sub
```

The `SetGridPosition` procedure inserts the grid at the bottom of the form. The width of the grid is adjusted to within 100 twips of the edge of the form and the height is set for three or fewer

visible rows. If the grid has more than three rows, only three are visible, and the user can scroll to see the other parts of the grid.

```
'
'Position the grid on the form.
'
Sub SetGridPosition ()

    'Provide a 100-twip border all around.
    frmMDIGraph.grdMonthly.Width = frmMDIGraph.ScaleWidth - 2 * GRID_BORDER
    frmMDIGraph.grdMonthly.Left = GRID_BORDER

    'Determine the number of grid rows to display
    If frmMDIMain.WindowState = MAXIMIZED Or frmMDIGraph.grdMonthly.Rows < 4
    ➥Then
        'If the window is maximized or grid is 3 rows or less, display all rows.
        frmMDIGraph.grdMonthly.Height = (frmMDIGraph.grdMonthly.RowHeight(0) +
        ➥15) * frmMDIGraph.grdMonthly.Rows
    Else
        'Display only 3 rows of grid
        frmMDIGraph.grdMonthly.Height = (frmMDIGraph.grdMonthly.RowHeight(0) +
        ➥15) * 3
    End If

    frmMDIGraph.grdMonthly.Top = frmMDIGraph.ScaleHeight -
    ➥frmMDIGraph.grdMonthly.Height - GRID_BORDER
    DoEvents
End Sub
```

The `ResizeChartAndGrid` procedure resizes just about everything on the form. It first sets a flag to prevent recursion. This procedure changes the size of things, which would cause a resize event, which would cause this procedure to be executed again. The flag prevents that from happening. The procedure then resizes `frmMDIGraph` to fill the active area of the MDI parent form. It then calls `SetGridPosition` to resize the grid, then `SetGraphPosition` to adjust the graph. Finally, it resizes the banner and the pie chart.

```
'
'Resize and redraw the existing chart.
'
Sub ResizeChartAndGrid ()
    'Note: This function is recursive without the flag.

    Dim intLeft As Integer   'Left distance from client edge.

    'Prevent recursion and don't try to change an icon's size.
    If fInhibitResize Or frmMDIMain.WindowState = MINIMIZED Then
        Exit Sub
    End If

    fInhibitResize = True   'Prevent recursion.

    'Resize the graph form to fit the full window on the main form.
    If frmMDIGraph.WindowState = NORMAL Then
        'Window is in normal mode, so resizing is valid.
        frmMDIGraph.Top = 0
        frmMDIGraph.Left = 0
```

Day 8: Coding the Application, Part 1

```
        frmMDIGraph.Width = frmMDIMain.ScaleWidth
        frmMDIGraph.Height = frmMDIMain.ScaleHeight
    End If

    DoEvents    'Give the window a chance to change size.


    'Scale the grid.
    Call SetGridPosition

    'Set the widths of the grid columns.
    Call SetColWidths

    'Scale the graph.
    Call SetGraphPosition

    'Set the size of the banner to just fill the screen.
    frmMDIGraph.picBanner.Width = frmMDIGraph.ScaleWidth
    frmMDIGraph.picBanner.Top = 0
    frmMDIGraph.picBanner.Left = 0
    frmMDIGraph.picBanner.Height = frmMDIGraph.ScaleHeight


    'Resize pie chart.
    frmMDIGraph.chtPieChart.Width = 1.2 * frmMDIGraph.Width
    frmMDIGraph.chtPieChart.Left = -(frmMDIGraph.chtPieChart.Width - 
    ➥frmMDIGraph.Width) / 2
    frmMDIGraph.chtPieChart.Height = 1.2 * frmMDIGraph.Height
    frmMDIGraph.chtPieChart.Top = -(frmMDIGraph.chtPieChart.Height - 
    ➥frmMDIGraph.Height) / 2

    'Reset the recursion flag.
    fInhibitResize = False
    DoEvents
End Sub
```

Summary

This completes the first day's coding. So far, most of the main procedures are coded, leaving several minor procedures, the drill-down grid, and the printing procedures for tomorrow. In addition, we will consider Modification Notes and Debugging the Process tomorrow, after the project is completely coded.

The files for today's work are in the \DCNSPT1 directory on the included CD.

Coding the Application, Part 2

Day 9

Coding the Application, Part 2

Yesterday you learned about good programming practice and programmed the main procedures in the decision support application. Today you continue with the decision support application, coding the drill-down data and printing the charts.

Today you will

- ☐ learn to fill the drill-down grid
- ☐ learn to use the common dialogs to print and save a chart

The Decision Support Application Project

We continue now with the decision support application, exploding a pie wedge to select the data to display on the drill-down grid.

Note: You might want to refer back to the figures in Day 5 when reading this chapter.

Exploding a Pie Wedge

As shown in Figure 5.20, when a pie chart is visible, you can drill down to the information that makes up one of the wedges by double-clicking on it, or, as shown in Figure 5.19, double-click outside of the pie chart to go back to the previous chart. Since the Graph control doesn't have hot spots on the pie wedges, use the methods from the section in Day 7 titled "Adding Hot Spots to Controls" to add hot spots to the wedges. The DblClick event on the pie chart doesn't return the location of the point where you double-clicked. To get this information, place code to save the mouse location in the chart's MouseUp or MouseDown event procedures, and then process that information in the DblClick procedure.

MouseUp or *MouseDown*?

Both the MouseUp and MouseDown event procedures are executed before the DblClick event, so you could use either of them to save the mouse location. It's common practice to execute a clicked-on command when you release the mouse button, which is why we use the MouseUp procedure here, although either will work.

The chtPieChart_MouseUp procedure watches for clicks on the pie chart. If the click was done with the left mouse button, the procedure saves the location of the mouse click in two global variables.

```
'Save the coordinates of a mouse click.
'
Sub chtPieChart_MouseUp (intButton As Integer, intShift As Integer,
➥sngX As Single, sngY As Single)
   If intButton = LEFT_BUTTON Then
      sngMouseX = sngX
      sngMouseY = sngY
   Else
      sngMouseX = 0
      sngMouseY = 0
   End If

End Sub
```

The double-click event on a pie chart finishes the work started by the MouseUp event. The procedure first calls the intPieHotHit() function to see if a pie wedge was clicked on and to return the number of the wedge. If intPieHotHit returns a 0, the double click was outside the pie chart and the user wants to restore the previous chart. If a pie wedge was hit, the procedure explodes that wedge and removes the labels and label lines from the other wedges. Next, the procedure tests the wedge angle and shifts the pie chart left or right, depending on which side the label is on, and displays the drill-down options form as a modal form. A modal form must be closed before a program can continue. The drill-down options form allows the user to select the type of data to display.

When the drill-down options form returns, the procedure unloads the form and checks its return value. If the returned value is IDCANCEL, the procedure redisplays the pie chart. If it returns IDOK, the procedure calls DisplayDDData to fill the drill-down grid and display it.

```
'
'Detect a double click on a pie segment.
'
Sub chtPieChart_DblClick ()

   Dim intCtr As Integer     'Generic counter.
   Dim intHotHit As Integer  'The number of the selected wedge.
                             'A 0 indicates no wedge selected.
   intHotHit = intPieHotHit(CInt(sngMouseX), CInt(sngMouseY))

   If intHotHit = 0 Then
      'An area outside the pie chart was double-clicked.
      'Redisplay the previous chart.
      frmMDIGraph.chtMonthly.Visible = True
      frmMDIGraph.chtPieChart.Visible = False
      If fShowGrid Then
         frmMDIGraph.grdMonthly.Visible = True
      End If
      DoEvents
   Else
```

Day 9: Coding the Application, Part 2

```
            'An area inside the pie chart was double-clicked.
            'Loop to explode selected wedge and implode the others.
            'Remove the labels of the imploded wedges
            For intCtr = 1 To frmMDIGraph.chtPieChart.NumPoints
                frmMDIGraph.chtPieChart.ThisPoint = intCtr
                If intCtr = intHotHit Then
                    frmMDIGraph.chtPieChart.ExtraData = G_EXPLODED
                    frmMDIGraph.chtPieChart.LabelText = strLabels(intCtr)
                Else
                    frmMDIGraph.chtPieChart.ExtraData = G_NOT_EXPLODED
                    frmMDIGraph.chtPieChart.LabelText = ""
                End If
            Next intCtr
            DoEvents

            'Remove the label lines from the pie chart.
            frmMDIGraph.chtPieChart.GraphStyle = G_NO_LINES

            'Redraw the chart with the exploded wedge.
            frmMDIGraph.chtPieChart.DrawMode = G_DRAW
            DoEvents

            'Shift the pie chart left or right to
            'make room for the drill-down options.
            If intWedgeAngle <= 180 Then
                'Shift the chart to the right (the pie chart is larger than the form).
                frmMDIGraph.chtPieChart.Left = 0
            Else
                'Shift the chart to the left.
                frmMDIGraph.chtPieChart.Left = frmMDIGraph.Width - _
                    frmMDIGraph.chtPieChart.Width
            End If

            'Display the drill-down options form as a
            'modal form and wait for it to return.
            frmDrillOptions.Show MODAL

            'Unload the form instead of just hiding it to cause the form_load
            'event to occur whenever the form is made visible.
            Unload frmDrillOptions
            DoEvents

            'Check for OK or Cancel return from the drill-down options form.
            Select Case intDDReturnValue
                Case IDOK
                    'Get and display the detail grid.
                    Call DisplayDDData(intHotHit) 'in DRILL_DN.BAS
                Case IDCANCEL
                    'Restore the labels of the pie chart.
                    Call RestorePieChart
            End Select

        DoEvents

        End If
End Sub
```

The intPieHotHit() function checks the location of the double click and returns 0 if the double click occurred outside the pie chart or returns the selected wedge if the double click is within the chart. You'll have to dust off your trigonometry knowledge to know exactly what's going on. The procedure first calculates the location of the chart's origin and radius. It then calculates the position of the double-click point relative to the origin. If the double-click point is outside the chart, the value of intPieHotHit and intWedgeAngle are both set to 0. If the double click is within the pie chart, the procedure proceeds to calculate which quadrant the click occurred in. The quadrants are numbered starting with 1 for the top-right quadrant and proceed clockwise.

```
'Calculate geometric coordinates of mouse clicks on the pie chart.

Function intPieHotHit (intMouseX As Integer, intMouseY As Integer) As Integer
    'intPieHotHit is the number of the selected wedge.
    Dim intCtr As Integer          'Generic loop counter.
    Dim intOriginX As Integer      'Mouse X position.
    Dim intOriginY As Integer      'Mouse Y position.
    Dim intRadius As Integer       'Radius of pie chart.
    Dim intRelX As Integer         'Mouse X relative to origin.
    Dim intRelY As Integer         'Mouse Y relative to origin.
    Dim intQuadrant As Integer     'Polar quadrants, 1-4.
    Dim sngPi As Single            'Value of pi (3.1416).
    Dim dblSumData As Double       'Sum of data.
    Dim sngTheta As Single         'Hit angle in radians.
    Dim intDegrees As Integer      'Hit angle in degrees.

    'Calculate value of pi.
    sngPi = 355 / 113

    'Create a local array to hold accumulated data.
    ReDim dblData(frmMDIGraph.chtPieChart.NumPoints) As Double

    intOriginX = frmMDIGraph.chtPieChart.Width \ 2
    intOriginY = frmMDIGraph.chtPieChart.Height \ 2 - Int(.025 *
➥frmMDIGraph.chtPieChart.Height)
    intRadius = Int(frmMDIGraph.chtPieChart.Height / 4.5)
    intRelX = intMouseX - intOriginX    'Positive right of origin
    intRelY = -intMouseY + intOriginY   'Positive above origin

    If Sqr(intRelX ^ 2 + intRelY ^ 2) > intRadius Then
        'Mouse is outside the pie.
        intPieHotHit = 0
        intWedgeAngle = 0
    Else
        'Mouse is within the pie's perimeter.
        'Determine the quadrant in which the double click occurred.
        'Quadrants are I to IV, clockwise.
        If intRelX >= 0 Then
            If intRelY >= 0 Then
                intQuadrant = 1
            Else
                intQuadrant = 2
            End If
```

Coding the Application, Part 2

```
    Else
      If intRelY >= 0 Then
        intQuadrant = 4
      Else
        intQuadrant = 3
      End If
   End If
```

After the quadrant is determined, the rotation angle is calculated by calculating the arctangent of the ratio of the relative x and y values. The arctangent gives the angle within a quadrant, so the procedure uses a `Select Case` statement to select the quadrant and add the appropriate offset to the calculated angle.

```
'Get the angle from the arctangent of the mouse position.
'The angle is measured clockwise from 12 o'clock (ratio
'of the opposite (X) to the adjacent (Y) side).
sngTheta = Atn(Abs(intRelX) / Abs(intRelY))    'Radians.

'Convert radians to degrees within quadrant.
Select Case intQuadrant
   Case 1
      intDegrees = sngTheta * 180 / sngPi
   Case 2
      intDegrees = 180 - (sngTheta * 180 / sngPi)
   Case 3
      intDegrees = 180 + (sngTheta * 180 / sngPi)
   Case 4
      intDegrees = 360 - (sngTheta * 180 / sngPi)
End Select
```

The procedure now knows the angle to the point where the mouse clicked on the chart. Next, it calculates the angles subtended by each of the pie wedges by multiplying the fraction of the total pie a wedge subtends and multiplying by 360. Note that the pie wedges count counterclockwise, while the angle is calculated clockwise.

```
'Loop to accumulate the data values counterclockwise.
For intCtr = frmMDIGraph.chtPieChart.NumPoints To 1 Step -1
   'Set the point counterclockwise.
   frmMDIGraph.chtPieChart.ThisPoint = intCtr

   'Put the accumulated data from the point into the array.
   dblSumData = dblSumData + frmMDIGraph.chtPieChart.GraphData
   dblData(intCtr) = dblSumData
Next intCtr

'Convert the chart data into degrees.
For intCtr = 1 To frmMDIGraph.chtPieChart.NumPoints
   dblData(intCtr) = dblData(intCtr) * 360 \ dblSumData
Next intCtr
```

The next block compares the angle of the clicked point with the upper and lower bounds of the wedges to determine what wedge was clicked on. When the clicked wedge is found, its number is stored in `intPieHotHit`, and the angle of the center of the wedge is stored in `intWedgeAngle`.

```
            'Loop to test the click angle versus the angle of the data wedge.
            For intCtr = frmMDIGraph.chtPieChart.NumPoints To 1 Step -1
                If intDegrees <= dblData(intCtr) Then
                    If intCtr < frmMDIGraph.chtPieChart.NumPoints Then
                        intWedgeAngle = Int(dblData(intCtr + 1) + (dblData(intCtr) -
                        ➥dblData(intCtr + 1)) \ 2)
                    Else
                        intWedgeAngle = Int(dblData(intCtr) \ 2)
                    End If
                    intPieHotHit = intCtr
                    Exit For
                End If
            Next intCtr
        End If
```

This last block is used while designing this procedure to test the results. The block checks the SHOW_TEST_FORMS flag to see if it's True. If it is, the frmTestTrig form is displayed and filled with data. The test forms are described later in this chapter.

```
    'See if we are in test mode.
    If SHOW_TEST_FORMS Then
        'Display the TestTrig form.
        frmTestTrig.Show
        'Put the values in the TestTrig form.
        frmTestTrig.txtRelX = intRelX
        frmTestTrig.txtRelY = intRelY
        frmTestTrig.txtTheta = sngTheta
        frmTestTrig.txtDegrees = intDegrees
        frmTestTrig.txtWedge = intCtr
        frmTestTrig.txtWedgeAngle = intWedgeAngle
        frmTestTrig.txtRelRadius = Sqr(intRelX ^ 2 + intRelY ^ 2)
        frmTestTrig.txtControlRadius = intRadius
    End If

End Function
```

Getting the Drill-Down Data

As shown in the structure chart in Figure 5.20 and also in Figure 5.21, selecting the drill-down data starts with the drill-down options form displayed by the chtPieChart_DblClick function. The form contains option buttons for the types of drill-down data available.

When the drill-down options form is loaded, the following Form_Load procedure is executed to position the form. Note that this is not an MDI child form like the chart and grid forms, but a separate form with no border or title bar. Because it's the same color as the main form below it, it blends into that form as if it were a part of it, but actually it sits just above it. The form is loaded as a modal form, so nothing can be done with any of the other forms or menus in this application until the drill-down options form is closed or hidden.

The Form_Load procedure first sets the Top and Left properties of the form so that it sits over the center of the left or right side of the MDI parent form. The side is selected to be the opposite

Coding the Application, Part 2

of that where the pie chart was shifted. The procedure then enables or disables the option buttons according to the code stored in the `DDFlag` field of the `tblDefinitions` table.

```
'
'Load the drill-down options form and shift it left or right.
'
Sub Form_Load ()
    'Note: This procedure must be in the Load event handler.
    '      Otherwise, the position is not set on the first
    '      change from left to right (or vice versa).
    Dim intCtr As Integer   'Generic counter.
    Dim tblDefs As Table    'Temporary table def to pass
                            'the global table to a form.
    Const FORM_TOP_HEIGHT = 1375   'Height of the title bar and
                                   'menus on the MDI parent form.
    Const EDGE_OFFSET = 500

    'Import the global table def. This is a bug workaround for VB-3.
    Set tblDefs = tblGraphs

    'Center form vertically.
    frmDrillOptions.Top = frmMDIMain.Top + FORM_TOP_HEIGHT + _
       (frmMDIMain.Height - FORM_TOP_HEIGHT - frmDrillOptions.Height) / 2

    'Position the form horizontally, depending on the wedge selected.
    If intWedgeAngle <= 180 Then
        frmDrillOptions.Left = frmMDIMain.Left + EDGE_OFFSET
    Else
        frmDrillOptions.Left = frmMDIMain.Left + frmMDIMain.Width - _
           frmDrillOptions.Width - EDGE_OFFSET
    End If

    'Enable/disable appropriate options.
    'Disable all of them, then turn on the available ones.
    For intCtr = 1 To NUM_OPTS
        optDrill(intCtr).Enabled = False
    Next intCtr
    If InStr(tblDefs("DDFlag"), "P") Then optDrill(DDPRODUCT).Enabled = True
    If InStr(tblDefs("DDFlag"), "C") Then optDrill(DDCUSTOMER).Enabled = True
    If InStr(tblDefs("DDFlag"), "S") Then optDrill(DDSALESMAN).Enabled = True

End Sub
```

Whenever an option button on the drill-down options form is clicked, the following procedure stores the selected option in the global variable `intSelectedDDOption`.

```
'
'Save the selected option.
'
Sub optDrill_Click (intIndex As Integer, intValue As Integer)
intSelectedDDOption = intIndex
End Sub
```

When the user presses the Cancel or OK buttons, one of the following two procedures is executed to set the return value and hide the drill-down options form. The form was loaded as a modal form by chtPieChart_DblClick, so it must be hidden in order for the code in chtPieChart_DblClick to continue.

```
'
'Signal a cancel and unload the drill-down options form.
'
Sub cmdCancel_Click ()
   intDDReturnValue = IDCANCEL
   frmDrillOptions.Hide
End Sub

'
'Set the OK return value and hide the form.
'
Sub cmdOK_Click ()
   intDDReturnValue = IDOK
   frmDrillOptions.Hide
End Sub
```

When the user has selected the data to display, the chtPieChart_DblClick procedure calls the DisplayDDData procedure to write the SQL statement to get the data for the drill-down grid. The procedure first loads several fields from the tblDefinitions table. The fields include the name of the drill-down data table, the name of the field in the table that contains the data, the name of the description table, and so forth.

```
'
'Fill the details grid with data.
'
Sub DisplayDDData (intHotHit As Integer)
   'intHotHit is the selected wedge.
   Dim intCtr As Integer          'Generic loop counter.
   Dim tblDefs As Table           'tblDefinitions.
   Dim ssType As Snapshot         'Table that supplies the descriptive data.
   Dim ssDetail As Snapshot       'Created by SQL statement.
   Dim frmDrill As Form           'Alias for frmMDIGrid.
   Dim grdDrill As Control        'Grid that displays the data.

   Dim strDataTable As String        'Name of data table.
   Dim strDataField As String        'Name of data field of data table.
   Dim strTypeTable As String        'Name of tblType.
   Dim strTypeField As String        'Name of primary key field.
   Dim strTypeName As String         'Name of legend field.
   Dim strSQL As String              'Complete SQL statement.
   Dim strSQLSelect As String        'SELECT statement.
   Dim strSQLFrom As String          'FROM clause.
   Dim strSQLWhere As String         'WHERE clause.
   Dim strSQLGroupBy As String       'GROUP BY clause.
   Dim strMonth As String            'Month of data (01-12).
   Dim strCode As String             'Code of current level.
   Dim strCaption As String          'Caption for the form.
   Dim strOperation As String        'The type of operation to perform
                                     'in the SQL string.
   Dim strSummedVariable As String   'The name of the summed variable.
```

Coding the Application, Part 2

```
'Import the definitions table.
Set tblDefs = tblGraphs

'Get the rollup table and the field that contain the data.
strDataTable = tblDefs("DDDataTable")
strDataField = tblDefs("DDDataField")
'Get the caption for the table.
strCaption = tblDefs("DDCaption")

'Get the month. Months start in column 2.
strMonth = LTrim$(Str$(frmMDIGraph.grdMonthly.SelStartCol - 1))

'Get the table and fields that contain the descriptions.
strTypeName = tblDefs("DDTypeName")
strTypeTable = tblDefs("DDTypeTable")
strTypeField = tblDefs("DDTypeField")
```

The procedure next creates a snapshot of the description table, which contains the text descriptions of the objects being displayed. These are the same descriptions used to create the legends or the detail grid. The procedure then locates the description associated with the selected pie wedge.

```
'Open the description table.
Set ssType = dbGraphs.CreateSnapshot(strTypeTable)
ssType.MoveFirst

'Move to the entry for the chosen pie wedge.
ssType.FindFirst strTypeField & " = " & Chr$(34) & strDDID(intHotHit) &
➥Chr$(34)
If ssType.NoMatch Then
    'Error condition.
    MsgBox "Error, can't find wedge ID"
    Exit Sub
End If
```

The next block of code creates the caption for the drill-down grid by combining the text from the DDCaption field of the tblDefinitions table with the description of the selected wedge and the current date.

```
'Fix the month number.
If Val(strMonth) < 10 Then
    strMonth = "0" & strMonth
End If

'Create the caption for the form.
strCaption = strCaption & " " & ssType(strTypeName) & " for " &
➥strMonths(Val(strMonth), 2) & ", " & strYear
```

The next few blocks of code create the SQL statement to search the database for the drill-down data. The strings are created in pieces, depending on what data is being requested. Strings are created for each field of the SQL statement and then combined into the complete statement at the end. The first block creates the operational strings that define the operation (Sum or Average) to be applied to the data.

```
'Create the operation strings.
'The operation depends on the type of data being summed.
If tblDefs("Units") = "$" Then
    strOperation = " Sum("
    strSummedVariable = ") AS SumOf"
ElseIf tblDefs("Units") = "%" Then
    strOperation = " Avg("
    strSummedVariable = ") AS AverageOf"
Else
    strOperation = " Sum("
    strSummedVariable = ") AS SumOf"
End If
```

The second block creates the pieces of the SQL statement that are specific to the option button selected on the drill-down options form. The three options are By Product ID, By Customer, and By Salesman. The Select Case statement creates the strSQLSelect, strSQLFrom, and strSQLGroupBy strings. The strSQLSelect string tells the database what fields to return—for example, if you select the By Product ID option, it returns Product ID, Product Name, and the data item being summed or averaged.

The strSQLFrom string tells the database what tables to combine to get the data. For the By Product ID option, the data is obtained from an inner join of the inventory table and the data table. The two tables are joined with the Product ID field.

The strSQLGroupBy string tells the database what items to combine when creating the summations or averages. For the By Product ID option, the data is grouped by product ID and product name. Since each product name has a unique product ID, this amounts to a grouping by product ID. Both are required to prevent the JET database engine from complaining that you are specifying a field and not using it. In summation queries, every field must be either a group by field or a field to be summed.

```
'Create the table-specific components of the SQL statement.
Select Case intSelectedDDOption
    Case DDPRODUCT
        'Create the SQL statements for the product drill-down.
        strSQLSelect = "SELECT Inventory.[Product ID], Inventory.[Product
        ➥Name]," & strOperation & strDataTable & "." & strDataField &
        ➥strSummedVariable & strDataField
        strSQLFrom = " FROM Inventory INNER JOIN " & strDataTable & " ON " &
        ➥strDataTable & ".[Product ID] = Inventory.[Product ID]"
        strSQLGroupBy = " GROUP BY Inventory.[Product ID], Inventory.[Product
        ➥Name];"
    Case DDCUSTOMER
        'Create the SQL statements for the customer drill-down.
        strSQLSelect = "SELECT Customers.[Customer ID], Customers.[Company
        ➥Name]," & strOperation & strDataTable & "." & strDataField &
        ➥strSummedVariable & strDataField
        strSQLFrom = " FROM Customers INNER JOIN " & strDataTable & " ON " &
        ➥strDataTable & ".[Customer ID] = Customers.[Customer ID]"
        strSQLGroupBy = " GROUP BY Customers.[Customer ID], Customers.[Company
        ➥Name];"
    Case DDSALESMAN
```

Coding the Application, Part 2

```
    'Create the SQL statements for the salesman drill-down.
    strSQLSelect = "SELECT Employees.[Employee ID], [Employees].[Last
➥Name] & "", "" & [Employees].[First Name] AS [Employee Name],"
➥& strOperation & strDataTable & "." & strDataField &
➥strSummedVariable & strDataField
    strSQLFrom = " FROM Employees INNER JOIN " & strDataTable & " ON " &
➥strDataTable & ".[Employee ID] = Employees.[Employee ID]"
    strSQLGroupBy = " GROUP BY Employees.[Employee ID], [Employees].[Last
➥Name] & "", "" & [Employees].[First Name];"
End Select
```

The third block creates the strSQLWhere string that contains the Where clause. The Where clause tells the database which data items to select, and it includes the type of the selected pie wedge and the current month and year.

```
'Add Where clause to select the exploded category, segment, or region.
strSQLWhere = " WHERE " & strDataTable & "." & strTypeField & " = " &
➥Chr$(34) & ssType(strTypeField) & Chr$(34)

'Add the year and month to the Where clause.
strSQLWhere = strSQLWhere & " AND " & strDataTable & ".Year = " & Chr$(34) &
➥strYear & Chr$(34)
strSQLWhere = strSQLWhere & " AND " & strDataTable & ".Month = " & Chr$(34)
➥& strMonth & Chr$(34)
```

The last block of the SQL code concatenates all the SQL strings into an SQL statement and sends that string to the database engine to create a snapshot of the data.

```
'Concatenate the elements of the SQL statement and create the snapshot.
strSQL = strSQLSelect & strSQLFrom & strSQLWhere & strSQLGroupBy
Screen.MousePointer = HOURGLASS   'Set the mouse pointer to the hourglass.

Set ssDetail = dbGraphs.CreateSnapshot(strSQL)

Screen.MousePointer = DEFAULT   'Reset the mouse pointer.
'Handle errors caused if a table is missing.
If Err Then
    MsgBox "Rolled up data is not available.", MB_ICONSTOP, "Drilldown
➥Problem"
    Call RestorePieChart
    Exit Sub
End If


If ssDetail.RecordCount = 0 Then
    'Table missing or no records.
    MsgBox "No records returned for this query.", MB_ICONSTOP, "Drilldown
➥Problem"
    Call RestorePieChart
    Exit Sub
End If
```

If good data returns from the database engine, the last block in this procedure calls PopulateGrid to fill the grid with data and display it.

```
    'Change the values of these control variables to use another grid.
    Set frmDrill = frmMDIGrid
    Set grdDrill = frmDrill.grdDetail
    'Populate the grid with data from ssDetail.
    Call PopulateGrid(frmDrill, grdDrill, ssDetail, strCaption)

End Sub
```

The `PopulateGrid` procedure takes the selected data and fills the drill-down grid with it. This procedure loads the drill-down form and then hides it. The form must be loaded in order for the data to be inserted into it, but it proceeds much faster if it's hidden. The following blocks of code set up the drill-down grid and copy the selected drill-down data from the snapshot object. The setup includes setting captions, column widths, fixed columns, and fixed rows.

```
'
'Load the drill-down grid with data and display it.
'
Sub PopulateGrid (frmDrill As Form, grdDrill As Control, ssDetail As Snapshot,
➥strCaption As String)

    Dim dblDataTotal As Double    'Sum of data column for caption.
    Dim tblDefs As Table          'New instance of tblDefinitions.

    'Import the database and definitions table.
    Set tblDefs = tblGraphs

    frmDrill.Show                 'Load the form if not loaded.

    grdDrill.Visible = False

    'Get the dimensions of the grid
    ssDetail.MoveLast             'Get an accurate record count.
    grdDrill.Cols = ssDetail.Fields.Count
    grdDrill.Rows = ssDetail.RecordCount + 1

    'Create an array to hold the text widths for each row and column.
    ReDim intTextWidths(grdDrill.Rows, grdDrill.Cols)

    'Add the field names to row 0 (fixed headings).
    For IntCol = 0 To ssDetail.Fields.Count - 1
        grdDrill.Row = 0
        grdDrill.Col = IntCol
        grdDrill.Text = ssDetail.Fields(IntCol).Name

        'Center the field names.
        grdDrill.FixedAlignment(IntCol) = 2

        'Set the column width to 110% of the text width.
        intTextWidths(0, IntCol) = frmDrill.TextWidth(grdDrill.Text) * 1.1
    Next IntCol

    'Populate the grid with the data.
    ssDetail.MoveFirst
    For intRow = 1 To grdDrill.Rows - 1
        'Iterate the rows.
        grdDrill.Row = intRow
```

Day 9

Coding the Application, Part 2

```
For IntCol = 0 To grdDrill.Cols - 1
   'Iterate the columns and add data from the snapshot.
   grdDrill.Col = IntCol
   'Null values cause problems, so eliminate them.
   If IsNull(ssDetail.Fields(IntCol).Value) Then
      grdDrill.Text = " "
   Else
      grdDrill.Text = ssDetail.Fields(IntCol).Value
   End If

   'Set the column alignment.
   If intRow = 1 Then
      If IntCol = 0 Then
         If InStr(grdDrill.Text, " ID") Then
            'Center columns with ID.
            grdDrill.ColAlignment(IntCol) = 2
         End If
      ElseIf IntCol = grdDrill.Cols - 1 Then
         'Right-align the last data column (numeric).
         grdDrill.ColAlignment(IntCol) = 1
      Else
         'Left-align all other columns.
         grdDrill.ColAlignment(IntCol) = 0
      End If
   End If

   If IntCol = grdDrill.Cols - 1 Then
      'Accumulate the total of the data.
      If Not IsNull(ssDetail.Fields(IntCol).Value) Then
         dblDataTotal = dblDataTotal + ssDetail.Fields(IntCol).Value
      End If

      'Format the data in the last column.
      If tblDefs("Units") = "$" Then
         If intRow = 1 Then
            'Add a dollar sign.
            grdDrill.Text = Format$(grdDrill.Text, "$#,##0")
         Else
            grdDrill.Text = Format$(grdDrill.Text, "#,##0")
         End If
      ElseIf tblDefs("Units") = "%" Then
         If intRow = 1 Then
            'Use percent symbol.
            grdDrill.Text = Format$(grdDrill.Text, "###.0%")
         Else
            grdDrill.Text = Format$(Val(grdDrill.Text) * 100, "###.0 ")
         End If
      Else
         'General number formatting.
         grdDrill.Text = Format$(grdDrill.Text, "#,##0.00")
      End If
      DoEvents
   End If

   'Put the text widths in the array.
```

```
            intTextWidths(intRow, IntCol) = frmDrill.TextWidth(grdDrill.Text)
        Next IntCol

        'Go to the next record in the snapshot.
        ssDetail.MoveNext
    Next intRow

    'Size the grid's columns by finding the maximum width.
    For IntCol = 0 To grdDrill.Cols - 1
        For intRow = 0 To grdDrill.Rows - 1
            'Set the width of the columns to 110% of the maximum text width.
            If grdDrill.ColWidth(IntCol) < 1.1 * intTextWidths(intRow, IntCol)
            ➥Then
                grdDrill.ColWidth(IntCol) = 1.1 * intTextWidths(intRow, IntCol)
            End If
        Next intRow
    Next IntCol

    'Set the height of the grid.
    grdDrill.Height = grdDrill.RowHeight(0) * grdDrill.Rows * 1.08
    'Make sure there is still room for the label at the top of the form.
    'The label extends down 600 twips onto the form.
    If grdDrill.Height > frmDrill.ScaleHeight - 600 Then
        grdDrill.Height = frmDrill.ScaleHeight - 600
    End If

    'Set the width of the grid.
    grdDrill.Width = 0
    For IntCol = 0 To grdDrill.Cols - 1
        grdDrill.Width = grdDrill.Width + grdDrill.ColWidth(IntCol) - 15
    Next IntCol
    'Make sure the grid fits within 90% of the form.
    If grdDrill.Width > frmDrill.ScaleWidth * .9 Then
        grdDrill.Width = frmDrill.ScaleWidth * .9
    End If

    'Position the grid in the center of the form.
    'Leave 500 twips at the top for the label.
    grdDrill.Left = (frmDrill.ScaleWidth - grdDrill.Width) \ 2
    grdDrill.Top = 500 + (frmDrill.ScaleHeight - 500 - grdDrill.Height) \ 2

    'Set the form caption.
    frmDrill.Caption = strCaption
    'Set the label on the form to the caption plus the total.
    If tblDefs("Units") = "$" Then
        strCaption = strCaption & ", " & Format(dblDataTotal, "$#,##0")
    ElseIf tblDefs("Units") = "%" Then
        'Note: The percent format automatically multiplies by 100.
        strCaption = strCaption & ", Average: " & Format(dblDataTotal /
        ➥(grdDrill.Rows - 1), "##0.0%")
    Else
        strCaption = strCaption & ", " & Format(dblDataTotal, "#,##0.00")
    End If
    frmDrill.lblCaption = strCaption

    'Display the grid.
```

Day 9: Coding the Application, Part 2

```
    grdDrill.Visible = True
    DoEvents

    'Highlight the totals column by selecting it.
    grdDrill.SelStartCol = grdDrill.Cols - 1
    grdDrill.SelEndCol = grdDrill.Cols - 1
    grdDrill.SelStartRow = 1
    grdDrill.SelEndRow = grdDrill.Rows - 1
End Sub
```

The `RestorePieChart` procedure is used when the user presses the Cancel button on the drill-down options form. This procedure unloads the drill-down options form, centers the pie chart, and restores the labels.

```
'
'Remove the drill-down options form and redisplay the pie chart.
'
Sub RestorePieChart ()
    Dim intCtr As Integer   'Generic loop counter.

    Unload frmMDIGrid

    For intCtr = 1 To frmMDIGraph.chtPieChart.NumPoints
        frmMDIGraph.chtPieChart.ThisPoint = intCtr
        frmMDIGraph.chtPieChart.LabelText = strLabels(intCtr)
        frmMDIGraph.chtPieChart.ExtraData = G_NOT_EXPLODED
    Next intCtr

    'Restore the original left margin of the chart.
    frmMDIGraph.chtPieChart.Left = intPieChartLeft

    'Restore the label lines to the pie chart.
    frmMDIGraph.chtPieChart.GraphStyle = G_DEFAULT

    'Redraw the chart with all of the labels.
    frmMDIGraph.chtPieChart.DrawMode = G_DRAW

End Sub
```

Creating the Drill-Down Tables

The drill-down chart requires a set of drill-down tables in the Graphs database similar to the tables required for the charts in the application. Unlike those other charts, we don't know exactly what data is needed until runtime, so we create seven general tables and use the procedures discussed in the preceding section to select the data needed for a specific chart.

The seven tables are in the DDDataTable field of the tblDefinitions table. There is one for each chart class, except for Inventory, which requires two. The seven tables and the persistent queries needed to create them are listed in Table 9.1. The calculations involved in these tables are the same as for the monthly tables discussed on Day 4, so refer to that chapter if you want to see how something is calculated.

Table 9.1. The drill-down tables and the queries that create them.

Table	Query
tblSalesDetail	qrySalesDetail
tblMarginDetail	qryMarginDetail
tblOrdersDetail	qryOrdersDetail
tblBacklogDetail	qryBacklogDetail
tblCycleDetail	qryCycleDetail
tblInventoryDetail	qryInventoryDetail
tblTurnsDetail	qryTurnsDetail

qrySalesDetail

All the tables begin with the year and month. tblSalesDetail needs to include the Segment ID, Region ID, and Category ID for the three sales classes and Product ID, Customer ID, and Employee ID for the three possible drill-down options. The sales are calculated in the same manner as the monthly sales tables. The difference is the grouping of the table according to segment, region, and product.

```
SELECT Format(Invoices.[Shipped Date],"yyyy") AS Year,
Format(Invoices.[Shipped Date],"mm") AS Month, Inventory.[Category ID],
Customers.[Segment ID], Customers.[Region ID], [Order Details].[Product ID],
Customers.[Customer ID], Orders.[Employee ID],
Sum([Order Details].[Unit Price]*
[Invoice Details].[Units Shipped]*(1-[Order Details].[Discount])) AS Sales
INTO tblSalesDetail
FROM Invoices INNER JOIN ((Customers INNER JOIN (Inventory INNER JOIN (Orders
INNER JOIN [Order Details] ON Orders.[Order ID] = [Order Details].[Order ID])
ON Inventory.[Product ID] = [Order Details].[Product ID]) ON
Customers.[Customer ID] = Orders.[Customer ID]) INNER JOIN [Invoice Details] ON
[Order Details].[Order Detail ID] = [Invoice Details].[Order Detail ID]) ON
Invoices.[Invoice ID] = [Invoice Details].[Invoice ID]
GROUP BY Format(Invoices.[Shipped Date],"yyyy"),
Format(Invoices.[Shipped Date],"mm"), Inventory.[Category ID],
Customers.[Segment ID], Customers.[Region ID], [Order Details].[Product ID],
Customers.[Customer ID], Orders.[Employee ID];
```

qryMarginDetail

The tblMarginDetail table needs only the Category ID field for the pie chart wedge selection and the Product ID field for the drill-down option. The tabulated value is the average margin.

```
SELECT Format(Invoices.[Shipped Date],"yyyy") AS Year,
Format(Invoices.[Shipped Date],"mm") AS Month, Inventory.[Category ID],
Inventory.[Product ID], [Margin1]/[Margin2] AS Margin,
(Sum([Order Details].[Unit Price]*[Invoice Details].[Units Shipped]*(1-
```

Coding the Application, Part 2

```
[Order Details].[Discount]))-Sum([Inventory].[Unit Cost]*
[Invoice Details].[Units Shipped])) AS Margin1,
(Sum([Order Details].[Unit Price]*[Invoice Details].[Units Shipped]*(1-
[Order Details].[Discount]))) AS Margin2
INTO tblMarginDetail FROM Invoices INNER JOIN ((Inventory INNER JOIN
(Orders INNER JOIN [Order Details] ON Orders.[Order ID] =
[Order Details].[Order ID]) ON Inventory.[Product ID] =
[Order Details].[Product ID]) INNER JOIN [Invoice Details] ON
[Order Details].[Order Detail ID] = [Invoice Details].[Order Detail ID])
ON Invoices.[Invoice ID] = [Invoice Details].[Invoice ID]
GROUP BY Format(Invoices.[Shipped Date],"yyyy"),
Format(Invoices.[Shipped Date],"mm"), Inventory.[Category ID],
Inventory.[Product ID];
```

qryOrdersDetail

The `tblOrdersDetail` table is laid out much the same as the `tblSalesDetail` table. The only difference is that the tabulated value is the total orders instead of the total sales.

```
SELECT Format(Orders.[Order Date],"yyyy") AS Year,
Format(Orders.[Order Date],"mm") AS Month, Inventory.[Category ID],
Customers.[Segment ID], Customers.[Region ID], Inventory.[Product ID],
Customers.[Customer ID], Orders.[Employee ID],
Sum([Order Details].[Unit Price]*[Order Details].[Quantity]*(1-
[Order Details].[Discount])) AS Orders INTO tblOrdersDetail
FROM Customers INNER JOIN (Inventory INNER JOIN (Orders INNER JOIN
[Order Details] ON Orders.[Order ID] = [Order Details].[Order ID]) ON
Inventory.[Product ID] = [Order Details].[Product ID]) ON
Customers.[Customer ID] = Orders.[Customer ID]
GROUP BY Format(Orders.[Order Date],"yyyy"), Format(Orders.[Order Date],"mm"),
Inventory.[Category ID], Customers.[Segment ID], Customers.[Region ID],
Inventory.[Product ID], Customers.[Customer ID], Orders.[Employee ID];
```

qryBacklogDetail

The `tblBacklogDetail` table is also nearly identical to the `tblSalesDetail` table, except that the backlog is being tabulated instead of the total sales.

```
SELECT Format(Orders.[Order Date],"yyyy") AS Year,
Format(Orders.[Order Date],"mm") AS Month, Inventory.[Category ID],
Customers.[Segment ID], Customers.[Region ID], Inventory.[Product ID],
Customers.[Customer ID], Orders.[Employee ID],
Sum([Order Details].[Unit Price]*[Order Details].Quantity*(1-
[Order Details].Discount)) AS Backlog INTO tblBacklogDetail
FROM Invoices INNER JOIN ((Customers INNER JOIN (Inventory INNER JOIN
(Orders INNER JOIN [Order Details] ON Orders.[Order ID] =
[Order Details].[Order ID])
ON Inventory.[Product ID] = [Order Details].[Product ID]) ON
Customers.[Customer ID] = Orders.[Customer ID]) INNER JOIN [Invoice Details] ON
[Order Details].[Order Detail ID] = [Invoice Details].[Order Detail ID]) ON
Invoices.[Invoice ID] = [Invoice Details].[Invoice ID]
WHERE (((Format([Invoices].[Shipped Date],"mmyy"))<>
Format([Orders].[Order Date],"mmyy")))
GROUP BY Format(Orders.[Order Date],"yyyy"), Format(Orders.[Order Date],"mm"),
```

```
Inventory.[Category ID], Customers.[Segment ID], Customers.[Region ID],
Inventory.[Product ID], Customers.[Customer ID], Orders.[Employee ID];
```

qryCycleDetail

The `tblCycleDetail` table is also nearly identical to the `tblSalesDetail` table, except that the backlog is being tabulated instead of the total sales.

```
SELECT Format(Invoices.[Shipped Date],"yyyy") AS Year,
Format(Invoices.[Shipped Date],"mm") AS Month, Customers.[Segment ID],
[Order Details].[Product ID], Customers.[Region ID], Customers.[Customer ID],
Orders.[Employee ID], Avg(DateDiff("d",Orders.[Order Date],
Invoices.[Shipped Date])) AS Days, StDev(DateDiff("d",Orders.[Order Date],
Invoices.[Shipped Date])) AS StdDev, Count("Orders") AS Orders INTO
tblCycleDetail
FROM Invoices INNER JOIN ((Customers INNER JOIN (Orders INNER JOIN
[Order Details] ON Orders.[Order ID] = [Order Details].[Order ID]) ON
Customers.[Customer ID] = Orders.[Customer ID]) INNER JOIN [Invoice Details] ON
[Order Details].[Order Detail ID] = [Invoice Details].[Order Detail ID]) ON
Invoices.[Invoice ID] = [Invoice Details].[Invoice ID]
GROUP BY Format(Invoices.[Shipped Date],"yyyy"),
Format(Invoices.[Shipped Date],"mm"), Customers.[Segment ID],
[Order Details].[Product ID], Customers.[Region ID], Customers.[Customer ID],
Orders.[Employee ID];
```

qryInventoryDetail

The `tblInventoryDetail` table needs only the Category ID and the Product ID fields—the Category ID field to match the selected wedge and the Product ID field for the one available drill-down option. The other drill-down options, By Customer and By Salesman, have no useful meaning here and are not included.

```
SELECT tblInventoryHistory.Year, tblInventoryHistory.Month,
Inventory.[Category ID], Inventory.[Product ID],
Sum([tblInventoryHistory].[Unit Cost]*[tblInventoryHistory].[Units In Stock])
AS [Value] INTO tblInventoryDetail
FROM tblInventoryHistory INNER JOIN Inventory
ON tblInventoryHistory.[ProductID] = Inventory.[Product ID]
GROUP BY tblInventoryHistory.Year, tblInventoryHistory.Month,
Inventory.[Category ID], Inventory.[Product ID];
```

qryTurnsDetail

The `tblTurnsDetail` table also needs only the Category ID and the Product ID fields. As with the `tblInventoryDetail` table, the other drill-down options have no meaning here and are not available.

```
SELECT tblInventoryHistory.Year, tblInventoryHistory.Month,
Inventory.[Category ID], Inventory.[Product ID],
Sum([tblInventoryHistory].[Unit Cost]*[tblInventoryHistory].[Units Shipped])/
Sum([tblInventoryHistory].[Unit Cost]*([tblInventoryHistory].[Units In Stock]+
[tblInventoryHistory].[Units Shipped])) AS [Value] INTO tblTurnsDetail
```

Coding the Application, Part 2

```
FROM tblInventoryHistory INNER JOIN Inventory ON
tblInventoryHistory.[Product ID] = Inventory.[Product ID]
GROUP BY tblInventoryHistory.Year, tblInventoryHistory.Month,
Inventory.[Category ID], Inventory.[Product ID];
```

Restoring the Pie Chart

When the user finishes viewing the drill-down grid, he double-clicks on it to redisplay the pie chart. That restoration is accomplished with a double-click event procedure for both the drill-down form and the drill-down grid.

```
Sub Form_DblClick ()
   'Purpose: Restore the pie chart with a double click.
   Call RestorePieChart
End Sub

Sub grdDetail_DblClick ()
   'Purpose: Restore the pie chart with a double click.
   'Note:    Same as double-clicking form.
   Call RestorePieChart
End Sub
```

The Printing Procedures

When you select File | Print, the program structure shown in Figure 5.22 is initiated. In that structure, one of several procedures is executed, depending on what is currently visible on the MDI form. Printing for the charts is done by sizing the chart to fit on the printer object and then copying the image from the graphics server to the printer.

This first procedure is executed when the Print command is selected. The procedure prepares and displays the Printing common dialog, which returns the printing options. The procedure then calls the PrintVisibleChart procedure to print the current chart. A loop at the end of the procedure has been commented out. If your printer driver doesn't support multiple copies, these lines have to be uncommented and the PD_USEDEVMODECOPIES flag removed from the Flags option to create multiple copies.

```
'
'Display the Print dialog and print.
'
Sub mnuFilePrint_Click ()
   Dim intCtr As Integer   'Generic counter.
   cdgDialogs.CancelError = False
   cdgDialogs.Copies = 1
   cdgDialogs.FromPage = 1
   cdgDialogs.ToPage = 1
   'Set the flags for no print range and no print selection.
   'Use the printer drivers multiple copies capability.
   cdgDialogs.Flags = PD_NOPAGENUMS + PD_NOSELECTION + PD_USEDEVMODECOPIES
   cdgDialogs.Action = DLG_PRINT
```

```
        'Test to verify that the printer has been set as the default printer.
        If cdgDialogs.PrinterDefault Then
           'Important: EndDoc is needed to set the new orientation.
           printer.EndDoc
        Else
           MsgBox "The printer you use must be selected as the default printer.",
           ➥MB_ICONSTOP, "Printer Error"
           Exit Sub
        End If
        'Print the copies. Uncomment the For/Next loop and remove
        'the PD_USEDEVMODECOPIES flag above if the printer driver does
        'not support multiple copies.
    '    For intCtr = 1 To cdgDialogs.Copies
           Call PrintVisibleChart
    '    Next intCtr

    End Sub
```

The `PrintVisibleChart` procedure determines what is visible and prints it on the default printer. You could use the `PrintForm` method to print the contents of the form, but the images created by the graphs control are capable of much higher resolution. To make use of that higher resolution, redraw the chart on the printer object by copying the Windows metafile (.WMF) image from the chart control and pasting it onto the printer object.

The first block of the procedure determines what is currently visible and sets some control variables to point to the frontmost objects.

```
'
'Print the graph and grid.
'
Sub PrintVisibleChart ()
    'Purpose: Print the graph and grid to a single printer hDC.

    Dim intLeft As Integer
    Dim sngLeft As Single
    Dim intTop As Integer
    Dim sngTop As Single
    Dim intWide As Integer
    Dim sngWide As Single
    Dim intHigh As Integer
    Dim sngHigh As Single
    Dim sngGridLeft As Single
    Dim sngGridTop As Single
    Dim grdPrint As Control
    Dim chtPrint As Control
    Dim intGridLeft As Integer
    Dim intGridTop As Integer
    Dim sngScale As Single
    Dim SaveOld As typSave       'Structure for old chart data.
    Dim fPrintWhat As Integer    'Flag indicating what is being printed.

    Dim hWinMF As Integer        'Handle to the graph metafile.
    Dim hWinDC As Integer        'Handle to the printer device context.
    Dim intResult As Integer     'Result of WinAPI function call.
    Const INCH2TWIP = 1440       'Convert inches to twips.
```

Day 9

Coding the Application, Part 2

```
'Set control variables.
If (frmMDIGraph.chtMonthly.Visible = True) Then
    'The monthly chart is visible.
    Set chtPrint = frmMDIGraph.chtMonthly
    If fIsCrosstab Then
        fPrintWhat = LEVEL2_CHART_AND_GRID
        Set grdPrint = frmMDIGraph.grdMonthly
    Else
        fPrintWhat = LEVEL1_CHART_AND_GRID
        Set grdPrint = frmMDIGraph.grdMonthly
    End If
ElseIf (frmMDIGrid.grdDetail.Visible = True) Then
    'The detail grid is visible.
    fPrintWhat = DETAIL_GRID
    Set grdPrint = frmMDIGrid.grdDetail
    Set chtPrint = frmMDIGraph.grdMonthly
Else
    'The pie chart is visible.
    fPrintWhat = PIE_CHART
    Set chtPrint = frmMDIGraph.chtPieChart
    Set grdPrint = frmMDIGraph.grdMonthly
End If

'Set mouse pointer.
Screen.MousePointer = HOURGLASS
DoEvents

'Important: The following is required to obtain
'          valid hDC for PostScript printers.
Printer.Print   'PostScript printers need to be reset to return hDC.
```

The second block determines if the printer is in portrait or landscape mode and sets several position and scale factors. For paper sizes other than 8 1/2 by 11 inches, these factors will need to be adjusted in order for everything to be sized and centered correctly. All of the measurements are in inches, which are later converted to twips.

```
'See if the printer is in landscape or portrait mode.
If Printer.ScaleWidth > Printer.ScaleHeight Then
    'Landscape orientation.
    Select Case fPrintWhat
        Case LEVEL2_CHART_AND_GRID
            'Location and dimensions for the level 2 graph.
            sngTop = .5
            sngLeft = .75
            sngWide = 10
            sngHigh = 6
            'Top-left corner and scale factor for the grid.
            sngGridLeft = .8
            sngGridTop = 6
            sngScale = .89
        Case LEVEL1_CHART_AND_GRID, PIE_CHART
            'Location and dimensions for the level 1 graph.
            sngTop = .5
            sngLeft = .125
```

```
            sngWide = 10
            sngHigh = 6
            'Top-left corner and scale factor for the grid.
            sngGridLeft = 1.125
            sngGridTop = 7
            sngScale = 1
        Case DETAIL_GRID
            'Top-left corner and scale factor for the grid.
            sngGridLeft = .8
            sngGridTop = .5
            sngScale = 1
    End Select
Else
    'Portrait orientation in effect.
    Select Case fPrintWhat
        Case LEVEL2_CHART_AND_GRID
            'Location and dimensions for the level 2 graph.
            sngTop = 1
            sngLeft = 0
            sngWide = 7.5
            sngHigh = 5.5
            'Top-left corner and scale factor for the grid.
            sngGridLeft = .5
            sngGridTop = 7.5
            sngScale = .7
        Case LEVEL1_CHART_AND_GRID, PIE_CHART
            'Location and dimensions for the level 1 graph.
            sngTop = 1
            sngLeft = .25
            sngWide = 8
            sngHigh = 6
            'Top-left corner and scale factor for the grid.
            sngGridLeft = .65
            sngGridTop = 7.5
            sngScale = .9
        Case DETAIL_GRID
            'Top-left corner and scale factor for the grid.
            sngGridLeft = .5
            sngGridTop = 1
            sngScale = 1
    End Select
End If

'Convert grid units to twips.
intGridLeft = Int(sngGridLeft * INCH2TWIP)
intGridTop = Int(sngGridTop * INCH2TWIP)

'Overscale the viewport extension to expand the graph.
If Printer.ScaleWidth > Printer.ScaleHeight Then
    'Landscape scaling factors.
    Select Case fPrintWhat
        Case LEVEL2_CHART_AND_GRID
            sngWide = sngWide * 1.5
            sngHigh = sngHigh * 1.5
        Case LEVEL1_CHART_AND_GRID, PIE_CHART
            sngWide = sngWide * 1.7
```

Coding the Application, Part 2

```
            sngHigh = sngHigh * 1.7
         Case DETAIL_GRID
            'No scale change.
      End Select
   Else
      'Portrait scaling factors.
      Select Case fPrintWhat
         Case LEVEL2_CHART_AND_GRID
            sngWide = sngWide * 1.5
            sngHigh = sngHigh * 1.5
         Case LEVEL1_CHART_AND_GRID, PIE_CHART
            sngWide = sngWide * 1.3
            sngHigh = sngHigh * 1.3
         Case DETAIL_GRID
            'No scale change.
      End Select
   End If
```

The next block calls `PrintGrid` to draw the grid on the printer. The grid must be drawn first, because when the graph is copied onto the printer, the scale is changed, which makes drawing the grid difficult.

```
'Draw the grid on the printer hDC.
If fPrintWhat <> PIE_CHART Then
   Call PrintGrid(grdPrint, intGridTop, intGridLeft, sngScale, fPrintWhat)
   DoEvents
End If
```

Drawing the graph on the printer is accomplished by first rescaling the existing graph and then copying the image to the printer. First, the block saves the old size to use when rescaling the image on the form back to its previous size. Next, it copies the caption from the form to the graph object and sets the drawing style to monochrome. The next few lines rescale the image to fill the printed page.

```
'Process the chart.
If fPrintWhat <> DETAIL_GRID Then
   'Save the prior display dimensions.
   SaveOld.intWidth = chtPrint.Width
   SaveOld.intHeight = chtPrint.Height
   SaveOld.intLeft = chtPrint.Left
   SaveOld.intTop = chtPrint.Top

   'Add a title to the graph.
   chtPrint.GraphTitle = frmMDIGraph.Caption

   'Set the drawing style to monochrome.
   chtPrint.DrawStyle = G_MONO
   DoEvents

   If (fPrintWhat = LEVEL1_CHART_AND_GRID) Or (fPrintWhat =
   ↪LEVEL2_CHART_AND_GRID) Then
      'Turn horizontal and vertical grid lines on.
      chtPrint.GridStyle = G_HORIZONTAL + G_VERTICAL
   End If
```

```
'Rescale the metafile.
chtPrint.Left = 0
chtPrint.Top = 0
chtPrint.Width = sngWide * INCH2TWIP
chtPrint.Height = sngHigh * INCH2TWIP

'Draw the chart.
chtPrint.DrawMode = G_DRAW
DoEvents
```

With the graph rescaled to fit the printer object, the next block copies the rescaled image from the graphic server to the printer object.

```
'Add the graph to the metafile
hWinMF = GSGetMF(0)     'Call to the graphic server DLL
                        'to get the metafile handle.
hWinDC = Printer.hDC    'Return the handle of the
                        'printer's device context.

intResult = SetMapMode(hWinDC, 7)   'MM_ISOTROPIC mapping mode.
intLeft = Int(GetDeviceCaps(hWinDC, 88) * sngLeft)
intTop = Int(GetDeviceCaps(hWinDC, 90) * sngTop)
intWide = Int(GetDeviceCaps(hWinDC, 88) * sngWide)
intHigh = Int(GetDeviceCaps(hWinDC, 90) * sngHigh)

'Set viewport origin (left and top margins).
intResult = SetViewportOrg(hWinDC, intLeft, intTop)

'Set viewport extent (width and height).
intResult = SetViewportExt(hWinDC, intWide, intHigh)

'Copy the image of the chart to the printer.
intResult = PlayMetaFile(hWinDC, hWinMF)
DoEvents
End If
```

The image is now on the printer object, so execute the NewPage and EndDoc methods to print the image.

```
'Important: Both of these instructions are required.
Printer.NewPage
Printer.EndDoc
```

The image is sent to the printer, so the next procedure scales the graph back to its previous size and color.

```
If fPrintWhat <> DETAIL_GRID Then
   'Reset the chart to normal display mode.

   If (fPrintWhat = LEVEL1_CHART_AND_GRID) Or (fPrintWhat =
   ↪LEVEL2_CHART_AND_GRID) Then
      'Turn horizontal and vertical grid lines off.
      chtPrint.GridStyle = G_NONE
   End If
```

Day 9: Coding the Application, Part 2

```
        'Delete the graph title and set DrawStyle to color.
        chtPrint.GraphTitle = ""
        chtPrint.DrawStyle = G_COLOR
        DoEvents

        'Return the size to the original dimensions.
        chtPrint.Left = SaveOld.intLeft
        chtPrint.Top = SaveOld.intTop
        chtPrint.Width = SaveOld.intWidth
        chtPrint.Height = SaveOld.intHeight


    End If

    Screen.MousePointer = DEFAULT
    DoEvents
End Sub
```

The `PrintGrid` procedure draws a grid onto the default printer. The location and scaling is determined by the arguments to the procedure. The procedure first calls `FindWidth` and `FindHeight` to get the full height and width of the existing grid control. `FindFont` is called to see if the existing font is available on the printer. If it isn't, Arial is substituted.

```
'
'Print a grid in the printer's picture box.
'
Sub PrintGrid (grdControl As Control, intTopMargin As Integer, intLeftMargin As
➥Integer, sngScale As Single, fPrintWhat As Integer)
    'Substitute shading lines for colors in grid legend.
Dim intTextHeight As Integer
Dim intTextWidth As Integer
Dim intGridWidth As Integer
Dim intGridHeight As Integer
Dim intCol As Integer
Dim intRow As Integer
Dim strFontName As String
Dim intStartWidth As Integer
Dim intStartHeight As Integer
Dim intCharWidth As Integer
Dim intAlignment As Integer
Dim intLegendX As Integer
Dim intLegendY As Integer

    intGridWidth = FindWidth(grdControl)
    intGridHeight = FindHeight(grdControl)
    strFontName = grdControl.FontName

    'Use the printer font corresponding to the display font if available.
    If FindFont(strFontName) Then
        Printer.FontName = grdControl.FontName
        Printer.FontBold = grdControl.FontBold
    Else
        'If TrueType Arial is available, use it.
        If FindFont("Arial") Then
            Printer.FontName = "Arial"
            Printer.FontBold = True
```

```
        Else
            'Otherwise, use the first available printer font.
            Printer.FontName = Printer.Fonts(0)
            Printer.FontBold = True
        End If
    End If
```

The next block scales the font to fit the grid to be printed on the printer and prints a light gray color on the fixed rows and columns.

```
    'Scale the font size.
    Printer.FontSize = grdControl.FontSize * sngScale
    intTextHeight = Printer.TextHeight("0")

    Do While intTextHeight > grdControl.RowHeight(0) * sngScale
        'Reduce the font size if it exceeds the row height.
        Printer.FontSize = grdControl.FontSize * 3 \ 4
        intTextHeight = Printer.TextHeight("0")
    Loop

    'Add a block light gray background to the fixed rows.
    If grdControl.FixedRows > 0 Then
        'Print the grayed fixed row(s).
        Printer.CurrentX = intLeftMargin
        If fPrintWhat = LEVEL2_CHART_AND_GRID Then
            'Shading starts in column 2.
            Printer.CurrentX = intLeftMargin + grdControl.ColWidth(0) * sngScale
        End If
        Printer.CurrentY = intTopMargin
        Select Case fPrintWhat
            Case LEVEL2_CHART_AND_GRID
                Printer.Line -Step((intGridWidth - grdControl.ColWidth(0)) * _
                    sngScale, (grdControl.RowHeight(0)) * sngScale), _
                    RGB(224, 224, 224), BF
            Case LEVEL1_CHART_AND_GRID, DETAIL_GRID
                Printer.Line -Step(intGridWidth * sngScale, _
                    (grdControl.RowHeight(0)) * sngScale), RGB(224, 224, 224), BF
        End Select
    End If

    'Add a block gray background to the fixed columns.
    If grdControl.FixedCols > 0 Then
        Select Case fPrintWhat
            Case LEVEL2_CHART_AND_GRID
                'Add a block light gray background
                'to column 1 (columns start at 0).
                Printer.CurrentX = intLeftMargin + (grdControl.ColWidth(0) * _
                    sngScale)
                Printer.CurrentY = intTopMargin + (grdControl.RowHeight(0) * _
                    sngScale)
                Printer.Line -Step((grdControl.ColWidth(1) * sngScale * 1.1), _
                    (intGridHeight - grdControl.RowHeight(0)) * sngScale), _
                    RGB(224, 224, 224), BF
            Case DETAIL_GRID
                'Add a gray background to columns 0 and 1.
```

Coding the Application, Part 2

```
            Printer.CurrentX = intLeftMargin
            Printer.CurrentY = intTopMargin + (grdControl.RowHeight(0) *
            ↪sngScale)
            Printer.Line - Step(((grdControl.ColWidth(0) +
            ↪grdControl.ColWidth(1)) * sngScale), (intGridHeight -
            ↪grdControl.RowHeight(0)) * sngScale), RGB(224, 224, 224), BF
      End Select
   End If
   DoEvents
```

The next block draws the actual grid on the printer.

```
'Print the grid of the control.
Printer.CurrentX = intLeftMargin
Printer.CurrentY = intTopMargin
Printer.Line -Step(intGridWidth * sngScale, intGridHeight * sngScale), , B

'Print the horizontal lines.
For intRow = 0 To grdControl.Rows - 1
   If intRow = 0 Then
      intStartHeight = intTopMargin
   Else
      intStartHeight = intStartHeight + grdControl.RowHeight(intRow - 1) *
      ↪sngScale
   End If
   Printer.CurrentX = intLeftMargin
   Printer.CurrentY = intStartHeight
   Printer.Line -Step(intGridWidth * sngScale, 0)

   If fPrintWhat <> DETAIL_GRID And intRow > 0 And intRow < grdControl.Rows
   ↪- 1 Then
      'Print the shading for the legend boxes in the appropriate rows.
      Call PrintHatchLegend(grdControl, intTopMargin, intLeftMargin,
      ↪intStartHeight, sngScale, intRow)
   End If
Next intRow
DoEvents

'Print the vertical lines.
For intCol = 0 To grdControl.Cols - 1
   If intCol = 0 Then
      intStartWidth = intLeftMargin
   ElseIf intCol = 2 And fPrintWhat = LEVEL2_CHART_AND_GRID Then
      intStartWidth = intStartWidth + grdControl.ColWidth(1) * sngScale * 1.1
   Else
      intStartWidth = intStartWidth + grdControl.ColWidth(intCol - 1) *
      ↪sngScale
   End If
   Printer.CurrentY = intTopMargin
   Printer.CurrentX = intStartWidth
   Printer.Line -Step(0, intGridHeight * sngScale)
Next intCol
DoEvents
```

Finally, the text is printed on the grid just drawn on the printer.

```
'Print the text from the grid.
For intCol = 0 To grdControl.Cols - 1
   'Get the current width of grid.
   If intCol = 0 Then
      intStartWidth = intLeftMargin
   ElseIf intCol = 2 And fPrintWhat = LEVEL2_CHART_AND_GRID Then
      intStartWidth = intStartWidth + grdControl.ColWidth(1) * sngScale * 1.1
   Else
      intStartWidth = intStartWidth + grdControl.ColWidth(intCol - 1) *
      ➥sngScale
   End If

   grdControl.Col = intCol

   For intRow = 0 To grdControl.Rows - 1
      'Get the current height of grid
      If intRow = 0 Then
         intStartHeight = intTopMargin
      Else
         intStartHeight = intStartHeight + grdControl.RowHeight(intRow - 1)
         ➥* sngScale
      End If

      grdControl.Row = intRow

      'Save the text height and width of caption font.
      intTextWidth = Printer.TextWidth(grdControl.Text)
      intTextHeight = Printer.TextHeight(grdControl.Text)
      intCharWidth = Printer.TextWidth("0") / 2

      'Set the y-coordinate of the Printer object.
      Printer.CurrentY = intStartHeight + ((grdControl.RowHeight(intRow) *
      ➥sngScale) - intTextHeight) / 2

      'Set the x-coordinate of the Printer object according
      'to the Alignment property of the grid text.
      If intCol < grdControl.FixedCols Or intRow < grdControl.FixedRows Then
         intAlignment = grdControl.FixedAlignment(intCol)
         Printer.FontBold = True
      Else
         intAlignment = grdControl.ColAlignment(intCol)
         Printer.FontBold = False
      End If

      Select Case intAlignment
         Case GRID_ALIGNLEFT
            'Text aligned left.
            Printer.CurrentX = intStartWidth + intCharWidth
         Case GRID_ALIGNRIGHT
            'Text aligned right.
            Printer.CurrentX = intStartWidth + ((grdControl.ColWidth(intCol)
            ➥* sngScale) - intTextWidth) - intCharWidth
         Case GRID_ALIGNCENTER
            'Text centered.
            Printer.CurrentX = intStartWidth +
            ➥(((grdControl.ColWidth(intCol) * sngScale) - intTextWidth) / 2)
```

Day 9

Coding the Application, Part 2

```
            End Select

            'Print the grid text.
            Select Case fPrintWhat
                Case LEVEL2_CHART_AND_GRID
                    If intCol > 0 Then Printer.Print grdControl.Text
                Case LEVEL1_CHART_AND_GRID, DETAIL_GRID
                    Printer.Print grdControl.Text
            End Select
        Next intRow
        DoEvents
    Next intCol
End Sub
```

The following three procedures determine the height and width of the existing grid and determine if the font used on the grid is available on the printer. These procedures are all used by the `PrintGrid` procedure.

```
Function FindHeight (Ctrl As Control) As Integer
    Dim intCtr As Integer   'Generic loop counter.
    Dim intHeight As Integer
     intHeight = 0
     For intCtr = 0 To Ctrl.Rows - 1
         intHeight = intHeight + Ctrl.RowHeight(intCtr)
     Next intCtr
     FindHeight = intHeight

End Function

Function FindWidth (Ctrl As Control) As Integer
    Dim intCtr As Integer   'Generic loop counter
    Dim intWidth As Integer
    intWidth = 0
    For intCtr = 0 To Ctrl.Cols - 1
        If intCtr = 1 Then
           '10% extra for column 1 (bold font).
           intWidth = intWidth + 1.1 * Ctrl.ColWidth(intCtr)
        Else
           intWidth = intWidth + Ctrl.ColWidth(intCtr)
        End If
    Next intCtr

    FindWidth = intWidth
End Function

Function FindFont (Font As Variant) As Integer
    Dim intCtr As Integer   'Generic loop counter.

    For intCtr = 0 To Printer.FontCount - 1
        If Font = Printer.Fonts(intCtr) Then
            FindFont = True
            Exit Function
        End If
    Next intCtr
```

```
            FindFont = False

        End Function
```

The `PrintHatchLegend` procedure draws a series of hatched grids to match the hatching used by the chart control when it's displayed in monochrome. The hatching switches between horizontal, vertical, and diagonal hatching, depending on the data set number it applies to.

```
Sub PrintHatchLegend (grdControl As Control, intTopMargin As Integer,
➥intLeftMargin As Integer, intStartHeight As Integer,
➥sngScale As Single, intRow As Integer)
    Dim intCtr As Integer   'Generic loop counter.
    Dim intPitch As Integer
    'Print the hatching for the legend boxes in the appropriate rows.
    intPitch = 35   'Pitch (twips) between horizontal and vertical shading lines.

    For intCtr = 1 To Int(grdControl.ColWidth(0) * sngScale / intPitch)
        'Print horizontal, vertical, or diagonal lines in boxes.
        Select Case intRow
            Case 1, 4, 7
                'Horizontal shading lines.
                Printer.CurrentX = intLeftMargin
                Printer.CurrentY = intStartHeight + (intCtr * intPitch)
                Printer.Line -Step(grdControl.ColWidth(0) * sngScale, 0)
            Case 2, 5, 8
                'Vertical shading lines.
                Printer.CurrentX = intLeftMargin + (intCtr * intPitch)
                Printer.CurrentY = intStartHeight
                Printer.Line -Step(0, grdControl.RowHeight(intRow) * sngScale)
            Case 3, 6, 9
                'Print the diagonals across the top of the legend box.
                Printer.CurrentX = intLeftMargin + (intCtr * intPitch * 1.4)
                Printer.CurrentY = intStartHeight

                'Note: Adjust the pitch by Sqr(2) to maintain similar density.
                If (intCtr * intPitch * 1.4) < grdControl.ColWidth(0) Then
                    'Don't print past the edge of the legend box
                    Printer.Line -Step(grdControl.ColWidth(0) * sngScale - (intCtr *
                    ➥intPitch * 1.4), grdControl.RowHeight(intRow) * sngScale
                    ➥- (intCtr * intPitch * 1.4))
                End If

                'Print the corner-to-corner diagonal.
                If intCtr = 1 Then
                    Printer.CurrentX = intLeftMargin
                    Printer.CurrentY = intStartHeight
                    Printer.Line -Step(grdControl.ColWidth(0) * sngScale,
                    ➥grdControl.RowHeight(intRow) * sngScale)
                End If

                'Print the diagonals down the side of the legend box.
                Printer.CurrentX = intLeftMargin
                Printer.CurrentY = intStartHeight + (intCtr * intPitch * 1.4)
                If (intCtr * intPitch * 1.4) < grdControl.RowHeight(intCtr) Then
                    'Don't print past the edge of the legend box.
```

Day 9 Coding the Application, Part 2

```
            Printer.Line -Step(grdControl.ColWidth(0) * sngScale - (intCtr *
              intPitch * 1.4), grdControl.RowHeight(intRow) * sngScale
              - (intCtr * intPitch * 1.4))
         End If
      End Select
   Next intCtr
End Sub
```

Copying and Saving a Chart

Two procedures, shown in Figure 5.23, are available to copy the current chart to the clipboard or to a disk file. When you select Edit | Copy, the `mnuEditCopy_Click` procedure is executed. The Graph control has the built-in capability of copying the current graph to the clipboard. You simply set the `DrawMode` to the constant `G_COPY`.

```
'
'Copy the graph to the clipboard.
'This should change according to what is selected.
'
Sub mnuEditCopy_Click ()
   frmMDIGraph.chtMonthly.DrawMode = G_COPY
End Sub
```

The capability to save an image of the grid is also built in to the Graph control, but first you must select a filename and a location. Here, the common dialog control is used again, but this time it is the Save As dialog, set with the `Action` property. The common dialog control returns the filename and path, which are then inserted in the `ImageFile` property of the Graph control. When that property is set, the `DrawMode` property is set to the constant `G_WRITE`, and the image is written to the file.

```
Sub mnuFileSave_Click ()
   'Purpose: Display the Save common dialog to get a filename.
   cdgDialogs.CancelError = False
   cdgDialogs.DefaultExt = ".WMF"
   cdgDialogs.Filter = "Windows Metafile|*.WMF|All Files|*.*"
   cdgDialogs.Flags = OFN_OVERWRITEPROMPT
   cdgDialogs.DialogTitle = "Save Graph As A Windows Metafile"
   cdgDialogs.Action = DLG_FILE_SAVE
   'Test to verify that a file was selected.
   If cdgDialogs.Filename = "" Then
      Exit Sub
   End If
   'Create a Windows metafile file and store the chart.
   frmMDIGraph.chtMonthly.ImageFile = cdgDialogs.Filename
   frmMDIGraph.chtMonthly.DrawMode = G_WRITE
End Sub
```

Handling the Pop-Up Labels

The pop-up labels are displayed whenever the mouse is over one of the toolbar buttons. The `MouseMove` event occurs whenever the mouse moves over an active control. Two `MouseMove` procedures are used here—one for the graph class buttons and one for the graph type buttons. The two procedures operate by first turning everything off and then displaying the label for the selected button.

```
'
'Display the pop-up label when the pointer is over the button.
'
Sub gpbGraphClass_MouseMove (Index As Integer, Button As Integer,
➥Shift As Integer, X As Single, Y As Single)
    'Turn everything off, then turn one on.
    Call HidePopUpLabels
    lblPopUpClassLabels(Index).Visible = True
End Sub
'
'Display the pop-up label when the pointer is over the button.
'
Sub gpbGraphType_MouseMove (Index As Integer, Button As Integer,
➥Shift As Integer, X As Single, Y As Single)
    'Turn everything off, then turn one on.
    HidePopUpLabels
    lblPopUpTypeLabels(Index).Visible = True
End Sub
```

A problem with pop-up labels is making them go away when you move off the control. If the user moves fast enough, she will move across the 3D panel before Visual Basic can register a MouseMove event for that control. Because of that problem, the HidePopUpLabels procedure is called from several places, including both 3D panels, the MDI_Graph and MDI_Grid forms, the graph control, the pie chart control, and the grid control.

```
'
'Hide any button labels that were left visible when
'the user moved off the button bar too fast.
'
'
Sub Panel3D1_MouseMove (Button As Integer, Shift As Integer, X As Single,
➥Y As Single)
    Call HidePopUpLabels
End Sub

'
'Hide any button labels that were left visible when
'the user moved off the button bar too fast.
'
'
Sub Panel3D2_MouseMove (Button As Integer, Shift As Integer, X As Single,
➥Y As Single)
    Call HidePopUpLabels
End Sub
```

Both the MDI_Graph and MDI_Grid forms contain the following Form_MouseMove procedure.

```
'
'Hide any button labels that were left visible when
'the user moved off the button bar too fast.
'
```

Day 9: Coding the Application, Part 2

```
Sub Form_MouseMove (Button As Integer, Shift As Integer, X As Single,
➥Y As Single)
    Call HidePopUpLabels
End Sub
```

The `HidePopUpLabels` procedure simply loops over all the labels and sets their `Visible` property to False.

```
'
'Turn off all button labels.
'
Sub HidePopUpLabels ()
    Dim intCtr
    For intCtr = 1 To NUM_CLASS_BUTTONS
        frmMDIMain.lblPopUpClassLabels(intCtr).Visible = False
    Next intCtr
    For intCtr = 1 To NUM_TYPE_BUTTONS
        frmMDIMain.lblPopUpTypeLabels(intCtr).Visible = False
    Next intCtr
End Sub
```

Selecting a Chart Using the Menus

In addition to selecting a chart using the toolbar, you can select a chart using the View menu. All of the submenus on the View menu are control arrays, and the `Index` property of the control array is set to the chart code. Thus, all you have to do is check the `Index` property to see which chart the user wants to view. All of the menu event procedures are written like the one that follows. They simply get the `Index` property and pass it to the `SelectChartType` procedure.

```
'
'Select one of the margins charts.
'
Sub mnuViewMargins_Click (Index As Integer)
    Call SelectChartType(Index)
End Sub
```

The `SelectChartType` procedure, which is also on the `MDI_Main` form, extracts the chart class and type and simulates button presses by directly calling the chart class and chart type toolbar button event procedures.

```
'
'Select one of the chart types.
'
Sub SelectChartType (intIndex As Integer)
    'intIndex equals the chart code.
    Dim intTheClass As Integer
    Dim intTheType As Integer

    intTheClass = intIndex \ 10
    intTheType = intIndex Mod 10

    'Simulate button clicks to display the selected chart.
    gpbGraphClass(intTheClass).Value = True
```

```
    gpbGraphType(intTheType).Value = True
End Sub
```

Viewing the Detail Grid Using the Menus

You can also make the detail grid visible by selecting View | Details. The `mnuViewDetails_Click` procedure calls the `ToggleGrid` procedure to toggle the grid visible and cause it to be displayed.

```
'
'Toggle display of the grid.
'
Sub mnuViewDetails_Click ()
    Call ToggleGrid
End Sub
```

Initialization

The initialization structure, shown in Figure 5.24, is performed by the startup procedure, `Main`. The `Main` procedure opens and loads the .INI file, sets some text arrays, and displays the first chart. The procedure first calls `LoadAndParseINIFile` to open the .INI file and read its contents. Next, it loads three- and four-letter month abbreviations and the numeric month abbreviations and stores them in global text arrays. These arrays are used to label the chart and grid.

```
'
'Startup procedure.
'Open the database, initialize strings, etc.
'
Sub Main ()
    Dim intCtr As Integer   'Generic loop counter.

'Open the .INI file and load the database path and the current year.
    Call LoadAndParseINIFile

    For intCtr = 1 To 12
       'The year (1995) and day (1) used in DateSerial are dummy values.
       strMonths(intCtr, 1) = Format(DateSerial(1995, intCtr, 1), "mmm")
       strMonths(intCtr, 2) = Format(DateSerial(1995, intCtr, 1), "mmmm")
       If intCtr < 10 Then
          strMonths(intCtr, 3) = "0" & LTrim$(Str$(intCtr))
       Else
          strMonths(intCtr, 3) = LTrim$(Str$(intCtr))
       End If
    Next intCtr
```

Next, the procedure initializes some flags and then opens the database file and the `tblDefinitions` table. The database file and the `tblDefinitions` table objects are stored in global variables, so they are available everywhere in this application.

```
    'Clear the flags.
    fInhibitResize = False    'Don't inhibit resizing.
    fInhibit = False          'Don't inhibit button clicks.
```

Day 9: Coding the Application, Part 2

```
        fIsCrosstab = False    'Flag indicating a crosstab query.
        fShowGrid = False      'Don't display grid with graph.

        'Open the database and the operational tables.
        Set dbGraphs = OpenDatabase(strDataFile)
        Set tblGraphs = dbGraphs.OpenTable("tblDefinitions")

        tblGraphs.Index = "PrimaryKey"

        'Open the initial form.
        fInhibit = True
        frmMDIMain.Show
        DoEvents
        fInhibit = False
        frmMDIGraph.Show
        DoEvents
```

Finally, the procedure displays the first chart type by calling the event procedure for the first chart class button.

```
        'Put up the first chart type by clicking on the class button.
        tblGraphs.MoveLast
        frmMDIMain.gpbGraphClass(SALES_CLASS).Value = True
        'Force a redraw of the graph.
        frmMDIGraph.chtMonthly.DrawMode = G_DRAW
        'Hide the banner and display the first chart.
        frmMDIGraph.picBanner.Visible = False
        frmMDIGraph.chtMonthly.Visible = True

        DoEvents
End Sub
```

The LoadAndParseINIFile procedure loads the DCNSPT.INI file and parses its data. Currently, only three pieces of data are needed from the startup section of the file: the location and name of the rollup data file, the year to display data for, and the default help filename. If any of these values are missing, the procedure displays a message and ends the application.

```
'
'Load and parse the .INI file.
'
Sub LoadAndParseINIFile ()
    Dim strALine As String
    Dim fgotStart As Integer
    Dim intEqMark As Integer
    Dim strVariable As String
    Dim strValue As String

    'Assume that the file is in the Windows directory.
    Open "c:\windows\dcnspt.ini" For Input As #1
    Line Input #1, strALine    'Skip a line
    'Find [startup].
    fgotStart = False
    Do While Not EOF(1)
        Line Input #1, strALine
        If strALine = "[startup]" Then
```

```
            fgotStart = True
            Exit Do
        End If
    Loop
    'Bomb out if [startup] not found.
    If Not fgotStart Then GoTo Bombout
    'Read and parse the startup information.
    Line Input #1, strALine
    Do While InStr(1, strALine, "[") = 0 And Not EOF(1)   'Stop if EOF or
                                                          'a new section.
        intEqMark = InStr(1, strALine, "=")
        If intEqMark = 0 Then GoTo Bombout
        strVariable = Trim(Left(strALine, intEqMark - 1))
        strValue = Trim(Right(strALine, Len(strALine) - intEqMark))
        Select Case strVariable
            Case "DataFile"
                strDataFile = strValue
            Case "Year"
                strYear = strValue
            Case "Help"
                App.HelpFile = strValue
        End Select
        Line Input #1, strALine
Loop
    Close #1
    If strDataFile = "" Or strYear = "" Or App.HelpFile = "" Then GoTo Bombout
Exit Sub
Bombout:
    MsgBox "Corrupt INI file, can't continue."
    End
End Sub
```

When the `frmMDIMain` form is loaded, its `Form_Load` procedure initializes its default size on-screen. The size set fills a large part of the screen on a standard VGA monitor. If different monitors are to be used, this size might need to change or might need to be set dynamically according to the actual screen size.

```
'
'Set the initial dimensions of the main form.
'
Sub MDIForm_Load ()
    'Turn off resizing until we are done making changes.
    fInhibitResize = True
    frmMDIMain.Width = 8750
    frmMDIMain.Height = 6000
    frmMDIMain.Left = 400
    frmMDIMain.Top = 1100
    DoEvents
    fInhibitResize = False
End Sub
```

Initializing the `frmMDIGraph` form is handled by its `Form_Load` procedure. When the form loads, it displays the banner to hide the contents of the form while they are being initialized. The `frmMDIGraph` form has many controls that might confuse the user if he were to see them during startup. The banner simply hides everything while it displays the name of the program and the credits. Next, the procedure sets some of the default properties of the `chtMonthly` graph control.

Coding the Application, Part 2

```
'
'Initialize the graph form.
'
Sub Form_Load ()
    Dim intCtr As Integer   'Generic loop counter.
    'Hide the pie chart.
    frmMDIGraph.chtPieChart.Visible = False
    'Display the banner.
    frmMDIGraph.picBanner.Visible = True

    'Run mode settings for the monthly graphs.
    chtMonthly.FontUse = G_ALL_TEXT    'Set all fonts to the font
                                       'family and style.
    chtMonthly.FontFamily = G_SWISS    'Set the font family to Arial (Swiss).
    chtMonthly.FontStyle = G_BOLD      'Set the font attribute to bold.
    chtMonthly.AutoInc = G_OFF         'Turn off autoincrement.
    chtMonthly.NumPoints = 12          'Up to 12 months of data.

    DoEvents

End Sub
```

Ending the Program

Normally you end the program by selecting File | Exit. The event procedure attached to this menu command simply executes the End statement, which closes all open files and ends the program. A second event procedure must be included to end the program in the event that the user closes the main form.

Showstopper: If you close the main form for an application without ending the application, and another form was in memory and hidden, that other form remains in memory but is inaccessible. This state causes a problem, because the inaccessible form uses up memory that can't be reclaimed unless you quit Windows and start up again. To prevent this problem, place an End statement into the Form_Unload procedure for the main form of an application. Closing the main form should always cleanly end an application.

```
Sub MDIForm_Unload (Cancel As Integer)
    End
End Sub

Sub mnuFileExit_Click ()
    End
End Sub
```

The About Menu

Help | About generally displays the copyright and the program credits. Here, we redisplay the banner used at the beginning of the program. A second procedure hides the banner when the user clicks on it. (The other items on the Help menu will be discussed on Day 12.)

```
'Display the banner.
'
Sub mnuHelpAbout_Click ()
    'Display the banner.
    frmMDIGraph.picBanner.Visible = True
    'A mouse click on the banner hides it.
End Sub

Sub picBanner_Click ()
    'Hide the banner.
    frmMDIGraph.picBanner.Visible = False
End Sub
```

Using the Test Forms

Two test forms used in this program during design mode to ease the development of the procedures determine a double-click event on the chart or pie chart. The frmTestMonth form, shown in Figure 9.1, is displayed when the global constant SHOW_TEST_FORMS is True. The chtMonthly_MouseMove event procedure is where the test is made and the form is displayed. The test form shows the current mouse position and the month using the current logic set in the code. The form is used to determine how to select a month label and to see that the month selected in code is the same month that the mouse pointer is on.

Figure 9.1.
The frmTestMonth form.

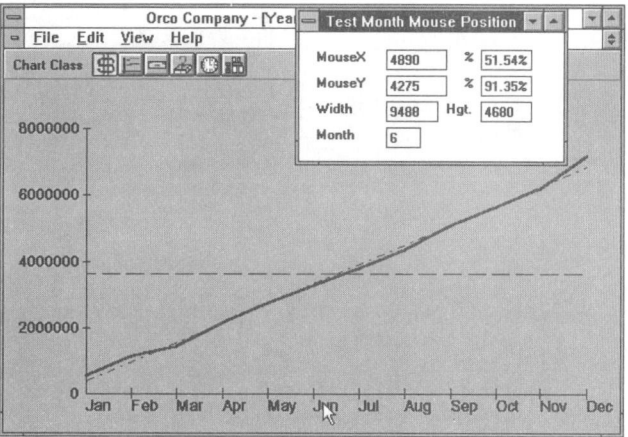

Day 9: Coding the Application, Part 2

```
'
'Hide any button labels that were left visible when
'the user moved off the button bar too fast.
'
Sub chtMonthly_MouseMove (Button As Integer, Shift As Integer, X As Single,
➥Y As Single)
    Call HidePopUpLabels
    'In design mode, display the test form to see what
    'values the x- and y-coordinates of the mouse are.
    If SHOW_TEST_FORMS Then
        'Global constant SHOW_TEST_FORMS determines appearance of form.
        frmTestMonth.Show
        frmTestMonth.txtMouseX = X
        frmTestMonth.txtMouseY = Y
        frmTestMonth.txtMouseXPct = Format$(X / frmMDIGraph.chtMonthly.Width,
➥"##0.00%")
        frmTestMonth.txtMouseYPct = Format$(Y / frmMDIGraph.chtMonthly.Height,
➥"###0.00%")
        frmTestMonth.txtWidth = frmMDIGraph.chtMonthly.Width
        frmTestMonth.txtHeight = frmMDIGraph.chtMonthly.Height
        frmTestMonth.txtMonthNum = intTestDblClickMonth(X, Y)
    End If

End Sub
```

The `frmTestTrig` form is displayed when the pie chart is visible, as shown in Figure 9.2. The form shows the current mouse position as well as the angle and the selected pie wedge. The form is displayed by the `intPieHotHit` function, but that function normally is run only when the user double-clicks on a wedge of the pie. To make it more useful, a call to `intPieHotHit` is made in the `chtPieChart_MouseMove` event procedure. In this way, the `MouseMove` event procedure continually updates the mouse position and the selected wedge.

Figure 9.2.
The `frmTestTrig` *form.*

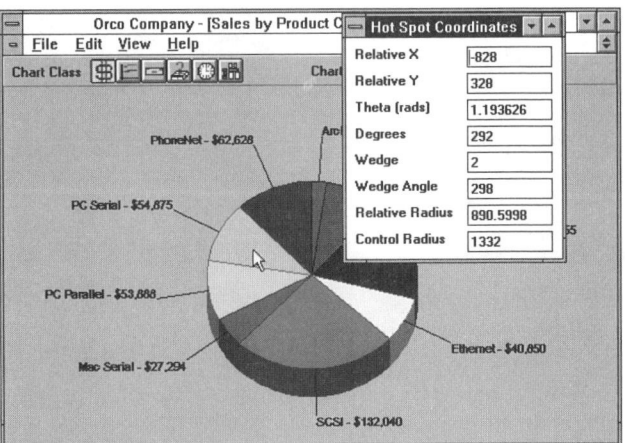

```
'Hide any button labels that were left visible when
'the user moved off the button bar too fast.
'
Sub chtPieChart_MouseMove (Button As Integer, Shift As Integer, X As Single,
➥Y As Single)
   Dim intDummy As Integer
   Call HidePopUpLabels
   If SHOW_TEST_FORMS Then   'Show test coordinates.
      intDummy = intPieHotHit(CInt(X), CInt(Y))
   End If
End Sub
```

Resizing Things

If the user changes the size of the MDI parent form, the graph and grid forms need to be resized to fill out the new size of the MDI parent form. This is handled by calling `ResizeChartAndGrid` in the `MDIForm_Resize` event procedure.

```
'
'The form has been resized.
'Adjust everything to fit.
'
Sub MDIForm_Resize ()
   Call ResizeChartAndGrid
End Sub
```

Modification Notes

Modifying an existing code can be a difficult experience if you don't know exactly what the code's author was doing. Before doing any revisions, study the code in detail until you understand how it works, and then make your modifications. If the modifications are major, you need to go through a structured design anyway, so why not go ahead and do it right. Additionally, if you do rewrite a program, that doesn't mean that you have to throw out everything and start from scratch. There's no reason not to reuse reasonably well-written debugged procedures from an existing code.

> **Note:** When modifying someone else's code, it might be simpler to recode an old procedure instead of trying to figure out how it works and then making changes to it. You must assess each case on its own merits and proceed accordingly.

Coding the Application, Part 2

Debugging the Process

Serious debugging starts here, as you code the procedure. Syntax errors show up immediately and are fixed as you write the code. Many other errors show up when the code is being compiled, especially if you put an `Option Explicit` statement at the beginning of each module.

When the code finally runs, the more difficult errors become evident. Errors in logic or in the actual execution of the code appear and cause the code to operate incorrectly. Problems with the Visual Basic system also show up, and work-arounds must be created. For example, in Visual Basic version 3, if a variable is declared as a global database or table object, it should be available in all procedures in all modules. Unfortunately, it is not. When the variable is accessed in another procedure, it works once, and after that it is treated as an ordinary variable and causes errors. The work-around is to declare a new object variable in the new module and then equate it to the global object variable. The local copy is then used in the procedures.

Bring in the Customer

When you reach a point where most of the code is running but not completely debugged, you might want to bring in the customer and let him see what you're doing. He might want to be assured that you're doing what he expects, and he also might be able to see errors in the output that aren't apparent to you. This is especially true in modeling situations where the results aren't obvious. Here it is the customer's experience with the mathematics and the process involved that might give him a feel for what the results should look like.

For example, numerical solutions of nonlinear differential equations are often extremely unstable. If you don't have a good feel for what the results should look like, you might waste a lot of time calculating with garbage.

Summary

Today you completed the initial coding of the application, creating the drill-down chart and using the built-in common dialog boxes to print and save files. The next chapter adds error traps to the existing code to prevent problems with the database from crashing your code.

The code as it stands at the end of this chapter is in the \DCNSPT1 directory on the included CD.

Adding Error Trapping to the Application

Adding Error Trapping to the Application

Thought you were done writing code, didn't you? Well, not quite. You still have to add error trapping to the application, and then you have to debug it, which is the topic of Day 11. Error trapping consists of inserting code blocks that capture runtime errors and handle them instead of letting your code crash.

Today you will learn

- how error trapping works
- how to create an error trap
- what to do when your application encounters an error

The Goal of Day 10

The goal of Day 10 is to learn the operation of and uses for error trapping. When a system that doesn't have error trapping encounters an error, it displays an error dialog box and then immediately ends the program. The goal of error trapping is to capture these error events and handle them instead of letting the system do it. Your code can then try to correct the problem or at least make a graceful exit from the application instead of just crashing.

Understanding Error Trapping

Error trapping is an *out-of-band operation* for capturing errors. Out-of-band means that the flow of control in an error trap proceeds outside of an application's normal flow of control. When an error occurs in a running application, the system halts the program, displays an error description, and then quits the program if it's compiled or drops into break mode if you're running in the interpreter. For example, in Figure 10.1, procedures A, B, and E are the active call chain. In other words, procedure A was executing and called procedure B, which began executing and called procedure E, which contains the current execution point. In a normally executing program, E would complete and return to procedure B, which would eventually complete and return to procedure A. If an error occurs while procedure E is executing, control flows outside of this active call chain to the system error handler, and the program ends.

As shown in Figure 10.2, when you turn on error trapping in a procedure, the error trap intercepts the call to the system error handler and directs it to your program's error handler instead. Since you know what your program is supposed to do, you can design into your error handler the capability to correct the problem and proceed. If you can't fix the error, you can at least save all your work and close all your files before ending.

Error trapping doesn't follow the object-oriented block structure of your code. It's an unstructured jump to the error handler. This jump is outside of the normal flow of execution in a procedure and can occur from anywhere in a procedure that an error handler is active. In this way, error trapping overlays your existing application and can be added during the original coding, or later after the coding is complete.

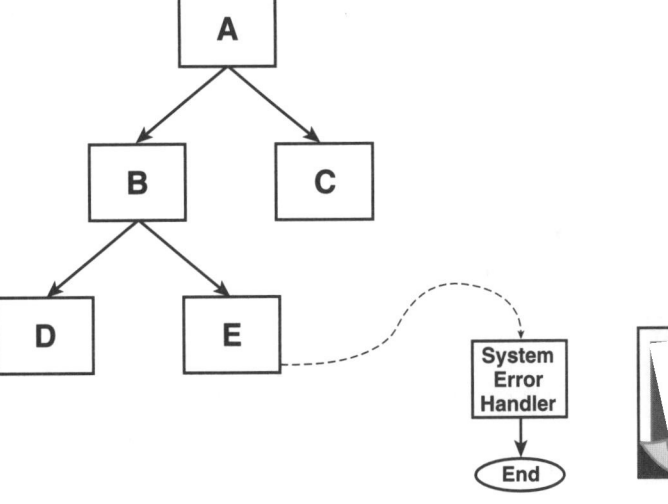

Figure 10.1.
The control flow for the system error handler.

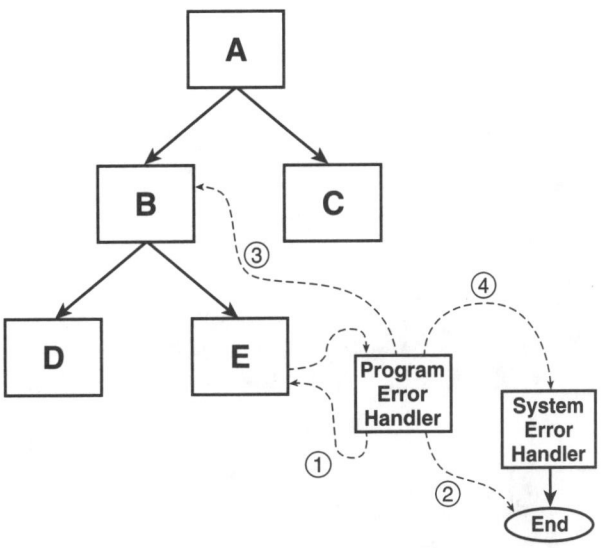

Figure 10.2.
The control flow for a program error handler. The marked paths indicate options available to the error handler.

When an error trap captures an error, it passes that error to your error handler. An *error handler* is simply a block of code whose task is to "handle" the error. Unlike an ordinary code block, an error handler knows

- that an error has occured
- the error number (`Err`)
- the line number of the error (`Erl` if you happened to number the lines)

Adding Error Trapping to the Application

- how to return to the statement that caused the error (Resume)
- how to return to the statement following the statement that caused the error (Resume Next)

Using this information, you write code to determine if the error is something you expected and can fix, or if it's something unexpected, requiring you to terminate the program.

For example, if you have a formula with a variable in the denominator and you get a divide-by-zero error, you would check that variable to see if it's zero and perform some action if it is. What you do depends on what result you expect from the formula when the variable is zero. You could make the variable be a very small but not quite zero value and recalculate the formula, or you could set the value of the formula and continue with the next statement.

For example, the following formula converges to the number 1 when x is zero:

```
y = Sin(x)/x
```

If you try to calculate this with x equal to zero, you will get a divide-by-zero error. You could set x equal to 0.00000001 and recalculate the formula, or set y equal to 1 and continue with the next statement.

Textbook Tip: The following are some error trap commands:

On Error Goto Label: Enables an error trap. Label is the first statement of the error handler. If 0 is used as the label, the error trap is disabled.

Err: A built-in variable that contains the error number of the last error that occurred.

Erl: A built-in variable that contains the line number of the closest numbered statement. Since lines are rarely numbered anymore, this isn't very useful.

Resume: A statement that causes execution to continue with the statement that caused the error.

Resume Next: A statement that causes execution to continue with the statement after the one that caused the error.

Resume Label: A statement that causes execution to continue at the indicated Label. Label can be anywhere in the current module.

Error$: A function that returns the text displayed by the system error handler when an error occurs. The error number is used as an argument to the function.

Error: A statement that simulates an error. The argument is the error number of the error to simulate.

As shown in Figure 10.2, you have several choices as to what to do after fixing or not fixing the problem that caused the error. In the figure, an error trap is active for procedure E. If an error occurs in that procedure, control flows to the error handler. After the error handler has processed the error, it can do one of the following:

- [ ] If it corrects the error, it can return control to the statement in which the error occurred (using Resume) and try again, or it can return control to the statement following the statement in which the error occurred (using Resume Next) (path 1).
- [ ] It can gracefully terminate the program (path 2).
- [ ] It can send control to another procedure in the same module using Resume Label (path 3).
- [ ] It can reissue the error and let the system error handler handle it using Error Err (path 4).

In many cases, the cause of an error can be corrected, and the program should continue without crashing. Other times, you have a situation in which the error must end the program, but some things need to be done before the program ends, like saving a file. Error trapping allows you to handle these abnormal situations in a much more controlled way.

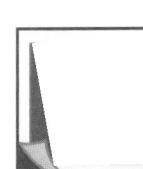

Showstopper: An error handler must end with a Resume or Exit (Sub or Function) statement. If the calculation point reaches an End Sub or End Function statement in the same procedure where the error occured, without executing Resume or Exit your error handler will generate an additional error.

Control Flow in an Error Situation

The flow of control in an application with active error handlers is quite different from the standard procedure call and return structure of a normally executing application. If an error handler is active in a procedure and an error occurs, control is immediately passed to the handler. If a procedure doesn't have an active error handler but another procedure in the active call chain does, control is passed to that handler instead. If more than one error handler is active in the active call chain, the first handler you encounter as you move up the call chain from the error location handles the error. If an error handler can't handle an error and passes it back to the system, the error is passed up to the next active error handler in the active call chain until it reaches the beginning. If it is again passed back to the system, the system error handler handles the error in its normal way.

For example, in Figure 10.3, procedures A and E have error handlers that are activated when the procedures are executed. If the current execution point is in procedure E and an error occurs, the procedure E error handler is given control (path 1). If D is the active procedure and an error

347

occurs, since no error handler is active in procedure D, procedure B (path 2) is checked for an active error handler. Because B doesn't have an active error handler, procedure A (path 3) is checked for an active error handler. Since procedure A has an active error handler, control is passed to the procedure A error handler (path 4). If an error occurs in procedure E and the procedure E error handler passes the error back to the system, procedure B is checked, and then A, and the procedure A error handler again processes the error.

Figure 10.3.
The hierarchy of control flow for call chains with more than one active error handler.

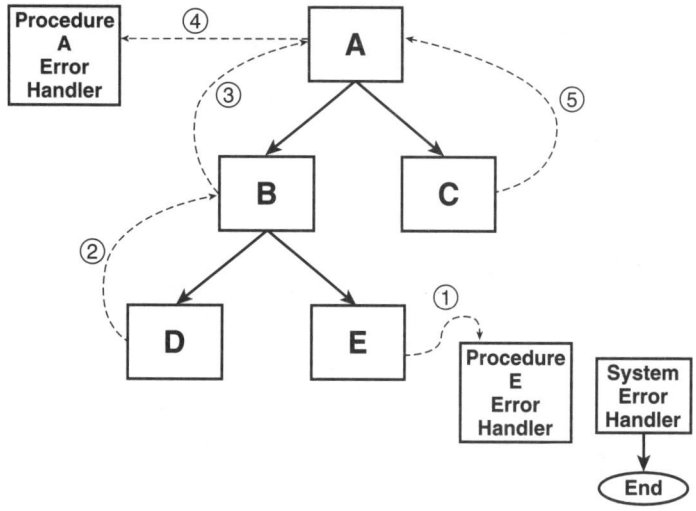

Error Handler Hierarchies

Error handlers can pass an error back to the system if the error handler can't do anything about it. Do this with the statement Error Err, where Err is the system variable that contains the error number. Use this capability to create a hierarchy of error handlers. Have error handlers in a specific procedure handle errors that are specific to that procedure. In the parent procedure, place an error handler to handle specific errors for the parent procedure and more general errors for the parent procedure and all its child procedures. At the top of the call chain, place the "If all else fails" error handler to do a graceful shutdown and end your program.

Common Locations for Error Trapping

There are two common locations for error trapping: input/output (I/O) and numeric procedures. The most common and necessary location for error trapping is in I/O procedures. I/O procedures are the most likely place for things to be different from what your program expects. When your program attempts to open a file, the file might be missing or might already have been opened by another application. When your program reads a file, the data might be less than what you expected. When your program attempts to write a file, the media might be write-protected, out of space, or any number of other possibilities. Instead of checking for every possibility before running the susceptible code, use an error handler and let it take control if there is an error.

Accessing external programs and databases is also an I/O procedure and is susceptible to unexpected problems. If you open a connection to an external application and that application returns an error, you generally want to just close the communication channel and give the user the opportunity to do something else. If you send a request to a database engine and the request is improper or the data is unavailable, you generally don't want your application to crash. You want it to issue a warning that there is a problem and then continue. Error trapping is how you manage these situations.

The second common place for an error trap is in high-powered numeric procedures that might process improper data. Improper data includes such things as dividing by 0 or taking the square root of a negative number. An error trap here allows you to continue or correct a calculation instead of crashing your application.

Toggling the Trap

During program development, you want an application to crash when an error occurs and drop into the debugger. When the application is finished, you want the error handler to take care of the errors instead of having your application crash. To make this change simple to accomplish, control the enabling of the error traps with a global constant. Then you only have to change the value of the constant to enable or disable the error traps.

For example, the following code fragment shows a generic implementation of an error trap:

```
...code...
...code...
'Enable the error trap and designate the code
'starting with the label MyTrap as the error handler.
On Error Goto MyTrap
'The following code is at risk of causing an error.
...code...
...code...
```

Day 10: Adding Error Trapping to the Application

```
'Use an Exit Sub statement to protect the
'error handler from accidental execution.
Exit Sub
MyTrap:   'The label marking the start of the error handler.
'Examine the variable Err to see if the error can be corrected.
...code...
If correctable Then
   'If the error can be corrected, do it and resume.
   ...code...
   Resume
Else
   'If the error can't be corrected, pass it back to the system.
   Error Err
End If
End Sub
```

The Decision Support Application Project

The decision support application doesn't change the contents of any files except when saving an image of the current graph, so if it crashes, it probably won't hurt anything. For this reason, the system error handler is sufficient for most problems. If the program crashes, it crashes, and you just have to start it again. The program does connect to a database, download tables, and execute queries. If any of these operations were to fail, the system error handler would end the program. Since it won't do to have the program crashing whenever a table is missing, error traps are needed in all the procedures that access the database engine.

Nine procedures access the database in a way that could fail. Opening a database, opening a table, and running a query are operations that are prone to failure. Accessing field contents of an already open table is unlikely to cause an error unless the field name is wrong, and that error should have been taken care of during the debugging stage. Here are the procedures that need error trap protection:

Main
DrawChartAndGrid
FillLegendArrays
GridColRowHeaders
GridColHeaders
SetGridCrossfoot
Form_Load (drill-down options form)
DisplayDDData
PopulateGrid

Out of this list, five procedures are subprocedures of other procedures on this list. The four subprocedures shown in a regular (nonbold) font don't need an error trap, because any errors are handled by the trap in the parent procedures. The procedures shown in bold need to have error traps added to them. `SetGridCrossfoot` is a subprocedure of the `DrawChartAndGrid` procedure. It could have its errors trapped by `DrawChartAndGrid`'s error trap, but because of the large amount of database access in that procedure, it has its own error trap to help localize a problem if one occurs.

The *DEBUGON* Global Constant

While the program is being debugged, you want it to crash whenever there is a database error so you can see what the problem is and correct it. Thus, the global constant DEBUGON is used to turn the error traps on and off. DEBUGON is defined in the test and debugging flags section of the declarations section of the DCNSPT.BAS module. The statement is shown in bold in the following code segment. Whenever DEBUGON is True, error trapping is turned off.

```
'Test and debugging flags
Global Const DEBUGON = True              'Turn debugging mode on or off.
Global Const SHOW_TEST_FORMS = False    'Display test forms.
```

Error Trapping in the Main Procedure

The `Main` procedure has two possible locations for I/O errors—the `LoadAndParseINIFile` procedure call, and the statements that open the GRAPHS.MDB database and the `tblDefinitions` table. The `LoadAndParseINIFile` procedure must open the .INI file and read it. If the .INI file isn't in the Windows directory where it's supposed to be or the file isn't readable for some reason, this procedure could fail. The statements that open the database and the table could also fail if the database or the table isn't where it should be.

To add an error trap to this procedure, insert the line

```
If Not DEBUGON Then On Error GoTo StartUpError
```

before the call to the `LoadAndParseINIFile` procedure. The `If Not DEBUGON Then` part of the statement tests the global constant DEBUGON to see if it's False. If so, the second half of the statement, `On Error GoTo StartUpError`, is executed. It turns on error trapping and designates the statement label `StartUpError` as the starting point for the error handler. If any error occurs in this procedure or in any of its subprocedures that don't have a local error trap, control jumps to the `StartUpError` label at the end of the procedure.

The error handler for this procedure is really very simple. When an error occurs, the handler displays a dialog box containing the error and then ends the program. At this point, forcing the program to end is the most reasonable alternative. If either the .INI file, the database file, or the `tblDefinitions` table has a problem, it's not possible to continue. The additions to the `Main` procedure are shown in bold in the listing that follows.

Day 10: Adding Error Trapping to the Application

Logging the Errors

An error handler is a good place to insert code to create a log of trapped errors while debugging an application. Include in the log any pertinent information to help you determine an error's cause. Add code to the error handler to open the log file and append an entry to it. Use the information in the log file to debug the application or any attached files, databases, or other attached applications. Normally you want to remove or disable this code in the released version of your application.

```
'Startup procedure.
'Open the database, initialize strings, etc.
'
Sub Main ()
    Dim intCtr As Integer   'Generic loop counter.

    'Turn on the error handler.
    If Not DEBUGON Then On Error GoTo StartUpError

'Open the .INI file and load the
'database path and the current year.
    Call LoadAndParseINIFile


    .
    .
    .
    ...skipped lines...
    .
    .
    .

    'Put up the first chart type by clicking on the class button.
    tblGraphs.MoveLast
    frmMDIMain.gpbGraphClass(SALES_CLASS).Value = True
    'Force a redraw of the graph.
    frmMDIGraph.chtMonthly.DrawMode = G_DRAW
      'Hide the banner and display the first chart.
    frmMDIGraph.picBanner.Visible = False
    frmMDIGraph.chtMonthly.Visible = True

    DoEvents

    Exit Sub

StartUpError:
    MsgBox Error$ & Chr$(13) & "Quitting application.", MB_ICONSTOP,
➥"Start-Up Error"
    End

End Sub
```

Protecting the Error Handler

The `Exit Sub` statement placed just before the label that starts the error handler not only supplies an exit point for the procedure, but it also protects the error handler from being entered during the procedure's normal execution.

Error Trapping in the *DrawMonthlyChartAndGrid* Procedure

The `DrawMonthlyChartAndGrid` procedure does a lot of database access, both in the procedure itself and in its subprocedures. The error trap is enabled near the beginning of the procedure and the error handler is located at the end. The errors expected here are generally caused by missing data in the database, so the error handler doesn't make any corrections. It just warns the user that there was a problem and then gracefully ends the procedure, cleaning up any loose ends. The program is still running, and the user can simply select another object to display.

One other statement in the procedure

```
If DEBUGON Then Clipboard.SetText strSQL
```

copies the `strSQL` string to the clipboard if debugging is enabled, making it easy to examine which SQL strings are being sent to the database engine. The statements added to `DrawMonthlyChartAndGrid` are in bold.

```
'
'Draw the monthly graph. If this is a crosstab chart, fill the
'grid with data. The grid is not displayed unless fShowGrid is true.
'
Sub DrawChartAndGrid ()

    'Local variables.
    Dim fPlotPoints As Integer     'Turn on plotting of points.
    Dim intDataSets As Integer     'Number of data sets.
    Dim intSet As Integer          'Data set counter.
    .
    .
    .
...skipped lines...
    .
    .
    Next intCtr
    If Not fPlotPoints Then
       MsgBox "Table '" & tblGraphs("DataTable") & "' not available.", 16,
       ➥"Programmer at Work"
       Exit Sub
    End If
```

Day 10: Adding Error Trapping to the Application

```
    'Turn on the error handler if not debugging.
    If Not DEBUGON Then On Error GoTo DrawError

    Screen.MousePointer = HOURGLASS   'Set the mouse pointer to the hourglass.
    .
    .
    .
...skipped lines...
    .
    .
    .
    'Create an SQL string for the rollup
    'table and create a snapshot with it.
    strSQL = strCreateSQL()
    'Paste the SQL statement to the clipboard.
    If DEBUGON Then Clipboard.SetText strSQL

    Set ssGraph = dbGraphs.CreateSnapshot(strSQL)

    'Fill the legend arrays for the grid and graph controls.
    Call FillLegendArrays
    .
    .
    .
...skipped lines...
    .
    .
    .
    'Draw the graph.
    frmMDIGraph.chtMonthly.DrawMode = G_DRAW

    'Reset the mouse pointer.
    Screen.MousePointer = DEFAULT

Exit Sub
'Process any errors drawing the chart.
DrawError:
    MsgBox Error$, MBICON_STOP, "Error Drawing Graph or Chart"
    Screen.MousePointer = DEFAULT   'Reset the mouse pointer.
    Exit Sub
End Sub
```

Error Trapping in the *SetGridCrossfoot* Procedure

The SetGridCrossfoot procedure is a subprocedure of the DrawChartAndGrid procedure. It could use that procedure's error trap to handle its errors. However, this procedure does a lot of database accessing, so it gets its own error trap to better localize any problems. The trap is enabled after the variables are declared, and the error handler is located at the end displays an error and exits the procedure. The additions to SetGridCrossfoot are in bold.

```
'Add the totals to the bottom of the grid.
'
Sub SetGridCrossfoot ()

    Dim intRow As Integer
    Dim intCol As Integer
    ReDim intNotNullRows(frmMDIGraph.chtMonthly.NumSets) As Integer
    ReDim intNotNullCols(frmMDIGraph.chtMonthly.NumPoints) As Integer

    'Turn the error handler on if not debugging.
    If Not DEBUGON Then On Error GoTo CrossfootError

    varColTotals(0) = 0
.
.
.
...skipped lines...
.
.
.
    Select Case tblGraphs("Units")
        Case "$"
            frmMDIGraph.grdMonthly.Text = Format$(varRowTotals(0), "$#,##0")
        Case "%"
            frmMDIGraph.grdMonthly.Text = Format$(varRowTotals(0), "##0.0%")
        Case "Avg"
            frmMDIGraph.grdMonthly.Text = Format$(varRowTotals(0), "##0.00")
        Case Else
            frmMDIGraph.grdMonthly.Text = Format$(varRowTotals(0), "#,##0.00")
    End Select
    Exit Sub

CrossfootError:
    MsgBox "Error computing totals.", MB_ICONSTOP, "Crossfooting Error"
    Exit Sub
End Sub
```

Error Trapping in the *Form_Load* Procedure

The Form_Load procedure of the drill-down options form, DDN_OPTS.FRM, obtains data from several database files, so you should protect it with an error trap. The trap is enabled after the variables are declared, and the error handler is at the end. The changes to Form_Load are in bold.

```
'
'Load the drill-down options form and shift it left or right.
'
Sub Form_Load ()
    'Note: This procedure must be in the Load event handler.
    '      Otherwise, the position is not set on the first
    '      change from left to right (or vice versa).
```

Day 10: Adding Error Trapping to the Application

```
        Dim intCtr As Integer   'Generic counter.
        Dim tblDefs As Table    'Temporary table def to pass
                                'the global table to a form.
        Const FORM_TOP_HEIGHT = 1375  'Height of form header, menu bar, and toolbar.
        Const EDGE_OFFSET = 500       'Offset from edge of form.

        'Turn on the error handler.
        If Not DEBUGON Then On Error GoTo DDNOptionsError

        'Import the global table def. This is a bug workaround for VB-3.
        Set tblDefs = tblGraphs
        'Center form vertically.
        frmDrillOptions.Top = frmMDIMain.Top + FORM_TOP_HEIGHT + (frmMDIMain.Height
        ➥- FORM_TOP_HEIGHT - frmDrillOptions.Height) / 2

        .
        .
        .
   ...skipped lines...
        .
        .
        .
        If InStr(tblDefs("DDFlag"), "P") Then optDrill(DDPRODUCT).Enabled = True
        If InStr(tblDefs("DDFlag"), "C") Then optDrill(DDCUSTOMER).Enabled = True
        If InStr(tblDefs("DDFlag"), "S") Then optDrill(DDSALESMAN).Enabled = True
        Exit Sub

   DDNOptionsError:
        MsgBox Error$, MB_ICONSTOP, "Drill Down Options Error"
        'Simulate a Cancel after the error.
        intDDReturnValue = IDCANCEL
        frmDrillOptions.Hide
        Exit Sub

   End Sub
```

Error Trapping in the *DisplayDDData* Procedure

The DisplayDDData procedure fills the drill-down grid with data from the database. If the database files are available, that data is copied into the grid. If not, the procedure makes a graceful exit.

The error trap and error handler for this procedure are much like those placed in the other procedures, except for a special case located near the middle of the procedure around the command to create a snapshot object of the returned drill-down data query. The On Error Resume Next statement causes an error to skip the offending statement and continue with the next statement in the program. In this case, an On Error Resume Next statement is placed before the call to create a snapshot. The next statement following the call to create a snapshot is an If statement that is testing for an error. If it finds one, it restores the pie chart and exits the procedure. Otherwise, it continues with the procedure. Since the On Error Resume Next statement clears the error trap, the trap enabling code must be run again to re-enable the trap for the code at the end of the procedure.

Changes to DisplayDDData are in bold.

```
'Fill the detail grid with data.

Sub DisplayDDData (intHotHit As Integer)
    'intHotHit is the selected wedge.
    Dim intCtr As Integer    'Generic loop counter.
    Dim tblDefs As Table     'tblDefinitions.
    Dim ssType As Snapshot   'Table that supplies the descriptive data.
    .
    .
    .
...skipped lines...
    .
    .
    .
    'Set error handler if not debugging.
    If Not DEBUGON Then On Error GoTo DrillDetailsError
    'Import the definitions table.
    Set tblDefs = tblGraphs
    .
    .
    .
...skipped lines...
    .
    .
    .
    'Concatenate the elements of the SQL statement and create the snapshot.
    strSQL = strSQLSelect & strSQLFrom & strSQLWhere & strSQLGroupBy
    Screen.MousePointer = HOURGLASS   'Set the mouse pointer to the hourglass.

    On Error Resume Next
    Set ssDetail = dbGraphs.CreateSnapshot(strSQL)

    'Handle errors caused if tables are not available.
    If Err Then
       MsgBox "Rolled up data is not available.", MB_ICONSTOP,
       ➥"Drilldown Problem"
       On Error GoTo 0
       Call RestorePieChart
       Exit Sub
    End If
    Screen.MousePointer = DEFAULT 'Reset the mouse pointer

    'Set error handler if not debugging.
    If Not DEBUGON Then On Error GoTo DrillDetailsError

    If ssDetail.RecordCount = 0 Then
       'Table missing or no records.
       MsgBox "No records returned for this query.", 16, "Drilldown Problem"
       Call RestorePieChart
       Exit Sub
    End If

    'Change the values of these control variables to use another grid.
    Set frmDrill = frmMDIGrid
```

Day 10: Adding Error Trapping to the Application

```
    Set grdDrill = frmDrill.grdDetail
    'Populate the grid with data from ssDetail.
    Call PopulateGrid(frmDrill, grdDrill, ssDetail, strCaption)

    Exit Sub

DrillDetailsError:
    MsgBox Error$, 16, "Drilldown Error"
    Call RestorePieChart
    Exit Sub
End Sub
```

Modification Notes

If you're modifying an existing code, you can't assume that the application has error trapping enabled. You must examine the application to locate the trap enabling statements and the error handlers.

Because error trapping operates outside of a procedure's normal control structure, adding error trapping to an existing application usually isn't difficult. If the existing code is modular and has most of the I/O statements in one place, surrounding that area with an error trap enabler and the error handler itself would take care of it. If the I/O statements are scattered throughout the code, an error handler would have to be placed at each I/O statement to do it correctly. An option here is to create an I/O procedure with an error trap and call that procedure whenever you need to do I/O instead of doing the I/O directly from several places in the program.

Debugging the Process

If a program is crashing with system-generated errors and the cause of those errors is out of your control, this is a good place to insert an additional error trap. Whether the trap skips over the problem procedures as is done in the decision support application or corrects the problem depends on your particular situation.

To test error trapping, use the Error statement. Place the keyword Error followed by an error number wherever you want to test an error trap. When the Error statement is executed, Visual Basic issues the error that corresponds to the number just as if that error had actually occurred. Using the debug window and the single-step commands, you can step through the error trap to ensure that it's doing what you expect.

Another thing to worry about is causing an error within the error handler. When the error trap is triggered and control shifts to the error handler, the local error trap is disabled. The local trap isn't re-enabled until the Resume statement is executed at the end of the error handler. If the error handler causes an error, such as when writing to an error log file, that error will be handled by the next higher error trap in your application, or by the system error handler. This shouldn't be

a problem while you're designing and debugging the application, because you should understand what's happening. However, you really don't want to have this happen in a released application. If your error handler is going to do something that could cause an error, you should enable a new error handler to protect that code. Be sure to disable the new error handler using the On Error GoTo 0 statement before executing the Resume statement to re-enable the previous error handler.

Showstopper: If an error occurs in your error handler, the values of Err and Erl will change, because they always contain the error number and the location of the last error. If you haven't saved their values before encountering the error, you might end up correcting the wrong error.

Summary

Today you learned about the uses of error trapping and how to add it to your code. You also completed the coding of the decision support application. Error trapping is a process by which you can capture errors generated by an application that would normally have caused a fatal crash, and handle them yourself. Especially with I/O procedures and numerical calculations, where the possibility of encountering an error is high, you generally don't want the application to crash, but to be restored to a stable state so that the user can continue and try something else.

You also finished coding the decision support application. Tomorrow you will start debugging.

The code created today, including the error traps, is in the \DCNSPT2 directory on the included CD.

11

Debugging and Testing

Day 11

Debugging and Testing

Now that the application is written, why doesn't it work? Or why does it work but give the wrong results? It's debugging time. Even the most carefully crafted applications have bugs. Some are obvious, and others are extremely difficult to detect. The next step in designing an application is debugging and testing to ensure that your application works as it should.

Today you will learn

- [ ] the role of debugging and testing
- [ ] debugging methods
- [ ] testing strategies

The Goal of Day 11

The goal of Day 11 is to ensure that the application works as expected. One of the last things you want to happen is to give your new application to your customer and then learn that it crashes all the time or, even worse, that it generates incorrect results. Your customer might forgive a subtle bug that rarely causes a problem, but a major bug might cost you this and any future projects for this customer.

The only way to ensure that everything works is to directly test the application in as many different environments and under as many different conditions as possible. Testing starts as soon as each line of code is typed, when the Visual Basic editor checks the syntax of each typed statement. When the application finally compiles without error, alpha testing begins inside your organization to find and remove the most obvious and easy-to-find errors. When the application gets close to being finished, beta testing begins, and you start distributing your application to trusted outsiders to try out. Beta testing should find most, and hopefully all, of the problems with your application. Finally, release candidate testing is done with what you believe is a complete, well-debugged application.

Testing Platforms

You should especially consider the lower-powered platforms when testing an application. The high-powered machine you use for development purposes might give you a distorted view of your application's operation and efficiency. Most businesses don't have the latest hardware, and most business applications don't need the power of a state-of-the-art machine anyway. Some applications that work well on a high-powered machine might be extremely slow or not work at all on a smaller machine.

Using the Built-In Debugger

You should have used Visual Basic's built-in source code debugger when you learned the Visual Basic language. The built-in debugger is very powerful. It allows you to step though a program one statement at a time and examine the values of different variables at each step. An application drops into the debugger whenever it's in break mode. You enter break mode by pressing Ctrl-Break, clicking on the Pause button on the Visual Basic toolbar, encountering a breakpoint or the Stop statement in an application, or encountering an error.

When an application goes into break mode, the debug window becomes active and a code window opens, displaying the next statement to be executed (see Figure 11.1). If the application didn't enter break mode because of an error, pressing the single step (F8) or procedure step (Shift-F8) buttons on the Visual Basic toolbar executes the single marked statement in the code window and moves the mark to the next statement. The difference between single step and procedure step occurs when the statement to be executed is a procedure call. The single step command causes the code window to switch to the called procedure and execute its first statement. The procedure step button executes all of the called procedure and stops on the next statement in the initial procedure. If the application entered break mode because it encountered an error, pressing any of the step buttons usually causes the error to occur again.

Figure 11.1.
The debug and code windows in Visual Basic.

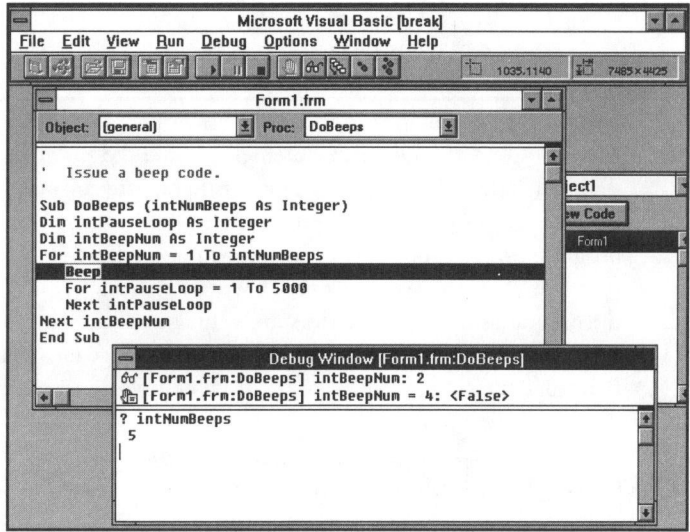

Whenever a program is in break mode, you can select a variable and click on the instant watch button (Shift-F9) to see the variable's current value. In addition, the variable can be made into a watch variable and displayed in the watch pane at the top of the debug window, as shown in Figure 11.1. A watch expression continuously displays its value as you execute the program a step at a time with the step buttons.

Debugging and Testing

You set breakpoints by selecting a statement in a code window and clicking on the breakpoint button (F9) on the Visual Basic toolbar. A running application stops and changes to break mode whenever it encounters a breakpoint.

Stepping Over a Loop

A common occurrence while stepping through a program is to encounter a loop. If the loop is iterated many times, you can spend all day trying to step through it. If you aren't interested in what happens inside the loop and just want to get beyond it, set a breakpoint in the statement that follows the loop and click on the toolbar's run button (F5). The loop executes, and the program stops on the marked statement. If you want to iterate the loop a certain number of times and then stop while still within the loop, set a watch expression on the loop variable that becomes True when the loop variable equals the value you want.

For example, to stop the loop shown in Figure 11.1 when the loop variable, `intBeepNum`, is equal to 4, add the watch expression `intBeepNum = 4` to the Add Watch dialog box and click on the Break When Expression Is True option button. The watch expression appears in the watch pane, as shown in Figure 11.1. Click on the toolbar's run button. The procedure runs until `intBeepNum` equals 4, and then drops into break mode.

Use all of these tools to examine a program's operation and locate and correct errors. With Visual Basic, you can change most statements while the program is in break mode. Exceptions are statements that define variable types or that create constants. You must restart your program if you change one of these statements. After you've made your corrections, you can continue the program from the point where it stopped by clicking on the Run button to see if you fixed the problem. If you need to back up a few statements to recalculate values prior to the point where the program stopped, select the statement where you want the program to start running and use the Debug | Set Next Statement command to change the starting point. When you click on Run, the program starts executing at the statement you just set.

Adding Debugging Code

You might wonder why you should add debugging code to an application when you can examine every step in an application using the built-in debugger. The reason is that dropping into the debugger changes the state of an executing application, and that change might hide the error. The biggest change to the operating environment when single-stepping through an application is that all system events get to execute between each statement. System events include updating the contents of windows and executing other triggered event procedures. If a bug occurs in a running application but not when you single-step through the same code, try testing the values using debugging code instead.

Debugging code consists of statements that tell you what's happening in an executing application. The most common debugging code is to insert a `Debug.Print` statement in a program to print the location of the current execution point or the current value of a variable as the program is executing. All values printed with the `Debug.Print` statement appear in the debug window. If you want to know where you are in an application, insert statements like

```
Debug.Print "In block 1"
```

whenever you want to print your location. Make the printed text tell you where you are.

> **Adding and Removing Debugging Code**
>
> There are two methods for adding or removing debugging code—using an `If` statement and using comments. If you have a lot of debugging code, place it in the body of a block `If` statement with a global variable as its argument. Setting the global variable to True executes the debugging code, and setting it to False turns it off.
>
> If you have only a few statements of debugging code, placing a single quote at the beginning of each statement turns it into a comment and makes it unexecutable. Remove the single quote to re-enable the debugging code.

You can also print values to a disk file, to the clipboard, or to the printer (although the printer is less reliable in the Windows environment because it doesn't print immediately). To put data on the clipboard, use the `Clipboard` object and the `SetText` method. This method was used in the preceding chapter to examine the SQL string being generated and sent to the database engine. The following statement tests `DEBUGON` to see if you're debugging. If you are, it places the contents of `strSQL` on the clipboard.

```
If DEBUGON Then Clipboard.SetText strSQL
```

In addition to printing, you can use sounds to tell you where you are in an application or what the values of different variables are. Use the `Beep` statement to create beep codes to tell you approximately where you are in an application without disturbing the desktop by writing to a window. Create a procedure like the following, and call it whenever you want to issue some beeps.

```
'
'Issue a beep code.
'
Sub DoBeeps (intNumBeeps As Integer)
Dim intPauseLoop As Integer
```

Debugging and Testing

```
Dim intBeepNum As Integer
For intBeepNum = 1 To intNumBeeps
    Beep
    For intPauseLoop = 1 To 5000
    Next intPauseLoop
Next intBeepNum
End Sub
```

The upper limit of the intPauseLoop loop should be set to a value that results in a recognizable pause on your machine. The size of that value depends on the speed of your processor, and it must be set by trial and error. If the pause is too short, the beeps run together, making them impossible to count. When you call this procedure, the argument you use determines the number of beeps it produces. For example, the following causes five beeps when the Command1 button is pressed:

```
Sub Command1_Click ()
    DoBeeps 5
End Sub
```

Testing the Procedures

You can test individual procedures in the debug window. This is especially useful for function procedures, because you can test them to make sure they produce the correct values. First, get into break mode so that the debug window is active. You can do this by running an application and clicking on the pause button on the Visual Basic toolbar or pressing Ctrl-Break. If you need to dimension some variables to use, put a command button on a form and insert the Dim statement, followed by the Stop statement, in the Click event procedure:

```
Sub Command1_Click ()
    Dim intAVariable As Integer
    Stop
End Sub
```

Run the procedure and click on the command button to dimension the variable and stop the program in break mode. You can then use the debug window to run procedures to test their operation. Test function procedures using a Print statement to print the value returned by the procedure. For example, to try out the Tan() function, type this line in the debug window of a stopped application:

```
? Tan(.5)
```

and the result appears:

```
.546302489843791
```

Any built-in or user-defined function can be tested in this way.

To test a normal procedure, simply type its name in the debug window and press Enter. Most commands and functions can be tested this way to ensure that they're doing what they should.

Testing

Where debugging is finding and fixing errors in an application, testing is determining if they exist. When you test an application, you not only try out all the application's options, but you also try out those options in as many different environments as possible. The more testing you do and the more thorough you are while testing, the less likely it is that some obscure bug will give your customer grief. And, as I have said all along, you don't want to give your customer grief.

> **Testing Is Boring**
> I admit it: Design is fun, and debugging is a challenge, but testing is a chore. However, it's a very important chore. Even if you hate testing, do it anyway. Force yourself. Do whatever it takes to do a good job of testing your application. Think of testing as a prelude to a debugging session, where you find a subtle bug that requires all your deductive abilities to puzzle out and fix (that's fun, right?).

As shown in Figure 3.1 on Day 3, a useful output of the design process is a test plan. A test plan is simply a list of all the things that an application is supposed to do, along with the expected result. In an application like the decision support application, the list is fairly obvious (each option has a button), so a formal test plan isn't really necessary. In a more complex numerical calculation, the options and values needed to exercise those options aren't obvious, so you need to produce a written test plan from the design of the system to be sure you don't miss anything.

> **Textbook Tip:** Here are the testing categories:
> *Alpha testing* is performed in-house on the parts of an unfinished application. Alpha-level code should never go outside of your organization.
> *Beta testing* is performed outside of your organization by a select group of beta testers. The code isn't necessarily complete, and it might have missing parts, but the parts that do work are close to being done.
> *Release candidate testing* is performed on a complete, well-debugged application that has all its parts in place. As the name suggests, this is code you believe is done (it isn't), but you're testing it one more time to be sure.

Debugging and Testing

> **Do Things Wrong**
>
> When you're testing, don't just use your application the way it's supposed to be used. Try things out of order and backwards. Push buttons when you're not supposed to. Use data fields with no data in them or numeric fields with text in them. Make sure you can do everything wrong and not cause your application to crash.
>
> If you don't do this, your users certainly will. Users are noted for using applications for many things they weren't intended for and, amazingly, often getting them to work.

Alpha Testing

The first testing stage after a program is written is the alpha test. You do the alpha testing yourself in-house, because the application often has missing options, is prone to crashing, and could damage your data if it crashes. Be sure that the application is well-marked as alpha-level, and include caveats that it might crash at any time. Alpha-level applications should never get outside your organization unless there's an extremely compelling reason to do so. Alpha-level applications seen outside of your organization can damage your reputation if you're not careful. Continue alpha testing until everything that has been installed in an application seems to work. You don't have to have all of the features installed to start beta testing, but all those you have installed should work reasonably well. If you add a new feature, start alpha testing again on that new feature before releasing the code for beta testing.

Beta Testing

Beta testing is where you finally let a copy of your code out of your organization for testing. You must test outside of your organization, because it's unlikely that you have access to all the different environments that a good group of beta testers can make available to you. The second reason for testing outside is that you know how your application should work, so you probably don't make it do things it's not supposed to do. A good beta tester will have his or her own agenda for using your code and will likely try to make it do things you never dreamed of. This is exactly what you need, because then you can find hidden problems and fix them.

Beta testers can give you a huge amount of help cleaning up your application. They will spend hundreds of hours fooling with it, working into the wee hours of the morning. They will hunger for the next release, bugs and all. They provide lots of free advertising as they spread the word about the neat new stuff you're doing. And the only pay they get is a preview of a new code before everyone else and usually a free copy of the code when it's complete.

Don't Stiff Your Beta Testers

Don't stiff your beta testers by forgetting to send them a copy of the final version of your code. Even the ones who don't send in that many bug reports still spent a lot of time trying things out. If you get a reputation for not sending the final code, your pool of eager helpers might dry up, leaving you to pay for the testing at the full contract programmer price. The cost of providing a copy of the final package is minimal compared to the amount of time that the testers put in.

Before sending code out for beta testing, be sure that it's already in relatively good condition and not prone to crashing all the time. If there are some known problem areas, be sure to tell your testers so that they can stay away from them.

Choose your beta testers with care. Not everyone is cut out to be a beta tester. Corporate officers are generally not good choices. What you want are computer weenies who delight in their machines and who understand what beta-level code is. Most executives don't appreciate the fact that a beta application isn't finished and will cause their machines to crash, possibly quite often.

Be careful when sending a beta application to your final customer. First impressions are very important. He might be turned off by problems with the beta code, especially if it eats all the data on his hard disk. He might not want to even try the final version, even though all the problems are fixed. Again, find someone who understands what a beta-level application is and the risks involved with using it.

Nondisclosure Agreements

A *nondisclosure agreement* (NDA) is often set up between a programmer and his beta testers. Since the beta testers don't work for you, you have little control over what they do with your product if you don't have an NDA in place. At a minimum, you want the beta testers to protect the copies of your application and not let them get into your competitors' hands.

Depending on your marketing strategy, you might or might not want to restrict your beta testers from talking to the press and others about your new application. If it's a new program, you might want to keep its existence a secret until you're ready to release it, in order to protect your investment in the application and to prevent copycat applications from invading the market too soon after you release your application. If it's a new release of an existing application and there are competitive products in the same market, you probably want your testers to tell all to get potential purchasers to wait for your product instead of buying the competitors'.

Debugging and Testing

The NDA Balancing Act

When writing your NDA, remember that your beta testers are working almost for free. If your NDA is too restrictive and has too-severe penalties in case of an accidental breach, they might tell you to forget it. Most beta testers understand the need for protecting your investment and are more than willing to go along with a reasonable set of restrictions. Then again, too-soft restrictions won't afford you the protection you seek for your product. You need to balance the restrictions in your NDA between your need for protection and your testers' convenience.

You need to ensure that the beta-test copies of your application are destroyed after the final version is ready. If people use the beta-test versions thinking they are the final version, they might get the wrong idea about the quality of your work. Include a provision in the NDA that the beta tester should destroy the beta documentation and erase the disks.

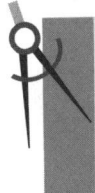

Schools Can Benefit

Your local schools can benefit from your beta test. Distribute the beta-test software on floppy disks and suggest that the testers donate them to local schools after the beta testing is done. Schools are always short on disks and disk boxes.

Provide a Testers' Forum

Beta testers like to discuss your new software with other programmers and with you, the developer. However, a restrictive NDA prevents them from doing that. If possible, provide a forum for the beta testers in which they can discuss your product among themselves and with you. This will satisfy their need to discuss the product with other testers.

There are lots of ways to set up the forum, from hosting a weekly in-person discussion group or an online discussion to using a bulletin board system (BBS) or a private CompuServe forum. What you use depends on your needs and resources. Keep in mind that beta testers often work odd hours, making an online forum or BBS of some sort preferable to in-person meetings.

Stress Written Reports

When a beta tester discovers a bug, request that she provide a written report describing the problem and how to reproduce it. To get the testers to do this, make it as easy as possible. An online electronic form is a good solution. There are many electronic forms programs that could be used for this purpose. Electronic forms are also useful in that the data they contain can be automatically transferred into a database program without having to be retyped.

To see a good example of an online bug reporting form, examine Microsoft's WinBug program. When using the WinBug application, you need to describe your system only once, and all future bug reports inherit that information. The bug report consists of the type and capabilities of your system, a statement of the problem, a statement of how to reproduce the problem or how to work around it, and any pertinent files that could help track down the problem.

Obtain the reports electronically using a BBS or an electronic online service such as CompuServe. This gets the information to you sooner and is less work for the beta testers, because they just e-mail you the reports. Provide telephone or fax numbers for those who don't have online access.

Dr Watson

Included with Windows is the DRWATSON.EXE program. It isn't automatically installed in any program group. You must install it yourself by creating a new program item and connecting it to the DRWATSON.EXE program in the Windows directory. Run the Dr Watson program before running a new Windows application. If the application crashes and causes a general protection (GP) fault, Dr Watson creates a record of where the fault occurred and what the state of your system was at the point of the crash. The log file that Dr Watson creates could help you locate a problem with a crashing application.

Microsoft's MSD Program

Another program included with Windows is Microsoft Diagnostics (MSD.EXE). This program is located in the Windows directory and runs in DOS mode. Running it gives you a complete description of your system, including hardware and software. A beta tester can run it and send the report to you to give you a description of his or her machine.

Time Bombs

Some organizations place *time bombs* in the startup procedures of their alpha- and beta-level applications to prevent them from starting up after a reasonable length of time. Although this won't stop a user from turning back his clock to get the code to run, it might prevent him from using the code after a newer version is available. A time bomb is easy to implement:

Day 11 Debugging and Testing

```
Sub TimeBomb ()
Const StopDate = "12-15-94"
If Date > DateValue(StopDate) Then
    MsgBox "This code is out of date. Get a new copy from your vendor.", ,
    ➥"Time Bomb"
    End
End If
End Sub
```

Call this procedure from your startup procedure or from the Form_Load procedure of the first form in an application. It compares the current date with the date stored in the StopDate constant.

Be Careful with Code Disablers

Be really careful with code disablers. Make sure you remove them before shipping an application. It can be extremely costly to replace all copies of an application that had a disabler left in.

Also, don't write code that self-destructs when it determines that it's out-of-date to prevent the user from turning back the clock. If you accidentally destroy more than you planned, at the least you will highly upset your users, and at the worst you could be liable for damages.

Release Candidate Testing

The last level of testing is for release candidate applications. A release candidate application has all its parts in place, and all those parts appear to work. You send the release candidate applications to your beta testers for this final bit of testing. You can enlarge your list of potential testers, because this version of the application is less likely to cause embarrassing problems.

The Decision Support Application Project

On Day 10, you finished coding the decision support application and released it for in-house alpha testing. After finding and removing all the obvious errors, it's time to send the code out to be beta-tested.

The beta testers consist of a group of local computer enthusiasts, plus the computer guru at the Orco company. Luckily, someone at the Orco company was of the correct temperament to do the beta testing on the actual target system. This person can then show off the software to his managers without making them do it themselves and exposing their personal systems to a crash or possible lock-up. The group uses a BBS to discuss issues and leave bug reports. The BBS was created using an old PC, a couple of modems, and some inexpensive BBS software.

A Beta Tester's Notebook

After a few weeks of beta testing, the following list of problems, feature requests, and questions was left on the BBS:

1. The buttons on the toolbar can be clicked on during initialization. They stay pressed, but the chart doesn't change to the selected type.
2. How do we change to a different year?
3. The type buttons can be clicked on during printing.
4. I would like to be able to display more than one graph at a time.
5. I would like to be able to compare this year with last year.
6. When the pie chart shifts to the left or right, sometimes the label shifts off the screen.
7. If the .INI file isn't in the C:\WINDOWS directory, the code won't start up.
8. After the pie chart prints, it doesn't return.
9. When the pie chart is displayed, it redraws twice, causing a distracting flash on the screen.

Resolve these problems, requests, and questions one at a time. Keep in mind that you don't have to do everything that's requested. You can divert some requests to the next revision.

The Buttons Don't Reset

"The buttons on the toolbar can be clicked on during initialization. They stay pressed, but the chart doesn't change to the selected type." This is definitely a bug. The fInhibit flag protects the class and type procedures from being executed while the current type or class is being changed. However, that flag can't prevent the buttons from being pressed, so they stay pressed even though the underlying procedures don't run. You need to add a way to either prevent the buttons from being pressed or reset them after the current graph is drawn.

You could disable all the buttons while the graph is being updated, but then each button would display the disabled icon instead of the class or type icon. You could also put up a modal form that would prevent clicks anywhere on the application until the modal form was hidden or unloaded. This has possibilities, but we don't want to put up a form every time a graph is changed. The last option is to check the buttons after the current chart is completed and reset them to the correct state. This last option appears to be the best choice, so implement it.

Add code to the gpbGraphClass and gpbGraphType_Click procedures to reset the buttons when the fInhibit flag is set. Find the button that should be down and set its Value property to True, which puts it in the pressed state. The changes in these two procedures appear in bold.

```
'Change the graph class and display the first type.
```

Debugging and Testing

```
Sub gpbGraphClass_Click (intIndex As Integer, fValue As Integer)
    'The graph class is in the Tag property.
    Dim strCode As String
    Dim intCtr As Integer    'Generic counter.

    'Prevent recursion.
    If fInhibit Then
       'Reset the button.
       For intCtr = 1 To NUM_CLASS_BUTTONS
          'Find the button that should be down, then push it down.
          If gpbGraphClass(intCtr).Tag = intGraphClass Then
             gpbGraphClass(intCtr).Value = True
          End If
       Next intCtr
       'Exit the procedure.
       Exit Sub
    End If

    'Disable changing the graph class and type.
    fInhibit = True

    'Hide the pop-up labels.
    Call HidePopUpLabels
    DoEvents

    'Set the global graph class according to the button pressed.
    intGraphClass = gpbGraphClass(intIndex).Tag

    'Set the global type to the first graph type.
    intGraphType = TOTAL_TYPE

    'Set the type buttons.
    Call SetInitialTypeButtons

    'Create the graph.
    Call CreateNewGraph

    'Show the form in case another form is on top.
    frmMDIGraph.Show

    'In case the user moved the mouse before this procedure
    'finished, hide the drop-down labels.
    Call HidePopUpLabels

    fInhibit = False    'Reset the inhibit flag.

End Sub

'
'Set the graph type and display the graph.
'
Sub gpbGraphType_Click (intIndex As Integer, fValue As Integer)

    Dim intCtr As Integer    'Generic counter.

    'Prevent recursion.
```

```
    If fInhibit Then
        'Reset the button.
        For intCtr = 1 To NUM_TYPE_BUTTONS
            'Find the button that should be down, then push it down.
            If gpbGraphType(intCtr).Tag = intGraphType Then
                gpbGraphType(intCtr).Value = True
            End If
        Next intCtr
        'Exit the procedure.
        Exit Sub
    End If

    fInhibit = True

    'Hide the pop-up labels.
    Call HidePopUpLabels
    DoEvents

    'The graph type number is stored in the button's Tag property.
    intGraphType = gpbGraphType(intIndex).Tag

    'Display the graph.
    Call CreateNewGraph
    DoEvents

    'Show the form in case another form is on top.
    frmMDIGraph.Show
    DoEvents

    'In case the user moved the mouse before this procedure
    'finished, hide the drop-down labels.
    Call HidePopUpLabels

    fInhibit = False   'Reset the inhibit flag.

End Sub
```

Changing the Year

"How do we change to a different year?" In this version of the code, the year to display is read in from the .INI file. It could be set from a menu. Save this as a feature request for the next version.

The Buttons Can Be Clicked on During Printing

"The type buttons can be clicked on during printing." This problem is similar to that in item 1. You need to protect the buttons somehow. You could set the fInhibit flag during printing. However, displaying a modal dialog box during printing is very common. It protects everything until the modal dialog box is hidden or unloaded. Therefore, solve this problem by displaying a modal dialog when printing.

Debugging and Testing

Add the form named frmPrinting, shown in Figure 11.2. Move the procedure calls to draw a new chart to the frmPrinting form so that they can be called by that form when it loads.

Figure 11.2.
The printing form.

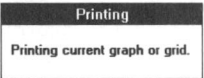

The mnuFilePrint_Click procedure previously called PrintVisibleChart to print the currently visible chart or grid. Comment out that statement and insert a statement to display the frmPrinting form as a Modal form. When the frmPrinting form is displayed, the frmPrinting_Activated procedure is executed. Insert code to call the PrintVisibleChart procedure to print the chart, and then hide the frmPrinting form when the printing is done. The changes to the mnuFilePrint procedure in the frmMDIMain form and the new frmPrinting_Activated procedure appear in bold.

```
'
'Display the Print dialog and print.
'
Sub mnuFilePrint_Click ()
   Dim intCtr As Integer   'Generic counter.
   cdgDialogs.CancelError = False
   cdgDialogs.Copies = 1
   cdgDialogs.FromPage = 1
   cdgDialogs.ToPage = 1
   'Set the flags for no print range and no print selection and
   'use the printer driver's multiple copies capability.
   cdgDialogs.Flags = PD_NOPAGENUMS + PD_NOSELECTION + PD_USEDEVMODECOPIES
   cdgDialogs.Action = DLG_PRINT
   'Test to verify that the printer has been set as the default printer.
   If cdgDialogs.PrinterDefault Then
      'Important: EndDoc is needed to set the new orientation.
      printer.EndDoc
   Else
      MsgBox "The printer you use must be selected as the default printer.",
      ➥16, "Printer Error"
      Exit Sub
   End If
   'Print the copies. Uncomment the For/Next loop and remove
   'the PD_USEDEVMODECOPIES flag above if the printer driver
   'does not support multiple copies.
'  For intCtr = 1 To cdgDialogs.Copies
'     Call PrintVisibleChart
   frmPrinting.Show MODAL
'  Next intCtr

End Sub


'
'Print the visible chart, and then hide this form.
'
Sub Form_Activate ()
```

```
    Call PrintVisibleChart
    Me.Hide
End Sub
```

Displaying Multiple Graphs

"I would like to be able to display more than one graph at a time." This is not an impossible task, but it would require reworking several of the procedures to handle a control array of frmMDIGraph and frmMDIGrid forms. Add this to the list of new features for the next version of the decision support application.

Displaying Multiple Years

"I would like to be able to compare this year with last year." This is also possible, but it too would require reworking the graphing procedures to either graph two years on two different graphs or overlay two graphs for two different years. Add this to the list of new features for the next version of the program.

The Pie Labels Move Off the Screen

"When the pie chart shifts to the left or right, sometimes the label shifts off the screen." This is a problem. Since we're drawing the graph oversized to make it larger on-screen, when we shift it to the left or right, there is a possibility that it might shift a label off the edge. This seems to happen only when the selected wedge of the pie chart is on the right or left side of the pie, as shown in Figure 11.3. The ones on the top or bottom don't seem to have a problem.

Figure 11.3.
The shifted pie chart with the label shifted off the edge of the screen.

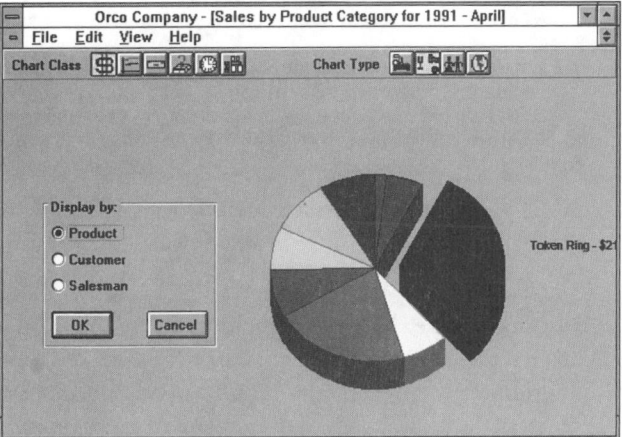

Day 11: Debugging and Testing

There are several options for fixing this. (Also, we could just ignore it, since it's just used to confirm the user's selection.)

1. Shorten the labels.
2. Fold the labels into two lines.
3. Don't shift the chart so far.
4. Reduce the size of the pie chart.

Shortening the labels isn't out of the question, but as more products are added, the problem will return. This is because the length of the text portion of the label comes from the database, not from the program.

The program adds the total dollars to the end of each text label. That could possibly be changed into a two-line label if the control will allow it. This needs to be tested to see if it would work.

To test it, change the lines in the DrawPieChart procedure that load the labels into the graph control to insert a return between the label text and the number. The following lines of code from DrawPieChart show that modification. The commented-out lines are the original code, and the bold lines following them are the replacements.

```
If tblGraphs("Units") = "$" Then
'    frmMDIGraph.chtPieChart.LabelText = frmMDIGraph.grdMonthly.Text & " - " &
     ➥Format(frmMDIGraph.chtMonthly.GraphData, "$#,##0")
    frmMDIGraph.chtPieChart.LabelText = frmMDIGraph.grdMonthly.Text & Chr$(13) &
     ➥Format(frmMDIGraph.chtMonthly.GraphData, "$#,##0")
ElseIf tblGraphs("Units") = "%" Then
'    frmMDIGraph.chtPieChart.LabelText = frmMDIGraph.grdMonthly.Text & " - " &
     ➥Format(frmMDIGraph.chtMonthly.GraphData, "#0.##%")
    frmMDIGraph.chtPieChart.LabelText = frmMDIGraph.grdMonthly.Text & Chr$(13) &
     ➥Format(frmMDIGraph.chtMonthly.GraphData, "#0.##%")
Else
'    frmMDIGraph.chtPieChart.LabelText = frmMDIGraph.grdMonthly.Text & " - " &
     ➥Format(frmMDIGraph.chtMonthly.GraphData, "#0.##.00")
    frmMDIGraph.chtPieChart.LabelText = frmMDIGraph.grdMonthly.Text & Chr$(13) &
     ➥Format(frmMDIGraph.chtMonthly.GraphData, "#0.##.00")
End If
```

When you run this variation, you find that it doesn't work. The graph control ignores the return in the middle of the label. Now we know that the graph control doesn't allow multiline segment labels.

Not shifting the chart so far would fix the problem, as long as there is still room for the drill-down form. This would result in a slightly off-center display, which might or might not be a good solution. To test this solution, comment out the lines that shift the pie chart. Just leave it in the center of the form and see what happens. In the chtPieChart_DblClick procedure, comment out the lines in the following listing, and then run the program. Figure 11.4 is the result.

```
'Shift the pie chart left or right to make room for the drill-down options.
'If intWedgeAngle <= 180 Then
```

```
    '   'Shift the chart to the right (the pie chart is larger than the form).
    '      frmMDIGraph.chtPieChart.Left = 0
    'Else
    '   'Shift the chart to the left.
    '   frmMDIGraph.chtPieChart.Left = frmMDIGraph.Width -
          ↪frmMDIGraph.chtPieChart.Width
    'End If
```

Figure 11.4.
The unshifted pie chart and the drill-down options. Not quite right.

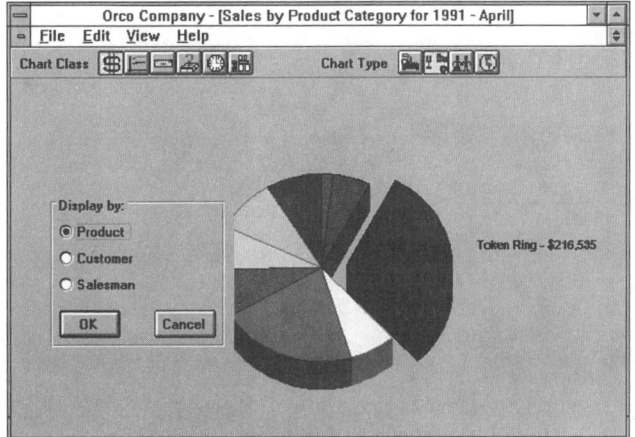

Well, this isn't quite right, but it has possibilities. Move the frmDrillOptions form into the upper corner on the side away from the exploded pie wedge. To do this, change the constants and one formula in the Form_Load procedure of the frmDrillOptions form. The changes are shown in bold. When you run this variation, Figure 11.5 is the result.

```
'
'Load the drill-down options form and shift it left or right.
'
Sub Form_Load ()
    'Note: This procedure must be in the Load event handler.
    '      Otherwise, the position is not set on the first
    '      change from left to right (or vice versa).
    Dim intCtr As Integer   'Generic counter.
    Dim tblDefs As Table    'Temporary table def to pass
                            'the global table to a form.
'   Const FORM_TOP_HEIGHT = 1375  'Height of form header,
                                  'menu bar, and toolbar.
    Const FORM_TOP_HEIGHT = 1075  'Height of form header, menu bar, and toolbar.
'   Const EDGE_OFFSET = 500  'Offset from edge of form.
    Const EDGE_OFFSET = 175  'Offset from edge of form.

    'Turn on the error handler.
    If Not DEBUGON Then On Error GoTo DDNOptionsError

    'Import the global table def. This is a bug workaround for VB-3.
    Set tblDefs = tblGraphs
```

Debugging and Testing

```
    '    'Center form vertically.
    '    frmDrillOptions.Top = frmMDIMain.Top + FORM_TOP_HEIGHT + (frmMDIMain.Height
         ↪- FORM_TOP_HEIGHT - frmDrillOptions.Height) / 2
    '    Place form at top of active area.
         frmDrillOptions.Top = frmMDIMain.Top + FORM_TOP_HEIGHT

         'Position the form horizontally, depending on the wedge selected.
         If intWedgeAngle <= 180 Then
            frmDrillOptions.Left = frmMDIMain.Left + EDGE_OFFSET
         Else
            frmDrillOptions.Left = frmMDIMain.Left + frmMDIMain.Width -
            ↪frmDrillOptions.Width - EDGE_OFFSET
         End If

         'Enable/disable appropriate options.
         'Disable all of them, then turn on the available ones.
         For intCtr = 1 To NUM_OPTS
            optDrill(intCtr).Enabled = False
         Next intCtr
         If InStr(tblDefs("DDFlag"), "P") Then optDrill(DDPRODUCT).Enabled = True
         If InStr(tblDefs("DDFlag"), "C") Then optDrill(DDCUSTOMER).Enabled = True
         If InStr(tblDefs("DDFlag"), "S") Then optDrill(DDSALESMAN).Enabled = True
         Exit Sub

    DDNOptionsError:
         MsgBox Error$, 16, "Drill Down Options Error"
         'Simulate a Cancel after the error.
         intDDReturnValue = IDCANCEL
         frmDrillOptions.Hide
         Exit Sub

    End Sub
```

Figure 11.5.
The unshifted pie chart and the drill-down options.

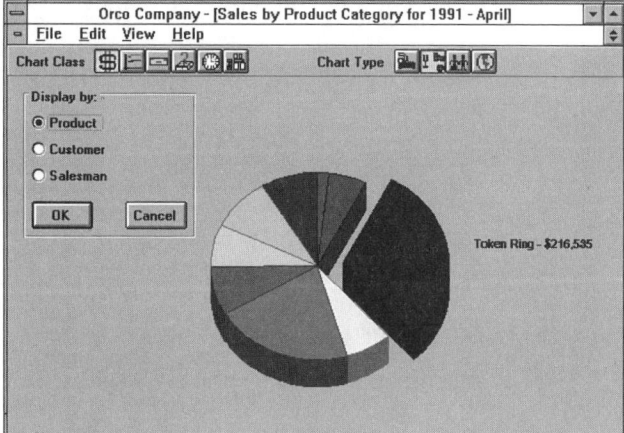

Commenting Out Comments

When using single quotes to comment out a block of statements, comment out every statement, including the comments. It's easier to comment out every line than to have to check every line to see if it's already a comment. Later, if you want to uncomment the block, it's also easier to remove the single quote from every line instead of trying to figure out which lines to uncomment and which to leave alone.

Figure 11.5 doesn't look too bad, but we still have one more variation to try before making a decision. Reducing the size of the pie chart to fit would work, but the pie would be somewhat smaller and less readable. To test this variation, add code to the chtPieChart_DblClick procedure to reduce the height of the pie chart. The pie's size is controlled by the height of the graph control. The added code (shown in bold) reduces the size of the pie chart by 20 percent and moves it down to center it. If we decide to use this option, the RestorePieChart procedure would need similar code to reverse the changes. Running this version produces Figure 11.6, which also is not too bad.

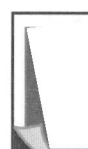

```
'
'Detect a double click on a pie segment.
'
Sub chtPieChart_DblClick ()

   Dim intCtr As Integer      'Generic counter.
   Dim intHotHit As Integer   'The number of the selected wedge.
                              'A 0 indicates no wedge selected.
   intHotHit = intPieHotHit(CInt(sngMouseX), CInt(sngMouseY))
.
.
.
...skipped lines...
.
.
.
      'Shift the pie chart left or right to
      'make room for the drill-down options.
      If intWedgeAngle <= 180 Then
         'Shift the chart to the right (the pie chart is larger than the form).
         frmMDIGraph.chtPieChart.Left = 0
      Else
         'Shift the chart to the left.
        frmMDIGraph.chtPieChart.Left = frmMDIGraph.Width -
        ➥frmMDIGraph.chtPieChart.Width
      End If
      'Change the height.
      frmMDIGraph.chtPieChart.Height = frmMDIGraph.chtPieChart.Height * .8
      frmMDIGraph.chtPieChart.Top = frmMDIGraph.chtPieChart.Top +
      ➥frmMDIGraph.chtPieChart.Height * .1
```

Debugging and Testing

```
        'Display the drill-down options form as
        'a modal form and wait for it to return.
        frmDrillOptions.Show MODAL
.
.
.
...skipped lines...
.
.
.
    DoEvents

    End If
End Sub
```

Figure 11.6.
The pie chart shrunk to fit.

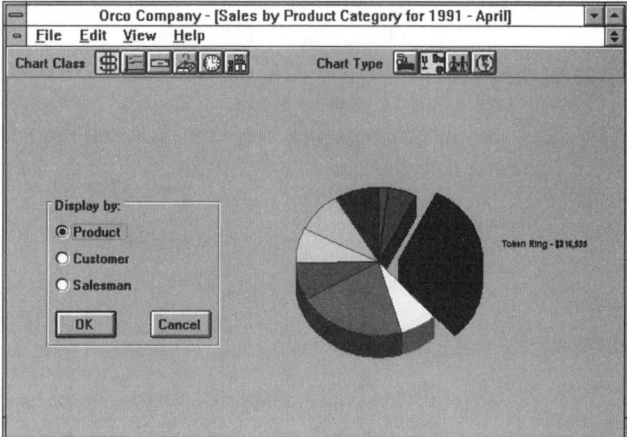

Of the three options tested, we chose the second one for the application, although the last one wasn't bad either. My preference is to keep the pie chart larger and move the drill-down options form to make room for it.

Problems Locating the .INI File

"If the .INI file isn't in the C:\WINDOWS directory, the code won't start up." This is a bug. The .INI file has been assumed to be in the C:\WINDOWS directory, the normal place for .INI files. If they aren't there, and you have a database with security options, the database driver won't be able to find it. However, the Windows directory doesn't have to be in C:\WINDOWS; it could be a different directory. An environment variable named WINDIR contains the location of the Windows directory. The application should obtain the path to the .INI file from the environment variable instead of assuming it's in the common location. Because of the future possibility of having security options added to the database, you want to force the user to put the .INI file in the Windows directory, wherever it is, so don't add an option to look elsewhere if it isn't found. Also, add code to the error trap to tell the user where the file belongs if it isn't found in the \WINDOWS directory. The following listing shows the changes to the LoadAndParseINIFile procedure in bold.

Note: Here is a good example of why you want to test your program on as many different machines as possible. If this program were tested only on standard setups, the problem with the location of the Windows directory wouldn't have been detected.

```
'
'Load and parse the .INI file.
'
Sub LoadAndParseINIFile ()
    Dim strALine As String
    Dim fgotStart As Integer
    Dim intEqMark As Integer
    Dim strVariable As String
    Dim strValue As String
    Dim strWinPath As String
    Const ERR_FILENOTFOUND = 53

    'Turn on the error handler.
    If Not DEBUGON Then On Error GoTo INIError

    'Get the location of the Windows directory.
    strWinPath = Environ$("WINDIR")

    'Assume that the file is in the Windows directory.
    Open strWinPath & "\dcnspt.ini" For Input As #1
    Line Input #1, strALine   'Skip a line.
    'Find [startup].
    fgotStart = False
.
.
.
...skipped lines...
.
.
.
    If strDataFile = "" Or strYear = "" Or App.HelpFile = "" Then GoTo Bombout
Exit Sub
Bombout:
    MsgBox "Corrupt INI file, can't continue.", 16, "INI File Error"
    End
INIError:
    If Err = ERR_FILENOTFOUND Then
        MsgBox Error$ & Chr$(13) & "DCNSPT.INI file must be in the Windows
        ➥directory.", MB_ICONSTOP, "INI File Error"
        End
    Else
```

Debugging and Testing

```
        'Reissue error for other handler.
        Error Err
    End If
End Sub
```

Pie Chart Missing After Printing

"After the pie chart prints, it doesn't return." This is a bug. After the program prints the pie chart, the screen looks like Figure 11.7. The pie chart was visible, and clicking on the form brings it back, so why did it go away? If you look at the caption in the title bar of the application, you see that the current active form on the MDI parent form is the drill-down grid, not the graph form. The graph form with the pie chart is probably there; it's just behind the drill-down grid form. Somehow, the drill-down grid form, with the grid hidden, has become activated and is now hiding the form with the pie chart on it.

Figure 11.7.
After the pie chart prints, it doesn't return.

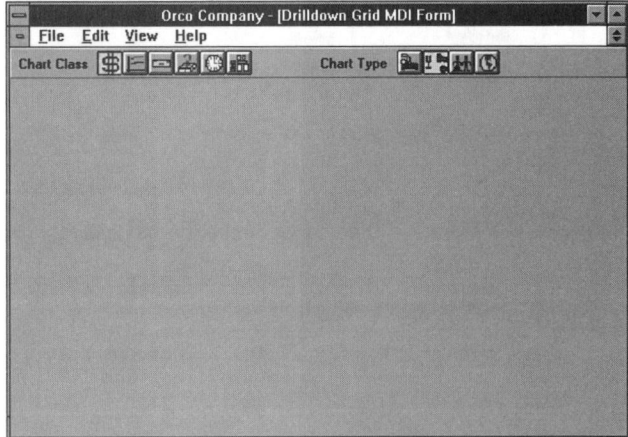

Open the PrintVisibleChart procedure and place a breakpoint on the first executable statement. The statement is at the beginning of a block If statement that determines what is currently active by testing the visible properties of the monthly graph, the pie chart, and the drill-down grid. The block If statement is shown in the following listing. The first bold statement is the one with the breakpoint set on it.

```
'Set control variables.
If (frmMDIGraph.chtMonthly.Visible = True) Then
    'The monthly chart is visible.
    Set chtPrint = frmMDIGraph.chtMonthly
    If fIsCrosstab Then
        fPrintWhat = LEVEL2_CHART_AND_GRID
        Set grdPrint = frmMDIGraph.grdMonthly
    Else
        fPrintWhat = LEVEL1_CHART_AND_GRID
```

```
        Set grdPrint = frmMDIGraph.grdMonthly
    End If
ElseIf (frmMDIGrid.grdDetail.Visible = True) Then
    'The detail grid is visible.
    fPrintWhat = DETAIL_GRID
    Set grdPrint = frmMDIGrid.grdDetail
    Set chtPrint = frmMDIGraph.grdMonthly
Else
    'The pie chart is visible.
    fPrintWhat = PIE_CHART
    Set chtPrint = frmMDIGraph.chtPieChart
    Set grdPrint = frmMDIGraph.grdMonthly
End If
```

Run the program and try printing the pie chart. The program stops at the breakpoint, as shown in Figure 11.8. Pressing single step causes the program to test the monthly graph to see if it's visible. You expect it to skip to the test in the second bold statement to see if the drill-down grid is visible, but instead it jumps to the resize event procedure for the drill-down grid. The top of the MDI parent form still indicates that the graph form is the active form, but the grid form appears to be trying to take its place. Stepping through the resize procedures doesn't seem to do much, and the graph is still the active form.

Figure 11.8.
Hitting the breakpoint in the PrintVisibleChart procedure.

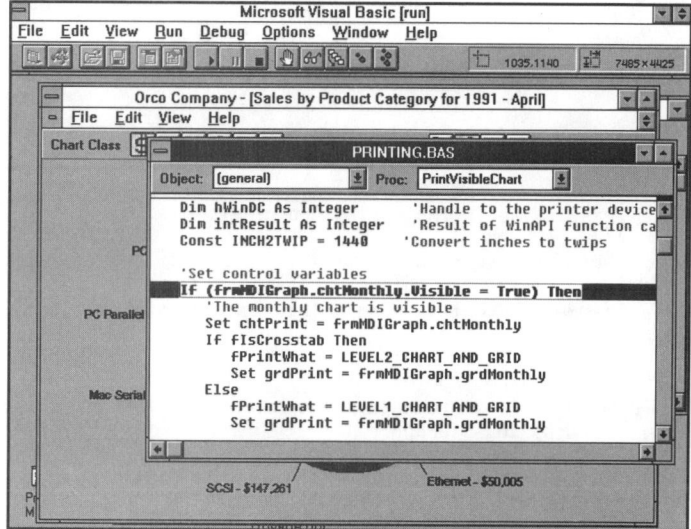

When the execution point finally returns to the PrintVisibleChart procedure, it is at the first statement in the Else clause of the block If statement, as shown in Figure 11.9. You would have expected it to be in the ElseIf clause to check to see if the drill-down grid is the active object. It appears that the act of testing the drill-down form to see if it was active made it into the active form, bringing it to the front. What is needed to correct this bug is to force the frmMDIGraph form

Debugging and Testing

with the pie chart back to the front. In the mnuFilePrint_Click event procedure, save the current active form before printing and then reactivate it after printing. The bold lines in the following listing perform this task. First create a form variable, then store the active form in it using the ActiveForm property of the frmMDIMain form. After the printing is done, use the Show method to restore the active form and bring it to the front.

Figure 11.9.
Returning from the resize event goes to the Else *clause of the block* If.

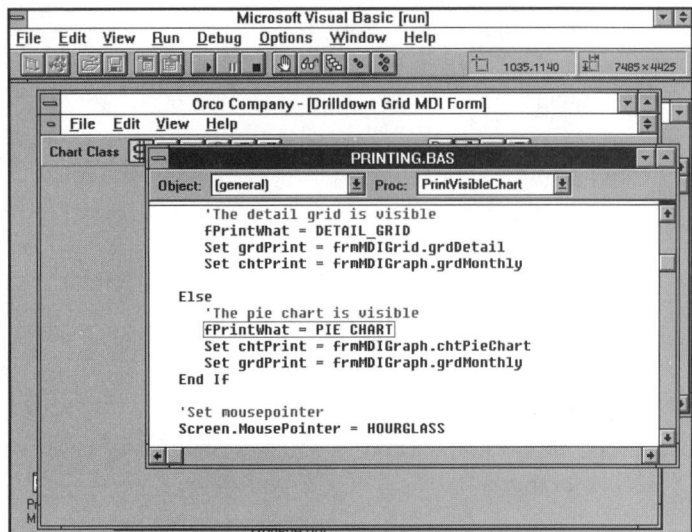

```
'
'Display the Print dialog and print.
'
Sub mnuFilePrint_Click ()
   Dim intCtr As Integer    'Generic counter.
   Dim frmFront As Form     'Stores current front form.

   cdgDialogs.CancelError = False
   cdgDialogs.Copies = 1
   cdgDialogs.FromPage = 1
   cdgDialogs.ToPage = 1
   'Set the flags for no print range and no print selection and
   'use the printer driver's multiple copies capability.
   cdgDialogs.Flags = PD_NOPAGENUMS + PD_NOSELECTION + PD_USEDEVMODECOPIES
   cdgDialogs.Action = DLG_PRINT
   'Test to verify that the printer has been set as the default printer.
   If cdgDialogs.PrinterDefault Then
      'Important: EndDoc is needed to set the new orientation.
      printer.EndDoc
   Else
      MsgBox "The printer you use must be selected as the default printer.",
      ➥16, "Printer Error"
      Exit Sub
   End If
```

```
'   Save the active form.
    Set frmFront = frmMDIMain.ActiveForm

    'Print the copies. Uncomment the For/Next loop and remove
    'the PD_USEDEVMODECOPIES flag above if the printer driver does
    'not support multiple copies.
'   For intCtr = 1 To cdgDialogs.Copies
'      Call PrintVisibleChart
    frmPrinting.Show MODAL
'   Next intCtr

    'Make sure the form is still visible.
    frmFront.Show

End Sub
```

Running these corrections gives the expected results.

The Pie Redraws Twice

"When the pie chart is displayed, it redraws twice, causing a distracting flash on the screen." This is a bug, but only a minor one. It doesn't cause any problems in functionality, just an annoying flash when the pie chart is drawn or redrawn. As with the last problem, insert a breakpoint and trace the execution of the procedure to see why the pie chart is getting redrawn twice.

There are four occasions where the pie chart is redrawn: the initial drawing of the pie chart, a cancel return from the drill-down options dialog box, a return from the drill-down grid, and a return from printing the pie chart. Testing these, we find that the initial drawing of the pie chart and the cancel return from the drill-down options dialog box don't have the double redrawing.

Putting a breakpoint in the RestorePieChart procedure used to restore the pie chart after displaying the drill-down grid, and stepping through the procedure, you find that the frmMDIGraph gets a redraw event when frmMDIGrid is unloaded. This redraw event causes the pie to be redrawn again after it's resized by the RestorePieChart procedure. To fix this, set the fInhibitResize flag to prevent the resize procedure from running, unload the form to trigger the Resize event, insert DoEvents to let the Resize event run and be canceled by the flag, and then clear the flag to allow normal resizing. The changes in the RestorePieChart procedure that follows are in bold.

```
'
'Remove the drill-down options form and redisplay the pie chart.
'
Sub RestorePieChart ()
    Dim intCtr As Integer   'Generic loop counter.

    fInhibitResize = True   'Disable resizing caused by unloading the grid.
    Unload frmMDIGrid
    DoEvents                'Let the redraw event occur.
    fInhibitResize = False  'Enable resizing.
```

Day 11: Debugging and Testing

```
For intCtr = 1 To frmMDIGraph.chtPieChart.NumPoints
    frmMDIGraph.chtPieChart.ThisPoint = intCtr
    frmMDIGraph.chtPieChart.LabelText = strLabels(intCtr)
    frmMDIGraph.chtPieChart.ExtraData = G_NOT_EXPLODED
Next intCtr

'Restore the original left margin of the chart.
frmMDIGraph.chtPieChart.Left = intPieChartLeft

'Restore the label lines to the pie chart.
frmMDIGraph.chtPieChart.GraphStyle = G_DEFAULT

'Redraw the chart with all of the labels.
frmMDIGraph.chtPieChart.DrawMode = G_DRAW

End Sub
```

To trace the problem in the printing procedures, insert a breakpoint in the `mnuFilePrint_Click` event procedure and step through the printing. The problem occurs at the `Show` statement we just inserted at the end of the procedure. Do the same things here that you did in the `RestorePieChart` procedure. Inhibit resizing, cause the event, let it occur with a `DoEvents`, and then enable resizing. The changes in the following procedure are in bold.

Note: The problem in this procedure occurs at the statement we just inserted to correct a previous problem. This is a good example of fixing one error and causing another.

```
'
'Display the Print dialog and print.
'
Sub mnuFilePrint_Click ()
    Dim intCtr As Integer   'Generic counter.
    Dim frmFront As Form    'Stores current front form.

    cdgDialogs.CancelError = False
    cdgDialogs.Copies = 1
    cdgDialogs.FromPage = 1
    cdgDialogs.ToPage = 1
    'Set the flags for no print range and no print selection and
    'use the printer driver's multiple copies capability.
    cdgDialogs.Flags = PD_NOPAGENUMS + PD_NOSELECTION + PD_USEDEVMODECOPIES
    cdgDialogs.Action = DLG_PRINT
    'Test to verify that the printer has been set as the default printer.
    If cdgDialogs.PrinterDefault Then
        'Important: EndDoc is needed to set the new orientation.
        printer.EndDoc
    Else
        MsgBox "The printer you use must be selected as the default printer.",
➥16, "Printer Error"
```

```
        Exit Sub
    End If

'   Save the active form.
    Set frmFront = frmMDIMain.ActiveForm

    'Print the copies. Uncomment the For/Next loop and remove
    'the PD_USEDEVMODECOPIES flag above if the printer driver does
    'not support multiple copies.
'   For intCtr = 1 To cdgDialogs.Copies
'       Call PrintVisibleChart
    frmPrinting.Show MODAL
'   Next intCtr

    'Make sure the form is still visible.
    fInhibitResize = True    'Turn resizing off while displaying the form.
    frmFront.Show
    DoEvents                 'Let any resize event occur.
    fInhibitResize = False   'Turn resizing back on.

End Sub
```

Testing these procedures again, we see that the pie chart is now redrawn only once, as expected.

Fixing Bugs in Your Own Programs

Your own programs will likely have totally different bugs from those shown in the examples in this chapter. The bugs you find are either cosmetic, serious, or disastrous. Cosmetic bugs, such as a misspelled word in a dialog box or the pie chart label moving off the side of the screen (as in the example), don't affect the operation of your application, only how it looks. You should fix cosmetic bugs if possible. A serious bug is anything that prevents your application from accomplishing its task, such as calculating incorrect values or crashing. You must fix serious bugs before you release an application for delivery. Disastrous bugs affect things outside of your application and its assigned task. Disastrous bugs include such things as crashing the system and wrecking or deleting files on the hard disk. Disastrous bugs absolutely *must* be fixed before you take the application off the machine you use for system development.

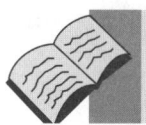

Textbook Tip: A bug is anything your program does that you didn't design it to do.

389

Debugging and Testing

Modification Notes

There is little difference between modifying an existing program and modifying a new one. You must still test the program and locate and fix problems. The biggest difference is that you might not be as familiar with the code in a modified program, making it more difficult to locate bugs. The more familiar you are with the code and structure, the easier it is to locate the source of a problem.

Additionally, when modifying a program, be sure to test the whole program, not just the part you modified. This is because changes in one part of a program can affect things in another part, especially if there's a lot of connectivity between the procedures. The sample application showed that two procedures that appeared to be independent of each other (the procedure to draw charts and the resize event procedure) actually were not. You must test the whole program if you modify any part of it.

Debugging the Process

This whole chapter described the process of locating and fixing bugs, so no additional debugging is necessary today. Take some time off to rest, sleep, eat—all those things you've been skipping because you haven't been able to tear yourself away from this book.

Summary

Today you learned about testing and debugging an application. Testing involves trying out all the different options in an application to be sure that they all work as you expect them to. With a moderately complex application, you need to create a test plan as part of the application's structured design. The test plan lists all the commands and options you should test to ensure that you test the whole application.

Testing must include use of the application by people who aren't familiar with it. You, as the developer, are too close to the application and are unlikely to try things out of order or with incorrect data. You need someone with a different machine and configuration and who doesn't know a thing about your application to test it for you. Hopefully this testing, known as beta testing, will find all the problems you missed.

Although minor bugs in software generally are tolerated, major ones are not. A major bug can destroy a package's marketability and a company's credibility. Even after the problem is corrected, a product's reputation as a product with a problem remains and can be very difficult to overcome.

Debugging involves fixing the problems you and your beta testers find. Visual Basic's built-in debugging tools are more than adequate for locating and fixing the problems with your application. As you find and fix bugs, you must retest the application to ensure that the problems are fixed. Retesting the application must include the whole application, not just the part with the problem, to ensure that fixing an existing problem didn't introduce a new one.

 The resulting code developed in this chapter is in the \DCNSPT directory on the included CD.

Amazingly, the coding and testing are done. The application is ready to ship—*not!* Even though the code is ready, it lacks documentation. Disks must be manufactured and labels printed. Plans for distribution, marketing, and support must be completed. Although it would be nice to be able to ship a code as soon as the last byte is typed, it isn't until all the administrative and support tasks are done that you can say you're truly done.

Documentation

In modern professional applications, documentation involves more than simply scribbling down a list of commands and options. Documentation now includes online documents and context-sensitive help as well as printed manuals. This part of the book shows you how to design and create a Windows help file and context-sensitive help.

Documenting the Application

Documenting the Application

The application is complete and does everything you want it to. You can make it display every graph and table. But what happens when you give it to a novice user? To get the point across and make the program usable, you must document it. Never mind that you've been designing an application that could be run without documentation. You must provide documentation for situations in which the steps aren't obvious.

Today you will learn

- about the documentation options
- how to design documentation
- how to create an online documentation system

The Goal of Day 12

The goal of Day 12 is to learn to document an application. A perfect application would need no documentation, because every operation and capability would be obvious, but since no application is perfect, you must document it. Documentation describes how to use an application, and it serves as a training guide to teach the user which options are available. Very often, alternative uses of an application aren't always as obvious to the user as special features.

Obvious Options

Time and again you will add a feature to automate some common operation, only to have the users do it the hard way—the way they've always done it. Use your documentation to highlight these new features and get the user to at least try them. If they still won't use them, maybe you should reconsider why they won't use them and if they are really useful.

Documentation Options

There are basically three different types of documentation for a computer application: printed documents, online documents, status bars, and online help. In addition, there are a lot of features that most people wouldn't think of as documentation, including pop-up labels and wizards. A *wizard* is a help window that tells you step-by-step how to achieve a certain task. The wizard might even set options for you as it leads you through the operations.

The documentation option or options you choose generally depends on the complexity of your application and the resources you have available to create documentation. For a small consulting project, a large, expensive printed document is unwarranted. For a mainstream application, good documentation is a requirement.

Printed Documents

Printed manuals are the original documentation option for computer programs. Older command-line and batch programs were useless without printed documentation. Because these older applications had no menus or buttons, it was almost impossible to know what to type at the prompt to get the system to do something useful. You might have been able to guess a command, but the number of possible options was much too large to figure out by trial and error. Documentation for these programs generally consisted of command lists and descriptions.

Newer applications have menus and buttons with names or pictures on them, making it generally obvious what you should do to make the program work. Picking a named option from a list eliminates the need for a printed list of commands. Documentation for these programs generally still lists the commands, but the documents themselves are more geared toward accomplishing tasks instead of listing commands.

Printed documents generally are necessary for any complex application. Even though the application's operation might be obvious, printed documents are needed and are often preferred by users. An unfortunate aspect of printed documents is that they must be printed, and printing takes time. To have the documents and the application ready on the same day, you have to send the printed documents to the printer a month or so early. Thus, any changes in the program interface will not be included in the printed description.

Supplements

Printed documents should be supplemented with printed or online updates to take care of changes and omitted material.

Online Documents

Online documents are simply documents that haven't been printed but are still on disk. If the user wants a printed copy, he must print it himself. Online documents are much more up-to-date than printed documents because changes can be made at the last minute as changes are made in the program. Online documents are useful in that they don't get lost as manuals do but are available with the program whenever they're needed.

Disadvantages of online documents are that they are slower to read and easy to pirate. According to the *Visual Design Guide* included with Visual Basic, people read about 30 percent slower online as compared to reading printed documents. The piracy issue comes about because the documents can be copied by simply copying the files along with the program. Printed documents are much more difficult to copy.

You have many options for online documents. The simplest are plain text files that can be read and printed on almost any computer. They're easy to produce but lack any special formatting or images. In Windows, both Notepad and Write can open and view plain text files.

Formatted documents require that you have the original application or a document reader such as Adobe Acrobat. The only application included with Windows that can open a formatted text file is Write, and it has only limited formatting capability compared to a program like Word. The Adobe Acrobat reader is a fully formatted document reader. It formats documents into Acrobat files that can be distributed to your users along with the reader application.

PostScript files allow you to print a fully formatted document, but your user must have access to a PostScript printer. PostScript files also tend to be quite large compared to the original document, especially if you use a lot of nonstandard fonts. Nonstandard fonts must be attached to the PostScript file so that the printer will know how to print them.

Online Help

Online help uses the Windows help program, WinHelp, to create a hypertext document. That document can then be linked to a running application using system calls. An online help system is the most modern of the documentation options and is available directly from within the application. More than a document, a Windows help file is a *hypertext* document in which words and phrases are linked to other topics in the help system, so a single click moves you to the new topic.

Online help is generally set up with a Help menu in the target application and also linked to the F1 key to give context-sensitive help. With context-sensitive help, the help topic displayed is determined by the object selected in the application when the F1 key is pressed.

Online help also includes pop-up labels over buttons and objects that explain the objects' use, and wizards that guide you through a complex task.

Designing a Help System

When you design a help system, especially a context-sensitive help system, you use much the same steps you used when designing the application:

- ☐ Determine what information is needed.
- ☐ Break the information into modular topics.
- ☐ Determine the connectivity between topics.
- ☐ Design the structure of the document.
- ☐ Create the document.

Determine What Information Is Needed

The first step is to determine what information is needed. Consider again who your users are and what they already know about their system. Are they administrators or administrative staff with little knowledge about how the system works and who only want to know how to turn it on? Or are they computer wizards who will figure out the easy stuff without help and who want to know the details of the internal workings? Presumably your users are somewhere in between.

When you know who your users are, determine what they need to know to make the system work. Most help packages include a user's manual to explain how to use the package and a reference manual to explain how the commands work. For upgrades, an upgrader's manual is useful. It explains how to do the upgrade, as well as the differences between the new and old versions of the program. Other manuals might be appropriate, depending on what the application is. The level of detail you use in these manuals is determined by who your users are.

Break the Information into Modular Topics

Whether you're writing a book or implementing an online help system, you still break the information into topics. In a book, the topics comprise the chapters and sections. In an online system, the topics comprise the pages of information presented to the user.

Start with an overview of the information and work down to the details. This is a top-down implementation, just like the structured design used to design the application. The techniques of structured design can be used if the documentation is complex.

After you've defined the overview of the information, break it into subtopics that provide the details. Break the subtopics themselves into subtopics until the information in a topic can be presented on a single page or less and can be easily understood. If you're writing a book, the top-level topics are the chapters, and the lower-level ones comprise the sections and subsections within the chapters. In general, a single topic should be no longer than two pages, and ideally it should fit on a single page.

Determine the Connectivity Between Topics

When you have your list of topics, define the connectivity between them. In a written document, the connectivity is usually sequential, from the beginning of the document to the end. A reference work is accessed randomly. It's not meant to be read from beginning to end, but selectively, as the topics are needed. An online help system is more flexible and can be read sequentially by paging from topic to topic or randomly using the hyperlinks.

Documenting the Application

Design the Document's Structure

When you have a good idea of what you want to say and in what order you want to say it, design the document's structure. Document design is most often done with an outlining tool, but it can also be done with diagrams and flowcharts. The final outline shows the document's main information flow—that is, the path the average user should take to get through the document. For a book, that flow is from front to back because of its rigid structure. For an online document, there is still a primary flow, but that flow doesn't have to be an ordered list of topics. It can be a list of hyperlinks.

Create the Document

When the design is done, you break the outline into separate topics and fill in the words and figures to complete it. Partitioning the outline is done somewhat differently, depending on if this is an online document or if needs to be printed. A printed document generally follows the outline directly, because each topic in the outline should flow to the next. An online document is treated somewhat differently, because the flow is from topic to topic without the restriction of having to go in sequential order.

Using the Outliner

The outliner in Word (or any other good word processor) is a useful design tool for any document, whether a book or an online help document. The design proceeds the same until you reach the last step, at which point the outline is partitioned into separate topics for writing. In a book, the topics and subtopics are left in the outline, and that document is expanded into a book. The order of the parts of the book is identical to the parts of the outline. For an online document, the ordering is somewhat different. Each heading and subheading in the outline is separated into a distinct topic and referenced to the original topic using hyperlinks.

The Windows Help System

The Windows operating system has a built-in help system. The WinHelp program reads help files and displays them for the user one topic at a time. Because the WinHelp program is part of Windows, any program can use it. For a complete description of the WinHelp system and creating Windows help files, see the *Help Compiler Guide* included with the Visual Basic package.

WinHelp has a considerable amount of capability, far more than is needed to create a reasonable help file. In addition to text files with hypertext links, a Windows help file can contain graphics with multiple hot spots and macro commands to create fully automated help procedures and online learning systems.

You can produce complex hypermedia documents with WinHelp, but it's not difficult to put together a simple custom help file for an application. Figure 12.1 shows a data flow diagram for producing help documents with WinHelp. The help package is designed in processes 1 and 2, and the help topic file is created in process 3. The help topic file is a rich text document file that contains all the text, links, formatting, and images necessary to create the help file. If an image will contain hot spots, they are added with the hot spot editor (SHED.EXE) in process 5. Images with hot spots are referenced by name in the topic file instead of being inserted directly into the file. To handle systems with different monitors (EGA, VGA, and so forth), you can create multiresolution bitmap files using the multiresolution bitmap compiler. If you don't do this, the system will stretch or shrink the single-resolution bitmap, which might or might not produce acceptable results. You can negate this problem by using Windows metafile images instead of bitmaps, because Windows metafiles are resolution-independent.

When the topic and image files are created, you create a project file that lists the files to combine into the help file in process 4 and then compile them into a help file in process 7.

To produce a simple help package consisting of text and a few small pictures, you need only the project file and the topic file. These two files are compiled into a help file using the help compiler. The WinHelp program then opens and displays the help file.

Day 12: Documenting the Application

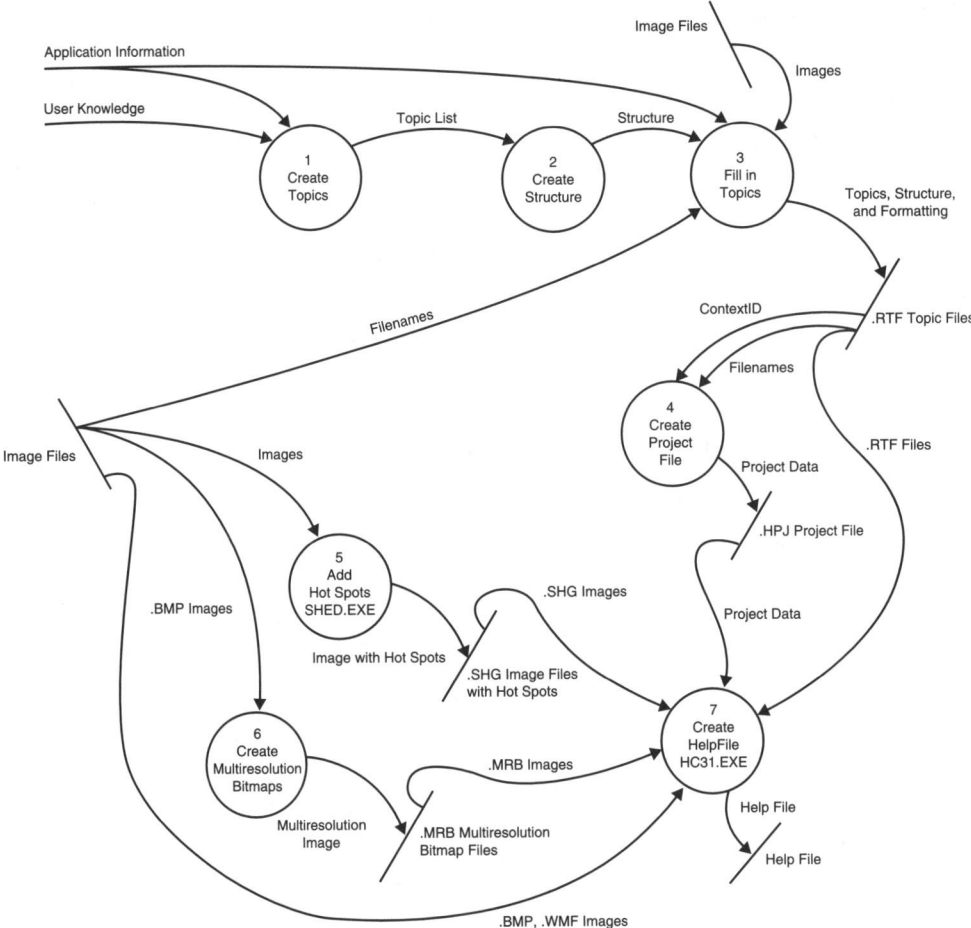

Figure 12.1. *The data flow diagram for creating a help file for use with the WinHelp system.*

Creating Help Topic Files

When you've completed the design of your help system, you need to convert it into topics stored in the topic file. The help topic file is a rich text format file containing one topic on each page. Automatic page feeds inserted by your word processor don't mark the end of a topic. Only inserted, hard-page feeds define the end of one topic and the beginning of the next.

Each topic has several attributes—Context ID, Caption, Browse Order Code, and Keywords. These attributes are attached to each topic using footnotes. The footnote character (the character placed in superscript next to the word you are footnoting) determines which attribute is contained in the footnote. Table 12.1 lists the attributes you can insert in a help topic file. The footnotes are all attached to the beginning of the topic, as shown in Figure 12.2.

Table 12.1. The attributes that can be assigned in a help topic file.

Attribute	Symbol	Description
Context ID	# footnote	The Context ID is a short string that names each help topic in the help topic file. This string is the name you use to create a jump to this help topic. This string can't contain spaces.
Title	$ footnote	This is a text string containing a title for the topic. The title is used with the search capability of help to list topics selected by a particular search. To place a title in the topic itself, type and format it there directly.
Keyword	K footnote	The keyword list is the list of words searched with help's search capability. When any keywords match a search, the topic's title is listed in the search dialog box. Multiple keywords are separated with semicolons.
Browse sequence number	+ footnote	The browse sequence is the order of the topics that the user sees when browsing through the help file using the browse keys. The browse sequence number is actually an alphanumeric string, and the sequence is determined by the location of that string in the list of all sequence numbers.
Build tag	* footnote	A build tag allows you to selectively include topics in a help file without having to create multiple help files. When you compile a help file, you tell the help compiler which build tags to include in the help file. Topics without build tags are included in all help files.
Jump text	Strikethrough or double-underlined text	Text marked with a strikethrough or double underline becomes a hypertext button for jumping to another topic. Place the Context ID of the topic to jump to as hidden text immediately following the jump text.

continues

Day 12: Documenting the Application

Table 12.1. continued

Attribute	Symbol	Description
Definition text	Single-underlined text	Text marked with a single underline becomes a hypertext button for displaying a definition window over the current topic. Place the Context ID of the topic containing the definition text immediately following the definition text. Note that a definition window does not replace the current topic as the jump text does. The definition window goes away as soon as you click elsewhere on the help document.

Figure 12.2.
A help topic file displayed in Word, showing the WhatIsDSA *help topic with its attributes in its footnotes.*

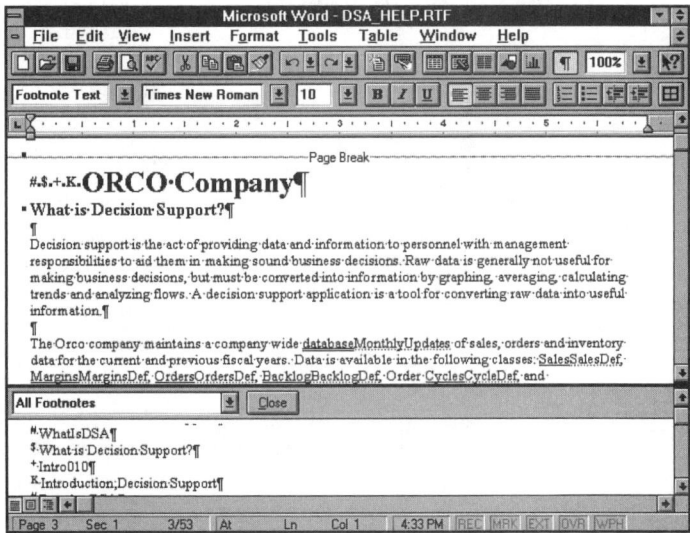

The primary attribute is the Context ID. In Figure 12.2, the Context ID for the topic displayed in the upper window is WhatIsDSA, displayed in the # footnote. Each help topic must have a unique Context ID that identifies it. Following the Context ID is the title in the $ footnote and the browse sequence number Intro010 in the + footnote. The keywords Introduction and Decision Support are in the K footnote.

To create a hypertext jump to a topic when a text string is clicked, double-underline the text and place the Context ID of the topic you want to jump to as hidden text immediately after the double-underlined text. In Figure 12.2, *database* is double-underlined, and the Context ID MonthlyUpdates immediately follows it. When the help topic is compiled, the double-underlined text is displayed as green underlined text, as shown in Figure 12.3. When you click on the word *database,* you immediately switch to the MonthlyUpdates topic.

Figure 12.3.
The WhatIsDSA *help topic displayed by the WinHelp program.*

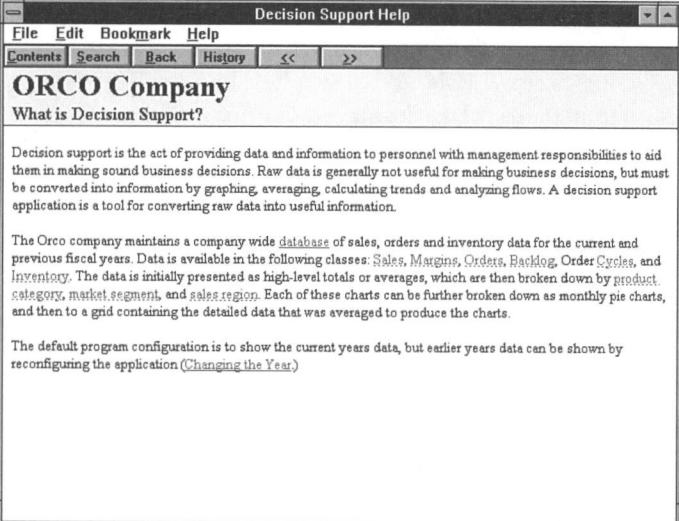

To display a definition instead of switching to a new topic, single-underline the text and place the Context ID of the topic containing the definition text as hidden text immediately following the single-underlined text. In Figure 12.2, `Sales`, `Margins`, `Orders`, `Backlog`, and `Cycles` are single-underlined, and the Context ID of the help topics to display immediately follows each. In the compiled help file, the single-underlined text is also displayed as green underlined text, as shown in Figure 12.3. But when you click on a single-underlined word, a window appears in front of the help topic window containing the definition text, as shown in Figure 12.4.

Figure 12.4.
The WhatIsDSA *help topic displayed by WinHelp, with the market segment hypertext button clicked.*

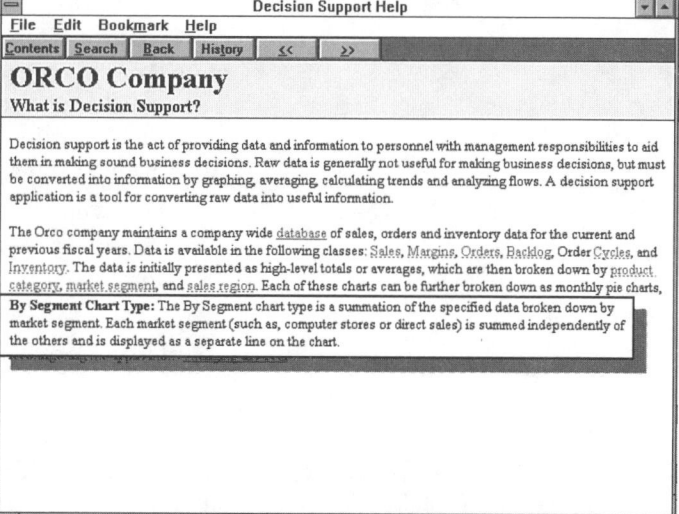

Documenting the Application

When a help topic is longer than a single page, a scroll bar appears at the right so that you can scroll through the topic. To lock some text at the top of the topic so that it doesn't scroll, format it as "Keep With Next" paragraphs. The color of this nonscrolling text can also be made different from the rest of the document. The first two lines of Figures 12.3 and 12.4 are nonscrolling text.

Creating Help Project Files

When the help topic file is completed, you must create a help project file with the .HPJ extension. The project file is a plain text file that specifies the files and options necessary to create a help file. The project file contains up to nine sections, separated with the section separators listed in Table 12.2. Each section has a specific function, as the table shows.

Table 12.2. The sections of the help project file.

Section Code	Required?	Description
[ALIAS]	No	Defines aliases (Context IDs) for a help topic.
[BAGGAGE]	No	Contains the names of files to be placed within the .HLP file.
[BITMAPS]	No	Contains the names of bitmap files to be placed in the .HLP file.
[BUILDTAGS]	No	Lists the build tags to include in this compilation.
[CONFIG]	No	Contains specifications for user-defined menus and special libraries.
[FILES]	Yes	Contains the topic files to include in this compilation.
[MAP]	No	Contains a mapping between the Context IDs used in the help file and the HelpContextIDs used in a Visual Basic program. The Context IDs in the help file are text strings, while the HelpContextIDs in a Visual Basic program are numbers.
[OPTIONS]	No	Contains options that control the compilation, such as the output filename, what to do about errors, and so forth.
[WINDOWS]	No	Contains definitions for the help windows, such as color and location.

At a minimum, you must specify the name of the help topic file for the help compiler to compile. You also usually define some options, such as an output filename for the error list. You need the [MAP] section if you're going to use context-sensitive help and the [WINDOWS] section if you plan to change the colors of the fixed and scrolling regions in the help file.

Compiling the Help File

Compiling the help file is easy. The help compiler is a DOS application, so type the compiler name (HC31.EXE) followed by the name of the help project file to compile that project. There is a restriction, though. The help compiler needs some protected-mode memory to run. The easiest way to supply this is to run the help compiler in a DOS box under Windows.

Linking the Help System with Visual Basic

There are two ways to link a help file with a Visual Basic application: use context-sensitive help or call WinHelp directly. Most applications use both context-sensitive help and a Help menu that opens WinHelp. To use context-sensitive help, you first set the variable App.HelpFile to equal the name of and path to the help file:

```
App.HelpFile = "d:\dcnspt\dsa_help.hlp"
```

You must do this before you can use context-sensitive help, so put this line in one of the start-up procedures for your application (Main). Then insert Context ID numbers in the HelpContextID properties of the controls you want context-sensitive help on. The Context ID numbers are defined in the help project file. When the user selects a control and presses F1, WinHelp is started, the indicated help file is loaded, and the topic indicated by the HelpContextID is displayed.

The easiest way to directly access WinHelp is to use the common dialog control. You can call WinHelp directly, but you must declare it first. The common dialog control takes care of that for you. The following listing shows how to implement the Contents command on the Help menu.

```
'
'Open the help file to the contents page.
'
Sub mnuHelpContents_Click ()
   cdgDialogs.HelpFile = App.HelpFile
   cdgDialogs.HelpCommand = HELP_CONTENTS
   cdgDialogs.Action = DLG_HELP
End Sub
```

The HelpFile property is set to the path to the help file. Here, that path is retrieved from the application's App.HelpFile property, which was set at start-up. The HelpCommand property is set to the constant HELP_CONTENTS, and the Action property is set to the constant DLG_HELP. When this menu command is executed, the common dialog control starts the WinHelp application, opens the indicated help file, and displays the table of contents topic. If the HelpCommand property is set to the constant HELP_PARTIALKEY, WinHelp is started with the indicated help file, and the Search dialog is displayed.

Day 12 — Documenting the Application

The Decision Support Application Project

Since the decision support application will be placed on only a few computers in the Orco Company, it doesn't make much sense to create a printed manual. The costs to do so would be much too high to make it worthwhile. Some Xeroxed briefing and setup instructions and briefing materials will be used when the new system is formally presented to the users and managers. The primary help facility will be an online help capability.

Designing the Help System

The help file is designed using Microsoft Word's outlining capability. The outliner lists the main sections and subsections. In addition, in each heading that defines an individual topic are listed the Context ID of the topic, the Name of the topic, the Browse Sequence Numbers, and the Keywords. A part of the outline in file DSA_HELP.OTL is shown in Figure 12.5. The outline shows a topic and two levels of subtopics.

Figure 12.5.
Designing the help file using the outliner in Microsoft Word.

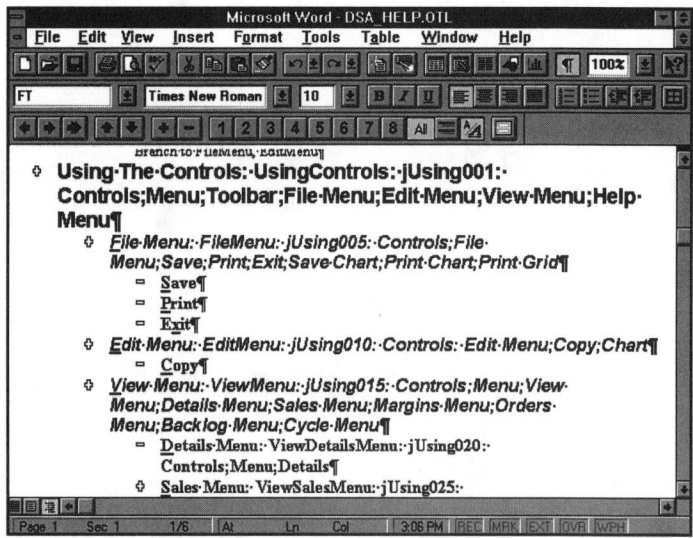

When the outline is complete, create a tracking table of topics, as shown in Table 12.3. This table makes it much easier to keep track of topic names and Context IDs.

Table 12.3. The topic tracking table in HELPTRAK.DOC.

Context ID	Title	Browse Code	Keywords
DSAContents	Decision Support Help Contents	Contents	
UsingDSA	Using Decision Support	Intro001	Introduction; Decision Support
WhatIsDSA	What Is Decision Support?	Intro010	Introduction; Decision Support
RunningDSA	Running the Application	Intro020	Introduction; Starting;Running
SelectingCharts	Selecting the Chart Class and Type	Intro030	Introduction; Charts;Selecting Chart Class; Selecting Chart Type;Type;Class
ViewingDetails	Viewing the Details	Intro040	Introduction;View Details;Grid
ViewingPieCharts	Viewing a Monthly Pie Chart	Intro050	Introduction;Pie Chart;Drill Down
DrillDownGrid	Drilling Down to the Details	Intro060	Introduction;Drill Down;Drill Down Grid;Grid
PrintingChartOrGrid	Printing the Visible Chart or Grid	Intro070	Introduction; Printing;Chart; Grid
CopyingAndSaving	Copying and Saving a Chart Image	Intro080	Introduction;Copy; Save;Chart
UsingControls	Using the Controls	jUsing001	Controls;Menu; Toolbar;File Menu;Edit Menu; View Menu;Help Menu
FileMenu	File Menu	jUsing005	Controls;File Menu; Save;Print;Exit; Save Chart;Print Chart;Print Grid

continues

Documenting the Application

Table 12.3. continued

Context ID	Title	Browse Code	Keywords
EditMenu	Edit Menu	jUsing010	Controls;Edit Menu; Copy;Chart
ViewMenu	View Menu	jUsing015	Controls;Menu;View Menu;Details Menu; Sales Menu;Margins Menu;Orders Menu; Backlog Menu;Cycle Menu
ViewDetailsMenu	Details Menu	jUsing020	Controls;Menu; Details
ViewSalesMenu	Sales Menu	jUsing025	Controls;Menu; Sales;Totals; Product;Segment; Region
ViewMarginsMenu	Margins Menu	jUsing030	Controls;Menu; Margins;Average; Product
ViewOrdersMenu	Orders Menu	jUsing035	Controls;Menu; Orders;Totals; Product;Segment; Region
ViewBacklogMenu	Backlog Menu	jUsing040	Controls;Menu; Backlog;Totals; Product;Segment; Region
ViewCycleMenu	Cycle Menu	jUsing045	Controls;Menu; Cycle;Average; Segment; Distribution
ViewInventoryMenu	Inventory Menu	jUsing050	Controls;Menu; Inventory;Totals; Product;Turnover
HelpMenu	Help Menu	jUsing055	Controls;Menu; Help;Help Contents; Help Search;Help About

Context ID	Title	Browse Code	Keywords
Toolbar	Toolbar	jUsing060	Controls;Toolbar; Buttons;Class Buttons;Type Buttons;Chart; Sales;Margin; Orders;Backlog; Cycle;Inventory; Total;Average; Product;Segment; Region; Distribution; Turnover;Disabled Button
TechNotes	Technical	Tech001	Technical;Year; Database;SQL; Troubleshooting
ChangeYear	Changing the Year	Tech005	Technical;Year; Changing The Year
ChangeDatabase	Locating the Database	Tech010	Technical;Database; Finding The Database
MonthlyUpdates	Doing Monthly Updates	Tech015	Technical;Monthly Updates;Updates
SQLStatements	The SQL Statements	Tech020	Technical;SQL; Database Queries
Troubleshooting	Troubleshooting	Tech030	Technical; Troubleshooting; INI;Missing INI; Database;Missing Database;Query Errors;Data Unavailable
NoINI	Can't Find INI File	Tech035	INI;Missing INI
NoDatabase	Can't Find Graphs Database	Tech040	Database;Missing Database
QueryError	Query Errors; Data Not Available	Tech045	Query Errors; Data Unavailable

continues

Documenting the Application

Table 12.3. continued

Context ID	Title	Browse Code	Keywords
Pop-Up Windows			
TotalDef	Totals	zDefs001	
CategoryDef	By Category	zDefs002	
SegmentDef	By Segment	zDefs003	
RegionDef	By Region	zDefs004	
AverageDef	Average Gross	zDefs005	
DistributionDef	Distribution	zDefs006	
TurnoverDef	Turnover	zDefs007	
ClassDef	Chart Class	zDefs008	
TypeDef	Chart Type	zDefs009	
SalesDef	Sales	zDefs010	
MarginsDef	Margins	zDefs011	
OrdersDef	Orders	zDefs012	
CycleDef	Order Cycle	zDefs013	
BacklogDef	Backlog	zDefs014	
InventoryDef	Inventory	zDefs015	

Note: The Browse Codes—jUsing005, for example—might look a little strange. Browse Codes are treated alphabetically when determining which code follows any other. The initial lowercase j makes the Using codes come between the Intro and Tech codes. Without the j, the Using codes would come after the Tech codes. The name Using tells you what group of topics this topic belongs to, and the number tells you where this topic appears in the Using group.

Leave Space for Additional Topics

Leave gaps between the numerical values at the ends of the Browse Codes, as shown in Table 12.3. These gaps make it easier to insert additional help topics without having to renumber all the existing ones.

Converting the Design to a Topic File

If this were a printed manual, you would fill in the outline with words and figures. For an online help file, you convert each heading into a topic and include in that topic all the first-level headings in that topic. Thus, in the part of the outline shown in Figure 12.5, Using the Controls becomes a topic that contains the subheads File Menu, Edit Menu, View Menu, and Help Menu (not shown in the figure). It doesn't contain the Save, Print, and Exit subheads of the File Menu topic, nor does it contain the Copy subhead of the Edit menu topic, as shown in Figure 12.6. File Menu becomes another, separate topic with the Save, Print, and Exit items, as shown in Figure 12.7. Thus, the outline is rearranged, with each heading and its first-level subheadings on separate pages.

When the outline is in the condition as that shown in Figures 12.6 and 12.7, the next step is to insert words, pictures, and formatting to create the body of each topic, as shown in Figures 12.8 and 12.9. In addition, the Topic Names, Context IDs, Browse Codes, and Keywords are cut from the topic headings and placed in footnotes attached to the topic headings.

Figure 12.6.
The Using the Controls topic outline.

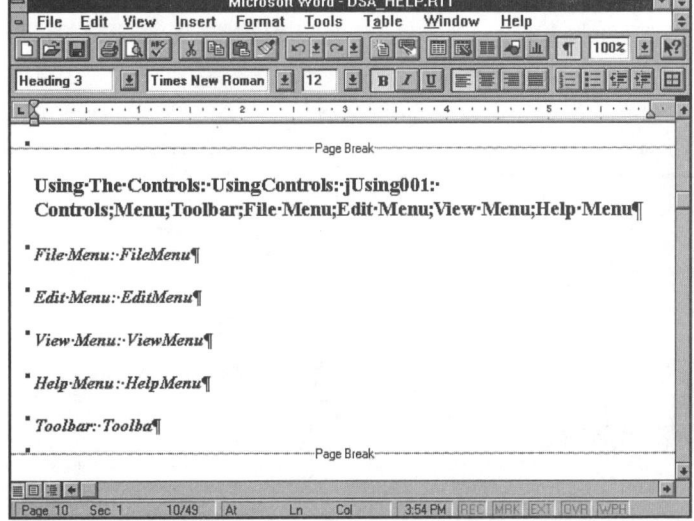
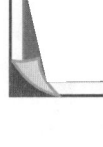

413

Day 12: Documenting the Application

Figure 12.7.
The File Menu and Edit Menu topics outline.

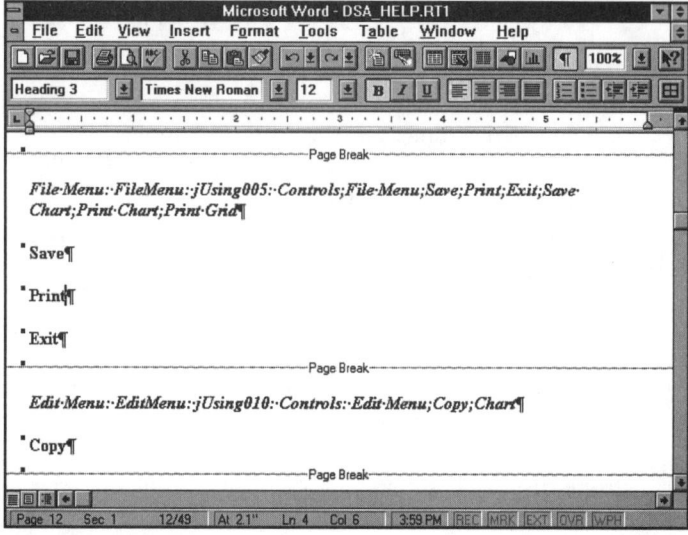

Figure 12.8.
The Using the Controls topic.

Figure 12.9.
The File Menu topic.

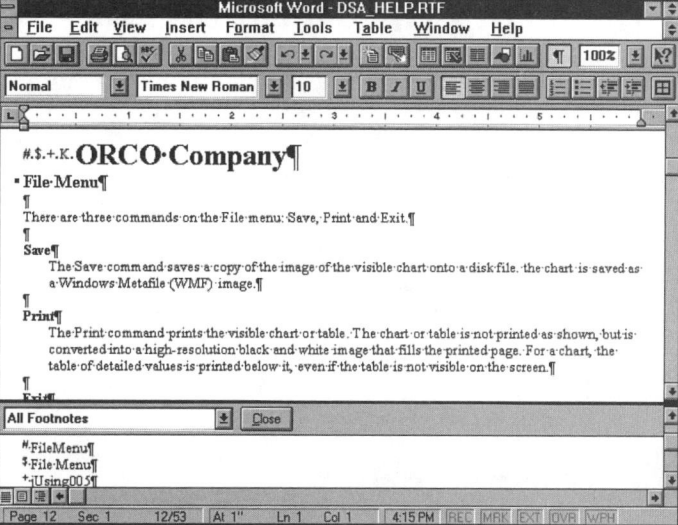

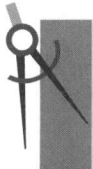

Help File Toolbar

When creating the help topic file, you continually need to format text with single and double underlines and mark some as hidden. To speed this work, create a custom toolbar for use in Word that contains buttons for these three commands. Create the custom toolbar by selecting the View | Toolbars command and clicking on the New button in the Toolbars dialog box. See the Word documentation for more information.

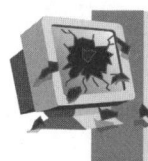

Showstopper: You must save the help topic file in rich text format (RTF) before the help compiler can compile it. To speed the opening and saving of the topic file, you can save the file in the editor's native format while you're developing it, but you must save it as RTF when you're done.

You must save the project file in text-only format before the help compiler can compile it. Saving it in the editor's native format won't significantly speed the opening and saving of the file.

Documenting the Application

Creating the Project File

With the topic file done, you need to create the project file. The project file isn't very complicated. A good starting point is the sample project file for the IconWorks program included with the help compiler. Rename and edit that file to create your own help file. The following help file, DSA_HELP.HPJ, compiles the DSA_HELP.RTF file.

```
;This help project requires hc 3.1.
[OPTIONS]
errorlog = dsa_help.err
title = Decision Support Help
contents = DSAContents
compress = false
oldkeyphrase = false
warning = 3

[FILES]
dsa_help.rtf

[MAP]
DSAContents 1
UsingDSA 2
WhatIsDSA 3
RunningDSA 4
SelectingCharts 5
ViewingDetails 6
ViewingPieCharts 7
DrillDownGrid 8
PrintingChartOrGrid 9
CopyingAndSaving 10
UsingControls 11
FileMenu 12
EditMenu 13
ViewMenu 14
ViewDetailsMenu 15
ViewSalesMenu 16
ViewMarginsMenu 17
ViewOrdersMenu 18
ViewBacklogMenu 19
ViewCycleMenu 20
ViewInventoryMenu 21
HelpMenu 22
Toolbar 23
TechNotes 24
ChangeYear 25
ChangeDatabase 26
MonthlyUpdates 27
SQLStatements 28
Troubleshooting 29
NoINI 30
NoDatabase 31
QueryError 32
TotalDef 33
CategoryDef 34
SegmentDef 35
```

```
RegionDef 36
AverageDef 37
DistributionDef 38
TurnoverDef 39
ClassDef 40
TypeDef 41
SalesDef 42
MarginsDef 43
OrdersDef 44
CycleDef 45
BacklogDef 46
InventoryDef 47

[WINDOWS]
main = "Decision Support Help", (0,0,1023,1023 ),,, (255,255,0)

[CONFIG]
BrowseButtons()
```

The file starts with an [OPTIONS] section to specify the compiling options. The compilation errors are logged to the file DSA_HELP.ERR. The title of the help file is "Decision Support Help." The table of contents Context ID is DSAContents. The compress option specifies no file compression. The oldkeyphrase option specifies that the old keyword table is not to be used, and that a new one should be created. The warning option specifies that all errors and warnings are reported.

The [FILES] section lists the one file to compile. Since all the images are imbedded in the topic file, no image files need to be listed.

The [MAP] section creates a mapping between the list of Context ID strings from the help topic file to a list of numbers. These numbers are used in the application to enable context-sensitive help. Only a few of these are actually used in the application, but numbering them all here ensures that all the numbers are unique.

The [WINDOWS] section sets the name, position, and color of the main help window. The color RGB code (255,255,0) specifies bright yellow. The position code (0,0,1023,1023) specifies that the upper-left corner is at 0,0 on the screen and specifies the size 1023x1023, which maximizes the window. The WinHelp system maps the whole screen onto a 1024x1024 grid.

Finally, the [CONFIG] section has a single command, BrowseButtons (), a macro command that enables the browse buttons on the WinHelp window. If you don't want to enable browsing, leave this command out, and you won't have to define the browse codes in the topic file.

Compiling the Help File

To compile the application, open a DOS window in Windows and run the help compiler by typing HC followed by the name of the project file. If you're going to be compiling the file several times (and you will as you debug the file), create a Windows icon that runs it with the correct option. When the compiler finishes, check the DSA_HELP.ERR file for error messages. The error messages list the errors and the topic numbers in the file. To find the topic in the file, count the hard page feeds from the beginning. When the compilation finishes, run WinHelp and open the new help file to check its operation, as shown in Figures 12.3 and 12.4.

Speeding the Compilation of the Help File

To speed help file development, create a Windows program group to compile the help file and view the results. Create a Windows program item to run the help compiler and compile the help file. Create another to open the error file with the Notepad program and another to start WinHelp and open the help file.

Linking the Help File to the Application

To link the help file to the help menu in the application and to add context-sensitive help, you must edit the application objects and add the Context IDs to the appropriate controls. First, in the initialization section of the program, read the name and path of the help file and place them in the App.HelpFile property. This is done in the LoadAndParseINIFile procedure. The bold line in the following listing performs that task. The actual path and name are placed in the .INI file.

```
'
'Load and parse the .INI file.
'
Sub LoadAndParseINIFile ()
   Dim strALine As String
   Dim fgotStart As Integer
   Dim intEqMark As Integer
   Dim strVariable As String
   Dim strValue As String
   Dim strWinPath As String
   Const ERR_FILENOTFOUND = 53

   'Turn on the error handler.
   If Not DEBUGON Then On Error GoTo INIError

   'Get the location of the Windows directory.
   strWinPath = Environ$("WINDIR")

   'Assume that the file is in the Windows directory.
   Open strWinPath & "\dcnspt.ini" For Input As #1
   Line Input #1, strALine   'Skip a line.
   'Find [startup].
   fgotStart = False
   Do While Not EOF(1)
      Line Input #1, strALine
```

```
        If strALine = "[startup]" Then
            fgotStart = True
            Exit Do
        End If
    Loop
    'Bomb out if [startup] not found.
    If Not fgotStart Then GoTo Bombout
    'Read and parse the startup information.
    Line Input #1, strALine
    Do While InStr(1, strALine, "[") = 0 And Not EOF(1)   'Continue until EOF
                                                          'or another section.
        intEqMark = InStr(1, strALine, "=")
        If intEqMark = 0 Then GoTo Bombout
        strVariable = Trim(Left(strALine, intEqMark - 1))
        strValue = Trim(Right(strALine, Len(strALine) - intEqMark))
        Select Case strVariable
            Case "DataFile"
                strDataFile = strValue
            Case "Year"
                strYear = strValue
            Case "Help"
                App.HelpFile = strValue
        End Select
        Line Input #1, strALine
Loop
    Close #1
    If strDataFile = "" Or strYear = "" Or App.HelpFile = "" Then GoTo Bombout
Exit Sub
Bombout:
    MsgBox "Corrupt INI file, can't continue.", MB_ICONSTOP, "INI File Error"
    End
INIError:
    If Err = ERR_FILENOTFOUND Then
        MsgBox Error$ & Chr$(13) & "DCNSPT.INI file must be in the Windows
        ↪directory.", MB_ICONSTOP, "INI File Error"
        End
    Else
        'Reissue error for other handler.
        Error Err
    End If
End Sub
```

Next, add Context IDs from the list in the help project file to the controls in the project. The menu window is shown in Figure 12.10, where HelpContextID 12, the FileMenu topic, is added to the File menu. Add the corresponding help topics to all the menus, and add ContextID 2, UsingDSA, to all the graph and grid objects.

Day 12: Documenting the Application

Figure 12.10.
Adding a HelpContextID to the File menu.

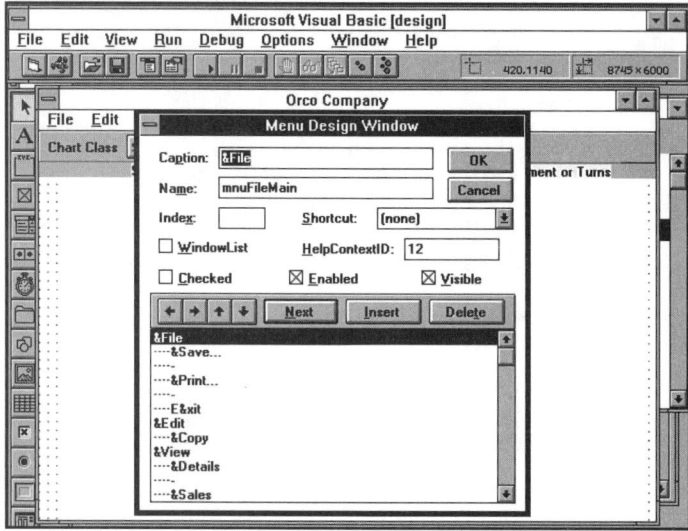

To add the Help menu, use the common dialog to make the connection in the Help menu. The Help menu has a Contents item and a Search item. We want the Contents item to bring up the help file's table of contents and the Search item to bring up the help search dialog. Use the common dialog control to handle both cases.

```
'
'Open the help file to the contents page.
'
Sub mnuHelpContents_Click ()
   cdgDialogs.HelpFile = App.HelpFile
   cdgDialogs.HelpCommand = HELP_CONTENTS
   cdgDialogs.Action = DLG_HELP
End Sub

'
'Open the help file search dialog box.
'
Sub mnuHelpSearch_Click ()
   cdgDialogs.HelpFile = App.HelpFile
   cdgDialogs.HelpCommand = HELP_PARTIALKEY
   cdgDialogs.Action = DLG_HELP
End Sub
```

The WinHelp program needs one more call to tell it when it is no longer needed. In the `mnuFileExit_Click` procedure, add another call to the common dialog to send WinHelp the quit command. WinHelp might not quit right then if some other application is also using it, but the close call tells it that the decision support application no longer needs it. When all programs that have opened WinHelp send it the close command, it will quit.

```
'
'End the program.
'
Sub mnuFileExit_Click ()
   'Tell Help we are done with it.
   cdgDialogs.HelpFile = App.HelpFile
   cdgDialogs.HelpCommand = HELP_QUIT
   cdgDialogs.Action = DLG_HELP

   'End the program.
   End
End Sub
```

Modification Notes

Modifying an existing help program is relatively easy if you have the original outline or the help tracking file. If you don't have these, you need to create a help tracking file so that you know what the topic Context IDs are. Once you have that, you can create your new help topics and add the appropriate hyperlinks to connect them to the rest of the file. Note that in Table 12.3 the Browse Codes aren't sequential but have big numerical gaps between successive codes. This is intentional to allow new help topics to be inserted without having to shift all the existing topics to make room.

Debugging the Process

The help file needs to be tested and debugged just like the application. A complex help file should be alpha- and beta-tested. A simple help file like the one for the decision support application can be adequately tested in-house. However, if the help file is available, include it with the application when you send the application to the beta testers.

Test the file by trying every hypertext link to ensure that it goes to the correct topic, fix the syntax errors identified in the error file, and read through the help file, looking for misspelled words and seeing if everything hangs together. Watch for underlined words that aren't green, which indicates that there is a hypertext link but that something is wrong with it. See if there is a space between it and the hidden Context ID. The errors listed in the error file tell you which Context ID was involved and which topic the error was in. The topics are located by number, counting from the beginning of the file. Each project is on a separate page, so just count pages to find the project involved.

The help compiler creates a help file even if it finds errors, so opening the file with WinHelp might find the error for you. A mistyped Context ID causes a "topic unavailable" error when you're running WinHelp.

Documenting the Application

Don't forget to check the search list to make sure all the words in it are correct. Typing a comma or a space instead of a semicolon between keywords will join two keywords as if they were one. It's usually obvious if any are joined as you search through the list.

Use the spell checker on your word processor to check the file for spelling errors. It will stop on all the Context IDs, so be careful not to correct the spelling on an ID, thereby making its spelling correct but making it the wrong ID.

Showstopper: Don't let your word processor correct the spelling of the Context IDs. Context IDs usually aren't real words, but run-together strings of words. A spell checker will always stop on them. If you accidentally correct one, you'll get a "topic unavailable" error when you try to view the file with WinHelp.

Summary

Today you learned to document your application, either as a printed document, an online document, or a Windows help file. We especially concentrated on the Windows help system and the WinHelp application, because it's easy and inexpensive to implement a Windows help file for a custom application. It's also always available to the user and doesn't get lost like printed manuals do. This doesn't mean that you shouldn't have any printed documents to go with an application. You almost always need some documents to describe the application's installation and capabilities, but you don't have to have a large, formal document.

The files used to create the help file described in this chapter are on the CD in the \HELP directory. The final version of the help file and the application files modified to use the help file are in the directory \DCNSPT.

Implementation

Implementation is the act of selling and supporting your application, including all the manufacturing, marketing, and sales that go along with selling. Implementation might be as simple as passing the rights to your application to your employer or as complex as developing your own distribution channels. This part of the book deals with these issues.

13

Manufacturing and Sales

Day 13: Manufacturing and Sales

Now that you've burned yourself out building your marvelous program, it's time to sit back and rake in the profits, right? Wrong. In all cases except the one in which you're writing the program for yourself, you must prepare the program for manufacturing. You might not actually do the manufacturing yourself, but you must still prepare the application and all its support files for the manufacturer.

Today you will learn

- to prepare a program for manufacturing
- the different avenues for manufacturing
- the different ways to sell a program
- a little about warranties, licenses, and copyrights

The Goal of Day 13

The goal of Day 13 is to learn to prepare a program for manufacturing and to consider how to go about manufacturing and selling the application. Your choices depend on who you are and who you wrote the program for. As I mentioned on Day 1, your situation should be one of the following:

- You are the customer.
- Someone else is the customer.
- A third person is the customer.

You Are the Customer

If you are the customer for this program, you probably are done. Use the program, enjoy it, change it—do whatever you want to it. It's yours. You don't have to satisfy anyone else, you don't have to manufacture it, and you don't have to sell it. You're done. You've finished this book. Good-bye and good luck.

On the other hand.... After doing all this work on a commercial-grade application, it would be nice to see some financial return for all your effort. Maybe selling it isn't such a bad idea.

Someone Else Is the Customer

When someone else is the customer, you generally are working under a contract of some sort that spells out your obligations. At a minimum, you must deliver the application to your customer. You might have to do the installation as well. If you're an employee of your customer, delivery might consist of simply copying the application to the company file server, where the other employees can get their electronic hands on it. If you don't have this avenue of delivery, or if you're a consultant and must take the application from your place of business to your customer's place of business, you need to make the application distributable.

In general, a distribution set consists of a set of floppy disks or a CD-ROM disk that contains all the files necessary to put your application on another machine. In addition, you might include a setup program on the disk to copy the files onto the user's hard drive. For a small application, you might get away with not using a setup program, but for anything else, you need one.

With most Windows applications, you don't just deliver an executable file, but also copies of shared libraries, custom controls, help files, and initialization files. If you miss any of these files, your application won't work. In addition, you might need to

- alter the Windows .INI files to register the program
- alter the program's .INI file to fit the system
- alter the AUTOEXEC.BAT and CONFIG.SYS files to handle the program
- create a program group with a program icon so that the user can run it by clicking on the icon

These are all good reasons for using a setup program, because it can be programmed to copy all the files into the right directories and to do all the editing.

A Third Person Is the Customer

If you're working for a software publisher who is going to sell your program to someone else, you probably won't have to deal with manufacturing and sales. Any good publisher has whole departments devoted to these tasks. However, you must deliver a gold master distribution disk to the manufacturing department. A *gold master* is the distribution set that is delivered to manufacturing for reproduction. It is the last beta-test copy of an application. Nothing short of an act of God (or a major program bug) can force any changes in this set.

Preparing an Application for Manufacturing

The first step in preparing a Windows application for manufacturing is to create and add a program icon. This is something we haven't done yet in this book. The program icon is what is displayed in the Windows Program Manager, and it's what is displayed on-screen when the running application is minimized. You also must scan all the program files for viruses to make sure you don't distribute an infected program. Finally, you must create an installation set that you will pass to the manufacturer.

Adding a Program Icon

The first step in creating a program icon is to draw it. The IconWorks sample program included with Visual Basic is a reasonable editor for creating icons. IconWorks functions much like a paint program, but it creates icon files (.ICO). There's a big difference between the images used for icons and those used on the tops of buttons. You want a button to blend in with the application's background so that it won't distract the user from the important information on the screen. On the other hand, you want an icon to be seen. You want the user to remember the icon so that she will use your application. An icon needs to be distinctive; it should stand out from the other icons on the desktop.

Scanning for Viruses

When all the files to create the distribution set are ready, perform a scan with a current antivirus scanner. A virus on your distribution set will wreck your reputation. Do a complete scan of your machine to ensure that no virus has slipped by you.

Showstopper: Distributing a computer virus with your application will do incredible damage to your reputation and to your pocketbook. If a virus is found, you must quickly recall all the disks and replace them with clean copies, all at your own cost.

Here are some things to consider when scanning a disk for viruses:

1. You must have a recent copy of the antivirus scanning software (less than six months old). If you don't have a recent copy of a scanner, you won't be able to detect any of the new viruses. Most antivirus packages offer regular updates to their software, which are available by mail or electronically (a BBS or the Internet).

2. Boot your machine with a clean, locked floppy disk before scanning your hard disk. A floppy is clean if you know it doesn't have a virus. You must lock it so that it can't be inadvertently infected. Many of the newer viruses have stealth capabilities that allow them to hide from an antivirus scanner. If you scan your disk with the virus in memory, your scanner might not be able to detect it, and the act of scanning your disk might infect every executable file on it.

3. When booting with the clean, locked floppy, be sure to do a cold boot. In other words, turn your machine off, wait 10 seconds, and then turn it on with the clean, locked floppy in the A: drive. You must do a cold boot to ensure that there is no virus in memory. Many viruses can survive a warm boot (Ctrl-Alt-Delete).

4. Scan any floppy disks you use regularly.

5. Don't put new software onto your machine until after you've made the distribution disks. You don't want to introduce a new virus after you've scanned your disk and before you create the distribution set.

6. Scan your disk again after creating the distribution set to be sure that a virus didn't sneak in while you were creating the disks. If you find a virus, dump your distribution set and start over. You can't scan the distribution set, because most of the files are compressed.

Showstopper: Modern stealth viruses can hide from you and from an anti-virus scanner, making them impossible to detect. For example, the One_half virus intercepts low-level read requests from the system and redirects those that access virus-infected sectors to other uninfected sectors on the disk.

Showstopper: Many viruses can survive a warm boot initiated with Ctrl-Alt-Delete. You must do a cold boot (power off for 10 seconds) to ensure that memory is clear before rebooting with a clean, locked floppy.

Showstopper: Beware of scanning with a virus in memory. You might infect your whole disk. A memory-resident virus normally watches for file accesses and infects files when they're accessed. An antivirus scanner opens every executable file to scan it. If a virus is in memory when you start scanning, the act of scanning might infect every executable file on your disk.

Creating a Distribution Set

You could write a Visual Basic program to create a distribution set for yourself and another to do the setup on the customer's computer, but why develop a new program to do what is already available in Visual Basic? Visual Basic includes the Microsoft Setup program and the Setup Wizard. Using these two programs, you can create a reasonably robust installation set.

The Setup Wizard scans your application and determines which controls it has and which libraries it needs to be able to run. Although it can't find everything, it does take care of all the controls delivered with Visual Basic. You might have to help it a little if you have custom controls from other vendors or homemade libraries that must be included with the application.

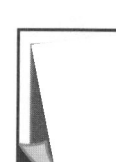

Manufacturing and Sales

When you run the Setup Wizard, it scans your application and its directory for needed files. It asks you about the application's database and imbedding capabilities and then displays a list of the files it thinks are needed in order for the application to run. You edit that list, adding or deleting files until you have a list of the files needed to make the application run. It then compresses the files and stores them on the floppy, along with the setup program. A second setup program (SETUP1.EXE) is created to do the actual installation. When you run the setup program on the floppy disk, it runs itself and copies itself and any files needed to run a Visual Basic program onto the hard drive. When the setup program finishes, it starts the SETUP1.EXE program to finish the installation. The SETUP1.EXE program is a Visual Basic program written by the Setup Wizard that installs the files in its file list. You edit this program to make any changes to the installation process.

Manufacturing: You Do It

You can do your own manufacturing, especially if you aren't selling a high-volume application. Custom applications created by a consultant often need only a few copies to a few tens of copies for delivery to the customer. Even 100 copies won't involve more than a couple of days sitting at your computer formatting and copying floppy disks. Doing your own manufacturing primarily consists of sitting at your computer, feeding it disks to format and copy. When the disks are copied, place labels on them, duplicate the documentation with a copy machine, and package the disks and documentation.

When copying the disks, use a disk duplicating and verifying program that stores the disk image in memory. Doing this saves you wear on your disk drive and on the master copy of your program. If you don't have a disk copying program that stores the image in memory, create a RAM disk in memory using the DOS VDISK.SYS driver and store the disk image there using the XCOPY program. You can then use a batch file to format and copy files onto the floppy disk.

Buying Disks

Buy your floppy disks in bulk to get a break on the cost. Most places give a pretty good break if you buy 100 disks or more at a time. However, don't buy unlabeled bulk disks. Buy brand name disks to ensure that the quality is good. Although unlabeled bulk disks might work just fine, it's more likely that they were marginal when tested, which is why they are unlabeled. Marginal disks often have bad sectors and are likely to become unreadable. The damage done to your reputation when you have to replace a disk that failed when the customer tried to install your new application will cost more than you saved buying inexpensive disks.

When you're considering the price of a disk, don't look at the cost of a box of 100 disks. Look at the cost of one disk compared to what you plan to sell your software

for. The ratio of those two numbers should tell you whether you're wasting money buying cheap disks.

You can make the labels using your printer, or you can send them out to be printed at a printer. Continuous-form labels are available for pin feed printers, and sheets of labels are available for laser printers. Alternatively, you can have your labels professionally printed by a commercial printer for a reasonable cost. If you have several low-volume products, you can get good-looking labels by having the background and company logo professionally printed and then printing the program title and copyright information using your home printer.

The manual can be printed professionally or Xeroxed, depending on the number of copies you need and the funds you have available. Xeroxing is more expensive per page. Printing has a fixed setup fee that is the same for any number of copies and that must be divided among all the copies made. Do some cost comparison analysis to determine which method to use. *Cost comparison analysis* graphs the cost per item versus the number of items sold for two different items or manufacturing methods. Be sure to include a fraction of the fixed costs and all of the variable costs when figuring out the cost of an item.

The packaging you use depends on the size of the printed manual. If the printed manual is only a few pages long, it can be folded and stuffed into a disk mailer with the disk, creating the package. Most applications that have a larger manual use a small box.

Subcontract It

When the number of copies of the software that you expect to sell reaches a high enough number, it becomes much more reasonable to subcontract the project out to a professional disk duplicating company. The risk in subcontracting the duplication of your disks is that the disk duplicator probably won't be as careful with the disks as you are. Subcontracting is very convenient, however. You can subcontract only the disk copying, or include the labeling, packaging, and shipping as well.

When to Buy a Disk Duplicator

You could buy a disk duplicator and do the mass duplications yourself. Before you buy one, consider whether you have enough duplication work to pay for the duplicator. In other words, take the cost of contracting a duplication and subtract the cost of doing it yourself, ignoring the cost of the disk duplicator. Divide that number into the cost of the disk duplicator to determine how many disks you must duplicate before you will save money using the duplicator.

Manufacturing and Sales

Use a Publisher

There are three ways to use a software publisher: subcontract the work to him, sell the product to him, or have him sell the product and pay you a royalty. What you do depends on many factors, including what you can sell your product for and how many copies you can sell. Negotiate with your publisher to get yourself the best deal possible, but realize that he probably has an existing sales channel that would take you years to develop.

Shareware

Shareware is another useful manufacturing option, since you don't really have to manufacture it. Upload the contents of your master disks to a popular BBS (bulletin board system) or to an anonymous FTP server on the Internet, and your application will spread widely if it's any good. Include with your application the standard shareware request that people should try it out and pay for it if they use it. Shareware is easy, because all you have to do is release it and sit back and collect the registration payments. However, it's unlikely that more than one copy in a hundred will be paid for.

Nag the User with a Shareware Banner

An apparently successful adaptation of the shareware request is to add it to a banner that displays while the program is starting up. Thus, the user sees the request every time she runs the program unless she pays the shareware fee and obtains a registration number. Add a button to clear the banner and an input box to insert a registration number. Use some sort of code to validate the registration number so that the user can't type in just any number. For example, add an extra digit to a serial number that makes the digits sum to a number ending in 0. If you added a 5 to 12345, that would be 123455, which sums to

1 + 2 + 3 + 4 + 5 + 5 = 20

Note: There are organizations that help shareware authors, such as the Association of Shareware Professionals on CompuServe (GO ASPFORUM).

Disk Selection Considerations

You might think that selecting a disk to use to distribute your application is a simple decision. Unfortunately, it is not. If you're under contract or are delivering an application to a specific company where you know what kinds of drives your customer's machines have, it's a simple decision. You use what they have or request. If you're selling to the general public, you need to consider your options and the problems they might cause.

Apple Macintosh Distributions

If you're distributing an Apple Macintosh application, the 800K double-sided 3 1/2-inch floppy can be read by all Macintoshes since the Mac Plus. Most newer Macintoshes also support the 1.44M 3 1/2-inch floppy.

MS-DOS/Windows Distribution

There are two standards for MS-DOS machines—1.2M 5 1/4-inch floppies and 1.44M 3 1/2-inch floppies. All newer machines are being built with the high-density 3 1/2-inch floppies, but many older machines, including the widespread PC/AT, can handle only the high-density 5 1/4-inch disks. A few of the really old PC and PC/XT machines can read only 360K 5 1/4-inch disks, but few if any of these machines can run Windows.

CD-ROM

A new distribution option is the CD-ROM. At less than $150 for a double-speed drive, they are rapidly becoming widespread as a popular distribution medium for large applications, multimedia files, and games. These drives have over 600M of space available, which should certainly hold any of the current applications with lots of space to spare. Also, in manufacturing lots of a few thousand, they are comparable in cost to a floppy disk. The current rule of thumb for a mass-produced application is that a single floppy disk is less expensive than a CD-ROM, but a CD-ROM is less expensive than two floppy disks. Note that this rule is changing rapidly and should be verified with a CD-ROM manufacturer at the time you manufacture a distribution.

Recordable CD-ROM (CD-R) drives are quickly dropping in price. I recently saw one for about $1,700, but most are in the $2,000 to $4,000 range. Recordable CD-R media cost less than $15 each. CD-R disks look much like CD-ROM disks and can be read in any CD-ROM drive, but they can be written to only once in a CD-R drive. With a CD-R drive, you can create your own CD-ROM distributions, which are useful for distributing a large application or database to a small number of customers. Note that CD-R disks aren't quite as robust as CD-ROMs and are somewhat susceptible to heat and excess sunlight, but with a little care, these restrictions shouldn't be a problem.

Manufacturing and Sales

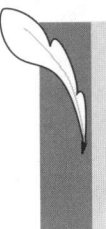

Note: An added benefit of having a CD-R drive is that it can be used for low-cost archival data storage. Although the recording drives are somewhat expensive, the CD-R disks are inexpensive and can be read in inexpensive CD-ROM drives. In addition, disks can be written that can be read by multiple platforms (Macintosh, MS-DOS, UNIX), making them a cross-platform solution.

Distribution Options

As applications become larger and new media types become widespread, choosing the distribution media for an application becomes harder, because there is no common media type. So what do you do if your customer's machine can't read the distribution disks for your application?

Most machines running Windows have 1.44M 3 1/2-inch drives, so a distribution of this type will satisfy most users. Another option is to include both 1.2M 5 1/4-inch and 1.44M 3 1/2-inch disks in the box. These dual-media distributions eliminate the need for stocking two versions of the same program and also eliminate the need for handling a service call when the user purchases the wrong size media. This is a reasonable option for high-priced applications, but not for inexpensive ones.

For a planned CD-ROM distribution, you need to consider what to do if the user doesn't have a CD-ROM drive. You must either stock two or more versions of the software with different media in each, or possibly include a coupon for users without a CD-ROM drive that lets them exchange the CD-ROM for floppy disks that fit their machines. This is a reasonable option only for applications that will fit on a reasonable number of floppy disks.

Distribution Media

I recently beta-tested a Visual Basic distribution on 360K disks. The distribution had 28 disks, which seems to be about the limit of what you should consider as a reasonable number of disks in a distribution. It's doubtful that you would want to stock a distribution set of this size. You probably would create one as needed when a customer requested it.

Legal Issues

There are some legal issues to consider when selling an application. Please realize that I am not a lawyer. What is printed here should not be taken as legal advice, but as a list of issues to discuss with your lawyer.

Disclaimers and Limits of Liability

No software is released without a disclaimer stating that the software is supplied without a warranty as to its accuracy, usability, or merchantability, although most disclaimers warrant the media to be defect-free and the program to be readable. Warranties of this type are a result of the complexity of software and the difficulty of proving that it works and has no bugs. Fully-warranted commercial software would cost tens of thousands of dollars instead of hundreds of dollars because of the additional testing that would be needed.

In most cases, the limit of liability is set at the cost of the software. Note that this doesn't limit liability due to negligence, but the problem would have to be pretty terrible and the cause would have to be pretty obvious for this to be used against you. For example, if your application deletes all the files on a customer's disk whenever it's installed, indicating that you never tested the gold master, you might be liable for damages. However, if the disk is erased by an obscure bug that is difficult or impossible to reproduce, it's unlikely that there would be any liability, because it's known that commercial software can occasionally do these things. Most users take these problems in stride and reinstall the last backup set.

License or Sale

The option to license or sell the software is one of protection. When a user purchases a software product at the local store, he believes he bought the software, no matter what the fine print on the box says. However, by licensing the software, you never pass title of it to your customer. For his money, he gets the disks, the manuals, and the right to use the software, but the software still belongs to you and you can say how it is used. When software is sold outright instead of being licensed, title passes to the user, and you lose any future control that isn't spelled out in the sales agreement or that isn't covered by federal law. About the only protection you have after a sale is copyright protection.

> **Licensing Strategy**
>
> When developing a licensing strategy, consider how things are, not how you would like them to be. Placing restrictive, unreasonable licensing provisions on an application might cost you more sales than you are protecting with your license. It makes sense to allow uses of your product in situations where you wouldn't make a sale if the use was disallowed.
>
> A case in point is Microsoft's license for some of its products that allows a user to take his work application home to use on his home computer. Even though the software resides on more than one computer, the one-computer-at-a-time rule in most licensing agreements normally wouldn't be violated, because the user is either using the software at work or at home. This use isn't allowed in the case where his

Day 13: Manufacturing and Sales

> family uses the software all day at home while he uses it all day at work, because that would violate the one-computer-at-a-time rule. Since the user is unlikely to buy another copy of an expensive software product to occasionally use at home at night, no sale is lost. If you required that the user remove the software from his work computer every afternoon before he put it on his home computer at night, and then remove it from his home computer before he could use it again at work, he would question your mental capacity. He would also look for another product with a more reasonable license to replace yours.
>
> Be a partner with your user instead of an adversary. Work out a reasonable use agreement that keeps everybody happy.

Copyrights

All written works, including software, are born copyrighted. In other words, as soon as you write it, a written work is copyrighted. Copyright protects the work from being copied, which means that no one can copy your work and call it their own. They can create a similar work; they just can't copy your work. Copyright doesn't protect how you make your program work, only the particular expression of your work. Patents protect how you do something. Copyrights last for the life of the copyright owner plus 50 years. Works done for hire are copyrighted for 75 years.

Copyright doesn't protect code that is dictated by the programming environment you're working in. For example, to open a database table, you open a database file with the OpenDatabase function and then open a table with the OpenTable function. Copyright protection doesn't protect the fact that you called these two functions in sequence, because this is a requirement of the environment you're working in.

Copyright doesn't protect code that is dictated by external factors such as the hardware, the operating system, or the particular task that the code performs if the sequence of steps is imposed on you by that external factor. For example, in an accounting program, debits to an account are subtracted from that account's balance. You can't claim a copyright violation because some other program also subtracts debits from an account's balance.

Copyright doesn't protect code that is in the public domain. If you import or copy blocks of code that are in the public domain, you can't claim protection for that code.

Copyright protection does protect how all this code is put together, and any blocks of code that don't fall into the unprotected categories just mentioned.

Although the current Copyright Act protects works as soon as they are "fixed in any tangible medium of expression," you have little practical protection from infringement unless you make an effort to provide notification and to register the copyright. Notification of a copyright

consists of the copyright symbol (©), the name of the copyright holder (which might not be the author), and the first year of publication. The word *copyright* isn't required but is often included. An example would be "© B. J. Orvis 1995." You would usually place this text in the About screen, as shown in Figure 13.1, and as remarks in the source code. In the figure, the copyright has been assigned to the developer's company, which holds the copyright in its name.

Figure 13.1.
The About screen (and the start-up banner), which shows the copyright notice.

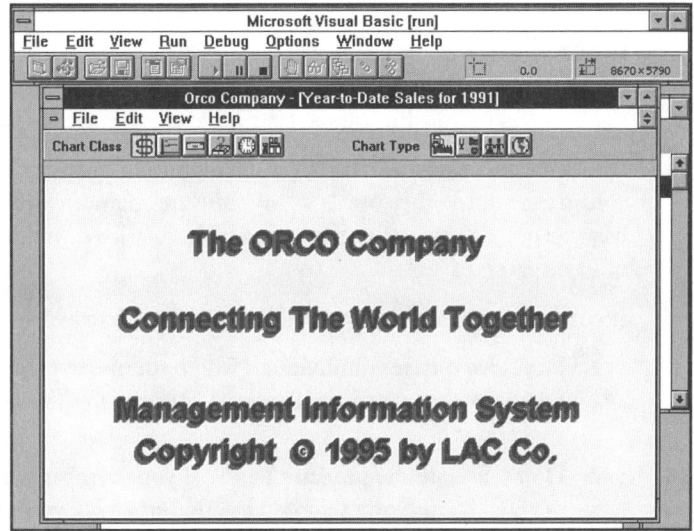

To register your copyright, contact the U.S. Copyright Office (note that there is a fee for this registration):

> Registrar of Copyrights
> Library of Congress
> Washington, DC 20559

Note: The requirements for obtaining foreign copyright protection used to differ from the requirements in the U.S. However, due to current international agreements (the Berne Convention and GATT), copyright protection obtained in the U.S. automatically extends to all signatory countries.

Manufacturing and Sales

Patents

In 1981, the Supreme Court decision in the *Diehr* case opened the door for software patents. Before that time, software was considered a mathematical algorithm, and thus couldn't be patented. Although it's possible to patent software, the time and expense involved and the limited likelihood of success largely limit the software patenting process to large corporations.

Keep in mind that a patent can't protect an idea or a mathematical algorithm, only the implementation of the algorithm as a process to do something. That is, the patent can't prevent others from using the mathematical algorithm. Only the process that happens to use the mathematical algorithm can be claimed and protected by the patent.

Patentable processes must be novel and useful and must not be obvious to someone knowledgeable in the art. In other words, if any software engineer would implement the process the same way you do, it's obvious and not patentable. As with copyrights, processes in the public domain can't be patented.

If you have a process that you think can be protected with a patent, do the following:

1. Have two different individuals who both understand the process sign and date the notebook that describes the initial conception of the process and any revisions to that conception.
2. Don't disclose the process outside of your company. Public disclosure of patentable material starts a one-year grace period in which you must submit a patent application. If you don't apply for a patent within that grace period, the process can't be patented.
3. Enlist the help of a good patent attorney to research the patent and prepare the application for you.

Foreign Patents

As with foreign copyrights, rules concerning foreign patents are changing, so enlist the help of a competent patent attorney if foreign patent protection is important to you. Be careful, though, because currently the rules are different in many foreign countries. For example, in many foreign countries, the first person to apply for a patent gets it, not the first person to develop a process.

Also, public disclosure might prevent you from obtaining a patent, because many foreign countries don't have a one-year grace period to apply for a patent after public disclosure.

Warranties

If a software product is defined as "good" under a software contract, the Uniform Commercial Code applies. Under Article 2 of the Uniform Commercial Code, express and implied warranties are automatically created for the product, including merchantability, adequate packaging, and fitness for the ordinary purposes for which the software is to be used. If the Uniform Commercial Code applies to a software product, it then becomes possible to obtain consequential and incidental damages against the seller of the software. These damages are not available if the Uniform Commercial Code does not apply.

Because of the potential liability for damages, warranties are largely lacking in the software industry. Except for guaranteeing the media to be readable, software isn't warranted to do anything useful. This is evidenced by the disclaimers that are shrink-wrapped to most distribution disks that exclude all of the requirements of the Uniform Commercial Code. Although disclaiming any warranty protects you if your software doesn't work, you can lose a lot of business if your products don't perform as advertised. The limit of most warranties is for the value of the software. In other words, you will return people's money if the software doesn't work, but you won't compensate them for the company database that the software damaged.

Registration

Software registration is primarily a good way to get addresses and demographics from the users of your software. Both items are useful. A list of addresses gives you a mailing list of interested people for future upgrades and companion products. The demographics tell you what kinds of people are buying your product so that you can tailor the features of future releases to them. You also get a mailing list that you can sell to other marketing organizations.

You can encourage registration by making it a requirement for technical support or by offering a premium (a company T-shirt, pen, coffee mug, and so forth) for a returned registration card.

Distributing Code Owned by Others

If you use copyrighted, patented, or licensed code in your application and you intend to distribute that application, generally you must pay a royalty to the code's owner and acknowledge that person in your application. The agreement between you and the owner of the rights to the code will spell out the cost and acknowledgment requirements necessary to distribute that code. For example, the Btrieve drivers included with Visual Basic require a separate license from Novell if you intend to distribute them with an application. Acknowledgments generally are placed in the About screen, along with the copyright information. The documentation you receive when you purchase the code should inform you of the need for any additional distribution licensing.

Day 13

Manufacturing and Sales

The Decision Support Application Project

You need to do three things to the decision support application to get it ready for manufacturing:

1. Add a program icon.
2. Scan for viruses.
3. Create a setup program.

Adding an Icon to the Application

To add an icon to the decision support application, first you need an icon. Use the IconWorks application included as a sample program with the Visual Basic package to draw your icon and save it as an icon (.ICO) file. Figure 13.2 shows the icon created for the decision support application. Note that there are several icons in the icon windows in the IconWorks application. Create several icons and choose the one that best fits the application.

Figure 13.2.
The IconWorks program with a custom icon for the decision support application.

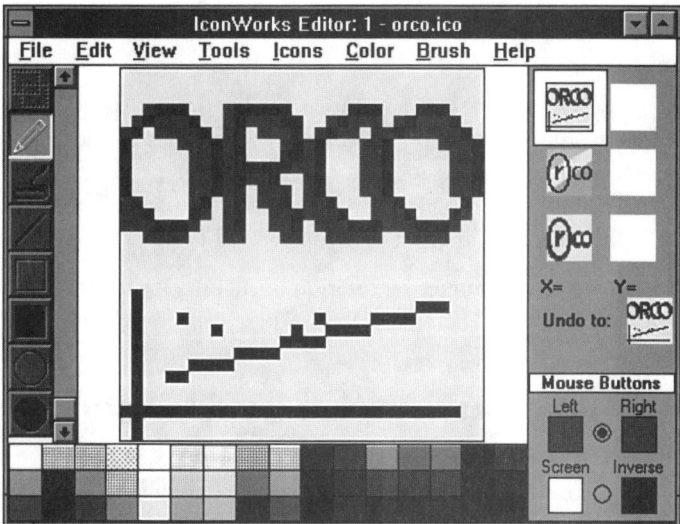

After the icon is created, start Visual Basic and display the `frmMDIMain` form. Select its `Icon` property and load the newly-created icon. The new icon will now show if the `frmMDIMain` form is minimized. When you create an .EXE file for the application, in the Make EXE dialog box, set the program icon to be the one from the `frmMDIMain` form.

If you want, you can now create a program item in Program Manager for the decision support application.

Scanning for Viruses

Now is the time to make sure your machine and your code are free of viruses before you create an executable application.

1. Obtain a clean, locked boot disk that contains a recent copy of your antivirus scanner.
2. Do a cold boot of your computer using the clean boot disk. In other words, turn the power off, wait 10 seconds, and then turn the power on with the boot disk in the A: drive. This ensures that no virus is lurking in memory.
3. Run the antivirus software and scan all the disks attached to your machine. If you don't find a virus, you can be reasonably sure that your machine is clean. There is a small possibility, though, that you have a new virus that your antivirus software won't detect. That possibility is very small if your antivirus software is up-to-date.
4. You can now reboot your machine from the hard disk and create the setup program.

Creating a Setup Program

All Visual Basic applications require multiple libraries and files to operate, so you need a setup program to install your application. The knowledgeable user could handle this with a simple list of files and directories, but most of your users probably don't have the technical knowledge or the time to do a manual installation of a complex package. And there's no reason why they should have to.

Showstopper: Don't forget to turn off debugging before compiling the final version of the application. Many applications have one or more debugging flags that change the way an application responds to errors. Be sure that debugging mode is disabled by setting or clearing the appropriate flags.

The Setup Wizard program included with Visual Basic makes quick work of creating an automatic setup package to install your application in whatever complex configuration you desire. Complete instructions for creating setup files and using the Setup Wizard are in Chapter 25, "Distributing Your Applications," of the Visual Basic *Programmer's Guide*.

The Setup Package

A setup package actually consists of two programs—the initial SETUP.EXE program and the user program SETUP1.EXE. The SETUP.EXE program creates a Visual Basic environment on the target machine by copying the Visual Basic libraries into the Windows directory. It then decompresses the program SETUP1.EXE and passes control to it. The SETUP1.EXE program

Manufacturing and Sales

is a Visual Basic program you create to copy your application and libraries to the target machine. The setup libraries contain functions to handle the copying of your files from the distribution media and decompressing them on the user's hard drive. Because it's a Visual Basic program, you can modify it with Visual Basic to do any special setup activities your particular application needs.

Creating a Setup Package

The easiest way to create a setup package is to let the Setup Wizard do it for you. Even with a complex configuration, use the Setup Wizard to create the initial cut of a setup package and then modify the result. The reason is that there are many special libraries that go with each of the custom controls, and if you miss one, your program won't work. The Setup Wizard knows which libraries go with which controls, and it includes them automatically. It compresses all of those files and stores them on floppy disks. It then writes the SETUP1.EXE program to copy and decompress all those files onto the hard disk of the target system. Since that program is a Visual Basic program, you can modify it to do any special setup that the Setup Wizard doesn't handle.

Using the Setup Wizard

The completed decision support application is on your hard drive, just waiting to be put onto floppies so that it can be distributed. To use the Setup Wizard, you must first save all the files in your application in text format. Use the File | Save As command and click on the Text box. When you run the Setup Wizard, you see the screen in Figure 13.3, asking you to locate the project file (.MAK) for your program.

Figure 13.3.
The Setup Wizard prompt for the project file of the application to set up. The project file for the decision support application is selected.

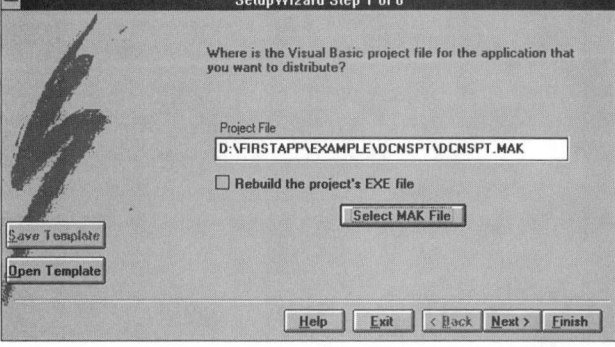

When you click on the Next button, the Setup program scans all the files in your project and determines which files and libraries are necessary. The program can't determine whether you're using data access, OLE, and some other special features, so it displays the screen shown in Figure

13.4, asking you which of these features you're using. The decision support application uses data access, so that box is checked. Click on Next to proceed to the next screen.

Figure 13.4.
The Setup Wizard prompt for special features, with the Data Access box checked. Data access is needed for the decision support application.

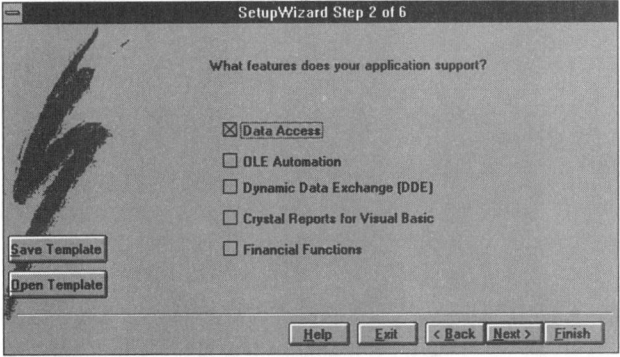

Since data access can use ODBC and other drivers, the Setup Wizard displays those drivers and lets you select the one you need (see Figure 13.5). The decision support application directly accesses the JET database engine, so it doesn't need an ODBC driver. Note that some of the listed drivers need a license to be distributed with an application. Drivers that need a special license have that fact noted in their documentation.

Figure 13.5.
The Setup Wizard prompt for ODBC and other drivers.

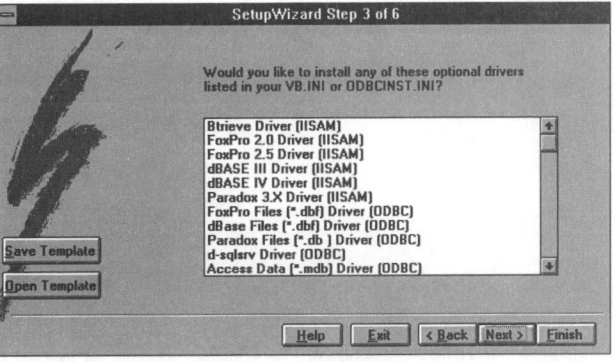

Click on the Next button. The Setup Wizard displays the screen shown in Figure 13.6, requesting the target drive and disk size for the setup files to go on. In the figure, the E: drive and 1.44M disks have been selected. This is needed so that Setup can organize the files on the disks to make best use of the space available.

443

Manufacturing and Sales

Figure 13.6.
The Setup Wizard prompt for the target drive and disk size. The E: drive and 1.44M disks are selected.

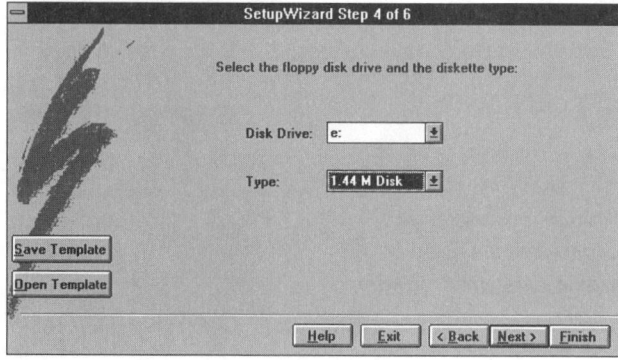

When this is done, Setup displays the screen shown in Figure 13.7. It contains all the files that the Setup Wizard thinks should be included on your setup disk. Look at this list closely to be sure that no files have been missed. This is where you can add the libraries that are needed by custom controls that were purchased separately from Visual Basic. Scanning the list, you see that the Setup Wizard has missed the help file and has included the copy of the .INI file stored in the source directory and not the correct one in the Windows directory.

Figure 13.7.
The Setup Wizard showing the selected files. The incorrect .INI file is highlighted.

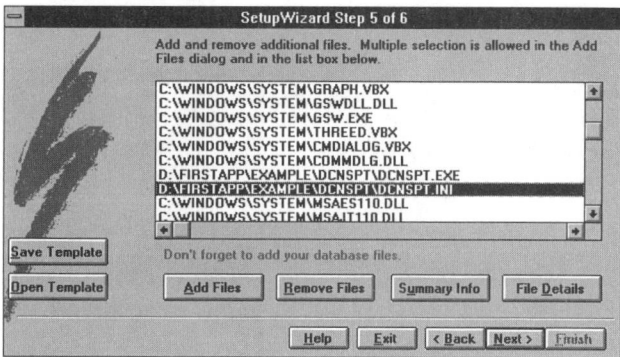

Select the incorrect DCNSPT.INI file and remove it, then use the Add Files button to add the DSA_HELP.HLP help file and the copy of DCNSPT.INI stored in the Windows directory (see Figure 13.8). Click on the Next button.

The Setup Wizard then opens a DOS window and compresses all the files. This can take several minutes for a large application. It then runs Visual Basic and creates the SETUP1.EXE program and compresses it. Finally, it asks you to insert a disk in the target disk drive so that it can create the setup set. As shown in Figure 13.9, all the files necessary for the decision support application will fit on one disk.

Figure 13.8.
The Setup Wizard showing the two new files added to the list.

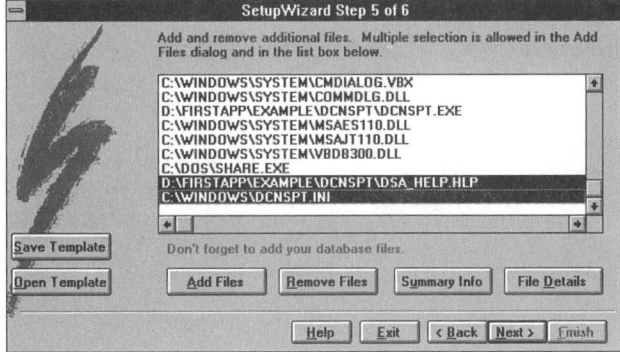

 **Showstopper:** If you don't have a formatted disk available when the Setup Wizard asks for it, it can't continue. However, you can Alt-Tab back to Program Manager, run File Manager, format a disk, and then Alt-Tab back to the Setup Wizard to continue.

Figure 13.9.
The Setup Wizard prompt for the first disk of the setup set.

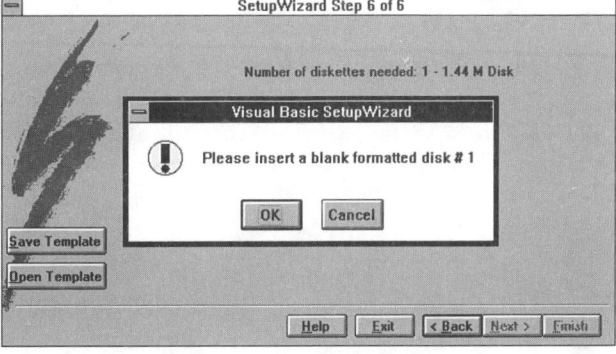

If you have only a simple application, and all the files are going in the correct place, you're done—you have a usable setup disk. However, you must still test it to make sure it works. Be sure to test it on a machine that doesn't have Visual Basic to ensure that you have gotten all the required libraries. A machine with a vanilla copy of Windows on it would be a good choice. A vanilla Windows machine is one with only DOS and Windows installed on it and nothing else.

445

Manufacturing and Sales

A Vanilla Testing Machine

You should test for missing files by doing a first-time installation of Windows and then installing the software being tested. To test a second time, you must delete all the files and reinstall DOS and Windows. To make this process go faster, use a backup utility to create a backup file on another disk or another partition of the same disk. That way, everything on the disk can be deleted and quickly restored for another test.

Another machine that is useful for this kind of test is running Soft Windows on a Power Macintosh. The "hard drive" for the Soft Windows PC is a file on the Macintosh. Set up the disk drive as you want it for testing in the DOS environment, and then switch to the Macintosh environment and make a copy of the disk drive file. When you're finished testing and want a fresh vanilla drive, delete the current disk drive file and replace it with a copy of the copy you made of the vanilla drive. After about five minutes, you will have a new drive for testing that is identical to the one you used for your first test.

Modifying the Setup1 Program

To do anything special or to check the installation, you need to examine or change the SETUP1.EXE program that the Setup Wizard creates. Start Visual Basic and open the SETUP1A.MAK project file in the \VB\SETUPKIT\SETUP1 directory. Select the Setup1 form and open its code window. The declarations section looks like the following listing.

Finding the Program Created by the Setup Wizard

To find the program just modified by the Setup Wizard, start Visual Basic after the Setup Wizard completes. Select the first program in the program list at the bottom of the File menu. That program is the one just created by the Wizard.

```
Const APPNAME = "ORCO DECISION SUPPORT"

Const APPDIR = "C:\DCNSPT"   'The default install directory.

Const fDataAccess% = True

Const fODBC% = False
Const fBtrieve% = False
Const fOLE2% = False
```

```
'Set the total decompressed file sizes
'by adding the sizes of the files.
Const WINSYSNEEDED = 1654460   'Files that go into the WINDOWS
                               'and SYSTEM directories.

Const OTHERNEEDED = 676386     'Files that don't go into the
                               'WINDOWS or SYSTEM directories.
```

The constants defined here were obtained by the Setup Wizard from the files in your application. APPNAME is the application name Setup uses when creating an application icon and group in the Windows Program Manager. APPDIR is a default directory for the application on the target machine, but the user can change this when doing the installation. The next four flags determine whether the application needs setup activities for data access, ODBC drivers, Btrieve drivers, or OLE 2.0 drivers. All of these are set according to the answers you gave to questions from the Setup Wizard.

The next two constants contain the total amount of disk space necessary for your application and all its files. The WINSYSNEEDED constant contains the total number of bytes of files that go in the WINDOWS and WINDOWS\SYSTEM directories. The OTHERNEEDED constant contains the total number of bytes needed for files outside of the Windows directory, such as the application directory. The total amount of disk space needed is split so that you can put the application directory on a different drive from the Windows directory. If you add files to this installation, don't forget to add the decompressed sizes to these constants. If you run the Setup Wizard again, these numbers are updated automatically.

Showstopper: If you make changes to the Setup1 program and then run the Setup Wizard again, all your changes will be lost. Be sure to save the Setup1 application and all its files in another directory if you want to keep them.

The main setup program is in the Form_Load procedure for the Setup1 form. Most of that code is identical from one installation to the next, but the following block of code does the actual installing of files and is changed whenever you run the Setup Wizard.

```
'----------
' Copy Files
'----------

If Not PromptForNextDisk(1, SourcePath$ + "DCNSPT.EX_") Then GoTo ErrorSetup
If Not CopyFile(SourcePath$, winSysDir$, "GRID.VB_", "GRID.VBX") Then GoTo
➥ErrorSetup
If Not CopyFile(SourcePath$, winSysDir$, "GRAPH.VB_", "GRAPH.VBX") Then GoTo
➥ErrorSetup
If Not CopyFile(SourcePath$, winSysDir$, "GSWDLL.DL_", "GSWDLL.DLL") Then GoTo
➥ErrorSetup
If Not CopyFile(SourcePath$, winSysDir$, "GSW.EX_", "GSW.EXE") Then GoTo
➥ErrorSetup
```

Day 13: Manufacturing and Sales

```
If Not CopyFile(SourcePath$, winSysDir$, "THREED.VB_", "THREED.VBX") Then GoTo
➥ErrorSetup
If Not CopyFile(SourcePath$, winSysDir$, "CMDIALOG.VB_", "CMDIALOG.VBX") Then
➥GoTo ErrorSetup
If Not CopyFile(SourcePath$, winSysDir$, "COMMDLG.DL_", "COMMDLG.DLL") Then
➥GoTo ErrorSetup
If Not CopyFile(SourcePath$, destPath$, "DCNSPT.EX_", "DCNSPT.EXE") Then GoTo
➥ErrorSetup
If Not CopyFile(SourcePath$, winSysDir$, "MSAES110.DL_", "MSAES110.DLL") Then
➥GoTo ErrorSetup
If Not CopyFile(SourcePath$, winSysDir$, "MSAJT110.DL_", "MSAJT110.DLL") Then
➥GoTo ErrorSetup
If Not CopyFile(SourcePath$, winSysDir$, "VBDB300.DL_", "VBDB300.DLL") Then
➥GoTo ErrorSetup
If Not CopyFile(SourcePath$, winSysDir$, "SHARE.EX_", "SHARE.EXE") Then GoTo
➥ErrorSetup
If Not CopyFile(SourcePath$, destPath$, "DSA_HELP.HL_", "DSA_HELP.HLP") Then
➥GoTo ErrorSetup
If Not CopyFile(SourcePath$, destPath$, "DCNSPT.IN_", "DCNSPT.INI") Then GoTo
➥ErrorSetup
```

Here, files are decompressed and copied to the target disk by the CopyFile function. The CopyFile function requires four arguments: the source path, the destination path, the source filename, and the destination filename. CopyFile's first argument contains the SourcePath$ variable, which is the path to the disk drive containing the distribution media. CopyFile's second argument is the destination path for the application on the hard disk. The three variables found in that argument are destPath$, winDir$, and winSysDir$. The string variable destPath$ contains the path to the application directory selected by the user. The string variable winDir$ contains the path to the Windows directory. The string variable winSysDir$ contains the path to the WINDOWS\SYSTEM directory. As you look down this list, you see that everything looks good except for the last entry. The DCNSPT.INI file is being placed in the program destination directory instead of the Windows directory. You need to change this entry to get the DCNSPT.INI file in the correct directory.

The next thing you need to do is to add code to edit the DCNSPT.INI file to insert the correct location of the help file and the database. The help file is in the same directory as the application, but you don't know where the database file is. You'll have to ask the user to supply that information.

Make the change to the last CopyFile command, and make the following additions (shown in bold) to the Copy Files block of the Form_Load procedure.

```
'----------
' Copy Files
'----------

If Not PromptForNextDisk(1, SourcePath$ + "DCNSPT.EX_") Then GoTo ErrorSetup
If Not CopyFile(SourcePath$, winSysDir$, "GRID.VB_", "GRID.VBX") Then GoTo
➥ErrorSetup
If Not CopyFile(SourcePath$, winSysDir$, "GRAPH.VB_", "GRAPH.VBX") Then GoTo
➥ErrorSetup
```

```
    If Not CopyFile(SourcePath$, winSysDir$, "GSWDLL.DL_", "GSWDLL.DLL") Then GoTo
➥ErrorSetup
    If Not CopyFile(SourcePath$, winSysDir$, "GSW.EX_", "GSW.EXE") Then GoTo
➥ErrorSetup
    If Not CopyFile(SourcePath$, winSysDir$, "THREED.VB_", "THREED.VBX") Then GoTo
➥ErrorSetup
    If Not CopyFile(SourcePath$, winSysDir$, "CMDIALOG.VB_", "CMDIALOG.VBX") Then
➥GoTo ErrorSetup
    If Not CopyFile(SourcePath$, winSysDir$, "COMMDLG.DL_", "COMMDLG.DLL") Then
➥GoTo ErrorSetup
    If Not CopyFile(SourcePath$, destPath$, "DCNSPT.EX_", "DCNSPT.EXE") Then GoTo
➥ErrorSetup
    If Not CopyFile(SourcePath$, winSysDir$, "MSAES110.DL_", "MSAES110.DLL") Then
➥GoTo ErrorSetup
    If Not CopyFile(SourcePath$, winSysDir$, "MSAJT110.DL_", "MSAJT110.DLL") Then
➥GoTo ErrorSetup
    If Not CopyFile(SourcePath$, winSysDir$, "VBDB300.DL_", "VBDB300.DLL") Then
➥GoTo ErrorSetup
    If Not CopyFile(SourcePath$, winSysDir$, "SHARE.EX_", "SHARE.EXE") Then GoTo
➥ErrorSetup
    If Not CopyFile(SourcePath$, destPath$, "DSA_HELP.HL_", "DSA_HELP.HLP") Then
➥GoTo ErrorSetup
    'If Not CopyFile(SourcePath$, destPath$, "DCNSPT.IN_", "DCNSPT.INI") Then GoTo
➥ErrorSetup
    If Not CopyFile(SourcePath$, winDir$, "DCNSPT.IN_", "DCNSPT.INI") Then GoTo
➥ErrorSetup


    'Decision Support Application.
    'Code to edit the DCNSPT.INI initialization file.
        ReDim INIFileLines(50) As String    'Array to hold .INI file contents.
        Dim intFileNum As Integer           'File number.
        Dim intLine As Integer              'Line number.
        Dim intNumLines As Integer          'Number of lines in the file.
        Dim intStartLine As Integer         'Line containing [startup].
        Dim intEndLine As Integer           'Line after startup containing [.
        Dim strPath As String               'String to hold new path.

        'Add a message to the status dialog.
        Statusdlg.Label1.Caption = "Editing DCNSPT.INI file. "
        Statusdlg.Label1.Refresh
        Statusdlg.Label2.Caption = "Edit this file by hand if an error occurs. "
        Statusdlg.Label2.Refresh


        'Open the .INI file and read its contents into the array.
        intFileNum = FreeFile
        Open winDir$ & "DCNSPT.INI" For Input As intFileNum
        intLine = 0
        intStartLine = 0
        intEndLine = 0
        Do While Not EOF(intFileNum)
          intLine = intLine + 1
          Line Input #intFileNum, INIFileLines(intLine)
          If INIFileLines(intLine) = "[startup]" Then intStartLine = intLine
          If intStartLine > 0 And intEndLine = 0 And intStartLine <> intLine And
➥InStr(1, INIFileLines(intLine), "[") > 0 Then intEndLine =
➥intLine
```

Manufacturing and Sales

```
    Loop
    Close intFileNum
    intNumLines = intLine
    If intStartLine = 0 Then
      MsgBox "[startup] missing from DCNSPT.INI file, edit by hand.", 64,
      ➥"Setup Error"
    ElseIf intEndLine = 0 Then
      MsgBox "No end section after [startup] in DCNSPT.INI file, edit by
      ➥hand.", 64, "Setup Error"
    Else
      'Find the help entry and set to the destination directory.
      For intLine = intStartLine + 1 To intEndLine - 1
        If InStr(1, INIFileLines(intLine), "Help=") <> 0 Then
          INIFileLines(intLine) = "Help=" & destPath$ & "DSA_HELP.HLP"
          Exit For
        End If
      Next intLine
      If intLine = intEndLine Then
        MsgBox "Help= missing from DCNSPT.INI file, edit by hand.", 64,
        ➥"Setup Error"
      End If
      'Find the data file entry and get the new entry.
      For intLine = intStartLine + 1 To intEndLine - 1
        If InStr(1, INIFileLines(intLine), "DataFile=") <> 0 Then
          intEQ = InStr(1, INIFileLines(intLine), "=")
          strPath = InputBox$("Input the path to the GRAPHS.MDB database.",
          ➥"Set Database Path", Mid$(INIFileLines(intLine), intEQ + 1))
          If strPath = "" Then
            MsgBox "Database path not set. Edit DCNSPT.INI file by hand.", 64,
            ➥"Setup Error"
          Else
            INIFileLines(intLine) = "DataFile=" & strPath
          End If
          Exit For
        End If
      Next intLine
      If intLine = intEndLine Then
        MsgBox "DataFile= missing from DCNSPT.INI file, edit by hand.", 64,
        ➥"Setup Error"
      End If
      'Open the .INI file and write the new contents.
      intFileNum = FreeFile
      Open winDir$ & "DCNSPT.INI" For Output As intFileNum
      For intLine = 1 To intNumLines
        Print #intFileNum, INIFileLines(intLine)
      Next intLine
      Close intFileNum
    End If
```

The added code first opens DCNSPT.INI and reads its contents, shown as follows, into the string array INIFileLines(). The array is dimensioned to 50 elements, which should easily hold the current .INI file and any future modifications to it. While reading the file, the code locates the line containing [startup] and the first line following the line containing [startup] that contains a [. This should be the beginning of a new section of the .INI file. The data that needs to be modified should be between the [startup] label and the first labeled line following it. The program tests to see that both of these lines exist. If they don't, it prints an error message and continues.

```
Decision Support Program INI File
[startup]
DataFile=D:\FIRSTAPP\EXAMPLE\ROLUPDAT\GRAPHS.MDB
Year=1991
Help=C:\DCNSPT\DSA_HELP.HLP
[end]
```

The next block locates the Help= entry and replaces it with one containing the destination path for the application and the name of the help file. If the Help= entry is missing, an error message is printed.

Following this is a very similar block of code that locates the DataFile= entry. Since we don't know where the database file is located on any particular machine, the code displays a dialog box that shows the existing path in the file and asks the user to type the correct path. The only testing done here is to see whether the result is blank or not. You could do more testing, but it won't hurt the application if the data file is wrong. The application will only complain a lot and not be able to load tables.

Note: Here are some possible variations: You could insert a common dialog open control and let the user search for the database file instead of having to type the file's path by hand. To make this work, though, you need to add the common dialog control and libraries to the SETUP.LST file so that they are loaded and expanded before trying to run SETUP1.EXE.

If the standard system has an environment variable that points to the database file, you could read and use it instead of trying to get the path from the user.

The last block of the modified file opens the DCNSPT file again and writes out the new contents. Test these modifications to be sure that they do what you expect them to do.

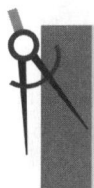

Speeding Testing

A way to speed testing is to comment out all the CopyFiles commands in the program so that they are skipped over. At the end of the tested code, you can stop or end the program to prevent it from doing all the other setup tasks.

Manufacturing and Sales

Adding the New SETUP1.EXE to the Setup

After you've made and tested the modifications, the new Setup1 program needs to be compressed and added to the setup files already on floppy disk. Select File | Make EXE file and create an executable file named SETUP1.EXE. Open a DOS window and run the compress program included in the setup kit.

```
\vb\setupkit\kitfiles\compress -r setup1.exe
```

The -r option causes compress to replace the last character in the file extension with an underscore. Thus, the file created by this command is SETUP1.EX_. Copy this compressed file to the first disk of the set of setup disks. In this case, there is only one disk, so the program goes on that one. It must be on the first disk so that the SETUP.EXE program can find it, copy it to the hard drive, decompress it, and run it.

> **Note:** Be sure to copy your source code for the SETUP1.EXE program into another directory from the \SETUPKIT\SETUP1 directory. Otherwise, the next time you run the Setup Wizard, the source code will be overwritten. Note that there is a SETUP1.MAC in that directory as well as the SETUP1A.MAC files created by the Setup Wizard. The SETUP1.MAC files are a sample set.

Testing the Setup

Test the new setup program to ensure that it installs all the files correctly, modifies the DCNSPT.INI file, and creates an appropriate program group. The program group is automatically created for the program and for the help file associated with it. Run the program to be sure it works.

If all works well, you have in your hand a gold master to send to manufacturing or wherever you plan to send your completed application.

Modification Notes

If you have an existing setup program, run the Setup Wizard anyway to get an updated list of files and directories. Then copy the special features of the old setup program into the new one.

If you're modifying a program that has already been offered for sale, you'll probably have all the licensing and warranty information in place. Now is a good time to make any necessary changes to the program. If the changes are significant, you might need to reregister the copyright and update the copyright date.

The manufacturing of a new version of an existing program generally must start from scratch, because the new files replace all the old ones and a new manual or help file replaces the old one.

Debugging the Process

You debug the setup program code exactly the same as any other Visual Basic program. The biggest difficulty is ensuring that you have the correct files available in your setup set. To check that, you must remove any files associated with Visual Basic from your test machine, install the program, and see if it works. Don't test on the machine you're using to develop the application, because it already has all the necessary files on it, and they will be there if your setup program installs them or not.

A Poor Man's Vanilla Machine

If you don't have access to a vanilla testing machine, but you don't want to throw away all your Windows files to adequately test an application, you can use the fact that all the files installed by most applications are in their application directory or in the Windows directory. To use this fact, install Windows again into a different directory, but don't let the Windows Setup program install any of your applications. Create new AUTOEXEC.BAT and CONFIG.SYS files that only reference the new Windows directory. Restart your computer and do your testing.

To return to your original system, change back to your original AUTOEXEC.BAT and CONFIG.SYS files and reboot. As long as the old Windows directory isn't in a path or environment variable, an application won't find files stored there and will give an error if needed files are missing.

Do quality control testing on your manufactured product by occasionally obtaining a manufactured copy of your program and running it through the same testing as the original copy. Make sure that it installs all the correct files and that the files work.

Summary

For any application that is to be more than a personal program, you need to consider manufacturing and sales of the application. And, in order to sell the application, you have to put it and all its necessary support files on a distribution set. Today you learned about creating distribution sets, selecting disks for distribution, and selecting distribution methods. A lot of what you do here depends on what your market is for this application and how many copies you need to support that market.

Manufacturing and Sales

The setup files created in this chapter are all in the folder SETUP on the CD. The final distribution set is in the \SETUP\DISK1 directory, which fits on a single high-density (1.44M) 3 1/2-inch disk.

Support, Upgrades, and Phaseout

Day 14

Support, Upgrades, and Phaseout

Yesterday you delivered your application to the customer. Are you done yet? Well, almost. You still must consider support, upgrades, and phaseout for your application.

Today you will learn

- about supporting your application
- about planning for upgrades
- how to phase out an application

The Goal of Day 14

The goal of Day 14 is to learn about the different ways to support your application, to plan for upgrades, and to consider when and how to phase out the application. Supporting an application is the act of supplying help for people who can't make your application work. How much support you supply should generally be guided by what a customer paid for the application.

Another part of support is planning for new versions of the application and deciding how or if you will let current owners of the application upgrade to the new version. New versions are of different types, and how you handle an upgrade depends on the type.

Finally, you need to consider when to phase out or abandon an application, and what to do for users who are still using that application.

Support

When you create an application by contract or for sale, you have to expect to supply some level of support for that application. If you want, you can support the applications you write for yourself, but not many people can call themselves on the phone.

Support is the help you give to the purchaser of your application after it has been purchased. Support tends to be of two types—installation support and features support. *Installation support* is the help you give your users when they have problems installing your application and getting it to run for the first time. *Features support* is the help you give your users after they have your application working and they're having problems getting a feature to work.

Installation Support

Installation support is important for any application, even the inexpensive ones. You lose a lot of credibility as a developer if a customer can't even get your application to install and run. In addition, you will lose any future sales to this customer and to anyone he tells about his problems with your software. If this customer happens to be a writer for a computer trade journal, the publicity can do a lot of

damage to your company. On the other hand, if you help him get it to work, or at least figure out why it can't work on his system (and maybe offer a refund), your customer is more likely to try your work again because he knows he will get help if he needs it.

As an aside, I have been told that in the book market, any publicity sells books, even bad publicity. I would assume that this rule of thumb would also apply to software titles, but I can't back up that supposition with any data.

Computer users have come to expect support for the applications they buy (even if they paid only $10 or $20 for them), at least to get the application installed. Support for low-cost applications is becoming a problem in the industry, because it consumes a large amount of the profits from the sale of an application. Inexpensive applications don't have much profit to consume.

Expensive applications and contract work are another matter. If you create a custom application for someone, you should have included a large amount of support in the contract. You will be expected to train the customer's people on how to use the application and how to administer it. You will also be expected to be on call for problems, especially for the first few months, when most of the problems and bugs show up.

Don't Go on Vacation Yet

When you finish your super application and deliver it to your customer, don't suddenly disappear on a month's vacation where no one can find you. Most of the problems with your application will show up in the first few months—configuration problems, bugs, things you didn't think of, things you never expected someone to try with your application, changes that occurred at the company between when you did the structured analysis and when you delivered the application. Problems will show up, and you will be expected to fix the serious ones as soon as possible.

If you've been paid a lot of money to develop this application, you need to be there to fix the problems as quickly as possible. A lot of your future earnings depends on how well you handle your current projects.

Problems with computer software tend to follow the same distribution as mechanical and electronic devices. The Weibull distribution function, shown in Figure 14.1, is well-known for its ability to fit fatigue and failure data, and software problems (at least in a statistical sense) should follow it as well. The curve shows that at the application's introduction, the number of problems discovered increases rapidly, peaks when most of the problems are found, and slowly

Support, Upgrades, and Phaseout

tapers off. You need to concentrate your support at the beginning, and relax a little after the problem occurrence rate passes over the peak.

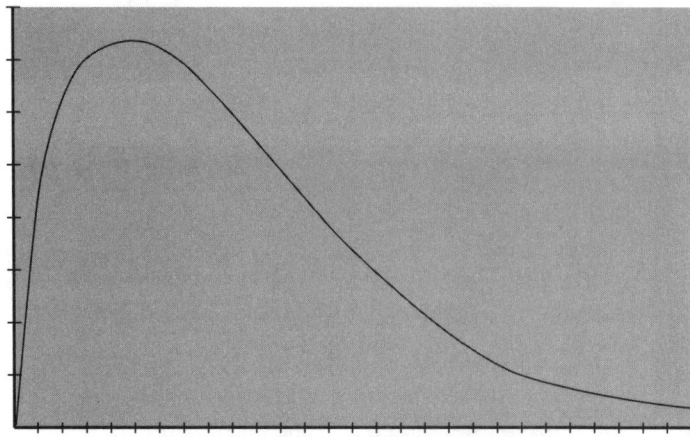

Figure 14.1.
The Weibull distribution function.

If you contract or sell your applications directly, you're generally expected to supply the support. If you sell your application to a manufacturer/distributor, that person or company generally must supply the support to the public, and you support the company. You might also get called in for problems that the regular support people can't handle.

No Support

The amount of support you can economically make available for an application depends largely on what a customer paid for it. For small, simple, inexpensive applications, it's not unreasonable to not supply support, or to supply a very minimal amount to help users through the initial installation. It's not acceptable to not offer support for a large, complex application.

Written Support

For small applications, you can supply your address so that users may write to you if they have a problem. Most users don't like this, because the turnaround for a letter is two weeks to a month, and they usually want the answers to their questions immediately. This is an economical way to do support, because you can save all your letters for a week and efficiently answer them all in a block. You can use form letters for common problems, which further cuts your expenses. The biggest cost is stamps to mail back the replies.

Fax Support

Fax support is the same as written support, but it's a lot faster. It's also more expensive, because it takes a couple of minutes on the telephone to fax a reply.

Another form of fax support is to store a list of frequently asked questions (FAQs) as faxes and to use an automated telephone gateway to select the fax to return by pressing buttons on your telephone. Several large software catalog stores are making their product descriptions available using a fax list like this. It's relatively inexpensive to operate, because the caller pays all the phone charges.

Telephone Support

Telephone support is probably the most common kind of support. When users have problems they can't figure out on their own, they generally want to hear from you immediately. This is especially true if they're having trouble installing or running the application. Nothing is more frustrating than to have a new application and to not even be able to get it to install correctly.

An alternative to free telephone support for smaller applications is a 900 number. With a 900 number, users pay for the time they spend on the phone talking to you.

Another alternative is a telephone gateway to a list of FAQs, where the users direct themselves to the answer using the buttons on a touch-tone phone. Many of the simpler questions can be answered this way, and the harder ones can be routed by the same system to a knowledgeable person.

> **Don't Talk Down to Your Users**
>
> Don't talk down to your users when they call for help, even if they're being incredibly stupid or are asking you a question that is answered on page 1 of the manual. Remember, most people today expect to be able to install and run an application without having opened the manual. After answering their questions, you can politely point out that the information they wanted was in the manual. Better yet, refer them to the page of the manual that has more information on the problem or feature.

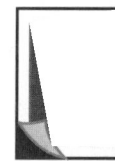

Video Support

Video support is relatively new to the software industry, but including a videotape showing how to install and use an application is relatively inexpensive, especially if it prevents several calls to your telephone support person. Short VHS videotapes cost only a couple of dollars to produce,

Support, Upgrades, and Phaseout

and a picture of what the users should see during installation and use might be informative enough that they can work out their own problems.

An alternative is a short video on the installation CD-ROM (if you're using a CD to distribute your application). If there's a lot of space left on the distribution CD-ROM, include a short video clip on installing and using your software. Distribution won't cost extra, because the space is unused anyway.

Online Support

Probably the largest form of support for applications is online support. Online support isn't quite as fast as telephone support, but it costs much less to implement. Online support includes e-mail, bulletin boards, and online services such as CompuServe, Delphi, and America Online. Probably the largest number of software support groups is on CompuServe. Many organizations such as Microsoft have forums on CompuServe where users can ask questions and download patches (corrections for programs with errors) and useful utilities. Forums also have users reading and answering the questions. If you're lucky, your users will handle a lot of your support for you.

Online Support Logs
Another benefit of online support is that you have a complete log of the conversations between your users and support people. Use these logs as a marketing tool to learn what the common problems are and what features your users want.

A bulletin board system (BBS) is relatively inexpensive and simple to set up. An old boat anchor of a PC and some modems can easily handle four or five simultaneous callers, and a hot 486 can handle 30 to 60 at once. Your only expenses are the incoming phone lines and managing the board. The BBS software takes care of everything else.

Buy Good BBS Software
If you set up a BBS system, skimp on the hardware and buy good BBS software like TBBS from eSoft. The amount of time you save administering the board easily pays for the software. RBBS software is freeware, but it's very difficult to administer because it was created by many independent software developers. (You pay for your copy of the software by adding to it.) BBS software that is easy to administer costs several hundred dollars but is well worth it.

Here are some administration issues to consider:

> How difficult is it to add a new file and its description to the system? Must you shut down the BBS and edit a directory file, or is it inserted automatically from within the BBS using dialog boxes?
>
> How difficult is it to add new sections (menus) to the BBS? Is a menu editor supplied, or must you create cryptic menu description files using a text editor?
>
> Is a menu compiler available so that you can describe the whole system in a single source file? (This is a nice feature.) Most BBS programs have each menu in a different file. To change things, you must edit each file separately. A menu compiler lets you create your BBS in a single file using a simple menu description language. The compiler then turns that file into all the menu files that the BBS needs.
>
> Does the system automatically remove files from the BBS directory if the files are no longer available on disk?
>
> Does the system allow easy configuration of user access to files and menus?
>
> Does the system automatically add new users?
>
> Can the system be administered remotely, or must you be sitting down at the console to make changes?
>
> Is good support offered?

Users of a BBS expect to find lists of answers for FAQs, patch files, upgrades, utility software, and an e-mail capability so that they can ask you questions about your software. E-mail is also useful in that it forces users to keep their questions short and to the point.

A newer online service for users with Internet access is a World Wide Web (WWW) home page. WWW looks much like the WinHelp program discussed on Day 12, except that the data comes from sites on the Internet instead of from your hard disk. Users connect to a site and see a fully-formatted document describing what's available. Clicking on highlighted words takes users to other documents that contain the needed information or to lists of files that can be downloaded. Other Internet services include anonymous FTP and Gopher for finding and downloading files.

On-Site Support

If you're a contractor, it's likely that you will initially provide all your support on-site at your customer's facility. Support begins with the introduction and demonstration of the application, probably at an in-house seminar. Support continues with training sessions, even for the simplest applications. Realize that you'll be dealing mostly with computer illiterates who have no idea how the software works, only that it does work (at least, it's supposed to). A large part of your training is to ensure that these people don't get frustrated and quit using your application. If no one will use your application, you can forget about any future contracts with that company.

Support, Upgrades, and Phaseout

Watch Your Users

Keep an eye on your users during a training session. Keep track of what their questions are and what they don't understand, even if you think the answers are completely obvious. When you get the chance to revise the application or its documentation, use this list to see which things need to be changed. Listen for new feature requests as well and include them for consideration when you create the next version.

Upgrades

It wasn't too many years ago that software manufacturers almost never did upgrades. You bought your software and that was that. The software engineer went on to another project, and the software you bought never changed. As competition increased in the software industry, however, manufacturers had to add more features to their software to maintain their market share. As a result, they made new and improved versions of their software available, but few of the people who already owned the software would pay full price for the revised version. Also, since software doesn't wear out, the manufacturers couldn't look forward to future sales to existing customers, as is true with the automotive industry, for example.

How do you entice these existing customers to buy the new version? Offer them an upgrade at a greatly reduced price. You might think that offering someone a $400 piece of software for $50 is taking a big loss, but first consider that if you don't cut the price significantly, you'll have no sale at all, and $50 is a lot more than nothing. Second, you now have many satisfied customers who can show off your latest version to their friends, generating more sales. Third, you're not really losing anything, because the variable cost to duplicate a package is significantly less than $50. Fourth, if you treat your customers right, you can sell them another upgrade every year or so.

Modern production applications seem to be in a race to see who can upgrade the most often. And computer users have come to expect lower-priced upgrades to their applications. You could also sell at cost or give away new versions so that everyone is using the latest version of your application if this benefits the sale of another of your products. For example, Apple did this with their Macintosh operating system because it stimulated software development, and increased software development stimulated hardware sales. Another example is Adobe Acrobat, the formatted document reader. Adobe sells the document-creation software and gives away the readers. The more people who have the readers, the more likely someone else will buy the document-creation software.

> **Don't Upgrade Too Often**
>
> If you upgrade too often, your customers will start skipping upgrades to wait for the next one. Some developers of major applications ship upgrades every six months or so, causing users to wonder, "Why should I upgrade now for $100 and then do it again in six months? Why not just wait six months and buy the next version?" If you plan to upgrade more often than once a year, the changes must be sufficient to convince your users that the upgrade is worth it.

Maintenance Upgrades

There are several different kinds of upgrades, depending on the reason for the upgrade. The first is the maintenance upgrade. A *maintenance upgrade* generally consists only of minor bug fixes. As you learn about and fix problems with your software, occasionally freeze the application and release a maintenance upgrade. All future sales of your application should be the upgraded version. If a user has problems because of a bug that is fixed in the maintenance upgrade, give her a copy of the upgrade. You should not solicit your users to buy a maintenance upgrade since the changes and problems fixed are minimal.

Features Upgrades

Features upgrades are another matter. Here is where you add new functionality to your application to make it stand out above all the other similar applications. This upgrade generates new sales and upgrade sales from your existing customer base.

> **Make the Features Useful**
>
> Don't add features to an application just to be adding features. Find out what your users want and add those features. One class of features is *usability enhancements*. Your users might not ask for these enhancements, because they don't realize that they need them. To determine what would be a useful usability enhancement, examine how your users use the application. Step-by-step, how do they get things done? When you've determined this, figure out how to reduce the number of steps, and you have a usability enhancement. A good example of a usability enhancement is the toolbar, which saves the user from having to pull down a menu to select a common command.

463

Support, Upgrades, and Phaseout

Damage Control Upgrades

Damage control upgrades are every developer's nightmare. As you deliver a new application, there is always that nagging fear that you've forgotten something important. In the race to get new applications out, you miss things, and bugs make it into the production version of an application. If the bugs are significant, you will have to issue a free upgrade to all your users, which can be quite expensive. Microsoft had to do this once because of a buggy version of Word. Another time, Central Point Software and Norton were racing to get their new tools versions out, and they both released versions of their tools that contained bugs and had to replace them. Hopefully, the good programming practice and structured design you've learned in this book will at least reduce the chance that this will happen to you.

Competitive Upgrades

Something that is being seen more often are *competitive upgrades*. This involves giving an upgrade of your product to customers who own a competitor's product in order to woo those customers away from the competitor's product. It's unclear how useful competitive upgrades are for increasing your market share.

Phaseout

When sales of your product have slowed to almost nothing and you don't plan an upgrade, you need to consider phasing out your application. Something to consider, though, is that the costs to continue selling an existing product usually are minimal, and even a few sales generate income.

If you do decide to phase out an application, you want to do it gracefully so that you don't anger your users. Be sure to stop sales first, well before you start phasing out your support activities. When the usage of your telephone or other support decreases to a low level, you can consider discontinuing that as well.

You have a few other options when phasing out an application other than just quitting. One is to sell or turn over your application to another person or company and let them take over manufacturing, sales, and support. Another option is to offer your user list to a competitor with a similar product. You might be able to negotiate for your users a good upgrade deal on a competitor's application, especially if you're willing to recommend the application to your users. Whatever you do, try to not leave your users out in the cold.

The Decision Support Application Project

The decision support application was a contracted project, and part of the contract is the training and support of the users at Orco. An initial roll-out presentation shows off the new application and its capabilities to the company executives and some interested employees. Try to find out who the company's software gurus are, because they are the ones to spread the word about your new application and help others get it installed and start using it.

> **Software Gurus**
>
> The title "Software Guru" is not on the official organizational chart for most companies (although there are some enlightened exceptions). Most gurus do other work in the company but happen to enjoy fiddling with new machines and software whenever they get the chance. As such, they are the ones everyone else goes to when they have a computer question. Because the position of guru isn't officially sanctioned, you will probably have to do some searching before you find them.
>
> Be careful identifying your software gurus to company management, especially if software guru is not an official position. Some managers are still shortsighted enough to ignore the contributions of the software gurus and all the extra hours they put in learning and understanding new software packages and berate them for wasting time doing things that aren't part of their job description. Let the gurus know you appreciate their contributions, but don't get them in hot water because of it.

After the roll-out presentation, a series of classes is planned for each department in the company to teach them how to install and use the application. The first class is for the data processing department, because these people will do most of the installations and troubleshooting, and they are also in charge of the database and the file servers where the database resides. In addition to installation and operation, teach these people how to do the monthly roll-ups to the GRAPHS.MDB database and how to do troubleshooting. Since you have just finished this application, it's unlikely that you will have much troubleshooting information, but clue these people in to whatever you do know, and give them your beeper number so that they can call you when they get stuck. This strategy has two benefits. First, it places these people between you and the rest of the company for supplying support for all the simple questions. Hopefully, they can answer all the simple questions themselves and will call you only when they get a hard one. The second benefit is that when you do get a support call, you know that the person who is calling you is knowledgeable about the product.

Day 14: Support, Upgrades, and Phaseout

As I mentioned earlier, stay close to your customer for the first few weeks to ensure that you are available if a bug you missed crops up and causes problems for the company.

Throughout the next year, you visit the company occasionally and sit down with the users to listen to their wants, needs, and gripes. At the end of the year, you translate these wants, needs, and gripes into a list of revised features and present it to Mr. Orco to see if he's interested in a revision to the application. If he is interested, you go back to the beginning of this book and start the process over again. However, this time you have a working program with well-documented code to start from, as well as all your design notes and diagrams from the previous development effort.

Modification Notes

In addition to preparing a revision for the Orco company, you have been approached by another company's CEO who has seen your application and who wants to commission you to develop a similar one for him. For the most part, only the tblDefinitions table in GRAPHS.MDB needs to be revised to make significant changes to the number and type of graphs displayed in the application.

Debugging the Process

At this point, debugging consists of listening closely to your customer to ensure that no killer bug was left in the application. Fix any significant bugs immediately and maintain a list of minor bugs to fix when you get time.

When you have more than one version of a product in the marketplace, your support becomes more difficult because you must support two programs with different problems. Your support people must find out which product a customer has before they can supply the right answers. A reasonable upgrade policy helps to get the old versions of the product out of the marketplace. Phasing out the support for a product a reasonable amount of time after the product is phased out also helps your support organization by reducing the number of applications they have to support. You might want to maintain a list of consultants you could recommend to users who don't want to upgrade to the latest version of your product.

Be careful about phasing out support too soon. Keep track of the number of calls you receive for an earlier version of your software. That number compared to the number of calls you get about your current version should give you a good handle on how important support is for owners of the earlier version.

Summary and Conclusion

Is it finally done? *Yes!*

Today you learned about supporting your application, doing version upgrades, and phasing out. Hopefully, you won't be phasing out an application in the near future, but it helps to plan for that eventuality.

Phaseout is the end of an application (and it is also the end of this book), but the process of application development continues to the next project, starting over again with Day 1. You probably have already negotiated your next project, so you can now start the development process in earnest.

The application development process is more than just writing code. It includes contract negotiation, systems analysis, structured analysis and design, module design, form design, debugging and testing, documentation, manufacturing, and support. Tying all this together is the software developer. You might be part of a team, or you might work alone. No matter; the process is the same.

Before you do anything concerning a new application, you must negotiate the contract between the developer and the customer. What kind of contract is used depends on the relationship between the developer and the customer. If they are the same person, a contract isn't needed. If the work is for anyone else and you're being paid for it, a contract is needed.

When the contract is in place, the task of structured analysis begins. Structured analysis is where you discover how the current system works and translate that process into tables and diagrams. Structured analysis is also where you discover exactly what the customer wants and fill in all the details.

When the analysis is done, the structured design begins. Structured design uses the data obtained in the analysis phase to create a structure chart, data dictionary, and process description that describes what the program will do. Using these tools, the designer creates a program structure chart and a list of process descriptions. At the same time, drawings of the user interface are created and revised until they show a standard, easy-to-use interface to the program.

The structure chart and process descriptions are passed to the programmer, who turns the descriptions into code and the drawings into forms and buttons. When the code is finished, it goes into testing and debugging to wring out the last of the problems. This phase includes beta testing, where some selected customers get to try out the application to see if there are any holes or other problems in the completed application.

Support, Upgrades, and Phaseout

When the application is complete, you create the help file or manual and an installation set. The installation set can be a problem, because many libraries are involved when you're preparing the application for manufacturing. Help is available in the form of the Setup Wizard. The Setup Wizard asks all the right questions and automatically selects most of the support files needed to complete this operation.

When everything is ready, you ship your application and prepare your support staff to answer questions and handle problems concerning your application. As your support organization answers questions, they also gather lists of problems and requested feature enhancements. When it's time to revise the application, you use these lists to select the changes and new features to add to the application and start the development process again.

If you've made it this far, congratulations for sticking with it. I hope this book has been of some use to you and, in some small measure, helps you to succeed with your next development project. I realize that the process of structured analysis and design takes away a lot of the mystique of software development, and it can get a little tedious at times, but it works, and that's what counts when you're developing software for a living. If you intend to pursue software engineering as a profession, go for it. I hope you succeed.

If 20 years from now you pull this book off the shelf and the methods of designing and engineering software still apply to this fast-paced occupation, I have succeeded beyond all my expectations. If it at least helps you get started as a developer or improves your existing development skills, I again have succeeded and am happy that I could help.

Good luck in all your programming adventures!

William J. Orvis

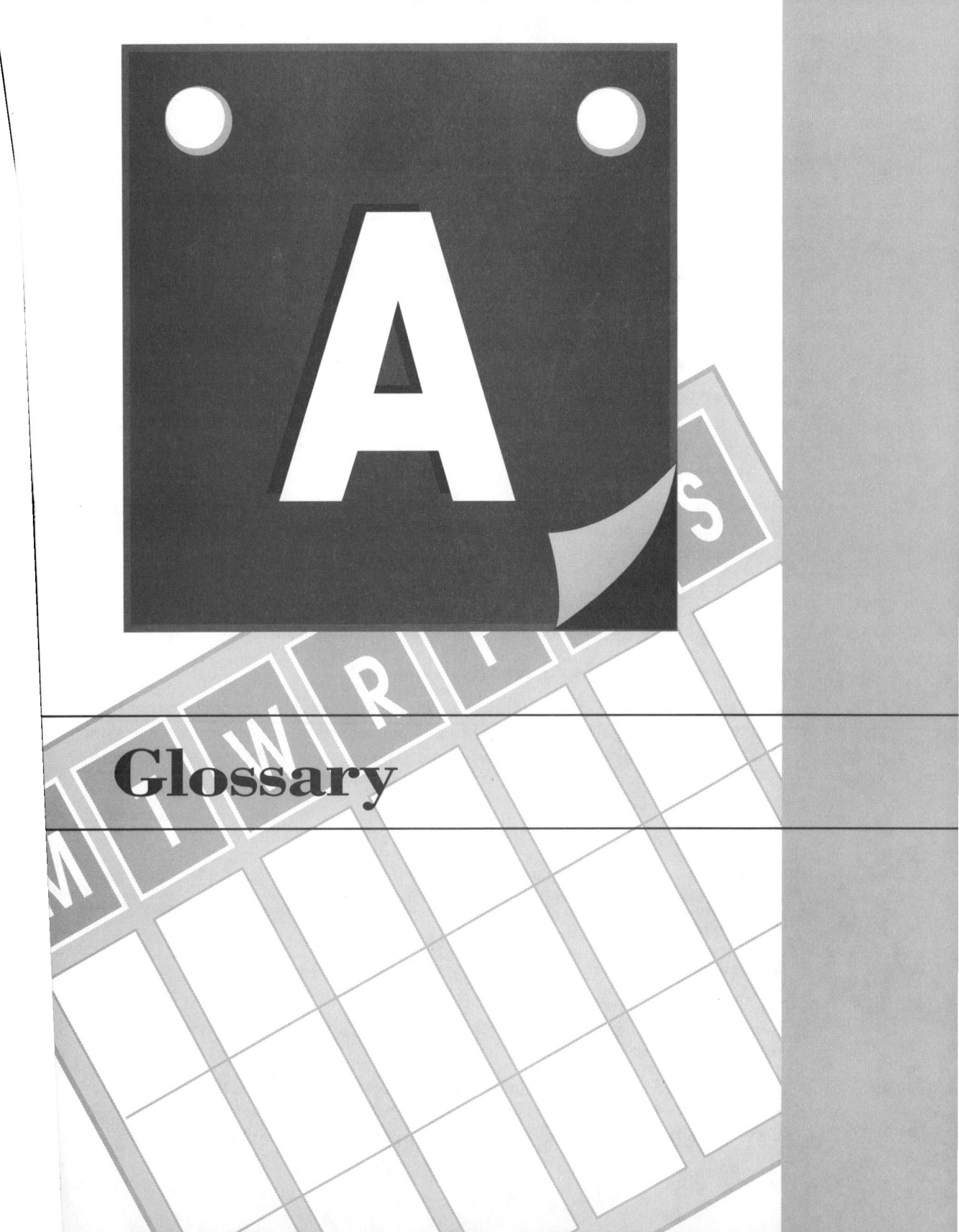

Glossary

Glossary

action modules   In structured design, action modules are a result of using transaction analysis to convert a data flow diagram into a program structure chart. Action modules fall below the first-level task modules and perform the tasks for the first-level modules. Functions needed by the action modules are available below them in a set of shareable detail modules.

alpha-level code   Code in which the framework is complete but has many nonworking parts. See also *beta-level code* and *alpha testing*.

alpha testing   In-house testing of a new application. The application still has lots of bugs, and it might be unstable and crash a lot.

attribute   In databases, each cell in a database table contains an attribute of the entity described by the record (row) containing the cell. Thus, the data in a record are known as the attributes of the entity described by the record. A column in the table is known as the attribute class for all the entities.

authentication   When referred to in terms of program or data security, authentication is the act of proving to the program or database that you are an allowed user. Authentication is usually performed by matching a username (UID) with a secret password (PID).

automated system   Performs the functions of the system using a machine. The machine is usually a computer, but it could also be a mechanical device such as a check printer or a card sorter. See also *manual system*.

backlog   The number of orders placed but not yet shipped.

batch mode   A method of running a program in which you give it all the commands and data at the beginning, and then it runs to completion without any other user involvement. When you start a batch program, you can go away and do something else while the program runs on its own, producing whatever results you requested. You pick up the results when it's done.

beta-level code   Code that is essentially complete, but that still contains a lot of bugs and nonworking parts. See also *alpha-level code* and *beta testing*.

beta testing   Combined in-house and outside testing of a new application. The application is essentially complete, but it's still prone to problems.

B.J.   Older son. Likes computers.

bottom-up design   Starts with the details and works up to the function of the process. See also *top-down design*.

breakpoint   A marked statement in a program. When an executing program encounters a breakpoint, the code pauses and goes into break mode.

brick wall   The situation that engineers abhor the most. Hitting a brick wall means that you've encountered a situation that you didn't expect and that can't be surmounted before you finish the project. These situations are usually caused by physical limitations and therefore can't be engineered around. They are rarely found in information management projects, but they do occur in modeling situations when a model is too large for a computer to hold or would take multiple lifetimes to calculate.

build   A completely assembled version of an application that is ready for testing. It doesn't necessarily have all its pieces in place.

category   See *product category*.

code   The written statements in a computer language that control the computer's operation. Visual Basic statements in a program are code, as are assembly language statements and the machine code that the compiler translates Visual Basic statements into and that the computer directly executes.

competitive upgrade   An upgrade to your product from a competitor's product.

construction   The act of taking your carefully crafted designs and turning them into a working application. Construction includes creating the visual interface by drawing the forms, and debugging and testing the code.

context chart   In structured analysis, the top-level data flow diagram in a stack of partitioned data flow diagrams. It is the highest-level data flow diagram, and it shows a global view of how data moves in an application.

cost comparison analysis   Graphs the cost per item versus the number of items sold for two different items or manufacturing methods. The cost of an item includes the variable cost per item plus a fraction of the fixed cost. Calculate the cost of an item from a manufacturing run of *n* items by dividing the total cost, including any fixed setup fees, by *n*.

cross-product join   In databases, a cross-product join isn't really a join, because no fields are joined between the two tables. By not joining the tables, you create a new table that combines each individual record in the first table with all the records in the second. A cross-product table can get very large if you're not careful.

cutting code   To start typing code on the computer. This term comes from punched card and paper tape days, where you input code by punching (cutting) holes in a card or tape.

cycle   See *order cycle*.

damage control upgrade   A free upgrade that fixes a bug found in an application after it was put into production.

data dictionary   In structured analysis, a table of all the data flows and their elements that defines the elements of each flow, and the data contained in each element. It may also contain the process descriptions. See also *process description* and *data flow diagram*.

data flow   In structured analysis, a group of data elements passing from one data transform to another or between a data store and a data transform.

471

Glossary

data flow diagram In structured analysis, a diagram of the movement of data within a system, showing where it goes and how it's transformed. It's an abstract description of how a system works. It doesn't contain any control or program flow information. See also *data flow, process description,* and *data dictionary.*

data store In structured analysis, a file or other temporary storage location for data. The user is also assumed to be a data store.

data transform See *process* and *structured design.*

database The file or collection of files that contain the data being stored. These files also contain information on the structure of the files and indexes to make it easier to locate data.

database engine The program that actually manipulates the files in the database. Usually, this is a driver such as Microsoft's JET engine, but it also can be an SQL server such as Oracle.

detail module In structured design, a detail module is a result of using transaction analysis to convert a data flow diagram into a structure chart. Detail modules perform individual subtasks for the first-level action modules.

documentation The act of telling the user how to install and use the application. Documentation can be either a written manual, an online manual, or a Windows online help file.

drill-down application An application that initially displays high-level data such as averages and totals. Clicking on an average or total displays more-detailed data that was used to create the average or total. Clicking again shows more-detailed data, until the original raw data is reached.

entity In databases, the object described by a single row in a database table.

entity identifier See *identifier.*

equijoin In databases, the same as an inner join.

error trapping The act of capturing an error before the system's error handler so that you can correct the error or at least end the program gracefully.

external consistency In interface design, external consistency insists that in different applications, commands, buttons, and menu items with the same name or icon work the same. See also *internal consistency.*

features support The help you give your users when they have problems getting one of your application's features to work. See also *support* and *installation support.*

features upgrade An upgrade that adds new functionality to an application.

field In databases, a column of a database, which contains a specific characteristic of each of the entities. Each field has a name that is not physically part of the table but that describes the table.

flat file database Consists of a single table with no dynamic links to other tables. All related information must be placed in this single table. See also *relational database*.

form The Visual Basic designation for a blank window. All controls, buttons, text, and pictures are attached to forms when they are displayed on-screen. See also *MDI form*.

freeware Software that is given to the world to use for free. The author generally retains the copyright and stipulates that the software not be sold or changed. See also *public domain software* and *shareware*.

functional primitive In structured analysis, a data transform that can't be partitioned again.

Gantt chart Used for project planning, a Gantt chart is a plot of task duration versus date. Tasks are listed on the vertical axis, and dates are listed on the horizontal. The duration of a task is signified by a horizontal bar to the right of the task name that stretches from the task's start date to its finish date.

gold master The final set of distribution disks for an application that is sent to manufacturing.

Golden Rule He who has the gold makes the rules.

graph class The class of a graph refers to the basic data type being plotted. Graph classes are sales, margin, orders, order cycle, backlog, and inventory. See also *graph type*.

graph type The type of a graph refers to how the data is rolled up. The top level, or type 1, graph is a monthly total or average. The next level down, the graph is split according to some criteria such as product type or sales region. The third type looks at the detailed data that makes up the monthly totals, and so forth.

hypertext A form of document that is not read sequentially, but is read by following links from the text on one page to other pages of related information. A Windows help file is a hypertext document.

identifier, entity identifier In databases, the one or more attributes in a database record that uniquely identify that record.

implementation The act of taking the application out of the development environment and preparing it to be sold in the outside world. Implementation topics include preparing the application for manufacturing, preparing an installation set, examining available sales channels, and considering revisions, upgrades, and eventual phaseout.

index In databases, an index is a data structure created on a particular column of a database table to make it easier to locate specific values in that column. For example, a dictionary is a database of word definitions indexed by placing the words in alphabetical order. Although it's not required, an index significantly speeds search operations involving large tables. A problem with an index is that it uses up a lot more space on disk, so you shouldn't index every field.

indexed field In databases, a field that has been processed to make it easier and faster for the database engine to locate a record based on a value in that field.

Glossary

inner join   In databases, an inner join connects records in the two tables with the same value in the joined fields. The inner join or equijoin is the most common way of joining two tables.

installation support   The help you give your users when they have problems installing your application and getting it to run for the first time. See also *support* and *features support*.

intellectual property   An intangible property (you can't touch it) that you develop with your intellect rather than with your hands. You might think that you created a computer program with your hands, but you only typed the code with your hands, which is a description of the property and not the property itself. The research, design, analysis, and data that lead to the development of a project are also intellectual property.

internal consistency   In interface design, within an application internal consistency insists that all commands, buttons, and menu items work the same. See also *external consistency*.

joining   In databases, a method of producing a new table by connecting two tables by comparing the values in one field in the first table to one field in the second. Fields that have matching values in both tables are connected. There is more than one way to join two tables. See *inner join, equijoin, outer join,* and *cross-product join*.

Julie   Wife. Takes care of everything, and wants to know when I'm going to get done so I can help too.

link   In databases, tables are linked by connecting a field in one table with a similar field in another. For example, a table of invoices might be linked to a table of customers with a customer number. Both the invoice table and the customer table would have the customer number field. Whenever you examine a particular invoice, you find the customer by looking up the customer number in the customers table.

link   In project management, a connection between the completion of one or more tasks and the start of another. A link signifies which tasks must be completed before another task can start.

maintenance upgrade   An upgrade that consists only of bug fixes, not feature enhancements.

manual system   A system in which the functions are performed by people. For example, writing checks by hand or inputting data at a terminal. See also *automated system*.

margin   The amount of profit on an item. That is, the difference between the sales price and the cost.

market segment   Any functional grouping of the market other than geographical. The segments could be male, female, children, or store type, such as novelty, department, grocery, and so forth.

MDI form   Multiple Document Interface form. This is a special variation of a form that is a parent form with one or more child forms attached to it. The parent form is the application window, and the child forms are the application's documents. Most commercial Windows applications are MDI forms. See also *form*.

milestone   In project planning, an event that signifies the completion of an important task or group of tasks. Milestones are usually included in the task list for a project.

module   In structured analysis, a single-purpose code element that most closely resembles a Visual Basic procedure.

module   In Visual Basic, a container file for one or more procedures (code modules) or a form definition and some procedures (form module).

nondisclosure agreement   An agreement between two parties in which one party agrees to protect and hold secret the confidential information or material of another party in exchange for being able to see or use that information or material.

normal connection   In structured analysis, the connections between modules in a program structure chart that flow in a tree structure, with no crossovers of the connections between parallel branches of the tree. See also *pathological connection.*

ODBC   Open Database Connectivity. A standard protocol for manipulating databases. Requires a special driver for each database type to translate between the standard ODBC commands and those the particular database expects.

order cycle   The amount of time between when an order is placed and when it is shipped.

out-of-band operation   Something that occurs outside of the normal communication channel. For example, error trapping occurs outside of the normal flow of control in an application.

outer join   In databases, includes all the records in one table plus any records in the joined table with matching values in the joined field. Because of this, an outer join has a direction that points from the table that includes all its records to the table that includes only the matching records.

pathological connection   In structured analysis, the connections between modules in a program structure chart that go in a circle, with top-level modules subordinate to modules below them. See also *normal connection.*

persistent object   An object that is physically part of the database file rather than something that is adapted from a database file.

persistent query   In databases, a query that is stored in an Access database so that it can be recalled and rerun when necessary.

primary key   In databases, the field or group of fields in a database that contains the identifier.

process   In computer operations, an executing code plus its environment.

process   In structured analysis, a systems component that combines, reorganizes, or changes data flows. Also called a data transform. See also *process description, data flow diagram,* and *data dictionary.*

Glossary

process description In structured analysis, a written description of how a process transforms data that is passed to it. See also *data flow diagram* and *data dictionary*.

product category Any functional grouping of products. Depending on what's important to a particular business, different product categories may be defined. For a business that sells clothing, each article of clothing would define a different category. For example, all shoes would be in the category *footwear*. For a shoe store, *footwear* would be too broad, so the categories might be *seasonal, formal, sport,* or even *color.*

program structure chart In structured analysis, shows all the modules in a program, how they are subordinated to each other, and what data flows between them. Used for grouping functions into appropriate modules that share the same data and function.

prototype A preliminary construction of an application, designed to show how an application will look and work, but without all the parts in place. An application used to test visual and algorithmic design elements.

pseudocode A written description of the workings of a procedure that is structured much like code, but without all the details. See also *structured English*.

public domain software Software that is given to the public with no strings attached. The author doesn't retain the copyright and doesn't limit the distribution or use in any way. See also *freeware* and *shareware*.

query In databases, a request passed to a database engine, asking it to do something such as select and return a table of values or create a new table.

real-time application An application that takes data and makes responses to a user or another machine, where the timing between receiving the data and making the response is important. A data logging application is a real-time application that interacts with a data I/O board.

record In databases, each row in a database table is known as a record. Contains attributes that describe a single entity or object.

relational database A database consisting of several tables. Related information in two tables is connected by joining a field in one table with a field in another. Joins may connect one record in a table with many records in another.

resource leveling In project planning, the task of extending the completion dates of parallel tasks to account for overcommitted resources. If the same person is the resource for two parallel tasks, the tasks must actually be done sequentially, which advances the completion dates.

rollup data Sums and averages of raw data combined according to some criteria.

rollup table A table of rollup data. See *rollup data*.

scope A range term that specifies how widely something is spread. In the case of an application, it defines the limits for different parameters associated with the application, such

as memory needed, screen size, and so on. For variables in a program, scope specifies where in the program the variables are available.

segment   See *market segment*.

Shane   Younger son. Video game expert, warrior.

shareware   A method of distributing software in which you try out the complete package and pay the author if you decide to keep it. See also *freeware* and *public domain software*.

Sierra   Younger daughter. Likes creating stories.

Skye   Older daughter. Athlete.

source code debugger   A debugger that steps through the source code of an application and allows you to see the statement being executed and obtain the values of the variables by name. Contrast this to an object code debugger, which steps through the machine language commands and accesses variables by memory address.

specification   A detailed list of the features and requirements that something, such as an application, must have in order to be acceptable. The specification doesn't tell how something works, only what it must do.

SQL   Structured Query Language. A special standard language for sending commands to database drivers.

structured design   A method of analyzing a system by breaking it down into its basic flows and transforms and designing a program to emulate the system.

structured English   A description of a procedure's operation that uses statements and code-like structure. See *pseudocode*.

support   The help you give to the purchasers of your application after they have purchased it. Support tends to be of two types. See *installation support* and *features support*.

systems analysis and design   The planning part of application development. Before you can build an application, you have to know what it's supposed to do. First you collect information about the system that the application will automate, and then you analyze its needs using structured analysis. When the analysis is complete, you use the methods of structured design to design the application.

table   In databases, a database consists of one or more tables of data. A table is a two-dimensional arrangement of cells, much like the cells in a spreadsheet.

task   In project planning, a statement that names part of a project that must be completed, such as "code the input" or "design the code." Tasks may also be broken down into two or more subtasks to further refine the list of things that must be done to complete a project.

time bomb   In software testing, a piece of code that prevents the testing versions of the software from working after a particular date.

Glossary

top-down design Top-down design starts at the top, with the function of the process, and works its way down to the details necessary to support the function. See also *bottom-up design*.

turnover The amount of time an item stays in inventory.

upgrade A new version of an existing software sold to an existing customer for a reduced price.

usability enhancement Rather than adding a new capability to an application, a usability enhancement is a software feature that decreases the work necessary to accomplish existing tasks. Thus, it makes the software easier to use rather than giving it new capabilities.

wizard A help window that leads you through a task step-by-step. Some wizards let you answer questions and then execute the application options for you.

Using the CD-ROM

Using the CD-ROM

Included with this book is a CD-ROM containing the source code for the sample application at two stages of completion, the complete final version of the application, the sample database files, and other files used in the planning and implementation of this project. To use this software, you must have the following:

- ☐ A 386 or better PC
- ☐ Windows 3.1
- ☐ Visual Basic 3

The following software is not required but is useful for fully examining all the files:

- ☐ Microsoft Access 1.1 to examine and manipulate the database files. If you have version 2.0, be careful not to convert the database to 2.0 format. Otherwise, Visual Basic version 3 won't be able to read it.
- ☐ Microsoft Excel. If you don't have Access, Microsoft Query (included with Excel) can be used to examine and manipulate the database files.
- ☐ A compiled version of the VisData sample program included with Visual Basic. This can also be used to examine the database files.
- ☐ Microsoft Project for examining the project planning files.

What's on the CD-ROM

The CD-ROM contains the following files and directories:

Files:

PACKING.TXT: A current listing of the files on the CD.

README.TXT: A description of the contents of the CD and how to use them.

Directories:

\BITMAPS: Contains all the images used for the buttons, icons, and startup banner.

\DCNSPT: Contains the source files for the final version of the application. Open the DCNSPT.MAK file with Visual Basic to view or modify the application.

\DCNSPT1: Contains the source files for the version of the application as of the end of
 Day 9.

\DCNSPT2: Contains the source files for the version of the application as of the end of
 Day 10.

\DESIGN: Contains files used during the design phase of the application, such as the data dictionary and the process descriptions.

\HELP: Contains the source files for the help compiler that create the help package used with the decision support application.

\ORCO: Contains the Access 1.1 database file ORCO.MDB, the sample of the Orco company database used to develop and test the application.

\OTHER: Contains sample files described in the text.

\PLANNING: Contains the project files created during the preliminary planning for the project.

\ROLUPDAT: Contains the Access 1.1 database file GRAPHS.MDB, which contains the tblDefinitions used by the decision support application and the rolled-up data from the Orco database. The source files for DOROLUPS.MAK are also in this directory. The DOROLUPS program does the monthly updates of the rollup data in GRAPHS.MDB by running persistent queries in the database.

\SETUP: Contains the source files for the setup application.

\SETUP\DISK1: The contents of the setup disk. The contents fit on a 1.44M floppy, which can be used to install the application.

Installing the Final Version and the Database Files

To install the source code, executable files, and database files for the final version of the sample application, insert the CD-ROM and follow these steps. You'll need about 4M of free space on your hard drive.

1. From the Windows File Manager or Program Manager, choose File | Run.
2. Type D:\INSTALL and press Enter. Replace the D with the drive letter of your CD-ROM. For example, if the disc is in your R: drive, type R:\INSTALL instead.
3. Follow the on-screen instructions in the installation program.

The installation program will create a Program Manager group named Professional VB Applications. It contains icons for Read Me First, ORCO Decision Support Program, and ORCO Decision Support Setup. This installation places three subdirectories (\DCNSPT, \ORCO, and \ROLUPDAT) in the root directory of the drive you indicated during setup.

The ORCO Decision Support Setup icon runs the \SETUP\DISK1\SETUP.EXE program on the CD-ROM, which is the final sample application packaged for distribution on floppy disk.

Using the CD-ROM

Note: If the setup program in \SETUP\DISK1 has a problem installing some of the files, especially those in the \WINDOWS or \WINDOWS\SYSTEM directories, you might need to move the existing version of the problem file to a backup area and then try installing again.

To run the sample application, double-click on the application's icon. If the program won't run, you might need to edit the DCNSPT.INI file in the \WINDOWS directory and change the `DataFile` entry to have a path to the GRAPHS.MDB file on the CD-ROM.

The Source Code Files

The source files for the three versions of the application can be opened and run directly from the CD-ROM. If you want to make changes and save the programs, you must copy them to a hard disk. To install the source files for the intermediate versions or the final version of the application, copy all the files from \DCNSPT, \DCNSPT1, or \DCNSPT2 to your hard disk. Copy the DCNSPT.INI file from the program directory you choose to the \WINDOWS directory. Edit that file so that the two paths in the file point to the help file and the GRAPHS.MDB database file. For example, the following listing of the DCNSPT.INI file has paths to the GRAPHS.MDB file in the ROLUPDAT directory on drive G: and the DSA_HELP.HLP file in the DCNSPT directory on the C: drive:

```
Decision Support Program INI File
[startup]
DataFile=G:\ROLUPDAT\GRAPHS.MDB
Year=1991
Help=C:\DCNSPT\DSA_HELP.HLP
[end]
```

The Sample Databases

Access database attachment files preserve drive and path names from their original attachment. The drive letter G is used in the files on this disc. G is an uncommon drive that won't conflict with other assignments on most systems. This provides most users with a way to access the files by mapping drive G: to the path where the files reside on their system.

If you don't map drive G:, you won't be able to access the attached tables in the ORCO.MDB database. You can still run the decision support application and access all the rollup tables. But you won't be able to run the rollup queries or the DOROLUPS program, which need to access the attached files.

To map drive G:, exit Windows and type SUBST G: C:\ and press Enter. This allows your system to see drive G: as equivalent to drive C:. If you installed the files to a drive other than C:, replace C:\ with the correct drive letter, followed by \. To make this mapping permanent, insert the SUBST command in your AUTOEXEC.BAT file.

If drive G: isn't available on your system, you will have to reattach the database files for the correct path on your system. You must also set the LASTDRIVE directive in the CONFIG.SYS file to a letter greater than G:

```
LASTDRIVE=H
```

The following tables in the ORCO.MDB database are attached to the GRAPHS.MDB database:

> Customers
> Employees
> Inventory
> Invoice Details
> Invoices
> Order Details
> Orders

The tables Regions, Product Categories, and Segments normally would also be attached to the GRAPHS.MDB database. However, these files have been moved to the GRAPHS.MDB database so that the decision support application can be run without needing to access an attached table.

You can use Access 1.1 to reattach the tables, or you can run the Visual Basic program ATTACHDB in the \SETUP directory on the CD-ROM to reattach the database tables. Start Visual Basic, and then open and run the ATTACHDB program. Follow the on-screen instructions to reattach the tables.

Using the Databases Directly from the CD-ROM

The GRAPHS.MDB database file expects to find the ORCO.MDB database file in the \ORCO directory on the G: drive. If your CD-ROM drive is installed as a different drive letter, you won't be able to access the attached tables on the ORCO.MDB database. Follow the instructions in the preceding section to map your CD-ROM drive to G:.

If you wish, you can change your CD-ROM drive to be drive G:. You do this by changing the arguments to the MSCDEX device driver in the AUTOEXEC.BAT file. A common installation might look something like this:

Using the CD-ROM

```
C:\CDROM\MSCDEX.EXE /D:MSCD001 /M:10 /V
```

To force the CD-ROM to be mounted as the G: drive (assuming that you don't already have some other drive mounted as the G: drive), add the /L:G switch to the command:

```
C:\CDROM\MSCDEX.EXE /D:MSCD001 /M:10 /V /L:G
```

You must also set the LASTDRIVE directive in the CONFIG.SYS file to a letter greater than G:

```
LASTDRIVE=H
```

After you reboot, your CD-ROM should be installed as drive G:.

If you don't use the MSCDEX.EXE driver, check your CD-ROM installation instructions for information on how to set the drive letter.

Index

() (optional operator)

Symbols

() (optional operator), 72
+ (concatenation operator), 72
. (dot syntax), 190
= (equivalence operator), 72
? (question mark), database object variable functions, 194
[] (selection operator), 72
{} (iterations operator), 72

A

About command (Help menu), 239, 339-341
Access database applications, 117-120
accessing
    databases, 104
        table contents, 122
        with SQL statements, 123-124
        with Visual Basic, 120-124
    high-resolution for program structure charts, 176
action modules, 470
algorithms (procedures), testing, 193-194
alpha testing applications, 368, 470
alpha-level code, 9, 470
Alt-Tab key command, 445
analyzing application specification, 39-40
antivirus scanners, 428-429
Apple Macintosh distribution (applications), 433
applications
    Access databases, 117-120
    alpha testing, 368, 470
    Apple Macintosh distribution, 433
    beta testing, 368-369, 373-391, 470
    builds, 471
    built-in debuggers, 363-364
    CD-ROM distribution, 433-434

charts, 55-57
competitive upgrades, 464, 471
contract proposals, 31-40, 49-52
control flows, 64
controls, placing, 33
copyrights, 436-437
crashes, preventing, 350-358
customer participation, 36
damage control upgrades, 464, 471
data displays, 49
data flow diagrams, 63-68
data forms, 38
data samples, 49-50
data storage, 50
databases, 105
debugging, 59, 180, 363-366
decision support
    contract proposals, 14-15, 25-27
    contracts, 27
    copyright/patent protection, 17-18
    cost estimates, 14
    data dictionaries, 85-93
    data flow diagrams, 76-85
    databases, 124-148
    defining, 7-8, 20-21
    documenting, 408-421
    error trapping, 350-358
    Gantt charts, 13-14
    graph classes/types, 41
    legal contracts, 15-16
    manufacturing, 440-452
    nondisclosure agreements, 17-18, 27
    ownership rights, 18-19
    pie charts, 302-307
    planning, 8-14, 21-25
    process specifications, 94-99
    program structure chart, 170-178
    project timelines, 12-13
    source code, 255-300
    task lists, 10-11, 21-22
    technical support, 465
    testing, 372-389
    user interfaces, 222-245

design changes, 37
design planning, 31-40
design questions, 48
development interviews, 35-39
disclaimers, 435
distributing, 434
distribution sets (disks), 427-430
documenting, 396-398, 472
drill-down, 8, 41, 472
drop-down button labels, 33
ending, 339
error trapping, 344-347, 389
external details, 35
features
    listing, 32-33
    upgrades, 463, 472
forms, designing, 213-214
gold master distribution disks, 427, 473
help systems, designing, 398-400
high-level data flow diagrams, 34, 47-48
icons, 427
implementing, 473
INI files, finding, 382-384
installation (technical support), 456
licensing, 435-436
limits of liability, 435
links, 474
maintenance upgrades, 463, 474
manufacturing, 430-431
    preparations, 427-430
    subcontracting, 431
    through publishers, 432
    through shareware, 432
MS-DOS/Windows distribution, 433
nondisclosure agreements, 369-370
online Help, 398
partitioning from data flow diagrams, 163-170
patents, 438
phasing out, 464

charts

pie charts, 46
prioritized updates, 33
procedures, testing, 366
program structure charts, 156-161
prototypes, 33-34
real-time, 476
redesigning, 27-28, 152, 342
   data flow diagrams, 99
   debugging, 390
   error trapping, 358
   help systems, 421
   manufacturing, 452
   program structure charts, 180
   specifying procedures, 203
   user interfaces, 245-246
release candidate testing, 372
replacing, 58-59
roll-up, 8
scoping, 31-32
security, 39
setup programs, 441, 453
source code
   breakpoints, 364
   comments, 253-254
   loops, 364
   maintenance, 255
   Structured English, 52
   variables, 254
specifying, 53-57
   analysis, 39-40
   background studies, 31-35
   surveys, 35-39
start-up time bombs (alpha/beta), 371-372
subcontracting manufacturing, 431
technical support
   BBS, 461
   faxes, 459
   features, 472
   installation, 474
   on-site, 461-462
   online, 460
   telephone, 459
   video, 459
   written, 458

testing, 362, 367-371
top-level modules, 170
upgrading, 462-464, 478
usability enhancements, 33
user interfaces, 41-46
user registration, 439
using licensed code, 439
variables
   declaring, 254
   displaying values, 363
viruses, scanning, 428-429
walk-throughs, 204
warranties, 439
writing specifications, 52-59
Association of Shareware Professionals, 432
atomic properties (fields), 114
attaching tables (databases), 128
attributes (database tables), 107, 114, 470
authentication, 470
automated systems, 470
average gross margin query (decision support application), 137-138
average order cycle query (decision support application), 142

B

background studies (application specification), 31-35
Backlog by Market Segment query, 141
Backlog by Product Category table, 140-141
Backlog by Sales Region query, 142
backlogs, 470
banners, 240
batch mode (programs), 470
beta testing
   applications, 368-369, 373-391, 470
   forums, 370

   nondisclosure agreements, 369-370
   online bug reporting forms, 371
beta-level code, 9, 470
BMP (bitmap) files, 217
bottom-up designs, 157, 470
breakpoints, 470
builds (applications), 471
built-in debuggers, 363-364
bulletin board systems (BBS), technical support, 460
business relationships (software development), 5-6
buttons (toolbars)
   pop-up labels, 333-334
   Tag properties, 271
bypassing loops, 364

C

calendar displays, resetting, 375
Cartesian joins (database tables), 133
cascading events, 180
CD-R (Recordable CD-ROM) drives, 433
CD-ROM distribution (applications), 433-434
cells (grids), clearing, 283
Chart Class procedure, 271-273
ChartBuilder graph control, 247
charts
   active forms, restoring, 384-387
   application data values, 55-57
   bottom-up designs, 157
   context, 69
   copying, 332
   creating, 274-280
   data requirements, 42-44
   definitions tables, 256-260
   drill-down tables, 316-320
   Gantt, 473

487

charts

charts
  graph controls, 235
  labels, troubleshooting, 377-382
  legends, 292
  printing, 200-201
  program structures, 476
  redrawing errors, 387-389
  sales by product category, 134
  saving, 332
  selecting with menus, 334-335
  switching between, 198
  top-down designs, 158
  year-to-date sales, 130-133
  see also graphs; grids
Class event procedures, 196-197
ClearGrid procedures, 283
clearing grid cells, 283
Close command (File menu), 211
code, *see* source code
cohesion (modules), 162-164
colors (user interfaces), 209
combining procedures into modules, 193
commands
  Debug menu, 364
  Edit menu
    Copy, 177, 332
    Relationships, 124
  Erl, 346
  Err, 346
  Error, 346
  error traps, 346
  Error$, 346
  File menu
    Close, 211
    Copy, 201
    Exit, 177, 201, 339
    Make EXE file, 452
    Print, 176, 200, 320
    Save, 176, 201
    Save As, 442
  forms, 213
  Help menu, 239, 339-341
  menus, 212
  On Error Goto Label, 346

Options menu
  Image Attributes, 217-218
  Project, 202
  Resume, 346
  Resume Label, 346
  Resume Next, 346
  Sort, 85
  Tools menu, 254
  user interfaces, 211
  View menu
    Details, 335
    Toolbars, 415
    Zoom In, 217
  see also key commands
comments (source code), 253-254, 381
commercially-employed developers
  contract considerations, 16
  nondisclosure agreements, 17
  ownership rights, 19
competitive upgrades (applications), 464, 471
compiling help system project files, 407, 417-418
compressing setup program files, 452
Compuserve Association of Shareware Professionals, 432
concatenation operator (+), 72
connections
  databases, 120-121
  program structure chart modules, 160
consultants
  contract considerations, 16
  nondisclosure agreements, 18
  ownership rights, 19
context charts, 69, 471
Context IDs (help topic files), 404
contract proposals
  accepting/refusing, 10
  customers, defining, 5-6
  decision support application, 14-15, 25-27

contractors
  contract considerations, 16
  nondisclosure agreements, 18
  ownership rights, 19
contracts (legal), applications, 15-16, 27
control arrays, 236-238
control flows (applications), 64, 169
  error handlers, 347
  errors, 347-348
control structures
  button graphics, 217-218
  decision support application, 222-233
  delineating, 190
  hot spots, 220-222
  user interfaces, 214-222
controls
  decision support application
    hiding, 297
  placing, 33
converting
  data flow diagrams to program structure charts, 168-170
  data forms, 38-39
  database formats, 38
Copy command
  Edit menu, 177, 332
  File menu, 201
Copy procedure, 201
CopyFile function, 448
copying charts, 332
copyright protection, 17-18, 436-437
cost estimates (applications), 14
cost margins, 474
couples (program structure chart modules), 161-162
crashes (applications), preventing, 350-358
CreateNewGraph procedure, 273-274

decision support application

creating
  applications
    distribution disk sets,
      429-430
    icons, 427
  bitmap files, 217
  charts, 274-280
  data dictionaries, 71-73
  data flow diagrams, 63-71
  graphs, 274
  grids, 274-280
  help system topic files,
    402-406
cross-product joins (database tables), 109, 471
Ctrl-Break key command, 363
cutting source code, 252

D

damage control upgrades (applications), 464, 471
data dictionaries, 63, 471
  creating, 71-73
  decision support application, 85-93
  operators, 72
data displays, 49
data flow diagrams, 62, 472
  components, 64
  converting to program structure charts, 168-170
  creating, 63-71
  data transforms, 165
  debugging, 100
  decision support application, 76-85, 170
  partitioning applications, 163-170
  processes
    partitioning, 68-71
    specifying, 75
  transaction processors, 167
  WinHelp utility, 401
data flows, 34, 63, 471
  digraphs, 64
  naming, 66
  parallel, 66

data forms, converting, 38-39
data samples (applications), 49-50
data sinks, 64, 67-68
data sources, 64, 67-68
data stores, 34, 50, 63, 472
data transforms, 34, 63, 67, 165-166, 472
  see also processes
Database Developer's Guide with Visual Basic 3, 104
databases, 104-106, 472
  Access applications, 117-120
  accessing, 104
    with SQL statements, 123-124
    with Visual Basic, 120-124
  connections, 120-121
  cross-product joins, 471
  decision support application, 124-148
  Definitions table, 152
  designing, 113-116
  E-R (entity-relation) diagrams, 116
  engines, 472
  entities, 472
  equijoins, 472
  fields, 472
  flat file, 105-106, 473
  formats, converting, 38
  indexes, 473
  inner joins, 474
  joining, 474
  layout, 50-52
  links, 474
  outer joins, 475
  persistent objects, 121-122
  primary keys, 475
  queries, 109-114, 476
    debugging, 153
    testing, 194
  records, 476
  registering, 121
  relational, 105-106, 476
  relational table diagrams, 116
  search engines, 105
  specialized applications, 105
  TableDefs collection, 151

  tables, 106, 122-123, 477
    attaching, 128
    attributes, 107
    Cartesian joins, 133
    decision support application, 125-127
    entities, 107, 115
    equijoins/inner joins, 108
    fields, 107
    indexes, 109
    joining, 107-111
    records, 107
    roll-up tables, 130
  virtual objects, 121-122
DateDiff function, 142
Debug menu commands, 364
debuggers, 477
debugging, 28
  applications, 59, 180
    setup program, 453
    with built-in debugger, 363
  data flow diagrams, 100
  error trapping, 358-359
  help systems, 421-422
  procedure specifications, 203
  queries (databases), 153
  source code, 342
  user interfaces, 246-247
debugging code (applications), adding/removing, 364-366
DEBUGON global constant (error trapping), 351
decision support application, 19-27
  average gross margin query, 137-138
  average order cycle, 142
  Backlog by Market Segment query, 141
  Backlog by Product Category table, 140-141
  Backlog by Sales Region query, 142
  banners, 240
  Chart Class procedure, 271-273
  charts
    copying, 332
    definition tables, 256-260

489

decision support application

drill-down tables, 316-320
legends, 292
saving, 332
selecting with menus,
  334-335
ClearGrid procedure, 283
contract proposals, 14-15,
  25-27
controls
  arrays, 236-238
  hiding, 297
  structures, 222-233
copyright/patent protection,
  17-18
copyright/programming
  credits, 339
cost estimates, 14
CreateNewGraph procedure,
  273-274
data dictionaries, 85-93
data flow diagrams,
  76-85, 170
databases, 124-148
defining, 7-8, 20-21
detail grids, viewing, 335-338
DisplayDDData procedure,
  error trapping, 356-358
Do Rollups program,
  149-151
documenting, 408-421
Draw Chart and Grid
  module, 172
DrawChartAndGrid
  procedure, 274-280
DrawMonthlyChartAndGrid
  procedure, error trapping,
  353-354
drill-down
  grid form, 240-242
  options form, 242-247
error trapping, 350-358
events, 173
FillLegendArrays
  procedure, 288
Form_Load procedure,
  307-316, 355-356
Gantt charts, 13-14
global variables, 262-271

graphs
  classes/types, 41
  form, 234-240
  positioning, 298-300
  type buttons, 282-283
GridColHeaders
  procedure, 289
grids, 283-291, 298-300
help
  project files, 416-417
  systems, 408-412
  topic files, 413-415
HideEverything procedure,
  297-298
HidePopUpLabels
  procedure, 334
icons, 440
initialization structure,
  335-338
installing, 442-446
Inventory by Product
  Category table, 148
Inventory Turnover
  query, 148
items, resizing, 341
legal contracts, 15-16
Main procedure, error
  trapping, 351-353
manufacturing, 440-452
MDI parent form, 222-233
menus, 230-233
Monthly Backlog table, 140
Monthly Ending Inventory
  table, 144-147
MouseDown procedure, 302
MouseMove procedures,
  333-334
MouseUp procedure, 302
nondisclosure agreements,
  17-18, 27
Order Cycle by Market
  Segment query, 142-143
Order Cycle Frequency
  Distribution table, 143
Orders by Market Segment
  query, 139
Orders by Product Category
  query, 139

Orders by Sales Region
  query, 140
ownership rights, 18-19
pie charts, 293-297
  drill-down options,
    307-316
  exploding wedges, 302-307
  restoring, 320
planning, 8-14, 21-25
pop-up labaels (toolbar
  buttons), 228-230
PopulateGrid procedure,
  313-316
printing procedures, 320-332
procedures
  error traps, 350
  specifying, 195-203
  test forms, 340-341
process specifications, 94-99
programs
  files, 260-262
  structure chart, 170-178
project timelines, 12-13
queries, running automatically, 148-152
ResizeChartAndGrid
  procedure, 299
RestorePieChart
  procedure, 316
sales by market segment
  query, 135
sales by product category
  chart, 134
sales by sales region
  query, 137
SelectChartType
  procedure, 335
SetColWidths procedure, 287
SetGraphPosition
  procedure, 298
SetGridCrossfoot procedure,
  285, 354-355
SetGridPosition pro-
  cedure, 298
SetGridValues pro-
  cedure, 284
SetInitialTypeButtons
  procedure, 282-283

external consistency (interfaces)

setup program
  compressing files, 452
  testing, 446-452
source code, 255-300, 342
SQL statement, 280-282
tables (database), 125-127
task lists, 10-11, 21-22
technical support, 465
testing, 372-389
ToggleGrid procedure, 285
Type Button procedure,
  271-273
user interfaces, 222-245
virus scans, 441
year-to-date sales chart,
  130-133
Year-to-Date Orders query,
  138-139
declaring variables, 254
Definitions table (databases), 152
designing
  applications
    forms, 213-214
    help systems, 398-400
  databases, 113-116
  toolbars, 213-216
  toolboxes, 216-217
detail grids, viewing, 335-338
detail modules (structured design), 472
Details command (View menu), 335
digraphs, 64
disclaimers (applications), 435
disk duplicators, 431
DisplayDDData procedure
  error trapping, 356-358
  specifying, 199-200
DisplayDDOptions procedure, 199
displaying
  drill-down grids, 199
  icon files, 218
  variable values, 363
distributing applications, 434
distribution disk sets (applications), 427-430
Do Rollups program, 149-151

docking toolboxes, 216
documenting
  applications, 396-398, 472
  decision support application,
    408-421
dot syntax (.), 190
Draw Chart and Grid module, 172
DrawChartAndGrid procedure,
  195-196, 274-280
DrawMonthlyChartAndGrid procedure, 353-354
DrawPieChart procedure, 198
drill-down
  applications, 8, 41, 472
  grids, 78
    decision support application, 240-242
    displaying, 199
    viewing, 175
  options form, 242-247
  pie charts, 307-316
  tables, 316-320
Drill-Down Options menu, 176
drop-down button labels, 33
DRWATSON.EXE utility, 371
dynasets (virtual database objects), 122

E

E-R (entity-relation) diagrams, 116
Edit menu commands
  Copy, 177, 332
  Relationships, 124
enabling error traps, 349
ending applications, 339
entities (database tables), 107, 115, 472
Environment Options command (Tools menu), 254
equijoins (database tables), 108, 472
equivalence operator (=), 72
Erl command, 346
Err command, 346

Error command, 346
error flows, 169
error handlers, 345, 352
  control flows, 347
  heirarchy, 348
  Main procedure (decision
    support application), 351
  protecting, 353
error trapping, 344-347, 472
  activating/deactivating, 351
  debugging, 358-359
  decision support application,
    350-358
  DisplayDDData procedure,
    356-358
  DrawMonthlyChartAndGrid
    procedure, 353-354
  enabling, 349
  Form_Load procedure,
    355-356
  global constants, 349
  I/O procedures, 349-350
  Main procedure (decision
    support application),
    351-353
  numeric procedures, 349-350
  SetGridCrossfoot procedure,
    354-355
Error$ command, 346
errors
  applications, 389
  control flows, 347-348
  logging, 352
  pie charts, 384-387
  troubleshooting, 347
events
  cascades, 180
  decision support application, 173
  procedures, combining into modules, 193
Exit command (File menu), 177, 201, 339
Exit procedure, 201
exploding pie chart wedges, 302-307
external consistency (interfaces), 472

491

FS key command

F

F5 key command, 364
F8 key command, 363
fax technical support (applications), 459
features technical support (applications), 472
features upgrades (applications), 463, 472
fields, 472
  attributes, 114
  primary keys, 107
  properties, 114
File menu commands
  Close, 211
  Copy, 201
  Exit, 177, 201, 339
  Make EXE file, 452
  Print, 176, 200, 320
  Save, 176, 201
  Save As, 442
files, metafile format, 176
FillLegendArrays procedure, 288
finding application INI files, 382-384
flat file databases, 105-106, 473
floppy disks, purchasing for manufacturing needs, 430
flowcharts (procedures), 191-192
fonts (grids), 327-331
footnotes (help topic file attributes), 402-403
Form_Load procedure, 307-316, 355-356
formats
  databases, converting, 38
  metafile, 176
forms, 473
  commands, 213
  designing, 213-214
  drill-down grid, 240-242
  drill-down options, 242-247
  graphs, 234-240
  MDI parent, 222-233
  see also user interfaces

freeware, 473
full-screen graphs, 44
function procedures, *see* procedures
functional primitives (processes), 69, 473
functions
  CopyFile, 448
  DateDiff, 142
  intPieHotHit( ), 303
  OpenDatabase, 120, 149
  testing, 193-194
  Weibull distribution, 457

G

Gantt charts, 13-14, 473
global variables, 262-271
gold master distribution disks, 427, 473
graphics (control buttons), 217-218
graphs
  classes, 473
  creating, 274
  decision support application, positioning, 298-300
  drawing on printers, 324
  full-screen, 44
  type breakdowns, 42
  type buttons, 282-283
  types, 473
  see also charts; grids
graphs form, 234-240
GridColHeaders procedure, 289
grids, 78
  cells, clearing, 283
  controls, 236
  creating, 274-280
  decision support application, 283-291, 298-300
  detail grids, viewing, 335-338
  drawing on printers, 324
  fonts, 327-328, 330-331
  hiding/revealing, 197-198
  printing, 200-201
  see also charts; graphs

H

Help menu commands, 239, 339-341
help systems
  applications, designing, 398-400
  debugging, 421-422
  decision support application, 408-412
  project files, 406-407
    compiling, 417-418
    decision support application, 416-417
    linking to applications, 418-421
    linking with VB applications, 407
  topic files
    creating, 402-406
    decision support application, 413-415
    toolbars, 415
  Windows, 401-407
HideEverything procedure, 297-298
HidePopUpLabels procedure, 219, 334
hiding
  decision support application controls, 297
  grids, 197-198
  pop-up labels (toolbar buttons), 220
high-level data flow diagrams, 34, 47-48
high-resolution (program structure charts), 176
hot spots
  control structures, 220-222
  images, 401
hypertext, 473

I

I/O (input/output) procedures, error trapping, 349-350

492

NDA (nondisclosure agreement)

icons
  applications, 427
  files, 218
IconWorks program, 218
identifiers (entities), 107, 115, 473
Image Attributes command (Options menu), 217
images (hot spots), 401
implementing applications, 473
indexes (database tables), 109, 473
INI (initialization) files, 178, 382-384
initialization
  procedures, 202-203
  structures, 335-338
inner joins (database tables), 108, 474
installing applications, 442-446, 456
intellectual property, 474
interfaces
  external consistency, 472
  internal consistency, 474
  MDI, 474
  program consistency, 206
  see also user interfaces
intPieHotHit( ) function, 303
Inventory by Product Category table (decision support application), 148
Inventory Turnover query (decision support application), 148
iterations operator ({}), 72

J–K–L

joining database tables, 107-111, 474
key commands
  Alt-Tab, 445
  Ctrl-Break, 363
  F5, 364
  F8, 363
  Shift-F8, 363
  Shift-F9, 363

key fields (relational databases), 105
keyboard prioritized updates, 33
labels
  application distribution disks, 431
  charts, troubleshooting, 377-382
legends (charts), 292
licensing applications, 435-436
limits of liability (applications), 435
linking help project files
  to applications, 418-421
  with VB applications, 407
links (applications/ databases), 474
listing application features, 32-33
LoadAndParseINIFile procedure, 351
logging errors, 352
loops, bypassing, 364

M

Macintosh GUI, 206
Main procedure, 351-353
maintenance upgrades (applications), 463, 474
Make EXE file command (File menu), 452
manufacturing
  applications, 430-431
    through publishers, 432
    through shareware, 432
  decision support application, 440-452
  preparations, 427-430
many-to-many relationships (records), 110
market segments, 474
MDI (Multiple Document Interface), 474
MDI parent form, 222-233
memory-resident viruses, 429

menus
  commands, 212
  decision support application, 230-233
metafile format, 176
Microsoft
  Diagnostics utility, 371
  Query (Access database application), 50, 118
  WinBug application, 371
modules, 475
  program structure charts, 158-159
    cohesion, 162-164
    connections, 160
    couples, 161-162
    pulling up sequentially, 187
  startup, 177
monitors (system capabilities), 401
Monthly Backlog table (decision support application), 140
Monthly Ending Inventory table (decision support application), 144-147
mouse prioritized updates, 33
MouseDown procedure (decision support application), 302
MouseMove procedures (decision support application), 333-334
MouseUp procedure (decision support application), 302
MS-DOS/Windows distribution (applications), 433
multiresolution bitmap files, 401

N

naming
  data flows, 66
  program structure chart modules, 159
NDA (nondisclosure agreement), 369-370

nondisclosure agreements

nondisclosure agreements, 475
  applications, 369-370
  decision support application, 17-18, 27
numbered processes, 70
numeric procedures, error trapping, 349-350

O

object-oriented programming (OOP), 68
objects
  persistent (databases), 121-122, 475
  virtual (databases), 121-122
ODBC (Open Database Connectivity), 475
On Error Goto Label command, 346
on-site technical support, 461-462
one-to-many relationships (records), 110
one-to-one relationships (records), 110
online bug reporting forms (beta testing), 371
online documentation (applications), 397-398
online Help (applications), 398
online technical support (applications), 460
OOP (object-oriented programming), 68
OpenDatabase function, 120, 149
operations (user interfaces), 210
operators, 72
optimizing programming, 252-255
optional operator (()), 72
Options menu commands
  Image Attributes, 217
  Project, 202
Order Cycle by Market Segment query, 142-143
Order Cycle Frequency Distribution table, 143
Orders by Market Segment query, 139
Orders by Product Category query, 139
Orders by Sales Region query, 140
out-of-band operations, 344, 475
outer joins (database tables), 108, 475
outliner utility, 400
ownership rights (applications), 18-19

P

packaging program structure charts, 169
parallel data flows, 66
partitioning
  applications from data flow diagrams, 163-170
  processes, 68-71
  program structure charts, 185-188
patent protection (applications), 17-18, 438
pathological connections (program structure chart modules), 160, 475
persistent
  objects (databases), 121-122, 475
  queries, 475
phasing out applications, 464
picture description files, 176
pie charts, 46, 293-297
  drill-down options, 307-316
  errors, 384-387
  exploding wedges, 199, 302-307
  hiding/revealing, 198
  restoring, 320
Pinnacle Publishing, 247
pop-up labels (toolbar buttons), 218-220, 228-230, 332-334
PopulateGrid procedure, 313-316
preventing application crashes, 350-358
primary keys (fields), 107, 475
Print command (File menu), 176, 200, 320
printed documentation (applications), 397
PrintGrid procedure, 326-327
PrintHatchLegend procedure, 331-332
printing
  charts, 200-201
  grids, 200-201
  procedures, 320-332
PrintVisibleChart procedure, 200-201, 321-322
prioritized updates (applications), 33
procedures
  algorithms, testing, 193-194
  applications, testing, 366
  class button arrays, 196
  ClearGrid, 283
  combining into modules, 193
  CreateNewGraph, 273-274
  decision support application
    specifying, 195-203
    test forms, 340-341
  DisplayDDData, 356-358
  DrawChartAndGrid, 274-280
  DrawMonthlyChartAndGrid, 353-354
  error trapping, 344, 349-350
  FillLegendArrays, 288
  flowcharts, 191-192
  Form_Load, 307-316, 355-356
  GridColHeaders, 289
  HideEverything, 297-298
  HidePopUpLabels, 334
  LoadAndParseINIFile, 351
  MouseDown, 302
  MouseMove, 333-334
  MouseUp, 302
  PopulateGrid, 313-316
  PrintGrid, 326-327
  PrintHatchLegend, 331-332

494

printing, 320-332
PrintVisibleChart, 321-322
program structure chart modules, 184-193
pseudocode, 189-191
ResizeChartAndGrid, 299
RestorePieChart, 316
SelectChartType, 335
SetColWidths, 287-288
SetGraphPosition, 298
SetGridCrossfoot, 285, 354-355
SetGridPosition, 298
SetGridValues, 284
SetInitialTypeButtons, 282-283
source code functions, 253
specifying (flowcharts/pseudocode), 189
step breakpoint command, 363
strCreateSQL, 280-282
testing, 194
ToggleGrid, 285
type button arrays, 196
processes, 67, 475
decision support application, specifying, 94-99
descriptions, 63
functional primitives, 69, 473
numbering, 70
partitioning, 68-71
specifying, 75
see also data transforms
program structure charts, 476
decision support application, 170-178
design evaluation, 161-163
high-resolution, accessing, 176
modules, 158-159
cohesion, 162-164
connections, 160
couples, 161-162
procedures, 184-193
pulling up sequentially, 187
packaging, 169
redesigning applications, 180

saving, 176
partitioning, 185-188
programming, optimizing, 252-255
programs, *see* **applications**
Project command (Options menu), 202
project files (help systems), 406
compiling, 407, 417-418
decision support application, 416-417
linking
to applications, 418-421
with VB applications, 407
properties (fields), 114
protecting
error handlers, 353
toolbar buttons during printing, 375-377
prototypes (applications), 33-34, 476
pseudocode, 189-191, 476
public domain software, 476

Q

queries, 476
databases, 109, 111-114, 153
decision support application, 148-152
persistent, 475
qryBacklogDetail query (drill-down tables), 318-319
qryCycleDetail query (drill-down tables), 319
qryInventoryDetail query (drill-down tables), 319
qryMarginDetail query (drill-down tables), 317-318
qryOrdersDetail query (drill-down tables), 318
qrySalesDetail query (drill-down tables), 317
qryTurnsDetail query (drill-down tables), 319-320
testing, 194

R

real-time applications, 476
Recordable CD-ROM (CD-R) drives, 433
records, 476
identifiers, 107, 115
many-to-many relationships, 110
one-to-many relationships, 110
one-to-one relationships, 110
reading, 123
sorting, 70
redesigning
applications, 27-28, 152, 342
data flow diagrams, 99
debugging, 390
error trapping, 358
help systems, 421
manufacturing, 452
program structure charts, 180
specifying procedures, 203
user interfaces, 245-246
redraw errors (charts), troubleshooting, 387-389
referential integrity, 124
registering databases, 121
registration (users), applications, 439
relational databases, 105-106, 476
relational operators, 72
relational table diagrams, 116
Relationships command (Edit menu), 124
release candidate code, 9
release candidate testing (applications), 372
replacing applications, 58-59
resetting
calendar displays, 375
toolbar buttons, 373-375
ResizeChartAndGrid procedure, 197-198, 299
resizing decision support application items, 341

resource leveling

resource leveling, 476
RestorePieChart procedure, 316
restoring charts, 320, 384-387
Resume command, 346
Resume Label command, 346
Resume Next command, 346
rich text format (RTF), 415
roll-up
   applications, 8
   data, 476
   tables (databases), 130, 149-151, 476
RTF (rich text format), 415
running decision support application queries automatically, 148-152

S

sales by market segment query, 135
sales by sales region query, 137
Save As command (File menu), 442
Save command (File menu), 176, 201
Save procedure, 201
saving
   charts, 332
   program structure charts, 176
scanning applications for viruses, 428-429
scoping applications, 31-32
search engines (databases), 105
security (applications), 39
SelectChartType procedure, 335
selection operator ([ ]), 72
Set Next Statement command (Debug menu), 364
SetColWidths procedure, 287
SetGraphPosition procedure, 298
SetGridCrossfoot procedure, 285, 354-355
SetGridPosition procedure, 298

SetGridValues procedure, 284
SetInitialTypeButtons procedure, 282-283
setup programs (applications), 441-442
Setup Wizard utility, 429, 442-446
shareware, 432, 477
Shift-F8 key command, 363
Shift-F9 key command, 363
single step breakpoint command, 363
snapshots (virtual database objects), 122
software, 476
Sort command, 85
sorting records, 70
source code, 471
   alpha-level, 9
   beta-level, 9
   breakpoints, setting, 364
   code blocks, 190
   comments, 253-254
   cutting, 252
   debugging, 342
   decision support application, 255-300
   loops, bypassing, 364
   maintenance, 255
   procedures, 253
   release candidate, 9
   Structured English, 52
   variables, 254
specifying
   applications, 53-57
      analyzing, 39-40
      background studies, 31-35
      surveys, 35-39
   procedures
      decision support application, 195-203
      flowcharts/pseudocode, 189
   processes, 75
SQL (Structured Query Language), 477
   accessing databases, 123-124
   decision support application, 280-282
starting code blocks, 190

startup modules, 177
stealth viruses, 429
strCreateSQL procedure, 280-282
string variables, 254
Structured Analysis and System Specification, 62
structured design, 24, 62-63, 477
   action modules, 470
   detail module, 472
structured English, 52, 189-191, 477
subcontracting application manufacturing, 431
surveys (application specification), 35-39
switches (module cohesion), 163
switching between charts, 198
systems analysis and design, 477

T

TableDefs collection (databases), 151
tables (databases), 106, 122-123, 477
   attaching, 128
   attributes, 107
   Cartesian joins, 133
   cross-product joins, 109
   decision support application, 125-127
   entities, 107, 115
   equijoins/inner joins, 108
   fields, 107
   indexes, 109
   joining, 107, 109-111
   outer joins, 108
   records, 107
   roll-up tables, 130
Tag properties (buttons), 271
task lists, 10-11, 21-22
technical support, 477
   applications, 456-462
   decision support application, 465

Zoom In command (view menu)

telephone technical support (applications), 459
test forms, 340-341
testing
    applications, 362, 366-371
    decision support application, 372-389, 446-452
    functions, 193-194
    procedures, 193-194
    queries, 194
third-party applications, ChartBuilder graph control, 247
time bombs (alpha/beta application start-up), 371-372, 477
ToggleGraphVisible procedure, 198-199
ToggleGrid procedure, 285
toolbars
    buttons, 216
        pop-up labels, 218-220, 333-334
        protecting during printing, 375-377
        resetting, 373-375
    designing, 213-216
    help topic files, 415
Toolbars command (View menu), 415
toolboxes, 216-217
Tools menu commands, 254
top-down designs, 158, 478
top-level modules, 170
topic files (help systems)
    creating, 402-406
    decision support application, 413-415
    toolbars, 415
transaction processors, 167-168
troubleshooting
    application errors, 389
    charts
        labels, 377-382
        redrawing errors, 387-389
    errors, 347
    pie charts, 384-387

Type Button procedure, 271-273
Type event procedures, 196-197

U

Uniform Commercial Code (software warranties), 439
updating roll-up tables, 149-151
upgrading applications, 462-464, 478
usability enhancements (applications), 33, 478
user interfaces, 206
    applications, 44-46
        features, 208
        graphs/charts, 41-44
    colors, 209
    commands, 211
    control structures, 214-222
    debugging, 246-247
    decision support application, 222-245
    design elements, 211-212
    design rules, 207-212
    external consistency, 211-212
    forms, 209
    internal consistency, 210-211
    operations, 210
    redesigning applications, 245
    see also forms; interfaces
utilities
    DRWATSON.EXE, 371
    Microsoft Diagnostics, 371
    outliner, 400
    Setup Wizard, 429, 442-446
    WinHelp, 401-407

V

variables
    declaring, 254
    global, 262-271
    values, displaying, 363

video technical support (applications), 459
View menu
    commands
        Details, 335
        Toolbars, 415
        Zoom In, 217
    selecting charts, 334-335
viewing
    detail grids, 335-338
    drill-down grids, 175
virtual objects (databases), 121-122
viruses
    memory-resident viruses, 429
    scanning applications, 428-429
    stealth viruses, 429
VisData (Access database application), 118-124

W

walk-throughs (applications), 204
warranties (applications), 439
Weibull distribution function, 457
WinHelp utility, 401-407
wizards, 478
writing application specifications, 52-59
written technical support (applications), 458

X–Y–Z

Year-to-Date Orders query, 138-139
year-to-date sales chart, 130-133
Yourdon, Ed, 62

Zoom In command (View menu), 217

Add to Your Sams Library Today with the Best Books for Programming, Operating Systems, and New Technologies

The easiest way to order is to pick up the phone and call
1-800-428-5331
between 9:00 a.m. and 5:00 p.m. EST.
For faster service please have your credit card available.

ISBN	Quantity	Description of Item	Unit Cost	Total Cost
0-672-30440-6		Database Developer's Guide with Visual Basic 3 (book/disk)	$44.95	
0-672-30619-0		Real-World Programming with Visual Basic (book/CD-ROM)	$45.00	
0-672-30621-2		How to Create Real-World Applications with Visual Basic (book/CD-ROM)	$39.99	
0-672-30448-1		Teach Yourself C in 21 Days, Bestseller Edition	$24.95	
0-672-30308-6		Tricks of the Graphics Gurus (book/2 disks)	$49.95	
0-672-30507-0		Tricks of the Game Programming Gurus (book/CD-ROM)	$45.00	
0-672-30485-6		Navigating the Internet, Deluxe Edition	$29.95	
0-672-30413-9		Multimedia Madness! Deluxe Edition (book/2 CD-ROMs)	$55.00	
0-672-30473-2		Client/Server Computing, Second Edition	$40.00	
0-672-30467-8		Sybase Developer's Guide (book/disk)	$40.00	
0-672-30364-7		Win32 API Desktop Reference (book/CD-ROM)	$49.95	
0-672-30338-8		Inside Windows File Formats (book/disk)	$29.95	
❏ 3 ½" Disk		Shipping and Handling: See information below.		
❏ 5 ¼" Disk		TOTAL		

Shipping and Handling: $4.00 for the first book, and $1.75 for each additional book. Floppy disk: add $1.75 for shipping and handling. If you need to have it NOW, we can ship product to you in 24 hours for an additional charge of approximately $18.00, and you will receive your item overnight or in two days. Overseas shipping and handling adds $2.00 per book and $8.00 for up to three disks. Prices subject to change. Call for availability and pricing information on latest editions.

201 W. 103rd Street, Indianapolis, Indiana 46290

1-800-428-5331 — Orders   **1-800-835-3202** — FAX   **1-800-858-7674** — Customer Service

Book ISBN 0-672-30596-8

The MCP Forum on CompuServe

Go online with the world's leading computer book publisher! Macmillan Computer Publishing offers everything you need for computer success!

Find the books that are right for you!
A complete online catalog, plus sample chapters and tables of contents give you an in-depth look at all our books. The best way to shop or browse!

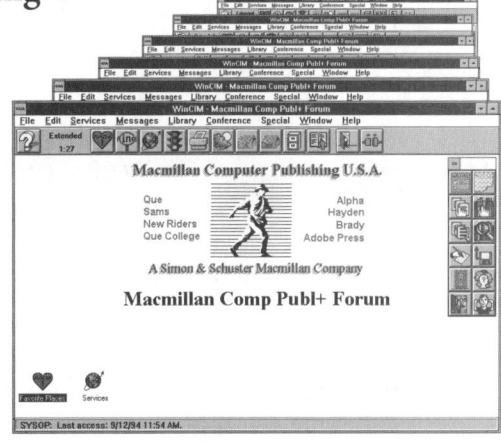

➤ Get fast answers and technical support for MCP books and software

➤ Join discussion groups on major computer subjects

➤ Interact with our expert authors via e-mail and conferences

➤ Download software from our immense library:
  ▷ Source code from books
  ▷ Demos of hot software
  ▷ The best shareware and freeware
  ▷ Graphics files

Join now and get a free CompuServe Starter Kit!

To receive your free CompuServe Introductory Membership, call **1-800-848-8199** and ask for representative #597.

The Starter Kit includes:
➤ Personal ID number and password
➤ $15 credit on the system
➤ Subscription to *CompuServe Magazine*

Once on the CompuServe System, type:

GO MACMILLAN

for the most computer information anywhere!

PLUG YOURSELF INTO...

THE MACMILLAN INFORMATION SUPERLIBRARY™

Free information and vast computer resources from the world's leading computer book publisher—online!

FIND THE BOOKS THAT ARE RIGHT FOR YOU!

A complete online catalog, plus sample chapters and tables of contents give you an in-depth look at *all* of our books, including hard-to-find titles. It's the best way to find the books you need!

- **STAY INFORMED** with the latest computer industry news through our online newsletter, press releases, and customized Information SuperLibrary Reports.
- **GET FAST ANSWERS** to your questions about MCP books and software.
- **VISIT** our online bookstore for the latest information and editions!
- **COMMUNICATE** with our expert authors through e-mail and conferences.
- **DOWNLOAD SOFTWARE** from the immense MCP library:
    - Source code and files from MCP books
    - The best shareware, freeware, and demos
- **DISCOVER HOT SPOTS** on other parts of the Internet.
- **WIN BOOKS** in ongoing contests and giveaways!

TO PLUG INTO MCP:

GOPHER: gopher.mcp.com
FTP: ftp.mcp.com

Installing the CD-ROM

The software on the CD-ROM can be used without installing it on your hard drive. If you want to modify the source code, however, you must install it to your hard drive. Please read Appendix B before using the software.

Insert the disc in your CD-ROM drive and follow these steps to install the software. You'll need about 4M of free space on your hard drive to install the files.

1. From the Windows File Manager or Program Manager, choose File | Run.
2. Type D:\INSTALL and press Enter. Replace D with the drive letter of your CD-ROM. For example, if the disc is in your R: drive, type R:\INSTALL instead.
3. Follow the on-screen instructions in the installation program.

When the installation is complete, the file README.TXT will be displayed for you to read. This file contains information on the files and programs that were installed.

The installation program will create a Program Manager group named Professional VB Applications. It contains icons for Read Me First, ORCO Decision Support Program, and ORCO Decision Support Setup.

This installation places three subdirectories (\DCNSPT, \ORCO, and \ROLUPDAT) in the root directory of the drive you indicated during setup. Be sure to read Appendix B or the Read Me First file before proceeding.